Nineteenth-century society

Essays in the use of quantitative
methods for the study of
social data

A PUBLICATION OF
THE CAMBRIDGE GROUP FOR THE HISTORY OF
POPULATION AND SOCIAL STRUCTURE

Nineteenth-century society

Essays in the use of quantitative methods for the study of social data

edited by E. A. Wrigley

Cambridge
at the University Press 1972

Published by the Syndics of the Cambridge University Press
Bentley House, 200 Euston Road, London NW1 2DB
American Branch: 32 East 57th Street, New York, N.Y.10022

© Cambridge University Press 1972

Library of Congress Catalogue Card Number: 71–174258

ISBN: 0 521 08412 1

Printed in Great Britain by
Alden & Mowbray Ltd
at the Alden Press, Oxford

Contributors

MICHAEL ANDERSON
Lecturer in Sociology, University of Edinburgh

ALAN ARMSTRONG
Senior Lecturer in Economic and Social History,
University of Kent at Canterbury

DUDLEY BAINES
Lecturer in Economic History, London School of Economics

BRUCE COLEMAN
Lecturer in History, University of Exeter

MICHAEL DRAKE
Professor in the Faculty of Social Sciences, The Open University

VIC GATRELL
Fellow and Lecturer in History, Gonville and Caius College, Cambridge

TOM HADDEN
Lecturer in Law, The Queen's University of Belfast

ROGER SCHOFIELD
Director of the Cambridge Group for the History of Population and
Social Structure, and Fellow of Clare College, Cambridge

PETER TILLOTT
Director of Continuing Education, University of Auckland

Contents

Contents

Introduction

E. A. Wrigley

During the nineteenth century the state became involved in gathering more and more information about its subjects. To the traditional interests in trade, taxable wealth, religious schismatics and war potential, were added many new interests which resulted in immense compilations of data. Some of these were eventually tabulated and published, though far more were not. Even the material which was published was so bulky that it is seldom consulted. Anyone, for example, who has worked with the hundreds of heavy volumes of the *Statistik des Deutschen Reichs* and other similar series produced by the Statistical Office in Berlin must occasionally have felt his spirits droop at their oppressive combined mass. And in all economically advanced countries the trend was similar. Because so much information was collected by the state during the course of the last century, there are great opportunities for studying nineteenth-century society in depth, but also special difficulties in doing so.

The main focus of attention in this book is the census – what information was required on census night; how the information was collected; how accurately and completely population characteristics were recorded; the problems which arise in attempting to use either the published census volumes or the enumerators' books; and the techniques which have proved useful in analysis. The census is too big a topic to be covered exhaustively in a single volume but in spite of this it is a good point of entry into the whole sweep of state-collected data about social, economic and demographic affairs. It was the most ambitious exercise of its type, covering every family in the land and requiring the co-operation of every household head, and work on the census exemplifies both the fascinations and frustrations of using nineteenth-century descriptive statistics.

There is a delusive clarity and apparent authority in the printed word or digit. But what is printed in a census volume or any other statistical publication represents the last operation in a long chain of data collection and collation, subject to error, omission and misinterpretation at every stage from the phrasing of the original enquiry to the proof-reading of the printer's galleys. This is a problem as old as administration itself, evident in eighteenth-century Scandinavia (where Drake has shown that the death rate in Norway in 1742 was inflated by a clerical error in making up totals of deaths to 70 per 1,000 where the true figure is about 50 per 1,000),[1] and in Britain in 1969 (where it became evident that the

1

under-recording of exports had for some years been on a scale sufficient to make a significant difference to the appearance of the balance of payments).

In some respects close examination of the accuracy of the census is reassuring; in others it shows how unsafe it is to trust any straightforward inferences drawn from the published figures. Tillott's work in unravelling the ways in which inaccuracies creep into census materials bears eloquent witness to the extreme difficulty of ensuring that there is exact correspondence between legislative intention and administrative action. He investigates both the circumstances in which information was originally obtained and the ways in which it was subsequently altered. And he shows that deficiencies were not uniform throughout the country. Local registrars sometimes indulged in highly idiosyncratic interpretations of their briefs and as a result there might be a spurious boost in the number of, say, lodgers at the expense of visitors or vice versa. Census checkers could be equally arbitrary.

The history of the census at the national level is described by Drake. He draws heavily upon contemporary comment to show how certain questions came to be regarded as normal on census schedules while others were taboo. Some remained long in doubt. The furious swaying battle over the taking of a religious census makes an instructive and exciting story – an epitome of the many nineteenth-century struggles between the Nonconformists and the Established Church. The appendixes to Chapter 1 provide in summary or tabular form an inventory of the contents of the nineteenth-century censuses, making it easy to discover which tabulations were made consistently and which appeared only sporadically.

The chapters written by Tillott, Anderson, and Coleman in different settings all underline the promise of micro-studies based on enumerators' books. It is a matter for regret that under the hundred years' rule enforced by the General Register Office these books can at present be consulted only down to the 1861 census, but it is significant that in spite of this restriction they are attracting many scholars who find the printed tabulations of the censuses unsuited to their purposes. Working from enumerators' books offers two great advantages over using census volumes; that the information can be extracted to fit the problem in mind, and that each entry concerns a named individual.

The significance of the first point will be recognised immediately by anyone who has been obliged to depend upon printed census tabulations, for it is always and inevitably the case that detailed cross-tabulations are available for very large populations only, while for small areas or socio-economic groups the tabulations are much simpler. At the parish level little more than the crude total of population may be printed. Yet to study the interlinkage of social, economic and demographic characteristics in a population, the gross statistics of large populations are usually of very little help because they refer to complex groups within which smaller and more homogeneous groups are submerged. Consider, for example, the history of the decline in fertility in the late nineteenth century.

The fertility tabulations of the 1911 census show well enough how national fertility fell gradually from about 1860 and also how wide was the difference in the timing and extent of the fall between different socio-economic groups. The professional classes were at one extreme: miners and agricultural workers at the other. Family limitation clearly percolated down through the ranks of society quite slowly so that high fertility groups in the 1890s might be at the same point as low fertility groups in the 1860s.

But to know these general characteristics of the fertility fall only serves to set the stage for work which might yield an adequate appreciation of the circumstances in which behaviour changed. For example, it would be valuable to know whether members of groups in which fertility fell early were responsive to local conditions as well as national trends. Did school-teachers, clerks and shopkeepers in coalmining districts conform to the local high fertility pattern, for instance, or did they behave like others in similar employment elsewhere in the country? Was there a difference between, say, school-teachers who came from local mining families and those who were of middle-class origin, or who moved into the district from elsewhere? To what extent did the family background of the wife influence matters? Or work opportunities for married women outside the home? And so on.

The ramifications of this topic are intricate and fascinating, and there are many similar topics. Yet the essential point is simple. The understanding of historical change depends upon using an appropriate framework within which the evidence can be marshalled. Often the appropriate framework is the individual family or household. These can then be combined and re-combined to suit the task in hand. But whereas it is always possible to build up in this way from the primary record in the enumerators' books, it is not possible to reverse the process and adapt the printed tabulations by sub-division. Hence the importance of work based on the enumerators' books.

That each entry in these books concerns a named man, woman or child is also very important. Recent advances in historical demography are very largely due to the development of a logic of nominal linkage between records of baptism, burial and marriage which concern the same individual or family.[2] There is no reason why this logic should not be extended to a wider range of nominal sources (such as enumerators' books at successive censuses, or enumerators' books and other nominal sources like vital registration,[3] wills, directories, tax lists, Poor Law records, etc.). The elucidation of some of the points listed above either requires the use of additional nominal sources or would be greatly helped by it. The enumerators' books provide an excellent central nexus from which to branch out in this way. For each person they give age, sex, occupation, place of birth, marital status, and relationship to head of family. In addition there is information about each household, its size, presence or absence of kin, number of servants living-in, and so on. Nominal linkage between enumerators' books and vital records may add such details as age at marriage, rank of birth in the family of orientation, father's occupation, information about earlier marriages, and occupation at a younger age. More complex operations may produce data about proximity of residence to that of kin by blood or marriage, or enable one to follow individuals through their successive life-cycle stages. Only a few substantive studies which illustrate the potential of work in this vein have been published as yet,[4] but the success which has attended family reconstitution in a similar data environment promises well for the future.[5]

Every research opportunity has its attendant disadvantages. In this case the bulk of the data is the most obtrusive problem. Schofield's chapter on sampling historical material is directed to this issue since the use of a suitable sampling method may radically reduce the amount of work entailed in sifting through bulky sources without appreciable cost in loss of detail and accuracy. He is at pains to show how research may be planned with this point in mind and also to emphasise that sampling theory is a much more flexible instrument than is sometimes supposed, adaptable to historical data which may seem at first sight too cumbersome to be sampled easily. Clustered sampling theory, for example, may be very helpful where the units of population which one wishes to sample are approached indirectly, as in the case of individuals within households. When the population to be sampled is clustered in this way, the precision of sample estimates for any given size of sample is less, but by an amount that can be specified. There are many instances of historical sources where it would be extremely tedious and time-consuming to sample directly but where indirect sampling may save the day.

Some difficulties are common both to the use of printed census volumes and to work on enumerators' books. In one section of his chapter, for example, Armstrong describes the method of occupational classification developed by Charles Booth to enable comparison to be made of the numbers engaged in industrial groupings at successive censuses. The trades comprising the sub-groups varied from census to census, as individual trades, crafts or occupations were combined or sub-divided, or occasionally reallocated between the sub-groups. To achieve the greatest possible consistency over time some reworking of published census data is necessary. Armstrong's discussion is framed chiefly in terms of the census tabulations but the long lists of allocations of trades to industrial groups should prove equally valuable to those working on enumerators' books.

In the other section of his chapter, which is chiefly concerned with the enumerators' books, Armstrong explores a further aspect of a difficulty which is encountered by most historians who use census data – that the information is collected by census officials with one purpose in mind, whereas the historian wishes to use it for another. In this case the information given is a general classification of occupations, the object in mind is the study of social stratification. There are few easy or fully satisfactory 'answers' in a matter of such complexity, but, as Armstrong insists, even though each historian may devise *ad hoc* schemes tailored to his own needs, it is most important that he should also make a number of tabulations in a standard form to facilitate comparative work.

Each author where appropriate has tried to indicate the limitations of the available data, their dependability, common sources of error in handling them, and the methods which may be used to produce uniform results. Baines tackles the measurement of migratory flows in this vein, proposing a method which yields both a 'best' estimate of net migration between counties decade by decade, and sets upper and lower bounds to the size of the flow. He also discusses other methods of measurement and the vexed problems which follow on boundary changes, or arise from differences in mortality rates between residents and migrants.

Gatrell and Hadden's chapter is devoted to a description of the statistics of criminal behaviour which are available for the nineteenth century, and to the inferences which can properly be drawn from them. They suggest that the relationship between the trade cycle and rates of certain classes of crime has been misconceived in the past, and show how the comparison of regional and national crime rates may throw light on the varying local incidence of economic misfortune. Coleman's review of the sources which may be used in the study of educational provision is of a similar character. In both cases the statistics pose teasing problems. They were less accurate, less consistent and less detailed than most census tabulations (though the enumerators' books are themselves important in studying local schooling), and demand a judicious wariness if they are not to be misleading.

This volume is but a small beginning. Both within the context of the census and more generally in relation to state-collected data, many more topics might have been discussed (some indeed were planned for this volume but for various reasons proved stillborn). The authors share the conviction that the remark that Disraeli is alleged to have made about statistics, tells us more about Disraeli than about statistics. No doubt all tools can be misused and powerful tools will then produce more damage than weak ones. But this is not a good argument against using powerful tools. Quantitative studies whether of society today or in the past can be as elegant, penetrative and illuminating as any others. For some purposes they are to be preferred to other methods. To be successful they require a scrupulous knowledge of the sources to which they are applied. Often, indeed, the intrinsic rigour of some statistical concepts, like sampling, imposes a greater care and precision in using sources than would otherwise be the case. It helps to ensure, too, that the distinction between illustrating a hypothesis and testing it (not always well observed in the past) is better understood.

As with an earlier volume published by the Cambridge Group for the History of Population and Social Structure, *An Introduction to English Historical Demography*, very few results of research are published in this book. It deals with sources and methods of research rather than with the end product. Where substantive results are mentioned it is usually to illustrate a point of technique.

The book is therefore a beginning in a second sense also. I hope that it will prove useful to those who are drawn to the study of the recent past, who are attracted by the vast bulk of information available about nineteenth-century society and its fascinating detail, and who are impressed by the opportunity it affords to study social, economic and demographic structure and behaviour. The Victorian age was not the first period in English history of which it can be said that there remains written evidence about every man who then lived. That had been true of many English communities since just before Elizabeth's reign when parish registers first came to be kept. But in the Victorian age the volume of information compiled for every individual mounted fast. This is a challenge to historical imagination as much as to historical technique. When the challenge is successfully met we shall know much more than we do now about the nature of industrialisation, urbanisation and rapid social change, and the response of men and women to them.

1. The census, 1801–1891

M. Drake

> INCIDENT OF THE CENSUS. The following specimen of womanly assumption was given in one of the census returns not a hundred miles from College Street, Portsea:
> 'Jane – wife, head of the family, mangle woman
> John – husband, turns my mangle.'
>
> *Portsmouth Times*[1]

How much a government should know about its subjects has long been a matter of controversy. There is, therefore, nothing archaic about the altercation given below, between a supporter and an opponent of a bill to take an *annual* census of England and Wales, a bill that was hotly debated in the House of Commons in the spring of 1753.

[A census], it is said, can answer no purpose but that of an insignificant and vain curiosity, as if it were of no consequence for the legislature to know when to encourage and when to discourage or restrain the people of this island, or of some particular part of it, from going to settle in our American Colonies. Do gentlemen think, that it can be of no use to this society, or indeed to any society, to know when the number of its people increases or decreases; and when the latter appears to be the case, to enquire into the cause of it and to endeavour to employ a proper remedy...Even here at home do not we know, that both manufactures and the number of people have in late years decreased in some parts of the Kingdom? Would it not be of advantage to us to know, whether this affects the whole, or if it be only a removal from one part of the island to another?

George Grenville[2]

It has been said, Sir, that an authentic knowledge of the number of our people, and of their annual increase or decrease, will instruct us when to encourage, and when to restrain people from going to settle in our American Colonies. Sir, our going or not going to America does not depend upon the public encouragement or restraint, but upon the circumstances they are in at the time. Let the number of our people be never so much increased, those who can easily find the means of subsistance at home neither will go, nor ought we to encourage them to go to America: and let that number be never so much diminished, we ought not to restrain those from going thither who can find no way of subsisting at home...

William Thornton[3]

The depth of feeling on this, and other issues, is reflected in the fact that at the Committee stage of the bill every single clause was debated and there were many divisions.[4] Nevertheless the bill passed the House of Commons, only to be rejected by the Lords.[5]

The question of a census does not appear to have been raised seriously again until the closing years of the eighteenth century. The controversy at that time as to whether or not the population of the country was rising, together with the suffering associated with the harvest failure of 1795 were no doubt important factors in providing a climate of opinion favourable to a census. However, the more immediate steps leading to the first census appear to have been taken rather casually by John Rickman.

In 1796, while Rickman was still in obscurity at Barton, (he was living in his father's house near Christchurch), he wrote a paper entitled 'Thoughts on the Utility and Facility of a general Enumeration of the People of the British Empire', extracts from which are given in the memoir by W. C. Rickman (in the *Gentleman's Magazine*). These extracts set forth in a very dry manner, the economic advantages of ascertaining the number of the population, the probability of its being far higher than the usual estimate, and the facility of arithmetically deducing it from the parish registers. This paper was communicated by Mr (afterwards Sir George) Rose, the Member for Christchurch, to Charles Abbot, the future Speaker, who was also interested in the subject. Abbot introduced the Population Bill in 1800, and on its being passed offered to Rickman the supervision of the returns.[6]

It seems therefore that Rickman was the sponsor of the first census as well as its organiser. Certainly Rickman believed this to be the case. In a letter to the poet Southey, dated 27 October 1800, he writes, 'At my suggestion they have passed an Act of Parliament for ascertaining the population of Great Britain.'[7] It is a rather interesting coincidence that at this time when Rickman, still without a career, was residing in his father's house, Malthus, also as yet without a career, was living in his father's house not sixty miles away as the crow flies at Albury in Surrey,[8] preparing the occasion piece that was to make him the father of modern demographic studies.

The censuses which were taken at the beginning of each decade throughout the nineteenth century fulfilled a number of functions. The early ones, for instance, helped to boost morale during the struggle with France. *The Times* commented in 1811: 'These returns of increased population must afford high satisfaction to every patriotic mind as shewing that the radical resources of the country have not been affected by the war which has lasted so long.'[9] Later, however, they provided the opportunity for a wry self-mockery. Thus *The Times* in 1850 noted: 'If it is a privilege to be born, and another privilege to be born an Englishman, the human race may be congratulated on the large increase of the privileged members which it has witnessed during the last half century.'[10]

On occasion the census results were received with a sense of shock. Take for example this comment which appeared in *The Times* on the return of the 1891 census of Liverpool. 'Liverpool still heads the list as the second city in these Kingdoms so far as population goes, with a population of 617,116 (we presume that five, the first figure in the printed returns should be six)...'[11]

On the census office confirming that the figure five was not a misprint, 'Something like dismay' was caused amongst the members of the Liverpool Municipal Authority, 'for the figures' made a 'vast difference to the rate of mortality per thousand – making it over 27 instead of 23'.[12]

Just how wide of the mark 'informed' public opinion could be of population size is illustrated by *The Times* estimate on 18 June 1851 of the population of Ireland as not 'much over 8,000,000'.[13] On 4 July 1851, however, *The Times* had to report the 'painful but authentic communication...that the population of Ireland is at this moment very little more than six millions and a half.'[14] Thus, the report continued 'it appears that the aggregate population of these islands is only about a half a million more than it was ten years ago, and that instead of increasing at the rate of a thousand a day, as is generally supposed, we have only increased at the rate of a thousand a week...'[15]

A sense of surprise, if not of shock, was also manifested by an 1811 commentator who compared the populations of some London parishes with those of leading provincial towns. 'By such a reference' he noted, 'it will be seen that the inhabitants of Marylebone outnumber those of Birmingham by 5,000 souls; Shoreditch is equal to Bath; Bethnal Green to Nottingham; St Pancras has 10,000 more than Sheffield; Kensington is equal to Cambridge; St Giles contains only 1,200 fewer than Leeds; and Islington equals the population of Canterbury.'[16] Shocks like this only served to strengthen the desire for more precise information of population conditions. True, there were those who still felt that the census served 'the purposes rather of natural curiosity than public advantage'.[17] 'Masses of figures are by themselves of little profit, except to gratify the same curiosity which is pleased by reading the pages of a directory or almanack.'[18] However, the case for a periodical census as a legislative aid was never strongly challenged.

Two-thirds of the political measures introduced into either House of Parliament are argued either with especial reference to the numerical divisions of the population, or at least upon the assumption that these divisions have been ascertained with sufficient accuracy for the purposes of debate.[19]

For want of such information as the census yields [our ancestors] legislated in the dark, so that our chief business of late years has been, not to make laws but to un-make them.[20]

On the social bearing of such an investigation, it is hardly necessary to dwell; it is only by learning what, as a people, we have been doing that we can learn what remains for us as a people to do. The command of data is the one circumstance which separates our legislation from the legislational code or mistaken principles which even great men were compelled to accept in former times. It was the opinion of Bacon that the plough should be kept in the hands of owners; in other words the farm should be infinitely small. It was the opinion of Johnson that population always progressed in a tolerably even ratio. It was a common belief in the eighteenth century that the number of a people constituted their wealth. It is now scarcely fifty years since Pitt supported a state provision for every labourer's child. It may be too much to say that we are guaranteed against similar or equal errors; but there is no doubt that in this case, as in others, knowledge is power, and that we acquire by our selfinquisition a larger grasp of the future.[21]

The only idea and object of such a roll-call is not that we may boast of our fecundity, which only the oriental views as in itself a subject for pride, nor that we may contrast the total of our bone and sinew with the resources of neighbouring peoples, but simply to acquire a series of facts which may illustrate the necessities and guide the legislation of a new lustrum.[22]

These arguments it will be noticed are in marked contrast with the points made by opponents of the census in 1753 who among other things asked: 'Can it be pretended that by the knowledge of our number, or our wealth, either can be increased?'[23] When, as happened with increasing frequency, members of the public urged the Government to extend the range of the census, they did so on the ground of its utility. For example, a correspondent in *The Times* in suggesting that those provisions of the Scottish census of 1861, designed to ascertain the number of rooms in each house, the number of persons in each family and whether the houses had or had not windows, should be included in the census of England and Wales for 1871, argued that the data were 'not only instructive but [had] given a great impulse to social and sanitary reform in [Glasgow and Edinburgh]'. He went on: 'If similar details were now given for every city and town and empire, and if they were continued every ten years, we should not only lay a solid basis for social science in regard to disease, pauperism and other evils, but we shall be able to compare one town with another, and from time to time the Kingdom with itself...'[24]

But it was not only the detailed results of the census that fascinated the Victorians; they appeared to be equally enthralled by the detailed mechanics of the operation itself. For as each census approached, the magnitude of the task the nation set itself was painstakingly presented to the public.

About 33,000 [enumeration books] of various sizes, each capable of holding from 400 to 3,000 names have been sent out from the Central Office...In addition to these books and forms various other returns have been dispatched, among which may be mentioned 100,000 special schedules for vessels, 1,200 enumeration books for the large institutions, and 3,000 special schedules for the small institutions of the country, 300 enumeration books for the Royal Navy, 33,000 instruction and memorandum books for the use of enumerators themselves. The weight of all these documents exceeds 55 tons. Before the 6,500,000 weekly executed household schedules – with which the public are now familiar – left the printers (Messrs Ford and Pilt of Long Acre), each of them passed through nine distinct processes – viz. printing (two at once), cutting in half, folding, tying, counting once, cutting again, checking twice, pressing with 150 tons of pressure and packing. The printed circular letters and elaborate books of instruction recently issued to various local offices, in order to set the gigantic local machinery successfully in motion, already number about 80 different kinds.[25]

Once it was agreed that a periodic census was desirable, the question of what it should cover became a major issue and one which led to considerable debate throughout the century. The early censuses, from 1801–31 were organised by John Rickman at the centre and carried out by overseers of the poor and the clergy in the various English parishes and by schoolmasters in Scotland. Rickman had a particularly low opinion of the overseers of the poor, who were responsible for the enumerated information; the clergy being responsible for making returns of baptisms, marriages, and burials. Writing to his friend Thomas Poole in 1803 on a proposed inquiry into the poor, which was to be carried out by the overseers, Rickman noted 'You know, I have some experience in the gross amount of the dullness of all probable overseers and can the better provide accordingly; I wrote the schedule and questions at some length and have promised to superintend the printing upon which much depends.'[26] Because of his low regard for the overseers of the poor, Rickman was loath to put too many questions on the census schedule. During his time the schedules were changed somewhat from census to census but the amount of information they provided was meagre. Rickman's handling of the census was criticised on this count, and the 1841 census was organised on a very different basis. For the first time householders were required to provide information about each individual in their household, including names. This nominative mode of census taking was continued throughout the century, although alterations to the schedule itself were relatively modest. Such a conservative approach was the subject of much criticism each time the census was debated and many suggestions were made as to how its scope could be widened. A list of rejected suggestions makes interesting reading.

Those in the abortive census Bill of 1753 included 'an annual account of the total number of people and of the total number of marriages, births and deaths; and also of the total number of poor receiving alms from every parish and extra-parochial place in Great Britain'.[27] In 1841 an attempt was made to obtain a valuation of property.[28] In 1851 it was proposed 'to collect some statistics of the labour market by taking down the rate of wages during the preceeding week and year in each locality, and to distinguish the infirm and the sick from the healthy members of the community...a column to mark the presence or absence of rudimentary education, and a column for the average price of provisions, which vary incredibly in the country districts would also seem to suggest themselves'.[29] It was also suggested that the census should include detailed agricultural returns, it being pointed out that 'such returns were collected under every government in Europe except those of Turkey and Russia'.[30] This suggestion for an agricultural census was included in a list of suggestions by the Statistical Society in 1860.[31] Among other suggestions of the Society was that information should be collected 'respecting the incomes of charitable and beneficent societies and institutions, such as exist in nearly every parish and in connection with every place of worship'.[32] A motion to instruct enumerators to ascertain the number of persons who could read or write was negatived in 1860, on the grounds that 'the information which would be obtained...would not compensate for the expense of obtaining it'[33] – an argument used not infrequently.[34]

An indication of how narrowly some proposals were defeated is given by the fate of a motion put in 1870 to include in the 1871 census of England and Wales a clause which had appeared in the 1861 census of Scotland, requiring house-holders to give details of their accommodation. It was argued in support of the motion (which was opposed by the Government) that the information supplied would act as 'a basis for future legislation, and as an incentive to local authorities and owners of house property to remedy the defects in the house accommodation of so large a proportion of our labouring classes', since it was 'estimated that the provision of adequate house accommodation would in many over-crowded districts lower the present average mortality by 10 to 25 per cent'. The motion was defeated in the Commons by the narrowest of margins: 56 to 57 at 2 a.m. on 22 July 1870.[35] The motion was brought in again at the Report stage, when the Government pointed out that it was 'useless' since 'under the Act of 1866 it was the duty of local authorities to procure information and prevent overcrowding, and sanitary reform would not be assisted by the inquiry which would cost £15,000'. This time the voting was 45 in favour of the motion and 60 against.[36]

Also in 1870 the Statistical Society suggested that 'the census of the following year should include an account of the number of industrial establishments of various kinds; the number, sex, and age of persons employed in them, dis-tinguishing masters from men, and the agents employed in the several processes of production – viz., animals, tools, machines, vessels; as well as information concerning the capital employed, wages paid, etc.'[37] It also wanted enquiries on religious, educational and housing conditions. In the debate on 26 July 1870, Sir J. Lubbock proposed that the census include a query of 'persons married to first cousins', since it was of great social importance to ascertain the number of consanguineous marriages and the result on the health of their offspring.[38] The motion was defeated by 92 votes to 45.[39]

In 1880 the National Association for the Promotion of Social Science, made a number of recommendations regarding the census of 1881. One was that the same questions should be asked 'as far as practicable' in all the various parts of the United Kingdom. These should include a statement on the householders' schedule of the religious persuasion of each inhabitant. The schedule should also include a column for 'sickness' or 'injury'. There should also be a 'return of the number of rooms in each house'. Houses intended for habitation should be distinguished from those not intended for this purpose. Further there should be a return of houses intended for habitation which were unlet. The occupational query should be 'amended in order to show the nature of the employment with greater precision'. There was also an interesting request that 'for every city and town the concentrated population and the area which it occupies should be returned, whether its boundaries be coincident or not with any legally defined boundary or boundaries'. Finally the Association asked that the census be quinquennial rather than decennial.[40]

This last demand was made repeatedly from 1880 onwards. In a leading article on the matter, The Times noted in 1880, that 'the Austrian Empire takes a fresh census every six years, France and Italy every five, Germany and Spain every three'.[41] A strong argument in favour of a quinquennial census was that an accurate population figure was required in order to calculate the death rate – 'practically...our sole measure of the health of a district'.[42] An article in the *Lancet* as early as 1871 contained the information that, using estimates of the population of Aberdeen, the crude death rate in 1871 was reckoned to be 32 per 1,000. The census of that year revealed, however, that the town had a population of 88,000 not 76,000 as had been thought. Hence the death rate was only 28 per 1,000.[43] A similar error was noted for Birmingham where the population was 10 per cent *less* than estimated.[44] On the other hand as the Registrar-General pointed out, 'the population of London estimated in the weekly tables, for the middle of the year 1871 was 3,258,469. The population enumerated on 2 April 1871 was 3,251,874. Calculated for that Sunday night, the estimate by the same method was 3,247,631 which differs only 4,173 from the enumerated population. This slight difference will not affect the rate of mortality which, as given for all London since 1861, may be considered correct...'[45] As noted below, however, not such a happy result emerged in 1891. In fact, as was remarked in 1880, so far as most large towns were concerned, the census figure was only accurate within three or four years of the census itself.[46] The calculation of death rates in smaller areas within cities was even more liable to error.[47] The 1881 census revealed that estimates based on the 1871 returns of the population of some of the largest towns in the country 'were wide of the mark by between 11 and 18 per cent'.[48] The Registrar-General in fact ceased publishing estimates of the size of some fifty smaller towns because of the degree of error involved.[49] *The Times* observed:

The purposes, political, social, sanitary, educational, physical, industrial, for which exact and detailed population statistics are required have vastly increased in number and complexity during the 87 years that have witnessed our eight decennial censuses. Altogether the rate at which we live and work nowadays is so much more rapid than it was in the infancy of the century that a census of the population taken more frequently than ten years seems an absolute necessity, if a census is a necessity at all.[50]

The census of 1891 showed that the total estimated population of the twenty-eight largest towns – at 10 millions – was as much as 600,000 too high. The most marked differences were (estimated populations in each case given first), London, 4,493,000–4,221,000: Brighton, 126,000–116,000: Portsmouth, 145,000–160,000: Nottingham, 252,000–213,000: Salford, 251,000–199,000.[51] All in all, there were seventeen large towns where the estimated populations were higher than the actual and as a correspondent to *The Times* noted they had all 'been credited in recent years with death rates more or less below the truth and to that extent have been living in a fool's paradise'.[52] Again, in 1900, the real death rate in Burnley was 3·8 per 1,000 higher than that based on the estimated population, while in Southampton it was 2·4 per 1,000 lower.[53]

The gap between estimated and actual populations could cause problems in other directions too. For instance, in January 1901 'Eastbourne invited applications from investors for a corporation stock, which, on the faith of the official figures showing the estimated population to be in excess of 50,000 was described as a trustee security (under the Trustee Act of 1893). The publication of the census of 1901 showed the population to be considerably less than 50,000 – a source of much embarrassment no doubt to the town's officials.'[54]

Among other proposals for additional queries was one designed to elicit the amount of industrial sickness in the country by putting the question 'If a wage-earner, were you yesterday (or "on the date of the census") prevented by actual bodily sickness from earning a wage?' Such an enquiry it was argued would produce 'an approximation to the true average of industrial sickness unobtainable by any other conceivable method and gain a safer basis for calculating exact rates of insurance (whether local or general, individual or national) against want in sickness'.[55]

On 11 December 1888, perhaps one of the most distinguished deputations to approach the Government on the question of the census waited upon Mr Goschen, the Chancellor of the Exchequer. It included several MPs, as well as Charles Booth and Professor Alfred Marshall. The deputation urged the taking of a quinquennial census and 'the importance of having an occupation census of a genuine character'. Goschen, who had been President of the Statistical Society, was sympathetic but he urged on the deputation that additional queries were expensive. It had been argued earlier that each additional enquiry increased the cost of the actual taking of the census by £6,000.[56] Goschen also pointed out that the 'Registrar-General held that a great subdivision in an occupation census did not lead to accuracy but to inaccuracy, and that he had less confidence than the deputation in either the willingness or the capacity of people to answer the questions that would be put to them'. 'There certainly would not be the same keen desire', he alleged, 'on the part of the great bulk of the public to give information as there was on the part of the statisticians to obtain it.'[57] *The Times* ruefully remarked: 'What a flood of light would be thrown on the condition of the people if a band of workers were to do for all our cities what Mr Booth had done in papers read before the Statistical Society, for Hackney, Tower Hamlets and the East End of London generally.'[58]

The deputation did have one effect: the setting up of a Treasury Committee, the first departmental committee on the census. Charles Booth was a member.[59] Its report was published in the summer of 1890. It recommended that a census should be held midway between decennial censuses, confined to the number, age, sex and distribution of the population. It also urged that there be a reduction in the type of areas for which the enumeration was tabulated; that a permanent census office be set up; that census clerks be appointed by open competition; that special attention be paid to the selection of enumerators; that in the householder's schedule persons should be returned as employers, employees or neither; that the term 'rank' be omitted from the columns hitherto provided for 'rank, profession and occupation'; that persons following no occupation but deriving an income from property and other sources of a permanent character should be returned as such and separately tabulated in the published report. Among the matters referred for further consideration were several administrative changes, one being the 'use of mechanical appliances to aid the work of tabulation'. This was a reference to the Hollerith process first used by the United States census in 1890. Hollerith had written to the committee offering to pay the travelling expenses if someone would come to examine his process. The invitation does not appear to have been taken up at the time. The Committee also asked for more information on industrial status, and 'the inclusion in the published reports of any instructions to enumerators likely to throw light on the statistics obtained'.[60]

From the Committee's point of view, these labours bore little fruit. For although in 1891 'the only new question to be put [was] one recommended by the Census Committee, namely where the occupier was in occupation of less than five rooms, the number of rooms occupied by him was to be ascertained',[61] its other recommendations were ignored, except for the minor one that 'rank' was omitted from the householder's schedule.[62] In Scotland a new enquiry was introduced as to whether one spoke Gaelic only or both Gaelic and English.[63]

The century closed with plans being laid for the 1901 census. *The Times* reported: 'We are afraid whatever proposals are made, statistical experts will be profoundly disappointed. It is almost a certainty that a list of the reforms for which they had been pressing will not be carried out. On this matter, public opinion has not been educated, and the official view is, broadly speaking, that the less information is given the better.'[64] *The Times* went on to give the reasons for the conservatism of the authorities. 'Chief among these reasons is cost – figures which are worth much cost much; next comes the necessity of obtaining returns expeditiously; and thirdly, there is liability to error which increases in a geometrical ratio with the increase of detail.'[65]

Of all the various 'might have beens', the enquiry which consumed most parliamentary and extra-parliamentary attention was undoubtedly the proposal for a religious census. This question is an intriguing one because it had such wide ramifications. The core of the matter, of course, was the relationship between the Anglicans and the Nonconformists. But one should not neglect its impact upon party political behaviour and the constitutional position of the Government. The subject was consequently surrounded with controversy from the start. Action commenced in 1851. Under the Census Act of 13th and 14th Victoria, Chapter 53, the Secretary of State for Home Affairs was given the power to ask for 'information required for the purpose of the Act'. He was bound to issue instructions for the purpose of obtaining this information and could 'inflict penalties on persons who either made false returns or neglected to make them'. Under these powers the Secretary of State asked for detailed educational returns from every headmaster in the country, an inquiry which Lord Stanley 'conceived to be...of the most inquisitorial character and altogether unjustifiable in point of principle;' for enquiries were to be made as to the pay of masters and assistants and their hours of work! There were also questions on religious matters. Critics were quick to note that here there was a difference between the particulars required from the Church of England and those required from the Dissenters.[66] For example, 'the Church of England was asked the number of her free sittings. The Dissenters were only asked the amount of standing room'.[67] Initially, however, the main attack was on the constitutional issue: 'that when a Secretary of State received authority for a specific purpose he should [not] be permitted to strain that authority'.[68]

The Government conceded that on these matters 'there were considerable legal doubts if the penalties of the Act could be enforced for refusing to give information'.[69] Nevertheless, they were still keen that the questions be asked. However, it was argued that if no penalty was involved, returns would be only partial and therefore 'of no practical use'.[70] The veteran statistician Lord Brougham refused to accept this argument, pointing out that 'the returns that were obtained in 1818 from schoolmasters and clergymen on the subject of education...contained a vast mass of valuable statistical details...upon which the Educational Committee was afterwards founded'.[71]

Some Anglican clergy carried their opposition to the religious census to the eleventh hour and beyond. For on 27 March, that is after the census forms had been delivered, the Bishop of Oxford presented a petition from a body of clergy in his diocese 'complaining of their being called upon to answer certain questions issued from the Registrar-General's office'. This petition laid great emphasis on the inevitably inaccurate nature of the census: the Bishop citing Canning's dictum that 'nothing was so fallacious as facts except statistics'.[72] Earl Granville speaking for the Government, said that the Registrar-General had now distinctly informed the public that replies to the queries could not be enforced by any legal obligations.[73] This was as far as the Government was prepared to go. It would certainly not meet the Bishop's request to withdraw the enquiry, and he commented 'if all other bodies of persons in the State, except the clergy, returned the information which was required from them, it would not redound to the credit of the latter'.[74] Earl Fitzwilliam added, no doubt with tongue in cheek, that 'clergymen ought not to be called upon to state the number of persons attending their Churches, that being a point on which it would be better for them to be ignorant than well informed in some cases'.[75]

In a leading article *The Times* attacked the negative approach to the census of the Bishop of Oxford, noting that 'there is no concealment without a motive'. The view that many clergy would refuse to fill up the forms, because no penalty was involved, which was implied by the Bishop, was countered by *The Times* on the grounds that 'they had received assurances from sources on which we can place confidence that great numbers of the *working* clergy have expressed their perfect willingness to comply with the wishes of the Government'. *The Times* added that 'all the Dissenting bodies are promoting the return in the most creditable manner'.[76]

The religious census was taken and whatever its shortcomings, which were considerable, they do not appear to be ascribable to gross negligence on the part of the clergy of the Church of England. However, in the Bill for the 1861 census, a clause appeared in the householder's schedule requiring all individuals to state their religion – under penalty. Both the question itself and the sanction were strongly opposed by the Nonconformists. This was hardly surprising for the 1851 census of religion had been in essence a census of attendance at a religious service on census Sunday. The result had been a very happy one for the Nonconformists as the attendance at their services had been almost as high as that at the Church of England services. They were, therefore, always happy to repeat this form of census. A census of religious persuasion, however, was likely to produce a much less favourable result for the Nonconformists as the great mass of people who did not attend religious services were as likely as not to profess themselves to be members of the Church of England.

Opposition to a census of religious persuasion, as opposed to one of attendance at a religious service, went a stage further at a meeting of 'about a dozen Members of Parliament and several leading Nonconformist ministers' chaired by Sir M. Peto in June 1860. This meeting passed a motion to the effect that the 'proposal to compel by means of a penalty, a statement of the "religious profession" of every inhabitant of the country is regarded...as an unwarrantable exercise of authority, and as repugnant to the spirit of modern legislation'. The meeting concluded that the proposal was intended 'to further the designs of an ecclesiastical party who seek to cast discredit on the census of 1851'.[77] The group then took the matter to Parliament and presented a memorial to Lord Palmerston on 30 June 1860 signed by no less than 167 Members of the House of Commons, all of whom belonged to the Liberal Party, asking him to withdraw the enquiry.[78] At the Committee stage of the Bill, Baines the prominent Nonconformist Member for Leeds, attacked clause 4, which required householders to state their religion, noting that many petitions against it had been received from Dissenting bodies throughout the country. He deemed it 'a duty to resist an authoritative demand on the part of the Government upon a point which they regarded as beyond the legitimate scope of civil interference'.[79] Baines went on to summarise the results of the 1851 census noting that the number of seats in the Church of England was given as 5,317,915 and in the Chapels of the Dissenting denominations, 4,894,648. The estimated attendance on the census Sunday in the Church of England was 3,773,474 and in the Chapels belonging to other denominations, 3,487,578, 'the attendance in each case bearing to the Church accommodation as near as possible to the proportion of 71 per cent'. A census conducted on these lines in 1861 would, he argued, 'be of use to the statesman and most of all the philanthropists and men of religion'. He ended by noting that 'between 1831 and 1851, there was an increase in population in England and

Wales of 27 per cent and of accommodation for religious worship of 42 per cent.'[80]

Although the Government spokesman, Sir G. C. Lewis urged that a census of religious persuasion should be taken, remarking that the query was included in the censuses of most civilised countries, he agreed to withdraw the proposal on account of Nonconformist pressure.[81]

Supporters of the established Church were not unnaturally enraged at the Government decision to bow before the storm created by the Nonconformists. And indeed there was a great deal of opportunism hidden behind the high-flown sentiments of the Dissenting spokesmen. As Lord R. Cecil pointed out, one hadn't heard much about the 'impropriety of examining into religious opinions' in 1851 'when it was proposed to frame the census upon a plan which it was thought might be favourable to the religious body which has the greatest political organisation, and could apply the sharpest whip to its members'.[82] He was glad the Dissenters had been exposed, for it could now be seen that 'it was Churchmen who wished for facts, and the Dissenters who did not'. He also observed that 'ever since the census of 1851 was published it had been made the basis of reproaches against the Church of England, and attempts to undermine her position as an Establishment'.[83]

Cecil, however, went further than this, alleging fraud on the part of the Dissenters in 1851. He remarked for instance:

In many cases the congregations of Dissenting Chapels were returned at larger numbers than the buildings would hold. At Bradford the Wesleyan Reformers had a Chapel capable of holding 810 persons. The number returned as attending religious worship was 1,061 in the morning, 1,483 in the evening. At Halifax the Chapel would hold 400 persons; the numbers returned were 460 in the morning, 526 in the evening. At Leeds the Chapel would contain 200; the numbers returned were 650 in the morning, 723 in the afternoon, and 1,030 in the evening. A Right Rev. Prelate, whose impartiality was well known, and who entertained no strong views upon religious questions [sic] stated in the other House that in his diocese Sunday school children had been driven from Chapel to Chapel at various times of the day, and that when two or three denominations had each a Chapel they clubbed their congregations at different services so that all three might count for each.[84]

The issue at stake between the Anglicans and the Dissenters had, of course, strong financial implications – which were brought out in the debates. For example, the annual grants for education were dependent upon the number of Dissenters and Anglicans in the populations. Also when such a matter as Church rates came up, it was convenient for the Dissenters to draw upon the findings of the 1851 census to support their argument that the Church of England was only a sect. The fact that 80 per cent of the marriages of the country took place in the Church of England and that 78 per cent of school children were in establishments run by the Church, might be thought to demolish this argument, but the Anglicans realised that a census of religious persuasion would strengthen their position still further.[85]

The question of a census of religious persuasion was brought up yet again in the debate on the census Bill for 1871. At the Committee stage an amendment to this effect was defeated by thirteen votes (the voting being 77 to 90).[86] On the Bill going to the Lords, however, this voting was reversed (43 to 39).[87] The Bill was then returned to the Commons which again refused to have a census of religious persuasion, this time by a larger majority, the voting being 101 to 40. On the Bill being returned to the Lords 'the Earl Morley moved that their lordships should not insist on their amendment to this Bill as to a religious census, the Commons having disagreed to it'.[88] His motion was accepted.

In 1880 the Government sponsor of the census Bill in the House of Lords, Viscount Enfield, rejected a religious census on the by this time familiar grounds (he also opposed 'an enquiry as to wages [as it] would be resented by the working classes who might think it a prelude to additional taxation' as well as an enquiry into sickness and injury as 'it would be of little value two years after a date to know who were or who were not in good health on a certain day').[89]

Viscount Cranbrook regretted that no religious census was being taken, noting: 'If it came to impertinent questions, it seemed to him, at all events much less impertinent to ask a man of what religion he was than to ask him whether he was insane or an imbecile.'[90] The religious question led to yet another division in the House of Commons. On the Committee stage a motion which proposed to amend the Bill to allow a census of religious persuasion was defeated by 97 votes to 20.[91] When the issue was again debated in 1890, the voting was, on the Committee stage, 288 to 69; a majority of 219 being thus against a religious census.[92]

The failure to get a national census of religious persuasion was partly made good by a variety of local censuses.[93] The development of partial censuses, on particular issues or areas, was a feature of the later nineteenth century. For instance, censuses of the population of prisons were taken in 1862 and 1873.[94] One of the most interesting of these extra-census counts was the day census carried out on a number of occasions by the City of London. The origin of this seems to have been the rather childish desire on the part of the City authorities to show that, although the resident population of the City had fallen from 157,000 in 1801 to 112,000 in 1861 and to 53,000 in 1881, this did not mean that the City was declining in importance. It was, of course, the first modern city to experience the by now commonplace movement of people to the suburbs as commerce pushed up land values in the city centre.

The first of these day censuses in 1866 showed that some 509,611 people entered the City on census day as clients and customers, whilst there were 170,133 merchants, shopmen and clerks or other people engaged in warehouses and shops. This compared with a resident population of only 74,732.[95] On 25 April 1881, between 5 a.m. and 5 p.m. some 589,468 persons entered the City on foot or in vehicles. This was an increase of 39,855 over the number entering between 6 a.m. and 6 p.m. on census day in 1876. Over the period 5 a.m. to 9 p.m. the number entering the yCit in 1881 was 739,640 and over the same period in 1876, 679,744.[96] During the hours 5 a.m. to 9 p.m. on census day in 1881, 71,893 vehicles of all kinds entered the City, '10,733 being credited to London Bridge alone'. Twelve railway stations brought in 176,009 passengers.[97]

The Times report of the day census of 27 April 1891 and of the vehicular census of 4 May 1891, reads as follows:

Nearly 800 enumerators were employed. The total number of 'employers' and 'employed' in 1881 was 261,061 and in 1891 it was 301,381, an increase of 40,320. The number of women engaged in the City during the day was 50,416 against 44,179 in 1881 and the number of children under 15 years of age 21,305 against 19,235. A census of the street traffic taken on 4 May for a period of 24 hours shows that 1,121,708 persons entered the City at 80 different points on foot or in vehicles, against 797,563 in 1881. The number of vehicles entering the City in the same time was 92,488 as against 71,893 in 1881. On the same day 52,413 persons came into the City to Liverpool Street Station, as against 33,890 in 1881; through Broad Street there came 43,042 as against 30,444 in 1881, and through the Metropolitan Railway at Bishopgate, 13,180 as against 9,325 in 1881. In the taking of this census 36,568 forms were used and the cost has been over £1,200.[98]

Having examined the role and scope of the nineteenth-century censuses it is now appropriate to turn to the most important feature of all: their accuracy. The value of any census very much depends upon the extent to which errors arising from the collection and processing of the data are minimised. The possibilities of error are enormous.[99]

In assessing the accuracy of any census one's first enquiry must be of the people who were being counted. Were they cooperative or suspicious? In the debate of 1753 much play was made by opponents of the census Bill of the alleged unwillingness of the population to be counted. For example, William Thornton, chief opponent of the Bill, expressed himself as follows:

As to myself, I hold this project to be totally subversive of the last remains of English liberty, and therefore, though it should pass into law, I should think myself under the highest of all obligations to oppose its execution. If any officer, by whatever authority should demand of me an account of the number and circumstances of my family, I would refuse it; and if he persisted in the affront, I would order my servants to give him the discipline of the horse-pond; nor would I fail to exert every faculty and power of my body and mind, all the influence which I derive from my fortune, or my attachments, to produce the same opposition in my neighbours, my tenants, and my friends.[100]

There is very little evidence in fact that many members of any social group did what William Thornton said he would do in the event of a census, though there are one or two examples recorded in the nineteenth-century press. Thus a 'Captain —— of —— Regency Square, Brighton' refused to co-operate with the enumerator of the 1841 census. He got a summons against him which the Captain's servant 'took up and threw...into the square'.[101] At the same census a case was heard at Marylebone Police Court concerning an 'elderly lady...who, instead of filling up the paper properly, had, at the bottom of the column in which her age should have been inserted, drawn with a pencil a human head and written against it the word "guess" '.[102]

Court cases arising from the census were however extremely rare in the nineteenth century. But this, of course, does not mean that everyone complied with the census law. There were many stages between overt defiance of the law on the one hand and following it to the letter on the other. *A priori* there were many reasons for not complying with the law. For example in both 1801 and 1811, the fear that the census was a prelude to 'some capitation tax or conscription' can hardly be said to have been unfounded.[103] 'Prejudice and ignorance' remained throughout the century. As J. A. Baines remarked in a paper before the Royal Statistical Society in February, 1900, 'as to ignorance which could not appreciate what was wanted in the return or which did not possess the information, all that need be said was that "custom cannot stale its infinite variety" '.[104]

No doubt the extent of prejudice and ignorance can be exaggerated, although now it is impossible to know to what extent. How, for instance, can one assess the value of a report from Ireland in 1841 that 'the census inspired such feelings of alarm on Sunday night the 6th inst. in the counties of Limerick and Clare, that the whole country was illuminated, hill and valley, with lighted firebrands. In the county of Westmeath there was scarcely a head of poultry left alive, an opinion having gone abroad that a tax or rate was to be levied upon them.'[105]

Another possible source of underenumeration was referred to in correspondence appearing in *The Times* in 1891. This concerned an allegation by a clergyman in 'one of the poorest and worst' parishes of the East End of London that in 1881 there were many instances of 'absolutely incorrect returns' made 'in order to avoid subsequent disagreeable proceedings ... for "over-crowding"... one house of six rooms [was] returned in the census paper as having eighteen residents, whereas there were in fact twenty-eight. Another with twenty-two inhabitants was returned as ten'.[106]

A similar distortion of the returns was alleged to have occurred in the 1891 census as a result of the query on the Welsh language. Many more people, it was said, returned themselves as 'monoglot Welsh and duoglot Welsh' than was in fact the case because in the Press 'attention was incessantly called to our responsibility as a nation, and to the approaching opportunity of doing an invaluable act of kindness to the Celtic race'.[107]

Inability to recall one's precise age for the purposes of the census was common throughout the nineteenth century, in Britain as in other countries. Indeed the Report of the 1891 census went so far as to say that 'not improbably the greater proportion of adults' did not know their precise age, and therefore gave an approximation, often in some multiple of ten.[108] In general this tendency does not appear to have been more common amongst one sex than another, although some women in their late teens overstated their age somewhat to bring it over

21. The alleged tendency of women over a certain age to understate it for reasons of vanity does not appear to be borne out by the statistics, despite the report of a French official who 'had taken down the age of every female that appeared at his Bureau, and, on one of them declaring herself thirty-five, started back with amazement, saying that 17,000 women had given him their ages and he had never yet seen a woman of thirty-five'.[109]

One indication of the degree of co-operation expected from the public is to be found in the preparations – which were laudably painstaking – for the census of 1841. On 15 April 1841 the Commissioners of the Census sent a circular to the 125 metropolitan registrars asking if they thought it 'absolutely requisite' that a policeman accompany the enumerators on the day of the census. In only fifteen instances was the assistance of the police thought necessary or desirable. A similar circular to the superintendent registrars of Manchester, Birmingham, Liverpool and Bristol, and two or three other provincial districts elicited the same sort of response.[110] The Commissioner of Police acting under the orders of the Government, agreed to provide an escort in London. In the event, 'in most of the parishes in and around the metropolis very little difficulty', it was reported, 'was experienced by the enumerators in obtaining the popular returns, with the exception of certain portions inhabited by the lower orders'.[111] A disgruntled enumerator, complaining that he had not been paid and perhaps, therefore, not too reliable a witness alleged, however, that 'the duties in some parts of the districts of Whitechapel, Spitalfields, Bethnal Green, St Giles, Westminster, etc., were...anything but enviable'.[112] Outside London little difficulty was reported in getting the household returns.[113]

It would appear likely that as, with the passage of time, the census became a familiar institution, and as general standards of education rose, its accuracy would improve. Some evidence to support this comes from comments made in 1851 by enumerators who had carried out both the census of that year, and also that of 1841. In London and the large towns it was noted that fewer 'operatives' had to appeal to their neighbours for assistance in filling in the schedules. It was also remarked that 'a large number of the schedules were filled in by the sons and daughters of the people with whom they were left', and that 'generally among the labouring class it was by the care of the women that the required information was secured'. One registrar in particular stated that his enumerators 'noticed that they had not much of the "rough work" which they had to perform in 1841'.[114]

The Census Commissioners were, naturally, well aware of the need to maintain the public's confidence in the census and were quick to investigate any irregularities, especially, of course, complaints that forms had not been left at particular houses. At every census the Registrar-General had to apologise for or explain why mistakes had occurred. Naturally, when reports appeared in the press that houses in such prominent places as Grosvenor Square,[115] Peckham-Rye (this one with 'a frontage of 200 feet to a main rural road and that on an omnibus route!'),[116] and Victoria Street,[117] were missed, the anti-census lobby had a field day.

The Census Commissioners also used every means they could to give publicity to the census. Increasingly, newspapers were important here. But the Church of England clergy also were asked – tactfully, through their bishops[118] – to encourage their flocks to co-operate. In 1881 the Bishop of Lincoln not only authorised the use of appropriate psalms (20, 33, 39, 90) and Lessons (Deuteronomy vii, viii, xxii to xxxii; St Matthew xiv, xxv), but also issued a special collect for use on the Sunday before census day.[119]

In 1901, the Board of Education issued

a circular inviting the co-operation of managers and teachers of the public elementary schools throughout England and Wales in the coming census...The circular [stated] that an event of such national importance [might] properly form a subject of special lessons and lectures in the Government day schools and these lessons in the case of older children [might] be turned to the practical advantage of the state in ensuring the accurate filling up of the census schedule in the families to which they [belonged]. The suggested instructions it [was] added [might] also be usefully extended to the scholars in the evening continuation schools'.[120]

To help the enumerators still further, the Census Commissioners tried to get local authorities to adopt a more rational numbering of houses. The complete absence of planning in the construction of most towns produced by the industrial and commercial developments of the nineteenth century, created some quite chaotic numbering systems. The following is perhaps one of the most remarkable examples.

There are many towns containing long lines of cottage streets, formed by the gradual coalescence of buildings erected by several small proprietors; and in such streets it is not uncommon for each proprietor to give his little road a distinctive name and to number the houses it contains from one upwards, without the smallest regard to the numbers in the vicinity! In Nottingham there was formerly a long street which was said to repeat its numbers up to three no less than thirty times, and which was the despair of relieving officers and parish doctors. A resident there would give his address as 'the fifth number three on the right hand side as you go up', for such names as 'Matilda-Place' or 'Eliza Cottages' had long been swept away.[121]

Although, as I have argued, the success of a census depended ultimately on the co-operation of the public, hardly less important was the efficiency of the enumerator. For the first four censuses, the enumerators were picked by the overseers of the poor, who were the local officers responsible for seeing that the census law was followed. Little appears to be known about how they carried out their assignment, apart from the fact that they did so in a variety of ways. There was little or no guidance from the central authorities. Evidence of the greater or lesser degree to which these officers attended to their duties is to be found in the fact that some areas made their returns far ahead of others. For example, up to 26 June 1801 complete returns were in the hands of central authorities from only fourteen English counties, and two Welsh counties. Several hundred returns were still awaited from other counties.[122] As late as 23 April 1802 no returns had been received from 'two of the remote counties' of Scotland,[123] although they should have been made by 10 November of the previous year.[124]

Rickman, in evidence before the Select Committee on the Census Bill in 1830, said that the overseers of the poor were 'not educated men' but that they could answer 'plain questions with much sincerity'. The danger of asking more involved questions was that one would incur the risk of 'retrograding instead of advancing in knowledge; that is, of arriving at misinformation instead of resting in acknowledged ignorance'.[125] In this Rickman was confirming what the opponents of the 1753 census Bill had said, namely that to ask the overseers of the poor to take an account of the population in writing could be an 'extreme cruelty' as it was 'well known, that in this Kingdom, many hundreds are annually elected to that office, who are so far from being able to write, that they cannot read; neither can they always afford to pay those who can'.[126] Rickman did, however, make one point in favour of the overseers of the poor being responsible for taking the census: this being that '(especially in the southern counties) from the poor relief system, the overseers of the poor...being officially cognisant of every individual and the number of children of every individual, who from poverty and consequent obscurity may be supposed often to escape particular notice in other nations',[127] they were better qualified than more highly educated men might have been.

Local variation in the taking of the early censuses is also indicated by the returns made to a circular issued by the Census Commissioners in 1841 to superintendent registrars, in which the latter were asked to find out the cost of the 1831 census in their area. Although 618 circulars were sent out, only 288 returns were received 'and of these the greater portion were confessedly imperfect'.[128] The reasons given for the failure to make returns were that in many cases parish accounts had been destroyed. However, from the other returns it appears that enumerators were sometimes paid in cash, sometimes with a dinner, whilst elsewhere they provided their services voluntarily.[129]

The crucial role of the enumerator was obviously in the forefront of the mind of T. H. Lister, the Registrar-General who did the preliminary planning for the 1841 census. Lister, who took over from Rickman, changed the system of enumeration. He did this in several ways. First, he deemed it essential, in order to avoid duplication, that the census be taken in the shortest possible time, in one day or at most two.[130] Second, he believed it appropriate to use the 2,193 registration districts as the basis of the enumeration, partly because the population of each of these districts was required for the calculation of birth, marriage and death rates; partly, too, because he believed the majority of registrars were 'very efficient men...with scarcely an exception possessing all the intelligence requisite to perform such duties satisfactorily'.[131] Third, Lister recognised that if the census was to be taken over a short period he could not use the registrars as enumerators, partly because the areas they looked after were too

big, partly because 'many of them being medical men, cannot be required even for one day, to devote their *whole* time and attention to taking the census'.[132] Fourth, it follows from this that 'if the census is to be taken in a short time, the districts must be small, and the enumerators many, and therefore, perhaps in many instances, men of *very* moderate education'.[133] This meant, of course, that the details they had to record could only be simple and furthermore – and Lister was most insistent on this – all the work of 'abstraction, condensation, classification and arrangement' should be done at the centre.[134] 'To have abstracts made in the country,' he observed, 'to be afterwards sent up and used as the materials for other abstracts to be made in London, is only to divide and weaken responsibility, to make uniformity of system impossible, to increase the chance of error, and to lessen the means of correction'.[135] It was this last point, that is the possibility of checking the enumerators' work, that appears to have caused Lister to insist that the name of every individual should be entered on the schedules. 'The names should be written *at length*', as, he added, 'an enumerator may sit at home and make *marks* and no examiner could detect his errors'.[136] When the Census Commissioners came to advise the registrars on who they should choose as enumerators, they produced a thumb-nail sketch of the obviously ideal type.

He must be a person of intelligence and activity; he must read and write well, and have some knowledge of arithmetic; he must not be infirm or of such weak health as may render him unable to undergo the requisite exertion; he should not be younger than 18 years of age or older than 65; he must be temperate, orderly and respectable, and be such a person as is likely to conduct himself with strict propriety, and to deserve the goodwill of the inhabitants of his district. It would also be desirable that he should be well acquainted with the district in which he will be required to act; and it will be an additional recommendation if his occupations have been in any degree of a similar kind.[137]

Before the 1841 census was taken some 71 registrars 'presiding in all parts of England and Wales' were asked 'what number of persons of all ages in every thousand of the population in their respective districts might be found willing to fulfil for fair remuneration the duties of "enumerator"'.[138] The answers to this query are tabulated overleaf.

How successful were the Census Commissioners in recruiting suitable enumerators? Unfortunately, opinions vary widely. In 1860 *The Times* remarked in a leading article that many of the enumerators were 'no better than labourers in point of education'.[139] The following year, however, *The Times* reported that applicants for the post of enumerator in London were 'exceedingly numerous and instances occur in which clergymen, scripture readers and others, influenced by philanthropic motives have expressed a desire to enumerate districts, inhabited by the poorer classes'.[140] Of the 500 enumerators employed to take the 1861 census of Edinburgh, 300 were taken from the city's Volunteer Regiment who, at the suggestion of the Lord Mayor undertook the duty 'in order to band

B

*Estimated number of enumerators per 1,000 population**

From	3 registrars the answer was	1
	12	2
	8	2 or 3
	6	3
	2	3 or 4
	4	4
	1	4 or 5
	4	5
	1	5 or 6
	1	6
	2	6 to 8
	3	10
	1	10 to 12
	1	10 to 20
	1	30 to 40
	2	40
	18	Indefinite answers
	1	No answers

Total 71

* *History of the Census of 1841*, Library, General Register Office, CN.1.1, p. 17.

over the fees to the funds of the Regiment, an exception being made in the case of the artizan volunteers' who were allowed to deduct 10s of the 25s fee for loss of time.[141] In 1891, however, evidence given before the Committee on the Census appointed by the Treasury contained a most damning indictment of the quality of the average enumerator from Mr Ogle, the Superintendent of Statistics at the General Register Office.

Ogle had been closely involved with the census of 1881 so that his views must carry some weight. One hopes, however, that they need not be taken at their face value for he has scarcely a good word to say for any aspect of the census. The enumerators were 'on the whole rather a poor lot[142]...very unsatisfactory'[143] and 'their mere handwriting and the general aspect of their work showed that a great many of them were very illiterate men'.[144] As for the registrars who supervised them 'a very great deal' of their ordinary work was done 'very badly'[145] so one could not rely too much on them either. As for the clerks at the central office in 1881 'a very large proportion...turned out to be absolutely unfit for any work at all...it would [not] be possible to do the work at all satisfactorily with such a staff...as last time'.[146] Any move in the direction of a more elaborate schedule – as urged by Charles Booth – was given no chance of success by Ogle. 'The larger the number of questions that are asked, the less

accurately are the answers given' he said, and cited some damning evidence from Switzerland to prove his point.[147]

In their Report the Committee remarked that the appointment of enumerators was 'not always determined solely by reference to qualifications for the work'. Thus a master French polisher was appointed 'from motives of charity' and 'one unfortunate selection' was made when a registrar appointed 'a newspaper seller who used to sell newspapers at the starting point of the South Hackney omnibuses, and who lost a number of his schedules on the day of the census which led to great difficulty and inconvenience'.[148] We know no more than this about the newspaper seller, but in the evidence given to the Committee we learn something more of the French polisher and can therefore see his appointment in a wider context. This rather softens the impact the Committee no doubt intended to convey in its brief mention of him. It appears that he was appointed by the registrar of Clerkenwell, who in all appointed ten enumerators and had about another half dozen applicants whom he decided not to take. Of these ten, eight were clerks, one was a house decorator and one the above-mentioned French polisher. All did their work satisfactorily. In the case of the French polisher, the registrar, Mr Tupper, said his work was 'well done', although he made some mistakes arising from the peculiar difficulties of his district. He also noted that when he appointed the French polisher he was aware that he had a son who was a clerk in an engineer's office and would help with the clerical work, the father being 'competent to do the distribution and collection'.[149]

Whether or not the central authorities' suspicion of the enumerators was well founded will only be discovered after the extensive investigation of enumerators' returns, which this book is intended to foster, has been made. What is certain is that the suspicions were ever present and that therefore the Census Commissioners did all they could to facilitate the enumerators' task. Thus in 1840 the Commissioners carried out a sample census partly to test the layout of the schedule and partly to find out how much work an enumerator could be expected to do in a day. Undoubtedly valuable lessons were learned from this. For example the last column of the sample schedule was headed 'Immigration'. The instructions for filling in this column were anything but easy to follow. Probably for this reason they make no appearance in the census itself.

In the *sixth* column, headed 'Immigration' should appear the 'name of the county' in which each individual was born, if it be not the same in which the party is now residing; the word 'county' if it be the same while yet the individual was born in another parish; 'an entire blank' if the parish and county of birth are both those of present residence; and the name of the country in which each individual was born if born abroad, specifying whether the party be an 'alien' or a British 'subject'. When the parish and county of birth are the same as that of residence, a specification of the fact need not be entered, since it can be presumed, and much repetition will be thereby avoided.[150]

The results of that part of the trial census designed to show how much work an enumerator could get through in 'one whole day from morning till night' are

given below. It will be seen that the sample covered a densely populated metropolitan area, two manufacturing districts, two country areas with 'average
density', a thinly populated rural district and a mining district (in that order).[151]

Superintendent Registrar's district in which trial census taken	Number of houses enumerated	Number of persons enumerated	Number of hours employed	Distance traversed
Westminster	47	430	8½	¼ mile
Birmingham	55	253	8½	Not stated
Leeds	152	636	10	Not stated
Isle of Wight	120	689	8	—
Isle of Wight	85	226	8½	4 miles out
Wycomb	—	—	—	Return missing
Machynlleth	38	200	10	12¾ miles
Truro	78	426	7½	Not stated

It was obvious from this trial census that some enumerators would be able to
deal with far more people than others, and that the size of their districts would
have to be decided locally. In 1871, the average enumerator had an area of less
than 2 square miles containing 131 houses and 696 people. These averages,
however, embraced wide local variations. Thus one enumerator counted only
64 people, while in London one enumerator counted 3,599 people, another
3,860 and a third 4,800.[152]

In 1841 it looked as if the payment of enumerators might be varied according
to local conditions, for in order to ensure they were 'fairly remunerated' the
Census Commissioners sent a circular to about sixty superintendent registrars
in various districts, asking 'what in their opinion, and according to the prices
and wages of their respective neighbourhoods, might, be considered a fair and
adequate allowance'.[153] In the end it was decided to have a scale which allowed
the enumerator to choose whether he be paid according to the number of houses
he visited or the number of people he counted. This went from 10s for a district
containing less than fifty inhabited houses or less than 300 persons to £1 1s 0d for
one which contained between 150 and 160 houses or between 900 and 960
persons.[154] In 1861, enumerators received a fixed fee of £1 plus 2s for every
100 persons over and above the first 400 they enumerated.[155] In 1871 these sums
were raised to £1 1s 0d and 2s 6d respectively.[156] Some enumerators complained
that this rate was too low and meetings were held in London in May 1871 to
organize a lobby to bring pressure on the government. One enumerator calculated he earned only 4d an hour.[157] The rate was however maintained in 1881
and 1891.[158] In 1901 a fixed sum of £1 1s 0d was retained but for every 100
persons enumerated after the first 400, 3s 6d was to be paid.[159]

One of the factors which could make the task of the enumerator more arduous
than it need be arose from the timing of some of the censuses. For if a census fell
on a date when people were likely to be away from home, the enumerator
might have to make several fruitless journeys. The importance of timing, too,

for the accuracy of the census was remarked on in the aforementioned debate of the Census Bill of 1753.[160] The decision to hold the 1841 census on 7 June (it had originally been scheduled for 1 July) caused considerable adverse comment on the grounds that 'a great portion of the rural population [had] left their houses for the purpose of getting in the harvest and [were] sleeping in outhouses in the fields' whilst the influx of labourers from Ireland and elsewhere 'would also distort the returns'.[161] For this reason the censuses of 1861–1901 were all held in April – that of 1851 was held on March 31 – as being a month when the 'displacement' of the population was likely to be least. But even this month caused problems. Thus in 1891 complaints arose because it was said that April 5, falling a week after Easter Sunday found many parts of the metropolis denuded of their population, taking a ten-day Easter break![162]

Much of the foregoing suggests that one ought to approach the enumerators' returns with all one's critical faculties fully alerted. This is particularly so for those studying small areas where the idiosyncrasies of an enumerator might lead to a quite misleading set of returns. It might, therefore, be appropriate to close this chapter with one or two illustrations of what appear to be results of the various interpretations put upon the census schedules either by the enumerators or the enumerated.

In 1841, for example, there were in England and Wales 13,255 nurses enumerated. In Scotland there were none. 'The number of domestic servants in the metropolis...[was] about one for every forty-seven of the inhabitants: the proportion throughout Great Britain, one for every sixteen persons: that of the county of Westmoreland one for every three.'[163]

In 1844 *The Times* sported a splendid leading article in which the writer made great fun of the fact that half the population had been entered as having no occupation and therefore filled the 'residual' category. In the countryside this residual category was much greater than in the towns. The bulk of its membership consisted of women and children, many of whom were no doubt employed in agriculture for part of the year 'yet a country enumerator would never think of describing [them] formally as agricultural labourers'.[164] Thus in Northamptonshire there were only 199 female agricultural labourers or 'one to a parish and exactly at the rate of one to a thousand persons'. As there were 3,315 farmers, only one in sixteen, according to these returns, would appear to have employed female agricultural labour![165]

A correspondent in *The Times* commenting again on the 1841 census report noted that Somerset had 233 civil engineers, whilst England and Wales as a whole had only 854![166] Bass, the brewer, said in 1870 during a Commons debate on the census, that according to the census of 1861 there were only 15,000 landed proprietors in the whole country. In the large county in which he lived there were, according to the census, only 294, yet he believed there were nearly half that number in his own parish.[167]

One final illustration comes from the evidence of Ogle before the committee on the census in 1890. He noted that it had proved impossible to get people to state whether they were masters or journeymen. Attempts to do this had been made since 1841. 'I do not think there are a thousand people in the whole census' he remarked, 'who put themselves down as journeymen, though some few put themselves down as masters'.[168]

This account of the census has covered the period during which the English are said to have moved towards and away from the notion of *laissez-faire* as the guiding principle of state policy. In the passage from mercantilism to collectivism this period has been regarded as a real if rather freakish aberration. Others have denied that it ever occurred. The history of the nineteenth-century census provides support for both these views. For, to take this latter view first, it is difficult not to concede that the census developed primarily, if not solely, as a legislative aid, even if in the rather tortured sense of one designed as much to unmake as to make laws.[169] On the other hand, however, the extreme reluctance to extend the range of enquiries, the refusal to set up a permanent census office, the marked emphasis on the costs of the operation, all indicate a deliberate unwillingness to exploit the full potential of the census.

Much of the opposition to the census was of a pragmatic nature, rather than anti-collectivist. Thus the Nonconformist desire for a census of religious worship combined, as it was, with an adamant refusal to countenance one of religious persuasion, can more easily be explained in terms of the likely outcome of the two types of census than in any other way. Again the anger of the landowners at the census was due to its exaggerating the decline in the importance of agriculture in the national economy, or in the case of Mr Bass's outburst, cited above, to the support the census gave to agitators against the landed interest.

This pragmatism, together with the need to debate the census bill every ten years meant that public opinion was frequently being assailed on the role of the census. As those who wanted positive changes were invariably keener to put their case than those who did not, their views received the greater attention. However, as this review has shown, the conservative forces were cumulatively very powerful and, though the census returns became fatter,[170] little was done after 1851 to change the extent of the enquiry. Thus the spectre that so haunted William Thornton in 1753 was not to be raised until the twentieth century.

Appendix 1. Sources

1. UNPRINTED SOURCES

The original returns for the first four censuses (1801–31) were destroyed in 1931. A similar fate almost befell the enumeration books of the 1851 and 1861 censuses. For in 1891, according to a correspondent in *The Times* (4 August 1891, 6c) the Local Government Board contemplated the destruction of the books which had apparently for many years been stored in the clock-tower at Westminster. The corresponding books for 1871 and 1881 were stored at Somerset House. As the correspondent noted: 'It is easy to imagine the future House of Commons might order returns for the preparation of which the old books would be indispensable. Be that as it may, the present time, when the establishment of a permanent Census Office is under consideration, seems a most inopportune one for the destruction of such priceless records, merely in order to acquire a little storage space'.

The books were, of course, reprieved, and together with those for the 1841 census can be examined at the Public Record Office. The returns for all censuses from 1871 onwards are not available, being still protected by the so called 'hundred-year rule'. However, negotiations are in progress with the Registrar-General and some relaxation of the rule may be expected.

There are two other bodies of manuscript material which provide valuable evidence of demographic conditions in the early nineteenth century. These cover for the most part not the enumeration parts of the census – the census proper – but the registration process which was tagged on to the first four censuses. The first of these bodies of material is in the Public Record Office in the Home Office papers (HO 71). These give, for every parish, the number of baptisms, burials, and marriages for each year 1821–30: ages at death (in years 1–100) for each year 1813–30: the annual average number of baptisms, burials and marriages not entered in the Church of England parish registers, with specific comments, 1821–30: the number of burials entered in non-Anglican registers together with those entries in the Anglican registers which relate to burials in non-Anglican grounds, each year 1813–30; the number of illegitimate children, differentiated by sex, in 1830.

The second body of material consists of two large folio manuscript volumes in the British Museum (BM Additional Manuscripts 6896 and 6897). They contain transcripts of 'the answers given to questions addressed to the officiating ministers and overseers in England and Wales and the schoolmasters in Scotland, preparatory to the Population Act of 1811, relative to the non-entry of baptisms, burials and marriages in the parish registers and decrease of the population'. The volumes consist of a digest of those made by John Rickman, so that presumably not all the returns appear in the two volumes.

One volume (BM Additional Manuscripts 6897) contains information relative to the enumeration part of the Population Act of 1811, namely answers to question 6, ('Referring to the number of persons in 1801, to what cause do you attribute any re-

31

markable differences in the number at present?') and question 7 ('Are there any other matters, which you may think it necessary to remark, in explanation of your answers to any of the preceding questions in the schedule?'). An instance of the entries in the volume is given below (p. 112):

> *Saddleworth Wapentake*: The increase of population (from 10,665 to 12,579 from 1801–1811) originates from the increase of trade. It appears that the increase of building has not kept pace with the increase of population, but the reason is obvious, for upon a reference to the return made ten years ago, I find several houses occupied by four or more families returned as separate and distinct dwelling houses, which were in fact no more than one.

The other volume (BM Additional Manuscript 6896) contains information relative to the Parish Register Abstract of the Population Act of 1811, namely answers to question 3 ('Are there any other matters which you may think it necessary to remark, in explanation of your answers to either of the preceding questions, especially whether any and what annual average number of baptisms, burials and marriages may (in your opinion) take place in your parish, without being entered in the parish registers, assigning the reason for such non-entry?'). An example of this kind of entry is given below.

> *Cleckheaton*: The number of baptisms and burials unknown. The marriages take place at Birstall, Cleckheaton, being a Chapel of Ease under it. At one small village, Lower Wike, in this Chapelry there is a chapel and seminary of United Bretheren. Upper Wike is situated nearer Wibsey Chapel, which is in the parish of Bradford, to which chapel more I suppose are taken than to Cleckheaton Chapel; the dues are also less, our dues being double, one half is passed to Birstall, namely 10d each baptism and 10d each burial.

The documents discussed above are all in central archives. Undoubtedly, however, a not inconsiderable amount of evidence from the early censuses can be found in the archives of County Record Offices and in parish chests. For a list of parishes with surviving enumeration returns from the 1801, 1811, 1821 and 1831 censuses and their whereabouts see issues 2 and 3 of the *Local Population Studies Magazine and Newsletter*.

2. PRINTED SOURCES

A. CENSUS REPORTS IN PARLIAMENTARY PAPERS (*PP*)

1801. *England, Wales, Scotland*

Abstract of answers and returns, pursuant to Act 41 Geo. III, for taking an account of the population of Great Britain in 1801, and the increase and diminution thereof. *PP* 1801, VI, 813–; *PP* 1801–2, VI, VII.

1811. *England, Wales, Scotland*

Abstract of answers and returns, pursuant to Act 51 Geo. III, for taking an account of the population of Great Britain in 1811. *PP* 1812, XI.

Comparative statement of the population of Great Britain in 1801 and 1811. *PP* 1812, X, 171–.

1821. *England, Wales, Scotland*

Abstract of answers and returns, pursuant to Act 1 Geo. IV, for taking an account of the population of Great Britain in 1821. *PP* 1822, XV.

Comparative statement of the population of Great Britain in 1801, 1811 and 1821. *PP* 1822, xxi, 631–.

1831. *England, Wales, Scotland*

Comparative account of the population of Great Britain in 1801, 1811, 1821, 1831, with annual value of real property, 1815, also, statement of the progress of the inquiry regarding the occupations of families and persons and duration of life, as required by population act 1830. *PP* 1831, xviii.

Abstract of the population returns of Great Britain, 1831. *PP* 1833, xxxvi–xxxviii.

Number of inhabited houses, uninhabited and building; number of families residing in such as are inhabited; occupation of families; number of males and females in each county in England, 1801, 1811, 1821, 1831. *PP* 1833, v, 638–.

1841. *England, Wales, Scotland*

Population in 1841 of each county of Great Britain; distinguishing males and females, and showing the rate per cent increase or decrease in each county as compared with population, 1831; also the number of houses inhabited, uninhabited, and building, according to the census, 1841; similar returns for Channel Islands and Isle of Man; also comparative statement of the population, and number of houses, 1801, 1811, 1821, 1831, for each county in Great Britain; also, population of each city and royal and parliamentary burgh in Scotland. *PP* 1841, Sess. 2, ii, 277–.

Abstract of the answers and returns made pursuant to Act 3 and 4 Vict. c. 99 and 4 Vict. c. 7 (Enumeration Abstract, 1841). *PP* 1843, xxii.

Index of names of places in the enumeration abstract of England and Wales. *PP* 1843, xxii, 515–.

Index of names of places in the enumeration abstract of Scotland. *PP* 1843, xxii, 597–; 679–.

Abstract of the answers and returns made pursuant to Acts 3 and 4 Vict. c. 99, and 4 Vict. c. 7, for taking an account of the population of Great Britain; occupation abstract, 1841:

Part i, England and Wales, and islands in the British Seas. *PP* 1844, xxvii.

Part ii, Scotland. *PP* 1844, xxvii, 385–.

Tables of the rates of increase, and of the population, deaths, and rates of mortality at different ages, in the divisions, registration counties, and districts of England; of the male and female population at the several censuses 1801 to 1841; of the ages of the male and female population, 1841; and of the male and female population of the parliamentary counties as constituted in the years 1801 to 1841. *PP* 1849, xxi.

1851. *England, Wales, Scotland*

Instructions prepared for the use of the persons employed in taking an account of the population of Great Britain by virtue of the Act 13 and 14 Vict. c. 53. *PP* 1851, xliii.

Population and houses in the divisions, registration counties, and districts of England and Wales; in the counties, cities, and burghs of Scotland; and in the islands in the British seas. *PP* 1851, xliii, 73–.

Population and houses, according to the census of 1851, in the counties and divisions of counties, and in the cities, boroughs, and towns returning members to Parliament in Great Britain. *PP* 1852, xlii, 475–.

Population and number of houses, according to the census of 1851, in every county and division of a county, and in all cities and boroughs returning members to Parliament in Great Britain, with the number of members returned; also in towns containing upwards of 2,000 inhabitants not returning members to Parliament. *PP* 1852, XLII, 491–.

Population tables. Part I. Numbers of the inhabitants in the years 1801, 1811, 1821, 1831, 1841 and 1851.

Vol. I Report; objects of census and machinery employed; results and observations; appendix of tabular results and summary tables of England and Wales, Divisions I to VII; area, houses, 1841 and 1851; population, 1801, 1811, 1821, 1831, 1841 and 1851. *PP* 1852–3, LXXXV.

Vol. II England and Wales continued, Divisions VII to XI; Scotland; islands in the British seas; appendix; ecclesiastical divisions of England and Wales. *PP* 1852–3, LXXXVI.

Index to parishes, townships and places in Population tables of Great Britain. *PP* 1852–3, LXXXVII.

Population tables. Part II. Ages, civil condition etc., and inmates of workhouses, prisons etc.

Vol. I Report; results and observations; appendix of tabular results and summary tables; England and Wales, Divisions I to VI. *PP* 1852–3, LXXXVIII, pt. I.

Vol. II England and Wales continued, Divisions VII–XI; Scotland; islands in the British seas. *PP* 1852–3, LXXXVIII, pt. II.

Religious worship (England and Wales). Report; history and description of the various churches; spiritual provision and destitution; appendix containing summary tables and tabular results. *PP* 1852–3, LXXXIX.

Education. Report; summary tables etc. *PP* 1852–3, XC.

Religious worship and education (Scotland). Report and tables. *PP* 1854, LIX, 301–.

Comparative statement of the expenses of the census of Great Britain in 1841 and 1851, number of persons enumerated, heads of information comprised in enquiry, and cost per 1,000 of population. *PP* 1854, XXXIX, 333–.

1861. *England and Wales*

Tables of population and houses enumerated in England and Wales and in islands in British seas on 8 April, 1861. *PP* 1861, L, 855–.

Population tables

Vol. I Numbers and distribution. *PP* 1862, L.

Vol. II Ages, civil condition etc.; and inmates of workhouses etc. *PP* 1863, LIII, pt. I, 265–; and pt. II.

General Report; with appendix of tables. *PP* 1863, LIII.

Return of expenses of Census of England and Wales in 1861, number of persons enumerated, heads of information comprised in enquiry and cost per 1,000 of the population; with comparisons of former charges in 1841 and 1851. *PP* 1863, XXIX, 249–.

Population of England and Wales, and of Scotland in 1831 and 1861 with percentage of increase. *PP* 1866, LVII, 605–.

1861. *Scotland*

Tables of population etc., of houses, and rooms with windows, in Scotland and its islands, on 8 April 1861. *PP* 1861, L, 911–.

Population tables and report
Vol. I Numbers of inhabitants, families etc. in civil counties and parishes, registration counties and districts etc., and islands; also classification of families according to size etc. *PP* 1862, L, 945–.
Vol. II Ages, civil or conjugal condition, occupations etc. and inmates of poorhouses etc. *PP* 1864, LI, 49–.

1871. *England and Wales*

Census of England and Wales 1871, preliminary report, and tables of population and houses enumerated in England and Wales, and in islands in British seas on 3 April 1871. *PP* 1871, LIX, 659–.

Population tables: Areas, houses and inhabitants.
Vol. I Counties. *PP* 1872, LXVI, pt. I.
Vol. II Registration or Union Counties; with an index to the population tables. *PP* 1872, LXVI, pt. II.
Vol. III Population abstracts: Ages, civil condition, occupations and birthplaces of people. *PP* 1873, LXXI, pt. I.
Vol. IV General report. *PP* 1873, LXXI, pt. II.
Suggestions offered to Home Department by members of Statistical Society in relation to ensuing census. *PP* 1870, LVI, 585–.
Table of allowances to be made to superintendant registrars etc. employed in execution of Act for taking census of England and Wales, 1871. *PP* 1871, XXXVII, 143–.
Expenses incurred in taking census in 1871 for England and Wales, Scotland and for Ireland: with comparisons of former charges in 1841, 1851, and 1861. *PP* 1875, XLII, 155–.
Number of male persons, of ages 18 to 25, in United Kingdom according to census of 1851, and of 1871. *PP* 1876, LX, 239–.
Return relating to areas, inhabited houses, and male population of United Kingdom. *PP* 1876, LX 275–.

1871. *Scotland*

Tables of population, of families, of children receiving education, of houses, and rooms with windows in Scotland and its islands on 3 April 1871. *PP* 1871, LIX, 813–.

Eighth decennial census of population, taken 3 April 1871.
Vol. I With report. *PP* 1872, LXVIII.
Vol II With report. *PP* 1873, LXXIII.

1881. *England and Wales*

Preliminary report and tables of population and houses for England and Wales, and in islands in British seas on 4 April 1881. *PP* 1881, XCVI.

General report and tables. PP 1883, LXXX, 583–.
Area, houses and population: counties. *PP* 1883, LXXVIII.
Area, houses and population: Registration counties. *PP* 1883, LXXIX.
Ages, condition as to marriage; occupations and birthplaces of people. *PP* 1883, LXXX.

Islands in British seas; Isle of Man, Jersey, Guernsey and adjacent islands. *PP* 1883, LXXX, 707–.

1881. *Scotland*

Tables of population, houses, rooms with windows in Scotland and its islands on 4 April 1881. *PP* 1881, XCVI, 143–.

Ninth decennial census, taken 4 April 1881, with report.
   Vol. I. *PP* 1882, LXXVI.
   Vol. II. *PP* 1883, LXXXI.
   Return of the population at each decennial period from 1801 to 1881, increase or decrease at 1841 as compared with 1801, and in 1881 compared with 1841: (1) For the whole kingdom; (2) For each county; (3) For each parish; (4) List giving above particulars for each Royal and Parliamentary burgh places etc. *PP* 1883, LIV, 315–.
   Return of number of Gaelic speaking people by counties, parishes, and registration districts, under census of 1881. *PP* 1882, L, 855–.

1891. *England and Wales*

Preliminary report and tables of population and houses enumerated in England and Wales and in islands in British seas on 6 April 1891. *PP* 1890–1, XCIV.
   Vol. I Area, houses and population: administrative and ancient counties. *PP* 1893–4, CIV.
   Vol. II Area, houses and population: registration areas and sanitary districts. *PP* 1893–4, CV.
   Vol. III Ages, conditions as to marriage, occupations, birthplaces, and infirmities. *PP* 1893–4, CVI.
   Vol. IV General report, with summary, tables and appendixes. *PP* 1893–4, CVI, 629–.
   Index to population tables. *PP* 1893–4, CIV, 519–.
   Islands in British seas; Isle of Man, Jersey, Guernsey etc. *PP* 1893–4, CVII.
   Letter of Registrar-General, relative to a complaint against remarks of his (on question of Welsh speaking population) in Census Report, 1891. *PP* 1894, LXIX.

1891. *Scotland*

Tables of population, of families, of houses and of rooms and windows in Scotland and its islands on 5 April 1891. *PP* 1890–1, XCIV, 15–.

Tenth decennial census, taken 5 April 1891
   Vol. I. Report and tables. *PP* 1892, XCIV.
   Supplement to vol. I. *PP* 1893–4, CVII, 65–.
   Vol. II, pt. I. *PP* 1893–4, CVII, 215–; pt. II. *PP* 1893–4, CVIII.

B. OFFICIAL ENQUIRIES INTO WORKING OF THE CENSUS

Minutes of evidence taken (session 1830) before the select committee on the Population Bill. *PP* 1840, xv, 469–.
   Report of the committee appointed by the Treasury to enquire into certain questions connected with the taking of the census with evidence and appendices, and the Treasury minute appointing the committee. *PP* 1890, LVIII, 13–.

Appendix 2. Tables in the census reports 1801–91

What follows is a guide to the contents of the census tables. Essentially I have tried to show what information was tabulated for what areas at each of the ten nineteenth-century censuses. Where necessary amplification is provided in the footnotes.

Key to the table

The censuses 1801–91 are each represented in the table by a single figure, that for 1801 being 0, for 1811 being 1 and so on up to 1891, represented by the figure 9.
E = England; W = Wales; S = Scotland.
* = Urban districts with populations in excess of 50,000.
† = Selected boroughs.

	Population totals	Area (acres)	Age	Civil condition	Birthplace	Family occupation	Personal occupation
Ancient counties	0 1 2 3 4 5 6 7 8 9	3 4 5 6 7 8 9	2 4 7	—	4 6 7	1 2 3	0 3 4
Parliamentary counties	5 6 7 8 9	7 8 9	—	—	—	—	—
Parliamentary county divisions	5 6 7 8 9	7 8 9	—	—	—	—	—
Registration counties	5 6 7 8 9	7 8 9	5 6 7 8 9	5 6 7 8 9	5 6 7 8 9	—	5 6 7 8 9
Administrative counties	9	9	—	—	—	—	—
Boroughs	0 1 2 3 4	3 4	4	—	4	1 2 3	3 4†
Parliamentary boroughs	4 5 6 7 8 9	4 5 6 7 8 9	—	—	4	—	—
Parliamentary borough divisions	9	9	—	—	—	—	—
Municipal boroughs	5 6 7 8 9	5 6 7 8 9—		—	4	—	—
County boroughs	9	9	—	—	—	—	—
Wards of municipal boroughs	7 8 9	9	—	—	—	—	—

	Population totals	Area (acres)	Age	Civil condition	Birthplace	Family occupation	Personal occupation
Registration districts	4 5 6 7 8 9	5 6 7 8	5 6 7 8	5 6 7 8	5 6 7 8 9	—	5 6 7 8
Registration sub-districts	5 6 7 8 9	5 6 7	7 8	7	—	—	—
Registration divisions	5 6 7 8 9	5 6 7 8	7 8	5 6 7 8 9	5 6 7 8 9	—	—
Hundreds, wapentakes	0 1 2 3 4 5 6 7 8	3 4 5 6 7 8	2 4	—	4	1 2 3	0 3
Tythings, chapelries, townships, hamlets, precincts, extra-parochial places	0 1 2 3 4 5 6 7	3 4 5 6 7	4	—	4	1 2 3	0 3
Provinces	5 6 7 8 9	—	—	—	—	—	—
Dioceses	3 5 6 7 8 9	—	—	—	—	—	—
Ecclesiastical districts or new parishes	5 6 7 8 9	7	—	—	—	—	—
Poor Law unions	5 6 7 8 9	7	—	—	—	—	—
Petty sessional divisions	7 8 9	7 8	—	—	—	—	—
Boroughs having separate courts of Quarter Sessions and Commissions of the Peace	7 8 9	7 8	—	—	—	—	—
Civil parishes	7 8 9	7	—	—	—	—	—
Ancient parishes	0 1 2 3 4 5 6 7 8	3 4 5 6 7	4	—	4	1 2 3	0 3† 4†
Urban districts	8 9	—	8* 9*	8* 9*	—	—	8* 9*
Rural districts	8 9	—	8 9	—	—	—	—

	Language	Houses inhabited	Houses inhabited – by how many families occupied	Houses unin- habited	Houses building	Number of rooms in house- hold	Number of rooms with one or more windows
Ancient counties	—	0 1 2 3 4 5 6 7 8 9	0 1 2 3	0 1 2 3 4 5 6 7 8 9	1 2 3 4 5 6 7 8 9	—	—
Parliamentary counties	—	5 6 7 8 9	—	5 6 7 8 9	5 6 7 8 9	—	—
Parliamentary county divisions	—	5 6 7 8 9	—	5 6 7 8 9	5 6 7 8 9	—	—
Registration counties	5 8 9	5 6 7 8 9	—	5 6 7 8 9	5 6 7 8 9	*E W* 9	*E W* 9
Administrative counties	—	9	—	9	9	—	—
Boroughs	—	0 1 2 3 4	0 1 2 3	0 1 2 3 4	1 2 3 4	—	—
Parliamentary boroughs	*S* 8 9	5 6 7 8 9	—	5 6 7 8 9	5 6 7 8 9	—	—
Parliamentary borough divisions	—	9	—	9	9	—	—
Municipal boroughs	*S* 8 9	5 6 7 8 9	—	5 6 7 8 9	5 6 7 8 9	—	—
County boroughs	—	9	—	9	9	—	—
Wards of municipal boroughs	—	5 6 7 8 9	—	5 6 7 8 9	5 6 7 8 9	—	—
Registration districts	*S* 8 9	4 5 6 7 8 9	—	4 5 6 7 8 9	4 5 6 7 8 9	—	—
Registration sub-districts	*S* 8 9	5 6 7 8 9	—	5 6 7 8 9	5 6 7 8 9	—	—
Registration divisions	—	5 6 7 8 9	—	5 6 7 8 9	5 6 7 8 9	—	—
Hundreds, wapentakes	—	0 1 2 3 4 5 6 7	0 1 2 3	0 1 2 3 4 5 6 7	1 2 3 4 5 6 7	—	—
Tythings, chapelries, townships, hamlets, precincts, extra- parochial places	—	0 1 2 3 4 5 6	0 1 2 3	0 1 2 3 4 5 6	1 2 3 4 5 6	—	—
Provinces	—	5 6 7 8	—	—	—	—	—
Dioceses	—	5 6 7 8	—	—	—	—	—
Ecclesiastical districts or new parishes	—	5 6 7 8 9	—	5 6 7 8 9	5 6 7 8 9	—	—

	Language	Houses inhabited	Houses inhabited – by how many families occupied	Houses uninhabited	Houses building	Number of rooms in household	Number of rooms with one or more windows
Poor Law unions	—	5 6 7 8 9	—	5 6 7 8 9	5 6 7 8 9	—	—
Petty sessional divisions	—	7 8 9	—	7 8 9	7 8 9	—	—
Boroughs having separate Courts of Quarter Sessions and Commissions of the Peace	—	7 8 9	—	7 8 9	7 8 9	—	—
Civil parishes	S 8 9	7 8 9	8 9	7 8 9	7 8 9	—	—
Ancient parishes	—	0 1 2 3 4 5 6 7	—	0 1 2 3 4 5 6 7 8	1 2 3 4 5 6 7 8	—	—
Urban districts	—	9	9	9	9	E W 9	—
Rural districts	—	9	9	9	9	E W 9	—

	Education conditions	Religious conditions	Deaf, dumb, blind, lunatic	Baptisms, burials, marriages
Ancient counties	—	5	—	0 and E W 1 2 3 4
Parliamentary counties	—	—	—	—
Parliamentary county divisions	—	—	—	—
Registration counties	5	5	5 6 7 8 9	E W 4
Administrative counties	—	—	—	—
Boroughs	—	—	—	0 and E W 1 2 3 4 †
Parliamentary boroughs	—	—	—	—
Parliamentary borough divisions	—	—	—	—

	Education conditions	Religious conditions	Deaf, dumb, blind, lunatic	Baptisms, burials marriages
Municipal boroughs	5	—	—	—
County boroughs	—	—	—	—
Wards of municipal boroughs	—	—	—	—
Registration districts	5	5	5 6 7 8 9	4
Registration sub-districts	—	—	5 6 7 8 9	—
Registration divisions	—	5	5 6 7 8 9	—
Hundreds, wapentakes	—	—	—	0 and *E W* 1 2 3 4
Tythings, chapelries, townships, hamlets, precincts, extra-parochial places	—	—	—	—
Provinces	—	—	—	—
Dioceses	—	—	—	—
Ecclesiastical districts or new parishes	—	—	—	—
Poor Law unions	—	—	—	—
Petty sessional divisions	—	—	—	—
Boroughs having separate Courts of Quarter Sessions and Commissions of the Peace	—	—	—	—
Civil parishes	—	—	9	—
Ancient parishes	—	—	—	—
Urban districts	—	—	—	—
Rural districts	—	—	—	—

NOTE

AREAS

Ancient counties. Sometimes called the geographical counties. The boundaries of these areas in England were fixed before Domesday (AD 1086); those in Wales in the period from AD 1138 to the early sixteenth century. In the nineteenth century some slight alterations were made under the authority of an Act of 1844 'to annex detached parts of counties to the counties in which they are situated'.

Parliamentary counties. As a result of the parliamentary reform acts of 1832 and subsequent years the boundaries of the areas which formed the basis of parliamentary representation were redrawn. The size of the populations within these areas was of great interest to nineteenth-century reformers and they were frequently published in conjunction with other 'relevant' information e.g. value of property, amount of assessed taxes.

Parliamentary county divisions. Some counties were divided for the purposes of parliamentary representation e.g. East and West Kent.

Registration counties The civil registration of births, marriages and deaths began in England and Wales in 1837 and in Scotland in 1855. For the most part the Poor Law unions were used as the *registration districts.* These unions consisted of groups of parishes which combined for the purposes of poor relief under the Poor Law of 1834. The Registrar-General grouped the registration districts into *registration counties,* so called because they did not always coincide with the ancient counties. The registration counties were further aggregated into eleven topographical *divisions* consisting of groups of counties thought to possess a common distinctive character, namely:

1. London, comprising the portions of Middlesex, Surrey and Kent within the limit of the Registrar-General's Bills of Mortality.
2. South-Eastern Division, comprising Surrey and Kent (Extra-Metropolitan), Sussex, Hampshire, and Berkshire.
3. South-Midland Division, comprising Middlesex (Extra-Metropolitan), Hertfordshire, Buckinghamshire, Oxfordshire, Northamptonshire, Bedfordshire, and Cambridgeshire.
4. Eastern Division, comprising Essex, Suffolk, and Norfolk.
5. South-Western Division, comprising Wiltshire, Dorsetshire, Devonshire, Cornwall, and Somerset.
6. West-Midland Division, comprising Gloucestershire, Herefordshire, Shropshire, Staffordshire, Worcestershire, and Warwickshire.
7. North-Midland Division, comprising Leicestershire, Rutland, Lincolnshire, Nottingham, and Derbyshire.
8. North-Western Division, comprising Cheshire, and Lancashire.
9. York Division, consisting of Yorkshire.
10. Northern Division, comprising Durham, Northumberland, Cumberland, and Westmorland.
11. Welsh Division, comprising Monmouthshire, South Wales, and North Wales.

Administrative counties. These resulted from the Local Government Act of 1888. They sometimes coincided with the existing ancient counties but when an urban sanitary district extended into two counties, the whole of the district 'was accepted as within that county which contained the largest portion of the population of the district according to the census of 1881'. Certain ancient counties were also subdivided into administrative counties e.g. the three ridings of Yorkshire became administrative counties.

Boroughs. Until the Parliamentary Reform Act of 1832 all boroughs returned members to Parliament. That act took away representation from some boroughs and created new boroughs with parliamentary status. Therefore, whereas before 1832 *municipal boroughs* and *parliamentary boroughs* were coterminous, this was no longer the case after that date.

Parliamentary Boroughs. See previous note.

Parliamentary borough divisions. The redistribution of Seats Act of 1885 involved the creation of single member constituencies. It was thus necessary to divide up the multiple member boroughs.

Municipal boroughs. See note above on *Boroughs.*

County boroughs. The Local Government Act of 1888 which created the *administrative counties* also designated sixty-one large boroughs as county boroughs. These had their own administration separate from that of the administrative county.

Wards of municipal boroughs. Divisions for electoral purposes.

Registration districts. See note above on *registration counties.*

Registration subdistricts. See note on *registration counties.*

Registration divisions. See note above on *registration counties.*

Hundreds, wapentakes. A division of the ancient counties, already used in the Domesday Book.

Provinces. Aggregates of dioceses, those in the northern areas being in the province of York, those in the southern, that of Canterbury.

Dioceses. Aggregates of Church of England parishes.

Ecclesiastical districts or new parishes. These were created from 1818 onwards in an attempt by the Church of England to accommodate the rise and redistribution of the population. The census reports give the precise date when any new parish was created and the name of the old parish of which it was previously a part.

Poor Law unions. Groups of parishes brought together for purposes of poor relief, following the Poor Law Amendment Act of 1834.

Civil parishes. At the beginning of the nineteenth century parishes were units of both religious and civil life. In the course of that century the civil and ecclesiastical functions separated and as a result boundary changes were made by the church authorities (e.g. in creating new parishes) which were not followed by the civil authorities. In turn the civil authorities made changes not followed by the church. In 1866 compulsory church rates were abolished and the ecclesiastical parish ceased to have any local government functions. By the end of the century the term parish is used only for 'a place for which a separate poor rate is or can be made or for which a separate overseer is or can be appointed'. The census report of 1871 renamed those ancient parishes that had not been divided, civil parishes.

Urban districts and rural districts. Created under the Public Health Act of 1872 – first called 'urban sanitary' and 'rural sanitary' districts.

Tythings, chapelries, townships, hamlets, precincts, extra-parochial places. Tythings, chapelries, townships, hamlets, and precincts, were subdivisions of parishes. Extra-parochial places were outside the parish structure and thereby exempt from taxation, poor relief, militia service, and so on. Acts of 1857 and 1868 virtually ended the civil privileges of these areas, though some ecclesiastical privileges still exist.

HEADS OF INFORMATION

Population totals. Before the census of 1841 it is likely that both omissions and double counting occurred chiefly because the enumerators were left in some doubt as to whether to count persons normally living in their districts or only those actually there on census day. From 1841 onwards the instructions to enumerators were much more precise. Thus at that census only persons sleeping in a house on the night of 6 June 1841 were to be entered as living there, whilst the 1851 schedule contained the injunction: 'No person absent on the night of March 30th to be entered'.

Age. In 1821 ages given in quinquennia up to 20 years, then in decennia to 100. In 1831 the age of males over 20 years of age given for all areas. In 1841 ages given in quinquennia for ancient counties, hundreds and 'principal towns'. For all areas population divided into those under 20 and those over 20 years of age; males and females being listed separately. In 1851 and 1861 ages given for individual years up to 5 years, then in quinquennia to age 100. From 1871 to 1891 ages given for individual years to age 5, then quinquennia to age 100; also those over and under 20 years of age. Apart from areas in the table, ages given, in 1871, for populations of 'principal towns' and in 1881 and 1891 for urban sanitary districts with populations in excess of 50,000.

Civil condition. The number of unmarried, married, or widowed men and women, 1851–91, given in quinquennial age groups from 15 years upwards. Ages of husbands and wives cross-tabulated in single years from 15 to 20, and then in quinquennia for registration counties.

Birthplace. The 1841 enumeration abstract distinguishes, for all areas, between persons (sexes not listed separately) born in the county where they resided on census day and those born outside it. For the counties, hundreds and boroughs the category is further subdivided into persons (males and females listed separately) born in other counties of England and Wales, in Scotland, in Ireland, in British colonies and in other foreign parts. Those for whom no data available also given.

In the censuses of 1851–91 birthplaces given by counties of England and Wales, London, Scotland, Ireland, British colonies, islands in the British seas, foreign parts and at sea. Age-groups under 20 and over 20 given except in 1881 and 1891.

Family occupation. In 1811, 1821 and 1831 occupations were returned under the following heads: (1) Families chiefly employed in agriculture; (2) Families chiefly employed in trade, manufactures or handicrafts; (3) All other families not comprised in the two preceding classes.

Personal occupation. In 1801 personal occupations were returned under three heads: (1) Persons chiefly employed in agriculture; (2) Persons chiefly employed in trade, manufactures or handicrafts; (3) All other persons not comprised in the two preceding classes.

Occupations of males, twenty years of age and over were returned in 1831 in the following categories: (1) Occupiers (in agriculture) employing labour; (2) Occupiers (in agriculture) not employing labour; (3) Labourers employed in agriculture; (4) Employed in manufacture or in making manufacturing machinery; (5) Employed in retail trade, or in handicraft as masters or workmen; (6) Capitalists, bankers, professional and other educated men; (7) Labourers employed in labour not agricultural; (8) Other males 20 years of age, except servants; (9) Male servants 20 years of age and over; (10) Male servants under 20 years of age.

Category 5 was subdivided further. The enumerators were given a list of the hundred 'most usual denominations of retail trade and handicraft' (*Report*, p. x). A blank space was left at the bottom of the form for the entry of trades not mentioned in the list. In London as a result some 426 subdivisions were returned.

The totals in each of these subdivisions of Category 5 were published only for each county and for a number of smaller areas. There are footnotes to each of the tables giving information on particular trades in other parts of each county. These are of course by no means comprehensive but are worth investigating by those interested in a particular parish or occupation.

In 1841 males and females over and under 20 years of age distinguished by a wide variety of occupations. The lists of occupations given vary from area to area. From 1851–91, populations cross-classified by age and occupation. In addition to areas specified in the chart, this information also given for populations of 'principal towns'.

In 1851 employers classified by number of their employees – singly from 1 to 9 employees, then in units of 10 up to 50, then for those with 75, 100, 150, 200, 250, 300 and 350 or more employees. Farmers also classified by number of employees – singly 1–9, then by fives from 10 to 59, then 60 and upwards: this information being cross tabulated against the size of their farms in acres – under 5, 5–9, by tens to 50, by 25s to 100, by 50s to 400, by 100s to 1,000, 1,200, 1,500 and 2,000 upwards. This information on farms repeated for ten counties in 1861, and for seventeen counties in 1871.

Language. The numbers of those 'in the habit of making colloquial use of the Gaelic language' were given for various areas in Scotland in 1881. In 1891 the householder's schedule required information on all over 3 years of age who spoke Gaelic, or Gaelic and English.

A statement as to whether they spoke Welsh, or English or both languages was required of all inhabitants of Wales and Monmouthshire in 1891.

Number of rooms in household. In 1891 a statement of the number of rooms was required of houses with less than five rooms. Information was tabulated by number of persons occupying them.

Educational conditions. The number of scholars in various age groups was given in censuses 1851, 1861, and 1871. Apart from this the only major enquiry into education occurred at the census of 1851. The information tabulated (by registration county) included the number of male and female scholars in age groups under 5 years, 5–10, 10–15, 15–20, 20 upwards; dates at which existing schools were established (private and public distinguished) – before 1801, 1801–11, 1811–21, 1821–31, 1841–51, and in each year 1841–50 and by whom maintained: number of scholars on the books and in attendance on census day (by registration counties); ages of scholars in public and private day schools distinguished by sex (by registration counties); number of teachers and their salaries, number of paid monitors and pupils and their pay in public day schools distinguished by sex (by registration counties) and according to source of their income; number of scholars in public and private schools distinguished by sex and by whom schools maintained (by registration counties and principal towns); Sunday schools, with number of scholars and paid and unpaid teachers, classified by denomination in registration counties (Wales divided into North Wales and South Wales) and large towns; number of day schools, whether public or private, Sunday schools and number of scholars in total and in proportion to total population in all municipal cities and boroughs of England and Wales; number of evening schools, whether or not also used as day schools, number of scholars and teachers in them, payments by scholars (in pence), classified according to number of months a year they are open and number of hours each day, and subjects taught, by occupations of adult pupils (by counties).

By registration districts, number of schools and scholars, whether public or private, number of Sunday schools and evening schools: also by whom schools supported.

List of literary and scientific institutes classified by number and character of members (whether proprietary, annual, quarterly) and sex of members, amount of subscription, number of volumes in library, frequency of lectures and usual subjects of lectures. Locality and description of each institution also given.

Religious conditions. The questions under this heading were confined to the voluntary enquiry associated with the census of 1851.

Number of places of worship, whether or not in separate buildings; number of sittings whether free, appropriated or not distinguished; number of attendants at public worship on Sunday, 30 March 1851 in morning, afternoon and evening; number of places open for worship at each period (morning, afternoon, evening) on Sunday, 30 March 1851 and number of sittings thus available; dates at which the buildings were erected or appropriated to religious purposes (before 1801, 1801–11, 1811–21, 1821–31, 1831–41, 1841–51, not stated). All the above data categorised by religious denomination. Information given for registration counties, ancient counties and large towns.

Proportion of sittings to population and whether provided by Church of England, other Protestant churches or Roman Catholics in registration divisions, registration counties and registration districts. For a small number of these areas the numbers of additional sittings required on the assumption that accommodation should be provided for 58 per cent of the population, is also given.

Districts with the most and the least accommodation relative to population: comparative position of Church of England and the Dissenting churches in respect of proportion per cent of sittings to population in the counties and in the large towns; number of persons present at the most numerously attended services on 30 March 1851 in registration counties and divisions according to whether services were conducted by Church of England, Protestant dissenters, Roman Catholics, all other bodies.

For England and Wales as a whole a table showing number of services held by each religious body at different periods of the day and a table giving a comparative view of the frequency with which the various religious bodies make use of the accommodation provided for them.

Deaf, dumb, blind, lunatic

Questions as to lunacy not included in the schedules until the census of 1871. The information given for the registration counties also tabulated by age.

Baptisms, burials, and marriages

Parish Register Abstracts were associated with the censuses taken between 1801 and 1841. That of 1801 contains the baptisms and burials for the first year of each decade from 1700 to 1780 (i.e. for 1700, 1710, 1720 etc.), and then for each individual year up to and including 1800. Totals of marriages were also given for each year from 1754 up to and including 1800. A note was made of defective registers. The Parish Register Abstracts of 1811, 1821, 1831 and 1841 contain totals of baptisms, burials and marriages for each year of the preceding decade. Male and female baptisms and burials listed separately in each of the abstracts. The detailed notes associated with the tables, chiefly drawing attention to their defects, are essential reading. Ages at death in intervals of one year from 1 to 100 are in the abstract of 1831 for the years 1813–30. This information given for ancient counties only in 1831. In 1841 it was given for registration counties. The abstracts cover not only all counties and hundreds but also certain selected towns.

2. The study of family structure

M. Anderson

Dahrendorf has noted that 'Sociologists still like to invent their history so as to lend profile to their statements about the present.'[1] To a remarkable extent this is still true of the sociology of the family. Until recently our knowledge of family life in the past was usually derived from one or more of three kinds of sources: novels, usually by middle class writers; largely impressionistic writings, frequently reformatory or didactic in aim, by middle class contemporaries; and anecdotes recounted to investigators by elderly respondents, some of which they in turn had heard from others even older than themselves. The first two were inevitably rather impressionistic and based on incomplete knowledge; in addition their didactic aims encouraged an emphasis on social pathology. Their evidence is almost certainly not therefore representative of the population as a whole.[2] The anecdotal sources are subject to all the well known problems of long period recall which seem to blur away the harshness of the past and the sufferings of substantial minority groups, and lead people to portray the past through rose-coloured (or, occasionally, grimy) spectacles. This bias in recall data on the family appears to be common to all cultures at all periods of history.[3]

All these sources, then, tend to give a picture of family and social life in the past which exaggerates in one direction or the other, which portrays the historical family either as highly integrated, or, alternatively, as highly disrupted. Undue stress is inevitably laid on isolated cases which were almost certainly atypical. Little weight can be given to such sources taken alone as facts on which to base reliable generalisations.

And yet the sociology of the family, more than most branches of the discipline of sociology, is much preoccupied with change and with the impact of social changes on the family.

Thus, for example, a number of studies have suggested, mainly on the basis of the kinds of data considered above, that important changes have occurred in family life in Britain's towns over the past thirty or so years.[4] Our ideas of what went before are usually hazy in the extreme, but often seem to include some images, based on scattered contemporary material and on our over-fertile imaginations, of stable rural communities, cohesive nuclear family systems, and, perhaps, tightly knit kinship systems. Then there came sudden disruptions

47

brought about by migration to the towns, factory work, squalid social conditions, until the situation gradually stabilised again into the relatively integrated 'traditional' working class communities which some writers have suggested existed in the 1930s and before.[5] Laslett and his associates have already shown something of the falsity of the romantic picture of pre-industrial rural England,[6] but we have so far rather few studies which attempt to get at the facts about family structure in nineteenth- and early twentieth-century British towns.[7] If, however, we are to be able to say anything really useful about recent social changes then we must have much more 'hard' information about the past than we possess at present. Systematic historical research into family structure in past ages must therefore become an integral part of the sociology of the family.

Much of the work that is done in the field is focused on the impact of industrialisation and urbanisation on some aspect of family structure. Rigorous investigations of the course of changes in family structure in Britain over the past 400 years could make an important contribution to our theoretical knowledge of the effects of these social revolutions, for here we have the opportunity of studying the impact on a society of changes generated within that society on people with, comparatively speaking, a highly homogeneous culture regardless of their occupations and technology.

The nineteenth century provides an important focal point in any plan for systematic study of the impact of industrialisation on the British family, for it was above all in this period that Britain was transformed from a pre-industrial to an industrial society.

There is also one other more mundane but no less important reason to consider the study of family structure in nineteenth-century Britain as potentially fruitful. Particularly after 1841, data on at least some aspects of family life become very readily available in the census enumerators' books. At about the same time valuable descriptive sources suddenly blossom forth in ever-growing numbers.

This kind of research is obviously, then, important to the sociologist. And it is equally valuable to the historian. For example, data obtained on the causes of variation in the age of marriage in the nineteenth century between different groups of the population and between different areas suggest support for the birthrate theory of population growth in the eighteenth century.[8] Data on the roles played by kin and neighbours in crises, and on the important contribution made by the old in some areas to the standard of living of their married children by allowing young mothers to work, may well help to explain some of the variations in the loads of Poor Law Guardians in different parts of the country. Data on patterns of inheritance and land transfer between generations suggest the correctness of Habakkuk's suggestion[9] that the availability of a labour force not tied to the parental plot was at least one very important factor which made the industrial revolution in Britain possible at all.

In view of the importance of research in this area it is perhaps somewhat surprising that there should exist few published modern studies of any aspect of family life in the late eighteenth and in the nineteenth centuries. A certain amount is known about changes in the economic functions of the urban-industrial family, from the work of Collier[10] and Smelser.[11] Margaret Hewitt has discussed the effect that a factory-working mother could have on the family as a domestic group.[12] Ivy Pinchbeck has reviewed more generally the roles of wives and mothers in the period of industrialisation.[13] A number of studies are now in progress or nearing completion using census enumerators' books to study the social structure of nineteenth-century towns and these will obviously throw up many facts and ideas which are highly relevant to the family sociologist.[14] Dorothy Crozier has concluded an important investigation into London middle-class family structure,[15] and some limited statistical data from a wider study of the whole population have also appeared.[16] The only completed study which to my knowledge has considered kinship and family cohesion in any rigorous manner is that of Foster, though, mainly because this is incidental to his main purpose, he has confined himself to a few tables and some stimulating discussion.[17] My own work[18] is therefore almost unique in its attempt to study the family and social change in one area of nineteenth-century urban England in detail, though much of it should be seen as exploratory rather than as a definitive example of this kind of research. A major gap remains, then, to be filled.

This chapter suggests some of the possible ways of replacing what is at present little more than folk myth, by fact. It is not concerned with the history of individual families, though such histories may be of great help in building up the overall picture.[19] The aim is rather to seek out and describe *patterns and uniformities* in the family life of certain sectors of the population taken as a whole.

The discussion relies heavily on my own experience which has been based largely on a study of parent–child relationships and of people's relationships with kin outside the nuclear family. It would seem that these aspects of family structure will be the main concern of most future investigators since it is much more difficult to do any adequate study of husband–wife relationships in an historical context. Many of the principles and techniques discussed here would, however, also be useful to those looking at other aspects of family life. I shall be concerned particularly to look at sources and techniques for the study of lower-class family structure, meaning by lower-class that whole section of the population, 'the class of labourers and small shopkeepers',[20] which the Victorian middle-class saw as so clearly differentiated from themselves. Students of middle-class and trade families also have at their disposal other valuable sources, notably wills and business records. Those interested in this area should therefore also consult the work of Dorothy Crozier.[21]

It is important that investigations of this kind are not confined to the family in isolation from its social setting, nor to only some of the many functions that the family in any society performs. Descriptions should have a wider scope, encompassing as far as is possible all behaviour that was in any way influenced by the individual's memberships in his family and kinship systems. Any aspect of family life, at home, in leisure time, at work, or elsewhere, in which family members oriented their actions in any way by reference to their family memberships should potentially be considered as relevant for a full understanding of family structure, and must be investigated if a full picture of the *significance* of family relationships is to be built up.

For, beyond a first simple series of descriptions will lie for most students a more fundamental and unifying aim, to assess *how important* family membership at different levels – membership of nuclear family, membership of different wider kinship groups – was to the members of any given society and group within that society. The aim then, even if it will often be only implicit or half formalised, is to establish as far as possible, in a comparative perspective (comparative across the country, between countries, between groups at a point in time, and over time) how important were relationships with parents, children, and wider kin in influencing the life chances of members of that group or society.

If we are even to begin to approach this ultimate aim of assessing the importance of relationships, we must try to decide what we mean by 'important', and how we might try to assess it. Unfortunately, there is a wide range of disagreement among sociologists on both these matters, though a number of fruitful lines of action do seem to be emerging.[22]

For example, it is now becoming clear that it is totally inadequate to confine one's attention simply to the study of patterns of residence. The sharing of a home and of obligations incurred by commensality is only one sphere of family activity, and its significance can only be assessed in the context of a much wider review of all the functions provided by the family, and of the extent to which individuals see themselves overall as being dependent on family relationships. Two examples from Victorian Lancashire may help to illustrate this point.

Firstly, a comparison of the proportion of young couples in the silk-weaving village of Middleton, Lancashire, who in 1851 shared a home with a parent, with the comparable figure for the town of Preston (6 per cent compared with 16 per cent), might suggest far stronger family bonds in Preston than in Middleton. This interpretation is almost certainly erroneous. In both these communities, relationships with parents were of very considerable importance for young married couples. In Middleton, these couples were frequently highly dependent on their parents for employment and for the provision of a loom on which to work,[23] and there were strong normative pressures which would have made it very difficult to refuse to meet community prescribed obligations to parents.[24] In Preston, if my interpretation is correct, both these pressures were much less, but the young couples found their mothers very useful as baby minders while the young wife worked. In addition (and this must to some extent have been important in Middleton too), bonds of kinship were important for most of the population because relationships with kin provided the most effective social welfare service available in the face of the crises which so frequently affected their lives.[25] Other forces were at work too in Preston. The town had a severe housing shortage and rents were high. This made it more difficult and less economical for young couples to set up in a home of their own, particularly one near their parents. In Middleton, on the other hand, while there is no evidence that there was any norm against this kind of sharing, such sharing was much less necessary. It would be a very rash man, therefore, who asserted on the basis of the figures cited above, that relationships with kin were more important in Preston, let alone two and a half times as important.

Similarly, taken alone, the finding that, in Preston in 1851, well over four-fifths of all boys aged 15–19 were living with their families of orientation, in spite of high rates of inmigration among single boys in this age group and the presence of considerable numbers of orphans, is only one indicator, and not necessarily a very good one taken alone, of the importance of family bonds to this group. Only by considering their relationships with the economic system, backed up by descriptive evidence on the content of their relationships with their parents, can it be established that this relationship was for some largely a matter of convenience. Indeed the extent of dependence and the degree of subjugation to parental authority of this group as a whole was rather low. Their high wages, earned as individuals in employment to which they had been often recruited without reference to their family membership, and the existence of alternative accommodation in the form of lodging houses, meant that if too great attempts were made to control them they could threaten to leave home, and could if necessary back up this threat by going off to join others of their age group in the lodging houses. Contrast with this the situation of the son destined to inherit the family farm in Ireland or in the rural areas of Lancashire who was highly dependent for his whole future standard of living on inheriting the farm and was therefore highly dependent on his father. Yet in many areas he was, at the same age, more likely than his urban cousin, to be living away from home, as a farm servant or labourer earning money to extend the family plot or gaining experience on other farms.[26]

It is essential, in short, to seek information over as wide a range of activities as possible. People in all societies face many different problems, and require assistance from others in meeting them. Finding a home and domestic assistance are only two of these problems. One also needs to find a job, someone to care for one in old age, assistance in all kinds of crises – sickness or death of the wage earner or mother or other family member, unemployment, migration to a new community – and possibly quite simply someone to confide in and give advice. If the individual cannot solve these problems himself, and in as far as they are seen to be frequent or pressing, he must seek help from others. In most societies these others have usually been kin.

This leads on to the second emerging principle on the concept of importance of family relationships. Attention cannot simply be confined to the study of relationships with other family members.[27] The study of sources of assistance other than kin in the major problem areas of a person's life is also necessary. As a polar case, if there is no one but kin to help a man solve some crucial problem that life presents him, then his family must be of overwhelming significance to him for, if he terminates relationships with them, he will die or suffer some serious deprivation.[28] This means, incidentally, that it is of particular interest to study what happens to those who have no relatives to perform any particular function.[29]

It seems to follow, then, that ideally the investigator would want to gather information on the seriousness and frequency of the crises and needs of the members of the social group under study, the resources at their disposal which they could mobilise to help them meet these needs, and their attitudes to the various persons and organisations to which they could conceivably have turned for assistance. Kin are but one of these alternatives. We must therefore try to look at as many aspects of the social, physical and technical environment in which the population lived as is possible within the limitations of the availability of data. Environmental factors act as crucial constraints on possible family relational patterns. The occupational structure of the community, occupational recruitment patterns, housing conditions, the attraction of migration and distance migrated, the efficiency and rules of the various social welfare organisations, working hours, the turnover of population in neighbourhoods, ideally one would like information on all these topics, and many more besides. Unfortunately, it is precisely in some of these areas that data are most likely to be lacking or of uncertain reliability. This does not mean that the attempt to collect it should not be made. It does mean that a cast-iron explanation of patterns of family behaviour will seldom be possible.

Finally, it must be remembered that patterns of behaviour are not simply determined by the objective constraints of a situation, though these in poorer communities will seldom be far from people's minds. These constraints are only manifested in action after they have been mediated through people's normatively prescribed definitions of 'proper' or 'ideal' behaviour. It is in this area that the greatest problems arise in an historical context, for data on values, on affective behaviour, on how important people actually saw relationships to be, on their motivations for maintaining relationships, and on their perceptions of alternatives, are seldom obtainable in any quantity, and may often be very unreliable when they are found. Nevertheless, all scraps of information on this area must be systematically collected. Out of these scraps some overall if slightly hazy jig-saw picture can usually be made up.

This leads then, to a final introductory point, the importance of descriptive material of all kinds for a complete understanding of patterns of family relationships and of the factors which influence them. While much time will be taken up with detailed and systematic work on samples from the census enumerators' books, many other kinds of data will also have to be used if an adequate picture is to be obtained. The enumerators' books, suitably used, can provide us with figures, some fairly precise, others very sketchy, on such matters as where related families lived, age of marriage, household composition at different stages of the life cycle and at different ages, marital statuses and family sizes, the occupations of family members and their migration patterns. How this information may best be obtained is discussed in Section III of this chapter. Other sources amenable to statistical treatment can also be used, either alone, or in conjunction with each other, or with the enumerators' books. These will include firms' records of employees, workhouse and other poor relief documents, registers of vital statistics, wills and published demographic information. Finally, almost any contemporary document, tract, investigation, or even novel may provide insights into areas which statistical data either do not cover or cover only in part. The uses of data of this kind are discussed in Section IV.

II

Before going on to describe in more detail the sources which may be available for students of family structure, and some of the techniques which can be used to tease the most information out of them, it may be worthwhile noting briefly some of the considerations which should be borne in mind when planning a study of this nature.

Most studies will need to use the enumerators' books of the Victorian censuses as a major data source. The availability of these for public inspection must inevitably influence the periods that can be studied. In England the complete documents are only available at present for the years 1841, 1851, and 1861, though presumably the 'hundred years rule' will release the 1871 books shortly.[30] It has, however, proved possible in the past to have special tabulations made by the Registrar-General's office from the later census data,[31] and also to obtain photostats of enumerators' books with names and addresses erased.[32] Even where the costs of these special services are not considered prohibitive, however, these procedures may be less valuable for students of family structure than for some others. For example, it is clearly impossible to use the bowdlerised photocopies to trace individuals from census to census or from census to other records, and techniques of this nature, particularly if the procedures can be computerised,[33] seem potentially to have an exciting pay-off both in their own right and as a check against conclusions from our one-shot data, by allowing us to study processes of change and their impact on the family.

There is also a further factor to be noted when considering the time-span over which data should be collected. The enumerators' books taken alone do not provide all the information that we need. Supporting data, particularly of a descriptive kind, is also needed unless our concern is exclusively with demographic, occupational, or residential aspects of family structure. This descriptive material is, however, widely scattered, so that one is forced to describe not family structure in, say 1851, but family structure in the period 1841–61, or even

1831–71, in order to get enough background information to fill in descriptions and to support explanations. This implies the assumption that changes within the period reviewed were either very slow or, alternatively, proceeded in clearly defined and specified jumps. It is reasonable to assume that changes in family structure in the nineteenth century were, in most places, fairly slow, though obviously this is not so in areas subject to sudden major changes in the conditions of existence (e.g. the Irish famine), and is probably more true for some aspects of family behaviour (for example, the effects of migration on relationships with kin left behind) than others (for example the relationships between father and son in cotton spinning).[34] Data from periods further from some centre point of a study must clearly be treated with caution. Nevertheless, it seems pedantic and unrealistic to exclude them by some arbitrary line. To take a period extending 20 years on either side of the centre year (say 1851), seems not unreasonable, but this will depend greatly on the area and precise topic studied.

If, however, it is necessary to assume fairly long periods as homogeneous, this has other implications too. The most important is that it is unwise to attempt any study of gradual change in patterns of family behaviour over periods of less than about 50 years. Descriptive sources can usually only be used for work on very long-run or very major changes, because otherwise the range of variation within the data for any period is almost as great as the changes overall. Attempts to make comparisons over short time periods are therefore to be viewed with great reservation. If analysis of change is to proceed beyond mere description of data from enumerators' books, trends must either be inferred from comparisons between areas more and less developed in terms of the independent variable *at a point in time* (e.g. 1851), or must, where data are available, be derived from the long-run data. There is little doubt that a comparative study taking listings for a year in the mid-eighteenth century, and for, say, 1851 and 1970, combined with descriptive and supporting data for a period of 20 years on either side of the dates of the first two, and interview material for the last, might provide us with valuable insight into processes of change. If adequate descriptive material was available, many of the listings of the kind used by Laslett and his associates, particularly if they were combined with family reconstitutions to provide information on relationships between persons who were not co-residing, are detailed enough to make at least crude long-run comparisons possible. This is particularly so in rural areas where inconsistencies over definitions of houses and households are much less likely to cause difficulties.

In general then, to get an understanding of the family patterns we observe in nineteenth-century Britain, and of the factors at work on them, it is best to concentrate in detail on a small span of time, attempting to link individuals between censuses and to other data sources, and making an intensive search for literary background material. This is likely to prove more fruitful than attempts at comparison between one Victorian decade and another.

A few other observations may also be made on the censuses already available for public inspection. Firstly, and unfortunately, the enumerators' books of the 1841 census are of limited value for the study of family structure, for they omit the all-important 'Relation to Head of Family' column. The other columns are also less detailed and, frequently, appear to be less carefully completed. Of the other two censuses, that of 1851 is, from a technical point of view, perhaps slightly superior, because the division of the enumerators' books into houses and census families, though undoubtedly subject to some error, is considerably clearer and probably more consistent than in 1861 and thereafter.[35]

Difficulties in many ways similar to those discussed above arise also in the choice of an area for study. Statistical material is more readily assessed and more easily assembled if it is for a single town chosen because it is believed to be typical of the region or of communities with a particular occupational base,[36] though a sample of several villages in an area is probably best for a rural study. On the other hand, adequate descriptive evidence for one town will very seldom be found. Data from other, similar towns seems admissible, however, though once again caution is necessary. One should always ask oneself whether differences in workbase, size, location, death rates, migration rates, or other factors between these other communities and the chosen town have had effects on their family structure.

Finally, since census data are available for almost the whole country,[37] choice of area and size of area will depend on the theoretical or historical problem in view, and on the availability of supporting data. For some areas this last is so scanty that interesting projects will be stultified. Here as always thorough exploratory work and pilot studies save much wasted time and effort.

III

The basis of most projects, then, will surely be the census enumerators' books of the years 1851 onwards. Their layout and the information available in them has been described by Armstrong and Tillott.[38]

So far almost all studies which have used this source, have taken a simple proportional sample – say one in ten of the houses in the community. This seems an important preliminary step if one is to appreciate the broad parameters of the community's family and social structure, but it has certain disadvantages. For example, a 10 per cent sample of Preston (1,241 co-residing groups in 1,127 houses) produced only 93 men over the age of 65, only 158 childless couples where the wife was under 45, only 38 men classified as upper middle-class, and only 32 families definitely migrant from purely agricultural areas. If such groups are of special theoretical interest, all these totals are too few for adequate statistical manipulation if significant results are to be obtained. The possibility of further sampling of groups of particular interest should, therefore, always be borne in mind. In some cases, where minority groups or problems are to be a principal focus of study, some form of stratified sampling could well be adopted from the outset.[39]

When sampling it is important not to forget the occupants of workhouses and other institutions. In some areas, the workhouse may contain a considerable proportion of certain age/sex groups, notably the old, and care must be taken to include the relevant proportion of these (a tenth if the sampling fraction is one in ten) in tabulations controlled by age. Where, as will often be the case, the area sampled and the Poor Law union are not the same, workhouse inmates must be allocated arbitrarily in rough proportion to the relative sizes of the sampled community and union.

The exact procedure adopted in coding data for transfer to cards or tape will vary according to the questions to be asked. However, under all circumstances a trial run with a small subset of data is very useful as it is difficult to foresee all of the problems which may arise in coding, and the best arrangement for easy tabulation is not always obvious until some trial runs have been made.

Broadly, however, it may be anticipated that information may be required on five levels – co-residing groups[40] within a house, co-residing groups, kinship groups, nuclear families, and individuals.

The system finally evolved for my Lancashire study, using data on Preston, involved three packs of cards, certain pairs of which, under some circumstances, could be combined, and this proved reasonably satisfactory, and may be worth describing briefly at this point to show the general principles followed.

'*A*' cards are the basic cards:

Columns 1–19 contain

(a) a code number to identify the co-residing group;
(b) data concerning the co-residing group as a whole: whether there was one or more than one co-residing group in the house and any kinship relation-ship identifiable between members of one group and of the others in the house,[41] numbers of kin, lodgers, and servants present, family structure of the head's family;[42]
(c) data concerning the family of the head of the first listed (primary) family: number of children, whether, and when, the family had migrated to the town,[43] stage in life-cycle,[44] income level,[45] marital status of the head, presence of step-children, type of kin present in the family classified by their relationship to the head (spread over three columns, one for parental generation, one for sibling generation (and their children) and one for married children (and their children). Also data on marital status of kin and whether the relationship was by blood or by affinity or could not be ascertained.

Columns 20–43 contain data on the individual members of the primary nuclear family: for each member, age, sex, occupation, and whether the occu-pation was the same as that of the household head, birthplace, classified by type of community and distance, up to a maximum of six children.

Columns 44–59 contain data on up to four kinsmen: data as for children, with the addition of relationship to head of household in broad categories of relationships, and marital status.

Columns 60–71 contain data on up to three lodgers: data as for kin except that relationship to household head is, obviously, omitted.

Columns 72–80 contain data on age, sex, birthplace, and type of servant, for up to three servants.

'*B*' *cards* are supplementary individual cards. They supplement 'A' cards when data are required on all individuals in the population who fell into a given category. They contain data on individual children, kin, lodgers, and servants, who do not fit on to 'A' cards, located in the correct column (i.e. with data on the fourth, seventh and tenth lodgers commencing on column 60 of each card, and on the fifth, eighth and eleventh on column 64). The first twenty-five columns correspond with those on 'A' cards to allow cross-tabulation of the characteristics of these individuals with those of the head and his wife, and with details of the structure of the co-residing group as a whole.

'*C*' *cards* are supplementary nuclear family cards. They supplement 'A' cards when data are required on all nuclear families, and contain information on secondary nuclear families, that is on nuclear families whose members are listed in the census as kin of the head, or as lodgers. Those columns of columns 1–19 of the corresponding 'A' cards which deal with nuclear family data are replaced by information from the point of view of the secondary family in question.

This system was devised after much trial and error and proved the most economical and practical of those tried. Thus, for data on co-residing groups, run pack 'A', for data on individuals run the appropriate columns of packs 'A' and 'B', for data on nuclear families run the appropriate columns of packs 'A' and 'C'. Obviously different projects will require somewhat different information and different card arrangements, and space must be left for the inclusion of special independent variables, usually in the form of partly processed data; for example in the Preston study, pack 'A' contained a column giving data on the availability of different classes of person in the co-residing group who might have cared for children of under 10 if their mother were away at work.

From this system, information can be obtained under a number of heads. As a first step, for example, tabulations can be produced to show the proportion of co-residing groups which contain kin. This, however, should only be a first step because, though overall proportions of co-residing groups with kin as members may not differ greatly between two communities under study, the categories of kin involved may be very different in the two cases. The next stage, then, is to obtain simple listings of the kinship composition of co-residing groups.

As an example, data for Preston and for a sample of Lancashire farming villages[46] are given in table 1.

The kinship categories adopted here summarise reasonably most of the important differences noted between communities and between socio-economic

C

Table 1 *Structure of the families of 'occupiers', agricultural village and Preston samples, 1851*

	Preston %	Agricultural villages %
Head alone, or only with unrelated persons	4	5
Childless married couples only	10	12
Married couples (or widowed persons) with unmarried children only	63	56
'Stem families' (two lineally-related ever-married persons, plus other kin if any)	10[a]	6[b]
'Composite families' (other combinations of kin)	13[c]	21[d]
All members of the head's family absent	0	—
All	100	100
N =	1,241	855

Note: The difference between proportions a and b is significant $p < 0.01$ (chi^2 = 9.775), and that between c and d is significant $p < 0.001$ (chi^2 = 26.482).

groups at the aggregate level. There are some immediately obvious points to be explained. What is the cause of the huge number of co-residing groups falling into the 'composite family' category? This category, mainly comprising families with odd nieces, nephews, or grand-children as members, is almost empty in tabulations from present day surveys. How does one account for the differences, significant though rather small, between the two samples?

Within samples, too, very interesting aggregate differences emerge. Table 2 gives similar information for farmers with farms of different sizes from the Lancashire village sample.[47]

Many of the differences in this table are not significant, but two clear trends do emerge which require explanation. Small farmers were much more likely to

Table 2 *Structure of the families of 'occupiers', farmers only, agricultural village sample, 1851*

Farm size	Head alone %	Childless married couples %	Nuclear families with children %	Stem families %	Composite families %	All %	N
Over 50 acres	1($\pm$1)	9($\pm$5)	52($\pm$8)	14($\pm$6)	24($\pm$7)	100	140
20–50 acres	—	16($\pm$7)	53($\pm$9)	9($\pm$5)	23($\pm$8)	101	114
Under 20 acres	9($\pm$6)	6($\pm$5)	61($\pm$11)	3($\pm$4)	21($\pm$9)	100	76
All	2	11	54	10	23	100	330

Note: The figures in brackets give the confidence intervals of the percentages at the 5 per cent level.[48]

have to run their farms alone, and were much less likely to have married children to assist them. The next step is then to see whether these findings are merely artefacts resulting from differences in the age composition of the different groups, or from some other co-varying factors. If no such simple explanation can be found, one can turn to the task of explanation. It is here that descriptive and other similar evidence will play their part.

It is also probably useful at this stage to list all the kin present in the sample, tabulated in terms of their relationship to the occupier. If this is done systematically, comparison between communities and over time will undoubtedly give interesting results as more studies are completed.

There are, however, a number of disadvantages in the use of aggregate data in this way. Many of the gross differences between communities may simply be due to differences in the age composition of the populations and it is useful at an early stage to control for this kind of variation. To take one example, the fact that a larger proportion of households in Swansea in the late 1960s contained parent(s) and married children than did so in Preston in 1851 may be misleading.[49] unless it is also noted that 32 per cent of those over 65 in Preston lived with married child(ren), and 65 per cent with unmarried or married child(ren), compared with only about 20 per cent and 40 per cent respectively in Swansea, and this is arguably the more significant point. Similar, though smaller differences may occur between communities in 1851, particularly if areas which were net gainers of population through migration, and those which were net losers, are being compared.

Similar problems may occur in comparisons by socio-economic group, as a result of occupational mobility over the life-cycle, a problem which, indeed, may complicate all comparisons by socio-economic group. For example, taken in aggregate, there was no significant difference in the proportions in employment, between the wives of skilled factory workers in Preston and the wives of labourers. In fact, however, at all age groups taken separately, the wives of skilled factory workers were more likely to have been employed. The explanation of this is simple. Over the life-cycle, there was a steady decline in numbers in the skilled factory group, as a result of men gradually being found unsuitable for the work. At the same time there was a steady rise in numbers in the labouring group, due both to occupational mobility into this group by displaced factory workers, and to the fact that most of the adult inmigrants could only get labouring jobs. And the proportion of wives who worked fell steadily over the life-cycle. This, moreover, is not an isolated case; to some extent all analyses by socio-economic group are liable to this bias. Equally, the converse may occur from time to time and a relationship which is in the aggregate highly significant statistically disappears completely when controlled by age. Great care must therefore be taken to consider the possible effects of age differences between populations whenever comparisons between groups are being made. It should always be remembered that the establishment of a statistically significant correlation does not prove that one has located a casual relationship, only that there is some co-variance. The co-variance may be due to the operation of some third factor that has not yet been located.

Age is not always the most discriminating variable, however, in relation to the changes which occur during the course of a married couple's life-cycle. It is a particularly weak predictor where the populations of the areas or socio-economic groups which are being compared had very different marriage ages. It often proves better to classify one's data in terms of the 'life-cycle stage' which the couples have reached. This variable has been used to good effect in recent years by sociologists studying family relationships in modern communities.[50]

The underlying supposition here is that changes in the behaviour of individual families over time are not so much determined by time itself as by the changes which occur over the life-cycle in the number of members of a family, and in its role structure. Particularly important are the restrictions which the number and age of its members impose on the family's range of possible courses of action, and those of its individual members, and the way these constraints alter as the life-cycle proceeds. Changes occur not only because of changes in income and in necessary expenditure as the number of members of the family rises and falls, but also, for example, because as children grow up they make different and perhaps fewer demands on their parents, and this in turn changes the roles that it is feasible for them to take on. The role most affected is probably the mother's role as member of the labour force.

The life-cycle stage scheme requires some modification before it can be used in a historical context, since the usual practice requires some knowledge of children who have left home, which is not available in the mid-nineteenth century English census data, nor so relevant when one's dependent variable is primarily the co-residing group. The groupings used in the Preston study showed the existence of marked trends over time in a number of variables; the categories used were:

Life-cycle stage	Married couples where:
1	Wife under 45; no children at home.
2	Wife under 45; one child only at home; child aged under one year.
3	Others with children at home but none in employment.
4	Children at home and some, but under half, in employment.
5	Children at home and half, or more than half, in employment.
6	Wife over 45; no children, or one only aged over 20, at home.

In all cases 'children' means unmarried children. For many purposes categories can be combined. For example, couples in life-cycle stages 1 and 2 are both in the main recently married, but members of one group have a child, and of the other have not. For some purposes the two groups are best taken together; for others, couples in life-cycle stage 2 may better be combined with those in stage 3. A similar system could be devised for widowed persons' families. Table 3 shows an example from the Lancashire study of the life-cycle stage variable in action, and shows how it clearly points up interesting trends which will require explanation.

Table 3 *Residence patterns of married couples by life cycle stage, Preston sample, 1851*

Life-cycle stage	Head of own household			Not head of own household			Total	
	Whole house %	Sharing a house %	All %	Lodgers %	Kin %	All %	%	N
1	44(±7)	13(±5)	57(±8)	28(±7)	15(±6)	43(±8)	100	159
2	56(±13)	20(±10)	76(±11)	14(±9)	10(±7)	24(±11)	100	59
3	76(±4)	14(±4)	91(±3)	5(±3)	4(±2)	9(±3)	100	388
4	85(±6)	13(±6)	99(±2)	1(±2)	—	1(±2)	99	122
5	82(±5)	16(±5)	98(±2)	1(±2)	0(±1)	1(±2)	99	234
6	73(±9)	23(±8)	95(±4)	4(±4)	1(±2)	5(±4)	101	106
All	72	15	87	8	5	13	100	1,068

Turning now to other variables, it can be predicted that, after age, sex, and marital status, the most important single set of factors influencing family residence patterns will be those relating to the economic (class) position of the family. A number of sub-variables seem likely to prove important on theoretical grounds: the size of a family's income, the regularity of this income, the expected distribution of this income over the life-cycle, the number of family members who must work to obtain this income, and the ability of the head to offer employment directly to his children and kin. In most communities, the occupation of the family head will probably be a fairly good indicator of class position, at least while the children were young. Particularly in areas like Lancashire, however, where the earnings of the wife and even of quite young children made up a large proportion of family income, the occupation of the head appears not to have been so relevant for some purposes as the excess of a family's income over its subsistence minimum expenditure. This appears, for example, to have influenced the readiness with which families took in relatives (including parents in old age) who were unable to support themselves, the willingness of children to remain at home in their late teens, and whether or not the mother worked. This last, in turn, seems to have affected the likelihood of co-residence with (and probably also of residence near to) kin, particularly the wife's mother.[51]

It is useful, therefore, to attempt to make, for each family, or for as many families in the sample as possible, an assessment of standard of living relative to some absolute poverty level. The assessment of the standard of living of sample families requires two types of information: estimated mean incomes for a wide range of employments, and estimates of the cost of a minimum subsistence standard of living for families of different sizes. It will often be possible to obtain reasonably good estimates of average incomes for many of the commoner trades in an area, by a careful collection of all information on wages encountered in literary sources. A list of 'standard' wages for the different occupations should be made, to ensure consistency within the study, and this list should incorporate any known variations in wages paid to employees of different ages in the same occupation. Such figures are somewhat arbitrary. Moreover, there may be uncertainties over the precise nature of the occupations of some of the population (the data in the occupation columns of the enumerators' books are possibly the most unreliable of all). In addition, incomes of people in the same occupation undoubtedly varied considerably. Some occupations, furthermore, cannot be classified in this way – occupations (particularly women's occupations like dressmaking) where some people were employed full-time and others only part-time, trading occupations where the data are insufficient to establish the true nature of clientele and thus of income, and white collar and professional groups. This obviously limits the generality of any statements made about the influence of standard of living. Results suggest, however, that a meaningful variable can be derived in this way, and that it has considerable predictive power.

The aggregate income for each family is taken from these figures, and is then set against a standard cost of living measure for each family, based on the size of the family. One possible solution here is to use as a standard measure the cost of workhouse diets, priced for the year in question, plus allowances for rent, fuel and sundries taken from budgets and other contemporary sources.[52] Another, and simpler, method is to use Rowntree's standard minimum subsistence budgets,[53] either arguing that changes in the cost of living between mid-century and 1900 were not sufficiently great to invalidate the figures, or making some adjustments in pricing to allow for changes in the prices of the various constituent parts of the Rowntree budget over the period in question.

As an example I shall cite the family of William Finch, Dresser of Yarn, and family, who lived in Preston in 1851. William's earnings as a dresser were assessed at 20s per week, those of his wife, a power-loom weaver, at 11s, and those of his 14-year-old son, also a power-loom weaver, at 9s.[54] This gave a family income of 40s. According to the Rowntree scale the subsistence cost of living for a family of two adults and five children was 28s 10d. If the Rowntree scale is taken direct, this gives a surplus of income over expenditure of 11s 2d for this family. A more precise calculation, seeking to adjust for price changes, would probably increase the food element by about 10 per cent or 1s 9d,[55] decrease the fuel element by perhaps 20 per cent or say 5d,[56] and decrease the rent element by a shilling at least.[57] The overall difference between the two methods is insignificant in this case.

Alternatively, where this method is not practicable, a simple ratio between the number of family members in employment, and total numbers in the family, both suitably scaled down for the lower earnings and consumption patterns of children, can be used. In practice this latter method seems to give quite good results, though slightly inferior to those obtained by the former.

One other procedural technique may be mentioned at this point. Interest will often be centred on differences in behaviour between migrants and non-migrants. Ideally, one would wish to differentiate between those who had been in-migrants as adults or independent teenagers, and the rest of the population, since it is the former group whose family relationships would probably be most affected by migration. The enumerators' books, however, give only 'Birthplace', though they do give the precise parish of birth, which means that many of those who appear from the books to have been migrants had in fact come in with their parents and siblings as young children. The relationships of this group with parents and siblings in adulthood, though probably somewhat different from those of the native-born, will have been far less disrupted than those of persons who came in as adults and who will normally have left parents and siblings behind. It is thus necessary to attempt to differentiate between the two groups. For married couples, this can be done fairly readily, if with some margin of error, by separating those couples where neither of the parents *nor the eldest child* had been born in the community, from all other migrants. This then, at least, leaves two 'pure' groups: non-migrants (both spouses and *all* children born in the community); and migrants, as defined above. There is also a third 'mixed' group. On this basis one can then argue that any parents, uncles and aunts, siblings, or descendants of siblings, who are found living in the same household or near to a 'pure' migrant couple, had come either *with* them, or to join them, or they had come to join these relatives; in this case there is at least a strong suggestion that the potentially disruptive effect of the migration on family relations was being reduced by conscious action on the part of family members.

The enumerators' books make it possible to describe and compare residence and certain other behavioural patterns of different groups of the population in terms of a wide range of variables – age, standard of living, socio-economic group, family size, birthplace, life-cycle stage, and many others. One major problem remains, however, that of assessing the significance of one's findings. Suppose that, as in Preston, 65 per cent of the population aged over 65 were living with children, either married or unmarried. As it stands, this figure is rather meaningless – indeed it looks rather low; over one third were not living with a child. In fact, however, it may be estimated that only about two thirds of the population of this age group would have had a child alive at all. This makes the figure of 65 per cent look very impressive. Now, in a modern community study, when interviewing an old person living alone, one would normally ask such questions as 'Have you any children alive?', 'If so, where do they live?' This would enable tabulations to be drawn up showing the number of old people *with children alive and living in the community*, who nevertheless lived alone. This would provide one important, if partial, indication of the kind of relationships existing between parents and children. Similar questions might normally be asked of young married couples about their parents, siblings, and other kin.

When mid-nineteenth-century English census material is being used this is not possible, for the information is not provided in the census.[58]

This problem, moreover, arises quite frequently; indeed, it arises whenever there is a question of the survival or non-survival of a person who might be expected to be in an ongoing functional relationship with another where the two are not co-residing. How many of the young lodgers were orphans? How many of the old people living alone had children who might care for them? How many married children could have had a parent living with them?

Unfortunately, we can never know the answers to questions such as these in any precise way. All we can do is attempt to estimate what the figure would be on certain assumptions. The most important assumptions are that both the individuals in question and their relevant kin had demographic histories similar to those of a random sample of the population of the same age and marital status.

But the necessary statistical materials are not available in the form required to enable one to make such calculations in any absolutely precise manner. Approximations may, nonetheless, sometimes usefully be made, the conclusions being presented as indications only, acknowledging that the true answer was probably two, three, or even in some cases five, per cent different from the estimate. Quite large variations in some of the assumptions make only rather small differences to the final results, and confidence may sometimes be increased by what limited comparisons it is sometimes possible to make with known figures for wholly or partly comparable populations.[59]

Most of these calculations require that assumptions be made about a number of different parameters, but almost all of them will require estimations of age specific mortality. Unless the population under study has mortality characteristics very similar to those for England and Wales as a whole or for some other population for which life tables already exist, it is necessary to construct a life table for the community under study. Life tables for mid-nineteenth-century England and Wales were published by William Farr for the years 1838–44[60] and for 1838–54.[61] The differences between them are unimportant. In 1849 the Registrar-General published[62] tables showing the mortality of the different Registration Districts in England and Wales. These, however, only give mortality rates for decennial periods of life, except that for the first five years of life annual figures are given, and, for the next ten, quinquennial figures. As they stand, therefore, these data are too crude for use as the basis of regional life-tables. They do, however, give a good indication of the amount by which the mortality of any given age group in any Registration District exceeded or was exceeded by mortality in England and Wales as a whole. This information can then be used to adjust upward or downward the annual mortality rates provided by the figures for England and Wales as a whole.

The next question is to decide the Registration District for which the table is to be constructed. Registration Districts were frequently not coterminous with towns. Thus, if one is interested in the mortality rates for the towns only, the figures for the Registration District which includes and is named after the town will underestimate urban mortality to the extent to which rural areas with lower mortality rates are included. In this case figures for another town with similar socio-economic characteristics and overcrowding problems but which comprised most or the whole of a Registration District must be used. Thus, in the Preston study, Manchester death rates have been used when purely urban mortality rates were needed.

If, however, one is dealing with an urban population in which there were many immigrants from the rural hinterland, and if many of these spent a considerable proportion of their lives in rural areas, purely urban data will probably over-estimate mortality and it may be better to use a broader unit, perhaps the whole county, as the base.

An example of the beginning of such a local life-table is given in table 4.

Table 4   *Local life-tables for larger Lancashire towns 1838–58*

Age at beginning of year	Numbers alive at beginning of year Manchester (a)	Death rate for England and Wales in that year (per 100) (b)	Excess of Manchester death rate over England and Wales (per cent) (c)	Death rate for Manchester in that year (per 100) (d)	Survival ratio (per 100) (e)	Numbers surviving to end of year Manchester (f)
0	100,000	14·949	162·86	24·346	75·653	75,653
1	75,653	6·312	236·42	14·923	85·077	64,363
2	64,363	3·544	206·25	7·039	92·961	59,560
3	59,560	2·401	210·58	5·054	94·946	56,648

(b) From Farr, *English Life Tables*, 1838–44.   (e) $100 - $ Column (d)

(c) From *Registrar General: Report, 1849.*

(d) $\dfrac{\text{Columns (b)} \times \text{Columns (c)}}{100}$ (f) $\dfrac{\text{Column (a)} \times \text{Column (e)}}{100}$

This life-table, then, gives an indication of the mortality chances for any individual over any period of years, and obviously has wide applicability in investigations of this kind.

Other calculations will necessarily vary somewhat, depending on the particular problem under study. As an example, let us consider the calculation of the proportion of old people who had children alive but were not living with them.

For this it is necessary to estimate the proportion of the population over the age of, say, 65 who, if they had been a random sample of the population, and on the basis of certain assumptions, would have had no children alive on census day.

Unfortunately, precise data on most of the points required are not available, and so some assumptions have to be made. Some are little better than informed guesses, but quite wide variations in some of the assumptions make rather little difference to the final result, which, because of simplifications in the calculations, will only be approximate anyway. The following data were used (all calculations are for 'persons', males plus females):

1. The age distribution of the old people on census day. This can be obtained from the enumerators' books and is grouped here into quinquennial figures, each centred on the middle year (thus the 65–69 group are all assumed to have been aged 67).

Table 5   *Age distribution of sample population, persons aged 65 and over, Preston sample, 1851*

Age group	Assumed age	Percentage of all 65 and over
65–9	67	43·0
70–4	72	31·5
75–9	77	15·0
80–4	82	6·0
85 and over	88	4·5
All		100·0
	(*N* = 200)	

2. The proportion who had never had children either because they never married, or, if men, because they married women whose child-bearing period had ended. In the Preston sample 6 per cent of males aged 45–54 and 10 per cent of females had never married. It was assumed that 8 per cent of the population had not married at an age when they were likely to have had children. Against this should be set a small number who had illegitimate children, but many of these subsequently married, few women probably had more than one such child, and illegitimate children probably had above average mortality. Illegitimate children are, therefore, ignored.

3. The number of children that a woman had had is obviously a crucial variable under the prevailing conditions of high mortality. The more children she had had, the more likely it was that at least one would have survived. Data on the number of children born to a national sample of women married 1851–61 (the nearest years for which reliable figures exist) are available in the 1911 fertility census tables.[63] These data are subdivided by quinquennial age of marriage groups. In theory one should take each age of marriage group separately. Since women marrying young would have had many more children than those marrying in their thirties, and since one must also allow for the fact that the older children of those marrying younger would have been older by 1851 and therefore fewer would have survived, there is no simple way of deriving the required estimates. On the other hand, precise data on the distribution of ages of marriage of the population are not available (though they could be obtained from an analysis of marriage certificates). The calculation was therefore simpli-

fied by assuming arbitrarily that the true results would be the same as those obtained from an analysis based on the age of marriage group 25–29, the group into which both median and mean age of marriage for the population almost certainly fell.[64] The family size distribution for women marrying in the 25–29 age group in the years 1851–61 was then obtained from the 1911 census. The proportions for some of the larger family sizes were grouped.[65] These data are presented in table 6.

Table 6 *Distribution of completed family sizes for women married at age 25–29 in the years 1851–61 (per cent)*

Number of children	None	1	2	3	4	5–7	8–12	over 12	All
Per cent	8·6	4·1	6·0	7·3	8·8	35·2	28·7	1·3	100
				($N = 7,628$)					

Source: *Fertility census*, 1911, Vol. XIII, 416–17.

4. It is also necessary to estimate the number of years lived by the children still alive in 1851. For the individual this varied with the birth order of the child and with the age of the parent in 1851. In the absence of reliable contemporary data it was assumed that all children were born of parents married at ages 25–29, and were born when their parents were aged 32. For parents aged 67 in 1851, then, any individual child would have had to have lived for 35 years, for parents aged 72, 40 years, and so on. Reference to the life-table gives the proportions dying from birth to ages 35, 40, 45 and so on, and these data are given in table 7.

Table 7 *Mortality probabilities from birth to 1851 for a child born when parents were aged 32, for parents of ages 67, 72, 77, 82, and 88 in 1851, from the Preston survival-table*

Age of parent in 1851	67	72	77	82	88
Years of life of child to 1851	35	40	45	50	56
Probability of dying before this age	0·6132	0·6478	0·6847	0·7278	0·7726

5. The probability that any one child would die in the first 35 years of life is thus 0·6132. This figure is, then, the probability, on the assumptions made here, that a parent who had only one child ever born would be left without any children alive when he or she reached the age of 67. If the parent had two children, and if the mortality probabilities of siblings were independent of each other, then the proportion with no children surviving would be the product of the mortality probability of the first child multiplied by the mortality probability of the second. The probability for a person aged 67 that neither of his two children would survive would be the square of the probability for one child, or 0·3760. For a person with three children the probability would be the cube, or 0·2305, and so on.

6. We have so far assumed that no couples were widowed during the child-bearing period. The survival-table suggests, however, that, of persons marrying at age 27, slightly more than 27 per cent would have died before they reached the age of 45. If the mortality probabilities of spouses were independent, for couples marrying at age 27, in 8 per cent of cases both would have been dead by age 45, in 53 per cent both would have survived, and in 39 per cent one or other spouse would have died. This means that the probability that any one individual who reached age 45 was still married was 0·73.[66] It is difficult to calculate with accuracy the family sizes of persons whose child-bearing periods were interrupted by widowhood, and this problem is increased by the high contemporary remarriage rates. The following assumptions were made: that one-half of those widowed had one-half of the number of children of those surviving to the end of the child-bearing period, and that the other half had three-quarters. When these figures for the widowed 27 per cent are combined with the figures of table 6 applied to the 73 per cent whose spouses survived to age 45, the probabilities for any member of the population of having any given number of children are obtained. These figures are given in table 8.

Table 8   *Family-size probabilities for persons aged 45 and over, after adjustment for widowhood and remarriage*

Number of children	None	1	2	3	4	5–7	8–12	over 12
Probability of having any given number of children	0·0888	0·0557	0·0815	0·0979	0·1155	0·3305	0·2207	0·0095

Table 9 shows the working calculations necessary to obtain for the population of Preston in 1851 who had married during the wife's child-bearing period and were now over 65 years of age, the proportion who in 1851 had no children alive on the assumptions made here. For each age group the first row gives the estimated proportion of old people who were in any given age group and who had had any given number of children, as a proportion of the total population of old people (i.e. the sum of all figures in rows 1 = 100 per cent); this is the multiple of the proportion in any age group and the proportion with any given family size. The second row gives the chances that no children would have survived for each number of children. For those who never had any children the proportion is, of course, 100·000. The third row gives the products of the figures in the first two rows. The sum of the figures in all the third rows gives the overall proportion required.

Some 23·8 per cent, then, of those old people who had married during the wife's child-bearing period (92 per cent of the total population of the old) had no children alive. If one adds to this figure the 8 per cent who did not marry before the end of the wife's child-bearing period or who never married at all, the overall percentage of old people without living children is just less than 30.

Table 9 *Working calculations for the proportion of persons marrying during the child-bearing period who had no surviving children in 1851: persons aged over 65, Preston*

Age group	Row number	Number of children							
		None	1	2	3	4	6	10	14
67	1	3·818	2·395	3·505	4·210	4·967	14·212	9·490	0·409
	2	100·000	61·321	37·058	23·058	14·140	5·317	0·752	0·065
	3	3·818	1·469	1·318	0·971	0·702	0·756	0·071	0·000
72	1	2·795	1·755	2·567	3·084	3·638	10·411	6·952	0·299
	2	100·000	64·777	41·961	27·181	17·607	7·388	1·301	0·229
	3	2·797	1·137	1·077	0·838	0·641	0·769	0·090	0·001
77	1	1·332	0·836	1·223	1·469	1·733	4·958	3·311	0·143
	2	100·000	68·474	46·887	32·105	21·984	10·308	2·266	0·498
	3	1·332	0·572	0·573	0·472	0·381	0·511	0·075	0·001
82	1	0·533	0·334	0·489	0·587	0·693	1·983	1·324	0·057
	2	100·000	72·776	52·963	38·548	28·051	14·857	4·168	1·169
	3	0·533	0·243	0·259	0·226	0·194	0·295	0·055	0·001
88	1	0·400	0·251	0·367	0·441	0·520	1·487	0·993	0·043
	2	100·000	77·262	59·694	46·121	35·339	21·271	7·580	2·701
	3	0·400	0·194	0·219	0·203	0·184	0·316	0·075	0·001

Sum of rows 3 = 23·771

Note: to simplify calculation it was assumed that average family sizes in the last three columns of table 8 were 6, 10 and 14 respectively.

Thus one may conclude that some 70 per cent of the aged population of Preston in 1851 (or, allowing for errors in the calculations, perhaps somewhere between 65 per cent and 75 per cent) had a child alive on census day. When this is compared with the 65 per cent who were in fact living with a child, married or unmarried, the result is very striking. It suggests that between 88 per cent and 100 per cent of all old people with a child alive were in fact living with that child.

Comparison with a mid-twentieth-century population is possible. Stehouwer[67] found that almost exactly three-quarters of the present day population aged over 65 in Britain, Denmark, and the United States had one or more living children. Stehouwer's populations probably had a higher average age and certainly had a lower average family size, but this must be to a great extent offset by the much lower infant mortality rates which prevailed in these countries by the late nineteenth century, by the fall in adult mortality rates, and by the fact that these are national samples, not figures for a town with one of the highest mortality rates in the mid-nineteenth-century world.

This example, then, shows the sort of thing that can be done. The assumptions are admittedly rough, but attempts to make them more precise, while they may give an air of spurious accuracy, are unlikely to improve upon them significantly. It may be noted that a different analysis of the same problem, which took each age of marriage group separately and calculated the mortality chances for each child of each age separately, gave a figure of 67 per cent, a comparable figure.

More complex computer simulation techniques would improve some aspects of the model, but not the reliability of the data fed in which remains the prime limitation on improvement. The results of exercises like that used as an illustration, though subject always to a fair margin of error, provide some yardstick against which to assess the significance of one's findings; without such a yardstick, indeed, many of the findings are quite meaningless. Some such estimates, cruder, or less crude, seem, therefore, essential. If the true importance of family relationships is to be understood, alternatives to them must always be considered. Thus, in Preston, young married couples could, at least in theory, choose between lodging and living with parents, and between hired nurses and mothers-in-law for child care. The old might go to the workhouse, or live alone, instead of being cared for by children. Children could send mother to live in the workhouse or alone, or themselves provide her with a home and support. The rural–urban migrant could often turn to persons from the same village, and to co-lodgers instead of to kin when he needed help in finding a house, in adjusting to urban life, and to a job. Descriptive evidence is obviously crucial here, in suggesting why one alternative rather than another was chosen, but the sample data provides statistical evidence both on the existences of alternatives, and on the choices between alternatives actually made.

So far attention has focused mainly on residence patterns, but the sample provides data on many other matters as well, either directly or by suggesting maximal or minimal figures for patterns of behaviour. It can be used, for example, to obtain data on the relationship between the occupations of fathers and co-residing children, husband and wife, and kinsman and kinsman, and these figures, when taken together with data on how recruitment to jobs actually occurred, provide some insight into the role of family relationships in job placement.

A sample of a population at a point in time, however, unsupported as it must be by evidence about past events and future expectations, is unable to throw any light on some very interesting and important questions. For example, once children leave home and marry, where do they live? The effect on family relationships may be quite different if they live five yards or five miles away (though this will depend in part on the functions kin perform for each other).[68] What bases other than kinship exist on which residential propinquity may be organised? How often did people move house? How far did they go? At what age did children leave home in different socio-economic groups? The sample data cannot help greatly here.

Again, the answers suggested by sample data on trends over time may be false. It is not usually justifiable to draw conclusions concerning changes over a life-cycle from data which only gives a cross-sectional picture at a point in time. For example, the fact that many younger migrant couples are to be found living in lodgings while few couples in later life-cycle stages were doing this might suggest either that all migrants moved first into lodgings and later to a home of their own, or that there was a transient element in the population, consisting of young married couples who later moved away. Similarly, while it can be shown that more newly married couples (LCSs [life-cycle stages] 1 and 2) were living in lodgings than couples in later life-cycle stages, this might be due either to a movement of couples out of lodgings between LCS 2 and LCS 3, or to some sudden change or shift in behaviour patterns since the time when those in LCS 3 were in LCS 2 (as a result, for example, of an increasing shortage of housing). Or again, it would be incorrect to infer from cross-sectional data that, because a high proportion of under 30s and a low proportion of over 50s were employed in cotton, occupational mobility out of cotton necessarily occurred among men aged 30 to 50. Much of the change which is important for certain aspects of family structure, can be explained in two other ways. On the one hand, new inmigrants tended not to obtain employment in the cotton industry, and this inflated the number of non-cotton workers in the older age groups. On the other hand, the continued expansion of the cotton industry in Preston meant that, regardless of the loss of employees in their 40s, there would always be more young than old cotton workers.

It is plain, then, that an attempt to obtain life-histories of families is of considerable importance. Individual biographies may help here, but may not be representative. Some attempt to use census data for this purpose seems, then, essential.

If one is dealing with villages, and with low population turnover, and above all, if registration certificates, or parish registers are available, this becomes a comparatively easy task if somewhat laborious. One good example of the productive use of this technique on pre-industrial data is Laslett and Harrison's *Clayworth and Cogenhoe.*

If the community studied, on the other hand, is a town of 70,000 people, to cover the whole town and trace individuals and families from census to census becomes a well-nigh impossible task if done manually, though possibly feasible by computer.[69]

It is worth noting, however, that useful results, if of less generality, can be obtained from a manual analysis of a small area of a large town which seems to contain a fairly good cross-section of the population under study. If a small number of enumeration districts are taken, lists made of all residents at each of the censuses available, an index made, and then a search undertaken through each census to locate individuals named in the other two, useful material can be obtained even if attention is confined to the base districts and, say, all enumeration districts contiguous to them. It is true that residential mobility among the urban working class was high[70] but most people did not move far[71] and many can usually be traced.[72]

Access to a large scale Ordnance Survey map of the area is invaluable at this stage, both in defining areas, and in plotting move and residence patterns.

There are, of course, many problems. For example, there is no way of knowing the extent to which the family behaviour of those traced differed from those who were not traced. Certainly the lives of migrants were being more disrupted. Their age and occupation parameters can, however, be ascertained. Again, unless it is possible to trace all the marriages of sample members in local marriage registers girls who marry between censuses will be under-represented.

It may, nevertheless, be useful to describe briefly criteria which may be used to decide whether or not a person traced in one census should be considered to be the same as a person traced in another, and also to discuss a few other points about this technique.

For any individual the following information is given and may be used in differentiating between individuals: Surname, Christian name, age (plus or minus ten years) and birthplace. These should all in theory remain constant for the same individual over time. In addition there is occupation, but this may sometimes change over a ten-year period and can therefore only be used as an additional supporting criterion but never to reject an individual. For single individuals, I have usually used the criteria same surname, Christian name, age (within one year) and birthplace. If age was correct to within five years same occupation, name, and birthplace were considered adequate as criteria, as long as either occupation or birthplace was not that of over 10 per cent of the population. If birthplace was discrepant, name, age (to within one year) and occupation were considered adequate as long as the occupation was not that of over one per cent of the population. Note that as a result of these rules all occupations and birthplaces will not have an equal chance of representation in the final figures so that tabulations to show differences in behaviour patterns by occupation or birthplace will have to exclude any individuals included in the sample on the strength of them.

For Christian names and surnames it is much more difficult to draw up hard and fast rules, though precise criteria for doing this are urgently required.

Sometimes, where certain surnames are very common, the whole system may break down when it becomes impossible to differentiate one John Smith from another. Spelling of surnames often changes from one census to another. Different spellings which give phonetically similar names should be specially watched for. Even Christian names may undergo transformation, not only from Margaret to Peggy, or from Elizabeth to Betty or Lisa, but, as in one remarkable case, from Thomas to William and back to Thomas, the continuity only being assured by identical names of the rest of the family and by the man's age, birthplace, and occupation.

Where an individual is a member of the same family in two censuses, it is usually easier to be certain of his identity, and, except perhaps where tabulations are being made to show differences between sole individuals and those who are members of families, and between familes of different sizes, it seems legitimate to use the additional information provided by combinations of information for several individuals to improve the recovery rate. For a family of two, one has seven distinguishing criteria (one surname, two Christian names, two ages and two birthplaces). For a family of three the number is 10, for four 13, and so on. All the above rules are applicable here. A further relaxation of one error for every two members of a family may probably be made without seriously increasing the chances of error.

The 'life histories' which are drawn out by techniques such as these may well, in very mobile communities, cover little over half of the population, but taken together, they at least make it possible to suggest some interesting tentative conclusions. For example, the homes of married sons can sometimes be traced, and the use of registration certificates should make possible the tracing of a fair proportion of married daughters as well. In the Preston study, for example, it was possible to discover the whereabouts of 24 sons who had married and left home, and whose parents' homes could also be traced. No fewer than 10 of these 24 sons were living within 100 yards of their parents. This looks impressive, but just how impressive?

Before the full import of these figures can be seen, it is necessary to try to estimate the proportion of relatives who have been traced. It is known that 127 sons aged 5 and over disappeared in an intercensal period from families which could be traced in at least two successive censuses. It may be estimated from the mortality table that, if these sons were a representative sample of the population as a whole, given their age distribution, 116 would have been alive at the next census. Using information about the proportion of the population married in each age group a rough estimate can be made of the proportions of the population unmarried at one census who would have married by the next.[73] On the basis of these very rough assumptions it would appear that 50, and more certainly, under 55, of these sons who had left home in the intercensal period would have been alive and married at the later census. In 1851 the town of Preston contained about 11,000 houses.[74] The area searched contained 1,703 houses in 1851, about 16 per cent of the houses in the town. On this basis, if these surviving married sons had been scattered randomly over the town,[75] and even if, as seems very improbable, none had left the town at all, one would have expected to find only between seven and nine in the area searched. In fact, at least nine of these married sons were traced to houses within 100 yards of their parents, and 22, or $2\frac{1}{2}$ to 3 times the randomly predicted number were found in the area searched.

Moreover, even within the searched area, there was a noticeable tendency for related persons to congregate near together rather than to be scattered over the whole area, even though, with one or two minor exceptions, the area was apparently remarkably homogeneous in its types of housing. This clustering tendency was most obvious if the actual distribution of related persons over the area was compared with a population randomly distributed over the same area. For this calculation all houses in the searched area were allocated a number, and each half of each paired relationship was randomly plotted on a map with the aid of a table of random numbers,[76] no more sophisticated technique being possible because the streets were not laid out on the ground in any regular pattern, so that distances between successively numbered houses varied considerably. Since at least one out of a high proportion of the pairs was living in the base area, which was in the centre of the searched area, to have plotted both houses entirely at random would have biased the results in favour of the hypothesis. To avoid this, the first number selected was always taken from a universe restricted to the enumeration district in which one of the actual residences had been located. Where one of the pair came from the base area, this enumeration district was always used for this purpose; otherwise, selection was made at random. The results are shown in table 10. The difference between random and actual data appears very marked.[77]

Table 10 *Comparison of actual and expected distances between residences of related pairs of kin; Preston intensive survey, 1841, 1851, 1861*

			Distances between pairs (yards)					
	Contiguous*	0–24	25–49	50–99	100–199	200–399	Over 400	All %	N
Actual distance (per cent)	8	5	6	19	21	27	13	100	52
Cumulative (per cent)	8	13	19	38	60	87	100	100	52
Expected distance (per cent)	—	2	2	7	16	38	35	100	104
Cumulative (per cent)	—	2	4	11	27	65	100	100	104

* Next door, opposite, or back to back.

Other information may also be derived from the life histories. For example, it is often possible to trace migrants back to their families in their home villages and thus to show that migrants were tending to move in with, or near to kin. This suggests deliberate action by the migrant to reach a goal seen by him as likely to lead to some beneficial result. What these results were can then be discovered by reference to descriptive data.

Or again, comparison of the rates of disappearance from nuclear families of sons and daughters of different age groups, and with parents in different occupations, after making due allowance for mortality, suggested in Preston, for example, that the relationship between the occupation of the father and the occupation of the child may well have been a significant determinant of the age at which the child left home.

Sometimes still more can be done. Data on several branches of some families may well be found extending over a number of censuses. Particularly with the addition of wills, marriage registers, and other external sources pertaining to the families, fascinating life histories can be built up which may be very useful as examples, or in suggesting hypotheses or principles of behaviour. Information on patterns of succession to property among groups who did not customarily make wills might also be obtained, if one could make enough long-run linkages.

In all this, of course, much hinges on the accuracy of the census. The census authorities believed that the census was taken 'with a nearer approach to accuracy than has before been attained, here or elsewhere.'[78] On the other hand, evidence to the Committee on the census,[79] and the obviously low literacy of some enumerators, casts some doubt on the accuracy of their work.[80] The life histories throw some light on the true picture, by showing the extent of inconsistencies between entries at successive censuses, though these data may not be wholly representative of the books as a whole if the enumerators in the base districts were either particularly bad or particularly good compared with the average; there is, however, so far no evidence to suggest that they differed markedly from the rest. The results obtained understate the true errors in the books, because some discrepancies between data on the same individual in different censuses may have been so great that he was missed altogether in the searches, and some individuals may well, for various reasons, have given consistent but erroneous information in both years. Information derived from reconstitution work would undoubtedly help here.

Nevertheless, the results make it possible to compare the information recorded for 475 persons traced in both the 1851 and the 1861 censuses and it may be worthwhile briefly mentioning them here as a guide to further work. Of the 475 people, no fewer than 47 per cent have recorded for them in 1861 an age which is not exactly ten years older than that given in 1851.[81] Since the censuses were only eight days more than ten years apart, errors on this score are minimal. However, only 4 per cent were more than two years out, and under 1 per cent more than five years in error. Because this method to some extent compounds the errors of both the 1851 and 1861 censuses, true errors in any one census will be considerably less than those given above. 14 per cent had a discrepancy in birthplace between the two years.[82] Some of these were not of any great importance, but in half of these cases migrants became non-migrants and *vice versa*. In most of these cases the eldest child was given with the same (migrant) birthplace as the parents in one census, and as born in Preston in the other. The explanation for this is probably usually that the enumerator, while copying out his schedules into the book, jumped or dropped a line. This 'carry-over' effect also occurs elsewhere from time to time. Five-year-old children are given as married like their parents, and sometimes occupations and surnames are carried down, particularly where ditto marks are in use. As a result of this 'carry-over' effect in the Marital Status column, too many eldest children are probably recorded as married but with spouse absent. It may also be remarked in passing that there is strong evidence to suggest, both from the life histories and from other sources, that many of those given as married but with no spouse present were, in fact, widowed.

Finally, at least 5 per cent had a discrepancy in the column 'Relation to Head of Family'.[83] About half of these were of little importance or were so obvious that correction in coding would be automatic: son instead of daughter, where the child had a boy's name and an age in the 'male' column; son instead of grandson where the mother of the other sons was 70 and the child was 3 (see below); son instead of stepson. The rest were more important. In particular, relatives, notably siblings and nieces and nephews, but also parents and children, were recorded as lodgers. They are probably over-represented in the lower socio-economic groups, and among women. There is some evidence to suggest that this may in part reflect real differences in the relationships of these people to the household head, in that they were, indeed, seen only or mainly in the role of lodgers in the household, contributing only for their keep, and free from kinship obligations.[84] These errors, are, however, surely mainly due to enumerators failing to elicit adequate information about these people. Certainly, it would seem that any figures on kinship co-residence which are derived from census data will somewhat understate, rather than overstate, the actual situation.

The kinship system as recorded in census residence patterns is normally narrow in its range. Few relatives more distant than first cousins, uncles and aunts, and nephews and nieces, appear. This probably reflects a number of things: ignorance of the correct title of more remote kinship relationships on the part of respondent and enumerator, the enumerator's failure to record more obscure relationships, and possibly that more remote kin were not seen as having claims to the privileges and obligations normally associated with kinship. In particular, the kinship terminology used by the nineteenth-century working-class seems to have been at times imprecise. Cases occur both in the census and in descriptive material of brothers-in-law described as sons-in-law, of sons-in-law and fathers-in-law as step-sons and step-fathers, and vice versa, and of nieces and nephews as sisters-in-law and brothers-in-law. Another source of error is where relationships in enumerators' books are given to persons other than to the head of the household. This usually involves the giving of the relationship to the person previously listed, or to a child's parent who is not the head, instead of to the head. Thus the children of a married son who heads a secondary family are given as 'son' instead of 'grandson', or, in one case, the head's father, listed at the end of the family after the head's children, is recorded as 'grandfather'. These errors are usually spotted, because the ages recorded may make the relationship as stated impossible.

Problems arise in all these cases as to whether and when to correct the data, particularly when one remembers that it might be the age and not the relationship column which is at fault. The best solution is only to correct where absolutely necessary to maintain commonsense in one's tabulations, unless the relationship is quite impossible (as is often so with the step-son and son-in-law cases). A case can also be made for treating as impossible any situation in which a woman with several fairly old children is recorded as having also a child so young that the age difference between mother and child means that the mother would have had to have been over 45 when the child was born. This relationship would then be counted as 'grandson' or 'granddaughter'. Similarly, where there is less than 35 years' difference in age between grandfather and grandson, the converse adjustment could be made, but much more information about the frequency and nature of errors of this kind is needed before general rules can be formulated.

One other point should be mentioned on the topic of terminology, the frequency with which the word 'friend' is used in the nineteenth century instead of 'relative', particularly for more distant kin. Unfortunately, it is not usually possible to tell whether or not any given 'friend' is a kinsman or not. It would seem, however, that in some areas, and among some groups, particularly the Irish, it usually means relative.[85]

IV

Data of a statistical nature can only take the story so far. They must be filled out, and supplemented by other descriptive material, drawn from a wide range of sources.

A word of caution may be useful as a preliminary.[86] Great care must be taken when collecting and analysing descriptive material to ensure that one records not only data on the performance of any function by any family member or kinsman, but also data on the performance of that function by any other individual or agency, and on the refusal by anyone to perform the function. If this is not done, a totally one-sided picture will be built up in the research notes, and in the final analysis, the importance of family relationships will be greatly overstressed. Moreover, it should be remembered that the data themselves are likely to be somewhat one-sided. Just because a third of one's notes refer to kin performing any given function is no indication that kin performed this function in a third of all cases, even if the number of references is large. Sometimes, comment will be made because the action was seen by the observer as extraordinary. Often, no comment will be made, because the action was seen as unremarkable. Some cases of non-performance will anyway be missed. Even if all cases (of a fairly large number of cases) are either positive or negative, categorical statements cannot be made without a careful consideration of all possible explanations of this apparent unanimity. Above all one must ask whether or not it was likely that mention of deviant cases would be made at all. Wherever possible the data must be checked against quantifiable material for indications of their generality.[87]

Descriptive material fulfils two main functions. First, it helps in the interpretation of quantitative data. Second, it is the only type of source which will cover areas where statistical data are either entirely lacking, or are of only limited and often tangential nature. This is particularly likely to be the case where one is interested in people's motivations and in the ways in which they themselves perceived their situation.

Under the first heading three points may be noted. Firstly, descriptive data may often suggest hypotheses to be examined. Thus it was statements to the effect that the old in Lancashire were often provided for because they could perform useful functions when the wife was working away from home in factories,[88] which led me in my Lancashire study to see whether there was a relationship between the mother being in employment and the presence of a parent in the household. Such a relationship did indeed exist.[89] Secondly, relationships suggested by statistical analysis (for example, the finding that many single young inmigrant lodgers came from the same village and were in the same occupation as the heads of their co-residing groups), can be filled out, and the mechanisms by which such situations came about can be explored. In the case of the lodgers, this involves looking at evidence describing the processes whereby young men were invited by those who had earlier emigrated from their village to come to the town, and were then found jobs, and provided with semi-permanent homes.[90] Most statistical data, indeed, will require some support from non-statistical evidence, particularly if processes are being examined. Illustrations of such processes from descriptive data also give life and credulity to the statistical assertions. Thirdly, the motivations and underlying actions cannot usually be understood simply by reference to statistical data. For example, it was found in Preston that if their mother was dead, children were much more likely to leave home than they were if their father had died. One possible explanation of this, suggested by theory and supported by much descriptive data, was that children perceived their mothers and fathers very differently. They tended to see their fathers as cruel and egoistic, while their mothers were usually seen as self-sacrificing. As a result, bonds of affection and feelings of obligation to mothers were much stronger than bonds to fathers.[91]

Descriptive data also have a role uniquely their own. It is evident that there are many topics on which one would like information (because different aspects of family behaviour are intimately related, and the understanding of any one needs some insight into all), but which cannot, in a historical situation, be investigated directly by statistical analysis. Since only descriptive data can be used, assertions can usually be made only with much less certainty.[92] It is, unfortunately, rarely possible to use any rigorous form of content analysis on the kinds of data used in the study of family structure,[93] though always important to keep one eye open for data suitable for quantitative analysis in this way.

Descriptive data are the chief source of information on the following: qualitative and emotional aspects of family relationships; authority patterns; socialisation; an actor's conception of the family and its meaning to him, and the roles and obligations that membership imposes on him; his views on the relative strength of obligations to wife, children, parents, uncles, cousins, neighbours, friends, workmates, persons born in the same village etc.; many of the functions family members perform for each other in every-day life and in crises, and why, how, and when they do so. Data on these and many other topics must, in a historical context, come solely, or almost solely, from descriptive sources.

Descriptive materials useful for this subject can be divided into three broad categories: descriptions of how and why members of groups of other people in general behave; of how and why other individuals have behaved or behave; and of how and why they themselves behave or have behaved.

Tracts, reports of missionary and charitable societies, descriptions of crises, newspaper investigations into the condition of the people, parliamentary investigations, and the evidence of some witnesses to them, speeches in parliamentary debates, and some aspects of novels and other works, come under the first head. Descriptions of crises – epidemics and slumps, for example – are often of particular value, for it is at such times as these that the full services of a kinship system are likely to be mobilised.[94] Most of the above sources also contain examples which fall under the second head. Under the third head come, on the one hand, verbatim or semi-verbatim replies to enquiries or questions – particularly useful here are the occasions on which ordinary people gave evidence to parliamentary enquiries about themselves, above all when the same questions were asked to a large number of people. Biographies, autobiographies and diaries are another valuable source under this head. Such materials are the major source of evidence on motivations and on the more intimate aspects of family life. It must be remembered, however, when considering answers to questions, that these were usually recorded long-hand by members of the middle-class, who may have slightly altered the original words used and, in doing so, have often increased the sophistication or the affective content of the phraseology in such a way as to convey an incorrect impression of concern, attachment, or motivation.

As always when interpreting data, attention must be paid to its probable reliability and generality. In particular, three questions seem important for the study of family structure: did the reporter really know enough about a situation to report it accurately? was he biased? how far can his findings be generalised?

Under the first head, two comments are important. Many of those who reported aspects of family behaviour, above all if they were dealing with the working class, were middle-class people with little real understanding of working-class life. They were, moreover, often visitors to the region in question, reporting superficial impressions or even basing their conclusions on selections from documentary material produced by others. For Lancashire Peter Gaskell, Ashley, Engels, and a number of novelists (Tonna or Dickens, for example) fall into this category. A second group consists of those who, though more familiar with working-class life and reliable on some topics, still fail to understand properly the constraints operating on people to bring about certain aspects of behaviour and thus impute incorrect motivations to them. Criticisms of working wives, of parents seeking employment for young children, and of unemployed fathers, often fall under this head.[95]

The second head, that of bias, is less important in this field than in most areas of historical enquiry. Most of the topics covered by this kind of research were not the express concern of the investigator whose report is being considered. Evidence, rather, usually comes as by-products of such enquiries, and from odd comments, though certain topics – parental authority or the absence of care for kin in their old age, for example – are sometimes of more direct concern to the authors, and the possibility of bias should be borne in mind. The disadvantages which result from the data being in this form have been noted earlier when the reasons why any piece of behaviour might or might not be the topic of comment were discussed. Moreover, the scattered nature of so much of the evidence makes its gathering laborious – there is no one source for any one topic – and makes classification and filing somewhat of a nightmare. It does help, however, to ensure its reliability, particularly if information about behaviour can be cross-checked from a number of different kinds of source.

It is the third head that presents the most trouble. It was pointed out above that the literature always tends to report what struck the observer as out of the ordinary or shocking – Mayhew's costermongers, drunks, children who deserted their parents, cases of extreme self-sacrifice or devotion. A further problem is that many of the best sources from the point of view of detail and quantity of data, are primarily concerned with social pathology, with the very poor, the delinquent and the criminal. Sometimes, as, for example, with children who deserted their parents and went into lodgings, statistical data can be used to suggest that in spite of widespread comment in the literature, the frequency of such behaviour was, in fact, low[96] (though the forces which led to the cases where a break actually occurred may still have been active in changing the quality of relationships which continued). If statistical confirmation is not available, the extent to which data can be generalised must be carefully considered; whether or not the behaviour seems consistent with other forms of behaviour on which evidence is 'harder' is often a useful guide. Above all, the pitfall of assuming that all behaved like a conspicuous minority, that, for example, all working-class husbands were wife-beating, callous, selfish drunkards must be rigorously avoided.

One point on the presentation of data may also be mentioned. It will never be possible to quote in full all references to any aspect of behaviour which one traces; indeed, what is required is analysis, so overquotation should be avoided. Thus, a long list of references in support of a point can be made to look very impressive, when, in fact, each one applies only to one isolated case. Conversely, two supporting references to general statements by well qualified and perceptive commentators are probably a far more valuable source. It is desirable that the type of source used on any topic and its assumed generality should be systematically indicated. Asterisks might, for example, be put to all references which are to single cases only. Statements supported by references thus marked can then be treated with a proper caution.

v

To conclude, it may be useful to suggest a number of possible lines of future research. More studies of the family in all its aspects in regions with different economic and social characteristics are highly desirable. London, the Midlands, mining areas, and some rural counties, as well as Ireland, all seem to offer scope for interesting work on a broad front, and to have adequate descriptive data available. Studies of an area over time might also prove useful, for example, the comparison of the kinship structure of a town in the 1850s and in the present day, particularly if economic change has been rather slower there than elsewhere, would be very worthwhile. Studies comparing areas of similar workbase but in different economic circumstances might also prove very interesting. A study of a town involved in a big strike or a slump at the time of the census compared with another not so affected, for instance, might throw interesting light on the reactions of the family to crises. Intensive studies, concentrating on a group of villages and using registration and other locally available data; studies limited to middle-class groups to test the generality of Crozier's London findings; studies of migrants; of the relationship between marriage and the transfer of land; and many more, would be of considerable value. Above all, a sure foundation of facts presented in such a way that comparability with other studies is ensured, and preferably oriented to theoretical considerations, will surely be a useful contribution to the furtherance of knowledge and the replacement of folk myth by fact.

3. Sources of inaccuracy in the 1851 and 1861 censuses

P. M. Tillott

I

The exploitation of the enumerators' returns to the nineteenth-century censuses, whether by using computers,[1] mechanical data-processing machinery,[2] or simply many hands to make light of the work,[3] has in the past few years begun to reach sizeable proportions. Some indication of the quantity of work in hand may be found within the covers of the present book. It seems appropriate, therefore, to try to assess the quality of the returns as source material with particular reference to the way in which they were compiled.

The following commentary is derived from experience gained while investigating the social and economic history of various urban and rural communities in Yorkshire and Lincolnshire and adjacent counties with a combined total population of more than 50,000.[4] The method of analysis adopted was designed to investigate the total population of each community rather than a sample, so nearly 3,000 pages of enumerators' books (recording a population of about 56,000 persons) have been examined. Most of this work was on the 1851 returns; such comparative study as has been possible with those for 1861 suggests that while similar experience with them would be very desirable, much of the commentary applies equally to both censuses. Yet, while it may fairly be claimed that the work is numerically widely based, it is limited to a few areas. The returns for other parts of England, particularly for London, may exhibit variations in practice that go altogether unmentioned here; and the returns for Wales, Scotland, and Ireland do not yet seem to have been examined from this point of view.

Only the 1851 and 1861 returns are here treated. The 1841 returns were not used in the projects: the lack of any indication of relationship to the head of the household, the less precise statements of age, the omission of localised birthplaces, and other features, make them incapable of such sophisticated interpretation as is possible for 1851 onwards. They are, moreover, very much less easy to handle, being poorly written for the most part and less systematically arranged. From every point of view it is the greatest pity that this should be so, for most historians of the nineteenth century would agree that the early 1840s are a key period in the history of industrial and rural communities alike. In one important characteristic, however – the recording of occupations – the 1841 returns, though inferior to those of later censuses, are not entirely dissimilar to

82

the later ones and what is said below in this field may perhaps be found useful by users of the earlier material.

Two points should be made at the outset. First, the material can never be regarded as coming within the first order of evidence since it is a recension of prime documents. Second, continued examination of the returns suggests very strongly that they are reliable and that for almost all purposes the extent of error described in the following pages is slight. On the other hand censal cover was limited. The enquirer will seek in vain for information about such things as religious affiliation, or educational attainment (except in so far as that is indicated by the scholars[5]), or, as in a modern census enquiry, the accommodation and amenities available to the household. The English censuses of 1851 and 1861 compare ill in some respects with their American counterparts of 1850–70 which, in six detailed schedules, called not only for the usual information about each individual but also for economic and social statistics of the neighbourhood.[6]

For all that, the range of enquiry which the enumerators' books will sustain is very wide, as the present volume, amongst other work, shows. But their value is severely limited unless they are used on a fairly extensive scale and in a comparative manner. Sampling design and data processing methods deserve close attention.[7]

The censal process in 1851 and 1861 in England has been described elsewhere[8] but it is convenient here to recall the administrative procedure. The country was divided into registration districts based on the Poor Law unions set up under the Poor Law Amendment Act of 1834 and the sub-districts derived from them. The registrars and their staffs chose enumeration districts of a suitable size and enumerators to visit them and submitted their lists to the Census Office for approval. In the week preceding the census night (30 March 1851, 7 April 1861) the enumerators delivered blank forms known as schedules to every householder in their district. They collected them the morning after census night, checked them, entered up those with no return by enquiry on the spot, and took them home, where they copied them into books of forms which were very similar in design to the householders' schedules. It is these books which have been preserved and are made available for public inspection at the Public Record Office.

Every enumerator's book is thus a recension of the householders' schedules and errors of mere copying or illegibility were bound to arise. How and where they may be detected is described below: they are perhaps the least significant of the kinds of error and emendation to be found. Other sources of error are more serious. For example, in an unknown but probably large number of cases neither the householder nor any member of his family will have been able to read or complete the schedule. Even where a literate person was available, his understanding of the instructions and treatment of the facts must have been subject to a variation wider even than that reported by enumerators today.[9] Under such conditions it might be supposed that the returns from remote rural areas would show marked differences from those of, say, the middle-class suburb of a town, but this is not so. The reason can only be that before copying them into their books the enumerators had to correct and standardise many schedules that were, as the Census Report puts it, 'manifestly false'.[10] Most unfortunately no sample of the householders' schedules seems to have been preserved.

Besides the enumerator, two other persons may have emended the householder's original statement. First, the district registrars were instructed to revise the enumerators' books, using the schedules as a check;[11] one registrar in the districts which are the subject of this enquiry, did so minutely;[12] others appear to have been content to sign the declaration in the front of each book, making sure that the returns from each enumeration district had arrived, but no more. Secondly, the clerks in the Census Office were instructed to revise them but to content themselves with surveying the inherent consistency of the enumerators' books without, generally speaking, examining the schedules;[13] how successfully they did so is described below.

One good reason for supposing the returns to be accurate may be thought to lie in the quality of the enumerators themselves. Only half a dozen or so of the ninety or more enumerators who produced the returns of the sample area showed evidence of unsuitability for their task. Many were men of clerkly habit with a strong feeling for accuracy – schoolmasters, parish clerks and so on. According to the Reports they encountered little disposition on the part of the public to mislead them, at any rate intentionally.[14] No doubt embarrassing family relationships were sometimes obscured, though in a surprisingly large number of cases they were laid bare in the returns; no doubt, too, ages were often uncertain (comparative studies of the '51 and '61 returns show them to have been so) and some were intentionally obscured.[15] But the remaining censal information – name, sex, occupation, and birthplace – was less liable to falsification, intentional or otherwise. In the description of occupation, difficulties arose less from a desire to obscure than from the inherent problems of definition and the ambiguity and imprecision of the instructions issued to both householders and enumerators. For while these instructions were elaborate and specific about peers of the realm, clergymen, doctors and similar minority groups, they were laconic when it came to distinguishing the multifarious occupations of the labouring poor. Most unfortunate of all, the instructions omitted, except in the case of army officers and physicians and surgeons, any directions for determining whether the occupation was followed full-time, part-time, or not at all. In certain cases the enumerators took it upon themselves to indicate unemployment but on the whole the returns are silent upon this point and in that silence lies one of their chief weaknesses for economic analysis.

Nevertheless, all in all, the abiding impression after examining a large number of enumerators' books is admiration for the skill of nineteenth-century administration coupled with faith in the accuracy of the results. It is an impression supported by such checks as can be made. For the more prosperous artisans, the traders, and the professional and middle-classes, one may turn to contemporary local directories. They offer a check of that part of the censal information most liable to interpretative error by the householders and enumerators – the occupation. On the whole the directory entry tends to be more detailed but rarely differs from the census about the main occupation followed. Occasionally, certainly, there is an impression that the census occupation hardly suggested the status implied by the directory entry and in the case of blanket terms such as 'merchant' the directory may often prove a useful corrective. Generally speaking the tendency is to up-grade the status implied by the census occupation but this is a characteristic that should be regarded with suspicion since it is most probably a reflection of the advertising nature of the directories.

In the Sheffield area 42 per cent of heads of households were traced in the 1852 White's Directory of the city. As might be expected the bulk of those found in the directory were in the social classes which included large employers of labour, managers, large shopkeepers, the professions, retired persons and those of independent means. A second group of social classes, the ordinary shopkeepers and the clerks, was not far behind them. About a sixth of the directory entries offered information different from, or additional to, that found in the census. Some of the information was trivial – the different spelling of a name, the different numbering of a house – and clearly of no greater authority than the census; other directory entries – the more expansive treatment of occupations, notices of places of business separate from the home address – were of more value. But the most interesting feature was that in five-sixths of the cases, the directory (which must have been compiled within a few months of the census) confirmed the enumerators' books. Thus, the census information relating to name, address and occupation of 35 per cent of the heads of household in the Sheffield quota for 1851 (i.e. 83 per cent of the traced households) could be confirmed from the directory; and of another 7 per cent it could be said that the census was not so much wrong as incomplete in its descriptions of occupations.[16]

Secondly, the poll books, especially those for 1852 where occupations are given, may be interwoven with the directories for a cross check. But since the occupational descriptions in the poll books are usually succinct to the point of obscurity the more usual application is of the censuses and directories to the poll books rather than the reverse.[17] That the three sources in combination may be extremely productive in several fields of research will no doubt appear in due course:[18] as a check on the validity of the census returns the poll books are of limited value.

Thirdly, it is possible to check the quality of the family information and occasionally the occupations by an examination of contemporary parish registers. One limited experiment has shown that the complete omission of a person is unlikely to occur and misinformation about age not as common as might be supposed.[19] The work is extremely laborious, needless to say, and hardly to be undertaken for its own sake. The use of census material in kinship studies, where such checks are likely to occur as by-products of the general enquiry, is discussed elsewhere in this book.

The mode of conducting the censuses of 1851 and 1861 and the checks applied by the officials concerned may thus be said to lead to a high expectation of detailed accuracy in the enumerators' books; and the limited checks that the modern investigator may apply confirm that expectation. Nevertheless there is a wide variation in the enumerators' practice and it is clearly desirable that the interpretation of those variations should be agreed by all who seek to use the material. What follows is an attempt to formulate a guide to the enumerators' practice accompanied by suggestions for a standardised interpretation wherever necessary.

II

Four persons, as has been said, may have had a hand in framing the entries in the enumerators' books in the Public Record Office: the householder, the enumerator, the district registrar and the Census Office clerk. The enumerators' books give no explicit indication whether the original householders' schedule was filled in by the householder himself or by the enumerator acting for him on the doorstep. Very occasionally, the individuality of the schedule shows through in the returns as, for example, in the order in which persons are recorded. The common arrangement of each household is head, wife, and children in descending order of age regardless of sex; but from time to time, in an otherwise normal enumeration district, an eccentric order occurs – all the males followed by all the females and so on.[20] In other cases it is possible to detect the influence of the householder in phonetic spellings of personal or place names. But with no specific indication of provenance for each entry, little is to be learnt from an examination of this aspect of the returns.

For the most part it may be assumed that the enumerators distributed, collected, corrected and copied their own set of schedules. There was provision for them to employ substitutes for one stage of the work and there is occasionally an impression that they used copyists for making up their books though this was not permitted. But it seems unlikely that significant conclusions are to be drawn from any errors that may occur on this account. Few avoid copying errors completely: an occupation copied on to the wrong line where it is absurd for the person enumerated (figure 1); condition placed under relationship to head (figure 2); insoluble sets of relationships (figure 3) and so forth. Occasionally an enumerator omits to use a page in his book – an insignificant error unless the investigator happens to be using a photographic copy that fails to note the omission. It is sometimes suggested[21] that the difficulties of enumerating densely populated ghettoes in industrial towns would overwhelm the enumerators. Such districts were perhaps uncommon in the sample area but a Sheffield household of Irish immigrants may serve as an illustration of what might occur (figure 4). And the exasperation that an enumerator might feel may be judged by the occupation entry for the appropriately named Matthew Parker of Hanover

No.	STREET	NAME	Rel. to Head	COND.	AGE		OCCUPATION	BIRTHPLACE
					M	F		
100	Thomas St. Court 5 No. 2	William Wanfield	Head	Mar	28		Table blade Cutler	Yks. Sheffield
		Elizabeth do.	Wife	Mar		32	Labourer	do. do.
101	Thomas St. Court 5 No. 3	Thomas Rawson	Head	Mar	25		(blank)	Yks.Armthorpe
		(etc. wife and two children)						

Figure 1   (S/O/100–101). (This figure and subsequent similar figures in this chapter are exact transcriptions from the enumerator's book.)

No.	STREET	NAME	Rel. to Head	COND.	AGE		OCCUPATION	BIRTHPLACE
					M	F		
36	High Street	Jeremiah Phillip	Head	Widr	67		Innkeeper	Yks. Embsay
		(followed by family and two servants)						
		William Whitaker	U	U	31		Labourer	do. Cowling

Figure 2   (Sk/a/36).

No.	STREET	NAME	Rel. to Head	COND.	AGE		OCCUPATION	BIRTHPLACE
					M	F		
121	170 Fitz-william St.	John Cockayne	Head	Mar	43		Silversmith	Der. Ashford
		(followed by wife and 2 children)						
		Ann Ashton	Mother	U		23	Formerly Lady's Maid	Yks. Normanton

Figure 3   (S/O/121).

Square, Sheffield: 'Humbug (see schedule)'. In the registrar's hand above is recorded that Parker had described himself as 'Angel or Bishop of the Catholic and Apostolic Church, Victoria Street, Sheffield'.[22] These matters aside, the enumerators varied between themselves and even within their own districts in their interpretation both of the instructions issued to them and of the material presented to them by the householders. It is these variations in practice, more than those of the householders, the registrars and the checkers, which form the subject of the commentary, under each head of censal information, that follows.

Emendations by the registrars are less easy to trace and, as has been said, occur extensively only in one district in the sample area. Here, in north-west Lincolnshire, the registrar in '51 and '61, Lucas Marshall Bennett of Chapel Cottage, Winterton, may be presumed to have had special knowledge for he was by profession a doctor in general practice in the region.[23] Certainly his

No.	STREET	NAME	Rel. to Head	COND.	AGE M	AGE F	OCCUPATION	BIRTHPLACE
121	Court 9 Coalpit Lane	John Flannagan	Head	Mar	35 ~~70~~		Labourer (Bricklayer)	Ireland
		nk	(blank)		11		nk	nk
		Eady Roll	(blank)			8	nk	nk
		Martin ~~Munks~~ Marsden	Lodger	Mar	43		(blank)	nk
		M do.	Lodger	Mar		27	(blank)	Ireland
		W do.	Lodger	(blank)		2	(blank)	Ireland
		nk	Lodger	(blank)		1mo	(blank)	Yks.Sheffield

Figure 4 (S/U/121). The abbreviation 'nk' stands for not known; the enumerator has made emendations for Flannagan's age (probably inserting the median of three score years and ten as occurs frequently in similar circumstances) and for Marsden's name; the child of the last entry may be one month or two – the figure has been made blotted.

emendations suggest that he carried out the very thorough checking of house-holders' schedules against enumerators' books enjoined by the Census Office.[24] Even in a sub-district of only 9,000-odd population it can have been no easy task. Registrars' alterations to the books can be inferred only from handwriting: in the case of Bennett they occur only in the '51 returns, are in ink (as opposed to the checkers' crayon or pencil) and may be identified with his signature at the front of each enumeration book.

For the purposes of investigation and analysis the registrars' emendations clearly have no less force than the enumerators' recension of the householders' schedules and may have more. Unless they are frequent and in a distinctive handwriting they will in all probability go unnoticed; but where they do occur and display some inherent consistency they may be taken to indicate that the returns for the enumeration district concerned are of high authenticity.

Temporary clerks were employed in the Census Office for checking, abstracting and tabulating the enumerators' books. Several clerks handled each book and their initials and signatures appear in the '51 returns. Here they are all referred to as Census Office 'checkers'. For the most part, the marks they made on the returns are ticks and crosses in pencil and crayon, arising from the need to count. Even in photographic copies of the books the marks are easily identified. In the '51 returns, but very much less commonly in the '61 returns, the checkers also inserted emendations of the material itself. The emendations are often erratic. They could not be based on local knowledge, since they did not check the enumerators' books against the schedules,[25] and although they were 'instructed, assisted and checked', their practice varied considerably. They missed

No.	STREET	NAME	Rel. to Head	COND.	AGE		OCCUPATION	BIRTHPLACE
					M	F		
67	Broomhall Terrace	Thomas Collinson	Head	Mar	26		Newspaper Reporter	Leeds Yks
		Martha Collinson	Wife	Mar		20		do. do.
		Joshua B.R. Collinson	Son	Un	2			do. do.
		Henry P. Collinson	Son	Un	7months			Sheffield do,
		John R.H. Collinson	Brother	Un	10		~~Reporter's Brother~~ Son	Leeds do,

Figure 5   (S/J/67). The amendment *Son* is in the pencilled hand of the checker.

many clerical errors by the enumerators of ascription to sex or birthplace, or of absurd relationships. Occasionally they emended unnecessarily making a brother a son where the ages made the ascription absurd (figure 5) or by making an unmarried lodger a widow.[26] Their most frequent emendations in the '51 returns occur under the 'occupation' column and here they might reach the nadir of their activities as when a Doncaster taxidermist was labelled 'Rate Coll.' later emended to 'Tax Coll.'[27] As might be expected, the occupation of taxidermist does not appear in the '51 *Census Report*.

In view of the nature and quality of the checkers' emendations as demonstrated here and elsewhere, their comments are usually best disregarded. In the sample area the checkers' ascriptions to occupation were noted but were found to influence results significantly only in the case of the employment of boys in one area.[28]

The returns as they stand today provide information under nine heads about each individual – his address, name, relationship to the head of the household,

D

marital condition, age, sex, occupation, birthplace, and whether blind or deaf and dumb; and four persons – householder, enumerator, registrar and checker – are likely to have had some hand in recording that information. Additionally, the returns are divided into households and here too, the four hands may appear. The treatment of the returns here follows the arrangement of the censal enquiries in order across the page of the enumerators' books but it should be borne in mind that it is often unwise to consider any entry in the books as an entity by itself; for every mark in pen or pencil the whole context – the family, the household, even the enumerator's book itself – will often provide the vital clues to interpretation.

III

THE HOUSEHOLD IN 1851

In its attempt to define and analyse the way in which houses were occupied by households, the census of 1851 met its Waterloo and the battle was hardly reversed ten years later. That the intention was there at all is interesting enough and was perhaps a consequence of such reports as the Health of Towns Commission. In one part of their *Report* the census officials declared that their intention was a purely technical one 'to secure uniformity in the returns'[29] but the tenor of other parts of the *Report* suggests that they may have been influenced by the notion that 'The possession of an entire house is....strongly desired by every Englishman.'[30]

The results were chaotic. Up to 1851 the censal unit had been the somewhat ill-defined 'family'. 'In the Act for taking the Census of 1851' says the *Report*, ' "occupier" is substituted for "family" '; and the occupier with whom the enumerator was to leave a separate schedule, was defined in the instructions.[31] But, laments the *Report*, 'Upon examining the enumerators' books, it was found that the practice had not always been uniform, but that any attempt to correct, at the Census Office, the statements of the enumerators on this point, would be futile.'[32]

'Not always been uniform' is somewhat disingenuous: almost every combination of practice possible occurs within the sample area. For the Census Office had entirely failed to recognise the complexity and variety of possible living arrangements. The *Instructions for Census Enumerators* for the 1966 sample census spends eleven pages on its instructions for distinguishing households and dwelling houses.[33] For households the modern census official wisely concentrates in his definition on 'housekeeping' or 'catering'. For the enumerators of 1851 and 1861 no such definition was available and from this all their difficulties flowed. What, for example, were they to do with the house occupied by two nuclear families – the married son with his wife and child who paid no rent but occupied a separate part of the house and catered for themselves; or who helped with the rent, ate with the family, but slept in a separate apartment?

Or, – clearly a common source of difficulty – the single male lodger whose room was a separate apartment for which he paid rent but whose meals were taken with the landlord? Or the single female lodger who did for herself entirely? And what if any of these single persons were relatives?

The instructions to the enumerators and householders to assist them in recording these situations in 1851 were as follows.

Delivery of Householders' Schedules. In the course of the week ending March 29th, 1851, it will be the Enumerator's duty to deliver to each Householder and Occupier in his District, a Householder's Schedule. In order that this delivery may be complete, he must, at every house, enquire whether the same is inhabited by one Occupier only, or by more than one; and if the latter be the case, he must leave a seperate Schedule with each Occupier:— understanding by 'Occupier', either the resident owner or any person who pays rent, whether (as a tenant) for the whole of a house, or (as a lodger) for any distinct floor or apartment . . . The Enumerator must make a note in a memorandum book of all those houses where he may have left Schedules with one or more Occupiers, stating the number left at each house.[34]

The schedule which the enumerators were to deliver to the householders had, printed on the dorse, an instruction to the householder which said:

This Schedule is to be filled up by the OCCUPIER or Person in charge of the House; if the house is let or sub-let to different persons or families, in separate stories or apartments, the OCCUPIER or Person in charge of each story or apartment must make a separate return for his portion of the house upon a separate Householder's Schedule.[35]

Unfortunately, in the 'Examples of the mode of filling up the return' two quite separate families were listed, divided by a single line right across the page. The intention was probably to illustrate as many of the variables of family information as possible but it seems likely to have given rise to some confusion in the minds of those householders whose houses were occupied by a second, unconnected family. It should be noticed also that in the column headed 'Relation to Head of Family' the householder was asked to 'State whether Wife, Son, Daughter or other Relative, Visitor, or Servant' no mention being made of lodgers or boarders.[36]

It might be supposed that the delivery of the schedules would have to be performed by the enumerator himself but this was not so. While the Census Office thought it 'highly desirable' that he should undertake this duty, he was, if 'quite unable to perform the duty himself', permitted to appoint a deputy.[37] On the morning after census night, that is on 31 March 1851, the enumerator was to visit every house within his district, if possible all on the same day, and collect the householders' schedules:

The mode of procedure on calling at a house (by which must be understood a separate building) *should be this*: The Enumerator should first ascertain whether it is inhabited by one 'Occupier' only, or by more than one: if by one 'Occupier' only, he should ask for the Householder's Schedule left during the previous week; if by more than one 'Occupier', he should obtain a separate Schedule from each.[38]

Each schedule received was then to be numbered consecutively throughout the district and where there were several occupiers in one house the enumerator was to be careful to pin or tie together all the schedules collected from that house.[39]

On his return home the enumerator was to enter the schedules in his book and when doing so follow these instructions:

Under the last name in any *house* (i.e. a separate and distinct *building*, and not a mere story or flat), he should draw a line *across the page as far as the fifth column*. Where there is more than one Occupier in the same house, he should draw a similar line under the last name of the family of each Occupier; making the line, however, in this case, commence a little on the left hand side of the third column, as in the example in page vi. of his book...By the term 'house', he must understand 'a distinct *building*, separated from others by party walls'. *Flats*, and sets of chambers, therefore, must not be reckoned as *houses*.[40]

The example sheets in the enumerators' books contained two imaginary shared houses: in both cases the two co-residing groups in the house are given separate schedule numbers and are divided one from the other by the short line described above; the address is given only for the first element; and the first person listed in each element is designated 'head'.[41]

The effect of these instructions rarely causes the investigator any problems where a household or 'co-residing group' occupied one separate house and such households form the bulk of those occurring in the sample area and possibly in the census of England. Wales, both urban and rural, may have had a similar character but it seems likely that the two great urban areas of Scotland were much affected by tenement building. Even in these straightforward households, however, errors do occur. Occasionally a long line may be omitted altogether, either in the middle of a page[42] or, more frequently, when the list of the household happens to end at the foot of a page. The enumerators' practice in filling the page of their books varies: some follow the examples printed on pages vi and vii of the books; others use a space whenever they have to draw a line; yet others only begin a new household towards the foot of the page when they have sufficient lines on that page to complete it. Lines may be ruled or drawn freehand and may be drawn beyond the fifth column, even across the page; a line may appear under a new head instead of under the last person of the previous household and lines may be marked, either by the enumerator or the registrar, 'ruled in error'.[43] Fortunately all such omissions and variations in the sample area were found, from the evidence of addresses, relationships to heads and names, to be readily assignable to mere clerical error.

Again, even in the straightforward household of one co-residing group in one house, the first person listed in a new group may not be called head although all the other evidence – new schedule number, new address, new name, long line – suggests that the investigator is confronted with a new household. The frequency of this factor in Doncaster and fifteen districts of Sheffield in 1851 is shown in table 1.

The expression used instead of 'head' for the first person listed in such households – 'wife', 'daughter', 'servant' – may often be read as indicating the relationship of that person to an absent head; occasionally the fact of the absence is specifically stated by some such expression as 'Wife – husband away' or by implication when the wife is listed as, say, 'Travellers' wife'.[44] In other cases, where a child or servant heads the list, it may only be surmised, though often with some justification from other evidence, that the head of household is away;

Table 1 *Occurrence of 'head equivalents' in households other than those sharing houses*

District: Sheffield	Head equivalents: numbers	Total households*	District: Doncaster	Head equivalents: numbers	Total households*
G	10	237	1	0	161
H	9	242	2	2	183
J	11	153	3	0	179
K	0	160	4	2	121
L	6	245	5	3	136
M	0	188	6	0	90
N	2	145	7	3	176
O	0	211	8	4	119
P	1	169	9	0	68
Q	0	147	10	0	68
R	3	185	11	0	115
S	1	252	12	2	154
T	1	218	13	4	109
U	1	141	14	7	227
V	6	140	15	5	190
	51	2,833	16	0	103
			17	12	186
			18	0	167
				44	2,552

* I.e. other than those sharing houses.

some enumerators simply leave the space blank in such cases. Conversely it is not safe to assume that where no 'incomplete' households of this kind are recorded none existed: in Sheffield District K, for example, one household was headed by the traveller's wife mentioned above and another by a 9-year-old boy but the enumerator headed every household by a person designated head.[45]

Other difficulties occur. The way in which the schedules are numbered may be haphazard: numbers may be omitted from the series, houses empty or building may or may not be numbered, the numbered series may contain half numbers

(58, 58½) or lettered numbers (115a, 115b, 115c), and additions of inhabited houses at the foot of each page may be faulty. Therefore the enumerator's summary of houses inhabited, uninhabited and building on page iii of his book must never be taken at its face value. Equally the schedule numbers may not be a true indication of the number of householders' schedules issued or collected. It follows that the number of *occupiers* recorded in the summary must be regarded with the greatest circumspection.

A further source of error may lie in the nature of the 'house'. Instances occur in which a single co-residing group with one schedule number, one head, divided from adjacent households by long lines, is recorded as occupying two or three house numbers in a street.[46] Or other anomalies may occur. In figure 6, number 7 Clarence Street appears at first sight to be occupied by two separate households.

No.	STREET	NAME	Rel. to Head	COND	AGE M	AGE F	OCCUPATION	BIRTHPLACE
40	7 Clarence Street	John Turner	Head	M	26		Commercial Traveller	Silkstone Yks.
		Wife						
40½	7 Clarence Street	Josh.N.Retford	Head	M	37		Law Stationer	Balbro Yks.
		(Wife, five children and father-in-law)						
41	11 Do.	Eardley Brown	Head	M	54		Silver Smith	Sheffield Yks.

Figure 6   (S/L/40–40½).

Closer examination of the enumerator's book shows that household 40½ has been inserted in a hand different from the rest of the entries, the street name is differently spelt in each entry, and a number is missing from the street number series. One likely explanation is that '7' is simply a clerical error for '9' in household 40½; or it may be that the number '7' had been given to two separate residences by the local authorities, thus leaving the enumerator sufficiently puzzled to make him pause, check the situation, and have the household inserted later. There are countless instances in towns where the division between separate 'houses' – in courts, in back-to-back blocks, in tenements and so on – is impossible to discover from the address information in the enumerators' books. In rural areas, addresses are often absent altogether or so unspecific as to be valueless. Moreover, the enumerators nearly always count the institutions in their districts (apart from those of 200 persons or more which were enumerated separately) as 'houses'; thus Wesley College in Sheffield is included as a house in the district enumerator's summary.[47] However, the house has little value as a unit of analysis and therefore such ambiguities are of little account in studies of the co-residing group. But any investigation of housing provision within a given locality – not lightly to be undertaken without the contemporary 60 in. Ordnance Survey plan and the survival, largely unaltered, of the property itself – must take careful account of all these anomalies in the enumerators' books.

Nevertheless, in most instances, all these considerations will have little or no bearing. Household will succeed household, occupying a single house indicated by the address, given a schedule number in a straightforward series, divided from its fellows by long lines and with the first person listed in each household designated as head. Such a series may cover the whole of an enumeration district, as, for example, Sheffield K, where the enumerator recorded 160 houses, 160 occupiers, numbered his schedules from 1 to 160, listed a head as the first person in every case, indicated different addresses by street numbers wherever he could and divided each household from the next by a long line (though not always of the same length). Those whose experience has confronted them only with such districts might be forgiven for asking why so much attention is given here and elsewhere in this volume to the nature of the census household. The answer is plainly to be seen as soon as the nature of houses occupied by more than one co-residing group is examined.

Conditions were not like Sheffield K in every Sheffield district and Sheffield is far from typical of urban living conditions in the north of England, let alone in England as a whole. There was, as has been seen, provision in the enumerators' instructions for recording shared houses. Unfortunately, the ambiguities inherent in the instructions and the inability of many enumerators to interpret even the unambiguous part of them led to many divergencies of practice. In the first place only a limited number of enumerators used short lines at all, even where examination of the households suggests that there may have been houses to be indicated in this way. The use of short lines in the sample area is shown in table 2. An example of what might be called the 'correct' use of the short line is shown in figure 7. In such cases it must be assumed that the enumerator detected more than one occupier in the house, left the appropriate number of schedules, collected them, pinned them together, numbered them separately and finally entered them in his book exactly as had been illustrated in the sample sheets of his book; that is, with one address, two schedule numbers, two heads and divided by a short line. The number of houses divided in this way is also shown in table 2.

Even where the enumerators recorded shared houses in this way the modern investigator cannot be certain of the meaning of the record: all depends upon the enumerator's assessment of the nature of the 'house' and his interpretation of the expression 'separate occupier'. As has been seen, the instructions to the enumerators were ambiguous and, as is shown elsewhere by Anderson, the thought behind them was unclear. Moreover, as has been noticed before, this was the one part of his duties for which the enumerator was allowed to employ a deputy. It is impossible even to guess from the document where this occurred; but, where it did, the enumerator's first opportunity to assess occupation was on the Monday after census night when, on the one hand, most heads of household were likely to be at work and when, on the other, he himself was anxious to collect his schedules in the shortest possible time. Even the numbering of the schedules – and no instructions were given about the manner of numbering

Table 2 *Districts of the sample area in which the short line was used in 1851 to divide shared houses*

Place	Number of districts	Number of districts in which short lines are used	Number of houses so divided	Number of short lines used 'correctly'*
North-west				
Lincolnshire	25	11	18	18
Bradfield	3	1	1	1
Braithwell	1	0	—	—
Dalton	1	0	—	—
Doncaster	18	13	38	32
Sheffield	15	8	23	12
Crookes, Sheffield	4	2	6	6
Skipton	7	2	3	3
Tickhill	4	0	—	—
Farnsfield	2	0	—	—
Hathersage	3	0	—	—

* I.e. according to the enumerator's instructions: see p. 92.

No.	STREET	NAME	Rel. to Head	COND.	AGE M	AGE F	OCCUPATION	BIRTHPLACE
15	82 Wellington Street	Richard Beedham	Head	M	42		Joiner	Notts. Budley
		(Wife, 6 children and his father)						
16		Anthony Truit	Head	M	33		Tailor	Yorks.Brammon
		Ellen Do.	Wife	M		26	(blank)	Do. Sheffield

Figure 7   (S/Q 15–16).

them – was to be done during collection, thus relinquishing what might have been a valuable key to their distribution amongst occupiers. Above all, it can hardly be doubted that the variations in household structure confronting the enumerator were as manifold in 1851 as they are today.

To these difficulties must be added another, namely, that the enumerators did not always record shared houses in the manner set out in their instructions. A household otherwise marked as sharing with the preceding one – by a new head, the same address and a short line, is not given a new schedule number (figure 8); or, conversely, households not otherwise marked as shared are given schedule numbers (e.g. 102a, 102b; 58, 58$\frac{1}{2}$) of a type used elsewhere in the same enumeration district for shared houses (figure 9). Or a line may be omitted altogether between two otherwise independent houses (and households) leading the unwary to regard the two as shared. Addresses may be similar without other elements to suggest sharing; the address for a house otherwise marked as shared may be

No.	STREET	NAME	Rel. to Head	COND.	AGE M	AGE F	OCCUPATION	BIRTHPLACE
4	137 Broomhall St.	Elizabeth Baines	Head	Wid		65	(blank)	London
		Henry do.	son	U	23		Metal Smith	Sheffield Yks.
		Ann Lord	Dar.	M		30	Dressmaker	Sheffield Yks.
		Elizabeth Do.	Dar.			9	Scholar	do. do.
		Henry Do.	son		3		(blank)	do. do.

Figure 8   (S/L/4).

No.	STREET	NAME	Rel. to Head	COND.	AGE M	AGE F	OCCUPATION	BIRTHPLACE
102 a	Edmund St.	Lydia Briggs	Head	Wid		47	(blank)	Sheffield Yks.
		(4 children)						
102 b	"	George Challenger	Head	M	42		Mason	Darton Yks.
		(Wife, 4 children and servant (mason))						

Figure 9   (S/H/102a–102b).

repeated (or dittoed) for the second household or it may not (figure 7). The first person listed in the first household or even in the second may be one of those head equivalents who are named when the head is absent (figure 8). Most frequent of all, the first person listed in the second household of the shared house may not be designated as head or as the equivalent of head, but as 'lodger' (figure 10).[48]

In these, as in other difficulties of interpretation of the enumerators' books, the investigator must adopt a standard procedure. What is here recommended may be expressed by the formula that analysis should be conducted in terms of co-residing groups, that these groups should be those listed under each new head (or head equivalent, *excluding 'lodger'*) and that a new house should be counted as occurring after each long line (1851) or double oblique stroke (1861 and after). Only one exception may be allowed. From time to time lodgers are found as heads of households which are divided from the preceding household by a long line and with the household given a new address by the enumerator (figure 11). In such circumstances it can only be assumed that the head of the lodger's household is absent, and he therefore stands as a head equivalent. The rationale for these procedures is set forth by Anderson elsewhere in this volume.[49]

No.	STREET	NAME	Rel. to Head	COND.	AGE M	AGE F	OCCUPATION	BIRTHPLACE
72	165 Fitzwilliam Street	Ellen Spencer	Head	U		29	Letter of Apartments	Yks.Sheffield
		(Nephew, niece and houseservant)						
73		William Smith	Lodger	U	35		Curate at St. Mary's	Do.Kirk Bramwith

Figure 10   (S/Q 72–73).

No.	STREET	NAME	Rel. to Head	COND.	AGE M	AGE F.	OCCUPATION	BIRTHPLACE
46	Trafalgar St. 98	John Hounsell	Head	M	31		File smith	Bridport
		(wife and three children)						
47	Trafalgar St. Court	John May	Lodger	U	29		Journeyman Cooper	Newark

Figure 11   (S/R/46–47).

After what has been said about the enumerators and their instructions and the way they interpreted them, little difficulty should be found in applying this rule in most cases. There remain instances – fortunately forming a relatively small proportion of the total at any rate in the sample area – in which it seems impossible to interpret the enumerator's record, or alternatively a household structure may be inferred even though not ostensibly disclosed by the record.

What, for example, is to be made of 170 South Street, Sheffield, in 1851 (figure 12)? Here were three households, each separately numbered, each separated by full lines, but all living at the same address. All three were perhaps separate occupiers, either as owner or paying rent. The widow may be described as 'housekeeper' as a head equivalent because the head was away or simply because the enumerator was unwilling to designate a woman as head – an attitude for which there is some evidence in the rest of the district. Again, the 'house' may not have been all one building – a guess slightly supported by the fact that in the second and third households the house number, 170, appears to have been written in as an afterthought. The poverty of the neighbourhood and the humble occupations of the second and third households might support an interpretation that some of them lived in unnumbered outbuildings to which the enumerator gave the number of the nearest house. Occasionally, though not in this case, such problems may be solved by the survival of the buildings and by the use of large-scale maps and plans. In the absence of such assistance the rule must be applied, giving in this instance three co-residing groups in three 'houses', Sarah Illingworth being regarded as a head equivalent. Such an interpretation is consistent with the bulk of the evidence.

No.	STREET	NAME	Rel. to Head	COND.	AGE		OCCUPATION	BIRTHPLACE
					M	F		
136	170 South Street	George Critchlow	Head	M	32		Time Keeper	Manchester
		Mary Do.	Wife	M		29	(blank)	Handsworth Yks.
137	No. 170 South Street	Sarah Illingworth	House Keeper	Wid		56	House Servant	Silkstone Yks.
		George Willoughby	Lodger	U	50		File maker and hardener	Balbro Derbys
138	No. 170 South Street	William Fleeson	Head	M	52		Labourer	Wath Yks.
		Anne Do.	Wife	M		55	(blank)	Whitwell Derbys.

Figure 12   (S/L/136–138).

Examples of confusion of this kind are fortunately uncommon, at least in the sample area. More frequent, though still not sufficiently so as to invalidate the whole procedure of analysis, are those cases where the investigator may believe that he has detected an undisclosed household structure. This may derive from three types of consideration: first, social or other connections between otherwise unrelated households may be found; secondly, it may be suspected that lodger families are in reality separate occupiers; and, thirdly, the presence of more than one nuclear family in a household may suggest a type of sharing in the household not indicated in any way in the returns.

An example of the first category may be found in a case at Winterton (Lincs.) where a small farmer and his wife have two unmarried daughters living with them, both dressmakers, aged 21 and 15. The next household, separated by a full line, consists solely of the head, a girl of the same name as those in the first household, unmarried, aged 28, born in Winterton as they were, and also a dressmaker. It is hardly pressing coincidence too far to guess that she is a relative, possibly a sister. Does she then live the entirely separate existence that the enumeration suggests?[50] Or, to take a more complex example, the keeper of the New Ship Inn at Mill Bridge, Skipton, had, in 1851, one Susanah Bullock living in his household, described in her relationship to him as nurse but given the occupation of provision dealer. The two conflicting statements seem irresolvable until one turns to the next household and notices that the head is an unmarried girl called Mary Bullock living with the sister Susanah. Mary was a milliner and dressmaker and Susanah (the younger of the two) a heald knitter: both, like Susanah the elder next door, were born in Cracoe, a village five miles from Skipton, and were of an age to be daughters of the nurse/provision dealer.

No.	STREET	NAME	Rel. to Head	COND.	AGE		OCCUPATION	BIRTHPLACE
					M	F		
59	Mill Bridge New Ship	John Pearson	Head	M	51		Inn Keeper	Yks. Skipton
		(Wife and two children)						
		Margaret Pilkington	Aunt	Wid		65	Independent	Do. Thorlby
		James Edmonson	Visitor	M	40		Inn Keeper	Do. Bingley
		Susanah Bullock	Nurse	M		50	Provision Dealer	Do. Craco
60	Mill Bridge	Mary Bullock	Head	U		24	Milliner and Dressmaker	Do. Cracoe
		Susanah Do.	Sister	U		21	Heald Knitting	Do. Do.

Figure 13   (Sk/b/59–60). Household 59 ends at the foot of one page without a full line in the document, a practice used elsewhere by the enumerator.

Is it too much to suppose that Susanah the elder usually lived in the second household, keeping a street corner shop there which was looked after by the dressmaker's daughter while she was nursing (perhaps an invalid wife or the 65 year old aunt)? (Figure 13.) Shop premises may tempt the investigator to make similar interpretations. In figure 14 it might not be unreasonable to guess that the servants in household 3 attend upon either the bachelor chemist in household 2 or the shopman in household 1, or on both. Equally, of course, it might be suggested that the proprietor and his family were absent from no. 1 and possibly from no. 3 if that, as seems likely, were also a shop.

In certain contexts, when supported by a close knowledge of the locality and its population drawn from other sources, guesses of this kind can be informative. But in any extensive analysis of social structure such households form only a small proportion and any misinterpretation arising from the application of the general rules will be of small importance beside the advantages gained from uniformity of method.

Secondly, there is the question of the lodgers. As will be shown later[51] it may be that there are more lodgers in the returns than is indicated by the designation itself. But for the purposes of the present discussion this factor may be ignored. Single lodgers, men and women, living within households, present no great problem; they may be recorded within the list under the head of household or they may be given a short line, with or without a new schedule number but with the designation 'lodger' as their relationship to head. Thus a woman lodging-house keeper and her companion are divided by a short line from the lodger, a young bachelor clerk.[52] This was at 163 Fitzwilliam Street; next door, at 165, the female head called herself a 'letter of apartments' but her only lodger, separated by a short line and with separate schedule number, was the bachelor curate of

No.	STREET	NAME	Rel. to Head	COND.	AGE		OCCUPATION	BIRTHPLACE
					M	F		
	2 uninhabited houses being Sale Shops							
1	8 South Street	John Skidmore	Shop-man	U	22		Pork Butcher	Ashford in the Water, Bakewell Parish
2	10 South Street	Samuel Elliott	Head	U	27		Chemist & Druggist	Ecclesal British Subject
3	12 South Street	Elizabeth Atkin	Servant	U		16	Maid Servant	Yks. Gleadless Common
		Caroline Bohner	Servant	U		20	Maid Servant	Germany
	4 uninhabited houses being Sale Shops							

Figure 14   (S/V/1–3).

St. Mary's Church.[53] It may be assumed that both young men formed part of the households within which they ate their meals and thus should have more properly been called boarders. No difficulty arises in such cases, for these 'boarders' will be included within the co-residing group under the general rules. Even the enumerators themselves, or perhaps their registrars, sometimes had doubts about the wisdom of using a short line in these circumstances and so deleted them, marking them 'ruled in error'. But it must be added that while this is true of the 1851 returns, it is applicable only in part, as will shortly be shown, to those of 1861.

As well as these single lodgers there occur, of course, nuclear families of lodgers, with and without children and they may be recorded as living within the co-residing group or as sharing the house. Families of this kind listed within the head's household must be referred to again shortly in another context; for those divided from the head by a short line it might be argued that it was a matter of chance or the enumerator's whim whether the first listed person in the second element was called 'head' or 'lodger'. Against this it might be urged that the sample sheets in the enumerator's book used, in both illustrations, the expression 'head' for the first person in the second element and that enumerators using 'lodger' in a similar context were attempting to express some condition different from 'sharing' in the sense implied by the instructions. The two cases

No.	STREET	NAME	Rel. to Head	COND.	AGE		OCCUPATION	BIRTHPLACE
					M	F		
39	West End	John Carnaby	Head	M	61		Ag. Lab	Lincs. North Kelsey
		Ann Carnaby	Wife	M		61	(blank)	Yks. Hull
		William Jhonson (sic)	Lodger	Widr	69		Ag. Lab	Lincs. Barton
40		William Carnaby	Head	M	34		Ag. Lab	Lincs.Wintringham
		(wife and daughter)						

Figure 15   (Wham/a/39–40).

No.	STREET	NAME	Rel. to Head	COND.	AGE		OCCUPATION	BIRTHPLACE
					M	F		
19	4 Court Broomhall Street	Elizabeth Strother	Head	Wid		30	Lodging House Keeper	Yks.Sheffield
	" "	James W. Do.	son		6		(blank)	Do. Do.
	" "	Maryat Loye	Lodger niece			12	(blank)	Do. Do.
	" "	Harriot Loye	Lodger	U		27	Warehouse Woman	Do. Do.
20	" "	William Lidget	Head	M	35		Police Watchman	Lincs. Oasby
		(Wife and child)						

Figure 16   (S/M/19–20).

should be treated differently. Such a method is unlikely grossly to misrepresent the reality and may, if the enumerators were responsive to situations they observed and understood, give a true index of the co-residing units.

Finally, there is the question of more than one nuclear family – kin or lodger – within the co-residing group or sharing a house. The lodger family sharing has already been discussed; the lodger family within the co-residing group, or, in a few instances, more than one such family, may well leave the investigator feeling that he is confronted with a case of sharing rather than one of lodging or boarding. Such feelings are the stronger when the head of household is in other respects a solitary, perhaps an aged widower or widow, bachelor or spinster. Yet there is no way behind the enumerator's book and for all our guesses the householder's statement and the enumerator's recension of it may represent the truth faithfully. There are, indeed, cases where the enumerator appears to have made just these kinds of distinctions. The enumerator of Appleby in Lincolnshire, who shows himself in other respects to be a careful and thoughtful worker, records two widower paupers, formerly agricultural labourers, living with son and grandson, and sharing a house. A centenarian and her daughter living on annuities, share with an aristocrat of village labouring life, a foreman; and a widower annuitant and his housekeeper share with another foreman. Yet another foreman has an agricultural labourer sharing, but the waggoners of whom he was foreman live with him as agricultural servants. Agricultural foremen or bailiffs, may be presumed to live in farmhouses large enough to be divided, but cottages are only thus used by two ageing paupers.[54] In Winteringham near Appleby and in Sheffield the enumerators record shared houses with a lodger in the first co-residing group (figure 15) and another Sheffield enumerator carefully distinguishes between part of a house used as a lodging house and the remainder occupied by a sharing family (figure 16).

The nuclear family – kin of the head and within the co-residing group – is not specifically indicated by the enumerator but is readily discovered from the relationships to the head and from the names. There is no evidence in such cases, of course, that the families are sharing and the investigator has no recourse but to accept the record as it stands. There occur, however, instances where a lodger family, either within the co-residing group or sharing, may be suspected as being kin. The Winteringham household in figure 15 is a case in point for the second family may well be thought to be the head's married son with his wife and child. In such cases, it must be freely admitted, the investigator can never be sure of his ground: his identification must depend upon the evidence of names, ages and birthplaces and lacks the essential information about relationship to head. Moreover, even supposing such an identification can be made with confidence, it cannot be claimed that this is evidence of a shared house. As a consequence the investigator has no choice but to classify them by the rule already given, thus bringing together into one category the lodgers who are kin and those who are not, and into another the sharing co-residing groups who are kin of the head listed first in their house and those who are not.

THE HOUSEHOLD IN 1861

In 1861 the page of the enumerators' books was increased slightly in size but re-lined to take twenty-five instead of the twenty of the 1851 books; at the same time the long and short lines to divide houses and households were replaced by double and single oblique strokes respectively, drawn across the column immediately to the left of the names – a return to the practice of 1841. As a consequence of these two changes the 1861 books are generally less easy to read but the identification of houses is assisted by the introduction of columns in which their numbers were to be recorded, distinguishing between those inhabited in one column and those uninhabited and building in another.

At the same time the Census Office reconsidered the problem of the household and the family but failed either to define it or find suitable means for recording the nature of lodging and sharing. 'The family in its complete form' says the *Report*[55] 'consists of a householder with his wife and his children; and in the higher class with his servants; other relatives and visitors sometimes form part of a family; so do lodgers at a common table who pay for their subsistence and lodging.' In taking the Census the enumerator was directed to leave with each occupier a household schedule; the occupier by definition including the owner, or the person who pays rent whether (as a tenant) for the whole of the house or (as a lodger) for any distinct floor or apartment. Thus a lodger alone, or in company with another lodger, occupying common apartments, is an occupier and as such is classed as a family in the abstracts.

It will be noticed that in this passage the word lodger appears to be used first to indicate boarder and secondly the true lodger who rents an apartment, though the key question of catering was still not mentioned. In the householders' and enumerators' instructions it was made clear that a lodger 'with or without a family' was to be considered an occupier to whom a separate schedule should be issued. In the column headings of the householders' schedules the words 'visitors, boarders etc.' are used, though such persons are not among the examples for the enumerators. The last of these, however, is a single stroke household of which the sole occupier was an unmarried ship carpenter whose relationship to head was designated 'lodger'.

The enumerators of 1861 were thus faced with an even more confusing set of instructions than their predecessors in 1851. Strictly read, the instructions suggested that every lodger or lodger family was to receive a separate schedule and was then to be recorded as sharing a house but with the first person listed after the single oblique stroke designated 'lodger' not 'head'. Certainly the effects of such a reading are to be seen in the returns. Single male lodgers who, one may guess, boarded with the family, are recorded as occupying shared houses but with the relationship to head of 'lodger'.[56] Nine lodgers in a lodging house are regarded as a group sharing the house with the lodging house keeper or, conversely, three grooms lodging in one house are each made a separate sharing group of one.[57]

Against this, shared houses on the 1851 pattern are recorded throughout the returns with each element divided from the other by a single stroke and the first person listed in each designated 'head' and, indeed, an example of this pattern of recording was printed in the enumerators' books. At the same time the use of 'boarder' in the column headings of the householders' schedules (it was used nowhere in 1851) opened the way to some puzzling interpretations by the enumerators. An aged widower who was a pauper appears as a separate head in his grandson's house which also contains another family as a separate group with a boarder in it; apparent grandchildren become boarders; and many persons who in 1851 would probably have been called lodgers are now recorded as boarders.[58]

It will be clear that comparisons of the number of lodgers and boarders between the '51 and '61 returns are hazardous and that the same is true of shared houses though to a lesser extent. Equally it will be clear that the investigator can no more re-interpret the enumerator's record in the 1861 material than he could in that of 1851. The same rule for analysis must be applied and will lead broadly to the same results except perhaps where single lodgers have been given the status of head in shared houses. How often lodgers were treated in this way in 1861 it is impossible to say, but limited experience of the returns has so far discovered very few single heads forming a co-residing group of one and sharing a house. In all other respects the 1861 returns, in their treatment of houses and households may contain the same confusing errors as those for 1851 and the same care must be exercised in their analysis.

IV

NAMES AND ADDRESSES, AGE, SEX, BIRTHPLACE, INFIRMITY

None of the confusions and ambiguities arising from the returns is so complex as the nature of the shared house. Much of the censal information is subject to no more than relatively unimportant clerical error. Occasionally the information is simply missing and in any of the columns the investigator may find a blank or the expression 'NK' – the abbreviation the enumerators were instructed to use for 'not known'.

The types of address used vary according to the district and the enumerator. In the towns of the sample area most enumerators numbered each house, arranging their schedules first for one side of a street and then the other, or, less frequently, taking all the house numbers in sequence. More rarely, the enumerator will give no more than a street name. District 2 of Doncaster in 1851 covered the inhabitants of a stretch of the Great North Road as it passes through the town centre: the street was a warren of shops and houses but the enumerator identifies nearly 150 houses by no more than the address 'French Gate', and even this is written but once on each page of his book against the first entry.

Few enumerators are as cavalier as this but even the careful ones could not find precise addresses for many houses in the scores of back-to-back courts of Sheffield. In such cases the street off which the court led could be identified and the court itself usually had a number; but individual properties within the court were not further identified. Addresses, therefore, cannot be used consistently to identify houses when analysing household structure.

What is true for the towns is doubly so for rural areas. In country districts there was rarely a street number to give. The enumerators of Tickhill and Winterton, for example, give the street names but no numbers; in Tickhill the three main streets each formed an enumeration district. Both these places were large villages. Smaller communities were frequently enumerated without even street names. Outlying farms or other properties are usually named though a considerable collection of dwellings may take the name of the principal house in the area.

The nature of the address data in the returns thus allows the reconstruction of the residence pattern of any given locality only in the best conditions. When the addresses are precise and consistently given, when contemporary maps, street plans and directories are available, and where the properties themselves have survived relatively unchanged, such a reconstruction is possible and may incidentally reveal the actual process of enumeration. Such conditions are rare for rural areas but may be found for towns or parts of towns. One of the more frustrating hazards in such attempts as have been made in towns in the sample area was found to be that street numbering was subject to frequent change. It should also be noticed that enumeration district boundaries, especially when based on ward or similar boundaries, often cut across streets. For the rest, the only confusion likely to arise is from illegible handwriting or copying error; neither was an important factor in the sample area.

Little trouble is found with Christian and surnames. The enumerators were told that they might use initials for Christian names other than the first. Most record all names in full but an occasional enumerator will use abbreviated names or initials or a combination of both. Fortunately, the use of initials for the first name was rare in the sample area and it is to be hoped that it was generally so, for the loss of full Christian names greatly increases the difficulties of comparative work between the returns themselves or between the returns and other sources. Two examples of inexplicable difference between the head's surname and that of his family have been found: William Henry Simpson of Sheffield had Sarah Lee as his wife though his children were called Simpson; Henry Steel, also of Sheffield, had Hannah Hall as his wife but his son was William Hall.[59] A variety of explanations could be devised for both cases but none can be supported from the census itself.

From time to time the name column must be used as an important clue in interpreting and occasionally emending the age/sex column. When 'Ebenezer' has been deleted and 'Ellen' substituted, the description 'son' left, but the age written in the female column, the balance of probability is obviously for a daughter named Ellen (see figure 17). Errors of this kind are most likely to have been made by the enumerators when entering up their books: in the householders' schedules sex was indicated by writing 'M' or 'F' in one column whereas the enumerators indicated sex by marking the age in one or other of two columns. Some errors, one may suppose, were made because, as in the instance illustrated, a name was at first misread and later changed without the consequent alterations in other columns being made.

In seven out of eight instances of this kind in the sample area name and relationship to head agreed with one another but the age was entered in the column for the opposite sex; in the other the name was inappropriate for the relationship and the entry in the age column. In all cases the person was taken to be of the sex indicated by the two elements which agreed. None of the instances in the sample area had been noticed by the Census Office checker. In consequence the reported male and female population figures of individual districts were wrong by these very small numbers. Because such errors tend to cancel one another out this probably resulted in an overall error of one female too many and one male too few in a population of about 48,000 in the sample area. Such

.No.	STREET	NAME	Rel. to Head	COND.	AGE		OCCUPATION	BIRTHPLACE
					M	F.		
18	114 Trafalgar St.	William Gregory	Head	M	31		Table blade forger	Calver Derbys.
		Elizabeth Do.	Wife	M		32	(blank)	Doncaster
		Ellen ~~Ebenezer~~	Son	U		3	(blank)	Sheffield
		(and another child)						

Figure 17 (S/R/18).

errors are insignificant. Similarly, a boy entered in both male and female columns, though it represents an absolute error in total population, presents no difficulty.

No check can be made of the ages recorded except by comparative work. In two small communities in the sample area comparisons between the '51 and '61 enumerations and between the '51 enumeration and parish registers show errors of one or occasionally two years but rarely more. In Hathersage (Derbys.) a third of the 1851 population may be traced from one census to the next and their age intervals are shown in table 3. Only 60 per cent of the traced population were recorded with an interval of 10 years; a further 28 per cent had intervals of 9 or 11 years. A similar distribution was found for the traceable population of Braithwell (Yorks.). A small proportion of those showing an eleven-year difference might be accounted for by persons born in the week of the year between the two census dates of 30 March and 7 April; and there is some evidence from parish registers that persons with birthdays within a month or two of the census dates rounded off their ages either up or down. Most of the wrong intervals occur with persons over the age of 20 and there are perhaps rather more errors in the ages of women than in those of men.

Many infants of less than one year are recorded in the manner advocated in the householders' schedules and the enumerators' instructions, that is by writing 'months' or 'mo.' after the figure but this expression is often written outside the column itself and investigators should take care to observe this detail. From time to time the enumerators recorded the age as 'not known'. In some cases the registrar seems to have asked the enumerator for an estimate which was then inserted; in others the checker emends with an expression such as 'say 18' – the

Table 3 *Age intervals 1851/1861 Hathersage and Braithwell*

Hathersage		Interval	Braithwell	
Numbers	%	(years)	Numbers	%
1	0·3	0	—	—
1	0·3	1	—	—
3	0·9	6	1	0·6
6	1·7	7	1	0·6
7	1·9	8	5	3·2
47	13·3	9	20	12·8
214	60·6	10	106	67·5
52	14·7	11	15	9·6
16	4·5	12	3	1·9
3	0·9	13	5	3·2
—	—	14	1	0·6
2	0·6	19	—	—
1	0·3	20	—	—
353*	100·0		157*	100·0

* 353 was 33·5% of the 1851 population; 157 was 34·6% of the 1851 population.

subject being an apprentice – and in another makes a woman 35, presumably on the grounds that she has a son of 12 [60] (see also figure 4). But omission of age is rare, perhaps because it was a topic on which the enumerators felt justified in making a guess when a subject was uncertain of the facts or unwilling to give them.

The birthplace is similarly subject to clerical error rather than to anything more serious so far as may be judged from the returns themselves. The checkers may be a little uncertain of geography as when they insert 'Germany' after Milan or leave 'Scotland, Dublin' uncorrected.[61] More charming entries such as 'Upon the Occien' cause no problem. Birthplaces in Scotland and Ireland are, unfortunately, commonly given only by the name of the country or at most the county: householders were asked only for the country in such cases though no instructions were given about Wales. A not uncommon error arises from the use of dittos in the birthplace column and places become assigned to wrong counties for this reason; generally speaking there is little difficulty in emending the return on a firm basis of internal evidence.

In the rare cases where the birthplace is not known, haste may lead to the reading of 'U.K.' for 'N.K.' Both the householders' and enumerators' examples showed the county written first in the birthplace column, followed by the place: enumerators vary in their treatment, one in the sample area even going so far as to alter many pages of his book (with disastrous consequences) simply to write the birthplaces in the order shown in the examples. Identification sometimes depends upon a fairly wide local knowledge and the use of place-name lists for places smaller than villages and hamlets.

Of the column for the blind or deaf and dumb there is little to say. In the sample area the entry was always made by the appropriate word or words being written in the column, and investigators should beware that checkers' ticks against birthplaces of persons born outside the county under enumeration are often made in this column, giving a false impression.

v

RELATIONSHIP TO HEAD AND CONDITION

The relationship to head and condition columns must frequently be interpreted together. Taken by itself there are few problems in the condition column. Handwriting should be closely observed, for single letter abbreviations are sometimes very much alike. Treatment of young children varies, some enumerators leaving the column blank, as in their and the householders' examples, and others unfailingly writing 'U' even for infants. The information is occasionally interchanged between the two columns.

Against this, the relationship to head column gives rise to one major problem – that of visitors and lodgers – and a number of lesser ones. The lesser problems may be disposed of first. As has already been seen not every household is given a head by the enumerators. In some cases an explanation is offered in some part of the entry: 'Wife – supported by husband living in Darlington' or may be reasonably assumed from the context.[62] In Tickhill in 1851, the Lumley family were absent from the Castle and the first person in the enumerated household is their 3-year-old daughter, Algitha, who was being looked after by servants.[63] Elsewhere in Tickhill several households were headed by the wives of grooms who had no doubt accompanied the Lumleys to London or Bath. In many such instances the enumerators fortunately describe the wives in terms of the absent head's occupation. Sometimes the enumerator regards the first person in the household as head where it is clear from the context that the true head of household is away. At Winterton Hall in 1851 the head is the housekeeper and the household four servants.[64] A lack of heads in two of a row of shops in South Street, Sheffield, might suggest that the shopkeepers lived away from their business premises which at night they left in charge of shopmen or servants. But that Ann and Mary Dickinson of Alkborough, spinsters in their fifties, farmers of 150 acres, both put themselves down as head reveals no more than a family situation – a rare enough glimpse of humanity through the statistical curtain of the returns.[65]

Table 4 *'Head equivalents' used in households other than those sharing houses, Sheffield and Doncaster, 1851*

Head equivalent	Number of occurrences
Wife	33
Widow	13
Servant	12
blank	11
Son	5
Daughter	3
Father	2
Lodger	2
Married	2
Partners/sisters	2
Visitor	2
Brother-in-law	1
Grand-daughter	1
Mother to head	1
Shopman	1
Sister	1
Widower	1
Wife, head from home	1
Wife, husband absent	1
	95

The frequency of occurrence of these head equivalents in Sheffield and Doncaster has been shown in table 1; the relationships recorded for these instances are shown in table 4. In all cases the divisions between households indicated by these head equivalents should be accepted for the purposes of household count even though only two actually say that the head is away. As will be seen, they represent less than two per cent of all the households in the two areas examined. For purposes of tabulating such persons in their relationship to the structure of the household they should retain their recorded status.

Apart from the head, errors occur in other ascriptions of relationship to head. Very common is the slip of making the children of married children of heads, 'sons' and 'daughters' instead of grandchildren; the context generally makes the relationship clear. A similar slip is the use of 'son' or 'daughter' (or even 'wife') where it is clear that in-laws are meant. 'In-law' provides another trap for the unwary in that it is also, and frequently, used to mean 'step'; a Hathersage enumerator even goes so far as to alter his first and common-sense term 'wife's daur' to 'daur-in-law'.[66] Generally speaking the context of age, name and condition will make the matter clear but the married step-daughter may not always be distinguishable from the daughter-in-law in the modern sense of the expression. Outside the immediate family, relationship to head might be thought

No.	STREET	NAME	Rel. to Head	COND.	AGE M	F	OCCUPATION	BIRTHPLACE
19	(blank)	George Ross	Head	U	54		Blacksmith	Lincs. Winterton
		Maria do.	Mother in Law	W		55	(blank)	Lincs. Belton
		James do.	son	U	24		Blacksmith	Lincs. Winterton
		Henry do.	son	U	23		Far. Lab	do. do.
		Ann do.	dau	U		15	Dress Maker	do. do.
		Jane do.	dau			11	Scholar	do. do.

Figure 18   (W/a/19).

No.	STREET	NAME	Rel. to Head	COND.	AGE M	F	OCCUPATION	BIRTHPLACE
76	Mill Bridge	Mary Holdsworth	Head	U		54	Nurse	Yks. Skipton
		Elizabeth do.	Sister	Wid		48	Parish Relief	do. do.
		Martha Johnson	do.	Wid		45	Weaver	do. do.
		Alice Holdsworth	do.	U		43	Weaver	do. do.
		Joseph Butterworth	son	U	16		Tinner and Brazier	do. do.

Figure 19   (Sk/b/76).

of as indicating status within the household. 'Nurse child' is perhaps generally used for fostering; adopted children occur; a 14-year-old boy and an 8-year-old girl were said to be 'friends' of two spinsters, and perhaps stood in a fostered or adopted relationship.[67] 'Shopman', 'assistant', 'apprentice', 'housekeeper', 'journeyman', and 'governess' all occur as well as the universal 'servant'. Illegitimacy may often be guessed at and is occasionally stated by such expressions as (unmarried) 'daughter's child'. Occasionally no relationship is given: in some cases it appears to be clerical omission and a suitable entry can be supplied; in others the explanation probably lies in the inability of either householder or enumerator to think of a suitable formula. Some sets of relationships are quite inexplicable, as in figure 18, which must involve enumeration errors in some part of the entry. In figure 19 one might suppose that the enumerator has been strictly correct and that Joseph is Mary's illegitimate child, though Elizabeth must be considered 'sister-in-law' not 'sister'. But if the enumerator has made a mistake in Elizabeth's surname, or if she has reverted to her maiden name, Joseph may well be *her* son though his relationship to head ought then to be 'nephew'.

Fortunately, insoluble difficulties of relationship to head are rare and in any case affect only a small part of the material available for analysis in such cases.

VI

VISITORS AND LODGERS

A major problem in the relationship to head column arises with the ascriptions 'visitor' and 'lodger'. In this, it is clear, Census Office, registrars and enumerators suffered from lack of consistent definitions or concepts. Most unfortunately, it is a matter of especial interest, for, as with the shared house, the presence of lodgers may be taken as an indication of status within a given occupational or social group, or conversely, of the social impact of certain groups in terms of family or household responsibility.

As has been seen, lodgers may be found in many houses, and when they are designated 'lodger' (with one minor exception) the investigator would be well advised to consider them as members of the co-residing group however their entry may have been arranged by the enumerator. Additionally, there are persons, or more usually families, not designated 'lodger', who are recorded by the enumerator as sharing a house: such persons or families may be regarded as a special category of lodgers.

Analysis of household and family structure should normally include as lodgers only these persons.[68] But in addition to those so designated by the enumerators (or who share houses in the manner described) there are those who might be thought to have the characteristics of lodgers even though they are designated 'visitor'. The problem arises in an acute form if the distinction between a visitor and a lodger is clarified.

The visitor is one who calls upon or goes to see a friend or relative *for a short time*. The duration may be anything from 10 minutes to a few months, it is true, but the temporary and social nature of the visit is never in doubt. The visitor, moreover, does not pay for his privilege. The lodger, on the contrary, is one who hires a room and whose stay, though it may be short, and is perhaps usually temporary, is governed by matters quite external to his relationship with his landlord. Indeed, if that relationship is disturbed, he will not, as does the visitor, go home, but find another lodging. We might formulate a definition in the following terms: 'The true visitor is one who does not usually live in the household or community, is a non-paying guest of the household and makes more than half his social and economic contribution to society in another community. The true boarding lodger usually lives in the household, pays for his rent and keep, and makes more than half his social and economic contribution to society in that community. Occasionally, the visitor may pay for his stay in a private house, lodging house or inn; and the lodger may stand in such a relationship to his host that his rent and keep are remitted. The criterion, in all cases, must be the degree to which the person belongs to the community'. The definition depends upon our ability to measure an individual's contribution to society – perhaps an impossible task for the enumerated population of 1851; nevertheless the distinction is important if we wish to exclude visitors from calculations of household size and to determine the character of lodging.

The question therefore arises: How far did the enumerators, who use both terms in their books, distinguish between these two social groups; and how did they use the terms at their disposal to record what they found? First, it must be said that there are frequent instances of both terms being used to describe persons who appear from the context to occupy similar positions within the community. The confusion is perhaps epitomised in the case of Frank Mycroft who was living in Sheffield in 1851: his relationship to head was 'visitor', his occupation 'lodger'.[69] The checkers annotated him 'no occupation'. And many cases are found in which persons who appear to be of similar status to one another are called variously 'visitor' or 'lodger'. Sometimes the enumerator makes a distinction: a lodger agricultural labourer and his wife (so-called by the enumerator) in a Winterton house-and-land proprietor's household, born as they were in foreign parts – 'Suxex' and 'City of Chiester' – might reasonably be regarded as true lodgers; the names and other particulars of two other lodgers in the house were 'not known' because they were 'for that night' and these two one might accept as visitors.[70]

Occasionally the enumerator will recognise that a relative is only in the house 'on a visit' and it is not uncommon to find the relationship in the appropriate column but with the occupation 'visitor'. Instances occur which may be read reasonably as a whole family on a visit or friends staying the weekend to view the new baby of the household. Against this, many young children, born in the place under review, are found as visitors, unattended by parents or relatives. Here one is perhaps meeting the common Victorian habit of boarding out children for whom there is no room at home. They are often said to be scholars and, amongst the older ones, to have an occupation and all may reasonably be regarded as lodgers. For persons in institutions more guidance is available. Boys in a boarding school – 'pupils', 'boarders', 'scholars' – may reasonably be regarded as part of the community in which they spend their school life, but in any case will require special consideration in any educational analysis of the returns. Lodgers in lodging houses may be designated as 'for the night' or by the rubric 'traveller, not known' suggesting that they fall most suitably into the class 'visitor'. The drovers, cattle-dealers and farmers crowding the Skipton inns on 30 March 1851 were there for the Fortnight Fair and perhaps most inn guests are temporary members of a community however the enumerators designated them.

There appears to have been no semantic shift in the use of the terms lodger and visitor between 1851 and now: indeed there is some indication that the Census Office had it in mind to try to determine the number of persons in each district who were regular members of the community as opposed to the enumerated community which might be augmented by temporary visitors or diminished by the absence of some of its normal members. Over and above his actual enumeration each enumerator was asked to estimate the number of persons 'who have not been enumerated as inmates of dwelling houses, but who it is believed have slept or abode in the District on the night preceding the day of enumeration'. This was known as 'Table (b)' and asked the enumerators to specify where such persons slept. Secondly, the enumerators had also to return '(1) the estimated number of such persons who are returned in the subsequent pages as having slept in his district on the night of March 30th, but who were there only temporarily' ('Table (c)') and '(2) The estimated number of persons who were absent from the district on the night of March 30th, but who usually dwell in the district', ('Table (d)'). There are similar tables in the enumerators' books for 1861. No instructions were given to the enumerators, apart from those on the form itself, about how they should complete these tables. Their attitude to them in the sample area varies considerably. Table (b) perhaps caused the least difficulty but over half the tables (c) and (d) were left blank by the enumerators. In the Sheffield area all but two were blank and the two were simply marked with nil signs. Such a result is not surprising for the enumerators were being asked to make estimates of a most difficult kind. Where they did attempt an estimate, the results are hardly meaningful. It might be supposed that the figures in table (c) would equal the number of persons designated 'visitor' and that those in table (d) might be the same as those absent heads and others noticed by the means already described. In only two districts in the sample area was the number of designated visitors equal to the number of persons shown in table (c) as only temporarily in the district on the night of 30 March. A similar calculation for table (d) which would attempt to relate the missing heads of households already described to the persons the enumerator was asked to notice as temporarily absent, is subject to many imponderables and no kind of correlation has been established in any district in the sample area.

If, therefore, it is on the one hand uncertain how the householders and enumerators viewed the distinction between lodgers and visitors, and if, on the other, it is manifest that their instructions were ill-defined and for the most part lacking altogether, it is hardly surprising that the confusions already illustrated arose in the enumerators' books. There can be little doubt that there are cases, perhaps few in number, where persons designated lodger ought to have been recorded as visitors and many more cases where the designated visitor was in reality a lodger.

The safest analytic process must be that already advocated, namely, to accept the enumerator's designation of all such persons. But if an investigator wishes to emend his material in an attempt to make a nearer approximation of the lodging and visiting elements in his community, the following considerations might be borne in mind. First, in the interests not only of preserving the validity of his material but also of comparability with other work, the emended data should always be indicated. Second, in this as in all work on census returns, the practice of individual enumerators must be taken into account. The enumerator of Sheffield T, for example, recorded only one household with lodgers but 44 (20 per cent of all households) with visitors. In these 44 households were 94 visitors of whom 42 were young bachelor workers, mostly in the Sheffield light trades, and another 11 were widows or widowers. There were 8 nuclear families of visitors but the enumerator marked no shared houses of any kind in the district. There is good ground for considering that many of the 94 visitors might more properly be classified as lodgers.

An investigation was made of the 15 Sheffield districts in the sample area, including the exceptional District T. Only visitors specifically said to be 'on a visit' (or an equivalent phrase), visitors in inns or pubs, sailors, adult visitors unaccompanied by relatives and given no occupation and visitor families of which the head was given no occupation, were kept as visitors. All others, including the children of housekeepers and other servants, and pauper visitors, were regarded as lodgers. Under these rules visitors who might be regarded as lodgers were found in 5·7 per cent of the households (forming 2 per cent of the population); lodgers who had already been so designated by the enumerators (exclusive of persons sharing houses) were found in a further 9·5 per cent of the households and formed a further 4 per cent of the total population.

Even when the lodgers and visitors have been considered along these lines there is still another class of such persons. These are the relatives whose relationship to head is given without stating that they are temporary visitors only. Occasionally the enumerator notices these situations by such expressions as 'daughter and visitor' or 'sister' with the occupation 'visitor, milliner' or 'grandson, visitor'. *Per contra* relatives are sometimes noted as lodgers though it is usually in the context of a shared house. But if it is difficult to distinguish visitors and lodgers it is for the most part impossible to discover the relatives who are truly visitors rather than members of the family or lodgers.

When all is said, it will be seen that analyses of lodging and temporary populations can never be firmly based. The investigator must bear in mind the ambiguity of the enumerators' instructions, the fact that the householders' instructions effectively mention only visitors, the difficulties of establishing such facts in the terms of the limited censal questions posed, and the immense variety of family and household situations which may be involved in the lodger/ visitor/boarder relationship.

VII

OCCUPATIONS: ADULT EMPLOYED MALES

For some, the most interesting column of the enumerators' books is that in which the occupation is given; all must classify their material by reference to it. For the great bulk of the employed male population few difficulties arise. The names of certain technical operations may be difficult to decipher if the trade in question is little known. The distinction between master and man is often unclear and there is no indication, generally speaking, whether a man is in full or part-time employment or out of work. Indication of the place of work or the name of the industry or the employer occurs only by chance. The nature of the trade or industry in which a man was employed was in fact called for by the Census Office both in the householders' and enumerators' instructions, but many unspecified clerks, labourers, porters, merchants, commercial travellers and so forth are to be found, though the ill effects of this feature of the returns are more noticeable in urban than in rural returns. Nevertheless, in this, the overwhelmingly greater proportion of the employed population, the investigator's problems are those of classifying his material rather than interpreting the document.

Certain special cases may be mentioned. The Census Office checkers were 'instructed, assisted and checked' in their work of handling the occupational statistics. Some picture of their methods emerges from an examination of the returns. Their corrections, in this as in other parts of the census material, were not always of the happiest. In an attempt to specify trade more closely one writes against 'Hand spinner (Hemp)' the word 'flax'; and against 'line worker' (who certainly worked with flax) the word 'rope' (which was probably made of hemp). Along the same lines, a 'silver-plate worker' becomes a 'goldsmith' or the producer's assistant, the 'cowman', becomes the producer/distributor, the 'cowkeeper'.[71] Less easy to deal with are emendations that could be true: the Sheffield 'moulder' who is annotated 'iron' rather than 'steel' or the 'engine stoker' in the same city who is labelled 'cutlery'. Elsewhere the checkers' emendations are superfluous as well as misleading – the specific 'pupil teacher' made the less well-defined 'governess' or the designation 'hawker' for all the travelling inhabitants of a Doncaster lodging house. Against this, the addition of 'agricultural' to unspecified labourers in rural districts (of rare occurrence) seems not unreasonable; or again it is likely that the 'machine makers' of Winterton were engaged in making 'agricultural implements.[72]

In all such cases the checkers' emendations were made in the course of his work of arranging the occupations for the highly idiosyncratic tabulation of the *Census Report* and not as a result of special knowledge or of a re-examination of the householders' schedules. Such emendations should be disregarded.

A further factor sometimes affected employed adult males: they might have more than one occupation. Both householders and enumerators were instructed to list occupations in order of importance; the *Census Report* claims that 'the first occupation was generally taken'[73] but some checkers in the sample area in fact inserted an indication of their choice by numbering the occupations, basing themselves apparently on such contextual evidence as the presence of employees in the trade and so on. Where the checkers give no guidance, investigators will frequently be able to use similar tests; otherwise, the rule that the first mentioned is of prime importance must generally be followed. Occasionally the case is one not so much of dual occupation as description by two words: 'house and land proprietor', for example. A checker who in one such instance underlined the word 'land' had no basis for assigning the primacy. Very occasionally, the investigator may notice an undisclosed dual occupation: an innkeeper with a farm servant in his household for example; and such situations may also be disclosed on comparison with directory, poll book or other parallel sources.[74]

No.	STREET	NAME		Rel. to Head	COND.	AGE		OCCUPATION	BIRTHPLACE
						M	F		
29	Gloucester St.	Susannah Thornton		Head	Wid		55	Manufacturer of Awl Blades Employing 28 Men, 12 Women, 7 Boys	Yks; nr Thorne
		John	do.	son	U	22		Warehouseman	do. Sheffield
		Eliza	do.	dau	U		16	Scholar	do. do.
		Jane	do.	dau	U		12	Scholar	do. do.
		Elizabeth Fletcher		serv	U		18	House servant	do. do.

Figure 20   (S/G/29).

As has been said, the difference between master and man is often difficult to determine. Both enumerators and householders were instructed (the enumerators slightly more fully) to distinguish masters, journeymen and apprentices. Additionally the numbers employed by masters were to be given (figure 20). The *Census Report* describes the returns as imperfect,[75] probably basing its judgement on the differential between the gross employed population and the numbers returned by masters. The matter was a good deal more complicated than the Census Office ostensibly understood. In Sheffield, thousands of men might be masters in the sense that they had long since learnt their craft in some branch or other of the steel finishing trade; but they might be employers one day and employed the next or even both together. Nor does it seem to be clear what the censal question really aimed at. On the one hand it seems to demand information about the difference between employers and employed – a question for which it is possible to see the rationale even if the subtleties involved appear to have been imperfectly understood. On the other hand to pose the question in the status terms of the apprenticeship and gild system is a glance backwards to conditions of labour that one feels men like Mann or Farr must have known to be anomalous over wide stretches of the employed population. Yet it was done and the consequence is a high degree of confusion. Generally speaking in older communities – market towns like Doncaster – the employers in traditional trades and crafts are given as masters and the number of their employees declared.

By no means all traditional craftsmen were classed in accordance with instructions. In Tickhill in 1851, 250 persons were employed as butchers, bakers, whitesmiths and all the like long-standing country trades and crafts. Of these, two are described as masters, three as journeymen, and fifteen as apprentices or the equivalent. What was the status of the remaining 230? The twenty-three children of 14 years or less may safely be regarded as employed persons; there were also ninety-one persons who were not heads of their own households and no doubt most of these were employed. We are left with 116 heads of households about whom it is impossible to say whether they were masters or journeymen (insofar as those terms mean anything) or whether they were employers or employed. It is also impossible to determine from the returns how many craft or trade establishments there were in Tickhill in 1851.

It will be understood from this that it is unwise to use the enumerators' books to determine the distribution of craft status amongst the employed population. Similarly, the returns cannot be said to record consistently the difference between employers and employed; and, finally, although many employers of labour record the numbers they employed, in accordance with the instructions, many did not.[76]

VIII

OCCUPATIONS: FARMERS

For one class of employers – farmers – the returns are fuller though hardly less confusing. The instructions to farmers read: 'The term FARMER to be applied only to the occupier of land, who is to be returned – "*Farmer of* (317) *acres*, employing (12) labourers"; the number of acres, and of in and out-door labourers, on March 31st, being in all cases inserted. Sons and daughters employed at home or on the farm, may be returned – "Farmer's son", "Farmer's daughter".'[77] The enumerators' instructions were the same except that a note was added: 'The *numbers* of *labourers* returned should include waggoners, shepherds, and all kinds of workmen employed on the farm, whether they sleep in the house or not; and when *boys* or women are employed, their number should be separately given. The male and female farm servants who sleep in the house will be returned in the Household Schedule, and their particular employments as waggoner, dairy maid etc. inserted in the column headed "Occupation".' There seems little doubt that the Census Office wished to discover the total labour force on each farm. The *Report* declares that 'Some uncertainty prevails as to whether the farms returned all their indoor farm servants; and women and boys were included in some cases and not in others.'

In the sample area there is ample confirmation of this confusion. The number of farm servants named in the schedule is frequently greater than the work force said to be employed. On just over half the farms in Tickhill in 1851, for example, no labour force was said to be employed at all though in five of these cases farm servants were named in the schedules. Tickhill appears to have been unusual in the number of holdings of unspecified acreage and employees; in the north-west Lincolnshire group almost all the farms are given an acreage and the employees stated and here again farm servants were sometimes more numerous than the labourers said to be employed. There is some evidence that confusion arose over nomenclature, for 50 years after the census the expression 'labourer' was used in one south Yorkshire village to indicate precisely those who were not in 'farm service', to distinguish, in fact, outdoor from indoor labour. Certainly everywhere one finds the agricultural labourer as a head of his own household, married and with a family, and the farm servant as the young bachelor, rarely, if ever, a head of household. The distinction was also in the minds of the checkers for where one finds an agricultural labourer living on a farm, many checkers annotate such a person 'fs' – farm servant.

In attempting to establish the labour force of farms, therefore, the enumerator's interpretation of his instructions must be considered together with the number and nature of the farm servants enumerated in the schedule. It would also be as well to consider the size of the family labour available: the practice of calling farmer's children 'farmer's son' etc. varies considerably and in some districts the young men of a farmer's household have no occupation assigned them. The female servants of a farm are also something of a problem. In the sample area milk-maids or dairy maids were not encountered; but it is hard to believe that female servants on farms were necessarily confined to domestic duties, and the checkers thought the same for from time to time, though not consistently, they marked such persons 'fs'. Occasionally, as in figure 21, an enumerator will distinguish between female domestic and farm servants. The same example, however, demonstrates the difficulty of assessing the farm labour force, for it is unclear whether or not the '16 labourers' include the three male and one female farm servants enumerated.

Farmers present one more difficulty for the investigator. What, it may be asked, is a farmer? 'The term FARMER' said the instructions 'is to be applied only to the occupier of land'. Strictly applied one might find oneself with men whose agricultural activities were confined to mere extensions of the cottage garden. Conversely, though a man might occupy 5 or 10 acres, he might cultivate it in his spare time with the help of his wife or son while his occupation remained that of an employed agricultural labourer. Precisely this latter situation is disclosed by the enumerator of Normanby in Lincolnshire. In this estate village many of the agricultural labourers, even an assistant footman at the hall and the village schoolmaster, had smallholdings of 4 to 15 acres. Such men were enumerated as 'agricultural labourer; occupier of 7 acres of land', not as farmers. The eight chief farmers of Normanby cultivated 2,698 acres between them in farms ranging between 175 and 515 acres; two others had small farms of 16 and 28 acres. The farmers of Normanby must be regarded as 10 in number; but in a less carefully enumerated district the total might have included the 17 smallholders.

No.	STREET	NAME	Rel. to Head	COND.	AGE M	AGE F	OCCUPATION	BIRTHPLACE
91	Castlethorpe	John Clark Foster	Head	U	26		Farmer of 382 acres employing 16 labourers	Lincs. Castlethorpe
		Hannah Smith	Parent	Wid		47	(blank)	do. Nettleton
		Mary Dan	Serv			19	House Serv.	do. Gokewell
		Ann Drinkell	Serv			16	Farm Servant	do. Broughton
		(and three male farm servants)						

Figure 21   (Br/a/91).

Other oddities occur. There are men recorded as agricultural labourers who have farm servants in their households who stand in the relationship 'servant' to them.[78] One of these even had a female domestic servant as well, and agricultural labourers with servants occur sporadically everywhere, suggesting a degree of prosperity not generally associated with employed farm labour even in the north and in 1851.

One final caution should perhaps be voiced. Investigation in the sample area suggests very strongly that the agricultural labour force of all kinds (apart from family or domestic servants) in a given enumeration district is rarely even roughly equal to the numbers indicated as employed by the farmers; it is often greater, sometimes very much so, and occasionally smaller, though usually by a small proportion. These anomalies are no doubt largely the result of the lack of coincidence between enumeration-district (usually parish) boundaries and the agricultural units of an area, and to some extent the result of mobility of hired labour working in a region of reasonably easy communications and 'open' communities. But some of the difference must also be due to under-recording of the labour force by the farmers in their returns of employees and to the prevalence of seasonal or part-time working.

Despite these difficulties, attempts have been made to relate the acreage farmed in a given locality to the labour force said to be available. Experience in the sample area shows that if such a study is made on a wide enough region (it is demonstrably impossible for a single parish or village) the relationship between the declared acreages and the strength of the labour force as declared by the farmers themselves is similar for areas of roughly equivalent farming conditions.[79] Yet in the north-west Lincolnshire area where the calculations were made there remained a body of agricultural labourers, forming rather more than one-fifth of the total, who were surplus to the labour force declared by the farmers.

IX

OCCUPATIONS: WOMEN'S EMPLOYMENT

The remaining difficulties to be found in the entries in the occupation column relate to classes of persons outside the adult male employed or employer population. Chief among these are women. 'The titles or occupations of ladies who are householders' say the instructions 'to be entered according to [*the instructions for men*]. The occupations of women who are regularly employed from home, or at home, in any but domestic duties, to be distinctly recorded.'[80] For the enumerators was added the note 'The rules which have been laid down for the return of rank and profession of men, apply generally to all women in business, or following specific occupations', and adds with some charm 'The occupations of the mistresses of families and ladies engaged in domestic duties are not expressed – as they are well understood.'[81] These instructions were faithfully and unambiguously carried out for thousands of women in the sample area. The returns record the hundreds of wives who were dressmakers and milliners, the widows who kept lodging houses, or maintained their late husband's businesses with the aid of his assistants or the son of the family as in figure 20; or who, less fortunate and only too common, made ends meet by keeping a mangle. Most such women must in one sense be regarded as following the occupation part time. The wives among them did not abdicate from the well-understood but unexpressed domestic duties and the spinsters and widows who were heads of their own households must equally have experienced the problems of the working housewife. Any analysis of the number of 'housewives' in the returns must take account of such persons.

Most wives did not have occupations and the enumerators usually left their entry in the occupation column blank or referred to them in terms of their husband's occupation – 'groom's wife', 'cutler's wife', and so on. A few enumerators in the sample area, not heeding, perhaps, the injunction about domestic

E

duties, called each wife a housekeeper or even, though rarely, added the words 'domestic duties'.[82] But the term 'housekeeper' is used by the enumerators in another context. In the households of widowers, of bachelors, and of married men whose wives were absent, some appropriate person – unmarried daughter, sister, mother and so on – is often designated housekeeper by the enumerators.[83] Such persons are the natural housewives in such households, and these too, must be included in any count of this section of the population. But they are by no means consistently noted as such by the enumerators and the checkers sometimes reacted to this designation by striking it out.[84]

Investigators may find that the wives of innkeepers, farmers, small shop-keepers, shoemakers and butchers are sometimes marked by some sign such as a ditto in the checker's hand to indicate that they follow their husband's occupation.[85] It appears that the Census Office believed that these, more than any other wives, assisted their husbands[86] and unless an investigator is prepared to accept this assessment the checkers' marks are best ignored. Women, however, were not uncommonly employed as labourers in the fields – the census found nearly 71,000 of them – and a few occurred in the sample area.

Many women – apart from wives of heads of households – are recorded with no occupation. One particular group may be singled out as presenting a special difficulty: these are heads of household, mostly widows, who not only have no occupation but for whom no means of support is indicated in the returns. In some households the presence of wage-earning adults may be regarded as sufficient indication of the source of the widow's livelihood. Indeed, many such cases are merely a result of the way in which the household has been enumerated: with the wage-earning son as head, the widow becomes a dependent relative of no occupation. Enumerators occasionally record such situations: 'supported by her daughter' – a dressmaker; or 'lives on her son's earning' – though in this case the son was not a member of the household.[87] But there are many for whom nothing is recorded. The difficulty with these women lies in the fact that although their condition is recognisable they can be given no classification by occupation. They are perhaps best described as of independent means but the social and economic status those means afford varied widely. In the Sheffield area investigated they formed 0·4 per cent of all the households, and if so small a proportion is generally found it is unlikely to affect the validity of any analysis which omits them. But their presence should no doubt be noted as part of the income-receiving population.

X

OCCUPATIONS: CHILDREN

Children usually form a third of the population of any district and the treatment of them by the enumerators varied considerably. The householders' and enumerators' instructions declared that the occupations of children and young persons occupied from home or at home on any but domestic duties were to be recorded;[88] but neither here nor elsewhere did the census officials define 'child' or 'young person'. In the sample area all persons of 14 years or less were regarded as children and it is this that is meant in the following commentary. The recording of the occupations of most children under about the age of 10 was straightforward. For most of them the enumerators had only to state whether or not they were scholars. The instructions read 'Against the names of children above five years of age, if daily attending school or receiving regular tuition under a master or governess at home, write "Scholar", and in the latter case add "at home" '.[89] Many enumerators in the sample area recorded scholars below the age of five – schoolchildren of four and three are not uncommon and infants of two and one occur. Whether the infants of very tender years really attended some kind of nursery or whether the enumerators allowed their dittos (frequently used in the books when recording scholars) to proceed too far, is a question that cannot be answered from the returns. Occasionally in the sample area, persons of 15 years and more were recorded as scholars but such cases should be treated with caution for many have the appearance of clerical error.[90] Scholars at home are usually found alongside an employed governess or an elder daughter who may be presumed to fulfil the function, though sometimes no such person is mentioned.[91]

Most commonly the designation 'scholar' presents no difficulty: what educational reality it represents is not a matter to be discovered from the returns and is discussed elsewhere in this volume. Children who were not scholars were not generally given any designation in the occupation column unless they were employed. One enumerator in the sample area uses the expression 'home' to indicate such children; others will occasionally use a nil entry mark (often easily confused with dittos) or record every child by the father's occupation – 'blacksmith's daughter' and so on. Employed children are less easy to identify. Throughout the sample area children of 14 years and under are found with occupations: the greater proportion are boys though there were many girls of 12 to 14 who were domestic servants. In rural areas the minimum age for employment of boys was usually 10, but in Sheffield 9- and even 8-year-old workers occurred. Generally speaking the occupations assigned to these children were plausible enough and it would be possible simply to record such children, noting only that one may wish to observe them both as children and as employed persons. But in this, perhaps more than in any other feature of the returns, the checkers have exerted a strong influence. In the sample area the checkers frequently assigned to boy non-scholars of approximately 10 to 14 years of age who were not recorded with an occupation, the occupation followed by the father. Many of these occupations were marked by roughly pencilled dittos but some were written in with the appropriate words and care should be taken, especially when working with photographic copies of the enumerators' books, to distinguish these emendations.

It will be seen from this that the figure of 400,000-odd boys of 10 to 14 noticed as employed in the *Census Report* for 1851[92] may overstate the number actually returned by the householders and enumerators. All depended on the abstractor or checker who tabulated the district concerned. Thus, in the Doncaster registration district the checker was much given to assigning occupations in this way, his enthusiasm so far outrunning his judgement as to make a 10-year-old boy a railway engine driver like his father.[93] As a result there are in Tickhill (which lay in that district) in 1851 twice as many such boys given occupations by the checker as by the enumerator. In north-west Lincolnshire, in Brigg registration district, such ascriptions are never made. In Sheffield, where householders appear to have distinguished carefully between those of their children who were employed and those who were not, the checkers rarely inserted an occupation in this way.

While the investigator may feel that these boys were indeed employed in some way or another there is, of course, no evidence in the enumerators' records for such occupations. The checkers' emendations are guesses and as such must be first distinguished and then disregarded.

XI

OCCUPATIONS: SERVANTS

The girls in the sample area are never so treated. They are scholars, they have occupations or they are left blank; and even the Doncaster checker never emended their occupation entry. Unfortunately there is a further difficulty about the employment of girls, though it refers not only to children but to adults as well. The commonest employment for girls of all ages between 10 and 25 was that of domestic servant. Most of these lived in their employers' houses and they are to be found throughout the returns as house servants, maid servants, maids of all work, and under a dozen or more other names and grades down to plain 'servant'. With these there is no difficulty, though investigators should remember that some will have the dual status of child and servant. But in some districts in the sample area daughters living at home, usually but not always over 14, were fairly consistently said to be house servants. Bearing in mind the nature of the servant's calling in 1851, an immediate reaction to this is that the girls are helping at home, that they are part of the vast domestic labour force the census officials described as 'well understood'.

For the majority this was no doubt the case and investigators have therefore only to distinguish between employed servants and those home helps whose position was in fact no different from the 2,700,000-odd girls and women who were returned in 1851 simply as daughter, grand-daughter and so forth. Occasionally the enumerator makes the position clear by some expression such as 'housemaid to father' and some checkers delete such ascriptions when they notice them.[94] But in this as in other matters the checkers are inconsistent, and one who was faced with 'servant at home' deleted 'at home' and presumably added the girl to his tabulation of employed domestic servants.[95] Others simply fail to notice the distinction. The matter is complicated by the occurrence, though in the sample area it was infrequent, of another phenomenon – that of the girl servant who sleeps at home but is employed elsewhere. Of two Sheffield girls, 15 and 11 years old, two enumerators make the statements 'in service – sleeps at home' and 'out service'; a 13-year-old Normanby girl is described as 'house servant to a neighbour'.[96] But there are others where an investigator might find such an explanation more appropriate than that the girls were helping at home, as in the Doncaster 14-year-old 'nurse girl' (deleted in this case by the checker) where there were no young children in her own family. What was more than likely was that the girl was a child minder by day, returning home when her charges' parents came back from their work; thousands of girls no doubt regularly performed the same service for a small sum. Even a boy of 13 is recorded as 'in farm service but sleeps at home'.[97]

Once aware of these ambiguities, it is possible to distinguish those servants who are employed for gain from those who are not. Clearly, all girls who are living as servants in houses other than their own are employed; equally, all those who are living at home must be regarded as not employed unless the enumeration specifically says that they are employed elsewhere, though an exception might be made for nurse girls where there was no child in the house.

Apart from the ambiguities that may arise on farms or in the employment of girls at home, servants present few difficulties in the returns. Investigators who wish to distinguish the employed *domestic* servants should bear in mind that trade employees, apprentices, and journeymen often stand in the relationship of servant to the head of household. The use of the term 'housekeeper' for wives and other relatives not employed by the head of household has already been mentioned. Employed housekeepers are usually distinguishable from the context; even where the expression may be thought to cover what the *Census Report* was pleased to call, though in another connection, a concubine, the lady can only be classified with the employed housekeepers for her status is unlikely to be overtly disclosed by the enumeration.

It should be noticed that apart from young girls sleeping at home, some adult servants did live out. The Tickhill grooms have already been mentioned and elsewhere in the sample area superior servants were occasionally noticed as heads of their own households like Joseph Watson, a Sheffield 'gentleman servant' who lived in a court off Broomhall Street with his wife and child.

The position of the governess in the 1851 household was just as anomalous as contemporary novels might lead us to expect. Sometimes she is governess, sometimes servant; one checker regarded pupil teachers in British schools and elsewhere as governesses. Occasionally the governess turns out to be an elder sister turned teacher for the nonce, leaving the investigator wondering how many more pass unnoticed amongst the unmarried daughters at home with no occupation.[98] Nurses, too, sometimes need careful scrutiny before classification: nurses and nursemaids or nurse girls in large establishments may usually be accepted as part of the servant population. But many nurses are found as heads of households, as housewives or as visitors or lodgers in other households.[99] These women, all either married or widows, usually in their middle years, are frequently found, when not at home in their own households, as visitors or lodgers in houses where their services have recently been of value in a confinement. They are, of course, the midwives or, as they were known and are sometimes called in the returns, the monthly nurses.

XII

PERSONS WITH NO OCCUPATION: THE RETIRED, WOMENFOLK, THE UNEMPLOYED AND PAUPERS

There remain four classes of persons without gainful occupation. One group, the retired persons, rarely presents any difficulty. Chelsea pensioners, superannuated excise officers, annuitants, and so on, are commonly recorded in the returns and from time to time the enumerators list men as retired from a trade or profession in conformity with their instructions. Some of the widows whose means of livelihood is not given might be considered to fall under this head and some men of advanced age for whom no occupation is given may also fall into this class. But the returns give no indication of retirement in such cases. One enumerator, however, was careful enough to note that, despite his age, a 79-year-old had not retired: he recorded him as 'journeyman shoemaker – at work'; and Alexander Aitken, 'a worn-out gardiner' was 'kept in pay for past services'.[100]

Of the many enumerated without occupation almost all are women who fall within the groups already mentioned. They are daughters, married and unmarried, and other dependent female relatives who, as one enumerator put it 'attend to domestic duties'. Occasionally a man of working age, even a head of household, is left without an entry for occupation with no explanation of his status. As with the widow heads with no recorded means of support, such men cannot be classified and have to be omitted from analysis. Most men enumerated without occupation are, needless to say, not heads of household but relatives dependent on their families by reason of age or infirmity. No enumerator in the sample area used the expression 'no occupation' but most checkers inserted it where they found a blank against an adult or a young adult.

Indication of unemployment, as opposed to lack of occupation, occurs only rarely. Some servants 'out of place' are recorded, or a lodger is described as 'out of business'; the expression 'late valet' is ambiguous, but may mean the same as 'out of place'. The actual word 'unemployed' is used of three men in two Winteringham households and of two girls, 9 and 11 years old, in a Sheffield household but these occurrences are quite exceptional.[101] Perhaps not surprisingly, only 17 years after the New Poor Law, the instructions to house-holders and enumerators made no mention of unemployment.

The instructions for enumerating paupers were specific enough. 'Almspeople, and persons in receipt of parish relief, should, after being described as such, have their previous occupations inserted: "Pauper (Agricultural labourer)".'[102] Many paupers are correctly recorded in the terms of the instructions: an 81-year-old widow of Winteringham is described as 'Pauper (Formerly Mistress of a Dame School)' and some enumerators are always careful to specify that the occupation mentioned was *formerly* followed. Others do not specify 'formerly' but use a form similar to that in the instructions with or without the brackets; in one case the order was reversed: 'Carpenter (Parish pay)'. Occasionally 'in receipt of parish relief' or similar expressions replace the word 'pauper' and the use of 'poor woman' and 'poor widow' occurs in a district in which the enumer-ator also uses 'receiving parish relief'.[103]

In addition to such instances some enumerators use a form which suggests that the paupers also had an occupation. Thus there occur entries such as 'in receipt of parish relief and straw-bonnet maker' and others who are 'pauper and charwoman' or who keep lodgers or are band-box makers.[104] Such com-binations are, of course, quite possible: out relief to aged widows (and many of these were such) continued throughout the century quite unaffected by the New Poor Law as the Webbs long ago pointed out.[105] Nor is it improbable that such relief was supplementary to a pittance earned charring. Nevertheless, such a form is hardly conclusive and may still indicate no more than the former occupation which would be followed if the individual were not pauperised. It should be noted also that not all the checkers appear to have understood the instructions and marked the former occupation for tabulation amongst the employed population.

Almsmen and women are generally recorded as such and with some identifi-cation of the almshouse or charity to which their benefit is attached. For in-pensioners it is usually possible to identify from the context the almshouse in which they live if this is not given. The inmates of St Thomas's Hospital in Doncaster were known as annuitants but there is no reason to suppose that annuitants found in the returns outside the context of charitable institutions were pensioners of this kind, even though many purchasers of annuities doubt-less received incomes just as small as the bedesmen.

XIII

THE ENUMERATORS' BOOKS AS SOURCE MATERIAL

What has been said about the interpretative difficulties, the anomalies and the plain errors in the enumerators' books may suggest that they do not warrant extensive analysis. Yet the fact that an increasing body of students are able successfully to use the returns to throw a powerful light on the social and economic history of the nineteenth century suggests a different conclusion. The point, of course, is that what has been said has been almost exclusively argued from the pathology of the material. It should be realised that a large proportion of the data is entirely unambiguous: page after page, household after household, sometimes in an almost unwelcome monotony, exhibits not one of the many difficulties described. Even where they do occur, many of the ambiguities and errors are of a trivial nature and easily and confidently emended.

The precautions that may be taken and the rules which will help to maintain a consistent treatment of the material and comparability with other workers in the field, are summarised in appendix 2.

Appendix 1

THE ENUMERATORS' BOOKS

Six sizes of book were issued to the enumerators in 1851, containing 24, 36, 48, 60, 72 and 84 pages (known as books A to F). Book C of 48 pages is illustrated in the *Census Report, 1851* (Pt. I, cxlviii–cliv) and was capable of enumerating (at 20 entries to a page) 960 persons or approximately the 200 households that was normally to comprise an enumerator's district. Densely populated urban districts used the 72- or 84-page books, recording roughly 300 or 350 households, though none in the sample area reached this number. The books for the 1861 census were differently arranged and contain 25 persons to a page.

It should be noticed that in both censuses the book pages are numbered, in 1851 by a stamp in the top centre of the page and in 1861 to the side and within the print area. This numbering, which is independent of the preliminaries of the books (which are numbered in lower-case Roman numerals), is on each side of each page or, more correctly, folio. A later number (by automatic stamp) numbers the folios only (i.e. one number to each folio), includes the preliminaries and refers to a series larger than the enumeration districts. Reference to the books is best made by place name, the letter and/or number of the district, and the schedule number of the entry, avoiding all reference to page numbering. But in obtaining copies of the books from the Public Record Office it will usually be necessary to specify place, enumeration district and the folios required, avoiding reference to either the schedule numbers or the pages.

Each enumerator's book in 1851 was prefaced by seven preliminary pages, numbered i to vii; for 1861 there were six pages. Pages v, vi, and vii in 1851, and ii and iii in 1861, are the instructions to the enumerators and the examples for entering up their books and have been discussed elsewhere. Page i in both censuses was the 'Description of Enumeration District'. In 1851 a series of six boxes shows the administrative divisions within which the place lay, the last three indicating the Superintendent Registrar's District, the Registrar's District and the Enumeration District. The same information is called for on page i of the 1861 books, though in a slightly different form. The three districts are commonly described not only in words but by numbers which may be understood by reference to the population tables of the *Census Reports* which are arranged by Division (a county or several counties), Registration District, sub-district and parish (or similar administrative division). In some cases the enumeration district is the parish and the numbers correspond to those of the *Census Report*; for many others the enumeration district number cannot be found from the population tables. It should perhaps be added that the arrangement of the books at the Public Record Office corresponds to neither of these numberings. The books are in two classes, HO 107 for 1851 and RG 9 for 1861; within these classes the books follow the arrangement of the *Census Report* but are bundled in collections which, more often than not, overlap the sub-districts of the registration districts. Thus Doncaster Registration District is number 510 in the *Census Report*. Sub-districts 1 and 2 (comprising 26 parishes and townships and many more enumeration districts) are in HO 107/2346; sub-district 3 (which contains the 18 enumeration districts of Doncaster town) is in another bundle; and 4 and 5 in yet another.

Besides the numbering according to this system, the enumerator was required to write on page i a description of his district which he either obtained from the Registrar or which the Registrar had already written there. In 1861 he was required to write any explanatory notes which would make the description more complete.

Page ii in 1851 and page v in 1861 were summary pages of the totals for each page of the enumeration book. The numbers entered on these pages and on the pages of the book itself were, of course, examined by the checkers at the Census Office and it might be supposed that they are always to be trusted. Experience in the sample area suggests that more errors occur than might be expected. In Doncaster five out of the eighteen districts contained errors in the numbers counted. The great majority of these appear to occur because the counts were made by adding the number of entries in the age columns. Of the twelve errors, two were simply wrong additions not noticed by the checkers; in seven cases the age had been omitted thus leading the enumerator to add up seven too few persons; in the remaining three cases the age had been written in both columns thus causing the enumerator to add one too many in each case. Sheffield showed only two such errors in two out of the fifteen districts examined.

It will be remembered that the summaries of houses and occupiers must be regarded with the greatest caution; they too, are subject to arithmetical error.

When complete, the totals on the summary page were transferred to page iii of the 1851 books and page iv of the 1861 books. These pages comprised four and three tables respectively, numbered (a) to (d) in 1851 and I, II and an unnumbered one in 1861. Tables (c) and (d) and I and II, which required an account of persons temporarily present and absent have already been described (section VI of this chapter). Table (b) in 1851 required the 'Estimated number of persons who have *not been enumerated* as inmates of any dwelling-house, but who it is believed have slept or abode in the District on the night preceding the day of Enumeration' and required them to be classified under three heads: 'in barges, boats, or other small vessels remaining stationary on canals or other navigable waters' and 'in barns, sheds, or the like' and 'in tents, or in the open air'. The table was not to include 'people in coasting or other sea-going vessels, nor persons *travelling* in railways through the district.'

The information in table (b) was to be given simply in terms of the number of males and females. The great majority of the enumerators made no entry in this table; some of the few who did also incorporated an age tabulation of their own devising for the persons mentioned.

It is clear from the instructions for table (b) that the enumerators were not to list these persons in the normal course of their enumeration in the books. It seems likely that for the most part they did not though one Lincolnshire enumerator listed six watermen and their families living in barges on the Broughton River; he did not, however, make any entry in table (b). For vessels of larger dimensions – coasters and ocean-going ships – ship schedules were issued in 1851 not to the enumerators but to the customs officers who enumerated not only those on board moored vessels but persons on the high seas. The distinction in size between barges and other moored vessels is not clearly stated but it seems unlikely that any were counted both by the enumerators and the customs officers. In 1861 persons in barges and boats of all descriptions were removed from enumeration in the equivalent of table (b) and issued with a separate enumeration schedule which they themselves filled up.

In both censuses the particulars of all those persons not dwelling in houses are missing except for the bare numbers of males and females, although occasionally the enumerator has mistakenly included them in the normal schedule. Clearly, if they only appear in table (b) or its 1861 equivalent they cannot be used in any way for analysis and even when they appear by error in the normal enumeration they should be omitted from household analysis. An exception may be made for those who in 1861 are enumerated on separate schedules ('Form A: Form for Vessels') who may be treated as if they were living in houses.

The general summary table (table (a) in 1851, unnumbered in 1861) is self-explanatory but it should be noticed that the persons living in barns, tents etc. are included in the population count. As a consequence the published population figures may be different from those obtained by the modern investigator who excludes such persons from his collection of data.

Pages iv (1851) and vi (1861) comprise the declarations signed by the enumerators, the registrars and the superintendent registrars on completion of their work. Quite apart from identifying the enumerator (who is not elsewhere named) the signatures may be of value in distinguishing any marks in the books that may have been made by the registrar. The tabulators and checkers of the Census Office usually add their signatures or initials to remarks on page iii (1851) and page iv (1861) of the books and these may assist in identifying the marks made in the body of the book.

A separate enumeration book was issued to the masters of public institutions – workhouses, prisons, asylums, hospitals – of 200 or more inhabitants. No householders' schedules were issued in such cases and the master entered the information directly into the book which, on completion, he sent to the registrar. The books take a form very like the general enumeration books but 'relationship to head' is replaced by 'position in the institution' and the occupation required was that of the inmates before admission. The summary sheets are adjusted to suit the special conditions of institutions.

The enumerators of 1851 also had the duty of delivering and collecting the forms for the enquiries into schools and places of worship made in that year. The results of these so-called religious and educational censuses are not preserved amongst the enumeration books.

The abbreviated references used for place names in the sample area are listed below.

Lincolnshire		*Yorkshire*	
Alkborough	Alk	Bradfield	Brad
Althorpe	Alt	Braithwell	Braith
Appleby	App	Dalton	Dal
Brigg	Bg	Doncaster	D
East Butterwick	EB	Sheffield	S
Burringham	Bu	Sheffield Crookes	Cr
Bottesford	Bo	Skipton	Sk
Broughton	Br	Tickhill	T
Burton Stather	BS		
Flixborough	Fl	*Nottinghamshire*	
Normanby	Norm	Farnsfield	F
Roxby	Ro		
Scunthorpe	Sc	*Derbyshire*	
West Halton	WH	Hathersage	Hath
Whitton	Whit		
Winterton	W		
Winteringham	Wham		

Appendix 2

THE USE OF ENUMERATORS' BOOKS

1. Poll Books, Directories and parish material should be used to supplement the census data.

2. The emendations of the registrars should be observed and usually accepted as part of the data. The emendations of the Census Office clerks and tabulators – the checkers – should be identified and disregarded since they are guides used for tabulating the data for the *Census Report* and not emendations of the enumerator's work after further enquiry.

3. The investigator should not seek to divide his material into houses but into households – better described as co-residing groups. These groups should be those listed under each new head or head equivalent, excluding lodgers. Exceptionally, where an entry for a lodger is preceded by a long line or double stroke and a new address, the lodger may be considered as a head equivalent. Where it is desired to find the number of houses these should be regarded as occurring after each long line or double stroke. The exceptional cases where lines are mis-drawn or omitted are covered by recommendations within the texts of this chapter and chapter 4.

4. In the columns relating to addresses, names, age and sex, relationships and birthplaces the following should be noted or observed:

Houses can only be identified with actual properties under ideal circumstances.

When the three elements in an entry – name, relationship, and sex, do not agree, the person should be read as being of the sex indicated by whichever two elements agree.

Entries for one person may be made in both age columns or neither.

Care should be taken to note the expression 'months' or 'mo' after the age of infants.

Birthplace counties may be misleadingly indicated by wrongly marked dittos. Checkers marks in the blind etc. column refer to their tabulation of birthplaces not to infirm persons.

A number of households will be found without a person designated as head: these (with the exception of lodgers in most cases) are to be regarded as head equivalents for determining co-residing groups but as having their recorded status for other purposes.

'In-law' is frequently used to mean 'step'.

'NK' is used as an abbreviation for 'not known'.

In analysing lodgers only those persons so designated by the enumerators should normally be included; visitors should be noted separately and household size counts shown with and without them. If an enumerator appears to have used the word 'visitor' for persons who were lodgers, tabulations showing how much this might increase the lodger population should be made. The transfer of visitors to the status of lodgers should be made with due regard to the idiosyncrasies of the enumerator involved and under a stated set of rules.

5. Special care should be taken to identify and disregard the checkers' marks and emendations in the occupation column: these include the addition of industrial classifications, marking the wives of certain tradesmen and craftsmen as engaged in their husband's occupation and assigning to boys of 10 to 14 years the occupations of their fathers.

Persons with more than one occupation should be regarded as chiefly following that first listed.

The enumeration of employment status in terms of master, journeyman etc. is inconsistent and should be regarded with caution.

The record of labourers employed on farms may or may not include the farm servants who live in the house and are enumerated with the household.

The absence of an acreage figure for a farm should not be taken to mean that the farm is necessarily a small-holding.

The word 'housekeeper' is used by some enumerators merely to mean 'engaged in domestic duties'. Housekeepers should only be regarded as following an occupation for gain if their relationship to head is that of servant (or in certain cases an equivalent relationship).

Heads of household not given an occupation must be excluded from those parts of the analysis which depend upon classification by occupation.

Only children marked by the enumerators as scholars should be so regarded.

Women and girl servants in their own households should be regarded as of no occupation unless it is specifically stated that they work away from home. Nurse girls may be regarded as an exception where there is no infant in the household.

Trade and craft employees who stand in the relationship of servant should be distinguished from domestic servants.

Paupers should always be regarded as having formerly followed the occupation recorded regardless of the form used in describing it.

The annuitant who was in receipt of alms should be distinguished from the purchaser of an annuity.

The summary totals of the enumeration should be carefully scrutinised and the total from table (b) or its 1861 equivalent deducted from the population total. The totals in tables (c) and (d) and their 1861 equivalents should be disregarded.

In 1861 and thereafter persons enumerated under the form for vessels should be treated as if they were co-residing units on land.

4. Standard tabulation procedures for the census enumerators' books 1851–1891

M. Anderson

I

Sociologists and social historians use the census enumerators' books for many different purposes. Quite frequently they simply want to amplify information obtained from the published reports on the number of persons in certain categories (numbers of migrants, miners, or married women, for example) in a community. In particular, it is often necessary to obtain information of this kind for areas different from (and usually smaller than) those for which details are published in the reports. Often, however, obtaining such information is only a beginning, for the enumerators' books suitably analysed can reveal very much more than simple counts of numbers in categories. The investigator may be interested in locating non-random regularities in the frequency with which persons in one category are also members of specified other categories (the proportion of lodgers who are also bachelor migrants, for example). Or he may be seeking information about the distribution in the population under study of patterns of group membership (the proportion of houses containing different numbers of persons, or the proportion of 'households' containing kin, lodgers, or servants). Or, finally, he may be interested in investigating the frequency with which persons who are members of both of a pair of categories (e.g. head of household and migrant) are found as members of the same group (e.g. household) as persons who are members of the same or other pairs of categories (e.g. lodger and migrant).

All these operations require the investigator to summarise, aggregate, or group in some way, the highly heterogeneous data with which he is faced. To do this he will define individuals in certain categories as members of discrete classes (at the simplest level, he will group his population into certain age groups). He will also define certain aggregates of individuals as comprising meaningful social groupings, and will present his analysis in terms of the number of members and patterns of relationships between members of these groupings (he may, for example, find that the average nuclear family size was 5·6, and that 60 per cent of all children were employed in the same trade or industry as their father).

Different investigators will, however, approach the data with somewhat different aims in view, and this will mean that they will frequently want to treat separately certain categories which another investigator, interested in a different problem, could reasonably treat as homogeneous enough to be taken together.

In another area, of greater interest to the second investigator, the reverse situation will occur. Nevertheless, there will be many occasions when investigators will seek to aggregate categories into groups and will have very similar aims. There is an obvious danger, in the absence of agreed procedures for analysis, that they will aggregate categories in different ways. As a result, it will be impossible to compare in any useful way the results of different studies. This would be unfortunate, since the answers to many problems of great historical and sociological interest will only be found when it becomes possible to compare findings from a large number of different studies of communities with different economic bases, employment opportunities, income levels, growth rates, migration patterns, and so on. This chapter seeks· to suggest standard tabulation procedures for one of the more difficult areas, the definition of houses, of different kinds of residential units, and of certain categories, notably that of lodger. It results from a series of discussions and meetings extending over several years between a number of people who, in their own work, have become painfully aware of the confusions and dangers in this area, and of the need for clear specification of standard procedures for analysis.[1]

II

Lack of comparability can be the result of two different but related sets of factors. Firstly, even if, which is not the case, the data were to present no problems of interpretation, different investigators might combine the same categories in different ways (for example, some might classify apprentices with servants, others with lodgers), or they might conduct their analysis of distributions and relationships in terms of differently bounded units (some giving the numbers of persons per house, others the numbers per 'household', for example). Secondly, though there was broad agreement on the classes of categories and on the groupings to be adopted, shortcomings in the data might lead different investigators to allocate doubtful cases to different groups or classifications, with the result that their published tabulations were not exactly comparable.

In deciding on the groupings and categories to be recommended, and on the solutions to be adopted in marginal cases, a number of considerations must be borne in mind. The most important appear to be:

(a) Which of the various alternatives is least likely to be subject to discrepancies both within the same enumerator's book and between different enumerators' books.

(b) Which provides the most internally homogeneous groupings.

(c) Which unit or classification provides us with the largest amount of sociologically or historically useful data.

(d) Which unit or classification is most likely to give us comparability between the census of 1851 and later censuses.

(e) Which is the grouping or classification most comparable with that used by historians of other periods and areas, and by sociologists and others in the study of modern societies. This may well be considered as the least important of these principles, since complete comparability can seldom be obtained.

(f) Which is the smallest unit which can be successfully and regularly identified and which is relevant to the purpose in hand, so that the maximum freedom to cross-classify and recombine data is preserved.

The enumerators' books for all nineteenth century censuses from 1851 onwards enable us to differentiate the members of different types of communities and also the co-residing members of nuclear families and kinship groups. In addition they make it possible to distinguish the occupants of one house from those of the next and to identify the members of 'census families'.[2] Almost all investigators will want, from time to time at least, to conduct analyses in terms both of houses and of 'census families'. The identification of both these units raises, however, some problems for the investigator, albeit in a rather small number of cases. It is the task of much of the rest of this chapter to provide reasoned standardised solutions to the commonest of these problems. It also considers the vitally important issue of the best residential grouping to take as the basic living unit in terms of which analysis of residence patterns and of relationships between the social characteristics of co-residing persons should be conducted.

The basic recommendations made here are:

1. Analysis of the composition of and relationships within residential units should normally be conducted in terms of 'census families'. Tillott's chapter in this volume gives something of the history of the census authorities' attempts to find an adequate definition of the 'census family', the group who, in the words of the 1851 instructions to enumerators, co-resided with an 'Occupier – understanding by "occupier" either a resident owner or any person who pays rent, whether (as a tenant) for the whole of a house or (as a lodger) for any distinct floor or apartment...'[3] This unit, the nearest approximation to the 'household', usually defined in terms of commensality[4] which is the unit normally used in present-day investigations, will henceforth be referred to here as a co-residing group, rather than 'household' to remind readers that its definition is rather different.

2. In the 1851 books a new house should be counted after each 'long line'; in the 1861 books a new house should be counted wherever a figure '1' appears in the column headed 'houses inhabited'.[5] The precise meaning to be given to these criteria in practice is discussed below where a number of minor exceptions to this rule are also noted. Where one wishes to refer in the aggregate to all people living in a house one might perhaps call them a 'houseful'.

3. For all nineteenth-century censuses from 1851 onwards the co-residing group should be defined as comprising all the names listed in an enumerator's book from one entry 'head' in the column headed 'relation to head of family' to

the last name preceding the next entry 'head'. The only exceptions which should normally be made to this rule are:

(i) Occasional cases where other words are used instead of and as the practical equivalent of 'head'. In some of these cases the head was absent from home on census night but the enumerator recorded relationships by reference to him, with the result that the first entry for a co-residing group in the 'relation to head of family' column reads, for example, 'wife', or 'servant' or, exceptionally, 'wife, head absent from home', or some such similar phrase. In other cases the head was at home on census night, but the enumerator chose to identify him by some other term instead of 'head'. For example, in the case of a business, the word 'partner' may appear, and widows are occasionally recorded not as 'head' but as 'widow'. In these cases the following rule should be used. Where in 1851 a long or short line, and in 1861 a single or double dash or a '1', is followed by an entry which suggests that the person first named is a head equivalent, a new co-residing group should be counted in spite of the general rule noted above that the word 'head' be the deciding criterion. This exception should not, however, be made in cases where the entry follows a short line or single dash, if this entry could reasonably refer to a relationship to the head of the previous co-residing group. In particular the word 'lodger' should never under these circumstances be taken as a head equivalent; all lodgers should be entered as part of the preceding co-residing group. This should also be done even in the occasional cases where a long line in an 1851 book is followed by an entry 'lodger', unless verification of the total number of houses at the foot of the page and, in areas where each house is clearly differentiated from the next by a new address, the recording of a new and distinct address in the address column in the hand of the enumerator, does indeed indicate that the enumerator intended a new house to be counted. Where the address and house total indicators disagree, the new address should be taken as decisive. Note that this case forms an exception to rule 2.

(ii) where two successive individuals are both listed as 'Heads' (or head equivalents), but no line or dash is drawn between them and there is no other indication of a new 'census family' (both, for example, have the same schedule number), both are to be included in the same co-residing group, it being assumed that they shared the headship.

Conceivable alternative rules (those not recommended here) seem to be in each case:

1. Unit of analysis: the house.
2. Definition of co-residing group: either, in 1851 the short line and in 1861 the single oblique mark; or, in both years, a new schedule number.
3. Definition of house: a new address given in the address column or, additionally, in 1861, the double dash.

Before proceeding to justify the recommended practices a number of other definitions and terms may perhaps also be usefully suggested:

1. A 'shared house' should be one in which there were two or more co-residing groups.
2. A 'primary family' should be the nuclear family of the head of the co-residing group.
3. 'Secondary families' should be all other nuclear families in a co-residing group; these may be subdivided as necessary into 'secondary lodger families' and 'secondary kin families', and these groups subdivided again if desired into different kinds of nuclear families.
4. Co-residing groups containing such secondary families are probably best described specifically, as for example, 'co-residing groups containing secondary lodger families, (or single lodgers)' or, where relevant, as 'stem families' or 'three generation families.'

The next three sections of this chapter look at the justifications for these recommendations, elaborate them somewhat, and note a number of cases where exceptions should be made to deal with inconsistencies or shortcomings in the original data.

III
DEFINITION OF 'HOUSE'

The 1851 enumerators were instructed to treat a house as 'a separate and distinct *building*'.[6] The census report elaborated this by noting that it was intended that each dwelling separated by a party wall be treated as a separate house,[7] but this elaboration was not contained in the instructions to enumerators and some confusion inevitably resulted. Some enumerators may even (quite logically) have included whole terraces as separate single buildings, but such errors will undoubtedly be very rare. In most large Scottish towns, however, and also probably in some other cities like Newcastle, where buildings were frequently clustered together behind and in part on top of others, where two front doors might serve the same block, and where one flat sometimes went over the top of or through into part of a neighbouring building, insuperable problems were sometimes found. In Scotland these problems were made worse because what the English called a 'flat' or 'apartment' was (and still is) referred to by the Scots as a 'house'. The almost hysterical protests of the Scots at having the English definition (which, they argued, 'was quite unintelligible in Scotland'[8]) thrust upon them continued until 1881 when a new definition was adopted in Scotland.[9] One important consequence of this is that the data on houses in all Scottish censuses before 1881 are quite meaningless.

The enumerator, in making up his book, was instructed to record the address of each house and, in his book, 'Under the last name in any *house*...he should draw a line *across the page as far as the fifth column*'.[10] It should therefore usually be possible for the investigator to distinguish each house by a new entry in the address column, and by what is normally known as the long line.

As Tillott notes in his chapter, occasionally lines are omitted, and occasionally also it seems that short lines, designed to be used to differentiate between census families, were drawn in error as long lines. It is, however, clearly impossible to be sure in any case that an error was in fact made and, since any alterations are bound to be based on largely subjective criteria and would therefore inevitably lead to inconsistencies between different investigators, the only reliable procedure seems to be to take all long lines as intended long lines and to agree that the few doubtful cases, which will almost certainly be randomly distributed over the population under study, will make no significant difference to the overall results.

Address data, the alternative criterion which might be adopted, are unfortunately even less useful. Particularly in rural areas, there is often no new entry in the address column for each house and it is essential to have a rule applicable to all areas. In towns, on the other hand, from time to time, what appear to be flats in the same building, are given separate numbers.

The long line seems therefore to be the most reliable indicator we can use in work on the 1851 books, and this will undoubtedly be valid in all but a tiny minority of cases.

The basic definition of a house remained the same in the nineteenth-century censuses after 1851. The definition was, however, elaborated somewhat further to conform to current international practice. Thus in 1861 'The enumerators of the United Kingdom were instructed to class under that category every habitation, each separate house comprising by definition all the space within the external and party walls of the building.'[11] In this and subsequent censuses a double oblique dash in the margin replaced the long line as the conventional indicator of a new house, and, in addition, each new house was indicated by an entry '1' in the 'houses inhabited' column. As was noted above it is this last indicator which is recommended for adoption here.

The only exceptions which it seems useful to allow are the following:

1. Where a long line is drawn (or (in 1861) a '1' appears) in the middle of a nuclear family (as indicated by relationships in the 'relation to head of family' column and by a similar surname) and where the entry for the 'head' of this family is not preceded by a long line (or (in 1861) by a '1') the marks may be deemed to be misplaced and suitable adjustments may be made to correspond with the sense. If this is not done members of the same family will appear to be living in the same co-residing group, but in different houses, which is clearly nonsensical.

2. Long lines in 1851 books are occasionally omitted at the bottom of pages. Where it is suspected that this has occurred, reference should be made to the total of inhabited houses at the foot of the next page and, where this total can only be correct if the first co-residing group on the page did indeed occupy a separate house, this may be taken as a substitute indicator, and a new house counted.

3. It may occasionally happen that a long line in 1851 books is followed by an entry 'lodger'. This should normally (see above) be taken to indicate a house where the head was absent so that the lodger should be taken as head equivalent. As noted above, however, this conclusion should always be verified against the total at the foot of the page and against the address data where these are given.

4. In the 1861 books, some urban enumerators occasionally omit the entry '1' in the inhabited house column in cases where they indicate a new house by a double dash and by a new and different address in the address column. Unfortunately, enumerators seem even more likely to omit double dashes from time to time and, as in 1851, address data are frequently lacking and so cannot be used as the general indicator. On pages where houses are being distinguished by number or house name in the address column, a new house should additionally be counted, therefore, wherever it is indicated by both a new and different address in the hand of the enumerator and by a double dash. In such cases it is deemed that a '1' has been omitted.

Persons entered in the main parts of enumerators' books as parts of families living in tents, barges (in 1851), caravans, and other temporary or movable accommodation should not be given houseful status, since they have been entered in error, and most such persons were probably not entered separately. Persons living in moored vessels, however, should have been systematically enumerated and are probably best treated in aggregate analysis as if they were living in separate houses, and the same should be done in 1861 books with persons living in boats and barges.[12] Lodging houses, hotels, prisons, workhouses and boarding schools should all be treated as houses, but, in the cases of schools, prisons, and workhouses, 'inmates' should usually be excluded *en bloc* from sample analysis, and, where desired, should be treated separately.[13]

IV

DEFINITION OF 'CO-RESIDING GROUP'

The 'co-residing group', what the census authorities call the 'family', is based on an attempt to differentiate groups of persons residing in distinct property or living space either owned by themselves or for which, as a group, they paid rent.

The instructions to enumerators for the 1851 census are superficially quite specific about the procedure to be used to differentiate between co-residing groups, both during the distribution and collection of the schedules and in the writing up of the enumerators' books.[14] Enumerators were to inquire, both during the distribution and during the collection of the schedules, whether a house had one or more than one occupier. Each occupier was to be given a separate schedule and a note made during distribution of all houses where more than one schedule had been issued. Each schedule was to be numbered separately. The instructions for making up the books noted:

Under the last line in any house...he should draw a line *across the page as far as the fifth column*. Where there is more than one Occupier in the same house he should draw a similar line under the last name of the family of each Occupier; making the line, however, in this case, commence a little on the left hand side of the third column, as in the example on page vi of his book.[15]

It is obvious from the detail of these instructions that all enumerators must have given some thought to the problem of differentiating between co-residing groups. Unfortunately, as chapter 3 amply illustrates, the decisions the enumerators actually arrived at were not wholly consistent. In part this was due to the imprecise nature of the definition which obviously led to confusion in marginal cases. The enumerator was instructed to 'leave a separate schedule with each Occupier – understanding by "Occupier" either a resident owner or any person who pays rent, whether (as a tenant) for the whole of a house or (as a lodger) for any distinct floor or apartment'.[16] But what were the precise criteria to be used to decide whether any given individual really paid rent for a separate floor or apartment? Did this refer merely to sleeping in a separate bedroom or did the person also have to eat in a separate room? What about a situation where two lodgers each paid to the landlord half the rent of a bedroom, which none of the landlord's family occupied? Many other doubtful cases can easily be imagined, particularly perhaps where kin occupied separate apartments but, formally at least, did not pay rent. One might suggest, however, that such marginal cases, because of their marginality, will not lead to highly misleading results.

Greater problems arise, however, from inconsistency in individual cases between the three possible criteria for defining a co-residing group, viz: the new schedule number, the short line, and the word 'head' indicating a new 'occupier'. For example, sometimes, though always in a small minority of cases, a short line is drawn between two families, but no new schedule number is indicated. Sometimes, following a short line, the first entry in the 'relation to head of family' column is given as 'lodger', not 'head', and so on. Sometimes, particularly at the bottom of a page, short lines are apparently omitted.[17]

The situation in 1861 is even more confused. In the 1851 instructions to enumerators, and in the examples given to guide them in making up their returns, new co-residing groups are always headed by 'heads' of 'families'. In 1861, in recognition of the fact that lodgers (who were not even mentioned on the schedule for 1851,[18] a fact that undoubtedly increased the confusion) had caused difficulty in 1851, the instructions and examples were changed. The full instructions to enumerators for the 1861 census were not published, but the report notes that, in addition to the 1851 definition, the enumerator was instructed that 'a lodger alone, or in company with another lodger, occupying common apartments, is an occupier, and as such is classed as a family in the abstracts'.[19] The exact meaning of the word 'common' in this statement seems unclear. It would seem, however, that no mistake should have arisen, because the instructions in the beginning of each enumerator's book were adamant: 'NOTE – a Lodger, with or without a family is to be considered as an Occupier'. In addition, the reverse of the schedule was amended to read:

If the house is let or sublet to different families *or lodgers*, each OCCUPIER *or* LODGER, must make a return for his portion of the house upon a SEPARATE PAPER [my italics, contrast 1851]. If the house is let or sublet to different persons or families, in separate stories or apartments, the OCCUPIER or Person in charge of each such story or apartment, must make a separate return for his portion of the house...[20]

Finally, one of the examples actually gave a separate 'family' containing just a single lodger, with the entry in the 'relation to head of family' column not as 'head' as was done for the other 'families', but as 'lodger.'

The underlying assumptions of the definitions for 1851 and 1861 remained the same, the occupation of separate apartments. Even this was somewhat compromised, however, by the insinuation of some concept of commensality, presumably as an aid to differentiation in cases where some apartments were shared even although others were occupied separately. Thus a distinction was apparently made even in 1861 (though once again we cannot be sure as the precise instructions to enumerators were not published), and certainly thereafter, between lodgers who boarded alone, and lodgers who boarded at the family table.[21]

The upshot of these changes was that in 1861 and thereafter many more schedules were issued to single lodgers and to small families.[22] One even finds occasionally (quite logically in a sense) each lodger in a house being given separate occupier status, with the paradoxical result that there are recorded more 'occupiers of separate apartments' in a house, than there were different rooms. In practice, of course, it must have been quite impossible for enumerators faced with a house where there were half a dozen lodgers each of whom ate separately, and who collectively shared a bedroom distinct from that used by any one in the family of the owner, to know what was required of them. Some appear to have grouped these lodgers together and entered them all as 'lodgers'; some to have done the same but arbitrarily defined one as 'head'; some allocated each to a separate 'family' and described each as a lodger; a few followed this procedure, but made each a separate 'head'; many ignored the change, followed the most prevalent 1851 practice, and simply included most lodgers, particularly if they were single, in the same census family as the head.

Inevitably, therefore, whatever definition of co-residing group is adopted the resulting aggregations will not be wholly homogeneous. Moreover, precise comparisons with the 1851 figures will never be possible. The question therefore arises as to which, in terms of the principles outlined above, is the best definition to adopt. In particular, should one follow the oblique marks and (usually, though by no means always, the schedule numbers) and thus classify many lodgers as household units, thus confusing the two categories?

It seems best that the word 'head' be taken as the indicator in both 1851 and

1861. It is probable that the resulting groups, in spite of the inclusion of a small number of lodgers entered as 'heads', will be more homogeneous, since many odd single lodgers will not then be raised to co-residing group status, with all the biases which would ensue.[23] The fact that a family was entered as lodgers of another family does suggest very strongly that they were (at least in most cases) in a different and inferior status, from those whose head was entered as 'head'. The fact that some persons who were really lodgers will have been entered as 'heads' seems little reason for combining and thus confusing what are (conceptually and also generally in practice) clearly different residential patterns.

What has been written above does not necessarily mean, however, that lodgers who are entered as separate 'occupiers' need necessarily be automatically grouped with other lodgers not given separate 'occupier' status. It may well be that as a group they show certain clear differences from other lodgers, but this, and its interpretations, is a question for empirical research.

V.

UNIT OF ANALYSIS

One consequence of the difficulties inherent in differentiating co-residing groups, might be to encourage investigators to use the house, rather than the co-residing group, as the unit of analysis. This seems undesirable for a number of reasons.

Firstly, as noted above, there may be inconsistencies even in the classification of houses.

Secondly, the house, as such, does not provide a sociologically meaningful grouping of individuals. The co-residing group even if, as I doubt, it were subject to widely different classification, does at least have the very important advantage that, in some sense, it was perceived as a real unit of some kind by the people asked by the enumerator how many occupiers there were in the house. Moreover, comparisons on the basis of the house are not really of much value. The number of people in each house does not, for example, give us any real index of overcrowding, because the size of houses varied so widely. On the other hand, comparisons on the basis of co-residing groups should at least give some idea of the numbers interacting on some kind of basis in a reasonably regular fashion; this becomes particularly relevant when the number of persons in a household falls to one.

It may also be noted that in, say, Edinburgh or Leith, and also in London and in many towns in the North of England in the middle of last century four- and five-storey tenement blocks each containing up to 20 completely self-contained residential units were common. Here, where 'house' might be occupied by 100 people, each in households of five, the house becomes a completely meaningless unit for analysis.[24]

Thirdly, if we are at all interested in the relationship of family members to the household head, the co-residing group is the only one which we can use, since such relationships are only given with reference to the head of the census family. Moreover, if we analyse in terms of houses how can we justify calling the head of the first co-residing group the head of the house as a whole; why not the second, or the third if there is one? In Preston, at least, there seems no systematic pattern according to which schedules were distributed.

VI

RECOMMENDED PROCEDURES FOR CERTAIN OTHER TOPICS

1. It would seem best to keep domestic servants, farm servants, shop assistants, trade servants, and apprentices in separate categories wherever possible.[25] If it is felt absolutely necessary to amalgamate any of these groups, apprentices are perhaps better amalgamated with servants, whom they are more like in terms of age and marital status, than with lodgers who otherwise represent a fairly distinct, meaningful and homogeneous category. Journeymen and shopmen may perhaps best be grouped with lodgers on the grounds of similar age, marital status and subordinate position. Children of servants are probably best classified as lodgers. Cooks, maids, and housekeepers are probably all best treated as servants, and governesses, although perhaps rather more different, are few in number in most areas and probably also fit best as servants.

2. Visitors, who have undoubtedly as a class somewhat different social characteristics from lodgers, should always be treated separately even though at the margin the two categories obviously overlap. Since any adjustments which are made by moving odd individuals from one category to another must inevitably be somewhat arbitrary and subject to different interpretations by different investigators, analysis in terms of the schedule entries should always be obtained, though, here as always, investigators with special interests in this group should obviously not be deterred from using their own classifications as well. Visitors have usually been excluded from household size counts. This certainly appears useful if we are mainly interested in ongoing residential units and long-term overcrowding, though perhaps both could be included in future work, and certainly, if so, the basis on which the calculations were made should always be indicated.

3. A number of other special cases arise on very infrequent occasions. As noted above, one or two co-residential units appear to have two heads – two spinsters, or two business partners with a housekeeper. Data are obviously lost by arbitrarily allocating the second individual in each case to the lodger category, but this may well be necessary. Such cases are, however, very rare, and will not greatly bias the category with which they are aggregated, while if they are of special interest, they are sufficiently few to be noted separately, and thus not to require mechanical tabulation.

4. Another problem arises where head equivalents are found in cases where the head is assumed to be absent from home. Should the first named person be

arbitrarily classified as 'head', or should one tabulate these co-residing groups as having no heads, and with the constituent members tabulated under their respective categories? It is recommended here that in all these cases the second course is adopted, even though some of the husbands who were not present may in fact have been more or less permanently absent, so that the status of their wives was very similar to those women given as 'head' in the 'relation to head of family' column, but whose marital status is given as 'married'. Note that in cases where head equivalents are members of families with co-residing kin, kinship relationships may have to be amended. For example, the 'mother' of a head equivalent 'wife' would have to be classified instead as 'mother-in-law', (her relationship to the absent head).

5. In conclusion, a general rule for all the topics covered in this chapter may be proposed. Consistency between investigators is most likely to be maintained if investigators take the data as they stand and make no attempts at re-interpreting doubtful cases, except in the ways described above. These will anyway be few in number and will surely never bias results to any significant degree. If the enumerators' books for any community are so badly compiled as to make nonsense if the rules outlined here are followed, then it may very well be better to study some other area rather than to begin to make what will inevitably be highly subjective guesses at what the enumerator might *really* have meant.

5. Sampling in historical research

R. S. Schofield

In some fields of history the quantity of evidence is so overwhelming that it would take an unacceptably long time to assess every item fully. Many of the subjects treated in this book fall into this category: for example a full evaluation of every household in the 1851 census returns for a large town would involve an immense amount of work. The usual strategy adopted in the face of an unmanageable quantity of evidence is a narrowing of the scope of the enquiry, in time, in space, or in subject matter. In many cases this may be an acceptable solution, but there are occasions when it is an unwelcome one. For example, interest may be precisely in the development of a large area over a long span of time, or the evidence may be quite manageable except for one vital series of documents of gargantuan size which alone would swallow up the time available for research.

There is, however, an alternative strategy open to us. If we can discover all we need to know by looking at only part of the evidence, that is by sampling it, we can radically reduce the time required to complete the research. As a result we may be able to embark upon research projects which would otherwise have been out of the question, or we may be able to extend either the range of our research by considering further evidence, or its depth by reflecting longer on the significance of our results. The feasibility of this alternative strategy in any particular instance clearly depends on how evenly information which is relevant to the research is spread amongst the documents to be sampled. If relevant information occurs in only a few documents, sampling is clearly inappropriate, as for example in a study of diplomatic correspondence, where crucial documents might fail to be included in the sample. On the other hand, if every document contains relevant information, and interest is centred on the typical rather than on the bizarre, then sampling will provide an acceptable summary of the evidence with an expenditure of only a fraction of the time and effort that a full perusal would entail. In general, therefore, the more important it is to discover evidence which occurs only rarely, the less appropriate sampling will be. Thus it may be sensible to sample a collection of documents for some questions, but not for others. A sample of railway company minutes, for example, may suffice for a study of the relative attention the company gave to a number of different issues, but it will be inadequate for a study of the formulation of a particular policy. Most of the subjects treated in this volume require an analysis of very large numbers of documents which are uniform in content. This is precisely the situation in which the greatest gains from sampling will accrue.

If an historian decides that it would be advantageous to sample a body of evidence, he is at present in considerable difficulty to know how to proceed. Books on the theory of sampling appear abstract and offer little practical advice, while books on the practice of sampling refer to alien disciplines, so that the historian may be left wondering in what way his evidence is analogous to six strains of wheat being subjected to five different fertilizers in seven counties.[1] Accordingly I have tried in this chapter to give practical advice on how a sample of historical documents should be drawn and how the results should be evaluated. I have chosen examples from the subjects and documents mentioned in this volume in the belief that familiar examples help to fix notions which may not be immediately clear when expressed in more general or abstract terms. I have also tried to explain something of the general principles behind sampling, albeit in a rather intuitive way, so that the reader can appreciate why he must take certain steps if his results are to be worth the paper they are written on, and so that he can make his own choice between alternative courses of action according to the nature of his evidence.

Although the exposition will be strictly non-mathematical in character, formulae will appear in the text because of their superiority over words in matters of economy and precision. I have thought it prudent, however, to assume that the reader may be unfamiliar with the conventions governing the way in which formulae are written, so I have provided in an appendix at the end of the chapter a brief guide to the more elementary conventions, which are all that are necessary for the present purpose. Mindful of my own difficulties in understanding other people's notation, I have thought it advisable both to explain the meaning of each symbol when it is first used in the text and also to provide in a second appendix a glossary of the symbols listed alphabetically, so that the reader can easily look up the meaning of any symbol which he does not understand. I have deliberately modelled my notation on that used by W. G. Cochran in *Sampling techniques*, 2nd ed. (New York, 1963). This is a comprehensive yet admirably clear standard textbook of a theoretical character, and to avoid confusion I shall wherever possible refer the reader to this work both for mathematical proofs and for guidance in matters which lie beyond the scope of this chapter.

DRAWING A SAMPLE

The aggregate of items to be sampled is known technically as the population, and the first step in drawing a sample is to define the population. There is seldom any difficulty about this in a historical context because the population is usually embodied in a document or series of documents. The next step is to specify how the population is to be subdivided so that it comprises an aggregate of items or units which can be sampled. This is often obvious in the context of the enquiry, but on occasion it requires a little thought. Let us suppose, for example, that the population at issue is a census enumeration district as described in the enumerators' books. We can subdivide this population into several kinds of units: into individuals, households, or areas such as streets or sub-districts; that is we can consider the enumeration district as comprising a population of individuals, a population of households, or a population of sub-districts.

The choice of an appropriate unit will depend on two considerations: the convenience of identifying the unit in the document and the objects of the enquiry. Sometimes these two considerations may lead to different conclusions. For example, we may be interested in the individuals enumerated in a census district, but we may find it impractical to sample so large a population of individuals. On the other hand we may find it easy to sample the smaller population of households comprising the same census district, thereby selecting individuals indirectly as members of the sample households. When elements are sampled indirectly in this way as members of a larger sampling unit, there are two points which should not be overlooked. Firstly, the sampling units must not overlap, that is each element must belong only to one sampling unit. The census books, for example, meet this requirement: each individual is assigned only to one household. Secondly, it is important to remember that elements in a sampling unit, for example individuals in a household, tend to be like each other. The selection of any sampling unit therefore involves the selection of a number of similar elements, known technically as a cluster. Thus a sample in which individual elements are selected indirectly in clusters will not be so representative as a sample in which the individual elements are themselves the sampling units, and accordingly some adjustment should be made to the sample estimates to allow for this.[2] It is therefore advisable to take as the sampling unit the smallest unit that is of interest in the enquiry, providing this is practicable from the point of view of selecting items for the sample. In the case of census studies, however, interest is usually directed towards the household, which makes this the obvious sampling unit, although estimates about individuals may also be required.

On the other hand interest may be centred on particular groupings of the sampling units, for example households grouped by the occupation of the head of the household, or, on a larger canvas, enumeration districts grouped by regional or economic characteristics. These groupings are known technically as domains of study, and where they are of overriding importance it may be worthwhile controlling the sample to ensure that each grouping is adequately represented. This will be discussed below under the headings *Subdivisions* and *Stratification*. For the present it will be assumed that there are no complications arising from either clustering or domains of study, so that all that we require is a simple sample of the items comprising the population.

Since the sample items have to represent the whole population, they should be chosen so that they reproduce, so far as possible, the *full range* of values occurring amongst the items in the population. The deliberate selection of certain items because they are thought to be average or extreme is therefore unlikely to be helpful. Indeed any kind of deliberate selection will probably do less than justice to the spread of population items, because human beings are unable to avoid bias, even when making simple judgements such as selecting a representative sample of stones displayed on a table.[3] We are therefore far more likely to get a representative sample if we avoid any kind of deliberate selection. A more promising approach would seem to be some procedure which would give each item in the population an equal chance of being included in the sample. This can be most effectively achieved if the selection of the sample items is left entirely to chance, thereby excluding all kinds of bias and subjective preference. Although we may feel intuitively that selection of the sample items with each item in the population having an equal chance of selection is likely to produce a representative sample, it could of course happen that by chance all the items selected for the sample come from one part of the population, producing a sample which is far from representative. But because the selection of each sample item has been left entirely to chance, the laws of chance can be used to estimate how probable it is that samples of different degrees of unrepresentativeness will occur in practice. That is for any sample that we may draw we shall be able to estimate how probable it is that the results it yields are unrepresentative of the population as a whole. Thus by abandoning all control over the selection of the sample items and leaving this entirely to chance, not only are we able to obtain estimates of the characteristics of the population which are free from bias, but we can also calculate how reliable these estimates are. No other method of selecting the sample items yields unbiased estimates of a calculable precision.

These advantages accrue only if we can ensure that chance alone determines the selection of the sample items. This is not so straightforward a matter to arrange as it might seem. Many ways of selecting items 'by chance', for example by drawing names or numbers out of a hat, turn out on close inspection to be biased, sometimes in rather subtle ways. The only sure way of excluding everything other than chance from the selection process is to choose the sample items with the help of a random number table.

Random number tables have been so designed that at any point in the table any number has an equal chance of appearing next. Thus to draw a sample so that each item in the population has an equal chance of selection it is only necessary to number each item in the population and then to read off a series of random numbers from the table, selecting for the sample the population items corresponding to these numbers. Random number tables are widely available and are very easy to use; one may begin at any point in the table and proceed in any direction, although it is usually more convenient to proceed vertically down columns.[4]

Three points, however, should not be overlooked. Firstly, it is important that the point of entry into the table should be determined arbitrarily before numbers are assigned to individual items, otherwise there may be a temptation to choose a starting point which will ensure the selection of a particular item, thereby violating the principle that each item must have an equal chance of selection. Secondly, this principle also requires that each number should have an equal chance of being encountered in the random number table, so that sufficient columns of figures should be taken together to accommodate the total number of items in the population. Thus if there are 7,843 items in the population, four columns should be taken together so that all numbers from 0000 to 9999 have an equal chance of occurring in the random number table. In practice this rule means that numbers can be encountered in the table for which there is no corresponding item in the population, in this example the numbers 7844–9999. When this happens the number is disregarded and the next number is taken. No harm has been done by this interruption because, by definition, each number and hence each item in the population has an equal chance of occurring *at any point in the table*. In the same way if the random number table indicates an item which turns out not to belong to the population being sampled, for example a prison in a sample of ordinary households from the census enumerators' books, the item can be disregarded and the next random number taken. Thirdly, there is no point in having the same item included several times in the sample, so if a random number occurs more than once it is ignored.[5]

Drawing a random sample therefore requires that at some stage each item in the population must be assigned a number. In some cases this causes difficulty: the population may be very large, or it may be impossible to write in the assigned number, for example when original documents are being sampled. There are several ways round problems of this kind. If the items to be sampled are grouped in units, for example in counties or on pages, and the total number of items in each unit is known, then adding up the unit subtotals cumulatively will immediately indicate the units in which the selected sample items lie. It will then only be necessary to number the items in the units concerned. On the other hand, if the items are listed in books with numbered pages, the page numbers can be used as the first part of the number for each item, the second part being given by the sequence of the item on the page. For example the ninth item on page 415 would have the number 4159. It is important in this case to allow sufficient numbers for the greatest possible number of items which can occur on the page, so that each item can have an equal chance of appearing. If in this example the maximum number of items appearing on a page were 14, then two digits must be provided in order to refer to the item; in this case the number corresponding to the ninth item on page 415 would be 41509. If random numbers are drawn for which there are no corresponding items, either because the first few digits are higher than the total number of pages, or because the last few digits are higher than the number of items on the page indicated, then the number is discarded and the next random number is taken as described above. Sometimes a large proportion of numbers has to be discarded as in the example cited, and in these cases this method is an inefficient way of drawing a random sample. An alternative, and usually more convenient, method is to draw the sample in two stages. The random number table is first used to indicate the page, or other larger unit, and then used again to indicate the item on the page to be selected for the sample.[6]

Although the random number table may seem to be a rather long-winded means of drawing items for a sample, it is well worth while taking some trouble over selecting items in this way because it is the only method which ensures that the choice of items is left entirely to chance. Strictly speaking it is only when the sample items have been selected by means of a random number table that we can make unbiased estimates of the characteristics of the population and give some indication of their reliability or precision. Nonetheless, in practice, samples are often drawn which are not random. The most common form of non-random sample, widely used in research on census enumerators' books, is the systematic sample.[7] A systematic sample is drawn by taking every kth item in sequence in the population. For example, a sample of households can be drawn from the census enumerators' books by taking every thirteenth household ($k = 13$). k, or the sampling interval, can be any size, depending on the number of items required in the sample. Systematic sampling therefore involves counting through the population as the sample is drawn, and in some circumstances, for example when working with original documents which cannot be numbered, it may be more convenient to draw a systematic sample than a random sample.

On the other hand, if the list of items contains items which do not belong to the population being studied, for example institutions listed in the census enumerators' returns when domestic households are being investigated, then a systematic sample may be more troublesome than a random sample. If a random sample is drawn and the random number table indicates an irrelevant item, the item is rejected, and the next random number is drawn. With a systematic sample, however, care must be taken to omit *all* irrelevant items when counting each sampling interval, whether or not the irrelevant items are indicated for selection in the sample. This means that every item in the population must be inspected to determine whether it is relevant, and therefore to be counted, or not. Failure to exclude irrelevant items will mean that their location will partly determine which relevant items are selected for the sample. If there is any connection between the irrelevant items and particular kinds of relevant items, for example institutions being located in poor areas, this will bias the sample results.[8] If excluding irrelevant items results in too few items being drawn a further systematic sample can be taken with a larger sampling interval, sufficient to acquire the number of items necessary to make up the balance.

Since systematic sampling is already established practice in historical research, it is important that the ways in which it differs from random sampling should be clearly understood.[9] The major difference lies in the fact that while in random sampling every item is selected by chance, in systematic sampling once the first item has been selected, the selection of all other items in the sample is predetermined by the sampling interval that has been adopted. Thus the character of a systematic sample depends firstly on which item is taken as the starting point, and secondly on the order of the items in the population.

The choice of which item is to be taken as the starting point not only determines which of all the other items will be included in the sample, it also determines the size of the sample whenever the sampling interval is not an exact fraction of the population size. Table 1 illustrates this point. Let us suppose that we wish to draw a systematic sample with a sampling interval of five, that is to take every fifth item, from a population of eighteen items. The columns headed A to E show which items will be included in the five possible samples we might draw, depending on whether we start with the first, second, third, fourth, or fifth item.

Table 1   *Five possible systematic samples from a population of eighteen items*

A	B	C	D	E
1	2	3	4	5
6	7	8	9	10
11	12	13	14	15
16	17	18		

It is clear from the table that out of the five possible samples three will contain four items (Columns A, B and C) and two will contain three items (Columns D and E). Thus the choice of the initial item in a systematic sample determines both the number and the identity of the other items in the sample.

It is therefore important that the choice of the initial item in a systematic sample should not be biased in any way, yet should still take into account the probabilities of obtaining samples of different sizes. These conditions can be met by selecting an item in the population by means of a random number table.[10] The initial item of the systematic sample in which the random number lies can be found in the following way. Divide the random number by the sampling interval, and the remainder indicates the initial item. If the remainder is 0, the initial item is indicated by the sampling interval itself. Let us suppose, for example, that we wish to draw a systematic sample with a sampling interval of five from the population of items in table 1 above, and that we have drawn a random number 12. We find the corresponding initial item for our sample by dividing the random number (12) by the sample interval (5) ($12 \div 5 = 2$, with a remainder of 2). The remainder indicates that the corresponding initial item is 2. A glance at table 1 will confirm that 12 is in the sample contained in column B, and that the initial item of that sample is indeed 2. If, on the other hand, we had drawn the random number 15, the division would indicate a remainder of 0 ($15 \div 5 = 3$, with no remainder). The corresponding starting item is therefore given by the starting interval itself, i.e. 5. Again table 1 confirms that 15 is in column E and that the initial item of this sample is 5.

In systematic sampling there are as many possible samples as there are items in the sampling interval. By choosing the initial starting item in a random way we can avoid bias in deciding which of the possible samples is to be taken. But the problem still remains of the order in which the items occur in the population, because this, together with the sampling interval we have chosen, determines which items will fall in which of the possible samples. The danger with all systematic samples is that the population is arranged in such a way that the sampling interval chosen results in an unrepresentative selection of items in the sample.

An example based on our population of 18 items contained in table 1 should make this clear. Let us suppose that this represents a list of wages of 18 individuals working in a small eighteenth-century factory, and that we wish to sample this list to discover something about wages at that date.[11] Let us further suppose that work in this factory is organized into groups of five men comprising 1 foreman and 4 workmen, and that the list of wages contains the names of the members of these groups, each group headed by the name of the foreman, with the groups running on consecutively. The first working group therefore comprises items numbered 1–5 in table 1, the second items 6–10, the third items 11–15. The fourth. group comprises only the three items 16–18, possibly because two members of this group have recently been killed in an accident and have not been replaced. Since each group is headed by the name of the foreman it is clear that the foremen will all be found in column A and no foremen will be found in columns B–E. In this case no matter which of the samples A–E we draw, it will be unrepresentative because we shall be systematically excluding either the workmen or the foremen.

This is a crude, and admittedly improbable, example, but it illustrates a fundamental weakness of systematic samples. If there is any rhythm or periodicity in the way the population has been listed, there is a danger that the sample interval chosen may be to some extent in phase with it, thereby systematically distorting the representativeness of the sample. If it is known that there is periodicity in the population this can be turned into an advantage by choosing a sampling interval which will ensure that each stage of the periodical cycle is properly represented. In most practical situations, however, for example in the sequence of houses as enumerated in the census returns, it is not at all clear whether periodicities are present or not, or if present how marked and regular they are. Consequently periodicity remains a possible source of bias in systematic samples which is difficult to evaluate. It may be trivial, or it may make the the results of the sample useless.[12]

A systematic sample is most like a random sample when the population to be sampled is listed in a random order. This can effectively be so for the purposes of the sample when the items are ordered by some characteristic, say alphabetically

F

by surname, which has no relation to the characteristics under investigation in the sample.[13] In this case systematic sampling is virtually equivalent to random sampling, and the estimates from systematic samples will be about as precise as those obtained from random samples of the same size.[14] This is encouraging, especially because of the great convenience of drawing systematic as opposed to random samples in many practical situations. On the other hand in most cases is it impossible to be certain that the items in the population to be sampled are effectively listed in a random order. If they are not, and especially if there are any periodicities in the way in which they are arranged, the results of the sample will be less precise than those of a random sample of the same size. Unfortunately there is at present no way of estimating the precision of systematic samples, and in practice this is estimated *as if* the sample had been drawn randomly. Since in almost every case this assumption is more or less untrue, it follows that the actual precision of a systematic sample is probably worse than the precision claimed *by some unknown factor*.[15] It is this uncertainty about the precision of results from systematic samples which constitutes their greatest drawback, and this needs to be offset against their greater convenience when deciding in any given instance whether to draw a random or a systematic sample. If random sampling is in practice impossible, and a systematic sample must be drawn, and there is reason to suspect that the population may not be effectively in a random order, the danger of bias from the systematic sample can be reduced by dividing the population into several strata and drawing two independent systematic samples from each stratum. This procedure presupposes that it is possible to stratify the population, which may not always be the case.[16]

The selection of the items to be included in the sample is clearly of critical importance for the representativeness of the sample results. It is therefore essential that a discussion of sample results should be accompanied by a detailed account of the nature of the population and of the methods used to select the sample items.

SAMPLE SIZE AND THE PRECISION OF SAMPLE ESTIMATES

'Systematic' and 'random' describe the two main ways of selecting sample items. Certain additions and refinements have already been mentioned, and they will be developed later, but for the moment it will be assumed that a simple random sample has been drawn. We shall now consider how the precision of the results of such a sample should be estimated in different circumstances, and what implications this has for the size of sample that should be drawn.

As we have already seen, when sample items have been selected entirely by chance it is always possible that all the items may come from one part of the population. For example, the sample may happen to contain only the largest items in the population, and would thus be unrepresentative of the population as a whole. The probability of getting representative results from a sample therefore depends on the chance that the sample items are in fact well spread over the population. Providing the sample items have been randomly chosen the laws of chance can be used to estimate the probability of any combination of items being selected.

Let us suppose that we wish to estimate a mean value for a population, say the mean size of household in a large city. If we were to draw a large number of similar random samples we would expect to get a different combination of items in the sample in each case, so that we would obtain a large number of different estimates of the mean population value. In the terms of our example, each of the large number of samples we might draw would contain a different combination of households, so we should obtain a large number of different estimates of the mean household size. The different sample estimates which might be obtained therefore themselves comprise a distribution, known as a sampling distribution. If we now imagine a sampling distribution which contains all possible samples of a given size, it can be shown that, providing the selection of the sample items has been left entirely to chance, the mean of all the sample estimates equals the true population value. In the terms of the example, if we were to draw all possible samples of a given size of the population of households in the city, and we were to take the mean of all the sample estimates of the mean household size, we should obtain the true mean household size for the population. It can also be shown that the individual sample estimates are more likely to occur near the true population value than far from it, and that they are normally distributed around the mean of the sample results.[17] Now it is a property of the normal distribution that, providing a quantity called the standard deviation of the distribution is known, it is possible to calculate the relative frequencies of values occurring within any specified range above or below the mean value.[18] Table 2 shows the percentage of sample estimates which can be expected to occur within a range defined as so many standard deviations either side of the mean of all possible sample estimates. The standard deviation in question is the standard deviation of the sampling distribution comprising the estimates of all possible samples of a given size. The numbers of standard deviations defining the different ranges are given on the line in the table labelled 'Normal deviate'.

Table 2   *Percentage of estimates of all possible samples of a given size falling within a range of values defined as the mean of the sample estimates ± normal deviate*[19]

	Range (mean ± normal deviate)					
Normal deviate	0·67	1·28	1·64	1·96	2·58	3·29
Percentage falling in range	50	80	90	95	99	99·9

Thus if we were to draw 100 samples, we should expect that the estimates of 95 of them would fall in the range 1·96 times the standard deviation of the sampling distribution either side of the true population value, and that the results of only five samples would fall outside this range. Normally when only one sample is drawn we express this result the other way round. We accept the sample estimate as the best available, and add a range within which we expect the true population value will lie. The range will depend on the degree of confidence with which we wish to be able to say that it includes the true population value. If we are willing to accept the possibility of being wrong five times out of 100, that is of being 95 per cent certain, then the range will be 1·96 times the standard deviation of the sampling distribution either side of the sample estimate we have obtained. If however we wish to be more certain, say 99 per cent certain, that we have specified a range which will include the true population figure, we shall have to increase the range to 2·58 times the standard deviation of the sampling distribution either side of the sample estimate.[20]

The range either side of the sample estimate, within which we expect the true population value to lie, is known as the *confidence interval*, while the upper and lower bounds of the range are known as the *confidence limits* of the sample estimate. The size of the range, or confidence interval, depends on two factors: the degree of confidence required, and the size of the standard deviation of the sampling distribution. The degree of confidence with which a range can be specified so as to include the true population value is largely a matter of personal taste, depending on such factors as the importance of the sample estimate being made and the probable scepticism of those who will be asked to accept it. The two confidence levels most usually adopted are those of 95 per cent and 99 per cent certainty.

The standard deviation of the sampling distribution appears to be a formidable quantity to estimate. Fortunately it is not necessary to draw all possible samples of a given size to obtain their distribution in order to calculate this statistic, indeed it can be estimated from the information contained in a single sample. This is done by calculating a quantity known as the standard error of the sample.[21] The standard error of a sample is in a sense a measure of the representative efficiency of the sample. This is determined by two factors: the variability of the items in the population, and the number of items in the sample. Clearly the more variable the population items, the more difficult it is for a sample of a given size to represent the full range of the population items. In the same way the larger the number of items in a sample, the better the sample can represent a population of a given level of variability. Thus the standard error of a sample will be high when the sample is unable to represent the full range of population values adequately, either because the population items are highly variable, or because the sample is small. The standard error of a sample will be low when the sample can represent the population items relatively well, because they are fairly homogeneous, or because the sample contains a large number of items. Accordingly when the standard error is high, because sampling is relatively inefficient, we should expect that random variation in the choice of individual sample items would produce a wide range of possible sample results, but when the standard error is low, because sampling is relatively efficient, we should expect that random variation in the choice of individual sample items would produce a narrower range of possible sample results.

The formula for calculating the standard error in any practical situation depends on the kind of estimate that has been made on the basis of the information in the sample. The two estimates most frequently derived from samples in historical research are those of the proportion of a population with a given attribute (for example the proportion of criminals unable to read and write), and the mean value of some characteristic of the population (for example the mean household size). The formulae for these two estimates and their standard errors will be given here, and for simplicity the discussion will be centred on them. The formulae for other kinds of estimates are similar in principle, and will be given in detail below.[22]

Formula 1. Estimate of a proportion of items in the population with a given attribute $(\hat{P})$[23]

$$\hat{P} = P$$

with standard error $(s_{(\hat{P})})$

$$s_{(\hat{P})} = \sqrt{\left(\frac{pq}{n-1}\right)}$$

where p = proportion of sample items with the attribute

q = proportion of sample items without the attribute

n = number of items in the sample

Note: This formula may be used with percentages instead of proportions.

Formula 2. Estimate of a mean value of the population items $(\hat{Y})$[24]

$$\hat{Y} = \bar{y}$$

with standard error $(s_{(\hat{Y})})$

$$s_{(\hat{Y})} = \frac{s}{\sqrt{n}}$$

where $\bar{y}$ = mean value of the sample items

s = standard deviation of the sample items $\left(\sqrt{\left\{\frac{\sum_{i=1}^{n}(y_i-\bar{y})^2}{n-1}\right\}}\right)$

It is clear from these two formulae that the size of the standard error depends on the two factors already mentioned: the variability of the items (measured by pq or s), and the number of items in the sample. Table 3 shows how differences in the degree of variability of the items affects the size of the standard error. It shows the standard errors that would be obtained if samples of one item each were drawn from populations with different proportions of items with a given attribute.

Table 3 *Standard errors of samples of 1 item (n = 1) from populations with proportion p possessing a given attribute (proportions expressed in percentages)*[25]

Proportion (p)	0	10	20	30	40	50	60	70	80	90	100
Variability (pq)	0	900	1,600	2,100	2,400	2,500	2,400	2,100	1,600	900	0
Standard error $\left\{ \sqrt{\left(\dfrac{pq}{1} \right)} \right\}$	0	30	40	46	49	50	49	46	40	30	0

The third line of the table shows that the standard error is greatest when the population is most variable, that is when 50 per cent of the items possess the attribute and 50 per cent do not. As the population becomes more homogeneous, that is as the proportion with the attribute tends towards 0 per cent or 100 per cent, the standard error becomes smaller. It reduces very little, however, until the proportion with the attribute is greater than 70 per cent or less than 30 per cent.

In this example we have assumed the sample size to be fixed in order to show the effect of changes in variability on the standard error. In practice, however, it is the variability of the population which is fixed, and the sample size which can be changed. It is clear from the position of n in the two formulae that any increase in the sample size will reduce the size of the standard error. But an increase in the sample size will not bring about a proportional reduction in the standard error. The fact that n occurs within a square root sign in the formulae means that in order to reduce the standard error by any desired factor we must increase the sample size by the square of that factor. Thus if we wish to halve the standard error, we must quadruple the sample size.

To illustrate the effect of changes in the sample size on the standard error of a sample, let us take an example where we wish to estimate a proportion, say the proportion of households where the head of household was born in the same community. If we assume that the proportion is 50 per cent, table 4 gives the standard errors for samples of 50, 100, 625 and 2,500 items.

Table 4 *Standard errors of samples from a population where p = 50 per cent*

Sample size (n)	Variability (pq) %	Standard error % (± 0.5)
50	2,500	7
100	2,500	5
625	2,500	2
2,500	2,500	1

The table shows clearly that increases in sample size are not matched by commensurate reductions in the standard error. A sample of 100 items from this population will have a standard error of 5 per cent, but if we wish to reduce this by a factor of five to 1 per cent we shall have to increase the sample size by a factor of 25 (i.e. 5^2) to 2,500.

The table also shows the effect of changes in sample size on the precision of the sample result. If we are willing to accept a confidence level of 95 per cent for our sample estimate, we can specify our confidence limits as 1·96 times the standard error. Thus if we had taken a sample of 50 items and had found a proportion of 50 per cent of heads of households were born in the community, our sample estimate would have been $50\% \pm 1\cdot96 \times 7\% = 50\% \pm 14\%$. That is we should say that from the sample we believe the proportion of household heads born in the community to be 50 per cent but that it could have been higher or lower than this. We are 95 per cent certain, however, that the true proportion is neither higher than 64 per cent nor lower than 36 per cent. This is an unsatisfactory result which illustrates the poor precision of estimates from small samples. If we now suppose that we had drawn a sample of 2,500 items, we should be able to specify the confidence interval as $50\% \pm 1\cdot96 \times 1\% = 50\% \pm 2\%$. We can now say that we believe the proportion of heads of households born in the community is 50 per cent and that we are 95 per cent certain that it was neither higher than 52 per cent nor lower than 48 per cent. With, a larger sample we have been able to estimate the proportion with much greater precision. In general, therefore, for any given degree of variability in the population and for any given confidence level, the size of the sample has a marked effect on the precision of the sample estimate.

It is perhaps worth emphasising that it is the actual number of items in the sample which is important, not the proportion of the population which is included in the sample. Many people find it puzzling that a sample of 100 from a population of 10,000,000 (1 in 100,000) will give as good an estimate as a sample of 100 from a population of 10,000 (1 in 100), providing the two populations are equally variable. The essential point is that the sample should be able to represent the variability in each population. Since by definition the variability of the two populations in the example is the same, from the sample's point of view the second population could be considered the same size as the first, the 10,000,000 people in the second population merely repeating several times over the information as to variability conveyed more succinctly by the first population. For both populations the precision of sample estimates depends on the sample items being able to represent the variability in the population, and because in each case the sample contains 100 items, the precision of the sample estimates will be the same.

The formulae which have been given for calculating the standard error and the confidence limits are of wide applicability, but the reader should be aware that there are certain circumstances in which the assumptions on which they are based no longer obtain, and alternative methods should be used. Although the calculation of confidence limits assumes that all possible sample results from a given population are normally distributed, it is not necessary that the population itself should be normally distributed, provided the size of the samples is large. If, however, the population distribution is very skew, the normal formula is likely to give a misleading impression of the precision of the sample and an alternative method should be used.[26] Unfortunately the binomial distribution of proportions and percentages, although approximately normal when sample sizes are large, becomes skew when sample sizes are small. This means that whenever the normal approximation formula (formula 1) is being used to estimate the standard error of a proportion or a percentage care must be taken to ensure that the sample size is not less than the figure indicated in table 5 below. The minimum sample size varies with the size of the proportion being estimated, and for this purpose the proportion taken should be either the proportion with the attribute or the proportion without the attribute, whichever is the smaller.

Table 5 *Smallest sample sizes for the use of the normal approximation formula for the standard error of an estimated proportion* $(s_{(\hat{p})})$

p or q (whichever smaller)		minimum sample size n
0·5	(50%)	30
0·4	(40%)	50
0·3	(30%)	80
0·2	(20%)	200
0·1	(10%)	600
0·05	(5%)	1,400

If the sample size is less than that indicated in the table for the proportion of p or q, then the standard error of the sample should be calculated from special tables.[27] But even when the sample size is sufficiently large for the normal formula to be used, it gives a slightly over-optimistic (i.e. narrow) estimate of the size of the confidence interval. The range *either side* of the sample estimate, defining the confidence interval, should therefore be increased by adding $1/2n$ (if the estimate has been made as a proportion), or $100/2n$ (if the estimate has been made as a percentage). This correction to the normal formula makes little difference if the sample size is large, but it will increase the confidence interval by ± 1 per cent if the sample has only 50 items.[28] Finally, for all kinds of estimates special steps should be taken in calculating the confidence limits if the sample contains less than 60 items. In these cases the factor by which the standard error is multiplied should not be the normal deviate, as given above in table 2, but the value of Student's t corresponding to $(n-1)$ degrees of freedom, where n refers to the number of items in the sample.[29]

If special action is not taken in the circumstances just outlined, the confidence limits will be set too narrowly, and the probability that they include the 'true' population value will not be as high as is claimed. There are other circumstances, however, in which application of the normal formula will result in needlessly wide confidence limits being set. Whenever the sample taken comprises a substantial fraction of the population, the standard error of the sample can be reduced by being multiplied by the factor $\sqrt{(1-f)}$, known as the finite population correction (*fpc*). In this factor, f stands for the sampling fraction, which is calculated by dividing the number of items in the sample by the number of items in the population n/N. Clearly when a high proportion of the population is included in the sample, the sampling fraction will also be large, so that the value $1-f$ and hence $\sqrt{(1-f)}$ will be small. When the standard error is multiplied by this factor it will be reduced. In practice a sampling fraction of less than 1 in 20 (5 per cent) reduces the standard error very little and in these circumstances it is scarcely worth while calculating the finite population correction factor.[30]

DETERMINING THE SIZE OF THE SAMPLE

It is well worth while at the outset considering the precision that will be required of the sample estimates. On the one hand there is no point in drawing a larger sample than is necessary to attain an estimate of sufficient precision, while on the other hand it is as well to ensure before drawing a sample that the largest practicable sample will in fact yield estimates that are precise enough to be useful. In most cases it is not difficult to decide upon the degree of precision appropriate to the context. If the field of enquiry is a new one, a fairly rough estimate may suffice. For example we may feel that at a first attempt to measure the proportion of heads of households born in the community a confidence interval of ± 5 per cent would be acceptable. In other circumstances, for example if we wish to discover whether the population being sampled is different from other populations, a greater precision in the sample estimates may be necessary.

The next step is to determine the confidence level for the sample estimate. Usually this means deciding between the two conventional levels of 95 per cent and 99 per cent certainty, and here too the choice depends on the context in which the sample estimates are to be used. Once the degree of precision and the confidence level have been specified, the simplest procedure is to calculate a quantity V, which is the desired variance of the sample, as follows:

Formula 3. Desired sample variance (V)[31]

$$V = \frac{d^2}{t^2}$$

where d = half the desired confidence interval (i.e. $\pm d$).

   t = normal deviate corresponding to confidence level (see table 2).

The estimated sample size can now be calculated as follows, depending on whether a proportion or a mean value is being estimated.

Formula 4. Estimated sample size for an estimated proportion (n_0)[32]

$$n_0 = \frac{pq}{V}$$

Note: If p and q are expressed as percentages, d must be expressed as a percentage in calculating V according to formula 3, above.

Formula 5. Estimated sample size for an estimated mean value (n_0)[33]

$$n_0 = \frac{s^2}{V}$$

If the sample size as estimated by either of these formulae proves to be a significant fraction of the whole population, say more than 5 per cent, it can be reduced by taking the finite population correction into account as follows.

Formula 6. Actual sample size reduced by finite population correction (n)

$$n = \frac{n_0}{1 + (n_0/N)}$$

Otherwise the estimated sample size (n_0) can be taken as the actual sample size to be drawn.

To illustrate the steps involved in estimating the sample size for a simple random sample, let us suppose that we wish to estimate the proportion of households in a community in which the head of the household was born in the community. We shall be satisfied with a 95 per cent certainty that our sample estimate lies within a confidence interval of ± 5 per cent. d is therefore 5 and t is 1·96 (the normal deviate corresponding to 95 per cent certainty, as given in table 2). V, the desired sample variance can now be calculated according to formula 3 as

$$V = \frac{d^2}{t^2} = \frac{5^2}{1·96^2} = \frac{25}{3·84} = 6·5$$

We have no idea what the proportion of heads of household born in the community will be, so we will play safe by estimating the population variability at a maximum, with p at 50 per cent and therefore q at 50 per cent also. We can now calculate the estimated sample size according to formula 4 as

$$n_0 = \frac{pq}{V} = \frac{50 \times 50}{6·5} = \frac{2500}{6·5} = 385$$

If the total number of households in the community is more than twenty times the estimated sample size, we shall not be able to take advantage of the finite population correction factor to reduce the estimated sample size, and we shall go on to draw a sample of 385 items. If, however, we suppose that the number of households in the community is 2,000, so that our estimated sample size is about a fifth of the population (20 per cent), we can use formula 6 to reduce the size of the sample we need to draw as follows:

$$n = \frac{n_0}{1+(n_0/N)} = \frac{385}{1+(385/2000)} = \frac{385}{1 \cdot 193} = 322$$

In this case we can achieve the same precision with a sample containing 63 fewer items.[34]

PILOT SAMPLES

Leaving aside the finite population correction for the moment, it is clear that the sample size depends on two elements, V (the desired sample variance) and pq or s^2, the variance of the population. V is determined by our requirements for the precision of our estimate. The variance of the population is outside our control, and may also be difficult to estimate. In the example we have just followed we hedged our bets by estimating the variance of a proportion at the maximum of 50 per cent. When values are at issue rather than proportions, we cannot take refuge in a similar device, because there is no upper ceiling to the variance of the population. Unfortunately it is difficult to estimate the variance of a set of values merely by casting an eye over the items in the population. One way round this difficulty is to estimate the population variance by taking a small pilot sample.[35] The formula for this estimate of the population variance is as follows:

Formula 7. Estimate of variance for a pilot sample (s_1^2)

$$s_1^2 = \frac{\displaystyle\sum_{i=1}^{n} (y_i - \bar{y})^2}{n_1 - 1}$$

where s_1^2 = variance of the pilot sample
 y_i = value of each item in the pilot sample
 $\bar{y}$ = mean value of the pilot sample items
 n_1 = number of items in the pilot sample

Since the number of items in a pilot sample is likely to be small, the variance of the pilot sample may not give an efficient estimate of the variance of the population. In calculating the required sample size therefore, the following formula should be used to estimate the required sample size, instead of formula 5.

Formula 8. Estimated sample size for an estimated mean value (n_0), variance estimated from a pilot sample and V from formula 3

$$n_0 = \frac{s_1^2}{V} \left(1 + \frac{2}{n_1}\right)$$

If the estimated sample size proves to be more than 5 per cent of the number of items in the population, it can be reduced by applying the finite population correction as in formula 6 above. Further sample items are now drawn, sufficient to bring the pilot sample up to the required sample size.[36]

To illustrate the steps taken in drawing a pilot sample, let us suppose that we wish to discover the mean age of heads of households in a community of 10,000 households. We require our estimate of the average age to be precise to within 2 years with 95 per cent certainty. The desired sample variance V is therefore calculated as $2^2/1 \cdot 96^2 = $ (say) 1. In the normal course of events we should substitute this value of V in formula 5 to discover the required sample size. Formula 5, however, requires some knowledge of s^2, the population variance. We have no means of knowing this, so we draw a small pilot sample of 20 items. From this we calculate an estimate of the variance (s_1^2) using formula 7. We will assume that s_1^2 is calculated to be 80. We can now estimate the required sample size by substituting our values for V and s_1^2 and n_1 (the number of items in the pilot sample) in formula 8.

$$n_0 = \frac{s_1^2}{V}\left(1+\frac{2}{n_1}\right) = \frac{80}{1}\left(1+\frac{2}{20}\right) = 80 \times 1 \cdot 1 = 88 \text{ items}$$

Since 88 items comprise nowhere near 5 per cent of the population of 10,000 items, the sample size cannot effectively be reduced by applying the finite population correction as in formula 6. We have already drawn 20 items, so we now draw a further 68 items, and pool the results.

The same two-stage procedure can be used when a proportion is to be estimated. Again a small pilot sample is taken to estimate p and q. The required sample size is now calculated as follows.

Formula 9. Estimated sample size for an estimated proportion (n_0), variance estimated from a pilot sample

$$n_0 = \frac{p_1 q_1}{V} + \frac{3 - 8p_1 q_1}{p_1 q_1} + \frac{1 - 3p_1 q_1}{V n_1}$$

where $p_1 = $ proportion of items in the pilot sample with the attribute

$\quad\quad q_1 = $ proportion of items in the pilot sample without the attribute

Note: This formula assumes that p_1, q_1, and V are expressed as proportions, not percentages.

Although this formula looks long and complicated, it is easy to evaluate. Again the estimate given by this formula can be reduced, if appropriate, by the finite population correction. Sufficient additional items are now drawn to increase the size of the pilot sample to the required level. Unfortunately the final sample gives a slightly biased estimate of the proportion of the items in the population with the attribute. It should be corrected as follows.

Formula 10. Corrected estimate of a proportion ($\hat{P}$), variance estimated from a
    pilot sample

$$\hat{P} = p_0 + \frac{V(1-2p_0)}{p_0 q_0}$$

where p_0 = proportion of sample items with the attribute
    q_0 = proportion of sample items without the attribute

Note: This formula assumes that p_0, q_0, and V are expressed as proportions,
not percentages.

It is important to remember that the whole of our discussion of the precision
of our sample estimates and of the appropriate sample size has been based on
the assumption that the sample items have been drawn in a strictly random
manner. If the sample items have been drawn systematically at some regular
interval down a list of items, the formulae given above will either over- or
under-estimate the precision of the sample estimates, depending on the way in
which the items are ordered in the list. These formulae should therefore only be
used in connection with a systematic sample if it can be shown that the population items are listed effectively in a random order.

SUBDIVISIONS: DOMAINS OF STUDY

So far we have assumed that we only require an overall estimate for the whole
population. In practice we may often wish to make separate estimates for subdivisions of the population, say for households classified into five different
socio-economic groups. We can do this by regarding the sample items relating
to each subdivision or domain of study as having been drawn from independent
subpopulations. The precision of these subpopulation estimates, and the required sample sizes, can then be calculated using the formulae given above.
Since the number of sample items relevant to any one subpopulation will be
relatively small, the precision of estimates for subpopulations will be less than
the precision of the overall estimate for the whole population. It is therefore
important to consider at the outset whether separate estimates will be required
for domains of study, and to specify an appropriate level of precision for each of
them. This will inevitably mean that a larger sample must be taken. As a rough
guide to the increase in sample size necessary, we can say that if estimates are
required for each of k subdivisions of the population, of a precision equal to that
originally required for the population as a whole, the sample size must be about
k times as large as originally planned.[37]

If a domain of study contains few items so that very few relevant items can be
expected to be drawn in the sample, the precision of the sample estimate for
this domain of study will be very low. This unfortunate result can be avoided
if the items in the population falling into the domain of study can be identified,
because they can then be sampled separately more intensively.

STRATIFICATION

'Systematic' and 'random' describe the two main methods of selecting items to be included in the sample. 'Simple' and 'stratified' describe the degree of control over the population being sampled. In the 'simple' sample, with which we have been concerned so far, no controls are placed on the population, and every item in the population has an equal chance of being selected for the sample. In a 'stratified' sample the population is divided into a number of subdivisions, or strata.[38] These subdivisions may be made at will, but they must be mutually exclusive and together they must comprise the whole population. Samples are then drawn independently for each subdivision, or stratum. Estimates are made separately for each stratum, and are then combined in the appropriate proportions to yield an estimate for the whole population. Thus in order to draw a stratified sample the number of items in each stratum in the population must be known.

Samples are drawn with the population stratified in this way for two reasons. The first has already been mentioned: we may be interested in separate estimates for subdivisions of the population, that is domains of study, which contain so few items that we may get too few sample items unless we draw separate independent samples. The second reason for drawing a stratified sample is that in certain cases the overall estimates for the population are much more precise than estimates derived from a simple sample. In a simple sample each item in the population has an equal chance of selection, so that it could happen by chance that too many or too few items are drawn from one part of the population. In a stratified sample, on the other hand, this possible source of unrepresentativeness is reduced because the number of sample items to be drawn from any part of the population, or stratum, is strictly controlled. The simplest form of control of this kind is to divide up the total number of sample items to be drawn amongst the different strata in the same proportion as the population items are divided between the different strata. This procedure is known as proportional stratified sampling. If, in addition, we can choose the way we subdivided the population items into strata so that the items in each stratum are as nearly alike as possible *with respect to the characteristic that is being estimated,* the overall estimate will be even more precise. This is because we have arranged that the individual strata are as nearly homogeneous as possible, and sample estimates become more precise the more homogeneous the population. Thus the independent estimates for each stratum will be more precise, and the wide variation which we have deliberately created between the strata will not detract from the precision of the overall population estimate, because we derive this estimate by combining the individual stratum estimates in the known correct proportions. Indeed if we have drawn a *proportional* stratified sample, the sample items for the different strata will already be in the correct proportions and the overall population estimate can be derived from the sample items, just as if a simple random sample had been drawn.

In practice, however, it is impossible to increase precision quite to this extent because dividing the population into homogeneous strata presupposes knowledge of the very characteristic of the population items that the sample is designed to discover. The next best step is to subdivide the population by some other characteristic which is known, or suspected, of being strongly correlated with the characteristic being estimated, and whose distribution in the population is known. Let us suppose, for example, that we are trying to estimate the average number of servants per household in an area, say a city, comprising several enumeration districts. Let us further suppose that the number of servants in a household is correlated with the socio-economic status of the head of the household, that residential location in the city is determined by socio-economic status and that we can use the printed census reports to group the enumeration districts by socio-economic status. We can now improve our estimate of the average number of servants per household for the whole area if we subdivide the area by grouping the enumeration districts into strata according to socio-economic status, so that there will be greater similarity in the number of servants per household in each stratum.

In the case where some strata are more variable than others we can further improve the precision of the overall population estimate if we abandon strictly proportional allocation and assign more sample items to the more variable strata, and fewer items to the less variable strata.[39] The following formula gives the optimal allocation of sample items to each stratum so that the precision of the overall population estimate is maximised.

Formula 11. Optimal allocation of sample items to each of L strata (n_h)

$$n_h = \sum_{h=1}^{n_L} \frac{N_h S_h}{N_h S_h}$$

where n_h = number of sample items to be allocated to a stratum (h)
N_h = number of items in that stratum in the population
S_h = standard deviation of items in that stratum in the population
n = total number of items in the sample

This formula presupposes not only that the numbers of items in each stratum in the population (N_h) are known, but also that some estimate can be made of the standard deviation of the items in each stratum in the population (S_h). Optimal allocation can therefore be used only where such an estimate can be made either on the basis of previous work or by inference from analagous evidence.

In general the kind of situation in which stratified sampling leads to large gains in precision over simple sampling is one where the population is composed of items of different sizes, which can be stratified conveniently by size, and where the principal variables to be estimated are closely related to the size of the items. In other circumstances, for example if the population is stratified by geographical region, or if proportions rather than variables are being estimated and the proportion lies between 30 per cent and 70 per cent, drawing a stratified sample leads to rather modest gains in precision over simple sampling, and may not be worth the extra trouble.[40]

Where it is expected that stratification will lead to large gains in precision and information is available on the distribution of the population items by size, it is worth while taking some care over the choice of the boundaries of the strata.[41] If in addition the population items vary widely in size, it will probably be advantageous to use optimal rather than proportional allocations of the sample items to the strata.[42] If, however, the gains from stratification are expected to be modest, there is no point in expending much effort either on choosing the stratum boundaries, or on optimal allocation which greatly complicates the arithmetic involved in calculating the sample estimates. Even when stratification brings a large increase in precision, little will be gained by having more than six strata.[43] We may, however, wish to subdivide the population into more than six strata because these are of interest as domains of study.[44] Indeed we may on occasion want to stratify the population one way to correspond with our domains of study, and another way in order to obtain a more precise overall population estimate. Unfortunately if we subdivide the population into strata to maximize the precision of the overall population estimate, the arithmetic involved in recombining the strata to correspond with the domains of study becomes rather tiresome.[45] In general therefore it is better to subdivide the population so that the strata correspond to the domains of study, accepting a lower level of precision in the overall population estimate than might otherwise have been achieved.

Stratified sampling presupposes knowledge of the number of items comprising each stratum in the population at large, so that the correct number of sample items can be drawn for each stratum, and so that the stratum estimates can be combined in the right proportions to yield an estimate for the whole population. In many historical contexts this information is imperfect or lacking, and this may restrict the number of ways in which the population can be stratified, or even prevent stratification altogether. Erroneous estimates of the numbers of items comprising each stratum in the population introduce a bias into the overall population estimate which may well outweigh any increase in precision which stratified sampling might otherwise yield.[46] If the precision of the overall population estimate is important, and the numbers of items comprising each stratum in the population are unknown, it is better to draw a simple sample without stratification.

Where the appropriate information is available, for example from printed census reports, and stratified sampling seems advantageous, the appropriate number of sample items may be selected for each stratum, either randomly or systematically. Where there is a separate list of population items for each stratum, the procedure is equivalent to drawing a simple systematic or random sample in each stratum. Often, however, there is no separate list of the population items in each stratum. In this case sample items should be drawn as if a simple sample were being selected for the whole population, each sample item as it is drawn being assigned to the appropriate stratum. The process continues until the required number of sample items have been drawn for all the strata, items drawn for strata for which the required number of sample items has already been attained being ignored. Alternatively a simple sample can be drawn from the whole population, without any control over the number of sample items in each stratum. The sample items are then assigned to the appropriate strata and estimates made for each individual stratum. Care must be taken, however, to combine these estimates in the correct proportions when calculating the overall population estimate.[47] This technique is known as stratification after selection and gives almost as precise an overall estimate as a normal proportional stratified sample, providing there are at least twenty sample items in each stratum.[48]

Since in a stratified sample the sample items in each stratum are selected independently, each stratum can be considered as an independent population, so the stratum estimates and their associated standard errors can be calculated using the formulae given above for simple samples.

Overall estimates for the whole population, however, require the following special formulae.[49]

Formula 12. Estimate of a population mean value from a stratified sample, with L strata ($\hat{Y}_{[st]}$)

$$\hat{Y}_{[st]} = \frac{\sum\limits_{h=1}^{L} N_h \bar{y}_h}{N}$$

where N = total number of items in the population
N_h = total number of items in a stratum in the population
$\bar{y}_h$ = mean value of sample items in a stratum

That is for each stratum the mean value of the sample items is multiplied by the number of items in that stratum in the population. The quantities obtained in this way for each stratum are added together and the result is divided by the total number of items in the population.

If the items in the stratified sample have been selected randomly, the standard error of the estimated population mean value is given by the following formula.

Formula 13. Standard error of an estimated population mean value from a stratified random sample, with L strata ($s(\hat{Y}_{[st]})$)

$$s_{(\hat{Y}_{[st]})} = \sqrt{\left\{ \sum_{h=1}^{L} \frac{W_h^2 S_h^2 (1 - f_h)}{n_h} \right\}}$$

where W_h = 'weight' of a stratum in the population, i.e. the number of items in the stratum in the population divided by the total number of items in the population (N_h/N)

s_h^2 = variance of the sample items in that stratum

$$\left\{ \frac{\sum\limits_{i=1}^{n_h} (y_{hi} - \bar{y}_h)}{(n_h - 1)} \right\}$$

y_{hi} = value of a sample item within that stratum
$\bar{y}_h$ = mean value of the sample items in that stratum
n_h = number of sample items in that stratum
f_h = sampling fraction in that stratum, i.e. the number of sample items in the stratum divided by the number of population items in the stratum (n_h/N_h)

That is the variance is calculated separately for each stratum. This is multiplied by the square of the stratum weight and a term representing the finite population correction $(1-f_h)$, and divided by the number of sample items in the stratum. The quantities obtained in this way for each stratum are added together, and the square root of the result gives the standard error of the estimated mean value of the items in the population. If the sampling fractions (f_h) are negligible, the term $(1-f_h)$ can be ignored.

If, however, a *proportional* stratified sample has been drawn, the sample already reflects the different number of items in each stratum in the population, so the mean can be estimated more simply as the mean of all the sample items, as follows.

Formula 14. Estimate of population mean value from a stratified sample, with *proportional* allocation ($\hat{\bar{Y}}_{[st]}$)

$$\hat{\bar{Y}}_{[st]} = \frac{\sum\limits_{i=1}^{n} y_i}{n}$$

where n = total number of items in the sample

With proportional allocation the standard error of this estimate can be calculated from a slightly simpler version of the formula given above.

Formula 15. Standard error of an estimated population average value from a stratified random sample, with proportional allocation of items among L strata ($s(\hat{\bar{Y}}_{[st]})$)

$$s_{(\hat{\bar{Y}}_{[st]})} = \sqrt{\left\{ \left(\frac{1-f}{n} \right) \sum\limits_{h=1}^{L} W_h s_h^2 \right\}}$$

where f = sampling fraction (n/N).

That is for each stratum the variance is multiplied by the stratum weight. These quantities are added together and the result is multiplied by a term representing the finite population correction $(1-f)$, and divided by the number of items in the sample. The square root of the result gives the standard error required.

If proportions are being estimated rather than mean values, the estimated population proportion and its standard error are calculated as follows.[50]

Formula 16. Estimate of a population proportion from a stratified random sample, with L strata $(\hat{P}_{[st]})$[51]

$$\hat{P}_{[st]} = \frac{\sum\limits_{h=1}^{L} N_h p_h}{N}$$

with standard error

$$(\hat{P}_{[st]}) = \sqrt{\left\{ \sum\limits_{h=1}^{L} \frac{W_h^2 p_h q_h (1-f_h)}{n_h - 1} \right\}}$$

where p_h = proportion of sample items in a stratum with the attribute

q_h = proportion of sample items in a stratum without the attribute

If a *proportional* stratified sample has been drawn a simpler formula can be used.

Formula 17. Estimate of a population proportion from a stratified random sample, with proportional allocation of the sample items among L strata $(\hat{P}_{[st]})$

$$\hat{P}_{[st]} = \frac{\sum\limits_{i=1}^{n} q_i}{n}$$

with standard error

$$(\hat{P}_{[st]}) = \sqrt{\left\{ \frac{(1-f)}{n} \sum\limits_{h=1}^{L} W_h p_h q_h \right\}}$$

In both these formulae percentages may be used instead of proportions, and the terms $(1-f_h)$ or $(1-f)$ may be ignored if the sampling fractions are negligible.

As with simple sampling, confidence limits can be calculated for overall population estimates from stratified samples, by multiplying the standard error by the normal deviate corresponding to the confidence level required. And again, as with simple sampling, provided we can make some estimate of the variability of the population, we can calculate the sample size necessary to yield an overall population estimate of any desired precision. With stratified samples, however, we must be able to estimate the variability of each stratum, as is clear from the following formulae for calculating the required size of a stratified sample.

Formula 18. Estimated sample size for a stratified random sample with L strata, to give an estimate of an overall population mean value of a desired precision (n_0)[52]

(1) Proportional allocation

$$n_0 = \frac{\sum\limits_{h=1}^{L} W_h S_h^2}{V} \qquad n = \frac{n_0}{1+(n_0/N)}$$

(2) Optimal allocation

$$n_0 = \frac{\left(\sum\limits_{h=1}^{L} W_h S_h\right)^2}{V+\left(\sum\limits_{h=1}^{L} W_h S_h^2/N\right)}$$

where $V =$ as defined in formula 3 above.

Formula 19. Estimated sample size for a stratified random sample with L strata, to give an estimate of an overall population proportion of a desired precision (n_0)[53]

(1) Proportional allocation

$$n_0 = \frac{W_h p_h q_h}{V} \qquad n = \frac{n_0}{1+(n_0/N)}$$

(2) Optimal allocation

$$n_0 = \frac{\left\{\sum\limits_{h=1}^{L} W_h \sqrt{(p_h q_h)}\right\}^2}{V} \qquad n = \frac{n_0}{1+\left(\sum\limits_{h=1}^{L} W_h p_h q_h/NV\right)}$$

Note: These formulae, with the exception of the formula for deriving n from n_0 for optimal allocation, can be used with proportions instead of percentages.

All formulae given above for stratified samples presuppose that the sample items have been selected randomly. Often, however, it is more convenient to draw a systematic sample in each stratum. Provided the population of items being sampled is listed in essentially random order the formulae given above will apply. If the population items are not in random order then fortunately stratification will still allow us to make an unbiased estimate of the sample error, provided we divide the population into at least ten strata and draw two systematic samples in each stratum, each with an independent random start.[54]

OTHER SAMPLE ESTIMATES

So far we have confined our attention to two kinds of estimates which we can make from the sample items: estimates of a mean value, and estimates of a proportion. In practice we may wish to estimate other characteristics of the population. We may be interested in the total number of items in the population with a certain attribute, or in the total value attained by the items in the population, for example the total wealth of a community. Or we may wish to estimate other parameters of the population, for example the median value or the standard deviation of the distribution of the population items. Formulae for a few estimates of this kind and for their standard errors are given below. In all cases it has been assumed that a simple random sample has been drawn.

Formula 20. Estimate of the total number of items in a population with an attribute $(\hat{A})$[55]

$$\hat{A} = Np$$

with standard error

$$s_{(\hat{A})} = \sqrt{\left\{ \frac{N(N-n)pq}{n-1} \right\}}$$

Note: The formula assumes that p and q are expressed as proportions, not percentages.

Formula 21. Estimate of the total value of the population items $(\hat{Y})$[56]

$$\hat{Y} = N\bar{y}$$

with standard error

$$s_{(\hat{Y})} = \frac{Ns}{\sqrt{n}}\sqrt{(1-f)}$$

where s = standard deviation of the sample items

$$\left\{ \sum_{i=1}^{n} (y_i - \bar{y})^2 / (n-1) \right\}$$

Formula 22. Estimate of the standard deviation of the population items $(\hat{S})$[57]

$$\hat{S} = \frac{\sum_{i=1}^{n} (y_i - \bar{y})^2}{n-1}$$

with standard error

$$s_{(\hat{S})} = \frac{\hat{S}}{\sqrt{(2n)}}\sqrt{\left(\frac{1+\beta_2-3}{n} \right)}$$

where the quantity $\sqrt{\{(1+\beta_2-3)/n\}}$ is a correction to allow for kurtosis in the population distribution. The quantity β_2 is tedious to compute.

Formula 23. Estimate of median value of population items, assuming the items
    arranged in order of magnitude[58]
    Where n is odd, median = value of item ranked $(n+1)/2$
    Where n is even, median = mean of values of items ranked $n/2$ and $(n+1)/2$
    Confidence limits: values of items with ranks $\{(n+1)/2\} \pm \{(t\sqrt{n})/2\}$

Alternatively we may be interested in the relationship between two characteristics of the population items. We might, for example, want to know the ratio
obtaining between the size of households and the number of resident unmarried
children in the household. Estimates of ratios between two values of the population items should be made using the following formula.

Formula 24. Estimate of a ratio obtaining between two values of the population
    items $(\hat{R})$[59]

$$\hat{R} = \frac{\sum\limits_{i=1}^{n} y_i}{\sum\limits_{i=1}^{n} x_i}$$

with standard error

$$s_{(\hat{R})} = \frac{\sqrt{(1-f)}}{\bar{x}\sqrt{n}} \sqrt{\left\{ \frac{\sum\limits_{i=1}^{n} (y_i - \hat{R}x_i)^2}{n-1} \right\}}$$

where x_i and y_i = the two values of the items whose ratio is to be estimated.

Note: This estimate is slightly biased; in certain circumstances the bias
becomes serious.[60]

On the other hand we may wish to measure the degree of association between
two values of the population items, for example between the size of the household and the age of the head of the household. The usual measure of association
between two variables is the product moment correlation coefficient, which is
estimated for the population items as follows:

Formula 25. Estimate of correlation coefficient between two values of the
    population items[61]

$$r_{(xy)} = \frac{\sum\limits_{i=1}^{n} (x_i - \bar{x})(y_i - \bar{y})}{s_{(x)} s_{(y)}}$$

where x_i and y_i are the two values of the items whose correlation is to be
    estimated
    $s_{(x)}$ and $s_{(z)}$ are the standard deviations of the x_i and y_i values

Unfortunately the closer the correlation between the x_i and y_i values, the more skewed the distribution of $r_{(xy)}$ becomes, making it impossible to estimate a standard error for an estimated $r_{(xy)}$ in the usual way. This can, however, be achieved by transforming $r_{(xy)}$ into the quantity z, either by reference to special tables or by using the following formula.

$$z = 1 \cdot 1513 \times \text{logarithm} \left(\frac{1 + r_{(xy)}}{1 - r_{(xy)}} \right)$$

z is normally distributed about the correlation coefficient ($r_{(xy)}$) of the population items with a standard error:

$$s_{(z)} = \frac{1}{n - 3}$$

Confidence limits can therefore be estimated for z, and the equivalent values of $r_{(xy)}$ can then be found most conveniently by reference to the special tables.[62]

INDIRECT ESTIMATES

If there is a strong correlation between two values of the population items, it may be possible to capitalise on this fact to make an indirect, but more precise, estimate of an average or total value for the population, than is obtained by any of the direct methods we have been discussing so far. When we make a direct estimate, say of an average value of the population items, we do so on the basis of the individual values of the sample items. Apart from the size of the sample, the precision of our estimate depends on the variability of the sample values. If, however, these values are highly correlated with another value for each of the sample items, the *ratios* between these values will tend to be much less variable because they will be more or less the same for each sample item. This means that we shall be able to estimate the ratio between the two values of the sample items with much greater precision than we can estimate the average value of either of the two sets of values. If, further, we happen to know the actual population average or total value for one of the sets of values, say from census material, we shall be able to apply our estimated ratio to this figure to derive a more precise estimate of the other set of values. The following two formulae define the ratio estimates of a mean and a total value of the population items.[63]

Formula 26. Ratio estimate of a mean value of the population items ($\hat{\bar{Y}}_{[R]}$)

$$\hat{\bar{Y}}_{[R]} = \hat{R}\bar{X}$$

where $\hat{R}$ = ratio estimated from the sample items.
$\bar{X}$ = known mean of the x values of the *population* items.

with standard error

$$s_{(\hat{Y}_{[R]})} = \sqrt{\left\{\frac{1-f}{n} \frac{\sum\limits_{i=1}^{n} (y_i - \hat{R}x_i)^2}{n-1}\right\}}$$

Formula 27. Ratio estimate of a total value of the population items $(\hat{Y}_{[R]})$

$$\hat{Y}_{[R]} = \hat{R}X$$

with standard error

$$s_{(\hat{Y}_{[R]})} = \sqrt{\left\{\frac{N^2(1-f)}{n} \frac{\sum\limits_{i=1}^{n} (y_i - \hat{R}x_i)^2}{n-1}\right\}}$$

where $X =$ known total of the x values of the *population* items.

Let us suppose, for example, that we wish to estimate the mean number of children resident in the household from the census enumerators' returns for 1851. Normally we would draw a sample of households and estimate the mean number of resident children in the population households by adding up the number of children in the sample households and dividing by the number of households in the sample. Let us, however, now suppose that we suspect from a preliminary glance at the enumerators' returns that the number of resident children is strongly correlated with the size of the household. If this is so we will find that the *ratio* of the number of children to the household size is fairly constant from one household to the next, and will vary less than the actual numbers of resident children. We will therefore be able to estimate this ratio more precisely than we can estimate the mean number of resident children. The ratio estimate is in fact very easy to obtain: we simply divide the total number of resident children in the sample households by the total of the sample household sizes, as in formula 24 above. Let us further suppose that we have an exact figure for the mean size of the *population* households available in the summary pages of the enumerators' returns.[64] We can now easily estimate the mean number of resident children in the population households by multiplying the known mean household size by the ratio we have just calculated between the size of household and number of resident children, as in formula 26 above. The total number of resident children in the population can also be estimated by multiplying the total of the household sizes, known from the enumerators' returns, by the estimated ratio, as in formula 27 above.

Indirect ratio estimates of this kind can only be used if information is available about the second, or auxiliary, variable for the whole population. Where this is so ratio estimates are more precise than the usual direct estimates providing two conditions hold.

(1) The two variables whose ratio is estimated are correlated.

(2) The coefficient of variation of the auxiliary variable $(s_{(x)}/\bar{x})$ is not more

than twice the coefficient of variation of the variable being estimated $(s_{(y)}/\bar{y})$.[65] Unfortunately the ratio estimate is biased, though the bias is negligible if the two variables are strongly correlated or if the sample size is large. In general therefore ratio estimates should not be used if the sample contains less than thirty items, or if the coefficient of variation of the sample estimate of the mean of the auxiliary variable $(s_{(x)}/\bar{x})$ is more than 10 per cent.[66]

INDIRECT SAMPLING[67]

So far we have assumed that we have been able to sample directly the units in which we are interested. Sometimes, however, this is impracticable. Let us suppose, for example, that we are interested in the proportion of men and women who could sign their names at marriage. Before 1838, when the Registrar-General began to collect this information centrally, the evidence is to be found in the ecclesiastical parish registers. Our population is therefore some 80,000 marriages registered every year in about 10,000 different parishes. Clearly in such a situation it is impossible to identify individual marriages, so in practice a random or systematic sample of marriages cannot be drawn. It is however relatively easy to use a list of the 10,000 parishes to draw a random or systematic sample of parishes. But drawing a sample of, say, 250 parishes, which register about 2,000 marriages annually, is not the same as drawing a sample of 2,000 marriages directly. We are in effect drawing our 2,000 marriages in 250 clustered sample items. If it happens that those getting married in a parish tend to be alike in their ability to sign their names, as is quite probable since many will have experienced the same schooling, much of the information in each clustered item is repeating itself. As a result the sample of clusters of marriages will be much less efficient than a direct sample of marriages in representing the general variability of the ability of brides and bridegrooms to sign their names. Expressed more formally, for a sample of a given number of elements selected indirectly in clustered items, the greater the homogeneity of the elements within the clustered items sampled, the poorer the precision of the sample estimates for the population of elements as a whole. Thus we can expect the standard errors of samples where elements are sampled in clustered items to be higher than where elements are sampled directly. Conversely, for a clustered sample to achieve the same precision as a direct sample, a larger number of elements must be taken. Because of their generally poorer precision clustered samples are drawn only when direct samples are impossible or inconvenient. It is worth emphasising that a sample may be direct for one set of estimates and indirect for another. A sample of households drawn from census enumerators' returns, for example, will be a direct sample if households are being studied, but an indirect sample if individuals are being studied, because the individuals have been sampled in household clusters. Where the elements under study have been sampled indirectly the normal formulae for calculating the population estimates and their standard errors should not be used because they will give misleading results. The following formulae should be used instead.

Formula 28. Estimate of a proportion of the population elements with a given attribute, when elements have been sampled in n clustered items of *equal size* $(\hat{P})$[68]

$$\hat{P} = \frac{\sum\limits_{i=1}^{n} p_i}{n}$$

with standard error

$$s_{(\hat{P})} = \sqrt{\left\{\frac{1-f}{n} \frac{\sum\limits_{i=1}^{n}(p_i-\hat{P})^2}{n-1}\right\}}$$

where n = number of clustered items in the sample
p_i = proportion of elements in each clustered item with the attribute

Formula 29. Estimate of a proportion of the population elements with a given attribute, when elements have been sampled in n clustered items of *unequal size* $(\hat{P})$[69]

$$\hat{P} = \frac{\sum\limits_{i=1}^{n} a_i}{\sum\limits_{i=1}^{n} m_i}$$

with standard error

$$s_{(\hat{P})} = \sqrt{\left\{\frac{1-f}{nm^2} \frac{\sum\limits_{i=1}^{n} m_i^2(p_i-\hat{P})^2}{n-1}\right\}}$$

where a_i = number of elements in each clustered item with the attribute
m_i = total number of elements in a given clustered item
m = mean number of elements per clustered item

$$\left(\frac{\sum\limits_{i=1}^{n} m_i/n}{}\right)$$

Estimates of mean and total population values from clustered samples can be made either directly or indirectly. In general indirect, ratio-type, estimates are more precise and the formulae for these will be given here.[70]

Formula 30. Estimate of a mean value of the population elements, when the elements have been sampled in n clustered items $(\hat{\bar{Y}}_{[R]})$

$$\hat{\bar{Y}}_{[R]} = \frac{\sum_{i=1}^{n} y_i}{\sum_{i=1}^{n} m_i}$$

with standard error

$$S_{(\hat{\bar{Y}}_{[R]})} = \sqrt{\left\{ \frac{(1-f)}{n} \frac{\sum_{i=1}^{n} m_i^2(\bar{y}_i - \hat{\bar{Y}})^2}{n-1} \right\}}$$

where y_i = total of the values of the elements in a clustered item

$$\left(\sum_{e=1}^{m_i} y_{ie} \right)$$

$\bar{y}_i$ = mean value of the elements in a clustered item

$$\left(\sum_{e=1}^{m_i} y_{ie}/m_i \right)$$

y_{ie} = value of an element in a clustered item

Formula 31. Estimate of a total value of the population elements, when elements have been sampled in n clustered items ($Y\hat{Y}_{[R]}$).

$$Y\hat{Y}_{[R]} = M_0 \frac{\sum_{i=1}^{n} y_i}{\sum_{i=1}^{n} m_i}$$

with standard error

$$S_{(YY[R])} = \sqrt{\left\{ \frac{N^2(1-f)}{n} \frac{\sum_{i=1}^{n} m_i^2(\bar{y}_i - \hat{\bar{Y}})^2}{n-1} \right\}}$$

where M_0 = total number of elements in the population
N = total number of clustered items in the population.

The following example illustrates the importance of using these special formulae when the elements have been sampled indirectly in clustered items. We will suppose that once more we wish to estimate the proportion of the population listed in the census returns who were born in the community. We will assume for the purposes of the example that there is a tendency for most members of a household to be alike with regard to their place of birth. We will also assume for convenience that all households comprise five individuals. We draw a random sample of ten households, and we find the following percentages of individuals born within the community.

Table 6 *Fictitious clustered sample*

Household no.	number of individuals m_i	number born in community a_i	percentage born in community p_i	$(p_i - \hat{P})$	$(p_i - \hat{P})^2$
1	5	4	80	+14	196
2	5	5	100	+34	1,156
3	5	1	20	−46	2,116
4	5	3	60	− 6	36
5	5	4	80	+14	196
6	5	1	20	−46	2,116
7	5	4	80	+14	196
8	5	1	20	−46	2,116
9	5	5	100	+34	1,156
10	5	5	100	+34	1,156
Total $\left(\sum\limits_{i=1}^{n}\right)$	50	33	660		10,440

We have therefore a clustered sample of ten items comprising fifty elements in all. If we proceed on the assumption that we have drawn the fifty elements directly in the ordinary way, we would estimate the percentage of individuals who were born in the community $(\hat{P})$ and its standard error according to formula 1, as follows:

$$n = 50$$

$$\hat{P} = p = \frac{\sum\limits_{i=1}^{n} a_i}{n} \times 100 = \frac{3300}{50} = 66\%$$

$$s_{(\hat{P})} = \sqrt{\left(\frac{pq}{n-1}\right)} = \sqrt{\left(\frac{66 \times 34}{49}\right)} = 6\cdot8\%$$

If we now take into account the fact that the fifty individuals were selected in ten clustered items, we would estimate the percentage born in the community, and its standard error, according to formula 28, as follows:

$$n = 10$$

$$\hat{P} = \frac{\sum\limits_{i=1}^{n} p_i}{n} = \frac{660}{10} = 66\%$$

This is the same result as we obtained using formula 1. However,

$$s_{(\hat{P})} = \sqrt{\left\{\frac{1}{n} \frac{\sum\limits_{i=1}^{n} (p_i - \hat{P})^2}{n-1}\right\}} = \sqrt{\left\{\frac{1}{10} \frac{10440}{9}\right\}} = 10\cdot7\%$$

which is more than half as much again as our previous estimate of the standard error.[71] Thus when elements have been sampled indirectly in clustered items the ordinary formula for the standard error (formula 1) can seriously underestimate its size, so one of the special formulae given above (formulae 28 to 31) should always be used instead.

An alternative method of deriving estimates when elements have been sampled in clustered items is to arrange matters so that the clustered items have a probability of being selected for the sample proportional to their size. Any measure of size will do, but it is normally convenient to take the number of elements in the clustered item. This method is not often practicable in historical research because the size of every cluster in the population is seldom known. Where this is the case, for example for the population of census enumeration districts, the first step is to compile a list of clustered items, entering the cumulative total of elements calculated from the top of the list successively against each clustered item. Random numbers are drawn from a random number table, and the clustered items are selected which contain the random numbers drawn. If more than one random number falls in any one clustered item, the item is still included each time in the sample, in order to keep the probability of selection proportional to the size of the clustered items.

The formulae for estimating the mean and total values of the population items, together with their standard errors, when clustered items have been selected with probability proportional to their size, are given below. They are somewhat easier to compute than the formulae already given for clustered items selected in a simple random manner.[72]

Formula 32. Estimate of a mean value of the population elements, when the elements have been sampled in n clustered items with selection of the clustered items proportional to their size ($\hat{\bar{Y}}_{[PPS]}$)

$$\hat{\bar{Y}}_{[PPS]} = \frac{\sum\limits_{i=1}^{n} \bar{y}_i}{n}$$

with standard error

$$s_{(\hat{\bar{Y}}_{[PPS]})} = \sqrt{\left\{ \frac{(1-f)}{n} \frac{\sum\limits_{i=1}^{n} (\bar{y}_i - \hat{\bar{Y}})^2}{n-1} \right\}}$$

Formula 33. Estimate of a total value of the population elements, when the elements have been sampled in n clustered items, with selection of the clustered items proportional to their size ($\hat{Y}\hat{Y}_{[PPS]}$)

$$\hat{Y}\hat{Y}_{[PPS]} = \frac{M_0}{n} \sum\limits_{i=1}^{n} \bar{y}_i$$

where M_0 = total number of elements in the population

with standard error

$$s_{(YY[PPS])} = \sqrt{\left\{\frac{M_0^2(1-f)}{n}\frac{\sum\limits_{i=1}^{n}(\bar{y}_i-\hat{\bar{Y}})^2}{n-1}\right\}}.$$

DIFFERENCES BETWEEN POPULATION ESTIMATES

So far we have been concerned with the question of how best to estimate different characteristics of the population on the basis of information contained in the sample. Sometimes, however, we may also be interested in differences between our population estimates. We may, for example, estimate that farmers had a larger mean size of household than labourers. The question now arises whether this represents a real difference between the two groups in the population, or whether the two groups are actually the same and the apparent difference in the estimates can be accounted for entirely in terms of the chance selection of the sample items. Fortunately we can estimate the likelihood of this second possibility, for just as we have been able to calculate the probability that any one sample result is more than a certain distance from the true population value, so we can calculate the probability that any two sample estimates of the same population value are more than a certain distance apart. In practice some level of probability, usually 5 per cent, 1 per cent or 0·1 per cent, is taken as critical, so that if the probability of the observed difference between the estimates occurring by chance is calculated to be less than the critical level, the 'chance explanation' is rejected as being unlikely, and it is concluded that it is more probable that the two estimates come from different populations. If, on the other hand, the probability of the observed difference between the estimates occurring by chance turns out to be more than the critical level, the 'chance explanation' cannot be ruled out, so no difference between the two estimates can be claimed. A difference between two estimates which is unlikely to have arisen because of the chance selection of the sample items from the same population is said to be 'significant'. Since the level of probability at which the 'chance explanation' is rejected is arbitrary, any statement about the 'significance' of a difference between two estimates should always specify the level of probability taken to be critical. Since not everyone will accept any given level as appropriate, it is also advisable to specify the calculated probability that the observed difference could have arisen by chance.[73]

There are a variety of methods which can be used to test the significance of differences between sample estimates. These are all fully described in standard textbooks on statistics, so only a few remarks on their appropriateness in different circumstances will be offered here. When values of the population items are at issue, the mean and the variance of the values are usually taken as the most convenient summary quantities to test. The two most powerful tests available are the t test and the F test, but they can only be applied if the population items from which the sample was drawn are approximately normally distributed.[74] If proportions or percentages are involved, alternative tests are available. All these tests, however, assume that the sample size is large enough to ensure that the estimates are reasonably precise. If this or other conditions, such as the assumption of an approximately normal distribution of the sample items, are not fulfilled, it is well worth while considering using one of the many nonparametric tests. These tests are less widely known, yet they are very easy to compute, and are only a little less efficient than the more usual tests. They can be made equally efficient by increasing the sample size by, in most cases, a matter of only 5 or 10 per cent.[75]

The logic of testing the significance of differences between two sample estimates can be applied in other contexts. We may observe, for example, that an estimate yielded by our sample seems inconsistent with what we would expect to find on the basis of a current theory. Again we may want to know whether this divergence is likely to be a real one, leading us to revise the theory which no longer fits the facts, or a freak result, arising from the operation of chance in the random selection of the sample items. In this case we would calculate how probable it is that so extreme a sample estimate could have been drawn from a population with the characteristics that the theory suggests that it should possess. The tests used are similar to those already mentioned for the case where two sample estimates are being compared, and are fully described in the standard textbooks.

SUMMARY

The purpose of this chapter has been to show how by taking care over the selection of items to be included in the sample and over the calculation of the results, we can with confidence estimate various characteristics of a body of documentary evidence after consulting what at first sight may appear to be a ridiculously small proportion of the documents concerned. This confidence in the results of a sample depends entirely on the exclusion of all factors other than chance from the selection of the sample items, for if any bias, conscious or unconscious, is allowed to creep in, the whole basis of the sample estimates and of the tests of significance is undermined. Sampling therefore requires constant vigilance, and a patent honesty in describing how the sample has been drawn, so that others may be in a position to judge the validity of the results.[76]

A historian reading this chapter may have found some of the procedures of sampling unusual, and, at times, even uncongenial. Yet he may perhaps be sympathetic to a discipline which, like his own, approaches its subject matter in a spirit of probability rather than of certainty. Indeed, mindful of the subjective basis of many of his own judgements, he may even welcome a set of procedures by which probability can be assessed objectively in a manner acceptable to all.

On the other hand it should be stressed that sampling is a technique, and that no amount of refinement in the way a sample is drawn can rescue evidence which is basically unreliable or which has become deficient through the accidents of survival. Sampling deserves serious consideration for the benefits it may confer; but it cannot in any way reduce the necessity for a strict appraisal of the evidence in its historical context. Indeed, by compelling a careful consideration of the objects of an enquiry and the nature of the evidence available, sampling should reinforce rather than replace the fundamental methods of historical research.

Appendix 1. Understanding formulae

Formulae are a convenient way of expressing ideas and relationships compactly and unambiguously. This is because they consist of a carefully defined set of symbols representing quantities or identities, which are shown to be related to each other by means of other symbols and conventions. These conventions comprise a kind of mathematical grammar. Some knowledge of the rules of this grammar is essential to an understanding of formulae.

MATHEMATICAL NOUNS

The symbol most frequently used to represent a quantity, or score, is X, although other letters, such as Y, are sometimes used instead. X and Y are also used to represent variables. For example, if income and age are two variables being recorded in a research project, X might be used to represent income, and Y to represent age. Another noun which is often used is the symbol N, which stands for the number of scores or quantities at issue. Thus if we have recorded the income and age of twenty individuals, $N = 20$.

The set of symbols used in this chapter to represent quantities or identities is defined in Appendix 2.

MATHEMATICAL ADJECTIVES

When we want to qualify a mathematical noun, in order to identify it more precisely, we usually write a subscript after the noun. Thus if we have a series of four quantities or scores, we can refer to each quantity individually by writing X_1, X_2, X_3, or X_4. We can also refer to an individual quantity or score indirectly by writing X_i, leaving i to be specified later by the context.

MATHEMATICAL VERBS

These are symbols which direct us to do something with the quantities defined by the nouns and adjectives. Most of these symbols, such as $+$, $-$, $\times$, $/$, will already be familiar. Another symbol, which is very common in statistics, is the summation sign, or Σ (sigma, the Greek capital S). This symbol means add up all the quantities or scores following the Σ. All the mathematical verbs relevant to the purposes of the chapter will be defined under *Arithmetical operations*, below.

MATHEMATICAL ADVERBS

In written language adverbs modify verbs, that is they define their action more precisely. In statistics the summation sign Σ is often modified by adverbial symbols. Let us suppose that we want to show that five quantities are to be added up. We could write $X_1 + X_2 + X_3 + X_4 + X_5$, or $X_1 + \ldots + X_5$ (where the three dots show that the intermediate terms have been missed out). Or we could write it more compactly as

$$\sum_{i=1}^{5} X_i$$

Here the notation above and below the summation sign qualifies it to mean that what are to be added together are the successive scores of X, beginning with the first score ($= 1$) and ending with the fifth (5). We can equally well write

$$\sum_{i=4}^{5} X_i$$

which means that only the fourth and fifth scores are to be added together.

As has already been explained, N is commonly used to denote the number of scores that have been recorded. If we want to add up all the scores recorded we can simply write

$$\sum_{i=1}^{N} X_i$$

In English expressions the words can often be written in several different orders. Some orders are not permissible because the sense of the expression is lost, while others are preferable because they bring out the sense more clearly. In mathematical expressions too, the symbols can be written in several different orders, and you may well find that some arrangements bring out the meaning of the expression much more clearly than others. It is quite permissible to rearrange the order of the symbols in a mathematical expression, provided you do not destroy the sense of the expression. The rules which allow rearrangement of the symbols while safeguarding the sense of the expression are the rules of algebra.

ARITHMETICAL OPERATIONS

Suppose that a and b are arbitrary numbers, but that n is a positive whole number (one of the numbers 1, 2, 3, ...), then

$a+b$ means   add b to a

$a-b$ means   subtract b from a

$\left.\begin{array}{l} a \times b \\ a(b) \\ a.b \\ ab \end{array}\right\}$ mean multiply a by b

$\left.\begin{array}{l} a/b \\ \dfrac{a}{b} \end{array}\right\}$ mean divide a by b

a^n means   raise a to the nth power, that is multiply n 'a's together, (e.g. $a^1 = a$; $a^2 = a \times a$; $a^3 = a \times a \times a$)*

a^{-n} means   the result of dividing 1 by a^n

$\sqrt{a}$ means   take the square root of a, that is find the number which, when multiplied by itself, equals a.

ORDER OF EXECUTION

Arithmetical operations must be executed in the following order of priority:
1. Raising to a higher power (for example, squaring), and taking a square root.
2. Multiplication and division.
3. Addition and subtraction.

Thus $a + b/c$ is executed as follows:
1. Divide b by c.
2. Add the result to a.

* We sometimes write $a^0 = 1$, which turns out to be a convenient usage.

Note: This is not the same thing as adding b to a, and dividing the result by c, as will be clear if you use numbers instead of a, b and c.

The rules of priority can, however, be overridden by the use of brackets. Brackets mean that all operations within the brackets must be given priority over those outside the brackets.

Thus $(a+b) \times c$ is executed as follows:
1. Add b to a.
2. Multiply the result by c.

Without the brackets this expression would have meant: multiply b by c and add the result to a. Again, if you use numbers instead of a, b and c, you will see that the presence or absence of brackets alters the meaning of the expression.

Sometimes brackets are implied in the layout of the expression. This is the case with division when the length of the division line indicates which symbols are to be taken together as comprising a single entity.

Thus $\dfrac{a}{b+c}$ can be written for $\dfrac{a}{(b+c)}$, where both expressions mean that a is to be divided by the result of adding b and c together.

Similarly when a square root sign encloses several symbols, any arithmetical operations under the sign must be executed before the square root is taken. Thus $\sqrt{(a+b)}$ is executed:
1. Add b to a.
2. Take the square root of the result.

Within any level of priority, however, arithmetical operations can be done in any order. For example, $\dfrac{4 \times 3}{2}$ gives the same answer regardless of whether the multiplication or division is done first.

The following example, which consists of an expression giving the value of a quantity x, illustrates most of the priority rules for arithmetical operations.

$$x = a - \frac{(b+c^2)d}{e-f}$$

Order of execution:
1. Multiply c by itself $\qquad\qquad\qquad\qquad c^2$
2. Add b to the result $\qquad\qquad\qquad\quad b+c^2$
3. Multiply this by d $\qquad\qquad\qquad\quad (b+c^2)d$
4. Subtract f from e $\qquad\qquad\qquad\quad e-f$
5. Divide the result of 3 by the result of 4 $\qquad \dfrac{(b+c^2)d}{e-f}$
6. Subtract this from a $\qquad\qquad\qquad\quad a - \dfrac{(b+c^2)d}{e-f}$

Finally it should be noted that the summation sign, sigma Σ, represents an arithmetical operation (i.e. add up all the quantities following the summation sign), and that in the order of priority of arithmetical operations, sigma comes *after* multiplication and division and *before* addition and subtraction.

Thus $\displaystyle\sum_{i=1}^{N} X_i Y_i$ is executed:
1. For each item, multiply the X score by the Y score.
2. Add up the results.

But $\displaystyle\sum_{i=1}^{N} X_i - Q$ is executed:

1. Add up the X scores of the items.
2. Subtract the quantity Q from the result.

Here too the brackets can override the normal order of priority so that

$$\sum_{j=1}^{N} (X_i - Y_i) \text{ is executed:}$$

1. For each item, subtract the Y score from the X score.
2. Add up the results.

A quantity or score can have more than one subscript. If a set of n items is subdivided into a number of subsets, the number of items in any subset can be expressed as n_h.

Thus $\sum_{i=1}^{n_h} Y_{hi}$ means add up the y scores in a subset.

Appendix 2. Glossary of symbols

$\hat{A}$	An estimate of the total number of items in the population possessing a given attribute (formula 20, p. 173).
a_i	The number of sample items, (or elements in a clustered sample item) with a given attribute.
β_2	A coefficient describing the shape of a distribution (see Yule and Kendall, *Introduction to the theory of statistics* (14th ed., London, 1950), pp, 151–60).
d	The range either side of an estimate, specifying the required confidence interval.
f	The overall sampling fraction (n/N).
f_h	The sampling fraction in a stratum (n_h/N).
M_0	The number of elements in the population (used when the elements have been sampled indirectly in clustered items).
m_i	The number of elements in a clustered item.
$\bar{m}$	The mean number of elements per clustered item $(\sum_{i=1}^{n} m_i/n)$.
N	The number of items in the population.
N_h	The number of items in the population in a stratum.
n	The number of items in the sample.
n_h	The number of items in the sample in a stratum.
n_i	The number of elements in a clustered item.
n_0	An estimate of the required sample size (formulae 4–6, p. 162).
n_1	The number of items in a pilot sample.
$\hat{P}$	An estimate of the proportion of items in the population possessing a given attribute (formula 1, p. 157).
$\hat{P}_{[st]}$	An estimate of the proportion of items in the population with a given attribute, from a stratified sample (formulae 16–17, p. 171).
p	The proportion of items in the sample possessing a given attribute.
p_h	The proportion of sample items in a stratum with a given attribute.
p_i	The proportions of elements in a clustered sample item with a given attribute.
q	The proportion of items not possessing a given attribute $(1-p)$.
q_h	The proportion of sample items in a stratum not possessing an attribute $(1-p_h)$.
$\hat{R}$	An estimate of the ratio between two values of the items in the population (formula 24, p. 174).
$r_{(xy)}$	The correlation coefficient of two values of the items (formula 25, p. 174).
$\hat{S}$	An estimate of the standard deviation of the population items (formula 22, p. 173).

S_h* The standard deviation of the items in the population in a stratum

$$\left(\sqrt{ \left\{ \frac{\sum\limits_{i=1}^{N_h}(y_{hi}-\bar{y})^2}{N_h-1} \right\} } \right)$$

$s*$ The standard deviation of the sample items

$$\left(\sqrt{ \left\{ \frac{\sum\limits_{i=1}^{n}(y_i-\bar{y})^2}{n-1} \right\} } \right)$$

s_1 The standard deviation of the items in a pilot sample.

s_h* The standard deviation of the sample items in a stratum

$$\left(\sqrt{ \left\{ \frac{\sum\limits_{i=1}^{n_h}(y_{hi}-\bar{y}_h)^2}{n_h-1} \right\} } \right)$$

$S(x), S(y)$ The standard deviation of the values x and y respectively.

s(subscript)   The standard error of the estimated parameter denoted by the subscript (e.g. $S_{(\bar{y})}$ = the standard error of an estimated mean value of the population items).

t The normal deviate corresponding to the required confidence level (see table 2, p. 155).

V The desired variance of a sample estimate (formula 3, p. 161).

W_h The stratum weight; i.e. the proportion of items in the population falling in the stratum (N_h/N).

$\bar{X}$ The sum total of an auxiliary value of the population items.

X The mean of an auxiliary value of the population items.

x_i An auxiliary value of a sample item.

$\bar{x}$ The mean of an auxiliary value of the sample items ($\sum\limits_{i=1}^{n} x_i/(n-1)$).

$\hat{Y}$ An estimate of the sum total of a value of the items in the population (formula 21, p. 173).

$\hat{Y}Y_{[PPS]}$ An estimate of the sum total of a value of the items in the population, when the elements have been sampled indirectly in clustered items, and the items have been selected with a probability proportionate to their size (formula 33, p. 181).

$\hat{Y}Y_{[R]}$ A ratio estimate of the sum total of a value of the items in the population, when the elements have been sampled indirectly in clustered items (formula 31, p. 179).

$\hat{Y}_{[R]}$ A ratio estimate of the sum total of a value of the items in the population (formula 27, p. 176).

$\hat{\bar{Y}}$ An estimate of a mean value of the items in the population (formula 2, p. 157).

$\hat{\bar{Y}}_{[R]}$ A ratio estimate of a mean value of the items in the population (formula 26, p. 175).

$\hat{\bar{Y}}_{[st]}$ An estimate of mean value of the items in the population, from a stratified sample (formulae 12–15, pp. 169–170).

$\hat{\bar{Y}}_{[PPS]}$ An estimate of mean value of the elements in the population, when the elements have been sampled indirectly in clustered items, and the items

$\hat{\bar{Y}}_{[R]}$ have been selected with a probability proportionate to their size (formula 32, p. 181).
A ratio estimate of a mean value of the elements in the population, when the elements have been sampled indirectly in clustered items (formula 30, pp. 178–9).

y_i A value of an item.

y_{ie} A value of an element in a clustered item.

y_{hi} A value of an item in a stratum.

$\bar{y}$ A mean value of the sample items

$$\left(\sum_{i=1}^{n} y_i \;\middle/\; (n-1) \right)$$

$\bar{y}_h$ A mean value of the sample items in a stratum

$$\left(\sum_{i=1}^{n_h} y_{hi} \;\middle/\; (n_h-1) \right)$$

$\bar{y}_i$ A mean value of a clustered item, when the item contains several elements

$$\left(\sum_{e=1}^{n_i} y_{ie} \;\middle/\; (n_i-1) \right)$$

z A transformation of the correlation coefficient $r_{(xy)}$ (formula 25, p. 174).

* More convenient versions of these formulae for the purposes of computation avoid having to find the deviation of the value of each item from the mean value, $(y_i - \bar{y})$, as follows.

$$s = \sqrt{\left(\sum_{i=1}^{n} y_i^2 \;\middle/\; n - \bar{y}^2 \right) \middle/ \left((n-1)/n \right)}$$

$$s_h = \sqrt{\left(\sum_{i=1}^{n_h} y_{hi}^2 \;\middle/\; n_h - \bar{y}_h^2 \right) \middle/ \left((n_h-1)/n_h \right)}$$

$$S_h = \sqrt{\left(\sum_{i=1}^{N_h} y_{hi}^2 \;\middle/\; N_h - \bar{y}_h^2 \right) \middle/ \left((N_h-1)/N_h \right)}$$

6. The use of information about occupation

W. A. Armstrong

PREFATORY NOTE

I

In these pages, consideration will be given to the best techniques for stratifying and grouping nineteenth-century communities in terms of economic function on the one hand, and social class on the other. The arguments put forward, and schemes to be discussed, are necessarily closely argued and even technical up to a point. It is therefore appropriate to deal with matters such as the need for grouping, and the nature of the basic material which we have to use in a preliminary note.

II

Ashton has written that economic historians (we might now add social historians) are concerned primarily with groups. Their subject is not Adam, a gardener, but the cultivators of the soil as a class; not Tubal-cain, a skilled artificer in brass and iron, but metal workers or industrialists in general. They deal less with the individual than with the type.[1] The now widely-agreed need to concentrate on the typical and the general rather than the unique or particular reflects perhaps the most fundamental influence of the social sciences on historical methods in this century. There will always remain those who dabble among the sources of history for the quaint and the unusual, and antiquarianism cannot be wholly condemned. But those who hope to see their researches make some contribution to the mainstream development of the subject must necessarily mark Ashton's words well.

In this case we are concerned with social and economic groupings on the national or local level, in the nineteenth century. Prospective research workers are likely to be concerned mainly with occupational distributions from the printed census on the one hand, or with the census enumerators' books (manuscript returns) on the other. It is with a view to helping such users in a practical way that this chapter has been written.

Specifically, we would wish to aim at allocating individuals according to two main principles, (a) by *industrial grouping* – so that we can trace the *economic* contours of a society and the bases on which these rest, and (b) by *social ranking*. From time to time research workers will feel the need to concentrate attention on an occupational group as such where sizeable numbers are concerned and there are important matters at issue (e.g. coal-miners, hand-loom weavers, railway engine drivers or farmers), but as a general rule, occupation may be said to be important only insofar as it enables us to allocate individuals to groupings (a) and (b) above.

To underline these distinctions, an example or two will be useful. An individual may be a clerk (occupation), but conceivably may be employed in an extremely wide range of manufacturing or service *industries*, or in local or central government. For many types of economic analysis it is the latter role that is important. But the fact that he is a clerk may, perhaps in conjunction with other variables if available, help us to place him in a *social class*, for occupation is itself considered to be a key variable in social class. Similarly, a carpenter (occupation) is likely to be employed in a wide variety of *industries*, and this is the important economic variable. But all carpenters, in whatever industry, constitute an *occupational* group, and persons of that occupation are generally viewed as falling under the heading of skilled manual workers, in the hierarchy of social class.

These distinctions are perceived and acted upon by social scientists and government institutions today, but this has not always been so. Nineteenth-century census schedules simply asked for 'Rank, Profession or Occupation', never succeeding in making it clear whether personal occupation, or industry of employment was actually being demanded. Similarly, the printed abstracts were neither consistently prepared on the basis of personal occupations, nor on that of industrial groups, but contained elements of both. It is therefore extremely important to examine the basis of the census work carefully at the outset.

III

At the first census (1801), only a very broad classification of occupations was attempted. Enumerators were required to answer the question 'What number of persons in your parish, township or place are chiefly employed in agriculture, how many in trade manufactures or handicraft; and how many are not comprised in any of the preceding classes?' The results of the question having been deemed a failure, its form was adjusted in 1811 to relate to families rather than persons. The revised question was repeated in 1821 and 1831, but in the latter case enumerators were also required to state the number of adult male persons (i.e. those aged 20 and over) falling into each of nine major categories. These were:

1. agricultural occupiers employing labourers
2. agricultural occupiers not employing labourers
3. labourers in agriculture
4. employed in manufacture or manufacturing machinery
5. employed in retail trade or handicraft as masters or workmen
6. capitalists, bankers, professional and other educated men

7. labourers, not agricultural
8. servants
9. others

The fifth class was also returned in detail for counties and large boroughs by means of a form containing 'one hundred of the most usual denominations of retail trade and handicraft', but enumerators were allowed to extend the list to meet local conditions. Apart from the lack of strict definition for each group, the degree of local initiative allowed led to the drawing up of lists on quite different principles, without uniformity of method. Consequently, no attempt was made to compile a classified list of occupations, and the national abstract consisted only of an alphabetical summary of very dubious value.[2]

From 1841, householders' schedules were in use, and at the census office an effort was made to group the occupations 'under definite rules and on uniform lines'. Nevertheless, although there was a great deal of rendering down and amalgamation of the many thousands of occupations mentioned on the schedules, the published figures for England and Wales covered 877 occupations, presented in alphabetical order, with very little attempt at further arrangement.[3]

A notable advance was caused in 1851 by the realisation of the deficiencies of an alphabetical return like that of the previous census. Some degree of categorisation was felt to be required, and with a view to providing this, a system of 'classes and sub-classes' of occupations (later, and more appropriately called orders and sub-orders) was devised.[4] These classes or orders were initially:

1. persons engaged in Imperial or local government
2. persons engaged in defence of the country
3. persons engaged in religion, law, medicine
4. persons engaged in art and literature, science, education
5. persons engaged in household duties (i.e. wives, children)
6. persons engaged in boarding, lodging, domestic service, dress
7. persons engaged in commercial pursuits
8. persons engaged in conveyance
9. persons engaged in agriculture
10. persons engaged in breeding, animal tending, fishing
11. persons engaged in numerous branches of manufacture
12. dealers and workers in animal substances
13. dealers and workers in vegetable substances
14. mineral workers
15. unskilled or unspecified labour
16. persons of rank, property or independent means
17. residual (especially those supported by the rest of the community – the disabled, paupers, criminals etc.)

In all, these amounted to 17 orders (or classes), which were broken down into 91 sub-orders. Each occupation, as it was separately stated in the census abstract, found its place here, and apprentices, assistants, labourers, porters etc. were generally included under the appropriate order or sub-order with which their work was connected. The number of orders was raised to 18 in 1871 and to 24 in 1881.

Otherwise, the general principles of classification adopted in 1851 were followed right down to 1911. Only minor adjustments were made in 1861 and 1871, but it is important to notice that persons described in the manuscript returns as 'retired' were generally (with one or two exceptions, such as army and navy officers, clergymen and medical practitioners until 1911) placed with the 'unoccupied' (census order 24) from 1881, whereas up to and including 1871 they were credited to the occupations concerned. Another important change (from 1881) was that clerks, porters, engine drivers, stokers, carmen, etc., who had formerly been grouped with the separate manufacture or trade with which their own work was connected, wherever possible, were now collected together under such headings as 'commercial clerk', 'messenger', 'porter' etc.

In 1901 there was considerable revision of the occupational headings with a view to bringing census statistics into closer harmony with those of other government departments. At the next census the same broad plan of occupational classification was retained (i.e. the 24 orders), but the number of separate occupations mentioned under these headings now rose to 472 (from 382 in 1901 and 347 in 1891), with a view to providing greater precision, and for 'occupations of recent growth'.[5]

To summarise; we have in the printed abstracts from 1851 a series of loose *groupings of occupations* (the orders), the principle of categorisation remaining on the same lines down to 1911, but with numerous alterations and refinements which obviously affect long-run (vertical) comparability. It seems clear that the census authorities were somewhat less concerned with this latter principle than with improved precision, and horizontal, or lateral comparability. Printed abstracts, drawn up on the lines we have described, were prepared for the nation, counties, registration districts and large towns, throughout the century. They were also broken down into sex and age-groups, though the constitution of the age-groups tended to vary slightly from census to census.

It is important to remember that all such abstracts were drawn up from the many thousands of different occupations originally stated in the census enumerators' books. Successive censuses provided ever more detailed instructions as to the filling in of the occupational column of the householder's schedule, but throughout the century respondents continued to describe their callings in an 'extremely inaccurate and inadequate manner'. They would state either the industry they worked in, in very general terms, (e.g. cotton-hand), or their personal position without reference to the industry ('foreman', 'weaver', 'spinner' etc.), or might use a local occupational term which the census clerks could not be expected to know (all-rounder, baubler, crowder, dasher, egger, fluker, Kell bulley, lurer, sand badger, walk flatter etc.).[6]

To meet the latter difficulty, from 1861 onwards a regularly revised book of instructions for the ordering of occupations was in use at the census office. It incorporated an occupational dictionary, enabling the clerks to treat the returns in a uniform manner, when rendering down the multiplicity of stated occupations, and was the direct ancestor of the 'Classification of occupations' volumes published regularly with the census since 1911.[7]

The former difficulty – that of inadequate description – was itself one reason why the nineteenth-century census authorities ultimately produced printed 'occupational abstracts' which as we have seen, were structured neither on a truly occupational basis, nor on the other hand, on a consistently industrial basis. It was clearly a matter of opinion as to which element tended to predominate, but all expert opinion was agreed, by the beginning of the twentieth century, that something more systematic was needed, and that *both* types of tabulation were required, since the occupational tabulation would be especially useful in connection with questions of vital statistics, and the industrial tabulation in connection with questions of economics.[8] Accordingly, the former occupational column was split into two parts in 1911; in the first column the respondent was to enter the 'nature of employer's business'. This was the first attempt at a specifically industrial classification, but the results left room for much improvement.[9] Nevertheless, the attempt to separate personal occupation from industrial role was persisted with in the twentieth century, and tables based on both principles were provided in successive censuses. In 1948 a *Standard Industrial Classification* was drawn up which with modifications of detail has been used at the censuses of 1951 and 1961.[10]

Meanwhile, occupational abstracts have continued to appear and another notable advance, also having its origins in 1911, has been the Registrar-General's attempt to use the census occupational data as the basis for a five-class scheme of social classification. This will be discussed in detail below and for the present it is simply necessary to note that whereas the nineteenth-century groupings of occupations were made to correspond roughly with industrial groups, but not without social-class overtones (in that the average level of prestige of some occupational orders was clearly higher than that of others), in the twentieth century the distinctions have been made highly specific, so that it is possible to examine in modern censuses tabulations drawn up on all three bases (simple occupation, industrial-grouping, social class). Each occupation is given a code number, and from 1921 onwards, published census volumes and decennial supplements show in detail all the groupings to which given occupations belong.[11] The extent to which we can make use of these developments will be considered below.

IV

Since trends in the development of historical method have an international character, it is not surprising that foreign scholars are currently facing up to the same difficulties as their English counterparts. In France a spirited debate is currently in progress centring round the difficulties of constructing a *codification socio-professionnelle* for French historical sources. Mlle Daumard has put forward a ten-category scheme based on the INSEE codification developed in France since the war.[12] These ten major groupings are agriculturalists, town workers, domestics, employees in service industry, those intermediate in status between employers and employees, business proprietors, public service, liberal professions, miscellaneous, and those without specified occupations. There are ninety-two subdivisions within these categories. A principal difference between her approach and that employed in this chapter is that whereas we shall attempt to distinguish clearly between social class or status on the one hand and industrial groupings on the other, Mlle Daumard's scheme appears to involve both dimensions at once, even though the declared purpose of the exercise is to group the occupied population into a limited number of large categories, each presenting a certain *homogénéité sociale*.[13]

In attempting to adapt a present-day classification, Mlle Daumard has laid herself open to numerous specific objections from historians – that her classification was developed for notarial sources and can only be applied with difficulty to other sources, especially where occupational descriptions are less exact; that the code is less applicable to rural society; that the diverse regional patterns found in France defeat its purpose. Still more fundamental questions appear to have followed from these. Is it possible to conceive of a scheme of classification which would be operative for eighteenth as well as nineteenth-century France? Again, would it not be preferable to define meaningful social categories by the tabulation of a wide range of variables such as occupation, judicial status, wealth and income levels, family size, age and birthplace etc., so that the elaboration of such a code would follow rather than precede detailed studies?[14]

These difficulties are in principle the same as those we face in this country, except that the French seem to be somewhat better placed with regard to sources. However rich these may be, however, some degree of categorisation must remain inevitable, as Mlle Daumard has remarked in her own defence. While we must guard against prejudging the results, we simply cannot work without some degree of classification.[15]

Any process of grouping, whether by age, birthplace, or in this case occupation, inevitably occasions some loss of detail. There are historians who instinctively object to the blanketing effect of all general schemes of classification, and on very much more reasonable grounds, those who prefer to use simple groupings of occupations, which are neither strictly hierarchical (social ranking) nor yet industrial groupings in the sense in which the term has been used above. They are likely to point to the difficulties of deciding what are the criteria of social classes (and the shortage of information on some of the relevant variables) and to the various practical difficulties involved. To such historians, there might seem to be virtue in simply considering individual occupations as such, unaffected or uncontaminated by modern systems of classification, and they may well be suspicious of what look like rigid and inflexible general schemes, conjured up without mature consideration.

We would not wish to claim that the schemes put forward later are fully comprehensive, entirely logical or perfectly suited to every scholar's purpose. Objections may very well be raised to the effect that this or that occupation ought 'obviously' to have been placed in an alternative group or social class. Nevertheless it would be widely agreed that if research is conducted with some common basis of classification, order and uniformity could be introduced into the field – and in view of the volume of work which will surely be carried out on the census in the years to come, this is surely a most important matter. By following the schemes suggested here, no one need feel that his hands are tied. There is no reason why particular occupations should not be singled out for special analysis where appropriate, and alternative schemes can and should be applied according to individual interest.[16] At the same time, if all would consider using these schemes *alongside* their own, their findings could be tabulated in forms which would be meaningful to other workers in the field. Anarchy might be avoided.

PART 1. A BASIS FOR SOCIAL STRATIFICATION

I

The kind of society which existed in western Europe prior to the industrial revolution was certainly hierarchical in character. The distinctions between men were described in terms of ranks, orders and degrees, or where attention was being drawn to particular economic groupings, of 'interest'.[17] Pre-industrial society is generally viewed as a kind of pyramid, with the monarchy at the apex, then the peerage, the gentry (major and minor nobility, in effect), yeomen and husbandmen (farmers), labourers and cottagers, and finally paupers. This was the fundamental structure of rural society and merchants, craftsmen, tradesmen and artificers might fit into the basic structure at various points (not generally as high as the gentry, certainly not as low as labourers, cottagers etc.). Between and within each of these very broadly defined groups there were later said to have existed 'chains of connection', and 'bonds of attachment'[18] which were associated not only with a network of social obligation but with the gentle slopes of social gradation. Such bonds were said to be strengthened by the element of social mobility supposedly present in England; while there were immense differences in wealth and income, and in the social esteem accorded to each rank or order, they were not buttressed by legal inequalities of the kind that were encountered in continental Europe of the *ancien régime*.

In eighteenth-century England the term 'class' was still reserved for the school-room and for scientific categories. Several writers have contended that the changes associated with the industrial revolution gave birth to new class-relationships, and an appropriate terminology, so that gradually the word became well-established as a social label. 'Middle classes', 'working classes', 'industrious classes', 'higher classes' were all terms which had come into fairly common usage among social commentators by the 1830s. It is fair to say that most of those who used the term 'class' (with or without qualifying adjective), were not very specific about what was meant by the term, except that many felt, consciously or unconsciously, that the older terms no longer applied in an urbanising and industrialising society which was breaking down the 'bonds of attachment' and 'chains of connection' supposed to have been so important in the past.

This criticism cannot however be extended to Karl Marx and Friedrich Engels, analysts of the trends of the times, prophets of the contradictions of capitalism and heralds of a new Socialist society. In their view, society was 'more and more splitting up into two great hostile camps, into two great classes directly facing each other: bourgeoisie and proletariat'. The bourgeoisie was strictly identified by its possession of the means of production, the proletariat by lack of the same. The petite bourgeoisie (smaller manufacturers, shopkeepers, artisans) was necessarily being forced by competition into the ranks of the proletariat. Parallel changes were taking place on the land, where the feudal aristocracy was in the process of being 'ruined' by the bourgeoisie, and polarisation had taken place between the capitalist farmer class and a landless agricultural labourer class, whose rights to land had been systematically dismantled over the centuries.[19]

Despite several important inaccuracies in this picture, much evidence to support these views can be cited, even beyond 1850. It must be remembered that this was a dynamic view of the overall tendencies of the time, not a static descriptive account. When we recall the deteriorating position of large groups of domestic producers, notably the hand-loom weavers, framework knitters, nail makers and the like, we bring to mind not merely small groups of individuals whose fate can be dismissed as irrelevant, but extremely large sections of the working-force, whose condition, in Hobsbawm's word, 'froze the blood of even the most flinty economist'.[20] Thompson has also pointed to the way in which established traditional skills in the metropolis were from the 1820s under siege from the competition of a morass of sweat-shops (furniture-making, tailoring, shoemaking, building) while on many fronts, as machinery lightened the burden of manual effort, it was found convenient and cheaper to use the labour of women and children. The tendencies which these authors have so graphically described may be taken as evidence for the Marxian view that the distinctions among workpeople, based on levels of skill, were diminishing, and that labour was everywhere being reduced to the lowest common denominator. As a consequence, Thompson argues, in the years between 1780 and 1832, most English working people 'came to feel an identity of interests between themselves, and against their rulers and employers'.[21]

On the other hand, it is also frequently pointed out that there was a brighter side to the Industrial Revolution – it produced new opportunities as well as destroying old skills. Engineers and machine builders of every kind and on all levels multiplied; white-collar occupations grew rapidly. Some important old skills remained distinctively well remunerated, and in the general field of manufacturing and mining there can be little doubt that a great many enjoyed larger real incomes than they or their forefathers could have expected in the past, even if this was often on account of enhanced *family* earnings. Again, it has been shown that these years saw 'the genesis of modern management'. The problems of conducting large-scale industry provided opportunities for men who made a wide range of practical day-to-day decisions, if not the strategic decisions about the running of a business which were still very much the province of the owner or entrepreneur in the nineteenth century. However, the future significance of this development could hardly have been foreseen by Marx and his contemporaries in early Victorian England, for at the beginning of that period (c. 1830), a managerial class 'could hardly be said to be in existence, though well-defined classes of managers had emerged in various specific industries'.[22]

At the beginning of the period with which we are concerned, the old and the new forms of economic activity and ways of life overlapped. It was manifestly obvious to most observers that the future development of England lay with the expansion of her industry, trade and commerce, and that her pre-eminence among the nations owed itself mainly to these. Yet in 1851 England was half-rural and half-urban, and the great industries of the industrial revolution employed only a minority of the total population. England was still a land where, according to the census, agricultural workers were by far the largest male occupational group, and domestic servants the largest female group. 'Handicraft blacksmiths were more numerous than the men of the great iron works . . . (and) more men were employed about horses on the roads than in all the work of the young railway system.'[23]

Consequently, it is not surprising that the older ways of characterising the social structure remained in use. Perhaps there were relatively few, in 1850, who would have insisted on talking in terms of 'ranks and orders', and a great many who would have been prepared to use the terms 'upper-classes', 'middle-classes' and 'working-classes'. On the other hand, for every single individual who adhered to the Marxian view that society was becoming polarised into two great classes, thousands would have insisted upon the gradations and status distinctions to be found within each of those groups. For every individual who asserted that the only significant movement between the classes was the downward projection of the petite bourgeoisie, thousands would have agreed with Samuel Smiles that it was possible for the man of talent who was prepared to nurture his gifts by practising diligence, thrift and self-help to climb the ladder which the shape of society seemed to resemble. Indeed the divisions within classes may well have been more keenly felt than those between them, and such dividing lines may well have seemed 'sharper at the base of the pyramid than towards the apex'.[24]

II

That global assessments and reassessments of the class situation, in both its measurable and non-measurable aspects, should be made by historians is obviously of the greatest importance; such studies as those which have been cited not only attempt to synthesise existing knowledge, but also generate new ideas and hypotheses to be tested by others, and so the progress of the subject is assured. They obviously contain a strong element of intuitive or subjective judgement, and many would agree that it is precisely those rare historians who are willing to deal in large-scale generalisations who most deserve our commendations.

Yet from the perspective of the would-be historian of Crewkerne, Malton or Wrexham, such generalisations may well appear remote and extremely difficult to apply to his community. While he should be sensitive to the implications of macrosopic studies for his own community, the local historian is much more likely to feel an immediate need for a working scheme of social classification to import order into the primary sources with which he is confronted, such as the census enumerators' books. His need, to paraphrase a pertinent passage from a recent sociological study, is for an invented scheme of classification to impose on the empirical data to further understanding and facilitate fruitful analysis.[25] This section is an attempt to meet that need.

The question is, however, which criteria should be employed to form a basis for differentiation between classes? As a help the local historian may at this stage turn to works of modern sociology, only to find that when sociologists use the terms 'class' and 'status' (although they may be quite specific in spelling out their respective meanings), they nevertheless appear to give an impression of speaking with many voices. There are in fact understandable differences of opinion about the relative weight to be attached to occupation, income level, education and position in the power structure when determining the social ranking of given individuals in modern society, to mention only those criteria which are more or less objective in character. Others have argued that class itself is a purely subjective phenomenon, a set of feelings by which some people feel a sense of identity which excludes others.[26] Many draw an important distinction between class and status, preferring to use the former only in its Marxist sense of relationship to the means of production, while viewing the status hierarchy rather as a reflection of the distribution of esteem in society.[27] It is not to be wondered at that the historian, perhaps lacking a training in the social sciences, will be bewildered by the complexity of the literature and the present emphasis on class as a relative concept, the essence of which may indeed vary in different types of society.

Certainly all local and regional historians should try to familiarise themselves with as much of this writing as circumstances allow, and should always be on the look out for opportunities to relate their own work to general theories and arguments. But in practice the range of information available for the great majority of nineteenth-century individuals is rather limited, extending in the census manuscripts to such details as name, age, sex, birthplace and occupation. Only the latter variable has direct relevance to social class. It is true that other indications of standing may sometimes be obtained from census data, such as the numbers employed in the case of an employer, or the number of domestic servants, but these do not enable us to make distinctions among that great majority of individuals who were not employers, and did not maintain domestic servants. The researcher may uncover other data (from wage-books, rate-books etc.) which can be matched with census data, and which may to some extent be relevant to social class, but for the most part, it is clear that he will have to rely on simple statements of occupation, not because this is the best or sole means of social classification, but as the only one which will enable him to place in a systematic way all individuals under consideration. This is not in itself distressing, for virtually every theorist of class sees occupation as an important determinant. As Thernstrom, facing up to the same problem in connection with American data, has written, 'The historical study of social mobility requires the use of objective criteria of social status. The most convenient of these is occupation. Occupation may be only one variable in a comprehensive theory of class, but it is the variable which includes more, which sets more limits on the other variables, than any other criterion of status.'[28]

If it is allowed that occupation is our best guide to social class, the difficulties do not end at that point. We are in the position of having either to determine a hierarchy of occupations for ourselves, or to take over some ready-made scheme, with or without modifications. By following the first course, the historian could flatter himself that he had used his innate judgement on each individual case, and taken full account of the nuances of the nineteenth-century class structure, but in practice, the outcome could well be that no two scholars would work on the same basis, which would be disastrous. On the other hand, no general scheme of classification (with published lists of attributions of individual occupations to social classes), exists for the nineteenth century, and we are bound to turn to what the twentieth century can offer.

It is necessary to rule out modern schemes of stratification which are too refined, e.g. the Hall–Jones scale.[29] This consists of arranging occupations under seven headings: 1. professional and high administrative; 2. managerial and executive; 3. inspectional, supervisory and other non-manual (higher grade); 4. inspectional, supervisory and other non-manual (lower grade); 5. skilled manual and routine grades of non-manual; 6. semi-skilled manual; 7. unskilled manual. Doubtless this is a useful tool for comparatively high quality present-day data, but the occupational terms stated in nineteenth-century sources are generally too laconic to allow of such distinctions being drawn, especially between groups 1 and 2, and 3 and 4. Similar objections apply to the 'socio-economic' groups introduced by the census authorities in 1951 and elaborated in 1961.[30]

Only one general scheme of social classification will be found to fit the two desiderata, i.e. not too refined for the data, and carrying with it published lists of occupations for easy allocation and comparability of classification, namely the Registrar-General's social classification scheme. Here all occupations are subsumed under five broad categories. So far as is practically possible, the basic aim is to ensure that each category is 'homogeneous in relation to the basic criterion of the general standing within the community of the occupations concerned'.[31] Vague though this may sound, we may assume that there would be in practice high correlations between these occupational strata and levels of education, income, social esteem and deference, authority etc., to mention just a few of the criteria which sociologists believe to be important in gauging social class. But the reader is entitled to require more details of the nature and details of the Registrar-General's scheme before he is likely to admit that it may have some practical application to nineteenth-century data, and because the scheme has itself gone through a process of evolution, a brief history seems appropriate.

<h3 style="text-align:center">III</h3>

In the Registrar-General's Decennial Supplements published from time to time in the nineteenth century, the mortality of males according to occupation was tabulated. The Decennial Supplement for 1911 attempted to extend the investigation to the fertility of married males in each occupation, along with occupational infant mortality rates. Presumably to avoid blinding readers with detail, the birth and infant deaths in the various occupations were 'summed into a number of groups, designed to represent as far as possible different social grades'. A stated social class assignment was given for each of the occupations separately distinguished in the 1911 census, on the following basis:

Class I. 'The upper and middle-class', included 'all occupational groups of which the majority of the members tabulated at the census could be assumed to belong to these classes.' White-collar occupations (including clerks) were included here, but the artisan was as far as possible excluded.

Class II. 'Intermediate between the middle and working-class because it consists of occupations, such as the shopkeeping trades, including many members of both.'

Classes III, IV, V. 'Working-class'. Class III included those occupations mainly consisting of skilled work-people, Class V of the census occupations consisting mainly of the unskilled. Those census occupations which included 'many men both skilled and unskilled' were listed as Class IV, and described as 'intermediate in type'.

Classes VI, VII, VIII. These were important sub-groups of the working-class which it seemed desirable to distinguish separately: VI, textile workers, VII, miners, VIII, agricultural labourers. Table 28 (A) of the Decennial Supplement gave the social class assignment of 373 principal census occupations and it was pointed out that by using the manual of occupations to be published along with the census it would be possible to ascertain the precise composition of every such occupational group.[32]

It will be understood that the 1911 social classification did not scrutinise the position of *individuals* – its basis was the wholesale assignment of occupations to social classes in a rough and ready way. Farmers (Class II) could be farmers of 10 or 1,000 acres; and while business proprietors could well be included in Class III or below, their clerks would go in Class I. Nevertheless, in spite of these known deficiencies, the incidence of infant mortality was found to be lowest in Class I and to increase regularly down to Class V, with no consistent gradation beyond this.

In 1921 the same basic five-class scheme was used, but the enhanced precision of the 1921 occupational census permitted the sub-division of the mining, textile etc. groups. Agricultural labourers were henceforth included in Class IV, and textile and mining workers were variously distributed, according to occupation, among Social Classes III to V; thus the Registrar-General's scheme now consisted of 'five great classes complete for the whole occupied and retired population'. Moreover, the improvement effected by what was now thought to be a 'genuinely occupational tabulation' had also provided much better means of assigning other individuals to their appropriate class. In 1911 many 'occupational' (so-called) headings had actually included members of all social classes, and 'assignment could only be made to the social class thought appropriate for the average member of a very diverse group'. The social class of individuals could now be assessed in accordance with the nature of their individual employment, which was 'far from being the case in 1911…the correlation, at all events, of mortality with assigned social class is now closer than it was in 1910–12'. Another readjustment made in the classification of particular occupations had been the relegation of clerks from Class I to Class II.[33]

The performance of the scheme on two successive occasions led contemporaries to conclude that the regularity of the mortality gradings provided a test of the success of the social grading involved, i.e. it generated results which accorded with the not unreasonable contemporary convictions upon the incidence of mortality and natality. (Comparative fertility was also discussed under these headings.) As the chief statistician at the General Register Office wrote, 'I would go so far as to suggest that the results now discussed not only prove that the social classification employed is substantially correct on the assumption of correlation of high mortality with low social status, but that…they are at the same time an indication both of success in the social grading of occupation, and of the association of mortality with low status. For…if the social classification used were without validity there would be no reason for correspondence with mortality…(and)…if there were no association between poverty… and mortality, the gradation of mortality by occupationally distinguished sections of society would be inexplicable.'[34]

In 1931 a certain amount of reallocation of particular occupations was carried out, but the changes were not generally as radical as those of 1921, when advantage had been taken of the general effort to place the occupational part of the census on a more strictly occupational basis. However, most clerks were relegated still further (to Class III), railway porters from Class IV to V, locomotive firemen, cleaners, ticket collectors from III to IV, and certain classes of textile workers from III to IV; while on the other hand farm bailiffs rose from III to II, agricultural-machine drivers and attendants, and dynamo and switchboard attendants from IV to III etc.[35] The next revision came in 1951, with the publication of the volume entitled *Classification of Occupations, 1950* (HMSO, 1951), which was reprinted in 1956.[36] This consisted of a complete directory of many thousands of occupational terms, with details of their subsumption into 981 occupational groups. Each of these groups found their place in the twenty-four census occupational orders, and more importantly from our point of view, were coded for social class. To give just one example, a balata-solution maker was coded (with spewing-machine attendant and about seventy others) under occupational code 541 (workers in rubbers, mixers, spreaders, moulders), all of whom were entered in Class III, and (incidentally, from our point of view) incorporated into occupational order 13.

Basically, the scheme of social classification was still one of five broad categories, 'homogeneous in relation to the basic criterion of the general standing within the community of the occupations concerned'. These were now stated (in general terms) to be:

Class I.   professional etc., occupations
Class II.   intermediate occupations
Class III. skilled occupations
Class IV.   partly skilled occupations
Class V.   unskilled occupations

Provision was made for Class III, for certain purposes, to be functionally subdivided between III(a) mine-workers; III(b) transport workers; III(c) clerical workers; III(d) armed forces; III(e) others. Class IV was divisible between IV(a) agricultural workers and IV(b) others; while Class V could be between V(a) building and dock labourers and V(b) others.[37]

IV

Having reviewed briefly the history of the Registrar-General's social classification, we need to consider the relative merits of the allocations of 1911, 1921, 1951, for our purposes. That of 1911 can be ruled out quite summarily. It is true that, as stated above, the composition of 373 socially classified occupational groups can be arrived at (by reference to the census volume x, entitled *Classified and alphabetical lists of occupations*) and there is no insurmountable practical barrier to its use. On the other hand, the 1911 classification bears all the marks of a first, hasty effort and lacks the detailed refinement of later attempts. (The classification of 1921 gives social class allocations for 989 separate occupational designations, that for 1951, 981.) Furthermore, the inclusion of all white-collar workers in Social Class I (including commercial travellers, clerks, schoolteachers, and those describing themselves as 'builders') is a most undesirable feature, reducing the credibility of a proposition that might otherwise seem sensible, namely that a scheme of social stratification produced in 1911 would accord more closely with nineteenth-century views than any scheme prepared at a later date in the twentieth century.

Thus, in practice, the issue resolves itself into a choice between the allocations of 1921 and 1951. We shall explore this question by examining how a range of occupations drawn from the York census enumerators' books in 1841 and 1851 would have been allocated under each of the two series of codings, but before embarking on this task it is important to stress two points:

(1) We shall not be examining the 1921 and 1951 schemes with a view to applying one or other to nineteenth-century data without further ado. Rather, the question is, which of the two provides the better basis for our proposed scheme of social stratification, a basis which can then be modified in a simple and unambiguous manner, to take account of the special problems which arise when working with nineteenth-century census data.

(2) The fact that only 1841 and 1851 occupations are used for this test does not mean that the findings are irrelevant to later census years. It is reasonable to assume that in the enumerators' books, a similar range and diversity of occupational terms will be found throughout the nineteenth century, and the fact that there would have been changes in the balance of occupations and in the principles by which they were grouped in the census office, does not affect the matter. Therefore, the principles of social classification that we shall eventually recommend may be applied to manuscript census data for the whole of the nineteenth century.

Listed in appendix A of this chapter are 239 grouped occupations encountered in samples of households drawn from the 1841 and 1851 returns for the City of York. We shall proceed to show in what respects the 1921 and 1951 systems of allocation would have treated them differently.[38]

Group A

The first nineteen occupations (accountant – vicar) were placed in Class I in both 1951 and 1921, with the sole exception of magistrate, which was stated as Class II in 1921, and archbishop's secretary, which was not listed at either date.

Group B

Of the next twenty occupations (auctioneer – veterinary surgeon) eighteen shared a common classification at both dates (Class II). Auctioneers and land agents were relegated from Class I to Class II between 1921 and 1951, and the vague term 'factor', while being allowed as Class II in 1921, was a case that had to be 'referred to the supervisor', according to the 1951 instructions – but brokers, agents and factors (unspecified) were actually included in Class II.

Group C

While there is a very close correspondence between the classifications for the two dates in respect of the occupations mentioned in groups A and B, the position with the next 150 occupations (forming group C) on first sight presents more complications. On the one hand there are a number of occupational terms (20 or 30) which give a reasonable idea of status, in that they clearly imply that the person so described was not self-employed. Police constable, various railway occupations, soldier, sailor, ship's carpenter, shopman, telegraph clerk etc. In another twenty or thirty cases the nature of the occupational term strongly suggests employee rather than employer or own account status, especially where the term implies work at a certain stage in the production of goods and articles (boot closer, brass fitter, car painter, coach-lace weaver or trimmer, coach-wheel maker, engine-spring maker, French-kid stainer, leather dresser, iron turner, millwright, bricklayer etc.). Unfortunately, there is a still wider range of terms which do not in themselves clearly indicate whether the person so described is an employer, employee, or own-account worker or one-man business proprietor (baker, basket maker, brush maker, cabinet maker, chair maker, chemist, clockmaker, coach maker, confectioner, coppersmith, cordwainer, draper, joiner, mason, saddler, shoemaker, slater, staymaker, tailor, and others, amounting to a hundred or more.)

Examination of appendix A will make it plain that the 1921 and 1951 classifications attempted to deal with the employer/employee question in slightly different ways. The 1921 census questionnaire demanded to know whether the respondent was an employer, or an employee. At the processing stage, the attempt was made to distinguish between employers and managers in industry on the one hand and work-people on the other, by means of separate code-numbers, e.g. bricklayer was coded 565 (Class III), but bricklayer (employer) was coded 560 (Class II). Similarly, butcher (employer or on own account) was coded 770 (Class II), while butcher's assistant was covered by 775 (Class III). We have set out these distinctions in Appendix A, where they applied. In 1951, it was laid down that where employers carried on undertakings covered by Orders III–XV (broadly speaking, the mining, manufacture and building sectors), they should, if engaged in small-scale enterprise, be assigned under the normal code for that occupation (e.g. blacksmith, 145 – Class III); if on the other hand their enterprises were on a large scale (10 or more employees), then the employer should be coded into a special order for administrators, directors, managers (Order XVI). However, where an employer's activities did not fall under those covered by Orders III–XV, they were to be assigned to the appropriate group making provision for proprietors, regardless of the number of workers employed. (This affected principally transport and service sectors.) It seems curious that the small-scale (under 10 persons) employer in pottery, engineering, metal-trades, articles of dress, leather, the small manufacturer of food, drink and tobacco etc. should be coded into the same class as his workers, but that the garage proprietor, fruiterer, or grocer should be coded differently (and generally classed above his workers and assistants). However, it is not essential to dwell on the irrationality of this, since the 1921 and 1951 codification procedure has been outlined mainly in order to emphasise that there is a problem here of distinguishing between employer and employee – which is a matter to which we shall have to return.

Reverting to consideration of the rest of the third group of occupations (assistant – writer) it will be noticed that we have included in group C a variety of retail and commodity dealers (fruiterer, greengrocer, grocer, tea dealer, pot dealer, cattle dealer, hay and straw dealer, innkeeper etc.). In 1921 all 'dealers' (employers or own-account) were coded 770 and entered as Class II, except stock and share-dealers (Class I) and hawkers and street-sellers (Class V). Their assistants were generally placed in Class III, as our schedule shows. Again, in 1951, wholesale and retail dealers were classed as II, with employees in Class III. There is thus no difference in the treatment of these people at the two dates, but here we have preferred to list them under group C rather than group B, for reasons which will be explained below.

In a general way, though without much attention to specific instances, we have touched upon the majority of the cases in group C of our list, and seen how they were classified at both dates. There remain several further points to which attention should be drawn. Clerks (all industries, including railway), were classified as II in 1921, III in 1951; cabmen, omnibus drivers and coachmen were classified according to the type of vehicle on both dates; eating-house keepers were placed in Class II at both dates. Firemen were variously classified at either date; while commercial travellers were downgraded from II to III between the 1921 and 1951, and soldiers rose from IV to III.

Group D

In the next group of thirty-four occupations (agricultural labourer – waterman) we find that all were classed as IV in 1951, except that a distinction was made between carters using horse conveyances (IV) and self-propelled vehicles (III). In 1921, cloth dressers, cork cutters, engine cleaners, gardeners, rail stokers and railway ticket collectors were all in Class III, as were the various types of domestic servant. Drovers rose from Class V to Class IV by 1951.

Group E

Lastly, the eleven occupations in this group (charwoman – scavenger) were all placed in Class V at both dates, with the exception that charwomen had been in Class IV in 1921. Within this group, only the porters represent something of a problem; although we have grouped them together here, the 1921 classification actually distinguished 34 types of porter, placing 3 in Class III, 17 in Class IV, 14 in Class V. That of 1951 referred railway-porters to V, and dock labourers (sometimes described as porters) to V; but various institutional porters (hotel, hospital, college, lodging house etc.) were in Class IV. Unspecified porters, as in 1921, found their place in Class V.

V

It seems clear that, in fact, there is little to choose between 1921 and 1951 as the basis of a working scheme. We have seen that the classes appear to have included broadly the same occupations at both dates, and the only really substantial differences are the relegation of clerks from Class II to Class III, and domestic servants from Class III to Class IV, between the two dates. This may reflect some decrease in the esteem in which such occupations have come to be held, but it is at least arguable that the general (i.e. non-specialist) clerk rarely enjoyed a higher level of social esteem than the skilled artisan even in the nineteenth century,[39] and on the other hand, in most situations the question of the social classification of domestic servants will not arise directly, since classification will usually be by household heads, and households headed by domestic servants are an extreme rarity.

There is, however, a purely practical point favouring the use of the 1951 classification as a basis, namely that the *one* printed volume required in order to make attributions will be widely available in libraries up and down the country. This is less likely to be the case if one chooses to work with the 1921 system, especially as two volumes are required (the *Decennial Supplement* for 1921 and the *Classification of Occupations*, 1921). This seems sufficiently important to decide the issue, since there are no strong reasons for favouring 1921.

In a study of the social structure of York, 1841–51,[40] the 1951 classification was used, with certain modifications as detailed below, and proved satisfactory. One likely practical objection may be disposed of forthwith – that a great many occupations have disappeared over the last hundred years, and that appropriate code numbers (and hence social classifications) will not be found in the 1951 volume. Those who suspect this may have their doubts set at ease when they find the following representative list of archaic occupations and titles still classified: street lamplighter, crossing sweeper, candle maker, yeoman, cordwainer, hand-loom weaver, town beadle, town crier, knocker-up, sword-blade forger, quill-pen cutter, pound keeper, postillion etc.

Using the 1951 classification as a basis, the first step in analysing data from the enumerators' books is to provide an *initial classification*, using the 1951 code-book, with only one modification at this point – an important one, however. All those described as dealers or merchants in this, that or the other, are best placed in Class III and not Class II (hay, straw, corn, cattle, sheep, pig, provision, coal, flour, pot, tea etc. to quote from our lists). Similarly, all those in retail shopkeeping trades (fruiterer, chemist, greengrocer, grocer, fishmonger etc.) should also be placed *initially* in Class III, irrespective of the fact that the 1951 classification would place only salesmen and assistants here, incorporating proprietors and managers in Class II. This should also be done with innkeepers, restaurant keepers etc. This has the initial effect of putting virtually all commercial persons in Class III and we make this recommendation because it seems evident that a great many persons who made their living in these ways, describing themselves as dealers or merchants, were far from being persons of substantial capital and often enjoyed only low standards of living arising out of their commercial operations.[41] The minority described as agent, factor or broker, may still be included under Class II, however, but those distinctively described as street-sellers, hawkers, pedlars, costermongers etc. should be consigned to Class V (following 1951 practice).

The initial social classification of household heads will thus be entirely along the Registrar-General's lines in the cases of Classes I, IV, and V, but Class II will be a little smaller and Class III somewhat larger, on account of the suggested modification. (Class III would at this stage comprise clerks, skilled workers, and a great variety of dealers and retailers.) Working from the initial classification, the following alterations may then be made, *upon consideration of individual cases.*

1. All employers of twenty-five or more persons (excluding domestics) should be placed in Class I. It is hoped that all such cases could be identified, and while it is not certain that all employers did fill in the answer to this query, there is nothing we can do to allow for those who did not. One of those who did not supply these details in 1851 appears to have been Benjamin Gott, the prominent Leeds textile manufacturer. Such a man might well, along with his household, fall to Class III, but in a sample of any size drawn from the enumerators' returns for Leeds, his exclusion from Class I and inclusion in, say, Class III, would not distort the global results for either class significantly. Of course this would not be true if there was evidence of a widespread failure to complete that requirement of the schedule satisfactorily, but at present there is no decisive evidence about the extent of failure to report fully. In 1851 there were apparently 'a certain number' of masters who did not state the number of men they employed,[42] but many respondents probably exaggerated their importance rather than understating it by omitting to record any such particulars. In later years, when the questionnaire attempted to distinguish between employers and employed, the authorities believed that many subordinates had returned themselves as 'employers' rather than 'employed', this being 'dictated by the foolish but very common desire of persons to magnify the importance of their occupational condition'.[43]

2. A distinction was made in the 1951 social classification between drivers of horse-drawn conveyances on the one hand, and self-propelled vehicle drivers on the other. The former were placed in Class IV, the latter in Class III. To eliminate this anachronism, one should treat all drivers of horse-drawn *passenger* conveyances as having the same status and classification as drivers of self-propelled vehicles in 1951. Carriers and carters are best left in Class IV.

3. To those firmly established in Class II on account of the 1951 occupational allocation (auctioneer, railway inspector etc.) one should add, by upgrading, all those whose initial allocation was Class III or IV, if they employed one or more

persons, not including members of their immediate family (wives, sons, daughters). For this purpose, apprentices should be counted, for there were a good many cases of household heads who did not actually return themselves as employers, but who had apprentices or journeymen living in. By this means all proprietors whose undertakings were at all substantial, whether in retailing, dealing or manufacture, would rise. Similarly, another important adjustment to be made is to upgrade innkeepers, lodging-house keepers, tavern and beer-house keepers, publicans and eating-house keepers from Class III to Class II, in cases where they employed at least one domestic servant or assistant other than members of their immediate family. (Incidentally, this procedure is not dissimilar to that used in the very latest available social classification of 1961; here, each occupation is given a basic social class, but persons of foreman or managerial status are raised.)

4. A number of entries of 'occupation' will be encountered which are not classified by the Registrar-General. These included (for York), 'house proprietor', 'house and land proprietor' or 'owner', 'living off interest', 'independent means', 'annuitant', 'pauper'. Although attributions are bound to be arguable and much would depend on the precise amount of land, houses, interest income etc., (which is not known), it seems best on the whole to place these in Classes I, I, I, I, II, V respectively. All persons described as retired should be classified on the basis of their previous occupations. Students should be classified according to the occupation for which they are training (e.g. medical student, law student), or consigned to the residual Class X (see below), if there is no clear evidence. Apprentices should be treated as the equivalent of journeymen in their respective trades, and in most cases it will be safe to assume that an 'apprentice' (so described), is bound to the trade of the head of the household in which he resides, unless there is specific evidence to the contrary. A few cases will not be allocable on the basis of the information given; in a sample of 781 household heads in York (1851), blank spaces, or such uninformative entries as 'husband away', 'gentlewoman', 'housewife', 'almswoman', 'spinster', were encountered in twenty eight cases ($3\frac{1}{2}$ per cent). Such households may be placed in a residual class (Class X).

VI

The reader is entitled to know how this scheme of stratification has performed empirically. The York study is the only completed work which uses it as yet, and for the purposes of interpreting some of the results (in respect of household and family size) we had to combine Classes I and II, and IV and V.[44] But this was not necessarily a reflection on the scheme of social stratification as such; rather, the necessity arose out of the small absolute numbers of cases which were encountered in some classes, in what was, overall, a fairly small sample. Our belief in the soundness of the scheme is strengthened by the results yielded by the 1851 sample of 753 classifiable household heads, as given in table 1.[45]

Table 1   *Distribution of Domestic Servants, 1851*

	Social class of household head				
	I	II	III	IV	V
Percentage of heads having one or more domestic servant (95% confidence limits in brackets)	81·4 (±9·9)	57·9 (±9·4)	9·1 (±2·9)	5·8 (±4·5)	—
Mean: domestic servants per household	1·88	0·75	0·12	0·10	—
Number of households	59	107	386	103	98

Table 1 demonstrates the kind of relationship between occupationally defined social class and the maintenance of domestic servants which might reasonably be expected, in the conditions of 1851.

Similarly, an inverse relationship appeared to exist between social class of household heads and the sharing of dwellings with another identifiable family unit (defined as a married couple, with or without children, or a person of either sex with one or more children). We say 'appeared to exist' because it is not possible to establish these differences with confidence, in the statistical sense.

Table 2   *Sharing of dwellings, in relation to social class, York, 1851*

	Social class of household head				
	I	II	III	IV	V
Percentage not sharing	98·3	98·1	94·0	92·2	88·8
Number of households	59	107	386	103	98

Despite this, a recurrent criticism of the Registrar-General's scheme of social classification is that it always tends to produce a swollen Class III.[46] The same is true when it is applied to nineteenth-century data. Table 3 illustrates this clearly, although we are not strictly comparing like with like.

Table 3

	Percentage in classes				
Social class distribution	I	II	III	IV	V
(a) Occupied and retired males, England and Wales, 1951[47]	3	14	52	16	15
(b) York, 1851. Household heads (3 per cent unplaceable)	8	14	49	13	13

Evidently we shall always tend to get a distributional pattern of this kind, and therefore some comments are called for.

It might be argued that there are a large number of persons whose occupations are not the final guide to their social status. Among those who are lumped into Class III, we might expect to find distinctions in a variety of individual factors – the person with a college education who did not succeed for some reason; the fact that iron-moulder A enjoyed a small legacy, while iron-moulder B did not; that railwayman C had happened to marry a virtuous wife devoted to 'keeping up appearances' while railway man D had married a slattern; or that bricklayer E was a temperate and sober individual, while bricklayer F drank to excess and so on. In other words, occupationally most of the Class III might very well be on much the same baseline, but the accidents of human life could well determine the social standing of given individuals, or individual families. Of course, personal circumstances might equally affect the esteem in which individual members of other classes were held too, and clearly there is no basis for weighing such things when handling historical evidence.

Yet we need to break down Class III on some basis, or so it is urged. To a greater extent than any of the other classes, it remains composed of disparate groups in that own account (non-employer) shopkeepers and workers will be found there, rubbing shoulders with traditional craftsmen, employees in the new industries of the industrial revolution, and workers in transport, building and services. Is this important?

It may not be important to attempt to distinguish between the component parts of Class III if this scheme of social classification is being used in conjunction with the scheme of industrial groupings discussed in the next section. By means of sorting punched cards (or processing data on computer tape, or even manual sorting where this is used) it will be possible to distribute the Class III cases among industrial groups. Let us suppose that we are interested in finding out the age structure of Class III. A simple run through of the data will elicit this information. But suppose further that we also require the age structure of Class III building workers only (the general run of skilled building workers). This could easily be arrived at by dropping all those members of Class III who were not coded as being in building. Thus, where the industrial classification is in parallel use, there is no need for concern about the excessive size of Class III. Comparative tabulations could be made between Class III shopkeepers, Class III clerks, Class III building workers, Class III transport employees and so on. For that matter, Classes I, II, IV, V could be broken down in a like manner and in as much detail as anyone could reasonably require. Apart from utilizing industrial sub-divisions in that way, it may often be helpful to distinguish between manual and non-manual workers within Class III, or between petty entrepreneurs, clerks and skilled workers, as Dyos has been able to do with reasonable accuracy.[48] The possibilities of splitting Class III, or any other Class, to suit individual needs are thus very extensive, although the importance of presenting material in a form whereby recombination is easy for comparative purposes must be stressed. Thus the criticism that Class III is too large, unwieldy and undifferentiated, may easily be dealt with by subdivision, without any implication that the ranking of one subsection is in any way superior to that of another.

To conclude: we have stated the need for employing an agreed common system of social classification for nineteenth-century occupational data. Reasons have been put forward for preferring the Registrar-General's 1951 scheme as a basis, and the necessary modifications have been detailed above, while in appendices B and C of this chapter we shall comment on the applicability of the scheme to 1841 data, and on the special problem of farmers. Used in the manner described, especially in conjunction with the industrial classification discussed in the next section, we believe that the modified Registrar-General's social classification is a reasonably flexible tool. Research workers should certainly feel free to single out occupations which particularly interest them, or to try out schemes of their own; but it will be greatly to the advantage of the subject if they will consent to use this form of classification alongside their own, to preserve a basis of comparability.

It is convenient to add that this system of social classification has been evolved with its application to the enumerators' books particularly in mind. Indeed, some of the suggested modifications to the Registrar-General's 1951 scheme require the scrutiny of individual cases, and access to information about individuals (such as the number of employees), which cannot be obtained from the printed census volumes. The aim, as suggested at the outset was merely to proffer a convenient arbitrary scheme of classification to render order and meaning into empirical data, and to try to secure its general acceptance. This scheme is not therefore designed for application to *printed* census data,[49] and in any case we would not assume that the 'class-structure' of a community had been established if its occupied population were merely to be assembled under these headings. By contrast, in the next section, we shall approach the question of industrial classification from the alternative starting point of printed occupational data, though that scheme can also be applied to the enumerators' books without much difficulty.

Appendix A. List of occupational terms encountered in samples drawn from the York enumerators' books in 1841 and 1851

This list is printed with two purposes in mind:

1. as an aid to the exposition of differences between the allocations of 1921 and 1951 (see text). Explanatory comments are added where necessary, generally following those given in the relevant census volumes.

2. as a check-list of some intrinsic value, in that it comprises many of the occupational terms most commonly encountered. The groups A, B, C, D, E in fact correspond with the *initial classifications* (Classes I–V) used in the study of York. As the text makes clear however, *individual cases* from Class III were upgraded to Class II (dealers and manufacturers who were employers, and all innkeepers etc. who had servants); while all employers of twenty-five or more persons were placed in Class I, irrespective of their trade.

	Social classification	
	1921	1951
Group A		
Accountant	I	I
Archbishop's secretary	not classified	not classified
Architect	I	I
Army officer	I	I
Attorney	I	I
Dentist	I	I
Independent minister	I	I
Magistrate (Stipendiary, i.e. paid magistrates are classified, but honorary magistrates such as JPs are not)	II	I
Museum curator	I	I
Naval officer	I	I
Ordnance surveyor	I	I
Rector	I	I
Reporter	I	I
Sharebroker	I	I
Shipowner	I	I
Solicitor	I	I
Surgeon or physician	I	I
Surveyor	I	I
Vicar	I	I

215

Group B	*1921*	*1951*
Auctioneer	I	II
Bookkeeper	II	II
Coal agent	II	II
Commercial teacher	II	II
Factor (unspecified)	II	II
Inland revenue collector	II	II
Land agent	I	II
Language professor	II	II
Music teacher	II	II
Professor of music	II	II
Proprietor of ladies' seminary	II	II
Police chief constable	II	II
Railway audit clerk	II	II
Railway inspector	II	II
Relieving officer	II	II
Schoolmaster/ Schoolmistress	II	II
Sculptor	II	II
Station master	II	II
Translator (languages)	II	II
Veterinary surgeon	II	II

Group C

Assistant (to linen draper)	III	III
Assistant (Ordnance office)	not classified	not classified
Baker	III (II if employer)	III (but if manager of retail business II)
Basket maker	III (II if employer)	III
Beer retailer	II	II
Blacksmith	III (II if employer)	III
Boiler maker	III (not employer)	III
Bookbinder	III (not employer)	III
Bookseller	II (bookstall clerk, keeper, manager)	II (but assistant III)
Bonnet maker	III (milliner: but employer II)	III
Boot closer	III	III
Brass fitter	III	III
Bricklayer	III (II if employer)	III
Brush maker	III (not employer)	III

Group C (cont.)	1921	1951
Builder	II	II
		(builder and contractor)
Butcher	III	III
	(assistant or slaughterer: but employer or own account, II)	(salesman, assistant: but proprietor or manager II)
Cabinet maker	III	III
	(not employer)	
Cabman	III	III
	(motor: but IV horse-drawn)	(taxi-cab: but IV horse-drawn)
Calico weaver	III	III
	(weaver, textile)	(weaver, textile)
Cattle dealer	II	II
	(see the heading 'dealers, employer or own account, not in stocks and shares or a street seller or hawker')	(retail and wholesale dealers: but hawkers and street sellers V)
Car (carriage) painter	III	III
Chair maker	III	III
Chemist	III	III
	(salesman and assistant: but own account or manager II)	(salesman, assistant: but retail proprietor, manager, pharmacist, etc. II).
Clerk (unspecified)	II	III
Clockmaker	III	III
	(II if employer)	
Coach builder	III	III
	(II if employer)	
Coach-lace weaver	III	III
Coachman	III	III
	(motor: but IV horsedrawn)	(motor: but IV horsedrawn)
Coach trimmer	III	III
		(coach finisher)
Coachsmith	III	III
Coach-wheel maker	III	III
Coal dealer	II	II
	(= dealer on own account, not hawker or street seller; but coalman, or coal hawker, III)	(coal merchant, retail: but coalman, coal hawker IV)
Compositor	III	III
Comb-maker	III	III
		(except celluloid IV)
Confectioner	III	II
	(pastrycook)	(proprietor, manager: but salesman, assistant III)
Cook	III	III
Cooper	III	III
Coppersmith	III	III

H

Group C (cont.)	1921	1951
Cordwainer	III	III
Corn, flour dealer	II	II
	(corn factor, agent)	(corn merchant, agent, factor)
Currier	III	III
	(II if employer)	
Cutler	III	III
	(not employer)	
Damask weaver	III	III
	(II if employer)	
Dentist's assistant	III	II
Draper	III	III
	(assistant: but II on own account)	(proprietor, manager II)
Dressmaker	III	III
	(II if employer)	
Eating-house keeper	II	II
Engine driver	III	III
Engineer	III	III
		(insufficiently defined – but most such workers come under this class)
Engine fitter	III	III
Engine-spring maker	III	III
Engraver	III	III
	(most engravers: but artists II)	(most engravers: but artists II)
Farrier	III	III
	(not employer)	
File cutter (maker)	III	III
Fireman	variously, III–V (21 types distinguished)	variously, III–V (36 types distinguished)
Fishmonger	III	III
	(II if employer)	(salesman, assistant: but proprietor or manager II)
Florist	III	II
	(grower: and probably assistant; but retail shop-keeper apparently II)	(shopkeeper: but assistant and grower III)
French-kid stainer	III	III
		(leather stainer)
Fringe weaver	III	III
Fruiterer	II	II
	(not assistant)	(proprietor, manager: but assistant III)
Gas fitter	III	III
Gilder	III	III
Girth weaver	III	III
	(web weaver)	(girth maker)
Glass blower	III	III
Glass maker	III	III
	(not employer)	

Group C (*cont.*)	1921	1951
Glass stainer	III	III
Glover	III	III
	(maker: but shopkeeper II)	(maker: but retailer II)
Greengrocer	II	II
	(not assistant)	(but salesman, assistant III)
Grocer	II	II
	(employer and own account: but assistant III)	(but salesman, assistant III)
Gun maker (gunsmith)	III	III
	(employer II)	
Gutta-percha merchant (broker)	II	II
Hairdresser	III	III
Hatter	III	III
	(journeyman)	(journeyman: but retailer II)
Hay and straw dealer	II	II
	(Dealer on own account not stocks and shares, nor hawker, street seller)	(all dealers excluding hawkers, street sellers)
Hosier	II	II
	(shopkeeper or own account: but frame-tenter III)	(but salesman, assistant or maker III)
Housepainter	III	III
Innkeeper (publican)	II	II
Ironmonger	III	II
	(employer or own account II)	(assistant III)
Iron-moulder	III	III
Iron turner	III	III
Joiner	III	III
	(employer II)	
Law stationer	II	II
	(stationer, dealer)	(proprietor, manager: but assistant III)
Leather dresser	III	III
	(employer II)	
Linen spinner	III	III
	(textile spinner)	(flax spinner)
Manure dealer	II	II
	(as for hay and straw dealer – see above)	(as for hay and straw dealer – see above)
Marble mason	III	III
	(employer II)	(not employer)
Master grinder	IV	III
	(grinder, metals)	(metal-grinder)
Master mariner	III	III
		(petty officer, seaman etc.: but master of ship and navigation officer II)

Group C (cont.)	1921	1951
Miller (flour and grain)	III (employer II)	III
Millwright	III	III
Muffin maker	III	III
Musician	III	III
Music seller	(not separately distinguished: shopkeeper, manager II: but assistant III)	II (music shop keeper)
Nail maker	III	III (forged: but stamped IV)
Nurse	III (sick or domestic)	III (nursing assistant: but qualified nurse II and nurse-maid IV)
Omnibus driver	III (motor: horse IV)	III (motor: horse IV)
Optician	III	II
Pawnbroker	II	II
Perfumer	III (employer or dealer II)	III (compounder: but maker IV)
Picture dealer	II (as for hay and straw dealer, see above)	II (as for hay and straw dealer, see above)
Picture-frame maker	III (employer II)	III
Pipe maker (tobacco)	III (not employer)	III
Plane maker	not given	III
Plasterer	III (employer II)	III
Police constable	III	III
Plumber	III (not employer)	III
Pot dealer	II (as for hay and straw dealer, see above)	II (as for hay and straw dealer, see above)
Pot maker (potter)	III (employer II)	III
Poulterer	II (employer, not assistant)	II (but assistant, III)
Printer	III (employer II)	III
Railway clerk	II	III
Railway fitter	not listed	III
Railway guard	III	III
Railway pointsman	III	III
Railway policeman	IV	III
Saddler	III (employer II)	III
Saddle-tree maker	III (not employer)	III

Group C (cont.)	1921	1951
Sailor	III	III
Sawyer	IV	III
	(wood: but metal V; stone III; employer II)	(wood and stone: but metal V)
Seamstress	IV	III
Seedsman	III	II
		(retail distributor: but assistant III)
Shipbuilder	III	(insufficient description: but
	(II if employer)	shipwright, etc. III)
Ship's carpenter	III	III
Shoemaker	III	III
	(employer II)	
Shopman	III	III
Silversmith	III	III
	(not employer)	(not a dealer)
Silver turner	III	III
	(silver chaser)	(silver chaser)
Slater	III	III
	(employer II)	
Soldier	IV	III
Stationer	II	II
	(dealer: but assistant III)	(but assistant III)
Staymaker	III	III
(corset maker)	(not employer)	
Stonemason	III	III
	(not employer)	
Stone sawer	III	III
Tailor	III	III
	(employer II)	
Tea dealer	II	II
	(as for hay and straw dealer, see above)	(tea grocer)
Telegraph clerk	III	III
Tobacconist	II	II
		(but assistant III)
Traveller (commercial)	II	III
Upholsterer	III	III
	(employer II)	
Victualler	II	II
	(provision agent)	(provision agent)
Waiter	III	III
Warehouseman	III	III
Watchmaker	III	III
	(employer II)	
Weaver (textile)	III	III
Wheelwright	III	III
Whitesmith	III	III
Wine and spirit dealer	II	II
		(but assistant III)

Group C (cont.)	1921	1951
Wire worker	III	III
	(not employer)	(wire goods worker)
Wood carver	III	III
Woodsman	III	III
Woodturner	IV	III
	(machinist)	
Writer	II	III
	(clerk)	(clerk)

Group D		
Agricultural labourer	IV	IV
Brazier	IV	IV
	(not precious metals)	(not precious metals)
Brewer	IV	IV
	(employer II)	
Brickmaker	IV	IV
	(employer II)	
Carter (or carrier)	IV	IV
(horse-drawn	(not farm or employer)	
conveyance)		
Cloth dresser	III	IV
Cork cutter	III	IV
	(not employer)	
Cowkeeper	IV	IV
	(if a farmer II)	(if a farmer II)
Drover	V	IV
Engine cleaner	III	IV
Flax dresser	IV	IV
Gardener	III	IV
General servant	III	IV
Gentleman's servant	III	IV
Goods deliverer (railway)	IV	IV
Groom	IV	IV
Herdsman	IV	IV
Horsebreaker	IV	IV
Horsekeeper	IV	IV
Hotel porter	IV	IV
Housekeeper	IV	IV
	(caretaker, houseminder: but	
	housekeeper (domestic), III)	
Housemaid	III	IV
Laundress	IV	IV
Office keeper	IV	IV
Ostler	IV	IV
Pavior	IV	IV
Quiltress	IV	IV
	(sewer)	(machinist)
Rail stoker	III	IV
Railway ticket collector	III	IV

Group D (*cont.*)	1921	1951
Rope maker	IV	IV
	(employer II)	
Steward (club)	IV	IV
Stoker	IV	IV
	(boiler stoker)	
Washerwoman	IV	IV
Waterman (boatman)	IV	IV

Group E

Charwoman	IV	V
Errand boy	V	V
Hawker	V	V
Labourer	V	V
	(general labourer, not on farm)	
Messenger	V	V
News vendor	V	V
	(newspaper seller)	
Porter	V	V
	(not otherwise described, but some porters in IV and III)	(not specified: but some in IV)
Rag and paper collector	V	V
	(rag gatherer, rag and bone man)	(rag and waste collector)
Rail porter	IV	V
Road labourer	V	V
Scavenger	V	V
	(road scavenger)	

Appendix B. Modification of the above scheme to suit 1841 data

The scheme of social classification outlined above is valid for 1851 and subsequent census years. We have seen that it is dependent in part upon the fact that those who were employers were asked to state this fact, and how many they employed. This information is not available in 1841, and for York it seemed that the best approach to solving the difficulty was to introduce the maintenance of domestic servants as a criterion of class. One scheme would have been to have had three classes:

Class A: Class I as constituted in our lists, less the large entrepreneurs (not identifiable).

Class B: Classes II–V, as in the lists, where they employed domestic servants.

Class C: Classes II–V, as above, without domestic servants.

Yet it seemed likely that a three-class scheme of this sort would lose too much detail. As applied to the York (1851) sample, the approximate distribution would have been Class A, 50 heads; Class B, 100 heads; Class C, 590 heads. The eventual scheme used in the study was to classify as follows:

Class (I): Occupations in group A of the list, less the handful of large entrepreneurs – not identifiable in 1841.

Class (II): Those having occupations listed under groups B and C above, provided that they employed at least one domestic servant.

Class (III): The residues of groups B and C, *not* employing domestic servants.

Class (IV): Occupations listed under group D above.

Class (V): Occupations listed under group E above.

Unfortunately use of this modification necessarily means that the social classifications adopted for the two dates are not strictly comparable. However, where it is essential to make comparisons involving 1841, there is no reason why data for 1851 and subsequent years should not at some later stage of the enquiry, be reclassified along the lines suggested for 1841. This is as far as one ought to be prepared to go in order to accommodate the 1841 data, however, which is deficient in several other respects.[50]

Appendix C. The problem of farmers

It will have been noticed that we have not yet referred to the special problem of the social classification of farmers and graziers. By and large, this is not serious where towns alone are considered: the few farmers who were encountered on the fringes of York were placed in Class II, which is the normal designation for farmers and graziers, both in 1921 and 1951.

This clearly will not do where a rural community is the focus of attention, for the term farmer is obviously one which comprehends a wide variety of meanings, economic circumstances and incomes. Farmers were asked to state in their returns the acreage worked and the number of employees, but such information was not always given. The census occupational returns of 1851 state the number of farmers and graziers as 249,431 (males and females), of which, according to the census authorities, 225,318 were masters actually occupying land (the others were presumably retired etc.). Of these, 91,698 made no return of the number of labourers on their farms, and it was believed that in the majority of such cases, no labourers were actually employed. (For 'it is certain...that in parts of the country, men who employ no workmen and have only a few acres of land, have always been called and returned at the censuses as farmers'.) However, the apparently frequent omission of this information renders it difficult to use this systematically as the criterion of status.

On the other hand, acreages were stated with relatively infrequent omission (only 2,047 farmers out of 225,318 did not give this information). In England and Wales farms averaged 111 acres, while for every 1,000 farms, 638 were under 100 acres, 205 of 100–199 acres; 154 of 200–999 acres; and only 3 of over 1,000 acres. Large holdings were most frequently encountered in the eastern and south-eastern counties, small farms in the North Midlands, Yorkshire, Wales and the North-West.[51] While we must be aware that the incomes yielded (and hence to some extent status conferred) by a given acreage of land varied, amongst other things, with its productivity, we have no option but to take acreage as the only practicable guide to status.

Where the focus of a study is a town, and farmers appear in only tiny numbers, it seems best to follow Miss Shepherd's convention[52] and consider only those with 5 acres or more as farmers in the full sense of the word. They should be placed in Class II, and farmers with less than 5 acres (or where acreage is not stated) in the Class below (III).

Again, however, this would not do if a rural society was being analysed, and this particular occupation is obviously one which would necessarily have to receive special consideration. For general purposes all farmers (except those with less than 5 acres) should be classed as II, but subdivisions (in terms of acreage) could be formulated for the *occupational group*, e.g. 5–, 10–, 20–, 40–, 80–, 160–; or 5–, 20–, 40–, 60–, 80–, 100– etc. and space would have to be found for recording these details on the cards or tape in use. Special local circumstances might call for modifications of these subdivisions.

PART 2. AN INDUSTRIAL CLASSIFICATION 1841–1891

VII

The prospective student of any nineteenth-century community, whether he wishes to examine region, town or village, will normally need to delineate its economic structure in relation to others, and to the national structure, at various points in time and over time. This will often apply even if his interest lies primarily in social or political history.

For the first thirty years of the nineteenth century, the principal source will be directories on account of the failure of the census to provide more than approximate estimates of the numbers employed in agriculture on the one hand and trade and manufacture on the other.[53] With a sense of relief, he will pass on to the detailed occupational data provided in the 1841 and subsequent censuses, only to find that if anything there is rather too much detail. How should occupations be combined into meaningful groups, and how can one make allowance for the obvious shifts in the constitution of census occupational classes? The student is likely to have recourse to sundry ill-defined conventions for amalgamation of occupations and bridging operations across the years, which, although they may well serve his immediate purpose, nevertheless somewhat detract from the comparative value of his work.

There are many obvious advantages in placing such calculations on a standard and uniform basis, whereby the structure of one community can readily be compared with another, and with the national. But on what basis can one best proceed? Bearing in mind that the stratification called for here is fundamentally by economic function (rather than by status, already discussed), the ideal would appear to be a scheme based on the modern conception of the industrial grouping.

VIII

As was pointed out in the prefatory note, the first attempt at a conscious industrial classification was made in 1911. On the printed schedules, householders were to enter personal occupations of inmates (col. 10), and in col. 11 the 'Industry or service with which worker is connected'. It was thus possible to produce tables showing which occupational groups were subsumed under each of twenty-two 'industrial groups', and for the first time it was found appropriate to publish a detailed list of occupations with code numbers.[54] (The latter had originated in 1861 as the census clerk's directory of occupational terms, and we have already had occasion to refer to it on p. 195.)

The 1911 attempt to distinguish between personal occupation and industry of employment was not, however, considered to be very successful, and further modifications were made to the census questionnaire of 1921 with a view to eliciting the twin pieces of information more precisely. Since that date the production of an industrial as well as an occupational classification, has been a regular part of census procedure. In 1948 a *Standard Industrial Classification*[55] was approved by the principal government departments, which consists of the following industrial groups or orders:

(1) agriculture, forestry, fishing; (2) mining and quarrying; (3) non-metalliferous mining products other than coal (glass, china, earthenware, cements); (4) chemicals etc.; (5) metal manufacture; (6) engineering, shipbuilding, electrical goods; (7) vehicles; (8) sundry metal products; (9) precision instruments, jewellery; (10) textiles; (11) leather and fur goods; (12) clothing manufacture; (13) food, drink, and tobacco manufacture; (14) manufactures of wood and cork; (15) paper and printing; (16) other manufacturing industries; (17) building and contracting; (18) public utilities (gas, electricity, water); (19) transport and communications; (20) distributive trades (wholesale and retail); (21) insurance, banking and finance; (22) public administration and defence; (23) professional services; (24) miscellaneous services.

Each major group is divided into subdivisions, and published lists containing above 10,000 separate designations permit research workers to place their studies on the same basis. Frequently, however, social scientists prefer to condense the twenty-four orders into somewhat broader groups. For example, Carr-Saunders, Jones and Moser[56] refer to eleven groups in comparing the industrial distributions for 1931 and 1951, namely:

(1) agriculture, forestry, fishing; (2) mining and quarrying; (3) manufacturing of all kinds; (4) building and contracting; (5) gas, electricity, and water; (6) transport and communications; (7) distributive trades; (8) insurance, banking and finance; (9) public administration and defence; (10) professional services; (11) miscellaneous services.

Deane and Cole[57] divide the twenty-four orders into eight groups, in order to link inter-war figures to those used for the nineteenth century in their study (agriculture, forestry, fishing; mining and quarrying; manufactures; building; trade; transport; public service and professional; domestic and personal).

The question which arises is, can the historian make use of the modern industrial classification (along with all the ancillary aids connected with it, such as the coded lists of occupations), to achieve order in nineteenth-century data? The obvious answer is that he cannot, for the simple reason that unless enquiry is made systematically into the individual's *field of employment*, as well as his personal occupation, no explicitly industrial classification can be made. We have seen that prior to 1911 this was not done. Nevertheless the modern industrial classification gives a clear idea of what is desirable for the analysis of economic structures, and our task must be to find the best possible approximation to it – to try to devise a scheme which will retain many of the characteristics of the modern industrial distribution and take us beyond the vague and formless 'occupational classes or orders' of nineteenth-century censuses. The basis of such a scheme is to be found in an early article written by Charles Booth.

IX

In the course of the preliminary studies which led up to his great survey of the *Life and labour of the people in London*, Booth found it necessary to address himself to the problem of census comparability, down to 1881. In his well-known paper entitled 'Occupations of the people of the United Kingdom, 1801–81',[58] the first few pages were devoted to criticisms of the system of occupational orders and sub-orders which had been in use since 1851, previously described in our prefatory note (p. 193).

Booth's main criticisms of the printed national abstracts ran along the following lines:

1. The number of separately stated occupations varied remarkably, even after the formulation of a standardised system of orders in 1851. Thus, in the census for 1851 many smaller divisions of labour were subsumed under broader or general headings, while by contrast in 1861 particularly detailed amplification of all minor forms of employment was given, rendering the tables very bulky. By 1871 the number of headings had been markedly reduced again. 'Here the pruning knife has been very busy: the tables are reduced to a third of their former size, numbers of small trades are spirited away...'

2. Although the broad plan of classification remained the same, huge transpositions of numbers had been made from one census order to another; 'the domestic class in one census includes the larger part of the population, and in the next is reduced by more than half; 350,000 persons in England alone (consisting of the wives and other relatives of farmers etc.) are taken from the agricultural class of one census and placed in the unoccupied of another; the partially occupied wives are in no two successive censuses treated alike'. Generally there was 'such a want of fixity of principle or method that even competent authorities have been seriously misled regarding the apparent results'.

3. Most paupers, criminals, lunatics etc. ('useless or disabled members of society') were actually included with the employed. Only those who failed to claim an occupation were included in the residual order (XVII). It seemed wrong to class as workers a vast number of persons who were not only outside the ranks of labour but 'a dead weight and burthen upon it'.

4. The censuses were not designed to throw light on the relative size and importance of the different branches of industry, and it seemed evident that 'to find out how many depend for their subsistence on any particular industry should surely be the final aim of an occupational census'. In the crudest possible form, the abstracts of 1801–31 had attempted this, but the principle had later been lost sight of.

Accordingly, in his paper, Booth set out to restate the census information in 'a more uniform and accessible shape', having regard 'less to occupation as such than to the industries within which people worked', so far as the nature of the information allowed. In his article, the occupied population, at each census date, was summed into eleven major categories with fifty-one sub-divisions, primarily on an industrial basis, with the global results given in table 1.[59]

Table 1   *England and Wales. Employment of occupied population by percentage 1851–81*

	1851	1861	1871	1881
Agriculture	20·9	18·0	14·2	11·5
Fishing	0·2	0·2	0·2	0·3
Mining	4·0	4·5	4·5	4·8
Building	5·5	5·8	6·3	6·8
Manufacture	32·7	33·0	31·6	30·7
Transport	4·1	4·6	4·9	5·6
Dealing	6·5	7·1	7·8	7·8
Industrial service	4·5	4·0	6·0	6·7
Public service and Professional	4·6	5·3	5·5	5·6
Domestic service	13·3	14·6	15·8	15·7
Others (Property owning and independents: Indefinite occupations)	3·7	2·9	3·2	4·4
TOTAL	100·0	100·0	100·0	100·0

We have thought it preferable to reduce the numbers of separate categories given in table 1 to nine, by combining 'agriculture' and 'fishing', and by dropping 'others' from the occupied population. Booth himself referred to the 'indefinite' class as at best 'a meaningless remainder', and the 'property owning' class as 'entirely delusive', since it was increasingly the fashion for men to claim some form of employment as their status.[60] They are best linked with 'dependents' in the residual (i.e. unoccupied) part of the population, and are so treated in table 6 and in appendix D. Restated in this modified form, the figures given in table 1 now become those in table 2.

By this approach, Booth expected to iron out to a large extent fluctuations in the numbers of separately stated occupations; he could set out the data in a more systematic manner (by using standard headings drawn up on a primarily industrial basis); and finally make transpositions of occupational groups from one census order to another irrelevant, by ignoring the census authorities' plan of arrangement. These improvements dealt with criticisms 1, 2 and 4 mentioned above. On the other hand, it is important to realise that there were certain inescapable limitations to what could be achieved. For instance, Booth could not meet criticism 3, for there was no way of knowing what proportion of the allegedly occupied population in the last six censuses had in fact been 'paupers, lunatics or otherwise useless and disabled'. A still more important limitation was that Booth operated only at the level of the printed abstracts, themselves the outcome of much condensation and processing at the census office. Therefore, he was not in a position to trace with absolute certainty the detailed *composition*

Table 2   *Employment of occupied population by percentage, 1851–81*

	1851	1861	1871	1881
Agriculture and fishing	21·9	18·7	14·8	12·3
Mining	4·1	4·6	4·6	5·0
Building	5·8	6·0	6·5	7·1
Manufacture	33·9	33·9	32·7	32·2
Transport	4·3	4·7	5·1	5·8
Dealing	6·7	7·3	8·2	8·3
Industrial service	4·6	4·1	6·2	7·0
Public service and Professional	4·9	5·5	5·6	5·9
Domestic service	13·8	15·1	16·4	16·4
TOTAL	100·0	99·9	100·1	100·0

of *individual* census occupations, at any single census, let alone their shifting composition across the years (e.g. it could only be a matter for surmise on his part that 'currycomb makers' and 'hairpin makers' (headings of 1861), were actually included under the 1881 census heading 'iron and steel manufactures'; or that the 'black ornament makers' of 1861 were actually covered by 'glass manufactures' in 1881). Booth's presumptions always look reasonable although it is not beyond the bounds of possibility that, in this case, black-ornament makers could have been later included under 'toy maker, dealer,' or 'furniture maker', or 'figure and image maker,' for example.[61] But these difficulties should not be exaggerated, and are likely to be of slight statistical significance. The whole purpose of Booth's study was to stand back from the morass of detail, and to attempt to view the national situation in terms of broader categories, based as far as possible on the industrial principle. It seems doubtful whether misallocations at the margin could have affected his results significantly.

X

Fairly clearly there are very many features of resemblance between Booth's groups and those of the modern industrial classification. This is especially the case when Booth's main sectoral groupings are compared (table 1) with those used by Carr-Saunders, Jones and Moser (see above, page 227). We have amplified Booth's headings to show the correspondence more clearly, e.g. to underline the fact that Booth's heading 'agriculture' actually comprises agriculture proper, forestry and breeding.

Figure 1   *Booth's major groupings compared with those in common usage today.*

Carr-Saunders, etc.	Booth
Agriculture, forestry, fishing	{ Agriculture and breeding { Fishing
Mining and quarrying	Mining and quarrying
Building and contracting	Building and contracting
Manufacturing of all kinds	Manufacture
Gas, electricity, water	No comparable category (Water comes under mining, gas under manufacture)
Transport and communications	Transport
Distributive trades	Dealing
Insurance, banking, finance	Industrial service (1) (Commercial)
Public administration and ⎫ defence ⎬ Professional services ⎭	Public service and professional
Miscellaneous services	Domestic service
No separate category	Industrial service (2) (General and unspecified labour)

The obvious differences between the two listings are that:

(1) Booth's 'general labourers' (a sub-category of 'industrial service') have no parallel in the modern scheme, where it is possible to distribute labourers by industry.

(2) Gas, electricity and water supply are not considered as a separate public utilities section by Booth, but come under a sub-branch of industry in the case of fuels, and under a sub-category of mining in the case of waterworks.

A second principal difference, less obvious from figure 1, is that whereas nowadays it is often possible to distinguish with some confidence between manufacture and the distributive trades, this was very much more difficult in the nineteenth century. Towards the end of that period, the census reports mentioned the pressure of interested government departments for a proper distinction between the two forms of activity, and the census authorities, while attempting to accommodate such requests, invariably spoke of the task as near impossible. The upshot is that many of the occupational groups added into Booth's *manufacturing* sector necessarily included *dealers* in a given material, as well as workers, e.g. tool maker, dealer: copper, copper goods manufacturer, worker, dealer: cork and bark cutter, worker, dealer etc. Hence, to assume that Booth's 'dealing' sector can be strictly equated with the coverage of the modern 'distributive trades' sector would be wrong, for it comprehends only a relatively restricted range of retail trading in coals, raw materials, clothing materials, dress, food etc. (See appendix D of this chapter).

Despite these qualifications, it is clear that there is a close similarity between Booth's scheme and the modern type of distribution, and it is notable that those who have wrestled with the question of the changing economic structure of England and Wales have relied heavily upon it. Most recently, Deane and Cole accept Booth's detailed tables as a starting-point in estimating an industrial distribution to 1881.[62]

XI

So far only a brief description of Booth's aims and global conclusions has been attempted, but the utility of his study goes beyond this, thanks to his thoughtfulness in preserving his worksheets. In the appendix to Booth's article, the following passage may be found:

> The full statement of the 400 occupations given in the census, with their addition into the groups given here, has been placed in the library of the Statistical Society and will be found useful for reference, giving, as it does, the complete information from the various censuses in parallel columns with uniform tabulation.[63]

Through the courtesy of the Society and its Librarian, it has been possible to examine this document very carefully, and in view of the uses which it is proposed to make of it, a detailed description is called for. It consists of one large bound volume, setting out the following information:

1. A series of 353 standard occupational headings, in the extreme left-hand column of each double-page spread. These are grouped vertically under industrial headings and subheadings, and have been reproduced in appendix D. Moving horizontally across the page, male and female totals for each occupation are stated by age-group (–15, 15–20, 20–, 25–, 65– for males; –15, 15– for females), for each census date.[64] Diagrammatically, the layout may be represented thus:

1831, 1841	1851								1861,1871,1881
	Males					Females			
	–15	15–20	20–	25–	65–	–15	15–	Total	
Bakers	X	X	X	X	X	X	X	T	
Confectioners, pastrycooks	X	X	X	X	X	X	X	T	
Total (baking)								Σ T	

It will be seen that there are seven entry points for each occupation at each census date, and these Booth filled by reference to the printed national abstracts, which normally stated the occupational data by age/sex groups (except in 1831 and 1841). Each individual census figure representing the number of persons in the given occupation and age/sex group was rounded to the nearest 100, and odd hundreds were expressed as decimals of 1,000. Thus, if there were 20,211 male bakers in the 25–64 age group, the entry would be 20·2; if 54,482 female confectioners aged 15–, 54·5 etc. Some of this rounding was done inconsistently where smaller occupations were concerned, however, and while the principle seems to have definitely been to round to the nearest 100, we have not invariably found that 50–149 would appear as 0·1, or –49 as nothing, etc. Furthermore, aggregative totals for each occupation (T) and industrial sub-group (ΣT) (e.g. baking as a whole), were derived from addition of the previously rounded age-group figures, and did not always represent with strict accuracy the rounded *census abstract total* for the occupation. These 'errors' are however, of minute significance.

2. Details of a number of 'estimates' prepared by Booth to cover situations where either data were missing for an occupation in a given census, or where it seemed necessary to split a few occupations (goldsmith, hatter etc.), are given in marginal notes on these same pages of the manuscript volume, and we have reproduced these in appendix D.

3. Similar details for Scotland and Ireland are laid out on subsequent pages, and details of the allocation of 'dependants' for all areas is shown. (In his paper, Booth split the dependants – all males under 20 and all females not returned as occupied – among the occupied groups according to certain assumptions, mainly that 'the whole number of wives and children in each group was proportionate to the number of males 25–65 years old'.) We have not used this part of his work, so it is unnecessary to discuss this further.

4. At the end of the manuscript volume, Booth set out lists of census abstract occupations included under his standard headings for 1881, 1871, and 1861, which cover virtually all occupations separately listed in the national census abstracts, for each date. Unfortunately no details are recorded of how the occupations of 1841 and 1851 were dealt with, though we may assume that the general principles of allocation must have been on much the same lines as for 1861.

Ideally, one would wish to have complete lists covering the allocation of every separately stated occupation at each census date, but the existence of even partial statements makes possible the following advances:

(1) A more certain knowledge of the composition of Booth's groups. Whereas in the published article, Booth's findings are broken down under a maximum of fifty-one headings (even in the detailed abstract on pages 351–67), we are able to amplify his breakdown under 353 census occupational headings (corresponding with those used in the 1881 census).

(2) Matching Booth's calculations against the data in the printed census volumes permits an arithmetical check, fully on 1881, 1871 and 1861, and partially on 1851 and 1841. Moreover, since a reworking could produce the same results only insofar as Booth's rules and conventions were both consistent and explicit, we have a parallel check on the 'principles of allocation'.

(3) By careful application of his conventions, the national analysis can be advanced to include 1891.

(4) The virtually complete lists of allocations for 1881 and 1861 may be presented under Booth's headings. This will be of particular value to local historians, in that local studies can be placed on Booth's basis to all intents and purposes, a matter to which we shall revert in section XVIII.

XII

Sections XII–XVI will embody the results of reworking the census data along Booth's lines, with a view to illustrating the composition of his groupings and carrying out checks on reliability (i.e. the first two 'advances' referred to above). In successive sections the procedure will be to treat each census individually, in some detail for 1881 and 1861 (for which years very full lists of allocations are available in the manuscript volume), and in rather less detail for 1871, 1851 and 1841.

We necessarily start at 1881, from which year Booth drew his 353 standard occupational headings. Our procedure was to compare each occupational heading separately listed in Booth's manuscript (353 headings) with the national occupational abstract, 1881, which actually lists rather more separate occupations than this (398). Booth's totals for each heading will be found in appendix D. They represent in each case the addition of a number of rounded totals, since, as already mentioned, he had previously split each occupation by age-group. These can usually be compared with the rounded total number for that occupation taken from the printed abstract. Since a few of Booth's occupational headings comprised more than one census occupation (usually where the numbers were small) the composition of a small number of his totals could only be arrived at by trial and error methods. For example, under agriculture (AG.3) Booth has apparently linked together vermin destroyers and dog, bird and animal keepers in a group termed 'Others engaged about animals'. The scope for misallocation is exceedingly small.

The following list comprises all those cases in which there was a divergence greater than 0·1 thousand (100) between Booth's figure and that arising from the procedure outlined above. Differences of 0·1 may be ignored, since they are usually simply the product of Booth's addition of previously rounded numbers.

Group

M.3. Clay, sand, gravel, chalk labourer, dealer, and fossil, coprolite digger, dealer (combined). Our calculation 5·5, Booth 5·1.

MF.23. According to the marginal notes in the manuscript volume (reprinted in appendix D), Booth allowed three-quarters of the 22·7 hatters in this group and one quarter in 'Dealing' (D.4). Three-quarters of 22·7 is 17·1 and not 17·5 (Booth).

MF.28. Booth claimed to have divided the occupation 'tobacco manufacturer, tobacconist' equally between this group and 'dealing' (D.6). Actually one half of the census occupation is 9·9 not 11·0.

D.4. See above, MF.23. Booth's figure should be 5·7 not 5·2.

D.6. See above, MF.28. Booth's estimate for 'dealer' tobacconists should be 9·9, not 8·8.

I.S.1. The total for 'officer of commercial company, guild, society etc.' should be 0·4 not 1·4 (Booth).

This schedule covers all the occupational headings used in the nine principal sectors of the occupied population. Otherwise, the category 'property-owning and independent persons' is 'estimated' by Booth at 254·8. This estimate was necessitated because the 1881 census did not supply separate details of the numbers in the various 'occupations' included by Booth under this heading (land and house proprietors, mine-owners, ship and boat owners, and persons of independent means). Booth does not give the basis of his estimate, except to observe that it was 'based on the figures given in the two earlier censuses'. The totals for these occupations in previous censuses had been (as stated by Booth):

	1861	*1871*
Male	55·7	49·3
Female	130·0	168·3
Total	185·7	217·6

Evidently Booth's estimate for 1881 (254·8) arose out of the application of the 1861–71 growth rate (17%), to the 1871 figure. The 254·8 was then apparently roughly split between males and females on the basis of the ratios pertaining in 1871. Finally he appears to have arrived at the total of 269·5 male persons 'of indefinite occupation' by deducting all male persons already accounted for as property owners (54·8) from all males (aged 20 and over) in the census occupational order 24 ('persons without specified occupations'). The calculation should yield 270·3.[65]

It is apparent that in a compilation of this scope, the number of errors is very limited, and they are exceedingly slight. Moreover, no census occupation of any significance whatever fails to be incorporated into Booth's 1881 calculations. We were able to verify this by ticking off each occupation on a Xerox copy of the census abstract as the reworking proceeded, and were left with only four occupations which apparently were not included in Booth's groups. These were 'others in books' (65 persons, or 0·1 in Booth's terms), 'others in arms' (28, or nothing in Booth's terms), 'others in food' (26 – again nothing), and 'Peer, MP, privy councillor' (600 or 0·6).

This exercise has enabled the reader to see how Booth's headings were based upon those used in 1881, and how the groupings were arranged, in considerable detail. It also suggests that the standard of accuracy in the rest of Booth's analysis is likely to be high, an impression confirmed by his 1871 tabulation.

XIII

This has been tested by the same means, i.e. comparing the data in the census occupational abstract with that under Booth's standardised headings, using his manuscript list of allocations (which was again virtually complete) as a guide. In the case of 1881 it was important to set out the comparison in detail to allow the reader to perceive how our checking procedure worked, but here we need only present the sectoral totals. In the first column of table 3 we set out the figures for each major sector according to our summation of the relevant census occupations; while in the second Booth's sectoral totals are given.

Table 3   *Test on the composition and size of 11 categories (1871)*

	Our total	Booth's total	Percentage discrepancy
Agriculture and fishing	1,525·2	1,524·9	—
Mining	477·7	474·6	0·7
Building	663·2	664·3	0·2
Manufacture	3,344·7	3,358·5	0·4
Transport	523·3	523·5	—
Dealing	836·7	838·1	0·2
Industrial service	635·6	635·6	—
Public service and Professional	576·2	578·1	0·3
Domestic service	1,682·6	1,683·5	0·1
Property owning and Independent	217·5	217·6	—
Indefinite	124·2	124·2	—
TOTAL	10,606·9	10,622·9	0·2

The discrepancies are all very small, the overall shortfall in our figures arising mainly from not having included a handful of occupations (five in all) for which Booth did not give a specific allocation in his manuscript listing for 1871. There were one or two minute errors in Booth's additions, but nothing which necessitated any correction to his figures, which are printed in appendix D of this chapter as stated in his manuscript volume. The test shows that Booth's work is arithmetically as correct as makes no matter, and we also found this to be the case when checking on the various subdivisions *within* each sector, although details are not shown here, for reasons of space.

XIV

For 1861, Booth had to hand a census occupational abstract of tremendous size, running to 24 pages of closely packed print, and covering some 1,500 different occupations. His manuscript volume shows how the great majority of these were added into his groups, and we were again able to reconstitute along the same lines, ticking off each item on a Xerox copy of the census abstract as it was accounted for. Eventually, having worked our way through Booth's headings, we were left on the one hand with some minor discrepancies between our results and his, and on the other short lists of residual occupations which did not appear to be already accounted for. By matching the two, some discrepancies could be eliminated, and by the same token, our lists of residual occupations reduced (e.g. 'carman, carrier, carter and drayman' – group T.5 – is stated at 67·7 in the census, 68·3 by Booth – without a doubt the 600 (0·6) 'hauliers' on the residual list were added here, although Booth's manuscript listing, not being perfectly complete, did not actually say so). By this means we were able to place all residual occupations of 150 or more (eight male, no female), care being taken to allocate in accordance with Booth's general plan, and also to see that in all such cases the allocations drew our reconstituted group totals *nearer* to Booth's, and not away from them. In appendix E (part A) of this chapter, the reader will find a list covering over 1,000 occupations *specifically allocated* by Booth in his manuscript volume, followed by the short list of allocations we made in the manner described, in appendix E (part B). Then in part C of the appendix there is a list of census occupations which were not allocated by Booth but which, because the numbers involved were individually so small (under 150), could be added in at any point without disturbing Booth's totals in any material respect (we have, however, suggested allocations for them). Finally in part D there is an alphabetical list of all the occupations mentioned in parts A–C and their allocations.

Having carried out these steps, we examined the remaining discrepancies and the points at which our estimates diverged by more than 0·1 from Booth's were as follows (our figures are given first, with Booth's in brackets afterwards):

1. engine and machine maker (MF.1) 69·8 (70·4)
2. domestic machine and bicycle maker (MF.1) 0·9 (1·1)
3. others about animals (AG.3) 2·2 (2·4)
4. mine service (M.1) 3·4 (3·6)
5. coal miner (M.1) 246·6 (248·6)
6. copper miner (M.1) 17·7 (20·7)
7. cutlery, scissor maker (MF.2) 17·1 (16·9)
8. typefounder etc. (MF.2) 3·7 (3·9)
9. iron and steel manufacture (MF.4) 138·9 (139·1)
10. nail, rivet etc: maker (MF.4) 31·0 (31·2)
11. copper manufacture (MF.5) 9·7 (6·8)
12. others (working in mixed metals) (MF.5) 2·4 (2·7)
13. earthenware, china etc. manufacture (MF.7) 38·1 (38·3)
14. others in coal etc. (MF.8) 3·7 (3·9)
15. matches, fuzees etc. (MF.9) 1·4 (1·8)
16. tanner etc. (MF.10) 10·9 (11·2)
17. cotton manufacture (MF.19) 457·6 (457·8)
18. crape, gauze etc. manufacture (MF.19) 6·5 (6·2)

19. weavers, spinners, factory hands (textiles) (MF.19) 17·5 (14·5)
20. flax and linen manufacture (MF.20) 22·3 (22·1)
21. others in flax and hemp (MF.20) 1·0 (0·8)
22. artificial flower makers and others (MF.21) 5·7 (5·9)
23. hatters (MF.24). Booth's stated allowance of three-quarters of the numbers of hatters here is incorrect and should be 10·5 (not 9·2), since there were 13·8 hatters
24. glovers (MF.24) 28·5 (27·8)
25. others in dress (MF.24) 1·0 (1·2)
26. leather goods manufacture (MF.25) 2·8 (3·2)
27. lithographic printer etc. (MF.30) 4·8 (4·6)
28. factory labour (undefined) (MF.31) 6·2 (6·4)
29. wheelchair etc. proprietor, driver (T.5) 0·7 (0·9)
30. coal labourer, heaver (D.1) 17·4 (15·4)
31. timber merchant (D.2) 9·9 (9·7)
32. hatter (D.4) (see 23 above) 3·3 (4·6)
33. greengrocer etc. (D.5) 19·7 (19·9)
34. hawkers, hucksters etc. (D.12) 40·4 (40·6)
35. general labour (IS.2) 309·8 (310·0)
36. government messenger, workman (PP.1) 16·4 (16·6)
37. figure and image maker (PP.9) 1·3 (1·6)
38. scientific pursuits (PP.12) 0·3 (0·5)
39. other teachers (PP.13) 59·3 (59·6)
40. club, college, institutional service (DS.1) 7·7 (8·0)
41. indefinite occupations (males) 82·1 (81·9)

Obviously, although there are a fair number of discrepancies, the magnitude of the error is in nearly all cases very slight. Discrepancies have doubtless arisen mainly from two causes – (a) Booth's system of addition, since as previously mentioned the addition of several rounded figures (the age groups), may result in a figure somewhat different from the rounded total census figure for the occupation which we took, and (b) the fact that in some cases it was not perfectly clear which (very minor) occupations were, or were not, included by Booth. Thus, in most of these cases, the Booth figure is slightly higher than ours. Further matching from the residual list (part C of appendix E) could no doubt have eliminated still more discrepancies.

Once again, Booth's arithmetic and close adherence to his stated principles of allocation stand up to the test well – in this case a most exhaustive and detailed test. We deemed it unnecessary to make minor corrections, so that, in appendix D, Booth's figures stand.

XV

When we pass on to the 1851 census we have to adopt a less rigorous procedure than that applied to 1861–81. In principle, the census occupational classification did not differ greatly from that of 1861, since it was prepared on the same plan of 17 orders. But where the 1861 national return was extremely detailed, the 1851 return telescoped a large number of relatively less important occupations. (A detailed return similar to that of 1861 was published, but only for Great Britain as a whole, i.e. England, Wales, Scotland.) Furthermore, Booth's manuscript does not contain a specific list of allocations for 1851.

Since it would be a lengthy task to trace the allocation of every occupation mentioned in the national abstract (especially for Booth's large and diverse manufacturing and dealing sectors), we set out to trace only the constitution of the other sectors, using the 1861 list as a guide. As for 1881, 1871 and 1861, the method was to check all occupational headings (of Booth's 1861 list) against those in the abstract. Once again, we wished to see whether our summation of what appeared to be the relevant occupations in each sector agreed with Booth's and that there were no occupations which had been ignored by Booth but which ought to have been included in one or other of these sectors. Again, perfect correspondence was not to be expected because of (a) the possibility of slight arithmetical mistakes by ourselves or Booth, (b) his usual practice of adding rounded figures, and (c) the absence of precise details of allocation for 1851 (not given in the manuscript volume). Even so, the discrepancies in nine sectors turned out to be exceedingly small, demonstrating once again the fundamental accuracy of Booth's arithmetical work and his close adherence to the principles of allocation which we have set out in detail for 1881 and 1861 (for, if there had been notable errors, or classification changes, the results of the reworking would have been very different).

Table 4 *Test on the composition and size of nine categories for 1851*

Sector	Our total	Booth's total	Percentage discrepancy
Agriculture and fishing	1,776·7	1,776·8	—
Mining	332·4	335·2	0·8
Building	459·7	460·7	0·2
Transport	346·2	345·3	0·3
Industrial service	376·5	376·6	—
Public service and professional	400·3	399·7	0·2
Domestic service	1,121·2	1,121·2	—
Property owning	211·3	211·4	—
Indefinite class	101·0	100·5	0·5
Total for these categories	5,125·3	5,127·4	—

Next, we established the size of the dependent class, within the scope of Booth's definition. (Our result, 9,497·4, compared with 9,499·0 by Booth.) Subtracting the sum of all these results (14,622·7) from the total population of

1851 (17,927·6), should yield the equivalent of the sum of the remaining Booth sectors, manufacture and dealing. Our figure for the combined group was 3,304·9, as against Booth's stated figure of 3,301·5 (discrepancy 0·1 per cent).

These results do not indicate that Booth's figures are necessarily correct for each subdivision *within* the major sectors referred to, but once again any discrepancies found were exceedingly small in the close examination of the detailed categories and we have no reason to suspect that they would be any larger in the manufacturing and dealing sectors, had we examined them in the same detail. His breakdown of the 1851 census thus passes our test with flying colours.

XVI

The census occupational abstract for 1841 is a formless alphabetical list of great size, covering some 900 stated occupations, many of which are very small. (aeronaut 1, bee-dealer 1, coral-carver 5 etc.) In this case, since once again no specific list of attributions is given in Booth's manuscript, we set out to test Booth's accuracy and consistency by summing all census occupations along the lines suggested by his 1861 list. Comparative results for ten categories are given in table 5.

Table 5   *Test on the composition and size of ten categories for 1841*

Sector	Our total	Booth's total	Percentage discrepancy
Agriculture and fishing	1,299·0	1,307·8	0·7
Mining	209·3	210·1	0·4
Building	350·5	352·5	0·6
Transport	146·7	148·4	1·1
Industrial service	352·6	359·6	1·9
Public service and professional	236·7	239·8	1·3
Domestic service	1,067·0	1,078·3	1·0
Manufacture ⎱ Dealing ⎰	2,130·0	2,149·2	0·8
Property owning	447·3	448·1	0·2

The discrepancies encountered are in all cases very small, again indicating that Booth's arithmetic was accurate and that the principles of allocation had been consistently adhered to. This was also found to be the case when we examined his various subdivisions for every category except manufacture and dealing. It will be noticed that our sectoral results are consistently slightly lower than his, but this is of no importance. Faced with multitudinous minor occupations which do not figure at all in *our* results (being individually less than 0·1 in size), Booth obviously departed from his usual practice of ignoring them (a procedure which was quite justifiable where the abstract was telescoped, and there were few such occupations, as in later censuses), and some allowance must have been made. We have not, however, been able to discover how Booth arrived at totals for the 'indefinite' group (336·9), and for dependents (9,281·1). In appendix D these two categories together form a total of 9,618·0. The residuum when our figures for the categories listed in table 5 are subtracted from the total population is 9,672·7, a discrepancy of 0·6 per cent when compared with the combined Booth figure for the indefinite and dependent groups.

XVII

In sections XII–XVI of this chapter, we have been following the first two of the four aims mentioned on pages 233–4. The third opportunity which the existence of Booth's manuscript offers is the extension of the national aggregative analysis to 1891. This is not a difficult task, since between 1881 and 1891 no fundamental changes in the principles of census classification took place. Not that the census authorities were insensitive to their critics inside and outside government departments – by using further columns on the householder's schedule, an attempt was made to distinguish between employers, employees and self-employed persons, but the results, it was held, were 'excessively untrustworthy'. (This does not affect our calculations in any way.) Some changes were also made in the age periods under which the persons engaged in any occupation were divided – whereas previously the groupings had been 5–, 15–, 20–, 25–, 45–, 65– (1881), these were now altered to 10–, 15–, 20–, 25–, 35–, 45–, 55–, 65– (1891). At first sight, this change would seem to invalidate any comparison between Booth's 1881 results and our 1891 results, not because the age groupings over 15 matter (we have not differentiated by age in our tables), but because employed males aged 5–9 are included in the 1881 (and earlier) series, but are completely excluded in 1891. However, this is not so serious as it might seem at first glance, for the census authorities commented that there were 'few if any children under 10 years of age in any occupation'. Since the occupied children aged 5–14 were to all intents and purposes the same as occupied children aged 10–14, valid comparison still can be made.[66]

A further attempt was made to cope with the dealer question to meet the old criticism that distribution was not kept separate from production. 'We would say that, though in economical treatises a broad line is drawn between production and distribution, in actual life the two are by no means so distinct, the maker and the retail seller being very frequently the same person: and further that, when the two are distinct persons, they very generally have one and the same title...Wishing, however, as far as possible to meet the views of our critics we have introduced into the classification fresh headings whenever it seemed probable that dealers might be separated, at any rate to some extent, from makers.'[67] It should be noted that in this study (as it concerns 1891) we have added such groups of dealers back into makers, in order to preserve comparability. Faced with an occupation such as 'trimming maker, dealer' (1881 and previous censuses), Booth perforce had to treat all as makers, adding them into the relevant subgroup of the manufacturing sector. In 1891 it would appear that trimming makers as such are listed under that heading, but that any dealers would have been included under the heading 'other dealers in mixed or unspecified materials'. Our purpose in making such adjustments is of course to attempt to keep the manufacturing section comparable with Booth's earlier sector, and to confine the 'dealing' sector in our 1891 calculations to the relatively restricted range of occupations which Booth had hitherto included there. But the point is actually much less important than might at first seem to be the case: the numbers separately distinguished as dealers by the census authorities are exceedingly small.

Lastly, although the census plan of classification of 1881 was adhered to, there was a certain amount of alteration of individual headings. Some of the 1881 headings were simply subdivided, as with the 1881 occupation 'harbour, dock, wharf, lighthouse – officials and servants'. Generally speaking, such subdivisions caused no difficulty since comparability could be arrived at by simply adding them back together. More frequent were amalgamations of occupations kept distinct in the previous censuses. Very often this was unimportant since it happened that the occupations being amalgamated had actually been in the same Booth group at earlier dates. For example, 'seaman (merchant service), pilot, ship steward and cook, boatman on seas', were amalgamated under one general heading; this causes no difficulty since all the occupations separately distinguished in 1881 were actually in the same Booth subdivision. (Transport, T.2)

There were, however, a number of cases where occupations hitherto placed in *different* Booth subgroups were amalgamated, and estimates had to be made, distinguishing the sexes where necessary.[68] The important difficulties, with their solutions are listed below:

(1) 'Nurseryman, seedsman, florist' (Booth group AG.1) and 'gardener – not domestic' (also group AG.1) were amalgamated with 'gardeners – domestic' (Booth group DS.2). We split the totals for 1891 in accordance with ratios suggested by the relative sizes for each occupation in 1881. Six estimates (3 male, 3 female) were thus obtained and we added those for 'nurseryman etc. and gardeners – not domestic', into group AG.1, removing the remainder (for 'gardeners – domestic'), to group DS.2.

(2) 'Horse proprietor, breeder, dealer' (Booth group AG.3 in 1881) was now combined with 'omnibus, coach, cab owner and livery stable keeper' (T.5). Again this was split by ratios suggested by their relative importance in 1881. Horse proprietors etc. were then placed in group AG.3 and 'omnibus, coach, cab owner, etc.' in T.5. In this case, all females (0·3) were placed in T.5, since there had been no female horse proprietors in 1881.

(3) 'Groom, horse-keeper, horse-breaker' (AG.3) was now amalgamated with

'domestic coachman, groom' (DS.2) and 'cabman, flyman, coachman – not domestic' (T.5). Again these were split by ratios suggested by their relative size in 1881 and placed in the appropriate Booth subgroups.

(4) 'Veterinary surgeon and farrier' had constituted one census occupation in 1881 (AG.3), but in 1891 farriers were included with 'blacksmiths' and 'white-smiths' (MF.4 and MF.5 – a further but distinct difficulty, see below). Veterinary surgeons were now separately distinguished. It seemed best to assume that the veterinary surgeon/farrier group had increased by the same percentage as horse-proprietors, breeders, dealers and omnibus, coach, cab owners, livery stable keepers, between 1881 and 1891 (it follows that our estimate for farriers and veterinary surgeons combined less the actual stated figure for veterinary surgeons, would yield an estimate for farriers.)

(5) 'Mining engineers' (M.1) and 'civil engineers' (B.1) are combined in 1891. We split these by the 1881 proportions and allocated to the appropriate groups.

(6) 'Contractor – undefined' (B.1) is amalgamated with 'manufacturer – undefined' (MF.31). The same procedure of splitting by 1881 proportions was used, all females (0·9) being placed in MF.31 since there were no female contractors in 1881.

(7) 'Blacksmith' (MF.4) is combined with 'whitesmith' (MF.5) and 'farrier'. Deducting our estimate for farriers (see point (4) above), we split the residue according to 1881 proportions and allocated accordingly. Since there were no female whitesmiths in 1881, all females in this group (0·5), were treated as blacksmiths.

(8) 'Currier' (MF.10) is amalgamated with 'leather goods, strap, portmanteau, bag maker and dealer' (MF.24). These were split according to 1881 proportions.

(9) The 1881 occupation 'timber merchant, dealer' (D.2) obviously contained many wood workers which Booth would undoubtedly have placed in group MF.13 if they had been separately distinguished. In 1891 these were distinguished and the further complication was added that the 1881 occupation 'cork, bark cutter, worker, dealer' (also MF.13) was split between workers and dealers, the latter actually being included under the heading of 'timber, wood merchant, dealer'. The problem is best understood if the numbers in the various relevant occupations are set out.

1881
(a) Timber, wood merchant, dealer	12·8	(11·8 M 1·0 F)
(b) Cork, bark cutter, worker, dealer	1·9	(1·7 M 0·2 F)
(c) Others (wood and bark)	0·3	(0·3 M 0·0 F)

1891
(a) Timber, wood, cork, bark merchant, dealer	8·4	(8·1 M 0·3 F)
(b) Cork, bark cutter, worker	2·1	(1·7 M 0·4 F)
(c) Others working in wood, cork, bark, etc.	8·7	(7·5 M 1·2 F)

First, we have assumed that the occupations 1881 (b) and 1891 (b) can be equated (there is no reason to suppose that the 1891 timber merchant category would be significantly smaller than 8·4 even if we were able to remove the cork dealers). This gave 2·1 for inclusion in MF.13. Secondly, we added together the occupations (a) and (c) for 1891 and split according to the proportions under these headings for 1881: thus 0·4 persons were retained in MF.13 and 16·7 were passed to D.2.

(10) 'cabinet maker' (MF.14), 'french polisher' (MF.14) and 'furniture broker, dealer' (D.9) were combined in 1891. Again, these were split on the basis of relative numbers in 1881 and allocated accordingly.

(11) 'accoutrement maker' (MF.24) was amalgamated with 'old clothes dealer' (D.4). These also were split according to 1881 proportions.

(12) 'Oil miller, oil cake maker, dealer' (MF.25) was split between workers and dealers, the dealers now being included with 'oil and colourmen' (D.5). This resulted in a small decline for the first-mentioned occupation. We assumed no decline, therefore adding a small allowance in group MF.25 (in effect, to regain the dealers), and subtracting the same from group D.5. (The numbers involved here were exceedingly small.)

(13) Coke, charcoal, peat cutter, burner, dealer (MF.8) was split between workers and dealers in 1891, dealers being included with 'coal merchants and dealers' (D.1). But since no fall is registered for 'coke etc. cutters and burners', it is difficult to believe that the modest rise in the number of coal merchants has been much affected by the addition of dealers in coke etc. No correction has been made.

(14) 'Army and Navy pensioners' (PP.4, PP.5) were simply included with all other pensioners and retired persons in 1891. Estimates were made by assuming that their numbers had grown by the same proportion as the active services (at home) during the decade. These estimates were deducted from the retired class (see below).

(15) In 1881, agriculture (AG.1), law (PP.7), medical (PP.8) art and theological students (PP.14) were separately distinguished, whereas in 1891 they were all incorporated into a new group 'students, 15 years or over'. However, this group obviously contained a great variety of students besides the specialist students mentioned above. Estimates for three of these were made by assuming that their numbers had risen by the percentage growth of the age-group 15–19 between the two census dates. For the medical students the position was more difficult, since in 1881 they had been included with medical assistants. The medical assistants (an unknown proportion of the combined group) were now subsumed (in unknown numbers) into 'subordinate medical service' in 1891. To arrive at a figure for these students, we assumed that their numbers bore the same relationship to principals in their profession (physicians etc.) as did law students to barristers, solicitors etc. (one-tenth). What would be an absurd assumption if one's attention was focused on the history of medical education becomes quite unimportant when we are dealing with aggregates of the magnitude of those

found in this study. (The sum of these estimates was 10·9, which was deducted from the general group 'students, 15 years and over').

(16) Were we to take the 1891 entry for indoor domestic servants at face value, the numbers would rise from 1,286·7 in 1881 to 1,444·7 in 1891; it was to fall again to 1,333·0 in 1901. However, the sharp rise between 1881 and 1891 was caused by a perverse decision to include with domestics all those *female relatives and daughters* returned as 'helping at home', 'housework' etc. In 1881, and again in 1901 and 1911, they were quite properly included in the unoccupied class. Thus 'the rate of increase for female domestic servants, which had been as low as 1·9 per cent in 1871–81, was returned as 12·7 per cent for 1881–91, and was followed by a decrease of 4·0 per cent in 1901 from the inflated number included in the previous census'.[69] We have made estimates for 1891 by averaging figures for 1881 and 1901, removing the excess to the dependent class (128·3 females), or indefinite class (6·4 males).

(17) In censuses prior to 1881, figures for the numbers of land and house proprietors, mine, ship and boat owners, were stated. Close reference to Booth's grouping of property owners for 1861 (in his manuscript volume) shows that he also included here those under such headings as peer, M.P., magistrate, capitalist, shareholder, gentleman (and woman), independent. Lacking this information for 1881, he constructed estimates 'based on the figures given in the two earlier censuses'. The estimate for property owners for 1881 was given as 254·8 (54·8 males, 200·0 females), and we saw that Booth's 1881 estimate arose out of the application of the 1861–71 growth (17 per cent) to the 1871 figure. If the same rate of increase were again applied between 1881 and 1891, the result would be an estimated size of 298·0 for this group. On the other hand, the census data actually refers to a category 'living on own means', to which 506·6 are allocated. We have preferred this figure for simplicity's sake, but obviously this is not comparable with the estimates for earlier years (1841–81), and these in turn are far from being reliably comparable among themselves. All statements of the size of such categories at any point in the nineteenth-century censuses are quite unreliable, and Booth himself pointed out that propertied class figures, even where (up to 1871) they were based on direct census statements rather than estimates, were 'entirely delusive'.[70] Many students will wish to throw the propertied and indefinite classes together in their final tables, as Booth himself did (see table 1), and we ourselves have preferred to class them with the unoccupied in the final analysis (see table 6 and appendix D).

(18) Retired persons were included with their respective trades until 1871, but in 1881 appear to have been included in census order 24 'persons without specified occupations'. Booth rated this distinction as of little practical importance, since it appeared to result in only a small increase in the size of the indefinite class.

In 1891 we are somewhat better placed to assess this, since 193·0 males and 68·0 females are distinctively listed as retired persons. 193·0 out of an occupied male population of 8,883·0 (aged 10 and upwards) is about 2·2 per cent: for females the totals are 68·0 and 4,016·0 or about 1·7 per cent. Clearly, while this difference between the earlier and later series of figures needs to be kept in mind (i.e. that up to and including 1871 the retired are classed in their trades and from 1881 are not), it is not a matter which gravely affects the figures for the other sectors. Booth appears to have been correct in attaching little importance to it.

The retired are one of the main components in the indefinite male class defined on Booth's principles. This comprises 'others', retired, pensioners and students (all 20 and over). We deducted 21·0 for military pensioners (see point 14 above), the residual figure standing at 353·8.

The dependent class, again following Booth, comprehended only persons of uncertain occupation under the age of 20, for males: (viz. 'others' 10–19, all males aged 0–9 and students 15–19 less the estimates for art, medical, law and agricultural students (see point 15 above). For females, the dependent class comprised all those of no specific occupation at any age i.e. the retired, pen-

Table 6   *Distribution of occupations according to Booth's principles, 1891*

| Sector | Absolute numbers | | | Percentage | |
	Male	Female	Total	(a) of occupied population	(b) of total population
Agriculture, fishing	1,244·5	51·9	1,296·4	10·2	4·5
Mining	669·5	7·6	677·1	5·4	2·3
Building	832·9	2·8	835·7	6·6	2·9
Manufacture	2,608·8	1,529·8	4,138·6	32·7	14·3
Transport	816·4	10·0	826·4	6·5	2·8
Dealing	851·3	298·0	1,149·3	9·1	4·0
Industrial service	885·6	20·8	906·4	7·2	3·1
Public service and Professional	563·0	265·2	828·2	6·5	2·9
Domestic service	358·9	1,632·4	1,991·3	15·7	6·9
Total (occupied)	8,830·9	3,818·5	12,649·4	99·9	43·7
Property owners: independent means (97·5 M, 409·1 F)					
Indefinite (353·8 M, 0·0 F)			16,353·1*		56·4
Dependants (4,771·0 M, 10,722·0 F)					
Total population			29,002·5		100·1

* N.B. A tiny adjustment has been made to this total, involving subtraction of 0·3 to ensure that the grand total can be equated with the population figure for the year. The discrepancy doubtless arises from the fact that estimates had to be made for certain occupations not separately stated (see text), but it should be realised that the error is only about 1 part in 90,000.

sioners, 'others' (10 and over), students and all females under 10 (again, following Booth's principles).

This list of adjustments and estimates may seem to be formidable but in fact there is a fairly high degree of comparability between the two census dates, and with only a few exceptions the major occupations can be said to have been comparable: it will have been noticed that our difficulties arose not with coal miners, workers in the textile and metal trades, agricultural labourers, food retailers etc., but with occupations of far less numerical significance.

We set out our findings on a sector-by-sector basis in table 6; fuller details under Booth's subheadings are given in appendix D.

XVIII

In these pages, we have been able to publish for the first time, virtually full details of the allocation of census abstract occupations under Booth's standardised headings. In sections XII–XVI it has been shown that in general his arithmetical working was highly accurate, so that in appendix D no attempt has been made to make minor corrections. This gives a detailed breakdown, by sex, of the national data at each census date (1841–81, with the addition of 1891), under Booth's headings. These are stated at three levels, viz:

(1) Nine major *industrial sectors* (agriculture and fishing, mining, building, manufacture, transport, dealing, industrial service, public service and professional, domestic service). The 'indefinite' and 'property owning and independent' categories have been included with the remaining part of the population (dependents), as the residual element in the population.

(2) Within the 9 major sectors, 79 *industrial subgroups*, following Booth. (agriculture and fishing 4, mining 4, building, 3, manufacture 31, transport 5, dealing 13, industrial service 2, public service and professional 14, domestic service 3).

(3) 346 occupational headings, based on those used in the 1881 census. (e.g. in MF.10, furriers and skinners: tanners, fellmongers, parchment makers: curriers). While some of these are clearly industrial in character, e.g. iron manufacture (MF.4), cotton manufacture (MF.19), we shall call these *occupational subheadings*, for simplicity's sake.

Our series of checks on Booth's results for 1841–81, serves to confirm the reliability of Booth's work for the national historian, but the main utility of the present study lies in its application to local, urban or regional history. Firstly, *printed* census data may now be arranged along Booth's lines without departing from his principles in any material respect at any date. This can be achieved by scrutiny of the details for 1881 (see above section XII) and for 1861 (appendix E). A uniform basis is thus made available for comparing communities with one another at any particular census date, while national tabulations are set out to correspond. Furthermore, such comparisons may be extended over time from one census to another in the knowledge that if perfect comparability is impossible this is the best available approximation to it.

It will be evident that the level of comparability which is attainable will be greatest at the level of the nine major industrial sectors. However much occupations were juggled at the census office, there is comparatively little danger of overlap or transpositions from one *sector* to another between census years, or of misallocations, given the details we have set out for 1881 and 1861. There may be some slight possibility of overlap between 'agriculture' and 'domestic service', (in respect of coachmen, grooms etc.), and possibly between 'dealers (unspecified)' and 'industrial service' where the world of agents, salesmen, buyers etc. inevitably shades over into that of commercial services. But the mining, building, transport, public service and professional sectors are well-defined, as is manufacture, apart from the unavoidable inclusion of a proportion of dealers.

Comparability at the level of the seventy-nine industrial subgroups will be rather less reliable, owing to two distinct causes. Firstly, some of Booth's industrial subgroups are conceptually not very sharply distinguished from others. For example, D.12 (general dealers) and D.13 (dealers unspecified) does not seem to involve a clear distinction, though reference to appendix E below suggests that Booth was trying to include petty businessmen in D.12, while D.13 includes many factors and agents. The distinctions made under MF.18, 19, 20 and 21 (textile industries), are sometimes rather arbitrary, while MF.1 (machinery) and MF.2 (tools), may well overlap to a certain extent. Secondly a separate kind of minor practical difficulty may emerge when arranging local data where the occupational headings used at the local level differ slightly from those of the national abstract. Usually, this will involve the more generous use of 'others' in a particular order for the local distribution. For example, if reference is made to the male occupational order IX (1861), 'persons engaged about animals', the national abstract distinguishes twenty-one subheadings, but the table for the West Riding of Yorkshire only eleven. Riding master, horse clipper, huntsman, castrator, knacker, dog dealer, rabbit catcher, animal and bird dealer, officer at menagerie or zoological gardens, and fish breeder would appear to have been subsumed under 'others about animals'. Or again, while no less than fifty-seven headings are used in the national abstract for census order X (10) 'in machines and tools', the return for Sheffield distinguishes only twelve, with a sizeable number under the heading 'others in tools, machines', raising some doubts about whether MF.1 (machinery) or MF.2 (tools) is the appropriate group.

At the level of the 346 occupational subheadings, comparability is least assured. As the national figures alone show (appendix D of this chapter) a given occupational heading across the years may exhibit erratic and improbable behaviour. Examples are given in the notes to appendix D. It follows that the series given under each such heading may not always faithfully represent the trend. On the other hand, shifts among the occupational subheadings will often leave industrial subgroup and sectoral totals unaffected. A case in point is probably to be found in MF.5 (copper, tin, lead etc. 1851), where Booth comments that an unduly large number under the occupational heading 'others in copper, tin, lead, etc.' is accountable for, and offset by 'a corresponding deficiency in the other items of the section' (see note xiii, appendix D). Similarly, the remarkably modest rise in the number of 'coal miners' (M.1) between 1861 and 1871 is almost certainly caused by the inclusion of many such miners under the heading 'miners in other or undefined minerals'.

As a general rule, these difficulties are best circumvented by operating at the level of the nine major industrial sectors, using judicious combinations among the seventy-nine industrial subgroups where overlap is suspected and where local conditions seem to require it. Essentially, this is what Booth himself did, for in the final published analysis, the number of separate sub-divisions was drastically reduced as follows:

1. *Agriculture and fishing*: here the number of industrial subgroups was (exceptionally) raised from 4 to 6, distinguishing the agricultural labourers and nurserymen, gardeners, etc. as separate entities.
2. *Mining*: reduction from 4 to 3 subdivisions, by combining M.2 and M.3 as 'quarrying and brickmaking'.
3. *Building*: no change.
4. *Manufacture*: reduction from 31 to 14 subdivisions, entailing the combination of MF.1 and MF.2 as 'machinery and tools'; MF.4, 5 and 6 as 'metal workers'; MF.8 and 9 as 'fuel, gas and chemicals'; MF.10, 11 and 12 as 'furs, leather, glue etc.'; MF.13, 14, and 15 as 'wood, furniture and carriages'; MF.16 and 17 as 'paper, floorcloth and waterproof'; MF.18, 19, 20, 21, and 22 as 'textiles and dyeing'; MF.23 and 24 as 'dress'; MF.25, 26, 27, 28 as 'food, drink and smoking'.
5. *Transport*: reduction from 5 to 3 subdivisions, entailing the combination of T.1, 2 and 3 as 'navigation and docks'.
6. *Dealing*: reduction from 13 to 6 subdivisions, by combining D.1 and D.2 as 'raw materials'; D.3 and D.4 as 'clothing materials and dress'; D.5, 6, 7 as 'food, drink and smoking'; D.9, 10, 11 as 'furniture, utensils, stationery'; D.12 and D.13 as 'general dealers and unspecified'.
7. *Industrial service*: no change.
8. *Public service and Professional*: reduction from 14 to 9 subdivisions, by combining PP.1, 2 and 3 as 'administration'; PP.4 and 5 as 'army and navy'; PP.9 and 10 as 'art and amusement'; PP.11 and 12 as 'literature and science'.
9. *Domestic service*: no change.

Sometimes the combinations which Booth himself employed will serve a particular purpose very well, but once having arranged the data along Booth's lines all sorts of alternative combinations among the seventy-nine industrial

I

subgroups may be tried. One of the outstanding properties of this scheme is, indeed, the flexibility which it offers while at the same time permitting systematic comparisons with other work drawn up along the same lines.

An example of the use of this scheme of industrial classification is given below where Booth's principles have been applied to Bath and to Sheffield (1861).

Table 7

	Percentage of total population		Percentage of occupied population	
	Male	Female	Male	Female
Bath (borough)				
Agriculture, fishing	4·81	0·05	7·57	0·12
Mining	0·34	—	0·53	0·02
Building	8·59	—	13·50	0·02
Manufacture	17·28	10·51	27·17	24·96
(MF.23, dress	5·11	9·31	8·03	22·11)
Transport	6·01	0·06	9·44	0·13
Dealing	9·44	2·78	14·84	6·59
Industrial service	5·34	0·14	8·40	0·32
Public service and Professional	7·70	2·44	12·10	5·78
Domestic service	4·10	26·13	6·45	62·06
Property owning, Independent	2·26	6·52	—	—
Indefinite	0·90	—	—	—
Dependants	33·24	51·37	—	—
TOTAL	100·01	100·00	100·00	100·00
Sheffield (borough)				
Agriculture, fishing	1·75	0·08	2·71	0·41
Mining	1·83	—	2·84	0·05
Building	4·53	—	7·03	0·03
Manufacture	41·29	7·35	64·05	38·50
(MF.1,2,4,5,6, metal manufacture	32·45	2·60	50·34	13·64)
Transport	2·93	0·98	4·55	5·13
Dealing	5·61	1·56	8·71	8·17
Industrial service	3·47	0·03	5·38	0·14
Public service and Professional	2·48	0·79	3·85	4·12
Domestic service	0·57	8·29	0·89	43·44
Property owning, Independent	0·21	0·62	—	—
Indefinite	1·00	—	—	—
Dependants	34·32	80·29	—	—
TOTAL	99·99	99·99	100·01	99·99

These examples were chosen with a view to testing how far the method would be successful in drawing out the differences between a centre of conspicuous consumption on the one hand, and a great industrial city on the other. Striking contrasts in fact emerge, notably in the manufacturing, dealing, public service and professional, and domestic service sectors. In manufacture, Sheffield's commitment to the metalworking trades is underlined, while 'dress' accounted for a large proportion of workers in the Bath manufacturing group. 'Dealing', i.e. the distributive trades, was significantly stronger in Bath, and the 'public service and professional' group was, relatively, about three times as well-represented there. While most occupied females were in domestic service in both communities, they were exceptionally numerous in Bath, where, by contrast, the proportion of 'dependent' females was much lower than in Sheffield. This suggests that one might expect to encounter large numbers of single females in Bath, attracted there to domestic service, and is borne out when other relevant census statistics are examined (sex ratios, 1,533 females to 1,000 males in Bath, 1,010:1,000 in Sheffield: percentage of females who were single, 48·9 in Bath, 28·4 in Sheffield).[71]

Obviously, arrangement of the occupational data along these lines, involving aggregative comparisons, need not mean that the student should stop at that point. In any study of Sheffield, it would obviously be important to proceed to consider the component occupations under MF.1, 2, 4, 5 and 6 in the fullest detail that the census allows, while the same industrial subgroups in Bath would hardly merit much attention. There are many further highly suggestive pointers in the printed volumes (e.g. of army personnel whose rank is known, in Bath there were 28 other ranks and 228 officers; in Sheffield 552 other ranks and 28 officers etc.).

XIX

Although Booth's analysis was initially designed only to take account of the national census abstracts, through elaborating the details we have shown how it may be applied to smaller units for which printed occupational data is available, such as counties, registration districts and the larger towns,[72] to produce interesting results.

Booth's scheme, however, can be applied not simply to printed census occupational data, but also to occupational data on *individuals*, as contained in the original enumerators' books. This may prove useful in two sets of circumstances,

1. Where the unit of study (a village, parish, or small town) is not sufficiently large to appear separately in occupational tabulations in the printed volumes.
2. Where the aim is not simply to describe and comment on patterns which the printed occupational data reveals, but rather to *relate* this data to other variables. It is one thing to show what proportion of the active population was employed in the transport sector, or in a subsection of it, such as rail

transport; the required information may be obtained straight from the census volumes, then arranged in the manner we have described. But if the researcher is equally, or more interested in, say, what proportion of the transport workers were immigrants, what proportion were aged below 30, what proportion were married etc. then it will be necessary to go back to the enumerators' books.

Both situations raise the question of how far Booth's categories can be applied to the *original* data, and since no attempt has yet been made to do so, only tentative comments can be made. Firstly, it is undoubtedly true that the researcher will encounter a number of occupational terms not listed by Booth even in the very detailed 1861 list given below in appendix E, which covers over 1,000 designations. But with equal certainty by far the greater *proportion* of individual respondents would have used terms which *are* contained in Booth's lists,[73] and it should not prove difficult to allocate the relatively small and probably statistically insignificant residue with the aid of a dictionary (e.g. cordwainer = shoemaker etc.)[74] Another point to bear in mind is that where occupations were split by Booth for the purpose of 'estimates', it would be necessary to allocate accordingly; e.g. the first goldsmith could go in MF.6, the second in D.11, and so on, in a systematic manner. Similarly, every fourth hatter would be placed in D.4 etc. (they could easily be recombined if necessary). This procedure would, at any rate, permit the allocation of occupations on a broad industrial basis from 1841 to 1861 and for 1871 and 1881 as the enumerators' books become available. On the other hand the relative complexity of the adjustments and splitting techniques we have used in advancing Booth's method to 1891 would seem at present to preclude its use for any purpose other than that for which it was drawn up, i.e. to facilitate the handling of *printed* census data.

In general of course, where the scheme is applied to data in census enumerators' books, it would again be advisable to conduct much of the analysis at the level of the nine sectors and seventy-nine industrial subgroups. This will tend to reduce the effects of misallocation under the 346 occupational subheadings, and on the other hand maximise comparability between studies carried out using Booth's scheme as a basis. This does not mean that *no* analysis should be carried out at the level of individual occupations. Tin-miners in Cornwall, for example, are too important for them to appear only as an indistinguishable element within industrial subgroup M.1, and separate identification of tin miners as a group would be necessary.

To conclude: it is believed that the scheme outlined above, with its nine major sectors and seventy-nine industrial subgroups, should meet many of the needs of those working on censuses. It possesses great flexibility, in that by using seventy-nine categories, a great variety of combinations are possible. Like the preceding social class section, it offers a basis of comparability which need not and should not inhibit experimentation with alternative schemes.

Appendix D. Detailed breakdown of Booth's occupational groups 1841–1891.

NOTES

1. The material in this appendix is drawn directly from Booth's manuscript volume, using his standardized occupational headings and aggregative groupings. He printed this data (for 1841–81) in a somewhat compressed form, entailing a reduction in the number of separate subdivisions, in the 1886 article, together with an important explanation of its coverage. 'All males over 20 years of age are counted as in some sense self-supporting, but no male under 20, or female of any age, is counted as self-supporting or occupied unless stated to be so in the census. The partially employed wives are throughout treated as *not* self-supporting, according to the principle adopted in the census of 1881. All males over 20 who are not returned as definitely employed or as independent have been placed in the indefinite class, which represents the residuum after all claims to definite occupations have been allowed. All males under 20, and all females who are not returned as occupied, have been considered as dependents.'

It will be seen that under such a system of classification, the whole of the population is covered for each census. Any person must be either 'definitely employed' (the area of employment being specified); or 'property-owner/independent'; or 'indefinite'; or, 'dependent'. The *definitely* employed are made up in Booth's study as follows:

	Subdivisions in original MSS. (Reproduced here)	Subdivisions in Booth's printed article
Agriculture ⎱ Fishing ⎰	4	6
Mining	4	3
Building	3	3
Manufacture	31	14
Transport	5	3
Dealing	13	6
Industrial service	2	2
Public service and Professional	14	9
Domestic service	3	3
Total	79	49

(For details of the combinations see page 249).

To these nine principal industrial divisions of the *occupied* population Booth added, as further sectors, the 'property-owning/independent' and the 'indefinite' categories,

253

both in his manuscript volume and in the published article. A major rearrangement which has been made in the following pages is to confine the occupied population to the industrial sectors mentioned above, and to place 'property-owners', 'indefinite' etc. with dependants in the residual part of the population (see above, pp. 229 and 245).

Apart from this adjustment, the only difference between the data given here and that in Booth's manuscript volume is that, for reasons of space, we have not provided an age breakdown.

2. No arithmetical corrections have been made to the figures given in Booth's manuscript, since it was evident that any errors of this nature were few and insignificant.

3. To Booth's figures for 1841–81 we have appended the results arrived at for 1891.

4. Most of the marginal notes in Booth's manuscript volume are printed here, the chief exceptions being his references to his series for 1831, which was not used. (Booth did not think it worthwhile including his 1831 tabulation in the printed article, since the census occupational returns for that year were of 'an incomplete character'.)

5. It will be noticed that the series of figures given under *individual occupational headings* is sometimes erratic, owing to changes in the census classification of occupations (see pp. 248–9 and notes to table), and no doubt to a series of seasonal and other factors. Cases in point are an apparent fall in the numbers of surveyors (B.1) between 1871 and 1881; fall in male domestic servants (DS.1), 1841–51 etc. That those described as 'weavers, spinners and factory hands (textile)', are always credited to the cotton industry (MF.19), may well affect the numbers in other branches of the textile industry. (e.g. MF.18, MF.20). It follows that scholars whose work focuses on the history of particular occupations should beware of using figures given at the level of the occupational subheading without a searching examination of the original census data. Our purpose, on the other hand, was to present the occupations in terms of broader industrial groups, so that many anomalies under individual occupational headings are likely to have been cancelled out. But it was essential to reproduce tables at this level of detail in order to inform the reader of how the broad groups were originally constituted by Booth.

[A] OCCUPIED POPULATION

Occupation	1841			1851			1861			1871			1881			1891		
	M	F	T	M	F	T	M	F	T	M	F	T	M	F	T	M	F	T
AGRICULTURAL SECTOR (incl. fishing)																		
1. Farming (AG.1)																		
Farm bailiffs, stewards	4·8	—	4·8	10·6	—	10·6	15·7	—	15·7	16·5	—	16·5	19·4	—	19·4	18·2	—	18·2
Farmers, graziers	229·3	19·2	248·5	226·5	22·9	249·4	226·9	22·8	249·7	225·6	24·3	249·9	203·3	20·6	223·9	201·9	21·7	223·6
Farmers' sons, grandsons, brothers, nephews	*	*	*	111·7	—	111·7	92·3	—	92·3	76·5	—	76·5	75·2	—	75·2	67·3	—	67·3
Agricultural labourers, farm servants	924·5	37·6	962·1	1,097·8	143·5	1,241·3	1,072·7	90·6	1,163·3	898·7	58·1	956·8	807·7	40·3	848·0	735·0	24·2	759·2
Shepherds	*	*	*	12·5	—	12·5	25·6	—	25·6	23·3	—	23·3	22·8	—	22·8	21·6	—	21·6
Woodmen	3·6	0·1	3·7	7·8	—	7·8	8·9	—	8·9	7·9	—	7·9	8·1	—	8·1	9·4	—	9·4
Nurserymen, seedsmen, florists	2·0	0·3	2·3	2·4	—	2·4	2·8	0·1	2·9	5·1	0·4	5·5	7·0	0·8	7·8	84·7	5·0	89·7
Gardeners (i)	45·6	1·0	46·6	69·6	2·2	71·8	76·7	1·8	78·5	95·8	2·2	98·0	63·6	2·3	65·9	2·6	0·1	2·7
Others in agriculture	0·1	—	0·1	3·8	0·1	3·9	0·9	0·1	1·0	1·2	0·1	1·3	1·5	0·1	1·6			
Total	1,209·9	58·2	1,268·1	1,542·7	168·7	1,711·4	1,522·5	115·4	1,637·9	1,350·6	85·1	1,435·7	1,208·6	64·1	1,272·7	1,140·7	51·0	1,191·7
2. Land Service (AG.2)																		
Agricultural machine proprietors, attendants	*	*	*	*	*	*	1·5	—	1·5	2·2	—	2·2	4·2	0·1	4·3	4·6	0·1	4·7
Land drainage service	*	*	*	*	*	*	1·7	—	1·7	1·3	—	1·3	1·7	—	1·7	—	—	—
Total	*	*	*	*	*	*	3·2	—	3·2	3·5	—	3·5	5·9	0·1	6·0	4·6	0·1	4·7
3. Breeding (AG.3)																		
Horse proprietors, breeders, dealers	2·2	—	2·2	1·3	—	1·3	1·3	—	1·3	1·4	—	1·4	2·2	—	2·2	2·8	—	2·8
Horse breakers, keepers, grooms (ii)	16·0	—	16·0	27·4	—	27·4	39·3	—	39·3	43·9	—	43·9	41·4	0·2	41·6	51·9	0·2	52·1

* No separate return.

[A] OCCUPIED POPULATION, Agricultural sector (cont.)

Occupation	1841			1851			1861			1871			1881			1891		
	M	F	T	M	F	T	M	F	T	M	F	T	M	F	T	M	F	T
Vet. surgeons, farriers	5·1	0·1	5·2	6·1	—	6·1	6·8	—	6·8	6·7	—	6·7	7·5	—	7·5	9·5	—	9·5
Cattle, sheep, etc. salesmen, drovers	4·9	—	4·9	7·5	—	7·5	9·3	—	9·3	8·8	—	8·8	8·4	—	8·4	8·1	—	8·1
Others engaged about animals	0·9	—	0·9	5·3	0·6	5·9	2·3	0·1	2·4	3·6	0·3	3·9	2·4	0·2	2·6	2·0	0·5	2·5
Total	29·1	0·1	29·2	47·6	0·6	48·2	59·0	0·1	59·1	64·4	0·3	64·7	61·9	0·4	62·3	74·3	0·7	75·0
4. Fishing (AG.4) Fishermen (iii)	10·2	0·3	10·5	16·9	—	16·9	17·0	0·3	17·3	20·7	0·3	21·0	29·4	0·3	29·7	24·9	0·3	25·2
Total	10·2	0·3	10·5	16·9	—	16·9	17·0	0·3	17·3	20·7	0·3	21·0	29·4	0·3	29·7	24·9	0·3	25·2
AGRICULTURAL SECTOR – TOTAL	1,249·2	58·6	1,307·8	1,607·2	169·3	1,776·5	1,601·7	115·8	1,717·5	1,439·2	85·7	1,524·9	1,305·8	64·9	1,370·7	1,244·5	51·9	1,296·4
MINING SECTOR																		
1. Mining (M.1)																		
Mine service (iv)	1·1	—	1·1	2·4	—	2·4	3·5	0·1	3·6	15·1	5·7	20·8	5·9	—	5·9	8·3	—	8·3
Coal miners (v)	100·0	1·6	101·6	183·4	2·5	185·9	246·6	2·0	248·6	268·1	—	268·1	378·7	3·1	381·8	513·8	3·3	517·1
Iron miners	8·1	0·4	8·5	19·4	—	19·4	20·6	—	20·6	21·0	—	21·0	25·9	0·2	26·1	18·2	0·1	18·3
Copper miners (v)	15·2	2·1	17·3	18·5	3·9	22·4	17·7	3·0	20·7	3·1	—	3·1	3·8	0·3	4·1	1·1	—	1·1
Tin miners	7·9	0·2	8·1	12·9	—	12·9	14·3	—	14·3	10·6	—	10·6	10·5	1·9	12·4	9·7	1·3	11·0
Lead miners	10·6	—	10·6	20·0	—	20·0	18·5	—	18·5	14·6	—	14·6	11·0	0·2	11·2	5·7	—	5·7
Miners in other or undefined minerals (iv)	25·6	0·9	26·5	*	*	*	8·0	—	8·0	38·7	—	38·7	2·7	0·1	2·8	2·4	—	2·4
Total	168·5	5·2	173·7	256·6	6·4	263·0	329·2	5·1	334·3	371·2	5·7	376·9	438·5	5·8	444·3	559·2	4·7	563·9

* No separate return.

Occupation	1841 M	1841 F	1841 T	1851 M	1851 F	1851 T	1861 M	1861 F	1861 T	1871 M	1871 F	1871 T	1881 M	1881 F	1881 T	1891 M	1891 F	1891 T
2. *Quarrying* (M.2)																		
Stone quarriers	10·8	—	10·8	18·2	—	18·2	21·0	0·1	21·1	25·7	—	25·7	28·9	—	28·9	52·6	0·1	52·7
Slate quarriers	3·1	—	3·1	7·4	—	7·4	9·4	—	9·4	9·8	—	9·8	14·9	—	14·9			
Stone and slate cutters	0·7	—	0·7	3·5	—	3·5	5·1	0·1	5·2	6·0	—	6·0	8·0	—	8·0			
Limestone quarriers, lime burners	2·4	—	2·4	5·0	—	5·0	5·5	0·1	5·6	5·2	—	5·2	3·3	—	3·3	2·7	—	2·7
Total	17·0	—	17·0	34·1	—	34·1	41·0	0·3	41·3	46·7	—	46·7	55·1	—	55·1	55·3	0·1	55·4
3. *Brickmaking* (M.3)																		
Brickmakers	16·7	0·5	17·2	27·8	—	27·8	37·7	1·9	39·6	36·2	2·5	38·7	47·3	2·8	50·1	41·0	2·7	43·7
Sand, flint, clay, gravel workers and others	0·5	0·1	0·6	4·7	2·0	6·7	5·6	0·3	5·9	6·6	0·6	7·2	5·0	0·1	5·1	5·9	—	5·9
Total	17·2	0·6	17·8	32·5	2·0	34·5	43·3	2·2	45·5	42·8	3·1	45·9	52·3	2·9	55·2	46·9	2·7	49·6
4. *Salt and water works* (M.4)																		
Salt makers	1·0	—	1·0	1·8	0·1	1·9	2·0	0·1	2·1	2·5	—	2·5	2·8	0·2	3·0	2·9	0·1	3·0
Waterworks service	0·6	—	0·6	1·6	0·1	1·7	2·0	—	2·0	2·6	—	2·6	4·0	—	4·0	5·2	—	5·2
Total	1·6	—	1·6	3·4	0·2	3·6	4·0	0·1	4·1	5·1	—	5·1	6·8	0·2	7·0	8·1	0·1	8·2
MINING SECTOR – TOTAL	204·3	5·8	210·1	326·6	8·6	335·2	417·5	7·7	425·2	465·8	8·8	474·6	552·7	8·9	561·6	669·5	7·6	677·1
BUILDING SECTOR																		
1. *Management* (B.1)																		
Architects	1·5	—	1·5	2·7	—	2·7	3·8	—	3·8	5·7	—	5·7	6·9	—	6·9	7·8	—	7·8
Civil engineers	0·9	—	0·9	2·6	—	2·6	3·3	—	3·3	5·2	—	5·2	7·1	—	7·1	7·3	—	7·3

[A] OCCUPIED POPULATION, Building sector (cont.)

Occupation	1841			1851			1861			1871			1881			1891		
	M	F	T	M	F	T	M	F	T	M	F	T	M	F	T	M	F	T
Surveyors (land, house, ships) (vi)	4·1	—	4·1	2·8	—	2·8	6·6	—	6·6	7·9	—	7·9	5·4	—	5·4	5·8	—	5·8
Contractors (vii)	0·3	—	0·3	1·2	—	1·2	2·4	—	2·4	1·5	—	1·5	5·5	—	5·5	6·9	—	6·9
Builders	8·4	0·1	8·5	11·7	0·7	12·4	15·7	0·1	15·8	23·1	0·2	23·3	30·6	0·1	30·7	37·6	0·2	37·8
Total	15·2	0·1	15·3	21·0	0·7	21·7	31·8	0·1	31·9	43·4	0·2	43·6	55·5	0·1	55·6	65·4	0·2	65·6
2. *Operative* (B.2)																		
Masons (viii)	63·6	0·2	63·8	78·7	—	78·7	82·4	0·1	82·5	94·1	—	94·1	97·4	0·1	97·5	84·6	0·1	84·7
Bricklayers (viii)	39·6	0·1	39·7	67·1	—	67·1	79·5	—	79·5	99·9	—	99·9	125·0	0·1	125·1	130·4	0·1	130·5
Plasterers, whitewashers (viii)	11·7	0·1	11·8	15·7	—	15·7	18·5	—	18·5	24·6	—	24·6	28·7	0·1	28·8	29·2	0·2	29·4
Slaters and tilers	4·0	—	4·0	4·4	—	4·4	5·2	—	5·2	6·1	—	6·1	7·5	—	7·5	6·8	—	6·8
Thatchers	3·7	—	3·7	5·9	—	5·9	5·3	—	5·3	4·1	—	4·1	3·7	—	3·7	3·6	0·1	3·6
Carpenters and joiners	136·6	0·4	137·0	156·1	—	156·1	177·8	0·2	178·0	205·6	0·2	205·8	235·0	0·2	235·2	220·7	0·3	221·0
Plumbers, painters, glaziers and paperhangers	43·6	0·4	44·0	58·3	—	58·3	76·5	0·4	76·9	106·8	0·5	107·3	141·0	0·8	141·8	169·7	0·7	170·6
Gasfitters	0·8	—	0·8	2·4	—	2·4	5·5	—	5·5	8·6	—	8·6	12·4	0·2	12·6	19·8	0·6	20·4
Locksmiths and bellhangers	5·4	—	5·4	6·2	—	6·2	5·4	0·1	5·5	7·2	—	7·2	7·3	0·4	7·7	*	*	*
Others	—	—	—	2·1	0·2	2·3	3·3	0·1	3·4	4·3	0·3	4·6	5·9	0·3	6·2	8·0	0·4	8·4
Total	310·1	1·2	311·3	396·9	0·2	397·1	459·4	0·9	460·3	561·3	1·0	562·3	658·9	2·2	661·1	672·8	2·6	675·4
3. *Roadmaking* (B.3)																		
Paviors (ix)	*	*	*	*	*	*	4·0	—	4·0	4·0	—	4·0	4·2	—	4·2	21·4	—	21·4
Road labourers (x)	8·0	—	8·0	7·9	—	7·9	9·5	—	9·5	8·3	—	8·3	10·9	—	10·9			
Railway labourers, navvies (x)	17·2	—	17·2	34·0	—	34·0	43·0	—	43·0	45·1	—	45·1	58·8	—	58·8	72·6	—	72·6
Others	0·7	—	0·7	—	—	—	—	—	—	1·0	—	1·0	0·5	0·3	0·8	0·7	—	0·7
Total	25·9	—	25·9	41·9	—	41·9	56·5	—	56·5	58·4	—	58·4	74·4	0·3	74·7	94·7	—	94·7
BUILDING SECTOR—TOTAL	351·2	1·3	352·5	459·8	0·9	460·7	547·7	1·0	548·7	663·1	1·2	664·3	793·8	2·6	796·4	832·9	2·8	835·7

* No separate return.

Occupation	1841 M	1841 F	1841 T	1851 M	1851 F	1851 T	1861 M	1861 F	1861 T	1871 M	1871 F	1871 T	1881 M	1881 F	1881 T	1891 M	1891 F	1891 T
MANUFACTURE SECTOR																		
1. Machinery (MF.1)																		
Engine and machine makers (xi)	8·6	0·2	8·8	48·2	0·5	48·7	70·4	1·8	72·2	106·5	0·2	106·7	102·9	0·3	103·2	134·1	0·8	134·9
Boiler makers	2·8	—	2·8	6·0	—	6·0	13·0	—	13·0	*	*	*	26·2	—	26·2	36·7	—	36·7
Domestic machinery and bicycle makers	0·8	—	0·8	*	*	*	0·9	0·2	1·1	*	*	*	2·7	0·7	3·4	12·8	1·1	13·9
Weighing and measuring machine makers	1·3	—	1·3	*	*	*	1·5	0·1	1·6	1·7	—	1·7	2·4	0·2	2·6	3·2	0·4	3·6
Agricultural machine and implement makers	1·3	0·1	1·4	*	—	*	1·0	—	1·0	3·6	—	3·6	4·0	0·1	4·1	3·2	0·1	3·3
Millwrights	6·9	—	6·9	7·6	—	7·6	8·2	—	8·2	7·6	—	7·6	6·9	—	6·9	6·1	—	6·1
Spinning and weaving machine makers	0·6	—	0·6	*	*	*	2·6	—	2·6	9·7	0·3	10·0	19·2	0·7	19·9	26·5	1·1	27·6
Total	22·3	0·3	22·6	61·8	0·5	62·3	97·6	2·1	99·7	129·1	0·5	129·6	164·3	2·0	166·3	222·6	3·5	226·1
2. Tools, etc. (MF.2)																		
Tool makers	10·0	0·2	10·2	13·3	0·6	13·9	18·3	0·9	19·2	17·3	1·2	18·5	18·9	1·5	20·4	21·6	2·0	23·6
Cutlery and scissors makers	10·3	0·4	10·7	8·0	—	8·0	16·1	0·8	16·9	18·1	1·2	19·3	16·6	1·6	18·2	17·7	2·3	20·0
Pin, needle, steel pen and pencil makers	2·8	1·9	4·7	2·8	2·8	5·6	3·0	3·4	6·4	4·7	4·3	9·0	3·0	5·2	8·2	3·0	5·4	8·4
Gunsmiths, sword, bayonet makers and ordnance manufacture	5·3	0·2	5·5	7·5	0·2	7·7	12·1	0·3	12·4	11·8	0·3	12·1	8·0	0·2	8·2	9·5	0·2	9·7
Typefounders, die, seal, coin, medal makers etc. (xii)	2·4	0·1	2·5	2·6	—	2·6	3·9	—	3·9	4·6	0·2	4·8	2·7	0·1	2·8	3·1	0·2	3·3
Total	30·8	2·8	33·6	34·2	3·6	37·8	53·4	5·4	58·8	56·5	7·2	63·7	49·2	8·6	57·8	54·9	10·1	65·0
3. Shipbuilding (MF.3)																		
Ship, boat, barge builders, shipwrights	19·9	—	19·9	23·4	—	23·4	34·8	—	34·8	41·1	—	41·1	45·7	0·1	45·8	62·6	0·1	62·7
Mast, oar and block makers	1·2	—	1·2	3·4	—	3·4	2·0	—	2·0	*	*	*	1·4	—	1·4	4·1	—	4·1
Riggers, fitters etc.	1·1	—	1·1				2·9	—	2·9	*	*	*	2·9	—	2·9			
Sailmakers	*	*	*	*	—	*	4·1	0·1	4·2	4·0	0·1	4·1	4·1	—	4·1	3·5	0·1	3·6
Total	22·2	—	22·2	26·8	—	26·8	43·8	0·1	43·9	45·1	0·1	45·2	54·1	0·1	54·2	70·2	0·2	70·4

* No separate return.

[A] OCCUPIED POPULATION, Manufacture sector (cont.)

Occupation	1841			1851			1861			1871			1881			1891		
	M	F	T	M	F	T	M	F	T	M	F	T	M	F	T	M	F	T
4. Iron and steel (MF.4)																		
Iron and steel manufacture	35·5	0·9	36·4	91·2	6·2	97·4	136·0	3·1	139·1	183·9	3·0	186·9	198·8	1·9	200·7	199·9	2·6	202·5
Anchor and chain manufacture	1·7	0·1	1·8	2·8	—	2·8	4·0	0·6	4·6	4·2	0·9	5·1	4·0	1·0	5·0	4·5	1·8	6·3
Bolt, nut, rivet, screw, nail manufacture	16·5	4·6	21·1	17·0	10·0	27·0	18·7	12·5	31·2	17·4	12·6	30·0	15·3	11·5	26·8	11·9	8·1	20·0
Blacksmiths	81·6	0·5	82·1	94·2	0·6	94·8	107·8	0·4	108·2	112·1	0·4	112·5	112·2	0·3	112·5	124·5	0·5	125·0
Total	135·3	6·1	141·4	205·2	16·8	222·0	266·5	16·6	283·1	317·6	16·9	334·5	330·3	14·7	345·0	340·8	13·0	653·8
5. Copper, tin, lead etc. (MF.5)																		
Copper and copper goods manufacture	3·1	0·3	3·4	4·4	0·1	4·5	5·8	1·0	6·8	5·6	0·2	5·8	7·3	0·1	7·4	8·5	0·1	8·6
Tin and tin goods manufacture	7·7	0·5	8·2	14·1	3·1	17·2	18·5	4·4	22·9	23·2	2·9	26·1	32·4	4·5	36·9	39·7	6·5	46·2
Lead and leaden goods manufacture	1·1	0·1	1·2	4·5	1·1	5·6	2·8	0·9	3·7	3·2	0·5	3·7	2·3	0·2	2·5	2·2	0·2	2·4
Zinc and zinc goods manufacture	0·2	—	0·2	0·5	—	0·5	0·7	—	0·7	1·7	—	1·7	2·3	—	2·3	3·4	0·2	3·6
Brass, bronze manufacturers, braziers	11·6	0·2	11·8	13·8	—	13·8	18·4	0·3	18·7	21·0	0·4	21·4	26·9	1·0	27·9	34·8	2·1	36·9
Wire makers, workers, weavers	2·7	0·1	2·8	3·9	—	3·9	5·7	0·3	6·0	7·4	0·5	7·9	8·7	0·5	9·2	10·2	1·0	11·2
Lamp, lantern and candlestick makers	0·5	0·1	0·6	*	*	*	1·1	0·1	1·2	1·5	0·2	1·7	2·5	0·5	3·0	3·1	0·7	3·8
Metal refiners, workers, burnishers	0·6	0·4	1·0	*	*	*	1·6	1·6	3·2	2·7	2·0	4·7	4·7	2·5	7·2	7·8	3·3	11·1
Pewter, white metal, plated ware manufacture	3·4	0·2	3·6	2·1	—	2·1	4·1	0·6	4·7	1·8	0·1	1·9	4·8	0·8	5·6	5·0	1·8	6·8
Whitesmiths	6·6	—	6·6	9·4	—	9·4	9·9	—	9·9	8·6	—	8·6	8·2	0·1	8·3	9·1	—	9·1
Others (xiii)	1·0	0·2	1·2	4·0	2·2	6·2	2·0	0·7	2·7	1·2	1·2	2·4	2·9	1·3	4·2	5·0	1·1	6·1
Total	38·5	2·1	40·6	56·7	6·5	63·2	70·6	9·9	80·5	77·9	8·0	85·9	103·0	11·5	114·5	128·8	17·0	145·8
6. Gold, silver and jewellery (MF.6)																		
Gold and silversmiths, jewellers (xiv)	4·0	0·2	4·2	5·3	0·9	6·2	7·1	0·8	7·9	9·5	1·5	11·0	10·5	1·9	12·4	10·3	1·7	12·0
Lapidaries and others	1·6	0·2	1·8	1·8	—	1·8	2·3	1·1	3·4	3·0	0·7	3·7	2·7	2·3	5·0	2·8	2·1	4·9
Total	5·6	0·4	6·0	7·1	0·9	8·0	9·4	1·9	11·3	12·5	2·2	14·7	13·2	4·2	17·4	13·1	3·8	16·9

* No separate return.

Occupation	1841			1851			1861			1871			1881			1891		
	M	F	T	M	F	T	M	F	T	M	F	T	M	F	T	M	F	T
7. *Earthenware etc.* (MF.7)																		
Earthenware, china, porcelain manufacture	16·7	7·1	23·8	23·6	10·7	34·3	26·3	12·0	38·3	29·3	16·0	45·3	28·7	17·9	46·6	34·8	21·8	56·6
Glass manufacture	6·7	0·3	7·0	11·2	1·0	12·2	14·5	1·4	15·9	18·4	1·7	20·1	19·9	1·7	21·6	24·1	2·1	26·2
Plaster and cement manufacture	0·2	—	0·2	*	*	*	1·7	—	1·7	2·0	—	2·0	3·6	0·1	3·7	5·4	—	5·4
Total	23·6	7·4	31·0	34·8	11·7	46·5	42·5	13·4	55·9	49·7	17·7	67·4	52·2	19·7	71·9	64·3	23·9	88·2
8. *Coals and gas* (MF.8)																		
Gasworks service	1·3	—	1·3	4·7	—	4·7	8·8	—	8·8	13·6	—	13·6	18·5	—	18·5	30·7	—	30·7
Others in coal, coke, peat and charcoal	1·2	0·1	1·3	3·2	0·9	4·1	3·8	0·1	3·9	4·6	0·2	4·8	5·2	0·2	5·4	5·7	0·2	5·9
Total	2·5	0·1	2·6	7·9	0·9	8·8	12·6	0·1	12·7	18·2	0·2	18·4	23·7	0·2	23·9	36·4	0·2	36·6
9. *Chemical* (MF.9)																		
Manufacturing chemists, alkali manufacture	0·9	—	0·9	8·5	0·8	9·3	7·5	0·3	7·8	10·7	0·6	11·3	15·0	1·1	16·1	19·7	1·8	21·5
Dye and paint manufacture	0·7	—	0·7	*	*	*	1·5	0·1	1·6	2·5	0·3	2·8	1·7	0·4	2·1	3·9	0·6	4·5
Ink and blacking manufacture	0·5	0·1	0·6	*	*	*	0·6	0·1	0·7	0·6	0·1	0·7	1·0	0·2	1·2			
Drysalters	0·3	—	0·3	*	*	*	0·6	—	0·6	0·7	—	0·7	0·9	0·1	1·0	1·2	0·2	1·4
Gunpowder manufacture	0·2	—	0·2	*	*	*	0·8	0·3	1·1	1·2	0·1	1·3	0·7	0·1	0·8	1·3	0·2	1·5
Matches, fuzees and fireworks manufacture	0·7	0·1	0·8	*	*	*	1·2	0·6	1·8	1·0	2·8	3·8	1·0	1·9	2·9	1·7	3·3	5·0
Total	3·3	0·2	3·5	8·5	0·8	9·3	12·2	1·4	13·6	16·7	3·9	20·6	20·3	3·8	24·1	27·8	6·1	33·9
10. *Furs and Leather* (MF.10)																		
Furriers and skinners	2·5	0·9	3·4	3·1	1·9	5·0	2·8	1·7	4·5	3·7	2·4	6·1	4·6	3·5	8·1	5·7	4·3	10·0
Tanners, fellmongers, parchment makers	7·7	—	7·7	9·7	—	9·7	10·9	0·3	11·2	10·7	—	10·7	10·5	0·1	10·6	10·6	0·1	10·7
Curriers	9·5	—	9·5	11·4	—	11·4	12·8	0·3	13·1	14·2	0·5	14·7	15·0	0·6	15·6	17·6	1·0	18·6
Total	19·7	0·9	20·6	24·2	1·9	26·1	26·5	2·3	28·8	28·6	2·9	31·5	30·1	4·2	34·2	33·9	5·4	39·3

* No separate return.

[A] OCCUPIED POPULATION, Manufacture sector (cont.)

Occupation	1841 M	1841 F	1841 T	1851 M	1851 F	1851 T	1861 M	1861 F	1861 T	1871 M	1871 F	1871 T	1881 M	1881 F	1881 T	1891 M	1891 F	1891 T
11. Glue, tallow etc. (MF.11)																		
Glue, size and gelatine manufacture	0·2	—	0·2	0·4	0·1	0·5	0·4	0·1	0·5	0·5	0·1	0·6	0·5	0·1	0·6	0·5	0·2	0·7
Tallow chandlers, candle and grease manufacture	3·1	0·1	3·2	4·8	0·2	5·0	4·6	0·3	4·9	3·7	0·3	4·0	3·0	0·2	3·2	2·5	0·3	2·8
Soap boilers and makers	0·7	—	0·7	1·2	—	1·2	1·6	—	1·6	1·8	—	1·8	2·0	0·3	2·3	2·9	0·9	3·8
Manure manufacture	*	*	*	0·2	—	0·2	0·8	—	0·8	1·2	0·1	1·3	1·2	0·1	1·3	0·9	0·1	1·0
Total	4·0	0·1	4·1	6·6	0·3	6·9	7·4	0·4	7·8	7·2	0·5	7·7	6·7	0·7	7·4	6·8	1·5	8·3
12. Hair etc. (MF.12)																		
Hair and bristle workers	0·5	0·4	0·9	1·0	1·6	2·6	1·1	1·9	3·0	1·0	1·8	2·8	0·9	1·7	2·6	9·7	6·2	15·9
Brush and broom makers	5·2	0·7	5·9	7·6	1·8	9·4	8·5	2·7	11·2	8·5	3·2	11·7	8·7	4·2	12·9			
Quill and feather dressers	0·1	0·1	0·2	0·6	0·4	1·0	0·3	0·6	0·9	1·1	1·4	2·5	0·4	2·1	2·5	0·5	2·4	2·9
Comb makers	1·6	0·2	1·8	1·8	—	1·8	1·3	0·2	1·5	0·9	0·2	1·1	0·6	0·2	0·8	2·8	0·6	3·4
Bone, horn, ivory, tortoiseshell workers	0·5	—	0·5	2·7	0·5	3·2	2·2	0·2	2·4	2·1	0·2	2·3	2·0	0·2	2·2			
Total	7·9	1·4	9·3	13·7	4·3	18·0	13·4	5·6	19·0	13·6	6·8	20·4	12·6	8·4	21·0	13·0	9·2	22·2
13. Wood workers (MF.13)																		
Sawyers	25·0	—	25·0	30·5	—	30·5	31·7	—	31·7	28·0	—	28·0	24·7	—	24·7	23·3	—	23·3
Lath, wooden fence and hurdle makers	1·4	0·1	1·5	1·7	—	1·7	2·7	—	2·7	3·0	—	3·0	3·0	—	3·0	2·4	—	2·4
Coopers, hoop makers and benders	15·6	—	15·6	15·9	—	15·9	19·7	0·1	19·8	19·2	—	19·2	18·6	0·1	18·7	17·1	0·1	17·2
Woodturners, box and case makers	7·9	0·6	8·5	9·1	1·5	10·6	10·1	2·0	12·1	12·4	5·4	17·8	11·4	2·6	14·0	12·7	1·9	14·6
Willow cane and rush workers	6·3	0·5	6·8	13·7	1·0	14·7	9·5	1·3	10·8	8·4	0·9	9·3	9·0	2·5	11·5	11·4	2·6	14·0
Cork and bark cutters and others	1·9	0·2	2·1	3·3	0·2	3·5	3·8	0·3	4·1	2·8	0·6	3·4	2·0	0·2	2·2	2·1	0·4	2·5
Total	58·1	1·4	59·5	74·2	2·7	76·9	77·5	3·7	81·2	73·8	6·9	80·7	68·7	5·4	74·1	69·0	5·0	74·0

* No separate return.

Occupation	1841			1851			1861			1871			1881			1891		
	M	F	T	M	F	T	M	F	T	M	F	T	M	F	T	M	F	T
14. *Furniture* (MF.14)																		
Cabinet makers and upholsterers	29.6	2.4	32.0	36.3	4.3	40.6	44.0	7.4	51.4	48.4	8.6	57.0	51.7	8.0	59.7	72.2	11.9	84.1
Carvers and gilders	5.2	0.1	5.3	5.8	—	5.8	6.5	0.1	6.6	7.3	0.2	7.5	7.8	0.3	8.1	8.2	0.5	8.7
French polishers	1.3	0.1	1.4	3.1	0.9	4.0	4.6	1.2	5.8	6.4	1.4	7.8	8.1	2.0	10.1	*	*	*
Undertakers and others	1.2	0.1	1.3	1.3	0.1	1.4	1.5	0.1	1.6	1.8	0.2	2.0	1.7	0.2	1.9	2.4	0.3	2.7
Total	37.3	2.7	40.0	46.5	5.3	51.8	56.6	8.8	65.4	63.9	10.4	74.3	69.3	10.5	79.8	82.8	12.7	95.5
15. *Carriages and harness* (MF.15)																		
Coach makers	11.8	0.2	12.0	15.4	0.2	15.6	18.7	0.2	18.9	22.7	0.3	23.0	23.8	0.2	24.0	41.5	0.5	42.0
Wheelwrights	25.1	0.2	25.3	28.0	—	28.0	30.0	0.1	30.1	30.3	—	30.3	28.6	0.1	28.7	27.8	0.1	27.9
Saddle, harness and whip makers	15.2	0.4	15.6	16.1	0.7	16.8	18.1	1.3	19.4	21.2	1.8	23.0	21.8	2.0	23.8	24.4	2.9	27.3
Railway carriage makers	*	*	*	*	*	*	1.3	—	1.3	2.3	0.1	2.4	9.4	0.2	9.6	*	*	*
Total	52.1	0.8	52.9	59.5	0.9	60.4	68.1	1.6	69.7	76.5	2.2	78.7	83.6	2.5	86.1	93.7	3.5	97.2
16. *Paper* (MF.16)																		
Paper manufacture	4.6	1.3	5.9	6.1	4.7	10.8	7.8	5.6	13.4	10.2	6.6	16.8	10.3	8.3	18.6	12.0	8.0	20.0
Envelope manufacture	*	*	*	*	*	*	0.2	0.9	1.1	—	1.5	1.5	0.2	1.9	2.1	0.3	2.5	2.8
Paper box and bag makers (xvi)	0.1	0.3	0.4	*	{2.2	*	0.3	1.7	2.0	—	2.1	2.1	1.2	8.7	9.8	2.1	17.2	19.3
Paper stainers	1.2	0.1	1.3	2.0		2.0	1.6	0.4	2.0	1.3	0.5	1.8	1.9	0.4	2.3	2.1	0.4	2.5
Others	0.4	0.9	1.3	2.7		4.9	1.3	0.4	1.7	2.7	0.5	3.2	3.0	0.6	3.6	4.3	1.0	5.3
Total	7.3	2.6	9.9	10.8	6.9	17.7	11.2	9.0	20.2	14.2	11.2	25.4	16.6	19.9	36.5	20.8	29.1	49.9

* No separate return.

[A] OCCUPIED POPULATION, Manufacture sector (cont.)

Occupation	1841 M	1841 F	1841 T	1851 M	1851 F	1851 T	1861 M	1861 F	1861 T	1871 M	1871 F	1871 T	1881 M	1881 F	1881 T	1891 M	1891 F	1891 T
17. Floorcloth and waterproof (MF.17)																		
Floorcloth and oilcloth manufacture (xvii)	0·3	—	0·3	2·8	1·4	4·2	0·8	0·1	0·9	0·8	—	0·8	1·3	—	1·3	1·5	0·1	1·6
Japanners	1·2	0·5	1·7				1·4	1·2	2·6	1·5	1·3	2·8	1·4	1·5	2·9	1·1	1·7	2·8
India-rubber, gutta-percha, waterproof goods makers	0·1	0·1	0·2				1·2	0·4	1·6	3·8	0·9	4·7	5·3	1·8	7·1	7·5	4·2	11·7
Total	1·6	0·6	2·2	2·8	1·4	4·2	3·4	1·7	5·1	6·1	2·2	8·3	8·0	3·3	11·3	10·1	6·0	16·1
18. Woollens (MF.18)																		
Woollen cloth manufacture (xviii)	67·3	21·4	88·7	76·9	45·4	122·3	81·2	48·8	130·0	71·7	56·8	128·5	57·3	58·5	115·8	61·6	61·3	122·9
Worsted and stuff manufacture	12·3	15·5	27·8	54·9	55·3	110·2	32·8	50·4	83·2	38·6	62·5	101·1	35·4	63·8	99·2	40·5	69·9	110·0
Flannel manufacture	0·5	0·1	0·6	*	*	*	0·7	0·4	1·1	0·8	0·4	1·2	0·6	0·5	1·1	2·4	3·0	5·4
Blanket manufacture	*	*	*	*	*	*	1·5	0·5	2·0	1·3	0·6	1·9	1·3	1·4	2·7			
Carpet, rug and felt manufacture	2·9	0·3	3·2	7·6	—	7·6	6·5	1·4	7·9	8·2	3·7	11·9	9·3	5·2	14·5	9·2	7·4	16·6
Woollen knitters	0·5	1·4	1·9	—	2·5	2·5	—	2·0	2·0	*	*	*	*	*	*	*	*	*
Others	—	—	—	9·9	5·4	15·3	1·0	1·6	2·6	0·2	0·6	0·8	0·4	0·6	1·0	0·6	1·2	1·8
Total	83·5	38·7	122·2	149·3	108·6	257·9	123·7	105·1	228·8	120·8	124·6	245·4	104·3	130·0	234·3	114·3	142·5	256·8
19. Cotton and silk (MF.19)																		
Cotton and cotton goods manufacture	100·5	116·9	217·4	178·7	194·8	373·5	198·4	259·4	457·8	188·4	279·9	468·3	185·4	302·4	487·8	213·2	332·8	546·0
Silk and silk goods manufacture	24·4	29·9	54·3	47·7	71·5	119·2	35·6	67·1	102·7	24·4	51·5	75·9	17·7	39·7	57·4	16·1	31·8	47·9
Ribbon manufacture	3·8	3·1	6·9	4·9	5·2	10·1	4·3	5·0	9·3	1·5	1·6	3·1	0·8	1·2	2·0	3·2	5·0	8·2
Fustian manufacture	2·2	1·3	3·5	3·3	2·2	5·5	2·7	2·8	5·5	3·2	4·2	7·4	3·0	5·2	8·2			
Crape, gauze, shawls, and fancy goods (textile) manufacture	4·3	1·3	5·6	2·7	4·9	7·6	1·5	4·7	6·2	2·8	7·2	10·0	1·8	7·6	9·4	4·0	9·0	13·0
Weavers, spinners and factory hands (textile)	65·8	33·2	99·0	7·1	6·3	13·4	4·7	3·6	8·3	7·4	12·5	19·9	8·0	10·4	18·4	3·7	5·7	9·4
Total	201·0	185·7	386·7	244·2	285·1	529·3	247·2	342·6	589·8	227·7	356·9	584·6	216·7	366·5	583·2	240·2	384·3	624·5

* No separate return.

Occupation	1841 M	1841 F	1841 T	1851 M	1851 F	1851 T	1861 M	1861 F	1861 T	1871 M	1871 F	1871 T	1881 M	1881 F	1881 T	1891 M	1891 F	1891 T
20. *Flax, hemp etc.* (MF.20)																		
Flax, linen and damask manufacture	10·4	6·4	16·8	13·1	13·2	26·3	9·3	12·8	22·1	7·4	10·6	18·0	4·2	7·8	12·0	2·6	5·6	8·2
Canvas and sailcloth manufacture	3·4	0·2	3·6	3·5	—	3·5	0·9	0·6	1·5	0·8	0·3	1·1	0·4	0·3	0·7	1·0	1·8	2·8
Sacking and bag manufacture	0·6	0·2	0·8	*	*	*	0·8	1·1	1·9	0·7	1·5	2·2	0·6	1·6	2·2	*	*	*
Hemp, jute and cocoa-fibre manufacture	0·4	0·2	0·6	—	0·5	0·5	0·9	0·2	1·1	0·7	0·1	0·8	1·2	2·3	3·5	1·2	2·3	3·5
Rope, twine and cord makers	8·9	0·5	9·4	11·6	1·5	13·1	11·8	1·7	13·5	10·3	1·4	11·7	9·7	2·1	11·8	8·4	2·4	10·8
Net makers	0·1	0·1	0·2	*	*	*	0·2	1·4	1·6	—	1·7	1·7	0·3	1·5	1·8	0·2	1·4	1·6
Mat makers	0·7	0·1	0·8	4·7	2·8	7·5	1·3	0·4	1·7	1·3	0·6	1·9	1·8	0·5	2·3	2·2	0·5	2·7
Others (xviii)	—	—	—	—	—	—	0·4	0·4	0·8	0·7	0·9	1·6	0·2	0·2	0·4	0·7	0·3	1·0
Total	24·5	7·7	32·2	32·9	18·0	50·9	25·6	18·6	44·2	21·9	17·1	39·0	18·4	16·3	34·7	16·3	14·3	30·6
21. *Lace* (MF.21)																		
Lace manufacture	6·5	20·3	26·8	9·4	52·3	61·7	8·9	45·1	54·0	8·5	40·8	49·3	11·4	32·8	44·2	13·0	21·7	34·7
Embroiders	—	0·8	0·8	—	2·6	2·6	0·1	2·2	2·3	—	1·4	1·4	0·1	2·3	2·4	1·3	7·7	9·0
Thread manufacture	0·4	0·4	0·8	—	0·8	0·8	0·4	0·7	1·1	0·3	0·9	1·2	0·5	1·7	2·2	0·6	2·1	2·7
Tape manufacture	0·5	0·4	0·9	*	*	*	0·6	0·9	1·5	0·6	0·8	1·4	0·8	1·1	1·9	0·9	1·5	2·4
Trimming manufacture	0·6	0·7	1·3	*	*	*	1·9	3·6	5·5	1·4	4·5	5·9	1·6	4·9	6·5	*	*	*
Artificial flower makers and others	0·3	0·9	1·2	0·5	2·9	3·4	1·2	4·7	5·9	1·0	5·9	6·9	1·2	4·7	5·9	2·8	5·2	8·0
Total	8·3	23·5	31·8	9·9	58·6	68·5	13·1	57·2	70·3	11·8	54·3	66·1	15·6	47·5	63·1	18·6	38·2	56·8
22. *Dyeing* (MF.22)																		
Fullers	1·2	—	1·2	1·5	—	1·5	1·0	—	1·0	1·9	—	1·9	2·5	—	2·5	2·3	—	2·3
Cotton and calico printers, dyers and bleachers (xix)	9·9	—	10·6	14·2	1·2	15·4	15·7	2·0	17·7	11·2	1·1	12·3	22·8	3·9	26·7	26·1	5·0	31·1
Wool, woollen goods, dyers, printers (xx)	1·4	0·3	1·7	*	*	*	1·9	—	1·9	2·6	—	2·6	2·7	0·1	2·8	6·1	0·1	6·2
Silk dyers, printers (xx)	1·2	0·1	1·3	*	*	*	2·7	—	2·7	1·6	—	1·6	1·6	0·1	1·7	1·7	0·1	1·8

* No separate return.

[A] OCCUPIED POPULATION, Manufacture sector (cont.)

Occupation	1841 M	1841 F	1841 T	1851 M	1851 F	1851 T	1861 M	1861 F	1861 T	1871 M	1871 F	1871 T	1881 M	1881 F	1881 T	1891 M	1891 F	1891 T
Dyers, printers, scourers, bleachers (undefined)	15·2	0·9	16·1	10·4	0·6	11·0	8·8	1·0	9·8	15·0	1·5	16·5	11·8	1·8	13·6	5·7	1·9	7·6
Total	28·9	2·0	30·9	26·1	1·8	27·9	30·1	3·0	33·1	32·3	2·6	34·9	41·4	5·9	47·3	41·9	7·1	49·0
23. *Dress* (MF.23)																		
Tailors and clothiers	113·3	6·7	120·0	121·7	17·5	139·2	110·3	27·5	137·8	111·8	38·0	149·8	107·7	53·0	160·7	119·1	89·2	208·7
Milliners and dressmakers	1·7	102·0	103·7	—	252·2	252·2	2·6	308·3	310·9	2·6	308·3	310·9	2·9	358·0	360·9	4·5	416·0	420·5
Shirtmakers and seamstresses	0·1	19·1	19·2	—	59·4	59·4	0·5	76·0	76·5	0·7	80·0	80·7	1·4	81·9	83·3	2·2	52·9	55·1
Hosiery manufacture	27·5	8·5	36·0	33·6	25·3	58·9	24·4	21·5	45·9	22·4	19·7	42·1	18·9	21·5	40·4	18·2	30·9	49·1
Hat manufacture (xxi)	11·7	2·7	14·4	9·4	6·7	16·1	7·2	2·0	9·2	10·1	6·2	16·3	9·5	8·0	17·5	12·3	9·5	21·8
Straw hat, bonnet and plait manufacture	1·5	17·7	19·2	—	46·5	46·5	4·1	44·2	48·3	3·6	45·3	48·9	3·0	28·0	31·0	3·4	15·0	18·4
Glove manufacture	3·1	6·1	9·2	4·5	25·3	29·8	3·8	24·0	27·8	2·7	20·3	23·0	2·3	13·2	15·5	2·8	9·2	12·0
Shoe and boot makers	176·7	10·8	187·5	211·0	29·3	240·3	211·6	39·5	251·1	197·5	25·9	223·4	180·9	35·7	216·6	202·6	46·1	248·7
Pattern and clog makers	3·2	0·1	3·3	3·7	—	3·7	5·0	—	5·0	1·2	—	1·2	7·4	0·1	7·5			
Others	0·3	0·8	1·1	6·3	2·9	9·2	0·3	0·9	1·2	1·3	1·5	2·8	—	—	—	—	—	—
Total	339·1	174·5	513·6	390·2	465·1	855·3	369·8	543·9	913·7	353·9	545·2	899·1	334·0	599·4	933·4	365·5	668·8	1,034·3
24. *Sundries connected with dress* (MF.24)																		
Accoutrement makers	0·1	—	0·1	*	*	*	0·5	0·3	0·8	0·4	0·2	0·6	0·3	0·3	0·6	0·5	0·5	1·0
Umbrella, parasol and stick makers	1·2	0·5	1·7	2·1	1·7	3·8	2·6	2·6	5·2	3·1	2·8	5·9	4·1	4·1	8·2	5·4	4·5	9·9
Button makers	2·3	1·7	4·0	3·0	3·9	6·9	2·8	3·8	6·6	2·4	3·4	5·8	2·3	4·1	6·4	1·9	3·1	5·0
Leather goods manufacture	0·9	0·5	1·4	2·2	0·5	2·7	2·9	0·3	3·2	3·5	1·1	4·6	4·0	1·4	5·4	4·7	2·2	6·9
Total	4·5	2·7	7·2	7·3	6·1	13·4	8·8	7·0	15·8	11·4	7·5	16·9	10·7	9·9	20·6	12·5	10·3	22·8

* No separate return.

Occupation	1841			1851			1861			1871			1881			1891		
	M	F	T	M	F	T	M	F	T	M	F	T	M	F	T	M	F	T
25. Food preparation (MF.25)																		
Oil millers, oil cake makers	0·3	—	0·3	0·9	—	0·9	2·0	—	2·0	3·5	—	3·5	4·5	0·1	4·6	4·4	0·1	4·5
Corn millers	21·9	0·5	22·4	32·0	0·5	32·5	31·7	0·4	32·1	29·7	0·4	30·1	23·2	0·3	23·5	22·4	0·4	22·8
Sugar refiners	0·9	—	0·9	2·0	—	2·0	2·8	0·1	2·9	2·8	—	2·8	2·9	0·1	3·0	3·5	0·2	3·7
Mustard, vinegar, pickles manufacture	0·2	—	0·2	*	*	*	0·6	0·3	0·9	1·1	0·8	1·9	0·8	0·7	1·5	1·3	1·2	2·5
Total	23·3	0·5	23·8	34·9	0·5	35·4	37·1	0·8	37·9	37·1	1·2	38·3	31·4	1·2	32·6	31·6	1·9	33·5
26. Baking (MF.26)																		
Bakers	33·4	3·7	37·1	45·6	6·1	51·7	47·9	6·2	54·1	53·4	6·5	59·9	63·4	7·6	71·0	74·5	9·6	84·1
Confectioners and pastry cooks	4·3	1·9	6·2	7·8	4·5	12·3	8·4	6·1	14·5	9·4	7·6	17·0	12·5	13·0	25·5	17·7	28·9	46·6
Total	37·7	5·6	43·3	53·4	10·6	64·0	56·3	12·3	68·6	62·8	14·1	76·9	75·9	20·6	96·5	92·2	38·5	130·7
27. Drink preparation (MF.27)																		
Maltsters	7·8	0·2	8·0	10·4	—	10·4	10·6	0·1	10·7	10·3	—	10·3	9·4	0·1	9·5	9·1	—	9·1
Brewers	9·1	0·2	9·3	17·1	—	17·1	20·7	0·5	21·2	25·5	0·3	25·8	24·2	0·4	24·6	25·9	0·4	26·3
Distillers, rectifiers	0·3	—	0·3	*	*	*	0·7	—	0·7	0·6	—	0·6	*	*	*	*	*	*
Ginger beer, mineral water manufacture	0·5	0·1	0·6	*	*	*	1·3	0·1	1·4	2·4	—	2·4	4·3	0·3	4·6	6·0	0·7	6·7
Total	17·7	0·5	18·2	27·5	—	27·5	33·3	0·7	34·0	38·8	0·3	39·1	37·9	0·8	38·7	41·0	1·1	42·1
28. Smoking (MF.28)																		
Tobacco manufacture (xxii)	1·6	0·9	2·5	1·6	0·4	2·0	3·9	0·9	4·8	5·2	2·2	7·4	5·4	5·6	11·0	6·5	8·0	14·5
Tobacco pipe and snuff box manufacture (xxiii)	2·4	0·5	2·9	3·5	0·9	4·4	2·8	0·9	3·7	1·8	0·7	2·5	1·7	0·7	2·4	1·5	0·7	2·2
Total	4·0	1·4	5·4	5·1	1·3	6·4	6·7	1·8	8·5	7·0	2·9	9·9	7·1	6·3	13·4	8·0	8·7	16·7

* No separate return.

[A] OCCUPIED POPULATION, Manufacture sector (cont.)

Occupation	1841			1851			1861			1871			1881			1891		
	M	F	T	M	F	T	M	F	T	M	F	T	M	F	T	M	F	T
29. *Watches, instruments and toys* (MF.29)																		
Watch and clock makers	13·3	0·2	13·5	17·1	—	17·1	20·2	0·6	20·8	20·7	0·6	21·3	22·6	0·8	23·4	22·5	1·4	23·9
Philosophical and surgical instruments and electrical apparatus makers	2·1	0·1	2·2	2·9	0·5	3·4	3·9	0·4	4·3	4·5	0·5	5·0	7·1	0·5	7·6	18·1	1·4	19·5
Musical instrument makers	2·3	—	2·3	3·5	—	3·5	5·7	0·1	5·8	7·2	0·2	7·4	9·0	0·2	9·2	12·2	0·4	12·6
Fishing tackle and toy makers	1·9	0·5	2·4	—	0·8	0·8	3·0	1·8	4·8	3·5	1·7	5·2	3·0	1·9	4·9	3·9	2·8	6·7
Total	19·6	0·8	20·4	23·5	1·3	24·8	31·8	3·9	35·7	35·9	3·0	38·9	41·7	3·4	45·1	56·7	6·0	62·7
30. *Printing and bookbinding* (MF.30)																		
Printers	15·6	0·2	15·8	22·2	—	22·2	30·2	0·4	30·6	44·1	0·7	44·8	59·1	2·2	61·3	82·0	4·5	86·5
Lithographers and copper-plate printers	1·0	0·1	1·1	2·5	—	2·5	4·6	0·4	5·0	5·6	0·3	5·9	6·4	0·3	6·7	9·2	0·4	9·6
Bookbinders	4·5	1·5	6·0	5·7	3·8	9·5	6·5	5·4	11·9	8·9	7·6	15·5	9·5	10·6	20·1	11·5	14·2	25·7
Total	20·1	1·8	22·9	30·4	3·8	34·2	41·3	6·2	47·5	57·6	8·6	66·2	75·0	13·1	88·1	102·7	19·1	121·8
31. *Unspecified* (MF.31)																		
Manufacturers, managers, superintendents	*	*	*	*	*	*	*	*	*	*	*	*	6·9	0·5	7·4	7·1	0·9	8·0
Apprentices	*	*	*	*	*	*	2·6	0·2	2·8	4·3	0·7	5·0	3·8	0·8	4·6	*	*	*
Engine drivers, stokers, firemen (in manufacturing) (xxiv)	21·3	0·1	21·4	*	*	*	9·6	—	9·6	31·0	—	31·0	66·1	—	66·1	82·1	—	82·1
Machinists, machine workers	*	*	*	*	*	*	0·1	0·8	0·9	—	21·0	21·0	4·7	7·5	12·2	8·8	21·5	30·3
Artisans, mechanics	*	*	*	12·6	*	12·6	12·5	—	12·5	17·5	—	17·5	28·8	2·2	31·0	52·3	6·3	58·6
Factory labourers	7·4	8·8	16·2	*	—	*	2·2	4·2	6·4	12·3	9·4	21·7	16·9	4·2	21·1	28·0	10·1	38·1
Total	28·7	8·9	37·6	12·6	—	12·6	27·0	5·2	32·2	65·1	31·1	96·2	127·2	15·2	142·4	178·3	38·8	217·1
MANUFACTURE SECTOR – TOTAL	1,314·0	484·2	1,798·2	1,728·6	1,026·2	2,754·8	1,925·5	1,191·3	3,116·8	2,089·3	1,269·2	3,358·5	2,243·2	1,355·8	3,599·0	2,608·8	1,529·8	4,138·6

* No separate return.

Occupation	1841 M	1841 F	1841 T	1851 M	1851 F	1851 T	1861 M	1861 F	1861 T	1871 M	1871 F	1871 T	1881 M	1881 F	1881 T	1891 M	1891 F	1891 T
TRANSPORT SECTOR																		
1. *Warehouses and docks* (T.1) (xxv)																		
Harbour, dock, wharf and lighthouse service	1·3	—	1·3	19·4	—	19·4	34·9		34·9	29·8	—	29·8	42·6	—	42·6	63·8	0·1	63·9
Warehousemen (not Manchester)	10·9	0·8	11·7	13·9	2·9	16·8	18·3	4·3	22·6	36·8	7·2	44·0	26·7	4·2	30·9	23·6	2·9	26·5
Meters, weighers	0·5	—	0·5	*	*	*	0·7	—	0·7	1·3	—	1·3	1·1	—	1·1	1·0	—	1·0
Messengers, porters and others	24·2	0·2	24·4	89·3	3·6	92·9	78·7	1·1	79·8	94·9	1·5	96·4	129·6	1·6	131·2	175·6	3·5	179·1
Total	36·9	1·0	37·9	122·6	6·5	129·1	132·6	5·4	138·0	162·8	8·7	171·5	200·0	5·8	205·8	264·0	6·5	270·5
2. *Ocean navigation* (T.2)																		
Pilots	1·8	—	1·8	2·6	—	2·6	3·0	—	3·0	3·1	—	3·1	3·0	—	3·0			
Seamen (merchant service) (xxvi)	36·9	—	36·9	74·9	—	74·9	94·7	—	94·7	94·4	—	94·4	95·1	—	95·1	107·4	0·4	107·8
Steam navigation service (xxvii)	*	*	*	*	*	*	3·6	—	3·6	6·6	—	6·6	*	*	*			
Ship stewards and cooks	0·1	—	0·1	*	0·2	0·2	1·4	0·2	1·6	3·5	0·2	3·7	6·4	0·4	6·8			
Boatmen-on-seas (xxviii)	*	*	*	*	*	*	1·3	—	1·3	1·3	—	1·3	1·6	—	1·6			
Total	38·8	—	38·8	77·5	0·2	77·7	104·0	0·2	104·2	108·9	0·2	109·1	106·1	0·4	106·5	107·4	0·4	107·8
3. *Inland navigation* (T.3)																		
Canal and inland navigation service	0·8	—	0·8	4·2	—	4·2	4·2	—	4·2	3·1	—	3·1	4·5	0·2	4·7	5·1	0·1	5·2
Bargemen, lightermen, watermen and others	23·5	0·1	23·6	32·6	2·5	35·1	31·3	0·2	31·5	29·8	0·4	30·2	29·9	0·3	30·2	30·8	0·6	31·4
Total	24·3	0·1	24·4	36·8	2·5	39·3	35·5	0·2	35·7	32·9	0·4	33·3	34·4	0·5	34·9	35·9	0·7	36·6
4. *Railways* (T.4)																		
Railway officials and servants	2·0	—	2·0	18·5	0·1	18·6	42·9	0·1	43·0	70·9	0·3	71·2	115·9	0·7	116·6	146·0	0·9	146·9
Railway engine drivers, stokers	*	*	*	6·6	—	6·6	10·4	—	10·4	13·7	—	13·7	22·9	—	22·9	40·0	—	40·0
Total	2·0	—	2·0	25·1	0·1	25·2	53·3	0·1	53·4	84·6	0·3	84·9	138·8	0·7	139·5	186·0	0·9	186·9

*No separate return.

(Note: In 1891 the Ocean navigation categories Pilots, Seamen, Steam navigation service, Ship stewards and cooks and Boatmen-on-seas are bracketed together giving a combined total of M 107·4, F 0·4, T 107·8.)

[A] OCCUPIED POPULATION, Transport sector (cont.)

Occupation	1841			1851			1861			1871			1881			1891		
	M	F	T	M	F	T	M	F	T	M	F	T	M	F	T	M	F	T
5. *Roads* (T.5)																		
Toll collectors	2·3	0·5	2·8	3·5	1·3	4·8	3·3	1·6	4·9	2·4	1·5	3·9	0·7	0·4	1·1	0·3	0·1	0·4
Livery stable keepers, cab and bus owners	2·4	0·2	2·6	3·2	—	3·2	4·1	0·2	4·3	5·5	0·3	5·8	6·6	0·2	6·8	8·2	0·3	8·5
Cabmen, flymen, coachmen (xxix)	13·4	—	13·4	20·8	—	20·8	26·3	—	26·3	40·0	—	40·0	30·5	—	30·5	37·2	0·1	37·3
Carmen, carriers, carters and draymen	26·0	0·5	26·5	43·7	0·6	44·3	67·7	0·6	68·3	74·5	0·7	75·2	124·6	0·7	125·3	169·3	1·0	170·3
Tramways service	*	*	*	*	*	*	*	*	*	*	*	*	2·6	—	2·6	6·9	—	6·9
Wheelchair proprietors, attendants, and others	*	*	*	0·7	0·2	0·9	0·8	0·1	0·9	0·8	—	0·8	0·9	—	0·9	1·2	—	1·2
Total	44·1	1·2	45·3	71·9	2·1	74·0	102·2	2·5	104·7	122·2	2·5	124·7	165·9	1·3	167·2	223·1	1·5	224·6
TRANSPORT SECTOR – TOTAL	146·1	2·3	148·4	333·9	11·4	345·3	427·6	8·4	436·0	511·4	12·1	523·5	645·2	8·7	653·9	816·4	10·0	826·4
DEALING SECTOR																		
1. *Coals* (D.1)																		
Coal merchants and dealers	5·9	0·4	6·3	10·7	—	10·7	11·6	0·7	12·3	15·3	1·0	16·3	19·2	1·2	20·4	22·4	1·4	23·8
Coal heavers and labourers (xxx)	8·4	0·4	8·8	12·3	0·7	13·0	13·6	1·8	15·4	24·7	3·3	28·0	13·7	—	13·7	18·4	0·1	18·5
Total	14·3	0·8	15·1	23·0	0·7	23·7	25·2	2·5	27·7	40·0	4·3	44·3	32·9	1·2	34·1	40·8	1·5	42·3
2. *Raw materials* (D.2)																		
Timber merchants, wood dealers	2·0	0·1	2·1	6·7	0·4	7·1	9·2	0·5	9·7	12·0	0·9	12·9	11·8	1·0	12·8	15·3	1·4	16·7
Hop merchants, dealers	0·2	—	0·2	*	*	*	0·5	—	0·5	0·6	—	0·6	0·4	—	0·4	0·4	—	0·4
Hay, straw and chaff dealers	0·5	—	0·5	*	*	*	2·1	—	2·1	2·6	—	2·6	2·6	—	2·6	0·9	—	0·9
Corn, flour and seed merchants, dealers	4·5	0·4	4·9	7·3	—	7·3	13·0	—	13·0	12·0	0·8	12·8	9·2	0·8	10·0	10·6	1·0	11·6
Woolstaplers	1·7	0·1	1·8	1·8	—	1·8	1·5	0·8	2·3	2·3	—	2·3	2·5	—	2·5	1·7	—	1·7
Total	8·9	0·6	9·5	15·8	0·4	16·2	26·3	1·3	27·6	29·7	1·7	31·4	26·5	1·8	28·3	28·9	2·4	31·3

* No separate return.

Occupation	1841 M	1841 F	1841 T	1851 M	1851 F	1851 T	1861 M	1861 F	1861 T	1871 M	1871 F	1871 T	1881 M	1881 F	1881 T	1891 M	1891 F	1891 T
3. Clothing materials (D.3)																		
Cotton and calico warehousemen, dealers	1·0	0·2	1·2	*	*	*	2·3	0·2	2·5	3·2	—	3·2	3·1	0·4	3·5	1·9	0·1	2·0
Manchester warehousemen	*	*	*	*	*	*	3·3	—	3·3	0·8	—	0·8	1·9	—	1·9	1·0	—	1·0
Cloth, worsted and stuff merchants, dealers (xxxi)	0·1	—	0·1	*	*	*	2·5	—	2·5	1·7	—	1·7	5·5	0·1	5·6	4·0	0·2	4·2
Silk merchants, dealers	1·7	0·1	1·8	2·0	—	2·0	1·5	0·2	1·7	1·4	—	1·4	1·2	0·1	1·3	0·8	0·1	0·9
Total	2·8	0·3	3·1	2·0	—	2·0	9·6	0·4	10·0	7·1	—	7·1	11·7	0·6	12·3	7·7	0·4	8·1
4. Dress (D.4)																		
Drapers, linen, drapers, mercers	24·6	2·7	27·3	37·5	6·1	43·6	45·7	12·0	57·7	55·3	19·1	74·4	53·5	28·8	82·3	60·7	46·3	107·0
Hosiers, haberdashers	2·6	0·9	3·5	3·2	2·5	5·7	4·4	2·1	6·5	4·4	4·1	8·5	4·9	4·7	9·6	5·7	6·8	12·5
Hatters (xxi)	3·8	0·5	4·3	3·1	0·9	4·0	3·6	1·0	4·6	3·4	2·1	5·5	4·1	1·1	5·2	4·1	3·1	7·2
Clothes dealers	0·4	0·2	0·6	*	*	*	3·2	2·0	5·2	*	*	*	0·6	1·7	2·3	1·1	2·7	3·8
Total	31·4	4·3	35·7	43·8	9·5	53·3	56·9	17·1	74·0	63·1	25·3	88·4	63·1	36·3	99·4	71·6	58·9	130·5
5. Food (D.5)																		
Butchers, meat salesmen	44·7	1·3	46·0	60·6	1·6	62·2	65·6	2·5	68·1	72·7	3·2	75·9	78·2	3·5	81·7	93·6	5·3	98·9
Poulterers, game dealers	1·2	0·2	1·4	2·0	—	2·0	2·2	0·6	2·8	2·7	0·7	3·4	2·9	0·7	3·6	25·6	4·1	29·7
Fishmongers	4·4	0·7	5·1	7·1	2·0	9·1	9·5	2·2	11·7	12·7	2·2	14·9	15·5	2·4	17·9	(braced)	(braced)	(braced)
Milksellers, cowkeepers	6·4	1·7	8·1	10·7	3·7	14·4	13·8	3·9	17·7	16·5	4·1	20·6	21·3	4·5	25·8	29·9	5·7	35·6
Cheesemongers	2·5	0·2	2·7	3·6	—	3·6	3·9	0·3	4·2	4·3	0·4	4·7	4·0	0·4	4·4	4·7	0·4	5·1
Provision curers, buttermen	1·1	0·4	1·5	0·6	—	0·6	7·8	3·6	11·4	8·7	4·5	13·2	11·3	5·3	16·6	11·3	4·8	16·1
Grocers, tea dealers	34·3	7·5	41·8	58·3	13·4	71·7	74·0	19·8	93·8	88·6	22·5	111·1	103·4	26·4	129·8	135·6	46·3	181·9
Greengrocers, fruiterers, potato dealers	5·6	2·8	8·4	8·7	4·7	13·4	14·4	5·5	19·9	19·4	6·9	26·3	22·8	6·8	29·6	30·5	10·5	41·0
Others dealing in food	0·4	0·1	0·4	12·9	4·8	17·7	—	—	—	—	0·1	0·1	—	—	—	*	*	*
Oil and colourmen	1·5	—	1·6	1·9	—	1·9	2·5	0·1	2·6	3·5	0·3	3·8	4·3	0·4	4·7	6·1	0·7	6·8
Total	102·1	14·9	117·0	166·4	30·2	196·6	193·7	38·5	232·2	229·2	44·8	274·0	263·7	50·4	314·1	337·3	77·8	415·1

* No separate return.

[A] OCCUPIED POPULATION, Dealing sector (cont.)

Occupation	1841 M	1841 F	1841 T	1851 M	1851 F	1851 T	1861 M	1861 F	1861 T	1871 M	1871 F	1871 T	1881 M	1881 F	1881 T	1891 M	1891 F	1891 T
6. *Tobacco (D.6)*																		
Tobacconists (xxii)	1·6	0·9	2·5	1·6	0·4	2·0	3·6	1·3	4·9	5·0	2·0	7·0	5·8	3·0	8·8	6·5	8·0	14·5
7. *Wines, spirits and hotels (D.7)*																		
Wine and spirit merchants	3·5	0·2	3·7	6·6	0·3	6·9	8·1	0·4	8·5	10·6	0·4	11·0	7·5	0·4	7·9	7·4	0·5	7·9
Inn and hotel keepers, publicans	43·4	9·5	52·9	64·0	14·9	78·9	52·7	13·6	66·3	61·1	15·9	77·0	57·4	12·7	70·1	55·2	22·8	78·0
Beersellers	4·1	1·5	5·6				11·7	4·0	15·7	13·8	3·2	17·0	12·9	3·7	16·6	11·8	5·8	17·6
Cellarmen	0·4	—	0·4	3·5	0·7	3·5	1·7	0·1	1·8	3·2	—	3·2	5·7	0·3	6·0	8·8	0·8	9·6
Total	51·4	11·2	62·6	70·6	15·2	85·8	74·2	18·1	92·3	88·7	19·5	108·2	83·5	17·1	100·6	83·2	29·9	113·1
8. *Lodging and coffee houses (D.8)*																		
Lodging and boarding-house keepers	1·2	6·3	7·5	2·7	14·9	17·6	3·5	17·2	20·7	3·8	22·1	25·9	4·5	32·9	37·4	6·0	45·2	51·2
Coffee and eating-house keepers	1·2	0·3	1·5	3·2	1·7	4·9	2·6	1·4	4·0	3·3	2·2	5·5	5·5	2·7	8·2	7·5	4·1	11·6
Total	2·4	6·6	9·0	5·9	16·6	22·5	6·1	18·6	24·7	7·1	24·3	31·4	10·0	35·6	45·6	13·5	49·3	62·8
9. *Furniture (D.9)*																		
Furniture brokers, dealers	0·3	0·1	0·4	2·8	0·7	3·5	3·2	0·8	4·0	3·7	0·8	4·5	5·1	0·9	6·0	6·0	1·2	7·2
Dealers in pictures and works of art	0·2	—	0·2	*	*	*	0·4	—	0·4	0·1	0·1	0·2	1·1	0·1	1·2	1·4	0·2	1·6
Pawnbrokers	2·3	0·3	2·6	3·5	—	3·5	4·7	0·8	5·5	6·5	1·1	7·6	7·6	1·3	8·9	9·8	1·7	11·5
Total	2·8	0·4	3·2	6·3	0·7	7·0	8·3	1·6	9·9	10·3	2·0	12·3	13·8	2·3	16·1	17·2	3·1	20·3
10. *Stationery and publications (D.10)*																		
Stationers, law stationers	3·4	0·4	3·8	3·9	1·0	4·9	7·1	1·8	8·9	7·9	3·0	10·9	10·0	5·2	15·2	12·7	9·1	21·8
Publishers, book-sellers, librarians	4·5	0·6	5·1	6·0	0·9	6·9	7·7	1·2	8·9	7·3	1·2	8·5	8·5	1·4	9·9	11·4	2·2	13·6
Newsagents	0·5	0·1	0·6	1·8	0·2	2·0	2·4	0·4	2·8	3·7	0·7	4·4	4·4	1·1	5·5	7·5	2·3	9·8
Music publishers, sellers	0·3	—	0·3	0·5	—	0·5	0·6	0·1	0·7	*	*	*	1·2	0·2	1·4	*	*	*
Ticketwriters, billstickers	0·1	—	0·1	*	*	*	0·2	0·1	0·3	*	*	*	0·6	0·5	1·1	1·1	1·3	2·4
Total	8·8	1·1	9·9	12·2	2·1	14·3	18·0	3·6	21·6	18·9	4·9	23·8	24·7	8·4	33·1	32·7	14·9	47·6

* No separate return.

Occupation	1841			1851			1861			1871			1881			1891		
	M	F	T	M	F	T	M	F	T	M	F	T	M	F	T	M	F	T
11. *Household utensils and ornaments* (D.11)																		
Earthernware, china and glass dealers (xviii)	1·9	0·7	2·6	3·2	1·4	4·6	3·9	1·4	5·3	3·5	1·5	5·0	4·3	1·9	6·2	4·7	2·5	7·2
Ironmongers, hardwaremen	6·0	0·3	6·3	7·7	—	7·7	10·3	0·6	10·9	15·9	1·5	17·4	15·2	0·9	16·1	20·1	1·4	21·5
Gold and silversmiths, jewellers (xiv)	4·0	0·2	4·2	5·3	0·8	6·1	7·1	0·9	8·0	9·5	1·5	11·0	10·5	1·9	12·4	10·3	1·7	12·0
Total	11·9	1·2	13·1	16·2	2·2	18·4	21·3	2·9	24·2	28·9	4·5	33·4	30·0	4·7	34·7	35·1	5·6	40·7
12. *General Dealers* (D.12)																		
General shopkeepers, dealers (xxxii)	15·3	10·0	25·3	19·9	17·8	37·7	9·6	15·5	25·1	29·9	26·2	56·1	29·1	25·8	54·9	28·0	25·6	53·6
Hawkers, hucksters, costers	11·2	3·7	14·9	16·5	9·2	25·7	27·3	13·3	40·6	30·6	19·2	49·8	29·4	17·7	47·1	42·4	16·6	59·0
Marine store and rag dealers	1·7	0·7	2·4	3·5	2·5	6·0	6·4	2·1	8·5	2·3	1·4	3·7	1·9	1·4	3·3	2·3	1·8	4·1
Total	28·2	14·4	42·6	39·9	29·5	69·4	43·3	30·9	74·2	62·8	46·8	109·6	60·4	44·9	105·3	72·7	44·0	116·7
13. *Unspecified* (D.13)																		
Merchants	11·8	0·1	11·9	7·9	—	7·9	13·7	0·1	13·8	15·9	—	15·9	10·3	0·1	10·4	8·4	0·1	8·5
Brokers, agents, factors (xxxii)	9·4	0·3	9·7	13·4	0·9	14·3	17·8	0·1	17·9	22·8	—	22·8	30·7	0·5	31·2	36·3	0·8	37·1
Auctioneers, appraisers, valuers house agents	3·0	0·1	3·1	3·5	—	3·5	5·3	0·1	5·4	6·3		6·3	10·0	0·1	10·1	11·7	0·1	11·8
Salesmen and buyers	1·6	0·1	1·7	1·4	—	1·4	1·2	1·1	2·3	2·6	1·7	4·3	3·2	1·4	4·6	3·8	1·0	4·8
Commercial travellers	1·3	—	1·3	8·4	—	8·4	10·8	—	10·8	17·9	—	17·9	35·5	—	35·5	43·9	0·2	44·1
Total	27·1	0·6	27·7	34·6	0·9	35·5	48·8	1·4	50·2	65·5	1·7	67·2	89·7	2·1	91·8	104·1	2·2	106·3
DEALING SECTOR – TOTAL	293·7	57·3	351·0	438·3	108·4	546·7	535·3	138·2	673·5	656·3	181·8	838·1	715·8	208·4	924·2	851·3	298·0	1,149·3

[A] OCCUPIED POPULATION (cont.)

Occupation	1841			1851			1861			1871			1881			1891		
	M	F	T	M	F	T	M	F	T	M	F	T	M	F	T	M	F	T
INDUSTRIAL SERVICE SECTOR.																		
1. Banking, insurance, Accounts (IS.1)																		
Bankers	1·6	—	1·6	1·5	0·1	1·6	1·4	—	1·4	1·3	—	1·3	1·7	—	1·7	1·9	—	1·9
Bank service	*	*	*	*	*	*	0·6	—	0·6	10·9	—	10·9	14·9	0·1	15·0	19·9	0·1	20·0
Insurance service	0·1	—	0·1	*	*	*	2·7	—	2·7	5·4	—	5·4	14·9	0·2	15·1	30·9	0·6	31·5
Accountants	4·4	—	4·4	5·7	—	5·7	6·3	0·1	6·4	9·8	—	9·8	11·5	0·1	11·6	7·9	0·1	8·0
Commercial clerks (xxxiii)	34·8	0·2	35·0	37·5	—	37·5	55·7	0·3	56·0	89·6	1·4	91·0	175·5	6·0	181·5	229·4	17·9	247·3
Officers of commercial companies and others	*	*	*	*	*	*	0·3	0·1	0·4	0·1	0·4	0·5	0·4	—	0·4	1·5	0·2	1·7
Total	40·9	0·2	41·1	44·7	0·1	44·8	67·0	0·5	67·5	117·1	1·8	118·9	218·9	6·4	225·3	291·5	18·9	310·4
2. Labour (IS.2)																		
General labourers (xxxiv)	306·3	12·2	318·5	324·6	7·2	331·8	306·5	3·5	310·0	509·5	7·2	516·7	556·9	2·8	559·7	594·1	1·9	596·0
INDUSTRIAL SERVICE – TOTAL	347·2	12·4	359·6	369·3	7·3	376·6	373·6	3·9	377·5	626·6	9·0	635·6	775·8	9·2	785·0	885·6	20·8	906·4

* No separate return.

Occupation	1841 M	1841 F	1841 T	1851 M	1851 F	1851 T	1861 M	1861 F	1861 T	1871 M	1871 F	1871 T	1881 M	1881 F	1881 T	1891 M	1891 F	1891 T
PUBLIC SERVICE AND PROFESSIONAL SECTOR																		
1. *Administration (central)* (PP.1)																		
Civil service officers and clerks	10·4	—	10·4	27·2	0·1	27·3	17·4	—	17·4	26·4	3·3	29·7	22·4	3·2	25·6	31·6	8·5	40·1
Civil service messengers (xxxv)	3·1	0·5	3·6	7·8	1·1	8·9	16·5	0·1	16·6	24·2	—	24·2	20·7	0·5	21·2	35·5	0·8	36·3
Post office	*	*	*	*	*	*	12·3	1·8	14·1	*	*	*	*	*	*	*	*	*
Telegraph, telephone service				3·4	—	3·4	2·4	0·2	2·6	2·7	0·2	2·9	7·2	2·2	9·4	10·6	4·4	15·0
East India service	0·5	—	0·5				1·2	—	1·2	1·0	—	1·0	0·2	—	0·2	0·2	—	0·2
Total	14·0	0·5	14·5	38·4	1·2	39·6	49·8	2·1	51·9	54·3	3·5	57·8	50·5	5·9	56·4	77·9	13·7	91·6
2. *Administration (local)* (PP.2)																		
Municipal, parish, union, district officers	5·1	0·4	5·5	9·8	1·0	10·8	8·4	1·5	9·9	11·0	2·4	13·4	11·9	3·0	14·9	13·7	5·2	18·9
Other local and county officials							0·3	—	0·3	0·2	—	0·2	6·1	—	6·1	6·1	—	6·1
Total	5·1	0·4	5·5	9·8	1·0	10·8	8·7	1·5	10·2	11·2	2·4	13·6	18·0	3·0	21·0	19·8	5·2	25·0
3. *Administration (sanitary)* (PP.3)																		
Town drainage and scavenging	0·5	—	0·5	1·5	—	1·5	2·1	—	2·2	2·2	—	2·2	4·1	0·2	4·3	6·3	0·2	6·5
Total	0·5	—	0·5	1·5	—	1·5	2·1	—	2·2	2·2	—	2·2	4·1	0·2	4·3	6·3	0·2	6·5
4. *Army* (PP.4) (xxxvi)																		
Army officers (effective and retired)	36·6	—	36·6	5·3	—	5·3	9·7	—	9·7	9·9	—	9·9	10·9	—	10·9	13·0	—	13·0
Soldiers and NCOs				36·5	—	36·5	66·8	—	66·8	70·7	—	70·7	56·9	—	56·9	78·5	—	78·5
Militia yeomanry, volunteers	*	*	*	*	*	*	2·8	—	2·8	5·7	—	5·7	10·7	—	10·7	*	*	*
Army pensioners	1·1	—	1·1	18·7	—	18·7	11·7	—	11·7	7·6	—	7·6	8·6	—	8·6	10·0	—	10·0
Total	37·7	—	37·7	60·5	—	60·5	91·0	—	91·0	93·9	—	93·9	87·1	—	87·1	101·5	—	101·5

* No separate return.

[A] OCCUPIED POPULATION, Public Service and Professional sector (cont.)

Occupation	1841			1851			1861			1871			1881			1891		
	M	F	T	M	F	T	M	F	T	M	F	T	M	F	T	M	F	T
5. Navy (PP.5) (xxxvi)																		
Navy officers (effective and retired)	6·2	—	6·2	4·2	—	4·2	4·4	—	4·4	4·4	—	4·4	3·9	—	3·9	3·5	—	3·5
Seamen, RN		—		6·7	—	6·7	17·7	—	17·7	18·9	—	18·9	16·8	—	16·8	22·0	—	22·0
Royal Marines (Officers and men)	1·8	—	1·8	6·3	—	6·3	8·7	—	8·7	8·4	—	8·4	7·7	—	7·7	9·5	—	9·5
Coastguards, RN	*	*	*	*	*	*	3·8	—	3·8	3·8	—	3·8	*	*	*	*	*	*
Reserve																		
Navy pensioners	1·0	—	1·0	8·0	—	8·0	6·2	—	6·2	7·3	—	7·3	8·9	—	8·9	11·0	—	11·0
Total	9·0		9·0	25·2		25·2	40·8		40·8	42·8		42·8	37·3		37·3	46·0		46·0
6. Police and Prisons (PP.6)																		
Prison officers	*			*			2·6	0·5	3·1	3·2	0·6	3·8	2·9	0·6	3·5	2·3	0·5	2·8
Police	13·5	—	13·5	16·4	—	16·4	22·0	—	22·0	28·3	—	28·3	32·5	—	32·5	39·9	—	39·9
Total	13·5		13·5	16·4		16·4	24·6	0·5	25·1	31·5	0·6	32·1	35·4	0·6	36·0	42·2	0·5	42·7
7. Law (PP.7)																		
Judges, barristers, solicitors	13·7	—	13·7	15·8	—	15·8	14·5	—	14·5	15·9	—	15·9	17·4	—	17·4	20·0	—	20·0
Law students							0·7	—	0·7	1·5	—	1·5	1·7	—	1·7	2·0	—	2·0
Law clerks and others (xxxvii)	14·7	—	14·7	16·4	—	16·4	18·5	—	18·5	21·3	—	21·3	24·5	0·1	24·6	27·4	0·2	27·6
Total	28·4		28·4	32·2		32·2	33·7		33·7	38·7		38·7	43·6	0·1	43·7	49·4	0·2	49·6
8. Medicine (PP.8)																		
Physicians, surgeons, practitioners	17·1	—	17·1	19·2	—	19·2	14·4	—	14·4	14·7	—	14·7	15·1	—	15·1	18·9	0·1	19·0
Medical students, assistants							3·6	—	3·6	4·5	—	4·5	6·1	—	6·1	1·9	—	1·9
Chemists, druggists	9·9	0·2	10·1	14·0	0·3	14·3	16·0	0·4	16·4	19·2	0·5	19·7	18·4	0·6	19·0	20·6	1·3	21·9
Dentists	0·6	—	0·6	*	—	*	1·6	—	1·6	2·3	—	2·3	3·6	—	3·6	4·6	0·3	4·9

* No separate return.

Occupation	1841			1851			1861			1871			1881			1891		
	M	F	T	M	F	T	M	F	T	M	F	T	M	F	T	M	F	T
Midwives	—	0·7	0·7	—	2·0	2·0	—	1·9	1·9	—	2·2	2·2	—	2·6	2·6	*	*	*
Medical services	0·3	13·6	13·9	0·8	24·0	24·8	0·5	24·9	25·4	0·5	28·7	29·2	2·0	35·2	37·2	4·1	54·0	58·1
Total	27·9	14·5	42·4	34·0	26·3	60·3	36·1	27·2	63·3	41·2	31·4	72·6	45·1	38·5	83·6	50·1	55·7	105·8
9. Art and amusement (Painting) (PP.9)																		
Painters (artists)	3·8	0·3	4·1	4·9	0·5	5·4	4·6	0·9	5·5	5·0	1·1	6·1	6·1	1·9	8·0	9·3	3·0	12·3
Sculptors (artists)	0·3	—	0·3	*	*	*	0·6	—	0·6	0·8	—	0·8	0·8	—	0·8			
Engravers (artists)	4·7	—	4·7	4·9	—	4·9	4·7	—	4·7	4·8	—	4·8	2·2	0·1	2·3			
Photographers	**	**	**	2·5	0·3	2·8	2·4	0·2	2·6	4·0	0·7	4·7	5·4	1·3	6·7	8·1	2·5	10·6
Art students							*	*	*	*	*	*	1·3	1·1	2·4	1·5	1·3	2·8
Figure and image makers	0·7	—	0·7				1·5	0·1	1·6	3·0	0·2	3·2	0·3	0·1	0·4	0·4	—	0·4
Animal and bird preservers, naturalists	0·2	—	0·2				0·3	—	0·3	*	*	*	0·7	0·1	0·8	0·8	0·2	1·0
Total	9·7	0·3	10·0	12·3	0·8	13·1	14·1	1·2	15·3	17·6	2·0	19·6	16·8	4·6	21·4	20·1	7·0	27·1
10. Art and amusement (music etc.) (PP.10)																		
Musicians (not teachers) (xxxviii)	3·4	0·2	3·6	5·3	0·8	6·1	8·0	1·6	9·6	8·9	2·0	10·9	10·6	3·4	14·0	10·7	10·5	21·2
Actors	1·0	0·4	1·4	1·2	0·7	1·9	1·3	0·9	2·2	1·9	1·7	3·6	2·2	2·4	4·6	3·6	3·7	7·3
Art, music and theatre service	*	*	*	1·4	—	1·4	0·2	0·1	0·3	2·4	0·2	2·6	1·1	0·3	1·4	2·0	0·5	2·5
Performers, showmen, exhibition service	0·1	—	0·1	2·7	0·2	2·9	0·7	0·1	0·8	0·9	0·3	1·2	1·4	0·5	1·9	8·1	1·0	9·1
Billiards, cricket and other games service	0·1	—	0·1				0·7	0·1	0·8	*	*	*	3·1	0·1	3·2			
Total	4·6	0·6	5·2	10·6	1·7	12·3	10·9	2·8	13·7	14·1	4·2	18·3	18·4	6·7	25·1	24·4	15·7	40·1

* No separate return.

[A] OCCUPIED POPULATION, Public Service and Professional sector (cont.)

Occupation	1841 M	F	T	1851 M	F	T	1861 M	F	T	1871 M	F	T	1881 M	F	T	1891 M	F	T
11. *Literature* (PP.11)																		
Authors, editors, journalists	0·6	—	0·6	1·5	—	1·5	1·7	0·1	1·8	2·2	0·2	2·4	3·0	0·4	3·4	5·1	0·7	5·8
Reporters, shorthand writers (xxxix)							0·6	—	0·6	2·0	—	2·0	2·7	—	2·7	2·4	0·1	2·5
Total	0·6	—	0·6	1·5	—	1·5	2·3	0·1	2·4	4·2	0·2	4·4	5·7	0·4	6·1	7·5	0·8	8·3
12. *Science* (PP.12)																		
Engaged in scientific pursuits	0·1	—	0·1	0·4	—	0·4	0·4	0·1	0·5	0·9	0·1	1·0	1·2	—	1·2	1·9	—	1·9
Literary and scientific instruction service	*	*	*	*	*	*	0·4	0·1	0·5	1·2	—	1·2	1·1	0·1	1·2	1·5	0·5	2·0
Total	0·1	—	0·1	0·4	*	0·4	0·8	0·2	1·0	2·1	0·1	2·2	2·3	0·1	2·4	3·4	0·5	3·9
13. *Education* (PP.13)																		
Schoolmasters	21·1	30·9	52·0	28·0	66·9	94·9	28·6	27·7	56·3	19·4	38·8	58·2	39·8	94·2	134·0	59·4	153·0	212·4
Teachers, professors, lecturers							14·2	45·4	59·6	16·2	60·3	76·5	9·9	36·6	46·5			
School service	*	*	*	*	*	*	0·1	0·1	0·2	0·2	0·2	0·4	1·8	1·1	2·9	3·6	2·0	5·6
Total	21·1	30·9	52·0	28·0	66·9	94·9	42·9	83·2	116·1	36·0	99·3	135·3	51·5	131·9	183·4	63·0	155·0	218·0
14. *Religion* (PP.14)																		
Clergymen (Established Church)	14·5	—	14·5	17·3	—	17·3	19·2	—	19·2	20·7	—	20·7	21·7	—	21·7	24·2	—	24·2
Roman Catholic priests	5·9	—	5·9	8·7	—	8·7	1·2	—	1·2	1·6	—	1·6	2·1	—	2·1	2·5	—	2·5
Ministers and priests of other denominations							7·9	—	7·9	9·3	—	9·3	9·7	—	9·7	10·1	—	10·1
Missionaries and service readers							2·0	1·1	3·1	2·1	1·2	3·3	2·9	1·7	4·6	5·1	4·2	9·3

* No separate return.

Occupation	1841			1851			1861			1871			1881			1891		
	M	F	T	M	F	T	M	F	T	M	F	T	M	F	T	M	F	T
Theological students	*	*	*	*	*	*	0·8	—	0·8	2·4	—	2·4	2·9	—	2·9	3·4	—	3·4
Nuns, sisters of charity	*	*	*	*	*	*	—	0·9	0·9	—	2·5	2·5	—	3·8	3·8	—	4·7	4·7
Church, chapel, cemetery officers and servants (xl)	*	*	*	4·1	0·9	5·0	4·4	1·1	5·5	3·4	1·4	4·8	4·6	1·7	6·3	6·1	1·8	7·9
Total	20·4	—	20·4	30·1	0·9	31·0	35·5	3·1	38·6	39·5	5·1	44·6	43·9	7·2	51·1	51·4	10·7	62·1
PUBLIC SERVICE AND PROFESSIONAL SECTOR – TOTAL	192·6	47·2	239·8	200·9	98·8	399·7	383·3	122·0	505·3	429·3	148·8	578·1	459·7	199·2	658·9	563·0	265·2	828·2
DOMESTIC SERVICE SECTOR																		
1. *Indoor service* (DS.1)																		
Indoor servants	212·7	772·8	985·5	74·3	751·6	825·9	62·1	962·8	1,024·9	68·3	1,204·5	1,272·8	56·3	1,230·4	1,286·7	52·1	1,257·8	1,309·9
Inn and hotel servants	*	*	*	23·4	31·9	55·3	24·4	14·2	38·6	28·5	20·6	49·1	35·8	26·5	62·3	46·4	44·3	90·7
College, club, hospital, institution and other servants	2·3	1·7	4·0	0·6	0·8	1·4	3·5	4·5	8·0	5·8	10·5	16·3	8·8	12·4	21·2	15·0	18·7	33·7
Total	215·0	774·5	989·5	98·3	784·3	882·6	90·0	981·5	1,071·5	102·6	1,235·6	1,338·2	100·9	1,269·3	1,370·2	113·5	1,320·8	1,434·3
2. *Outdoor service* (DS.2)																		
Coachmen and grooms (xxix)	*	*	*	22·3	—	22·3	33·3	—	33·3	37·4	—	37·4	73·2	—	73·2	89·3	—	89·3
Gardeners (i)	*	*	*	4·5	—	4·5	14·6	—	14·6	18·7	—	18·7	74·6	0·1	74·7	89·6	—	89·6
Park, lodge and gatekeepers (xii)	6·0	0·4	6·4	*	*	*	0·6	0·7	1·3	1·2	0·8	2·0	1·7	0·7	2·4	1·9	0·8	2·7
Gamekeepers				7·5	—	7·5	9·9	—	9·9	12·4	—	12·4	12·6	—	12·6	13·8	—	13·8
Total	6·0	0·4	6·4	34·3	—	34·3	58·4	0·7	59·1	69·7	0·8	70·5	162·1	0·8	162·9	194·6	0·8	195·4

* No separate return.

[A] OCCUPIED POPULATION, Domestic Service sector (cont.)

Occupation	1841			1851			1861			1871			1881			1891		
	M	F	T	M	F	T	M	F	T	M	F	T	M	F	T	M	F	T
3. *Extra service* (DS.3)																		
Cooks (not private)	*	*	*	*	*	*	1·2	0·1	1·3	2·4	—	2·4	2·9	1·7	4·6	4·9	9·2	14·1
Charwomen	—	20·1	20·1	—	53·7	53·7	—	65·3	65·3	—	77·7	77·7	—	92·5	92·5	—	104·8	104·8
Office keepers (not government) (xii)	*	*	*	*	*	*	0·2	0·3	0·5	0·8	3·2	4·0	2·9	4·3	6·2	7·2	10·2	17·4
Washing and bathing service	0·7	46·8	47·5	—	133·5	133·5	1·7	166·7	168·4	1·7	168·9	170·6	3·4	176·7	180·1	6·9	185·2	192·1
Hairdressers, wig makers	9·7	0·4	10·1	10·9	—	10·9	10·6	0·6	11·2	12·4	1·5	13·9	14·1	0·8	14·9	24·1	1·3	25·4
Chimney sweeps	4·6	0·1	4·7	6·2	—	6·2	6·5	0·4	6·9	6·2	—	6·2	6·7	0·1	6·8	7·7	0·1	7·8
Total	15·0	67·4	82·4	17·1	187·2	204·3	20·2	233·4	253·6	23·5	251·3	274·8	29·0	276·1	305·1	50·8	310·8	361·6
DOMESTIC SERVICE SECTOR – TOTAL	236·0	842·3	1,078·3	149·7	971·5	1,121·2	168·6	1,215·6	1,384·2	195·8	1,487·7	1,683·5	292·0	1,546·2	1,838·2	358·9	1,632·4	1,991·3
TOTAL OCCUPIED POPULATION (Sum of nine sectors given above)	4,334·3	1,511·4	5,845·7	5,714·3	2,402·4	8,116·7	6,380·8	2,803·9	9,184·7	7,076·8	3,204·3	10,281·1	7,784·0	3,403·9	11,187·9	8,830·9	3,818·5	12,649·4

[B] RESIDUAL POPULATION

	1841			1851			1861			1871			1881			1891		
	M	F	T	M	F	T	M	F	T	M	F	T	M	F	T	M	F	T
I. PROPERTY OWNING, INDEPENDENT (PO)																		
Landowners‡	17·0	13·0	30·0	17·0	13·3	30·3	15·2	15·6	30·8	14·2	8·8	23·0	15·0	10·0	25·0			
Housowners‡	10·0	15·0	25·0	10·6	18·1	28·7	11·4	24·7	36·1	4·4	12·7	17·1	8·0	20·0	28·0			
Mine owners‡	0·7		0·7	0·7		0·7	1·1		1·1	*	*	*	*	*	*			
Ship and boat owners‡	1·0	0·1	1·1	1·5	0·1	1·6	1·7	0·3	2·0	1·8	0·1	1·9	1·8	—	1·8			
Persons of independent means	96·9	294·4	391·3	31·2	118·9	150·1	26·3	89·4	115·7	28·9	146·7	175·6	30·0	170·0	200·0	97·5	409·1	506·6
Total (xliii)	125·6	322·5	448·1	61·0	150·4	211·4	55·7	130·0	185·7	49·3	168·3	217·6	54·8	200·0	254·8	97·5	409·1	506·6
II. INDEFINITE																		
Persons of indefinite occupation	265·2	—	265·2	65·9	—	65·9	69·5	—	69·5	123·0	—	123·0	269·5	*	269·5	353·8	—	353·8
Vagrants, paupers, lunatics, prisoners‡	71·7	—	71·7	34·6	—	34·6	12·4	—	12·4	1·2	—	1·2	*		*	*		*
Total	336·9	—	336·9	100·5	—	100·5	81·9	—	81·9	124·2	—	124·2	269·5	—	269·5	353·8	—	353·8
III. DEPENDENT CLASS	2,978·5	6,302·6	9,281·1	2,905·4	6,593·6	9,499·0	3,257·8	7,356·1	10,613·9	3,808·7	8,280·7	12,089·4	4,531·6	9,730·6	14,262·2	4,771·0	10,722·0	15,493·0
TOTAL 'RESIDUAL' POPULATION (Property owners, indefinite dependents)	3,441·0	6,625·1	10,066·1	3,066·9	6,744·0	9,810·9	3,395·4	7,486·1	10,881·5	3,982·2	8,449·0	12,431·2	4,855·9	9930·6	14,786·6	5,222·3	11,131·1	16,353·1†
ENTIRE POPULATION (total occupied plus total residual population)	7,775·3	8,136·5	15,911·8	8,781·2	9,146·4	17,927·6	9,776·2	10,290·0	20,066·2	11,059·0	11,653·3	22,712·3	12,639·9	13,334·5	25,974·4	14,053·2	14,949·6	29,002·5

* No separate return.
† See note appended to Table 6.
‡ Unless otherwise described.

K

NOTES TRANSCRIBED FROM BOOTH'S MANUSCRIPT
VOLUME

  (i) Gardeners in this class are apparently confused with those in domestic service.
      A correct comparison may be made by adding the two classses together.

 (ii) A number of those returned as grooms probably belong to transport, but as
      the census couples them with others who are connected with breeding it was
      necessary to place them here.

(iii) It is uncertain whether fishermen who were at sea on the census night are
      included in the returns, but it is believed that no considerable number escaped
      enumeration.

(iv) The returns in 1871 of 'mine service' and 'miners in other minerals' apparently
      include a large number who should have been returned in the specified
      branches of mining.

  (v) The females given in these lines for 1861 are described in the census for that
      year as 'coal labourers' and 'copper manufacturers', but the figures for the
      other decades make it obvious that they properly belong to mining.

(vi) House surveyors *only* are returned here in 1851.

(vii) All persons returned as 'contractors' have been placed here.

(viii) Masons', bricklayers' and plasterers' labourers are included in these three
      lines – paviors are included with masons in 1841 and 1851.

 (ix) In 1841 and 1851 paviors are returned with masons.

  (x) The figures for road and railway labourers, 1841, are estimates, deducted
      from 'general labourers' (see *Industrial services*).

 (xi) In 1871 this line includes, almost beyond doubt, the boiler and domestic
      machinery makers.

(xii) In the earlier censuses, pattern designers (about 1,000 to 1,600) are included
      in this line. In 1881 they appear to have been placed elsewhere.

(xiii) It will be noticed that where (as in 1851) there is an undue number in this line,
      it is accounted for by a corresponding deficiency in other items of the section.

(xiv) Goldsmiths have been equally divided between *manufacture* and *dealing*.

(xv) There appears to be some difficulty in the classification of fancy box makers,
      which are probably with this line in 1871 and with paper box etc. makers in
      other years.

(xvi) See note (xv) above.

(xvii) Those returned in this section in 1851 appear in the census as workers 'in
      oils, gums, resins etc.'

(xviii) This line in 1851 includes sacking, net, mat, sail makers etc.

(xix) In 1871 some of the cotton printers were apparently included in the general
      item, 'dyers, printers etc.'

(xx) Wool and silk dyers are, in the 1851 returns, included in woollen cloth and
      silk manufacture respectively.

(xxi) For the decades 1841–81 a proportion of one-fourth has been taken for those
      dealing only in hats.

(xxii) Tobacco manufacturers and tobacconists (or dealers) are together except
      in the 1861, 1871 and 1881 censuses. They have here been equally divided.

(xxiii) It is doubtful whether all those returned here in 1841, 1851, and 1861 are
      tobacco pipe makers, as a large portion of them are merely described as 'pipe
      makers'.

(xxiv) This section is unsatisfactory, particularly in 1841 and 1851. It is probable that some of the engine drivers here returned in 1841 belong to transport, and that some of those given in transport in 1851 belong here, but there is no means of ascertaining the number.

(xxv) These items are apparently confused, especially in 1871.

(xxvi) Only those seamen who were on shore or in port at the period of the census are returned.

(xxvii) In 1881 this item is probably merged in seamen.

(xxviii) With bargemen in 1841 and 1851.

(xxix) The distinction between coachmen – whether domestic or not domestic – has not been accurately maintained. (See *Domestic service*, section 2.)

(xxx) It is not unlikely that some of the persons returned here in 1871 are coal miners.

(xxxi) Cloth merchants only are returned here in 1871.

(xxxii) There were 15,000 described in the 1851 census as 'other general merchants, dealers and agents'. Here they have been divided between general shopkeepers and brokers, agents and factors.

(xxxiii) From the 1841 figures an estimated number has been deducted for law clerks. (See *Law*.)

(xxxiv) A proportion has been taken from the 1841 figures for railway and road labourers. (See *Building*, section 3.)

(xxxv) In the earlier censuses the artificers and labourers in HM Dockyards are here included, but in 1881 they have been returned in their proper trades. Post office employees are included in this line in 1871 and 1881.

(xxxvi) The Army and Navy stationed in England and Wales only on the census night are here returned.

(xxxvii) The total for 1841 is deducted from those described as commercial clerks.

(xxxviii) Musicians and music teachers are coupled together in the 1871 and 1881 censuses. They have here been separated by estimate.

(xxxix) Under literature, in census 1871, a line appears – 'students and others – males, 58,900; females, 77,800'. From these a proportion of 2,000 males has been taken for reporters, who are not separately returned; and the remainder have been relegated to the dependent classes.

(xl) Church officers, 1841, are included with the local officers, in *Administration*.

(xli) The figures for 1871 are estimates, taken from the census line 'others in service'.

(xlii) The figures for land and house owners are estimates in 1841, taken from those described as 'independent'. In 1881 the whole of the figures in this division are estimates, deducted from the 'unoccupied'.

Appendix E. The allocations of 1861

This list, which covers all occupations separately distinguished in the 1861 national occupational abstract, is divided into four parts.

Part A: Allocations for which we have direct authorisation from Booth's manuscript list. (Parts B and C constitute the residue.)

Part B: Occupations with 150 or more workers, for which the allocations have been inferred. (See text.)

Part C: All other census occupations, with details of the numbers involved and suggested allocations.

Part D: An alphabetical list of all occupations occurring in Parts A, B and C. Note that occasionally two allocations are given (e.g. hatter, silversmith). When working from the enumerators' books the context of the occupational information will often suggest the best allocation in cases of doubt.

Standard abbreviations used are as follows:

mcht	– merchant	govt	– government
dlr	– dealer	svt	– servant
mfr	– manufacturer, manufacture	lbr	– labourer
mkr	– maker	agt	– agent
wkr	– worker	kpr	– keeper

PART A

AGRICULTURE AND BREEDING

1. *Farming*

Agricultural lbr (outdoor); agricultural student; colonial planter; farm bailiff; farmer, grazier; farm servant (indoor); farmer's sons, grandsons etc; gardener (employed in gardens); hop grower; nurseryman (horticulturalist); others in agriculture; others (horticulture); shepherd; teazle grower; watercress grower; willow rod grower; woodman.

2. *Land service*

Agricultural engine and machine wkr; agricultural machine proprietor; land drainage service (not towns).

3. *Breeding*

Animal, bird dlr; castrator; cattle, sheep dlr; salesman; dog dlr, trainer; drover; horse breaker; horse clipper; horse keeper, groom (not domestic servant); horse proprietor, breeder, dlr; huntsman, whipper-in; knacker; others engaged about animals; pig mcht, dlr; rabbit catcher, killer; riding master; vermin destroyer; veterinary surgeon and farrier.

4. *Fishing*
Fisherman.

MINING

1. *Mining*
Alum miner; blende miner; charter master; coal miner; colliery viewer; copper miner; fossil digger, dlr; iron miner; jet miner; lead mine agt; lead miner; manager, receiver, clerk (coal mines); manganese miner; mine contractor; miner (not described); mining company's secretary, service; others connected with mines; sulphur miner; tin miner.

2. *Quarrying*
Limestone, lime quarrier, burner; slate mfr, mcht, dlr; slate quarrier; stone agt., mcht, cutter, dresser, etc.; stone quarrier.

3. *Brickmaking*
Beach lbr; brick mkr, dlr; chalk miller, digger, dlr; clay lbr; flint dlr; gravel digger, lbr; gun flint mkr; lime mcht; others working and dealing in stone and clay; quarryman (not otherwise described): sand mfr, wkr, dlr; stone dredger, digger.

4. *Salt and waterworks*
Salt mfr; waterworks service; well sinker.

BUILDING

1. *Management*
Architect; builder; civil engineer; contractor; contractor for sewers, docks etc.; land surveyor; estate agt; railway contractor; road contractor, surveyor, inspector; surveyor; surveyor, inspector of shipping.

2. *Operative*
Blind mkr; bricklayer; building materials dlr; carpenter, joiner; cornice and moulding mkr; gas fitter; hothouse builder; locksmith; bellhanger; marble mason; mason; others in houses and buildings; oven builder; painter; plumber; glazier; paperhanger; plasterer; sign painter; slater, tiler; staircase builder; stone, sea waller; thatcher; wood carver.

3. *Roadmaking*
Excavator, navvy; pavior; plate layer; railway lbr; road lbr.

MANUFACTURE

1. *Machinery*
Agricultural machinery and implement mkr; bellows mkr; block and print cutter; bobbin mkr; boilermaker; card mkr, cutter (for machines); comb mkr (for manufacture); doffer plate mkr; engine and machine mkr, dlr, agt; fire engine, fire hose and bucket mkr; flyer, fly mkr; frame mkr (cotton); framesmith; gas meter mkr, gasometer, retort mkr; gear and stay mkr; hackle mkr; hat, wig, bonnet, block mkr; heald, havel mkr, knitter; loom mkr; millmaker; millwright; others making and dealing in machines,

tools; picker mkr; pump mkr; reed mkr; roller mkr; scaleboard mkr; sewing machine mkr; shuttle mkr; sieve and riddle mkr; spindle mkr; washing machine mkr, mangle mkr; weighing machine, scale and measure mkr.

2. Tools etc.

Anvil mkr; armourer; awl mkr; blade mkr, forger; bayonet, lance mkr; coiner, coin stamper; cork screw mkr; cutler; cutlery, edge tool grinder; draughtsman; embosser; file mkr; fork mkr, grinder; gimlet mkr; gunsmith, gun mfr; knife mkr; medallist, medal mkr; mould mkr, die sinker; needle mfr; others connected with dies, medals; pattern designer; pencil mkr; pin mfr; razor mkr; sawsmith, mkr; scissors mkr; scythe, sickle mkr; shears mkr; shovel, spade mkr; steel pen mkr; sword cutler, mkr; thimble mkr; tool mkr, dlr; typefounder.

3. Shipbuilding

Block, oar, mast mkr; boat and barge builder; sailmaker; shipbuilder, shipwright; ship's chandler; ship's rigger; shipsmith.

4. Iron and steel

Anchor and chain mkr; blacksmith; bit mkr; bolt, nut mkr; curb, chain mkr; curry-comb mkr; fire-iron mkr; fender mkr; gridiron mkr; frying pan mkr; galvanised iron mfr; gas pipe, tube, retort mkr; grinder (undef.); hairpin mfr; handcuff, felons' iron mkr; handle mkr; hinge mkr; holloware mkr; iron box, safe mkr; iron mfr, moulder, founder; key mkr; latchmaker; nail mfr; others working and dealing in iron and steel; press wkr; rivet mkr; saddler's iron monger; screwcutter, wkr; scuttle mkr; skewer mkr; small ware mfr (steel); snuffers mkr; spring bar mkr; spring, door spring mkr; spring hook mkr; spur mkr; steel mfr; steel trap mkr; stirrup mkr; stove, grate, range mkr.

5. Copper, tin, lead etc.

Bath mkr; brass mfr, founder, moulder; brazier; burnisher; candlestick, chandelier mkr; castor, cruet frame mkr; chaser; coffin furniture (metal) mfr; copper mfr; copper plate mfr; coppersmith; electro-plate mfr; ferule mkr; gas apparatus, fittings mkr; gilt toy, watch key mkr; herald chaser; hook and eye, clasp and buckle mfr; lacquerer; lamp and lantern mkr; lead mcht, dlr; lead mfr; looking-glass silverer; metal gal-vaniser, stamper; metal refiner, wkr, turner, dlr; others in copper; others in lead, antimony; others in tin, quicksilver; others in mixed metals; pewterer, pewterpot wkr; plater, plated ware mfr; ring and fancy chain mkr; sinker mkr; spelter mfr; spoon mkr; tin foil mkr, dlr; tin man, tin wkr, tinker; tin mfr; tin plate wkr; tray-maker; urn, kettle, tea pot mkr; white metal mfr; whitesmith; wire mkr, drawer; wire weaver; zinc mfr, wkr.

6. Gold and silver

Assayer; gold beater; gold and silver lace mfr; gold and silver wire drawer; goldsmith, silversmith, jeweller; guard chain mkr; lapidary; orris weaver; others in gold and silver; pearl cutter, wkr; diamond cutter, wkr; pencil case mkr; water gilder.

7. Earthenware

Barytes mfr; bead and bugle mkr, dlr; black-ornament mkr; earthenware mfr; filter mkr; flint grinder, miller; gem and flint mkr; glass enameller, stainer, painter; glass mfr; glass, sand, emery paper mfr; millstone mkr, cutter; others in earthenware;

others working and dealing in glass; parian mfr; plaster, cement mfr, dlr; scagliola, artificial stone mkr; spar mfr, cutter; terra cotta mfr; whetstone, grindstone mkr.

8. *Coals and gas*
Charcoal burner, dlr; coke burner, dlr; gas engineer; gas works service; others working and dealing in coal; patent fuel mfr; peat, turf, cutter dlr.

9. *Chemicals*
Ammunition, cartridge wkr; asphalte mfr; blacking mkr, dlr; drug grinder, packer, wkr; drysalter; dye, colour mfr; dyewood cutter; emery mfr, wkr; fireworks mfr, pyrotechnics; fuzee mkr; gunpowder, percussion caps mfr; ink, printing ink mfr; manufacturing chemist and lbr; match mkr, seller; others in chemicals; shot, bullet mfr; starch mfr; varnish mkr.

10. *Furs and leather*
Currier; fellmonger; furrier; leather dyer, stainer; parchment, vellum mfr; skinner; tanner.

11. *Glue tallow etc.*
Bone crusher, boiler, calciner; gelatine, isinglass mkr, dlr; glue and size wkr; manure mfr, dlr; soap boiler; tallow chandler; wax refiner.

12. *Hair etc.*
Bone cutter, wkr, turner; brush and broom mkr, seller; comb mkr; feather dresser, dlr; haft mkr, turner; hair, bristle mfr; horn wkr, turner, dlr; ivory cutter, wkr, turner; others working in hair; others working in skins etc.; quill-pen mkr; shell wkr, dlr; tortoiseshell wkr, dlr; whalebone wkr, dlr.

13. *Woodworkers*
Basket mkr; birch broom, besom mkr; bowl and wooden spoon mkr; box mkr; cane dresser, dlr; cooper; cork cutter; crate mkr; fence, hurdle mkr; hoop mkr, bender; ladder mkr; press and safe mkr; last, boot tree mkr; lath mkr; others in bark; others in wood; others working, dealing in cane; packing case mkr; peg, clothes peg mkr; rush, sedge mfr; saddle tree mkr; sawyer; timber, wood, hewer, chopper, bender; toll handle mkr; trap, mousetrap mkr; turner (wood); willow cutter, weaver, dyer; wine cooper.

14. *Furniture*
Bedstead, mattress, bed tick mkr; buhl cutter, wkr; cabinet mkr, upholsterer; carver and gilder; chair mkr, mfr; door furniture mkr; dressing and writing case mkr; french polisher; fret cutter; looking-glass mkr; marquetry inlayer, veneerer; others in furniture; picture-frame mkr; plate chest mkr; Tunbridge ware mfr; undertaker.

15. *Carriages and harness*
Axletree maker; coach maker; others connected with carriages; perambulator, wheel chair mkr; railways carriage spring/buffer mkr; railway carriage, wagon mkr; railway wheel mkr; saddle harness mfr; wheelwright; whip mkr.

16. *Paper*
Card mkr; envelope mkr; fireplace ornament mkr; hat, band, match box mkr; machine, hand ruler; others in paper; paper bag mkr; paper box mkr; paper embosser; paper mfr; paper stainer; paper tube mkr; papier mâché mfr; pattern card mkr.

17. Floorcloth, waterproofs etc.
Floorcloth, oilcloth mfr; gutta-percha mfr, dlr; india rubber mfr, dlr; japanner; leathercloth mfr; oilskin mfr; waterproof articles mkr, dlr.

18. Woollens
Alpaca mfr; angora mfr; blanket mfr; carpet, rug mfr; felt mfr; flannel mfr; flock dlr, mkr; knitter; linsey weaver; listing, baize, serge mfr; mohair, angola mfr; moreen mfr; others in wool and worsted; quilter, quilt mkr; stuff mfr; woollen cloth mfr; woollen flock mfr, dlr; woollen yarn mfr, dlr; worsted mfr.

19. Cotton and silk
Berlin wool wkr, dlr; candle and lamp-wick mkr; chenille mfr; cotton band, mkr, spinner; cotton mfr; counterpane, coverlet mkr; crape mfr, dlr; crochet mfr; factory hand (undefined); fancy goods (silk) mfr; fancy wkr, dlr; fustian mfr; gingham mfr; gauze mfr; lint mfr; loom turner (silk, ribbon); muslin mfr; others in cotton and flax; packer and presser; plush, shag mfr; ribbon mfr; shawl mfr; shroud mkr; silk, satin mfr; small ware mfr (silk); spinner (not otherwise described); table cover mfr; velvet mfr (silk); weaver (undefined).

20. Flax, hemp, etc.
Canvas mkr, dlr; cocoa-fibre matting mfr; damask mfr; flax and linen mfr; hammock mkr; hemp mfr; jute mfr; mat mkr, seller; mop mkr; net mkr; oakum wkr, dlr; others in hemp; rope, cord mkr; sacking, sack, bag mkr, dlr; sailcloth mfr; tarpaulin mkr; tent, marquee mkr; tow mfr.

21. Lace
Artificial flower mkr; braid mfr; coach lace mkr, weaver; cotton velvet, velveteen mfr; embroiderer; elastic fabric wkr; fringe, tassel mkr; girth, web mkr, dlr; lace mfr; others in mixed fabrics; spinner; tape mfr, dlr; thread mfr; trimming mkr, dlr; wadding mkr.

22. Dyeing
Bleacher (undefined); cotton, calico dyer; cotton, calico printer; dyer, scourer, calinderer; fuller; fustian dyer; hot presser; silk dyer, printer; woollen printer; wool, woollen dyer.

23. Dress
Army and Navy contractor; baby linen mkr, dlr; bonnet mkr, dlr; boot-lace mkr; cap mkr, dlr; clothier; crinoline mkr; glove knitter; glover, leather glover; hatter, hat mfr; hose (stocking) mfr; list, carpet slipper mkr; milliner, dress maker; others in dress; patten, clog mkr; robe, cassock mkr; shirt mkr, seamstress; shoe, boot mfr; shoe heel, tip mkr; smock, frock mkr; stock tie, cravat mkr; straw hat, bonnet mkr; straw plait dlr; straw plait mfr; tailor; worsted, silk, cotton, cloth glove mkr.

24. Sundries
Accoutrement mkr; button mkr, dlr; fancy leather goods mkr; leather case, portmanteau, bag, trunk mkr; portfolio, pocket book, card case mkr; strop, strap, belt, thong mkr; umbrella, parasol, stick mkr.

25. Food preparation
Chicory mfr, dlr; chocolate, cocoa mfr; licquorice mfr; miller; mustard mfr; oil cake

mkr, dlr; oil miller, refiner; sauce, pickle, catsup mkr; seed crusher; spice mcht, dlr; sugar refiner; vinegar mfr.

26. *Baking*
Baker; confectioner, cook (pastry).

27. *Drink preparation*
Brewer; cordial mkr; distiller, rectifier; ginger beer, soda water, mineral water mfr; maltster; wine mfr; yeast mkr, dlr.

28. *Smoking*
Tobacco, cigar, snuff mkr; tobacco pipe mkr.

29. *Watches, instruments, toys*
Archery goods mkr; bat, ball mkr; billiard, bagatelle board mkr; bird-cage mkr; bowstring mkr; chess, backgammon (men, board) mkr; fish-hook mkr; fishing rod and tackle mkr; gut, catgut mkr; musical instruments mkr, dlr; music string mkr; optician, spectacle mkr; others connected with games, sports; others in musical instruments; philosophical instruments mkr; piano etc. tuner; steel toy mkr; surgical instruments mkr; toy mkr, dlr; truss, bandage mfr; watch and clock mkr.

30. *Printing*
Bookbinder; copper, steel plate printer; herald painter; letter, mark, stamp cutter; lithographer, lithographic printer; map and print colourer; map and print seller; others connected with prints and pictures; printer.

31. *Unspecified*
Apprentice; engine driver, stoker, fireman; factory lbr; foreman; furnaceman; machinist, sewing machine operator; machine lbr, wkr; manufacturer, manager, superintendant; mechanic; overlooker, manager, bailiff; timekeeper; winding machine operator.

TRANSPORT

1. *Warehouses and docks*
Ballast master, agt, heaver; corn, coal, fruit meter; cotton porter; courier; diver; harbour, dock service, dock lbr; lighthouse kpr, light dues collector; lumper, hobbler, beachman; messenger, porter, errand boy; meter (not distinguished); others (messengers); others (seas and rivers); others (storage); packer; ship lbr, watchman, kpr; shipping master; stevedore; storekeeper, storehouse lbr; warehouseman; water bailiff, sea reeve; wharfinger.

2. *Ocean navigation*
Boatmen on seas; pilot; seamen (merchant service); ship steward; steam navigation service.

3. *Inland navigation*
Bargeman, lighterman, waterman; canal, inland navigation service; others connected with canals and rivers.

4. *Railways*
Others (railways); railway agt; railway company svt, porter; railway engine driver, stoker; railway official, clerk, stationmaster; railway police.

5. Roads
Cabman, flyman; carman, carrier, carter; coachman (not domestic); coach, omnibus, cab owner; donkey kpr, driver; drayman; haulier; livery stable kpr; omnibus time kpr; others (conveyance); toll collector, contractor, agt; waterman (cabstand); wheelchair proprietor, drawer.

DEALING
1. Coals
Coal lbr, heaver; coal mcht, dlr.

2. Raw materials
Bark wkr, dlr; chaff cutter; corn mcht, dlr; flour dlr, agt; hay, straw dlr; hop mcht, dlr; sawdust, chip mcht, dlr; seed, meal mcht; timber mcht, dlr; timber, wood surveyor, valuer; wood dlr; wool stapler.

3. Clothing materials
Carpet dlr, warehouseman; cloth mcht, warehouseman; cotton, calico dlr, warehouseman; cotton fent dlr; cotton warehouseman; cotton waste dlr; fancy goods (silk) dlr; flax dlr, agt; lace dlr, agt, factor; linen dlr, agt, factor; Manchester warehouseman; mungo mcht; muslin agt, dlr; ribbon dlr, warehouseman; silk dlr, silkman; silk mercer; stuff mcht, warehouseman; waste dlr (wool, worsted); woollen mcht, dlr, salesman; woollen waste dlr; worsted mcht, dlr; worsted waste dlr; yarn dlr, warehouseman.

4. Dress
Clothes dealer, salesman, outfitter; draper, linen draper, mercer; hatter; hosier, haberdasher.

5. Food
Artist's colourman; butcher, meat salesman; cheesemonger; coffee roaster, dlr; egg mcht, dlr; fish drier, curer, fishmonger, dlr, seller; greengrocer, fruiterer; grocer, tea dlr; herbalist; milkseller, cow kpr; oil and colourman; others (vegetable food); oyster, shell fish dlr, seller; potato mcht, dlr; poulterer, game dlr; provision curer, dlr.

6. Tobacco
Tobacconist.

7. Wines, spirits, hotels
Beer seller; cellarman; inn kpr, hotel kpr; others in drinks, stimulants; porter, ale, cider, spruce agent; publican, licensed victualler; wine and spirit mcht.

8. Lodging and coffee houses
Coffee house, eating house kpr; lodging, boarding house kpr.

9. Furniture
Furniture broker, dlr; picture cleaner, dlr; pawnbroker.

10. Stationery and publications
Bill sticker, distributor; book agt, canvasser, hawker; bookseller, publisher; label writer, ticket writer; law stationer; librarian; music engraver, printer; music publisher, seller; newspaper agt, vendor, newsroom kpr; paper mcht, dlr; stationer.

11. *Household utensils, ornaments*
China, glass, earthenware mender; earthenware, china, glass dlr, importer; glass bottle mcht, dlr; glass factor, agent; gold and silversmith, jeweller; hardware man, dlr; ironmonger; iron, scrap iron dlr.

12. *General dealers*
Bazaar stall kpr; catsmeat dlr; fancy goods importer, warehouseman, dlr; fancy repository kpr; fruit, flower hawker, vendor; general dlr, huckster, costermonger; hawker, pedlar; marine store dlr; perfumer; rag gatherer, dlr; salt agent, mcht, dlr; shopkeeper (undefined); shopman; sponge mcht, dlr; water carrier, dlr; watercress gatherer, vendor; woollen rag dlr.

13. *Unspecified*
Agent, factor; auctioneer, appraiser, valuer; house agt, rent collector; broker; buyer; commercial traveller; coal, colliery agt, factor; iron mcht, agt; merchant; salesman; ship broker, agt; stock, share dlr, broker; underwriter.

INDUSTRIAL SERVICE

1. *Banking, insurance, accountancy*
Accountant; actuary; banker; bank officer, agt; bill discounter, money lender, dlr; commercial clerk; insurance, benefit society, agt, officer; loan office, manager, secretary; officer of commercial society or company; others (mercantile); public notary; scrivenor.

2. *Labour*
General lbr (branch undefined).

PUBLIC SERVICE AND PROFESSIONAL

1. *Central administration*
Artificer, lbr (HM Dockyard); civil servant (not GPO); customs; East India and Colonial service; govt messenger and workman; HM Court and Household; Inland Revenue; office keeper (govt.); other govt officers; Post Office; telegraph service.

2. *Local administration*
Mayor, alderman, municipal officer; fireman (fire brigade); officer of local board; other county and local officers; sheriff's officer and clerk; town crier, bellman; union, district, parish officer.

3. *Sanitary administration*
Crossing sweeper; dust collector, sifter, picker; scavenger, nightman; sewerman, lbr.

4. *Army*
Army agent; Army half-pay, retired officer; Army officer; Chelsea pensioner; militia; others connected with Army; soldier.

5. *Navy*
Coastguard; Greenwich pensioner; Navy agt; Navy half-pay, retired officer; Navy

hospital officer; Navy officer; others connected with Navy; Royal Marines; RN reserve; seaman (RN).

6. Police and prisons
Police; prison officer.

7. Law
Barrister, advocate, special pleader, conveyancer; judge superior or local; law clerk; law student; officer of law court; parliamentary agt; solicitor, attorney.

8. Medicine
Analytical chemist; chemist, druggist; corn cutter, chiropodist; cupper, bleeder; dentist; medical student, assistant; midwife; nurse (not domestic service); officer of medical society, medical agent, clerk; others in medicine; patent medicine vendor, herb doctor; physician; professor of hydropathy, homeopathy; surgeon, apothecary.

9. Art and amusement (painting)
Animal, bird preserver, taxidermist; artist in hair, hair worker; artist, painter; composition, ornament maker; engraver; figure, image maker; jet carver, worker; modeller; naturalist; others in carving, figures; photographic artist; sculptor; wax modeller.

10. Art and amusement (music etc.)
Actor; billiard table kpr, mkr; conjuror, performer, acrobat; cricketer; dancer; equestrian; exhibition kpr, svt; others connected with music; others in exhibitions; persons engaged about theatres; pugilist; skittle mkr, player; tennis-racket mkr; ventriloquist; vocalist, musician (not teacher).

11. Literature
Author, editor, writer; newspaper proprietor, editor, publisher; reporter, shorthand writer.

12. Science
Astronomer, observatory assistant; botanist, geologist; literary, private secretary; mineralogist; museum curator, keeper; other scientific persons; phrenologist; secretary, officer, literary and scientific societies; translator, interpreter.

13. Education
Drawing master, teacher; governess; general teacher; Head, Fellow of College; music master; others engaged in teaching; professor and lecturer on art, science; professor, teacher of languages; professor, teacher of mathematics; school college, secretary, officer, agt; schoolmaster; teacher of dancing, gymnastics; teacher of geography, navigation; teacher of writing.

14. Religion
Burial ground, cemetery svt; chapel keeper; chorister; church cleaner; church officer, sacristan; clergyman; missionary, scripture reader, itinerant preacher; nun, sister of charity; officer of religious society, clerical agt; other religious teachers, church officers; parish clerk, church clerk; pew opener; priest in other religions; Protestant minister; Roman Catholic priest; sexton, grave digger; theological student.

DOMESTIC SERVICE

1. *Indoor*

Clubhouse officer, manager, secretary; college servant; cook (domestic service); domestic svt, house kpr; hospital, lunatic asylum attendant; housemaid; inn, hotel, dining room svt; keeper of assembly, public rooms; laundry maid; mess contractor, messman; nurse (domestic service); officer of charitable institution; proprietor, officer, lunatic asylum.

2. *Outdoor*

Coachman, groom; gamekeeper; gardener; park, gate, lodge kpr.

3. *Extra service*

Bath kpr, attendant; charwoman; chimney sweeper; college porter; cook (not domestic service); frizette mkr; hairdresser, wig mkr; hairpad mkr; headdress mkr; mangler, laundry kpr; office kpr, porter (not govt); officer at menagerie, zoo; others (in attendance); servant's registry office keeper; shoeblack; washerwoman.

PROPERTY OWNING AND INDEPENDENT

Annuitant; boat owner; capitalist, shareholder; coalowner; copper mine proprietor; gentleman, independent; house proprietor; iron mine proprietor; landowner, proprietor; lead mine proprietor; magistrate; MP; mine proprietor and owner; peer; quarry owner, agt; shipowner.

PART B

List of occupations comprising 150 or more persons, which were allocated to occupational groups, notwithstanding no allocation by Booth.

Males		
Dressing, writing case mkr	168 (0·2)	MF.14
Dyewood cutter	215 (0·2)	MF.9
Hackle mkr	159 (0·2)	MF.1
Haulier	666 (0·7)	T.5
Steel toy mkr	557 (0·6)	MF.29
Straw plait dlr	239 (0·2)	MF.24
Varnish mkr	225 (0·2)	MF.9
Woollen rag dlr	193 (0·2)	D.12

Females. None

PART C

All census occupations other than those mentioned in Parts A and B, with national totals, and suggested allocations.

(Since all these are below 150 in size, Booth's totals would not be significantly affected wherever they were added in; however, they are listed for the sake of completeness).

Males	*National total*	*Suggested allocation*
Artificial-limb mkr	26	MF.29
Artificial-tooth mkr	38	MF.29
Artist's brush mkr	19	MF.12

Males	National total	Suggested allocation
Average adjuster	24	IS.1
Beehive mkr	22	MF.13
Bell founder	45	MF.5
Block printer	20	MF.30
Bombazine weaver	12	MF.18
Bone gatherer	111	D.12
Bronzer	74	MF.5
Bunting mfr	10	MF.18
Calico, cotton, print, salesman, dlr	19	D.3
Calico furniture glazer	55	MF.14
Clay mcht	59	M.3
Coach, carriage broker	19	D.13
Coal contractor	26	D.1
Coal shipper	21	D.13
Coprolite digger	139	M.1
Cork mcht	17	D.2
Cotton net mkr	19	MF.19
Curiosity dlr	49	D.12
Drabbet mfr	22	MF.20
Enameller	65	MF.7
Flax bleacher	29	MF.22
Flax dyer	12	MF.22
Fullers earth mfr	27	MF.9
Gimp mfr	123	MF.19
Glazier's diamond mkr	12	MF.6
Globe mkr	18	MF.30
Gravel mcht	12	M.3
Grindery dlr, wkr	14	MF.10
Guide	20	T.1
Gum mfr	30	MF.11
Gunpowder, flash, shot belt mfr	133	MF.2
Hair mcht	34	MF.12
Hame mkr	116	MF.15
Hide and skin dlr	73	D.2
Hot water apparatus mkr	13	MF.5
Ice mkr, mcht, dlr	23	MF.25
Inkstand mkr	30	MF.5
Lamp black mkr	19	MF.9
Leather embosser	7	MF.10
Leather japanner	52	MF.10
Leather-lace cutter	25	MF.10
Map mkr	23	MF.30
Marble mcht	16	M.3
Mill band mkr	34	MF.16
Morocco, patent leather mfr	75	MF.10
Mosaic tile mkr	53	MF.7
Naval architect	47	MF.3
Officer of military hospital	24	PP.4
Opera, theatrical agent	10	PP.10

Males	*National total*	*Suggested allocation*
Others connected with books	20	D.10
Others connected with fine art	36	PP.9
Others connected with law	4	PP.7
Others connected with literature	5	PP.11
Others connected with shipbuilding	32	MF.3
Others connected with surgical instruments	13	MF.29
Others connected with watches and scientific instruments	28	MF.29
Others (gums)	18	MF.11
Others (implements)	4	MF.1
Others in arms	30	MF.2
Others in board, lodging	9	D.8
Others in silk	52	MF.19
Others (skins)	26	MF.10
Others (water)	18	MF.4
Others (working and dealing in food)	18	MF.25
Peel mkr	15	MF.25
Pitch, tar, etc. wkr	39	MF.9
Playing card mkr	9	MF.16
Roasting jack mkr	63	MF.4
Sailor's society agent	17	IS.1
Saltpetre mkr	12	MF.9
Saw handle, frame mkr	75	MF.13
Seal engraver	44	MF.2
Secretary	107	IS.1
Sewing machinist	21	MF.31
Shawl warehouseman	27	D.4
Staple mkr	19	MF.2
Stenciller	12	MF.30
Sulphur, brimstone mkr	14	MF.9
Teacher of blind, deaf, dumb	23	PP.13
Theatrical property mkr, dlr	29	MF.23
Wafer mkr	10	MF.25
Waste dlr	28	D.3
Waste paper dlr	13	D.12
Wood screw mkr	46	MF.13
Woollen cord mfr	13	MF.18

Females		
Artificial-tooth mkr	37	MF.29
Artist's brush mkr	13	MF.12
Bone gatherer, dlr	15	D.12
Bronzer	35	MF.5
Bunting mfr	104	MF.18
Encaustic tile mfr	10	MF.7
Garter mkr	34	MF.23
Gold-beater's skin mkr	74	MF.10
Hair mcht	10	MF.12
Map mkr, publisher	111	MF.30

Females	*National total*	*Suggested allocation*
Muslin embroiderer	17	MF.23
Others (animal food)	3	MF.25
Others (arms)	51	MF.2
Others (board and lodging)	70	D.8
Others (canals, rivers)	2	T.3
Others connected with books	21	D.10
Others connected with fine art	10	PP.9
Others connected with law	4	PP.7
Others connected with literature	22	PP.11
Others (grease)	42	MF.11
Others (gums)	21	MF.11
Others (implements)	14	MF.1
Others (salt)	7	M.4
Others (sea, river)	14	T.2
Others (silk)	28	MF.19
Others (skins)	41	MF.10
Others (surgical instruments)	5	MF.29
Penholder mkr	17	MF.13
Pupils at convent	90	Dependent class
Theatrical properties mkr	19	MF.23
Valentine mkr	15	MF.16
Wafer mkr	12	MF.25
Wood screw mkr	62	MF.13

PART D

ALPHABETICAL CONSOLIDATION OF ALL OCCUPATIONS

Accountant, IS.1
Accoutrement mkr, MF.24
Acrobat, PP.10
Actor, PP.10
Actuary, IS.1
Advocate, PP.7
Agent, D.13
Agricultural engine and machine wkr, AG.2
Agricultural lbr (outdoor), AG.1
Agricultural machine proprietor, AG.2
Agricultural machinery and implement mkr, MF.1
Agricultural student, AG.1
Alderman, PP.2
Ale agt, D.7
Alpaca mfr, MF.18
Alum miner, M.1
Ammunition wkr, MF.9
Analytical chemist, PP.8
Anchor mkr, MF.4

Angora mfr, MF.18
Animal dlr, AG.3
Animal preserver, PP.9
Annuitant, PO
Anvil mkr, MF.2
Apothecary, PP.8
Appraiser, D.13
Apprentice, MF.31
Archery goods mkr, MF.29
Architect, B.1
Armourer, MF.2
Army agent, officer, retired officer, PP.4
Army contractor, MF.23
Art lecturer, professor, PP.13
Artificer (H.M. Dockyard), PP.1
Artificial-flower mkr, MF.21
Artificial-limb mkr, MF.29
Artificial-stone mkr, MF.7
Artificial-tooth mkr, MF.29
Artist, PP.9
Artist in hair, PP.9

Artist's brush mkr, MF.12
Artist's colourman, D.5
Asphalte mfr, MF.9
Assayer, MF.6
Assembly rooms kpr, DS.1
Astronomer, PP.12
Attorney, PP.7
Auctioneer, D.13
Author, PP.11
Average adjuster, IS.1
Awl mkr, MF.2
Axletree mkr, MF.15

Baby-linen dlr, mkr, MF.23
Backgammon board, men, mkr, MF.29
Bag dlr, mkr, MF.20
Bagatelle board mkr, MF.29
Bargeman, T.3
Basket mkr, MF.13
Bailiff (in industry), MF.31
Baize mfr, MF.18
Baker, MF.26
Ball mkr, MF.29
Ballast agt, heaver, master, T.1
Bandage mfr, MF.29
Bank agt, officer, IS.1
Banker, IS.1
Barge builder, MF.3
Barge owner, T.3
Bark dlr, wkr, D.2
Barrister, PP.7
Barytes mfr, MF.7
Bat mkr, MF.29
Bath attendant, kpr, DS.3
Bath mkr, MF.5
Bayonet mkr, MF.2
Bazaar stall kpr, D.12
Beach lbr, M.3
Beachman, T.1
Bead dlr, mkr, MF.7
Bed tick mkr, MF.14
Bedstead mkr, MF.14
Beehive mkr, MF.13
Beer seller, D.7
Bell founder, MF.5
Bell hanger, B.2
Bellman, PP.2
Bellows mkr, MF.1
Belt mkr, MF.24
Benefit society agt, officer, IS.1
Berlin wool dlr, wkr, MF.19

Besom mkr, MF.13
Bill discounter, IS.1
Bill distributor, sticker, D.10
Billiard board mkr, MF.29
Billiard table kpr, mkr, PP.10
Birch broom mkr, MF.13
Birdcage mkr, MF.29
Bird dlr, AG.3
Bird preserver, PP.9
Bit mkr, MF.4
Black ornament mkr, MF.7
Blacking dlr, mkr, MF.9
Blacksmith, MF.4
Blade forger, mkr, MF.2
Blanket mfr, MF.18
Bleacher, MF.22
Bleeder, PP.8
Blende miner, M.1
Blind mkr, B.2
Block and print cutter, MF.1
Block mkr, MF.3
Block printer, MF.30
Boarding house kpr, D.8
Boat builder, MF.3
Boat owner, PO
Boatman on seas, T.2
Bobbin mkr, MF.1
Boilermaker, MF.1
Bolt mkr, MF.4
Bombazine weaver, MF.18
Bone boiler, calciner, crusher, MF.11
Bone cutter, turner, wkr, MF.12
Bone gatherer, D.12
Bonnet block mkr, MF.1
Bonnet dlr, mkr, MF.23
Book agt, canvasser, hawker, publisher, D.10
Bookbinder, MF.30
Bookseller, D.10
Boot-lace mkr, MF.23
Boot mfr, MF.23
Boot-tree mkr, MF.13
Botanist, PP.12
Bowl mkr, MF.13
Bowstring mkr, MF.29
Box mkr, MF.13
Braid mfr, MF.21
Brass founder, mfr, moulder, MF.5
Brazier, MF.5
Brewer, MF.27
Brick dlr, mkr, M.3

Bricklayer, B.2
Brimstone mkr, MF.9
Bristle mfr, MF.12
Broker, D.13
Bronzer, MF.5
Broom mkr, seller, MF.12
Brush mkr, seller, MF.12
Buckle mfr, MF.5
Bugle dlr, mkr, MF.7
Buhl cutter, wkr, MF.14
Builder, B.1
Building material dlr, B.2
Bullet mfr, MF.9
Bunting mfr, MF.18
Burial ground svt, PP.14
Burnisher, MF.5
Butcher, D.5
Button dlr, mkr, MF.24
Buyer, D.13

Cab owner, T.5
Cabinet mkr, upholsterer, MF.14
Cabman, T.5
Calenderer, MF.22
Calico dlr, salesman, warehouseman, D.3
Calico dyer, printer, MF.22
Calico furniture glazer, MF.14
Canal navigation service, T.3
Candlestick mkr, MF.5
Candlewick mkr, MF.19
Cane dlr, dresser, MF.13
Canvas dlr, mkr, MF.20
Cap dlr, mkr, MF.23
Capitalist, PO
Card case mkr, MF.24
Card cutter (for machines), mkr, MF.1
Card mkr, MF.16
Carman, T.5
Carpenter, B.2
Carpet dlr, warehouseman, D.3
Carpet mfr, MF.18
Carpet-slipper mkr, MF.23
Carriage broker, D.13
Carrier, T.5
Carter, T.5
Cartridge wkr, MF.9
Carver, MF.14
Cassock mkr, MF.23
Caster mkr, MF.5
Castrator, AG.3

Cat gut mkr, MF.29
Catsmeat dlr, D.12
Catsup mkr, MF.25
Cattle dlr, salesman, AG.3
Cellarman, D.7
Cement dlr, mfr, MF.7
Cemetery svt, PP.14
Chaff cutter, D.2
Chain mkr, MF.4
Chair mkr, mfr, MF.14
Chalk dlr, digger, miller, M.3
Chandelier mkr, MF.5
Chapel kpr, PP.14
Charcoal burner, dlr, MF.8
Charitable institution officer, DS.1
Charter master, M.1
Charwoman, DS.3
Chaser, MF.5
Cheesemonger, D.5
Chelsea Pensioner, PP.4
Chemist, PP.8
Chenille mfr, MF.19
Chess board, men mkr, MF.29
Chicory dlr, mfr, MF.25
Chimney sweeper, DS.3
China dlr, importer, mender, D.11
Chip dlr, mcht, D.2
Chiropodist, PP.8
Chocolate mfr, MF.25
Chorister, PP.14
Church cleaner, clerk, officer, PP.14
Cider agt, D.7
Cigar mkr, MF.28
Civil engineer, B.1
Civil svt (not GPO), PP.1
Clasp mfr, MF.5
Clay lbr, mcht, M.3
Clergyman, PP.14
Clerical agt, PP.14
Clerk (coal mines), M.1
Clock mkr, MF.29
Clog mkr, MF.23
Cloth glove mkr, MF.23
Cloth mcht, warehouseman, D.3
Clothes dlr, outfitter, salesman, D.4
Clothes peg mkr, MF.13
Clothier, MF.23
Clubhouse manager, officer, secretary, DS.1
Coach broker, D.13
Coach-lace mkr, weaver, MF.21

Coach mkr, MF.15
Coach owner, T.5
Coachman, DS.2
Coachman (not domestic), T.5
Coal agt, factor, D.13
Coal contractor, dlr, heaver, lbr, mcht, D.1
Coal meter, T.1
Coal miner, M.1
Coal shipper, D.13
Coalowner, PO
Coastguard, PP.5
Cocoa-fibre matting mfr, MF.20
Cocoa mfr, MF.25
Coffee dlr, roaster, D.5
Coffee house kpr, D.8
Coffin furniture (metal) mfr, MF.15
Coin stamper, MF.2
Coiner, MF.2
Coke burner, dlr, MF.8
College agt, officer, secretary, PP.13
College Head, Fellow, PP.13
College porter, DS.3
College svt, DS.1
Colliery agt, factor, D.13
Colliery viewer, M.1
Colonial planter, AG.1
Colonial service, PP.1
Colour mfr, MF.9
Comb mkr, MF.12
Comb mkr (for manufacture), MF.1
Commercial clerk, IS.1
Commercial society officer, IS.1
Commercial traveller, D.13
Company officer, IS.1
Composition mkr, PP.9
Confectioner, MF.26
Conjurer, PP.10
Contractor, B.1
Conveyancer, PP.7
Cook (domestic service), DS.1
Cook (not domestic service), DS.3
Cook (pastry), MF.26
Cooper, MF.13
Copper mfr, MF.5
Copper mine proprietor, PO
Copper miner, M.1
Copper plate mfr, MF.5
Copper plate printer, MF.30
Coppersmith, MF.5
Coprolite digger, M.1

Cord mkr, MF.20
Cordial mkr, MF.27
Cork cutter, MF.13
Cork mcht, D.2
Corkscrew mkr, MF.2
Corn cutter, PP.8
Corn dlr, mcht, D.2
Corn meter, T.1
Cornice mkr, B.2
Costermonger, D.12
Cotton band mkr, spinner, MF.19
Cotton dlr, salesman, warehouseman, D.3
Cotton dyer, printer, MF.22
Cotton fent dlr, D.3
Cotton glove mkr, MF.23
Cotton mfr, MF.19
Cotton waste dlr, D.3
Cotton net mkr, MF.19
Cotton porter, T.1
Cotton velvet, velveteen mfr, MF.21
Counterpane mkr, MF.19
County officer, PP.2
Courier, T.1
Coverlet mkr, MF.19
Cow kpr, D.5
Crape dlr, mfr, MF.19
Crate mkr, MF.13
Cravat mkr, MF.23
Cricketer, PP.10
Crinoline mkr, MF.23
Crochet mfr, MF.19
Crossing sweeper, PP.3
Cruet frame mkr, MF.5
Cupper, PP.8
Curb mkr, MF.4
Curiosity dlr, D.12
Currier, MF.10
Currycomb mkr, MF.4
Customs, PP.1
Cutlery grinder, MF.2
Cutter, MF.2

Damask mfr, MF.20
Dancer, PP.10
Dancing teacher, PP.13
Dentist PP.8
Diamond cutter, wkr, MF.6
Die sinker, MF.2
Dining room svt, DS.1
Distiller, MF.27

District officer, PP.2
Diver, T.1
Dock lbr, T.1
Dock service lbr, T.1
Doffer plate mkr, MF.1
Dog dlr, trainer, AG.3
Domestic svt, DS.1
Donkey driver, kpr, T.5
Door furniture mkr, MF.14
Door spring mkr, MF.4
Drabbet mfr, MF.20
Draper, D.4
Draughtsman, MF.2
Drawing master, teacher, PP.13
Drayman, T.5
Dressing case mkr, MF.14
Dressmaker, MF.23
Drover, AG.3
Drug grinder, packer, wkr, MF.9
Druggist, PP.8
Drysalter, MF.9
Dust collector, sifter, picker, PP.3
Dye mfr, MF.9
Dyer, MF.22
Dyewood cutter, MF.9

Earthenware dlr, importer, mender, D.11
Earthenware mfr, MF.7
East India service, PP.1
Eating-house kpr, D.8
Edge tool grinder, MF.2
Editor, PP.11
Egg dealer, mcht, D.5
Elastic fabric wkr, MF.21
Electro-plate mfr, MF.5
Embosser, MF.2
Embroiderer, MF.21
Emery mfr, wkr, MF.9
Emery paper mfr, MF.7
Enameller, MF.7
Encaustic tile mfr, MF.7
Engine agt, dlr, mkr, MF.1
Engine driver, fireman, stoker, MF.31
Engraver, PP.9
Envelope mkr, MF.16
Equestrian, PP.10
Errand boy, T.1
Estate agt, B.1
Excavator, B.3
Exhibition kpr, svt, PP.10

Factor, D.13
Factory hand (undefined), MF.19
Factory lbr, MF.31
Fancy chain mkr, MF.5
Fancy dlr, wkr, MF.19
Fancy goods (silk) dlr, D.3
Fancy goods (silk) mfr, MF.19
Fancy goods dlr, importer, warehouseman, D.12
Fancy leather goods mkr, MF.24
Fancy repository dlr, D.12
Farm bailiff, AG.1
Farm svt (indoor), AG.1
Farmer, AG.1
Farmer's sons, grandsons, AG.1
Farrier, AG.3
Feather dlr, dresser, MF.12
Fellmonger, MF.10
Felon's iron mkr, MF.4
Felt mfr, MF.18
Fence mkr, MF.13
Fender mkr, MF.4
Ferule mkr, MF.5
Figure mkr, PP.9
File mkr, MF.2
Filter mkr, MF.7
Fire engine, hose, bucket mkr, MF.1
Fire place ornament mkr, MF.16
Fire-iron mkr, MF.4
Fireman (fire brigade), PP.2
Fireworks mfr, MF.9
Fish curer, drier, D.5
Fish dlr, seller, D.5
Fish-hook mkr, MF.29
Fishing rod, tackle mkr, MF.29
Fisherman, AG.4
Fishmonger, D.5
Flannel mfr, MF.18
Flash mfr, MF.2
Flax agt, dlr, D.3
Flax bleacher, dyer, MF.22
Flax mfr, MF.20
Flint dlr, M.3
Flint grinder, mkr, miller, MF.7
Flock dlr, mkr, MF.18
Floorcloth mfr, MF.17
Flour agt, dlr, D.2
Flower hawker, vendor, D.12
Fly mkr, MF.1
Flyer, MF.1
Flyman, T.5

Foreman, MF.31
Fork grinder, mkr, MF.2
Fossil dlr, digger, M.1
Frame mkr (cotton), MF.1
Framesmith, MF.1
French polisher, MF.14
Fret cutter, MF.14
Fringe mkr, MF.21
Frizette mkr, DS.3
Frock mkr, MF.23
Fruit hawker, vendor, D.12
Fruit meter, T.1
Fruiterer, D.5
Frying pan mkr, MF.4
Fuller, MF.22
Fuller's earth mfr, MF.9
Furnaceman, MF.31
Furniture broker, dlr, D.9
Furrier, MF.10
Fustian dyer, MF.22
Fustian mfr, MF.19
Fuzee mkr, MF.9

Galvanised iron mkr, MF.4
Game dlr, D.5
Gamekeeper, DS.2
Gardener, AG.1, DS.2
Garter mkr, MF.23
Gas apparatus, fittings mkr, MF.5
Gas engineer, MF.8
Gas fitter, B.2
Gas meter mkr, MF.1
Gas pipe, retort, tube, mkr, MF.4
Gas works service, MF.8
Gasometer mkr, MF.1
Gate kpr, DS.2
Gauze mfr, MF.19
Gear mkr, MF.1
Gelatine dlr, mkr, MF.11
Gem mkr, MF.7
General dlr, D.12
General lbr (branch undefined), IS.2
Gentleman, PO
Geography teacher, PP.13
Geologist, PP.12
Gilder, MF.14
Gilt toy mkr, MF.5
Gimlet mkr, MF.2
Gimp mfr, MF.19
Ginger beer mfr, MF.27
Gingham mfr, MF.19

Girth dlr, mkr, MF.21
Glass agt, dlr, factor, importer, mender, D.11
Glass bottle dlr, mcht, D.11
Glass enameller, mfr, painter, stainer MF.7
Glass paper mfr, MF.7
Glazier, B.2
Glazier's diamond mfr, MF.6
Globe mkr, MF.30
Glove knitter, MF.23
Glover, MF.23
Glue wkr, MF.11
Gold beater, MF.6
Gold beater's skin mkr, MF.10
Gold lace mfr, MF.6
Gold-wire drawer, MF.6
Goldsmith, D.11, MF.6
Govt messenger, workman, PP.1
Govt officers, PP.1
Governess, PP.13
Grate mkr, MF.4
Grave digger, PP.14
Gravel digger, lbr, M.3
Gravel mcht, M.3
Grazier, AG.1
Greengrocer, D.5
Greenwich pensioner, PP.5
Gridiron mkr, MF.4
Grinder (undefined), MF.4
Grindstone mkr, MF.7
Grindery dlr, wkr, MF.10
Grocer, D.5
Groom, DS.2
Groom (not domestic svt), AG.3
Guard chain mkr, MF.6
Guide, T.1
Gum mfr, MF.11
Gun flint mkr, M.3
Gun mfr, MF.2
Gunpowder mfr, MF.9
Gunsmith, MF.2
Gut mkr, MF.29
Gutta-percha dlr, mfr, MF.17
Gymnastics teacher, PP.13

Haberdasher, D.4
Hackle mkr, MF.1
Haft mkr, turner, MF.12
Hair mfr, mcht, MF.12
Hair wkr (artist), PP.9

Hairdresser, DS.3
Hairpad mkr, DS.3
Hairpin mfr, MF.4
Hame mkr, MF.15
Hammock mkr, MF.20
Hand rule mkr, MF.16
Handcuff mkr, MF.4
Handle mkr, MF.4
Harbour lbr, T.1
Hardware dlr, mfr, D.11
Harness mfr, MF.15
Hat block mkr, MF.1
Hat mfr, MF.23
Hatter, D.4, MF.23
Haulier, T.5
Havel knitter, mkr, MF.1
Hawker, D.12
Hay dlr, D.2
Headdress mkr, DS.3
Heald knitter, mkr, MF.1
Hemp mfr, MF.20
Herald chaser, MF.5
Herald painter, MF.30
Herb doctor, PP.8
Herbalist, D.5
Hide dlr, D.2
Hinge mkr, MF.4
HM Court and Household, PP.1
Hobbler, T.1
Holloware mkr, MF.4
Homeopathy, professor of, PP.8
Hook and eye mfr, MF.5
Hoop bender, mkr, MF.13
Hop dlr, mcht, D.2
Hop grower, AG.1
Horn dlr, turner, wkr, MF.12
Horse breaker, breeder, clipper, dlr, kpr, proprietor, AG.3
Hose (stocking) mfr, MF.23
Hosier, D.4
Hospital attendant, DS.1
Hot presser, MF.22
Hot water apparatus mkr, MF.5
Hotel kpr, D.7
Hotel svt, DS.1
Hothouse builder, B.2
House agt, D.13
House proprietor, PO
Housekeeper, DS.1
Housemaid, DS.1
Huckster, D.12

Huntsman, AG.3
Hurdle mkr, MF.13
Hydropathy, professor of, PP.8

Ice dlr, mkr, mcht, MF.25
Image mkr, PP.9
India-rubber dlr, mfr, MF.17
Ink mfr, MF.9
Inkstand mkr, MF.5
Inland navigation service, T.3
Inland revenue, PP.1
Inn kpr, D.7
Inn svt, DS.1
Insurance agt, officer, IS.1
Interpreter, PP.12
Iron agt, mcht, D.13
Iron box, safe mkr, MF.4
Iron dlr, D.11
Iron founder, mfr, moulder, MF.4
Iron-mine proprietor, PO
Iron miner, M.1
Ironmonger, D.11
Isinglass dlr, mkr, MF.11
Itinerant preacher, PP.14
Ivory cutter, turner, wkr, MF.12

Japanner, MF.17
Jet carver, wkr, PP.9
Jet miner, M.1
Jeweller, D.11, MF.6
Joiner, B.2
Judge (superior, local), PP.7
Jute mfr, MF.20

Kettle mkr, MF.5
Key mkr, MF.4
Knacker, AG.3
Knife mkr, MF.2
Knitter, MF.18

Label writer, D.10
Labourer (HM dockyard), PP.1
Labourer (sanitary), PP.3
Lace agt, dlr, factor, D.3
Lace mfr, spinner, MF.21
Lacquerer, MF.5
Ladder mkr, MF.13
Lamp black mkr, MF.9
Lamp mkr, MF.5
Lamp wick mkr, MF.19
Lance mkr, MF.2

Land drainage service (not towns) AG.2
Land surveyor, B.1
Landowner, PO
Language professor, teacher, PP.13
Lantern mkr, MF.5
Lapidary, MF.6
Last mkr, MF.13
Latchmaker, MF.4
Lath mkr, MF.13
Laundry kpr, DS.3
Laundry maid, DS.1
Law clerk, student, PP.7
Law court officer, PP.7
Law stationer, D.10
Lead dlr, mfr, mcht, MF.5
Lead-mine agt, miner, M.1
Lead-mine proprietor, PO
Leather bag, case, portmanteau, trunk
  mkr, MF.24
Leather-cloth mfr, MF.17
Leather dyer, stainer, MF.10
Leather embosser, japanner, leather lace
  cutter, MF.10
Leather glover, MF.23
Letter cutter, MF.30
Librarian, D.10
Licensed victualler, D.7
Licquorice mfr, MF.25
Light dues collector, T.1
Lighterman, T.3
Lighthouse kpr, T.1
Lime burner, quarrier, M.2
Lime mcht, M.3
Limestone quarrier, burner, M.2
Linen agt, dlr, factor, D.3
Linen draper, D.4
Linen mfr, MF.20
Linsey weaver, MF.18
Lint mfr, MF.19
List mkr, MF.23
Listing mfr, MF.18
Literary secretary, PP.12
Literary society officer, secretary, PP.12
Lithographer, MF.30
Lithographic printer, MF.30
Livery stable kpr, T.5
Loan office manager, secretary, IS.1
Local offices (other), PP.2
Locksmith, B.2
Lodge kpr, DS.2
Lodging house kpr, D.8

Looking-glass mkr, MF.14
Looking-glass silverer, MF.5
Loom mkr, MF.1
Loom turner (silk, ribbon), MF.19
Lumper, T.1
Lunatic asylum attendant, officer, pro-
  prietor, DS.1

Machine agt, dlr, mkr, MF.1
Machine lbr, wkr, MF.31
Machine ruler mkr, MF.16
Machinist, MF.31
Magistrate, PO
Maltster, MF.27
Manager, MF.31
Manager (coal mines), M.1
Manchester warehouseman, D.3
Manganese miner, M.1
Mangle mkr, MF.1
Mangler, DS.3
Manufacturer, MF.31
Manufacturing chemists (lbrs), MF.9
Manure dlr., mfr, MF.11
Map colourer, seller, MF.30
Map mkr, publisher, MF.30
Marble mason, B.2
Marble mcht, M.3
Marine store dlr, D.12
Mark cutter, MF.30
Marquee mkr, MF.20
Marquetry inlayer, veneerer, MF.14
Mason, B.2
Mast mkr, MF.3
Mat mkr, seller, MF.20
Match box mkr, MF.16
Match mkr, seller, MF.9
Mathematics professor, teacher, PP.13
Mattress mkr, MF.14
Mayor, PP.2
Meal mcht, D.2
Measure mkr, MF.1
Meat salesman, D.5
Mechanic, MF.31
Medal mkr, MF.2
Medallist, MF.2
Medical agt, assistant, clerk, student,
  PP.8
Medical society officer, PP.8
Member of Parliament, PO
Menagerie officer, DS.3
Mercer, D.4

Merchant, D.13
Mess contractor, DS.1
Messenger, T.1
Messman, DS.1
Metal dlr, galvaniser, refiner, stamper, turner, wkr, MF.5
Meter (not distinguished), T.1
Midwife, PP.8
Military hospital, officer, PP.4
Militia, PP.4
Milk seller, D.5
Mill band mkr, MF.16
Miller, MF.25
Milliner, MF.23
Millmaker, MF.1
Millstone cutter, mkr, MF.7
Millwright, MF.1
Mine contractor, M.1
Mine owner, proprietor, PO
Miner (not described), M.1
Mineral water mfr, MF.27
Mineralogist, PP.12
Mining company's secretary, service, M.1
Missionary, PP.14
Modeller, PP.9
Mohair mfr, MF.18
Money dlr, lender, IS.1
Mop mkr, MF.20
Moreen mfr, MF.18
Morocco mfr, MF.10
Mosaic tile mkr, MF.7
Mould mkr, MF.2
Moulding mkr, B.2
Mousetrap mkr, MF.13
Municipal officer, PP.2
Mungo mcht, D.3
Museum curator, kpr, PP.12
Music engraver, printer, publisher, seller, D.10
Music master, PP.13
Music string mkr, MF.29
Musical instruments dlr, mkr, MF.29
Musician (not teacher), PP.10
Muslin agt, dlr, D.3
Muslin embroiderer, MF.23
Muslin mfr, MF.19
Mustard mfr, MF.25

Nail mfr, MF.4
Naturalist, PP.9

Naval architect, MF.3
Navigation teacher, PP.13
Navvy, B.3
Navy agt, hospital officer, officer, PP.5
Navy contractor, MF.23
Needle mfr, MF.2
Net mkr, MF.20
Newspaper agt, vendor, D.10
Newspaper proprietor, PP.11
Newsroom kpr, D.10
Nun, PP.14
Nurse (domestic service), DS.1
Nurse (not domestic service), PP.8
Nurseryman (horticulturalist), AG.1
Nut mkr, MF.4

Oakum dlr, wkr, MF.20
Oar mkr, MF.3
Observatory assistant, PP.12
Office kpr (govt), PP.1
Office kpr, porter (not govt), DS.3
Officer of local board, PP.2
Oil and colourman, D.5
Oil cake dlr, mkr, MF.25
Oil miller, refiner, MF.25
Oilcloth mfr, MF.17
Oilskin mfr, MF.17
Omnibus owner, time kpr, T.5
Opera agt, PP.10
Optician, MF.29
Ornament mkr, PP.9
Orris weaver, MF.6
Others (agriculture), AG.1
Others (about animals), AG.3
Others (animal food), MF.25
Others (antimony, copper, lead, mixed metals, quicksilver), MF.5
Others (arms), MF.2
Others (army), PP.4
Others (in attendance), DS.3
Others (bark), MF.13
Others (in boarding), D.8
Others (books), D.10
Others (canals, rivers), T.3
Others (cane), MF.13
Others (carriages), MF.15
Others (carving), PP.9
Others (chemicals), MF.9
Others (church officers), PP.14
Others (coal), MF.8
Others (conveyance), T.5

Others (cotton), MF.19
Others (dies), MF.2
Others (dress), MF.23
Others (drinks), D.7
Others (earthenware), MF.7
Others (exhibitions), PP.10
Others (figures), PP.9
Others (fine art), PP.9
Others (flax), MF.20
Others (food), MF.25
Others (furniture), MF.14
Others (games), MF.29
Others (glass), MF.7
Others (gold), MF.6
Others (grease), MF.11
Others (gums), MF.11
Others (hair), MF.12
Others (hemp), MF.20
Others (horticulture), AG.1
Others (houses and buildings), B.2
Others (implements), MF.1
Others (iron), MF.4
Others (law), PP.7
Others (literature), PP.11
Others (lodging), D.8
Others (machine tools), MF.1
Others (medals), MF.2
Others (medicine), PP.8
Others (mercantile), IS.1
Others (messengers), T.1
Others (mines), M.1
Others (mixed fabrics), MF.21
Others (music), PP.10
Others (musical instruments), MF.29
Others (navy), PP.5
Others (paper), MF.16
Others (pictures), MF.30
Others (prints), MF.30
Others (railways), T.4
Others (religious teachers), PP.14
Others (salt), M.4
Others (scientific instruments), MF.29
Others (scientific persons), PP.12
Others (sea), T.2
Others (rivers), T.1
Others (shipbuilding), MF.3
Others (silk), MF.19
Others (silver), MF.6
Others (skins), MF.12
Others (sports), MF.29
Others (steel), MF.4

Others (stimulants), D.7
Others (stone and clay), M.3
Others (storage), T.1
Others (surgical instruments), MF.29
Others (teaching), PP.13
Others (vegetable food), D.5
Others (water), MF.4
Others (wood), MF.13
Others (wool), MF.18
Others (worsted), MF.18
Oven builder, B.2
Overlooker, MF.31
Oyster dlr, seller, D.5

Packer, T.1
Packing case mkr, MF.13
Painter, B.2
Painter (artist), PP.9
Paper bag, band, box, tube mkr, MF.16
Paper dlr, mcht, D.10
Paper embosser, mfr, stainer, MF.16
Paperhanger, B.2
Papier mâché mfr, MF.16
Parasol mkr, MF.24
Parchment mfr, MF.10
Parian mfr, MF.7
Parish clerk, PP.14
Parish officer, PP.2
Park kpr, DS.2
Parliamentary agt, PP.7
Patent fuel mfr, MF.8
Patent leather mfr, MF.10
Patent medicine vendor, PP.8
Patten mkr, MF.23
Pattern card mkr, MF.16
Pattern designer, MF.2
Pavior, B.3
Pawnbroker, D.9
Pearl cutter, wkr, MF.6
Peat cutter, dlr, MF.8
Pedlar, D.12
Peel mkr, MF.25
Peg mkr, MF.13
Pencil case mkr, MF.6
Pencil mkr, MF.2
Penholder mkr, MF.13
Perambulator mkr, MF.15
Percussion cap mfr, MF.9
Performer, PP.10
Perfumer, D.12

Pew opener, PP.14
Pewterer, MF.5
Pewterpot wkr, MF.5
Philosophical instruments mkr, MF.29
Photographic artist, PP.9
Phrenologist, PP.12
Physician, PP.8
Piano tuner, MF.29
Picker mkr, MF.1
Pickle mkr, MF.25
Picture cleaner, dlr, D.9
Picture frame mkr, MF.14
Pig dlr, mcht, AG.3
Pilot, T.2
Pin mfr, MF.2
Pitch wkr, MF.9
Plaster dlr, mfr, MF.7
Plasterer, B.2
Plate chest mkr, MF.14
Plate layer, B.3
Plated ware mfr, MF.5
Plater, MF.5
Playing card mkr, MF.16
Plumber, B.2
Plush mfr, MF.19
Pocket book mkr, MF.24
Police, PP.6
Porter, T.1
Porter agt, D.7
Portfolio mkr, MF.24
Post office wkr, PP.1
Potato dlr, mcht, D.5
Poulterer, D.5
Press mkr, MF.13
Press wkr, MF.4
Presser, MF.19
Priest, Roman Catholic, in other religions, PP.14
Print colourer, seller, MF.30
Print dlr, salesman, D.3
Printer, MF.30
Printing ink mfr, MF.9
Prison officer, PP.6
Private secretary, PP.12
Professor, art, languages, mathematics, PP.13
Proprietor, PO
Protestant minister, PP.14
Provision curer, dlr, D.5
Public notary, IS.1
Public rooms kpr, DS.1

Publican, D.7
Publisher, PP.11
Pugilist, PP.10
Pump mkr, MF.1
Pupils at convent, Dependent class
Pyrotechnics mfr, MF.9

Quarry agt, owner, PO
Quarryman (not otherwise described), M.3
Quill-pen mkr, MF.12
Quilt mkr, MF.18
Quilter, MF.18

Rabbit catcher, killer, AG.3
Rag dlr, gatherer, D.12
Railway agt, clerk, company svt, engine driver, official, police, porter, stationmaster, stoker, T.4
Railway buffer, carriage, spring, wagon, wheel mkr, MF.15
Railway contractor, B.1
Railway lbr, B.3
Range mkr, MF.4
Razor mkr, MF.2
Receiver (coal mines), M.1
Rectifier, MF.27
Reed mkr, MF.1
Religious society officer, PP.14
Rent collector, D.13
Reporter, PP.11
Retort mkr, MF.1
Ribbon dlr, warehouseman, D.3
Ribbon mfr, MF.19
Riddle mkr, MF.1
Riding master, AG.3
Ring mkr, MF.5
Rivet mkr, MF.4
Road contractor, inspector, surveyor, B.1
Road lbr, B.3
Roasting jack mkr, MF.4
Robe mkr, MF.23
Roller mkr, MF.1
Rope mkr, MF.20
Royal Marines, PP.5
RN Reserve, PP.5
Rug mfr, MF.18
Rush mfr, MF.13

Sack dlr, mkr, MF.20
Sacking dlr, mkr, MF.20

Sacristan, PP.14
Saddle mfr, MF.15
Saddle tree mkr, MF.13
Saddler's ironmonger, MF.4
Safe mkr, MF.13
Sailcloth mfr, MF.20
Sailmaker, MF.3
Sailors' society agt, IS.1
Salesman, D.13
Salt agt, dlr, mcht, D.12
Salt mfr, M.4
Saltpetre mkr, MF.9
Sand dlr, mfr, wkr, M.3
Sandpaper mfr, MF.7
Satin mfr, MF.19
Sauce mkr, MF.25
Saw frame, handle mkr, MF.13
Saw mkr, MF.2
Sawdust dlr, mcht, D.2
Sawsmith, MF.2
Sawyer, MF.13
Scagliola mkr, MF.7
Scale mkr, MF.1
Scaleboard mkr, MF.1
Scavenger, PP.3
School agt, officer, secretary, PP.13
Schoolmaster, PP.13
Scientific society officer, secretary, PP.12
Scissors mkr, MF.2
Scourer, MF.22
Scrap iron dlr, D.11
Screw cutter, wkr, MF.4
Scripture reader, PP.14
Scrivener, IS.1
Sculptor, PP.9
Scuttle mkr, MF.4
Scythe mkr, MF.2
Sea reeve, T.1
Sea waller, B.2
Seal engraver, MF.2
Seaman (merchant service), T.2
Seaman (RN), PP.5
Seamstress, MF.23
Secretary, IS.1
Sedge mfr, MF.13
Seed crusher, MF.25
Seed mcht, D.2
Serge mfr, MF.18
Servants' registry office kpr, DS.3
Sewerman, PP.3
Sewing machine mkr, MF.1

Sewing machine operator, MF.31
Sewing machinist, MF.31
Sexton, PP.14
Shag mfr, MF.19
Share broker, dlr, D.13
Shareholder, PO
Shawl mfr, MF.19
Shawl warehouseman, D.4
Shears mkr, MF.2
Sheep dlr, salesman, AG.3
Shell dlr, wkr, MF.12
Shell fish dlr, seller, D.5
Shepherd, AG.1
Sheriff's clerk, officer, PP.2
Ship agt, broker, D.13
Ship kpr, lbr, watchman, T.1
Ship steward, T.2
Ship's chandler, MF.3
Ship's rigger, MF.3
Shipbuilder, MF.3
Shipowner, PO
Shipping master, T.1
Shipsmith, MF.3
Shipwright, MF.3
Shirt mkr, MF.23
Shoe heel, tip mkr, MF.23
Shoe mkr, MF.23
Shoeblack, DS.3
Shopkeeper (undefined), D.12
Shopman, D.12
Shorthand writer, PP.11
Shot belt mfr, MF.2
Shot mfr, MF.9
Shovel mkr, MF.2
Shroud mkr, MF.19
Shuttle mkr, MF.1
Sickle mkr, MF.2
Sieve mkr, MF.1
Sign painter, B.2
Silk dlr, mercer, D.3
Silk dyer, printer, MF.22
Silk glove mkr, MF.23
Silk mfr, MF.19
Silkman, D.3
Silver lace mfr, MF.6
Silver wire drawer, MF.6
Silversmith, D.11, MF.6
Sinker mkr, MF.5
Sister of Charity, PP.14
Size wkr, MF.11
Skewer mkr, MF.4

Skin dlr, D.2
Skinner, MF.10
Skittle mkr, player, PP.10
Slate dlr, mfr, mcht, quarrier, M.2
Slater, B.2
Small ware mfr, (silk), MF.19
Small ware mfr (steel), MF.4
Smock mkr, MF.23
Snuff mkr, MF.28
Snuffers mkr, MF.4
Soap boiler, MF.11
Soda water mfr, MF.27
Soldier, PP.4
Solicitor, PP.7
Spade mkr, MF.2
Spar cutter, mfr, MF.7
Special pleader, PP.7
Spectacle mkr, MF.29
Spelter mfr, MF.5
Spice dlr, mcht, MF.25
Spindle mkr, MF.1
Spinner (not otherwise described) MF.19
Spirit mcht, D.7
Sponge dlr, mcht, D.12
Spoon mkr, MF.5
Spring bar mkr, MF.4
Spring hook mkr, MF.4
Spring mkr, MF.4
Spruce agt, D.7
Spur mkr, MF.4
Staircase builder, B.2
Stamp cutter, MF.30
Staple mkr, MF.2
Starch mfr, MF.9
Stationer, D.10
Stay mkr, MF.1
Steam navigation service, T.2
Steel mfr, MF.4
Steel pen mkr, MF.2
Steel toy mkr, MF.29
Steel trap mkr, MF.4
Steel plate printer, MF.30
Stenciller, MF.30
Stevedore, T.1
Stick mkr, MF.24
Stirrup mkr, MF.4
Stock broker, dlr, D.13
Stock mkr, MF.23
Stone agt, cutter, dresser, mcht, quarrier, M.2
Store kpr, T.1

Storehouse lbr, T.1
Strap mkr, MF.24
Straw bonnet, hat mkr, MF.23
Straw dlr, D.2
Straw plait dlr, mfr, MF.23
Strop mkr, MF.24
Stuff mkr, MF.18
Stuff mcht, warehouseman, D.3
Stone digger, dredger, M.3
Stone waller, B.2
Stove mkr, MF.4
Sugar refiner, MF.25
Sulphur mkr, MF.9
Sulphur miner, M.1
Superintendant, MF.31
Surgeon, PP.8
Surgical instruments mkr, MF.29
Surveyor, B.1
Surveyor, inspector of shipping, B.1
Sword cutler, mkr, MF.2

Table cover mfr, MF.19
Tailor, MF.23
Tallow chandler, MF.11
Tanner, MF.10
Tape dlr, mfr, MF.21
Tar wkr, MF.9
Tarpaulin mkr, MF.20
Tassel mkr, MF.21
Taxidermist, PP.9
Tea dlr, D.5
Tea pot mkr, MF.5
Teacher (general), PP.13
Teacher, blind, deaf, dumb, PP.13
Teacher, dancing, geography, gymnastics, languages, mathematics, navigation, writing, PP.13
Teazle grower, AG.1
Telegraphy service, PP.1
Tennis racket mkr, PP.10
Tent mkr, MF.20
Terra cotta mfr, MF.7
Thatcher, B.2
Theatres, persons engaged about, PP.10
Theatrical agt, PP.10
Theatrical property dlr, mkr, MF.23
Theological student, PP.14
Thimble mkr, MF.2
Thong mkr, MF.24
Thread mfr, MF.21
Ticket writer, D.10

Tie mkr, MF.23
Tiler, B.2
Timber bender, chopper, hewer, MF.13
Timber dlr, mcht, surveyor, valuer D.2
Time kpr, MF.31
Tin foil dlr, mkr, MF.5
Tin man mfr, wkr, MF.5
Tin miner, M.1
Tinplate wkr, MF.5
Tinker, MF.5
Tobacco mkr, MF.28
Tobacco pipe mkr, MF.28
Tobacconist, D.6
Toll agt, collector, contractor, T.5
Toll handle mkr, MF.13
Tool dlr, mkr, MF.2
Tortoiseshell dlr, wkr, MF.12
Tow mfr, MF.20
Town crier, PP.2
Toy dlr, mkr, MF.29
Translator, PP.12
Trap mkr, MF.13
Traymaker, MF.5
Trimming dlr, mkr, MF.21
Truss mfr, MF.29
Tunbridge ware mfr, MF.14
Turf cutter, dlr, MF.8
Turner (wood), MF.13
Typefounder, MF.2

Umbrella mkr, MF.24
Undertaker, MF.14
Underwriter, D.13
Union officer, PP.2
Urn mkr, MF.5

Valentine mkr, MF.16
Valuer, D.13
Varnish mkr, MF.9
Vellum mfr, MF.10
Velvet mfr (silk), MF.19
Ventriloquist, PP.10
Vermin destroyer, AG.3
Veterinary surgeon, AG.3
Vinegar mfr, MF.25
Vocalist, PP.10

Wadding mkr, MF.21
Wafer mkr, MF.25
Warehouseman, T.1

Washerwoman, DS.3
Washing machine mkr, MF.1
Waste dlr, D.3
Waste dlr (wool, worsted), D.3
Waste paper dlr, D.12
Watch key mkr, MF.5
Watch mkr, MF.29
Water bailiff, T.1
Water carrier, dlr, D.12
Water gilder, MF.6
Watercress gatherer, vendor, D.12
Watercress grower, AG.1
Waterman, T.3
Waterman (cabstand), T.5
Waterproof articles dlr, mkr, MF.17
Waterworks service, M.4
Wax modeller, PP.9
Wax refiner, MF.11
Weaver (undefined), MF.19
Web dlr, mkr, MF.21
Weighing machine mkr, MF.1
Well sinker, M.4
Whalebone dlr, wkr, MF.12
Wharfinger, T.1
Wheel chair drawer, proprietor, T.5
Wheel chair mkr, MF.15
Wheelwright, MF.15
Whetstone mkr, MF.7
Whip mkr, MF.15
Whipper-in, AG.3
White metal mfr, MF.5
Whitesmith, MF.5
Wig block mkr, MF.1
Wig mkr, DS.3
Willow cutter, dyer, weaver, MF.13
Willow rod grower, AG.1
Winding machine operator, MF.31
Wine cooper, MF.13
Wine mfr, MF.27
Wine mcht, D.7
Wire drawer, mkr, weaver, MF.5
Wood carver, B.2
Wood dlr, surveyor, valuer, D.2
Woodman, AG.1
Wooden spoon mkr, MF.13
Wood bender, chopper, hewer, MF.13
Wood screw mkr, MF.13
Wool dyer, MF.22
Wool stapler, D.2
Woollen cloth, flock, yarn mfr, MF.18
Woollen cord mfr, MF.18

7. The use of published census data in migration studies[1]

D. E. Baines

1. INTRODUCTION

A basic problem of social history is quantifying the available evidence. This is particularly true of migration studies. There is, of course, a great deal of statistical material available for the later nineteenth century but its handling has frequently masked many interesting features. For example, estimates of net intercensal migration are inherently highly accurate and commonly appear in modern census tables.[2] But they are of much less use to a student of social change than the far less accurate estimation of *flows* of migrants. That is, a 'snapshot' of the effect of migration upon the population growth of an area will tell us little about the *process* of migration because the bulk of movement is complemented by flows in the opposite direction.[3] Lancashire, for instance, was a net receiver of migrants throughout the nineteenth century and in fact gained 205,000 persons *net* in the 1870s. But the county lost (by the author's grossly understated estimation) at least 75,000 Lancastrians in the same period. Methods for estimating 'native' and 'net' outflows are discussed in section 3 below. Similarly, simple statements of the places of origin (the birthplaces) of a migrant group[4] are of little value unless the recent migrants – those who moved that decade – are distinguished.

2. THE NATURE OF THE EVIDENCE

The two main sources for the type of study described here are the 'birthplaces of the people',[5] published in the census tables which give the county of birth, and the annual reports of the Registrar-General.[6] The latter is needed because the difference between recorded changes in population size and calculated natural changes is an essential technique in migration studies. Great care has to be taken in using the two types of information.

The county of birth was enumerated in all censuses from 1851–1911. In 1841 a question enquiring whether the county of residence was that of birth was included.

Any comprehensive study based on this material must use the county as the basic unit of measurement. Some enumerations include birthplace data for smaller areas but this is not complemented by information on the *local* origins of the inhabitants of other counties. One could, for example, obtain the county of birth of the inhabitants of, say, Coventry, but not the Coventry-born inhabitants of adjacent towns. This restricts the study of individual towns to estimation of *net* intercensal movement. A similar problem is that it is impossible to trace the English by county of birth in Scotland and Ireland and vice versa. However, even to use the county as the basic unit poses many problems since in many cases the enumeration areas are not comparable over a period of time.

The history of the county as an administrative unit is long and complex.[7] Some of the so-called 'ancient' (or civil) counties of the nineteenth century were pre-Conquest principalities, some were old tribal areas or Danish units, and some were created in the twelfth century. These counties served for the early censuses but when the government wanted to divide England and Wales into small units for registration purposes (under the 1836 Act) they used the Old Poor Law unions created in 1782 and 1834. But these unions often crossed county lines so that the 'registration county' which is the summation of the registration districts was often very different from the county whose name it nominally carried. Part of the registration district of Stockport was in the ancient county of Lancashire, similarly part of the registration district of Stourbridge was in the ancient county of Staffordshire. Nor was the problem solved by the local government reforms of 1888. The 'administrative' counties then created were summations of units like urban sanitary districts etc., since to bring public health under one authority was the most important reason for the administrative reforms. Therefore, if these units crossed county boundaries, the administrative county would not conform to the ancient county. By the end of the nineteenth century attempts were being made to make registration counties conform to administrative counties but this was never done in the period under consideration.

Each county to be examined statistically must therefore be adjusted to a hypothetical 'standard' county. The ancient county is the only one for which data is continuously available, and moreover the only one whose area has any 'real' meaning for the period in question. The author adjusted all population data to conform to the civil (or ancient) county of 1891 which is essentially the area defined by the Counties (Detached Parts) Act of 1844 although there were many minor boundary changes subsequently. The adjusted total populations of these are in Mitchell and Deane.[8] 'London' is best defined as the area delineated by the Metropolis Management Act of 1855, which created an administrative unit out of parts of Middlesex, Surrey and Kent, because place of birth data are given for this area (1861–1901), and no other. The remainder of these three counties counted as extra-metropolitan areas which sometimes have to be calculated from the census if no 'London' column exists. Sufficient information is provided within each census to standardise civil counties and adjust administrative (1911) and registration (1851) counties as long as the assumption is maintained that the characteristics of the smaller areas 'transferred' from one county to another in the process of adjustment reproduce the characteristics of the counties of which they were a part. Thus, if a boundary change between 1861 and 1871 had increased the population of Hertfordshire by 2 per cent at the expense of Buckinghamshire, then all the components of the Hertfordshire population would be assumed to have increased by 2 per cent and all the components of the Buckinghamshire population would similarly be assumed to have decreased by the proportion of the population of the piece lost to the Buckinghamshire total population.

Assume, for example, that the population of Hertfordshire in 1861 is 100,000 with 40,000 under 20 years old and 60,000 over. Buckinghamshire has 50,000 population with 18,000 under 20 and 32,000 over. By 1871 Hertfordshire has gained territory from Buckinghamshire containing 2,000 people.

The new population of Hertfordshire aged under 20 will be

$$40,000 + \frac{2,000 \times 40,000}{100,000} = 40,800$$

and the new population 20 or over

$$60,000 + \frac{2,000 \times 60,000}{100,000} = 61,200$$

The new population of Buckinghamshire aged under 20 will be

$$18,000 - \frac{2,000 \times 18,000}{50,000} = 17,280$$

and the new population 20 or over

$$32,000 - \frac{2,000 \times 32,000}{50,000} = 30,720$$

The criteria for such boundary changes is therefore given by the identities:

$$\frac{P \text{ Herts (old area) } 1871}{P \text{ Herts (new area) } 1871} = \frac{P \text{ Herts under 20 years old (old area) } 1871}{P \text{ Herts under 20 years old (new area) } 1871}$$

$$\frac{P \text{ Bucks (old area) } 1871}{P \text{ Bucks (new area) } 1871} = \frac{P \text{ Bucks under 20 years old (old area) } 1871}{P \text{ Bucks under 20 years old (new area) } 1871}$$

It will be noticed that the actual *numbers* aged over and under 20 transferred to the two counties are different. This method assumes the 2,000 lost by Buckinghamshire to be distributed 720 aged under 20 and 1,280 aged 20 and above, whereas the 2,000 gained by Hertfordshire has 800 under 20 and 1,200 above. This is unavoidable because the age proportions differ in the two counties (36 per cent to 64 per cent in Buckinghamshire and 40 per cent to 60 per cent in

L

Hertfordshire). By strict logic it seems better to distribute the 2,000 by the characteristics of the *losing* county (Bucks.), or possibly by some average of the two distributions weighted by the two county populations. A practical disadvantage is that for a long time period this entails an innumerable number of separate calculations for each county whereas the simpler method is basically one operation per decade on the net population gain or loss. Moreover, to treat these transfers as 'real' is also illogical since the 1891 counties which I have suggested as a standard are themselves notional because they are what the county would have looked like with the boundaries of 1891 and it is therefore reasonable that their constituent parts mirror the whole area. Fortunately, the numbers that have to be adjusted are only a small proportion of the total populations but these adjustments can be particularly important since many migration estimates are residuals and boundary errors can seriously affect the estimates (see below, section 4).

Some 10 per cent of the Welsh at each census wrote 'Wales' as their county of birth. These entries must be distributed amongst the Welsh counties (and Monmouth is assumed to be one) on the same assumption used above. That is, that the natives of each Welsh county were equally liable to write 'Wales' instead of the county name. This may not be true, however, since those from the counties with proportionately the largest 'native' populations – those with presumably the least migration – were, probably more likely to know their county of birth. Only some 1 per cent of the English born wrote 'England' as their county of birth in 1911 but in some earlier censuses there was no provision for such an entry.

The main differences between the various enumerations are summarised below:[9]

1841: The proportion of the population of each English and Welsh registration county was given in four categories – whether they had been born in that county, in another English or Welsh county, in Scotland or Ireland.

1851: The civil counties of birth were given for the inhabitants of all registration counties. The two areas seldom coincided and there are some important discrepancies which makes the task of analysis very difficult in view of the objections raised above. The tables were not divided by sex although separate figures for 'over 20' and 'under 20' were given. There were also enumerations of the birthplaces of the inhabitants of the principal towns.

1861: Age distribution was given as before. This census (and all subsequent ones) divides the place of birth enumeration into males and females. The extrametropolitan counties must be calculated by summing the parishes which comprise the intra-metropolitan parts of the three counties in question. Some of these parishes are in more than one county.[10] Information on principal towns was included.

1871: Age distribution and 'London' totals were given but 'extra-metropolitan' still has to be calculated separately in all censuses to 1911.

1881: No age distribution. Extra-metropolitan has to be calculated. The enumeration was presented in two ways: (i) where those born in each county were to be found and (ii) the customary enumeration of the inhabitants of each county.

1891: No age distribution. Extra-metropolitan figures given. Presented as in 1881.
1901: No age distribution. No special problems of analysis but much fragmented and not presented in the customary order.
1911: No general age distribution statistics were given but the census included a special survey of the ages of the migrant groups in some areas. The place of birth statistics themselves were given in such a fragmented way that they are very difficult to use. Instead of the usual 53^2 county matrix given, this has to be produced from a matrix of approximately 300^2 urban and rural areas. Moreover, the figures were given in administrative and not civil counties. There was some information included on the origins of Scots and Irish migrants.
Post-
1911: There are no censuses containing equivalent birthplace data until 1951.

The numbers of births and deaths can be easily obtained from the Registrar-General's Annual Reports. They were, of course, given in registration districts and counties. These have to be converted to our 'standard civil counties'. If birth and death *rates* are used (these are usually obtainable in the Decennial Supplements) there is no problem since the error involved in applying a birth or death rate of any registration county to a civil county, is by definition the same error that converting *numbers* of births and deaths in registration counties to civil counties would involve.

This is because the Somerset House clerks in the nineteenth century did not actually calculate death rates for each decade but merely the average number of deaths expressed per thousand average population. This method can be shown by a hypothetical example:

Population of registration county	early 1861	180,000
Number of deaths	1861	5,000
	1862	4,900
	1863	5,100
	1864	5,200
	1865	5,400
	1866	5,200
	1867	5,400
	1868	5,600
	1869	5,500
	1870	5,500
Total number of deaths 1861–70		52,800
Population of registration county	early 1871	220,000

$$\text{Average Population} = \frac{180,000 + 220,000}{2} = 200,000.$$

$$\text{'Death Rate' 1861–70 for 10 years} = \frac{52,800 \times 1,000}{200,000}$$

$$= 264 \cdot 00 \text{ per } 1,000$$

$$= 26 \cdot 40 \text{ per } 1,000 \text{ per annum.}$$

Now, if the registration county overstated the civil county by an average of 20,000 people, to convert the deaths to those that occurred in the civil county only, each year's deaths must be reduced by 10 per cent. Total deaths would then be 47,520. The death rate of the civil county would then be:

$$\frac{47{,}520 \times 1{,}000}{180{,}000} = 264{\cdot}0 \text{ per } 1{,}000$$

$$= 26{\cdot}40 \text{ per } 1{,}000 \text{ per annum.}$$

So that to use the decennial 'death rates' is equivalent to converting actual numbers of deaths. Unfortunately, some abstracts of early county death rates do not distinguish males and females, so there is in those cases no alternative to summing the annual or even quarterly number of deaths. (Today, a well calculated decennial death rate will be adjusted to take into account the larger proportion of the average population alive at the *end* of the decade. If, for example, the death rate is falling and the population rising fast, the lower death rate in the later years could be affecting a much larger number of people so that a simple average death rate will be an overestimate, because there were more than average alive when there were less than average chances of dying. The *total number* of deaths will obviously be the same however death rate is calculated, but a modern rate cannot be simply grossed up to give those actual numbers.)

Although the numbers involved are always relatively large, a death rate correct to two decimal points is always sufficiently accurate. If this is doubted a recalculation of the example in section 7 will show that the final result when given to the nearest thousand cannot be affected. Such 'accuracy' would in any case be spurious. A more serious problem is the known under-enumeration of births before the 1874 act introduced penalties for failure to register. D. V. Glass[11] calculated on the basis of Farr's figures that 4 per cent of all births were unregistered in the 1850s and 2 per cent in the 1860s, but even this may be an underestimate.

3. NOTATION

The following notation will be used throughout this chapter: P – population, B – number of births, D – number of deaths, M – number of migrants, m – males, f – females (e.g. Df – number of female deaths).

County names,[12] Ireland, Scotland, overseas, OC ('other counties' which is all other English and Welsh counties than the one named in the expression) and 'all' (all destinations, birthplaces etc.) are used as superscripts to denote place of birth and in normal type to denote place of enumeration, and may in the case of migration also indicate direction of flow. When no superscripts are used in a migration expression this indicates a net figure and the net direction of flow is always given by the sign →. In other expressions the lack of superscripts indicates that the registration covers the whole population resident in the area indicated. Dates refer to a point in time in a P expression, but in other expressions to a period of time. For example:

P Cornwall 1861 = Population of Cornwall 1861.

P Cornwall 1861^{Cornwall} = Cornwall-born population enumerated in Cornwall in 1861 (the native population).

Pm Cornwall 1861^{Devon} = Male Devon-born population enumerated in Cornwall in 1861.

P OC 1861^{Cornwall} = Cornwall-born population enumerated in all other English and Welsh counties 1861.

D Cornwall 1861–70 = All deaths registered in Cornwall 1861–70.

M Cornwall 1861–70 = Net migration in or out of Cornwall (all persons) 1861–70.

M OC $1861–70^{\text{Cornwall}}$ = Cornwall-born population migrating to other English and Welsh counties 1861–70.

Mm Cornwall $1861–70^{\text{OC}}$ = England- and Wales-born males (except Cornwall) migrating to Cornwall 1861–70.

Mf overseas $1861–70^{\text{Cornwall}}$ = Female Cornwall-born population migrating abroad 1861–70.

M Devon→overseas $1861–70^{\text{Cornwall}}$ = Cornwall-born population migrating abroad from Devon 1861–70.

M Cornwall→OC $1861–70^{\text{Devon}}$ = Devon-born population migrating to other English and Welsh counties from Cornwall 1861–70.

4. METHOD OF CALCULATION

Most migration studies of the type discussed below rely on the concept that a population can only change in total as a result of births, deaths and net migration.

$P_1 + B_{1-2} - D_{1-2} \pm M_{1-2} = P_2$ is taken as an identity where P_1 and P_2 are the total enumerated populations at the first and second count and B_{1-2}, D_{1-2} and M_{1-2} are respectively births, deaths and net migration in the intervening time period. Therefore, net migration to and from any area which corresponds with a registration district or districts can be easily obtained. For example the 1861 enumerated population can be projected to 1871 by adding the numbers of births and subtracting the numbers of deaths in 1861–70. If this projection is more than the 1871 enumerated population there must be net out migration by the amount of the difference. If the projection is less there must be net in migration by that amount. Using our notation for Cornwall, that would be:

$$M \text{ Cornwall } 1861\text{-}70 = P \text{ Cornwall } 1861 + (B \text{ Cornwall } 1861\text{-}70$$
$$- D \text{ Cornwall } 1861\text{-}70) - P \text{ Cornwall } 1871.$$

Note that if M Cornwall 1861–70 is negative the balance of migration is inward. Conversely if it is positive, the balance is outward. A net measure of migration (including, it must be noted, elements of internal *and* overseas migration) can be produced with considerable accuracy since the only sources of error are those of the basic data or because the areas handled are not comparable over time. These are discussed above.

Two recent[13] methods of producing partially disaggregated migration statistics are discussed below. The first, devised by the author,[14] was used initially to estimate net intercensal overseas migration by county of birth. This can only be done, however, by initially estimating net internal migration by county of birth so that the method is appropriate for the examination of both internal migration and emigration. The second method, by Friedlander and Roshier[15] is a more extensive analysis of net internal intercensal migration flows by county of birth. The basic approach and main problems of the two methods are similar though in the case of internal migration, a greater degree of accuracy is necessary because estimates of overseas migration are less sensitive to errors in calculation since, as will be shown, many errors net out.

Estimates of net migration by county of birth can be obtained as follows. By the 'net migration' method described above, the net outflow of a *native* population (born in Cornwall) can be obtained. This outflow will virtually always be positive since normally more natives leave a county in a decade than return to their place of birth. Additions by birth to a native group will naturally be the total births for that county since all persons born there would be natives no matter what the origin of their parents. Thus, children born in Liverpool to Irish parents count as Lancashire born and swell the Lancashire emigration statistics if the whole family moves. The death rate of a native population is not the same as that of the total population since on the evidence of their age distribution their death rate will be *higher* than that for the county as a whole because there are invariably more children and more old people in a native group. This can be seen in the 'over and under 20' enumerations in the 1851, 1861 and 1871 censuses, and inferred from the well-known tendency for out migrants to be heavily weighted with young adults. This tendency was certainly apparent in the nineteenth century. The 'native' population of a county is therefore a biased group compared with the total population whose death rate is obtainable. The estimation of the death rate of migrant and native populations is the greatest single source of error and is discussed below. If, however, we assume at this stage that the death rate of the migrant (non-native) population of the county has been estimated, then the number of native deaths must be total deaths less migrant deaths.

Therefore:

$$D \text{ Cornwall } 1861\text{–}70 - D \text{ Cornwall } 1861\text{–}70^{OC+overseas}$$
$$= D \text{ Cornwall } 1861\text{–}70^{Cornwall}$$

Of course, the crude death rate[16] (as number of deaths) reflects the age distribution of the whole county and the native age distribution is therefore largely accounted for in it, since the native population obviously bulks large in the total population of that county. The native death rate must therefore be close to the crude death rate of any county.

The net outflow to all destinations of natives (Cornish born in Cornwall) can be obtained by adding the estimated increase of Cornish natives in say 1861–70 to the 1861 Cornish native population and comparing the result with the 1871 enumeration:

$$M \text{ } 1861\text{–}70^{Cornwall} = P \text{ Cornwall } 1861^{Cornwall} + B^* \text{Cornwall } 1861\text{–}70^{Cornwall}$$
$$- (D \text{ Cornwall } 1861\text{–}70 - D \text{ Cornwall } 1861\text{–}70^{OC+overseas})$$
$$- P \text{ Cornwall } 1871^{Cornwall}$$

The total Cornish-born in 1861–70 in all the other counties of England and Wales can be summed. This can then be reduced by a calculated 1861–70 death rate of the migrant population which has to be estimated. Both from contemporary and modern evidence[17] it can be assumed that actual migrants in any particular decade were heavily weighted towards the young-adult age groups. This bias can be induced into a hypothetical migrant group by weighting the numbers aged 15–34. I assumed that one half the actual migrants had these ages and the other half had the age distribution of the total population for that decade. But the death rate required to reduce a migrant population is that of the whole group, not just that of the arrivals in any one decade. Migrant populations have a skewed age distribution compared with the national one, but presumably it is less skewed than the age distribution of actual migrants because a migrant population includes one-time migrants who are ageing.

The hypothesis of age distribution can be tested for plausibility with known data by reducing a hypothetical migrant population by the appropriate death rates (P_x). Consider a group of female migrants (not just new arrivals) in a particular county in 1881–90. These are the survivors of earlier migrants but only a very small proportion could have been alive before 1840. We can, therefore, build up the 1881–90 migrant population on the assumption that the first migrants arrived in the decade 1841–50. If half of them were 15–34 and the rest

* +2 per cent for under-enumeration.

as England and Wales in 1846 (the mid-year of the decade) their age distribution would be:

	Migrants No. of women (per 1,000)	Natives England and Wales (per 1,000)
Age groups: 0–4	65	130
5–9	59	118
10–14	53	106
15–19	174	98
20–24	175	100
25–34	327	154
35–44	56	112
45–54	40	80
55–64	27	54
65–74	16	32
75–84	7	14
85 and over	1	2
	1,000	1,000

Now, if these migrants had arrived in a steady stream, about seventy-six would have died by 1851. That is, half the numbers in each age group (as the group was *arriving* throughout the decade) were reduced by the England and Wales age-specific death rate for that group. Another 1,000 migrants are added to the 924 survivors in the next decade (1851–60). Of those new 1,000 (whose age distribution and survival is determined by the England and Wales data for 1851–60), seventy-three would have died by 1861. And a further 132 of the original migrants would have died so that the migrant group of 1861 would number 1,719 women. (It must be remembered that the age specific mortality rates applied to the survivors of the original 1841–50 migrants in the decade 1851–60 are those of the 'next' age group – i.e. 10 years older than they were in 1841–50). The process can be repeated indefinitely, but errors are cumulative which means the longer the time span, the less reliable the final results.

The age distributions of the migrant group at various census dates obtained by this and similar tests were consistent with known data. That is, between one-third and one-quarter of the migrant group were under 20 years old in 1861 and 1871 which is consistent with the enumerations. There is also broad agreement with the 1911 age distribution which was given in that census for a very few selected areas.[18] Then, the proportion of young people was less than in 1861 and 1871 because the big receivers of migrants – which were the sampled towns – had high proportions of old migrants from previously heavy in-migration.

The crude death rates of the migrant group implied by a migration of 1,000 women per decade from 1841 to 1901 are as follows:

	Migrant arrivals	(5-year averages e.g. 1859–63)				
	1841–50	1861	1871	1881	1891	1901
Crude death rates (female) of migrant group	14·6	12·0	12·7	12·1	14·0	13·6
Crude death rates (female) England and Wales	21·6	21·3	21·0	18·9	17·8	15·8
Total number of migrants in hypothetical example	1,000	1,719	2,420	2,946	3,315	3,549

The death rates for 1841–50, 1861 and 1871 in this example are clearly too low to describe most migrant populations of the late nineteenth century. Very few of the migrants in the model population had reached old age. But around 1881 most of the surviving 1841–50 migrants would be in old age. The migrant group of that period could be described as mature; the rate of increase is slowing because earlier migrants are dying and being replaced by younger ones. The 1891 and 1901 death rates are clearly too high relative to the crude death rate for the country. Since the model only allows 1,000 new migrants each decade, migration is declining relative to deaths as a component of population growth. This can be seen from the very slow growth of total numbers. The age distributions of 1891 and 1901 are unrealistic in that large proportions of old people are swamping the young migrant arrivals with their low age-specific mortality. Thus 1881 would seem to approximate most credibly to conditions in a migrant receiving county for the period. The migrant population is growing fast but not excessively so, there are considerable numbers of new arrivals (one-third of the population) but there are also many survivors from previous migrations some of whom have been there a long time. The age distribution of 1881 as determined by this model implies a crude death rate of a migrant population of about two-thirds the appropriate England and Wales crude rate.

The 'death rate of migrant populations' is therefore assumed for the purpose under discussion to be two-thirds the crude death rate of England and Wales for the same period. It may appear that to use such a modified England and Wales rate is less logical than several possible alternatives – for instance a weighted average of the death rates of all the migrant receiving counties. But accepting the considerable margin of error in the statistics I believe that for an aggregative study the England and Wales rate can be fairly used and, in fact, that its use is as logical (or illogical) as any other (whether such a rate would be appropriate in *local* studies is discussed below). The reason for using a rate weighted by the death rate (or rates, if more detail can be obtained) of any particular county would be to include the effects of environment and occupation in that county. But there is no way of showing whether migrants were more or less susceptible than natives to the new environment or occupation. We cannot, therefore, know whether conditions in the county of *origin* were more or less severe than conditions in the county of *settlement*. So that to weight the 'death rate of migrant populations' in such a way is as arbitrary as not to. A modified

England and Wales rate does, of course, take general account of age distribution and we know from the Registrar General's evidence that in the nineteenth century this was the most important cause of variation in crude death rates.

Finally, the most important single element in variations in age-specific death rates – infant mortality[19] – is largely inoperative in this context since a migrant population is unlikely to include large numbers of children. And particularly is it unlikely to include many infants less than three months old (the most vulnerable period by far) if only because their mothers would be less willing or able to make the journey so soon after confinement.

The relative importance of these problems can be gauged from the worked example (see below). Emigration and net native outflow from Cornwall – a county with a consistently high proportion of its population migrating – is computed (a) using a death rate two-thirds the England and Wales rate in the same period (b) using a death rate that assumes *all* the migrant group were in the 15–34 age groups – not just those arriving that decade and (c) using the crude death rate for England and Wales for the period. The two latter rates represent the absolute lower and upper limit of the migrant death rate and the 'true' death rate must lie between. Assumption (b) – that all the migrant group are aged 15–34 – means that the two age groups with high mortality (infants and old people) are excluded. Assumption (c) implies that migrants are not selected positively by age at all, and therefore flies in the face of all the available evidence. The difference in the number of migrants calculated on the two assumptions is about 35 per cent for internal migrants and 8 per cent for overseas migrants. The two death rates differ by a factor of 2·5. Therefore some intermediate estimation is unlikely to be highly inaccurate, particularly since shorter life expectancy reduces the weighting of the older age groups as there were so few in them. It is obvious, however, that the aggregate error from this source, in *internal* migration estimates is of different sign which makes comparisons of internal and external flows rather more hazardous.

It is now possible to calculate the movement of Cornwall born into all the other English and Welsh counties. If the average enumerated migrant population of Cornish people in all the other English and Welsh counties in 1861–70 is reduced by our death rate of migrant populations for 1861–70 (two thirds of England and Wales crude rate) and the result subtracted from the enumeration of Cornish in all other counties in 1871 the difference must be net movement of Cornish born to all other English and Welsh counties.

Net movement of Cornish out of Cornwall (M 1861–70^{Cornwall})

$$= [\{P \text{ Cornwall } 1861^{\text{Cornwall}} + B \text{ Cornwall } 1861\text{–}70* - (D \text{ Cornwall } 1861\text{–}70$$
$$- D \text{ Cornwall } 1861\text{–}70^{\text{OC}+\text{overseas}\dagger})\} - P \text{ Cornwall } 1871^{\text{Cornwall}}].$$

* Converted for under-enumeration.

$\dagger$ [E & W death rate $\times \frac{2}{3} \times 10$] $\times \left(\dfrac{P \text{ Cornwall } 1861^{\text{OC}+\text{overseas}} + P \text{ Cornwall } 1871^{\text{OC}+\text{overseas}}}{2} \right)$.

Net movement of Cornish into other English and Welsh counties

$$(M \text{ OC } 1861\text{--}70^{\text{Cornwall}}) =$$
$$\{P \text{ OC } 1871^{\text{Cornwall}} - (P \text{ OC } 1861^{\text{Cornwall}} - D \text{ OC } 1861\text{--}70^{\text{Cornwall*}})\}$$

The residual – the net movement of Cornish-born out of Cornwall less the net movement of Cornish-born into all the other English and Welsh counties – must have gone overseas, or to Scotland or to Ireland. But we know that the movement of English to Scotland and Ireland was relatively small,[20] and to Scotland (the more important) mainly from northern counties where appropriate allowance can be made. It is therefore possible to give an estimate of net overseas movement by county of origin, i.e.

$$M \text{ } 1861\text{--}70^{\text{Cornwall}} - M \text{ OC } 1861\text{--}70^{\text{Cornwall}} = M \text{ Overseas } 1861\text{--}70^{\text{Cornwall}}$$

So far, we have been concerned with the *aggregate* movement of Cornish born out of Cornwall and into the other English and Welsh counties. There is no reason why Cornish movement into another county cannot be estimated in exactly the same way, that is:

$$P \text{ Devon } 1871^{\text{Cornwall}} - (P \text{ Devon } 1861^{\text{Cornwall}} - D \text{ Devon } 1861\text{--}70^{\text{Cornwall}})$$
$$= M \text{ Devon } 1861\text{--}70^{\text{Cornwall}}$$

But local (county to county) calculations create additional problems because the *average* characteristics of migrant groups discussed above may not be exhibited by the necessarily smaller migrant group examined in a local study. The calculation of a migrant death rate remains the most important problem – and the greatest source of error – and in a local study the investigator can never be as sure that the migrant death rate is appropriate. Because in a county-to-county calculation the actual migrants are a smaller group than in an aggregate study, assumptions about their age distribution may not be correct. The smaller the group, the more likely are its characteristics to be skewed (proportion of young, proportion of old etc.) compared with the *general* characteristics of migrants discussed above. Similarly, the averaging involved in boundary adjustments is more serious. Finally, although it may be safe to disregard the *experience* of a migrant group in the receiving county (effects of environment, working conditions etc.) when that group is comprised of many diverse groups in different counties it is less safe to do so in an individual case. To use a *national* death rate (less an estimated youth factor) is permissible for aggregate purposes since those counties where migrants flocked into a particularly unhealthy occupation or town are counterbalanced by those counties where migrants left similar occupations or towns. But the essentially unknowable effects of environment are far more distorting in a county-to-county study.

The arguments in favour of large units are, of course, equally valid for different inter-county migration flows as they are between these and aggregate flows.

---

* $[\text{E \& W death rate} \times \tfrac{2}{3} \times 10] \times \left(\dfrac{P \text{ OC } 1861^{\text{Cornwall}} + P \text{ OC } 1871^{\text{Cornwall}}}{2} \right).$

The larger the migration (other things being equal) the more valid the assumptions. So to calculate net movement of Cornish to Devon or London (where many went) is inherently more accurate than to calculate net movement to Norfolk or Hereford. It is doubtful if any decade flow of less than 1,000 can be greatly relied on. Of course, if there is local evidence of age of movement or of specific conditions in the receiving county, this can be used to give greater plausibility to the different assumptions. In all cases the best practice is to calculate the flows on the basis of various assumptions (as I have done in the worked example above) to estimate the limits between which the 'true' value must lie. The various assumptions chosen can then be seen in perspective.

5. AN ALTERNATIVE METHOD

The method used by Friedlander and Roshier[21] to show net inter-censal movement of natives between counties is a basically similar method of working the same data. They used a series of equations similar to the author's discussed above. These were expressed as a matrix to facilitate their solution (by computer). In their study Friedlander and Roshier faced the same major problem as the author – how to produce a death rate or survivorship factor for a group of sometime migrants residing in another county. Their chain of reasoning was as follows: such a death rate depends on three factors, the age specific mortality of the migrant group, the rate of previous migration and the ages at which migration takes place. None of these are known, but all can be estimated, particularly in the case when the migration in a previous period has been calculated. Now, if it is assumed that the age distribution of actual (current) migrants is *constant* – that is the actual migrants of the 1850s had the same age distribution as those of the 1890s – the variations in mortality of the migrant groups could be assumed only to depend on the rate of migration each decade. It has, of course, long been established that actual migrants are heavily biased towards the younger age groups. By maintaining this assumption and assuming the initial age distribution of the migrant group is known, it is possible to estimate the size of a migrant group (say, Herts. born in Bucks.) in the next census by applying a survivorship factor (P_x) – which is merely the probability of reaching the next age group – to each age group. The method of working is essentially the same as that used to reduce the hypothetical migrant population when the age distribution assumption was tested above. This survivorship factor is calculated from English life tables for each group in the decade in question. The residual – the size of the migrant group at the second census in excess of the reduced initial migrant group – is the net migration of, say, Herts.-born into (or rarely out of) the county in question.

The validity of this important assumption – and its corollary that initial age distributions of a migrant group can be estimated – was tested. The age distribution of the migrant group in some of those counties whose migrant age distribution was known from the 1911 census was projected by the above method from 1851 to 1911. It was found that the agreement between the calculated 1911 age distribution and the 'true' one was remarkably high. The calculated and 'actual' survivorship ratios that these distributions implied were in no case more than 4 per cent different. Thus it would seem reasonable to calculate net inter-county migration of natives by applying these survivorship ratios to the system of equations above, using the result of each decade's calculation (the migrant flow at the assumed age distribution) as the raw material for the subsequent calculation. In fact, the error produced in the final migration flows by using the same survivorship ratio for all counties of origin was found to be minimal in all but a few cases. For these cases a separate ratio was calculated but otherwise the survivorship ratio of England and Wales for that age group was used for the decade in question.

In order to do this it was necessary to establish the initial age distribution of the migrant group in 1851 in the same way as it is given for some areas in 1911. The only guide to the actual distribution is the '20 and over' and 'under 20' division of that census. Because of the problem of infant mortality the estimation of a breakdown of the 'under 20' group was the more important. This was done by looking back from the census of 1861.

The migrants aged 0–19 in 1861 (given in the census) are composed of the survivors of the migrants aged 0–9 in 1851 plus the new arrivals (aged 0–19) between 1851 and 1861.

So the number of migrants aged 0–9 in 1851 must equal the number in 1861 aged 0–19 who had survived, less any new arrivals aged 0–19 between the two censuses, i.e.

$$\text{migrant group } 0\text{–}9_{1851} = \frac{\text{migrant group } 0\text{–}19_{1861} - \text{new migrants } 0\text{–}19_{1851\text{–}60}}{\text{survivorship factor of } 0\text{–}9 \text{ age group (E \& W) } 1851\text{–}60}$$

Various age distributions of current migrants (which were held to be constant in all decades) were then projected from 1851 to see which would give the best prediction of the age distributions that were given in 1911 (see above). The best fit was given by the distribution below (these ages are at the time of the second census – e.g. 1861–70 migrants as distributed in 1870).

So, in all 10-year periods the age distribution of 1,000 *current* migrants was assumed to be:

0–9	340	10–19	150
20–29	280	30–39	230

Several criticisms may be levelled at this method. For example, it does not follow that because the 1911 age distribution can be predicted by projecting the authors' guesses as to the probable age composition of a migrant group in 1851, that the original guess was correct or that the assumption of constant age composition for actual migrants was correct. Firstly, constructing life tables for a period as long as 60 years is subject to many cumulative errors and especially so with nineteenth-century data. Secondly, it does not follow that if the data on age distribution had existed for the intermediate census years that these age distributions would have been predicted by these tests. A correlation between two series over a period of time does not prove or disprove any correlation between the two series at intermediate times. Therefore, that the migrants had a constant age distribution cannot be proved in this way. Thirdly, the survivorship ratio can only be adduced given the assumption of constant age distribution of migrants, but that actual distribution is the one which gives the best fit to the known data by using the same survivorship ratios. This introduces a dangerous degree of circularity into the whole argument. Fourthly, the 1911 data only exist for four counties (three of them in Wales) and for a few large towns the census authorities thought interesting.

With these reservations the historian might well fall back on one of his favourite weapons – plausibility. If the data present many problems is it not better to make a few critical assumptions on the grounds of plausibility and then try to estimate the limits of error that these assumptions imply? For example, Friedlander and Roshier are left with an age distribution of current migrants (see above) which is patently too young to satisfy tests which by their nature cannot be exact. Indeed, it is noticeable that despite the apparent refinement of the method, Friedlander and Roshier used a national series of survivorship ratios rather than trying to construct county ones (except in a few cases – which had to be decided on grounds of plausibility) without the excuse that they were considering migrants in *several* counties. They rightly decided that the additional effort was not worthwhile given all the other problems involved and given that by its nature the series of equations are giving estimate (best-fit) solutions. All in all, it seems unlikely, however, that any better *global* estimate of inter-county migration flows will be produced,[22] without an enormous amount of additional work which could not be justified by more 'accurate' results.

6. LIMITATIONS ON ACCURACY

It is important, at this point, to make clear exactly what is measured by a net inter-county migration flow. For even Friedlander and Roshier's method is not a 'true' picture of internal migration. Those who left their county of birth and returned before the next census are excluded (even those returning from overseas). Those who return to their county of birth at a subsequent census are masking the movement of another in the opposite direction. Seasonal migrants are missed since the *de facto* census was taken in April. Moreover, one must be careful not to assume implicitly that migration across a county line is more important than intra-county migration. Many English counties in the nineteenth century as now were not economic or social units and their boundaries divided centres of population in a quite arbitrary way. Because of this, and the problem of boundary changes, Friedlander and Roshier did not publish details of migration streams from adjacent counties.

Boundary changes are a major problem. For, further to the objections noted above, all of which are still valid, if Herts. absorbs enough of Bucks. to increase its population by 5 per cent does this not increase the Bucks.-born in Herts. without any of them actually moving? I assumed that enumerators altered the place of birth (usually a town) to the new county or that later inhabitants had allowed for the change themselves. Certainly, the enumerators were required to do it. Naturally, the Herts.-born population in all the other counties in England and Wales would have to be increased by 5 per cent since if Herts. is 5 per cent bigger, there will be more living outside it as they now come from a larger area. Whether they actually did or not is of course immaterial since as was suggested earlier, a hypothetical standard county must be used.

It must also be remembered that a Herts.-born man moving from Bucks. to Oxon. in 1865 counts as if he had moved from Herts. to Oxon., since he is enumerated as Herts.-born in Oxon. in 1871 but not in 1861. It is not claimed of course that these methods give 'true' measures of migration. But since by definition, more move from their place of birth than subsequently as 'secondary' migrants, the degree of distortion is acceptable. Of course, in an examination of movement overseas the above additional movements net out, but even here it must be emphasised that the movements are still net of people returning to their place of birth.

For example:

net native emigration
$$(M \text{ overseas } 1861\text{–}70^{\text{Herts.}}) = (M \text{ Herts.} \rightarrow \text{overseas } 1861\text{–}70^{\text{Herts.}})$$
$$- \{(M \text{ overseas} \rightarrow \text{Herts. } 1861\text{–}70^{\text{Herts.}})$$
$$+ (M \text{ overseas} \rightarrow \text{another English/Welsh county } 1861\text{–}70^{\text{Herts.}})\}$$

Moreover, the 'origins' of emigrants produced by this method is their county of birth, not the county they last inhabited before emigrating. Even if it were possible, however, to distinguish 'residence' from birthplace there are no criteria for distinguishing those who went to, say Liverpool, to earn their fare or wait for a (cheap) ship, from those who were 'real' secondary or tertiary migrants.

7. A WORKED EXAMPLE: TO CALCULATE MALE MIGRATION TO OTHER ENGLISH COUNTIES AND EMIGRATION OVERSEAS FROM CORNWALL 1861–70

(i) *Boundary changes*

Total population of Cornwall in 1861 (P Cornwall 1861^{all}) = 369,390.

Population of Cornwall in 1861 with boundaries of 1891 = 369,000 (from Mitchell and Deane).

No account need be taken of boundary changes since the area of Cornwall in 1861 was the same as the ancient county area of 1891 (standard county).

(ii) Data

Total male population of Cornwall 1861 (Pm Cornwall 1861 = 176,384).
Total male population of Cornwall 1871 (Pm Cornwall 1871 = 169,706).
Native male population of Cornwall 1861 (Pm Cornwall 1861^{Cornwall} = 160,876).
Native male population of Cornwall 1871 (Pm Cornwall 1871^{Cornwall} = 154,487).
Male deaths in registration county of Cornwall 1861–70 (Dm Cornwall 1861–70 = 38,363).
Male births in registration county of Cornwall 1861–70 (Bm Cornwall 1861–70 = 63,136).
Enumerated Cornwall-born males in other English and Welsh counties 1861 (Pm OC 1861^{Cornwall} = 23,408).
Enumerated Cornwall-born males in other English and Welsh counties 1871 (Pm OC 1871^{Cornwall} = 30,158).
Crude male death rate, England and Wales 1861–70 = 23·61 per 1,000 p.a.

(iii) Adjustments of registration data

Total population registration county of Cornwall   1861   364,848
Total population registration county of Cornwall   1871   358,141
Total population ancient county of Cornwall   1861   369,390 ⎫ with
Total population ancient county of Cornwall   1871   362,343 ⎬ boundaries
                                                                 ⎭ of 1831

$$\frac{364,848 + 358,141}{369,390 + 362,343} \times 100 = 98\text{·}8 \text{ per cent}$$

i.e. the registration county was only 98·8 per cent of the ancient county 1861–70 (parts of Cornwall were in the registration county of Devon).

Therefore if births recorded = 63,136 in the registration county there would be (63,136 × 100)/98·8 births in the ancient county
= 63,902
but these births are probably 2 per cent under-enumerated
= 63,902 + 1,278 = 65,180 male births 1861–70.
Similarly there would be (38,363 × 100)/98·8
= 38,826 male deaths 1861–70.

(iv) Calculation

Now, the average size of the male immigrant group in Cornwall (Pm Cornwall 1861–70^{OC}) =

$$\frac{Pm \text{ Cornwall } 1861 + Pm \text{ Cornwall } 1871}{2}$$

$$\frac{Pm \text{ Cornwall } 1861^{\text{Cornwall}} + Pm \text{ Cornwall } 1871^{\text{Cornwall}}}{2}$$

i.e. $\dfrac{176{,}384 + 169{,}706}{2} - \dfrac{160{,}876 + 154{,}487}{2} = 15{,}364^{*}.$

Now, by our previous hypothesis the death rate of the migrant population = two-thirds the crude death rate for England and Wales, i.e.

$$\frac{2 \times 23 \cdot 61}{3} = 15 \cdot 75 \text{ per } 1{,}000 \text{ p.a.}$$

So that the 15,364 members of the migrant group lost

$$\frac{15{,}364 \times 15 \cdot 75 \times 10}{1{,}000} = 2{,}420.$$

Therefore the deaths of natives in Cornwall

$(Dm \text{ Cornwall } 1861\text{–}70^{\text{Cornwall}}) = Dm \text{ Cornwall } 1861\text{–}70$
$$- Dm \text{ Cornwall } 1861\text{–}70^{\text{OC}}.$$

i.e. $38{,}826 - 2{,}420 = 36{,}406$ native deaths.

Now, if there were no migration the native male population of Cornwall in 1871 would be

160,876 (Pm Cornwall 1861^{Cornwall}) + 63,902 (Bm Cornwall 1861–70)
$- 36{,}406$ (Dm Cornwall $1861\text{–}70^{\text{Cornwall}}$) = 188,372

but only 154,487 native males were enumerated in the county in 1871 (Pm Cornwall 1871^{Cornwall}).

Therefore $188{,}372 - 154{,}487 = 33{,}885$ must have left for all destinations 1861–70.

Similarly, there were 23,408 male natives of Cornwall enumerated in other counties in 1861 and 30,158 in 1871.

Of these (assuming their age distribution is such that a death rate two-thirds that for England and Wales is appropriate)

$$\frac{2/3 \times 23 \cdot 61 \times 10}{1{,}000} \times \frac{30{,}158 + 23{,}408}{2} = 4{,}218$$

would have died between 1861 and 1871.

But in 1871, 30,158 natives of Cornwall were enumerated outside the county. Therefore 30,158 (Pm OC 1871^{Cornwall}) $- 23{,}408$ (Pm OC 1861^{Cornwall}) $+ 4{,}218$ (Dm OC $1861\text{–}70^{\text{Cornwall}}$) = 10,938 were new arrivals of Cornish natives into other counties 1861–70.

If 33,885 left the county for *all* destinations and 10,938 arrived in other counties

* This total includes those born overseas as well as those born in OC.

1861–70, then $33,885 - 10,938 = 22,947$ (23,000 to the nearest 1,000) must have gone abroad or to Ireland or to Scotland.

(v)

Now, if the death rate of the migrant population were the same as England and Wales (23·61 per 1,000) (see above), deaths of the migrant group in Cornwall would be 3,627 and deaths of natives in Cornwall would be 35,199. So migration to all destinations of Cornish natives would be

$$(160,876 + 63,902 - 35,199) - 154,487 = 35,092.$$

Deaths of migrant group in other counties would be 6,323. Migration of Cornish natives into other counties would be

$$30,158 - 23,408 + 6,323 = 13,073$$

and migration of Cornwall born overseas would be $35,092 - 13,073 = 22,019$.

Summary table

Death rate assumption	Net movement of Cornish males out of Cornwall to all destinations 1861–70 (to nearest 1,000)	Net movement of Cornish males into all other English and Welsh counties 1861–1870 (to nearest 1,000)	Net movement of Cornish males overseas 1861–70 (to nearest 1,000)
(a) that migrant group has same death rate as nation (23·61) (clearly too high)	35,000	13,000	22,000
(b) the preferred assumption that migrant group has $\frac{2}{3}$ death rate of nation (15·75) (based on assumption of age distribution)	34,000	11,000	23,000
(c) that migrant group is composed only of those aged 15–34 (DR = 8·60) (clearly too low)	33,000	9,000	24,000

(vi)

If the migrant population were *all* aged 15–34, their death rate would be 8·60 per 1,000 (by applying England and Wales age-specific death rates to a population x distributed as follows: $x/4$ age 15–19, $x/4$ age 20–24, $x/2$ age 25–34), deaths of the migrant group in Cornwall would be 1,321 and deaths of natives in Cornwall would be 37,505, migration to all destinations of Cornwall natives would be

$$(160,876 + 63,902 - 37,505) - 154,487 = 32,786.$$

Deaths of the migrant group in other counties would be 2,303 so migration of Cornwall natives into other counties would be

$$30,158 - 23,408 + 2,303 = 9,053$$

and migration of Cornwall-born overseas would be

$$32,786 - 9,053 = 23,733.$$

The results are presented in the accompanying summary table.

Assumptions (a) and (c) represent extreme limits of error. The 'true' death rate must fall in between. Note that in external migration, death rate fluctuations tend to net out as a high death rate increases the total migration out of a county *and* the total migration into all the other counties. External estimates are therefore less sensitive to assumptions about death rates than internal estimates.

8. SOME OTHER STUDIES

The method used by Brinley Thomas[23] to show flows of migrants into Glamorgan is as follows (it is very similar to the basic Friedlander and Roshier method, although of course done before the days of computers).

The study was based on two assumptions.[24] Firstly, that actual migrants were all aged 15–24 and, secondly, that the whole of the migrant population of Glamorgan (by county of birth) was aged 35–44 in 1861. Therefore, if the total migrant group of, say, Devon-born was reduced by the 35–44 death rate and the survivors subtracted from the enumerated 1871 Devon-born, the result would be net inward movement of Devon-born into Glamorgan 1861–70. In the next decade, if the survivors of the original migrant group were reduced by the death rate of the 45–54 age group and the new arrivals of the previous decade reduced by the death rate of 25–34 age group this could be subtracted from the 1881 enumeration to give net inward movement of Devon-born for 1871–80. This process was repeated for ten year periods to 1911, e.g.

$$M \text{ Glamorgan } 1871\text{--}80^{\text{Devon}} = P \text{ Glamorgan } 1881^{\text{Devon}} -$$
$$(P \text{ Glamorgan } 1871^{\text{Devon}} - D \text{ Glamorgan } 1871\text{--}80^{\text{Devon}})$$

where

$$D \text{ Glamorgan } 1871\text{--}80^{\text{Devon}} = (P \text{ Glamorgan } 1861^{\text{Devon}}$$
$$\times \text{ E \& W death rate } 45\text{--}54 \times 10)$$
$$+ (M \text{ Glamorgan } 1861\text{--}70^{\text{Devon}}$$
$$\times \text{ E \& W death rate } 25\text{--}34 \times 10)$$

(note that death rates are given per 1,000 population per annum, so that deaths of a population x with a death rate y over 10 years are $10xy/1,000$). H. A. Shannon[25] used the same method to show flows into London except he assumed the migrant group of 1851 were aged 35–44, on the grounds that migration to London was of longer standing.

The so-called 'Pennsylvania' study[26] examined net interstate movement in the USA by age group. It did not measure inter-censal migration flows. The basic method was a census survival technique but one sufficiently refined to yield data on net migration by age group. Such a census survival method measures, either the chance of surviving from one age group to the next, one census later (forward method) or the chances of having survived from one age group to the next since the last census (reverse method). The rate is a fraction calculated from the known national population at the two age groups.

(i) *Forward survival method:*

$$M \text{ (aged 20–24 in 1870) } 1870\text{–}80^{\text{Ohio}}$$
$$= P \text{ (aged 20–24) } 1880^{\text{Ohio}} - \left(\frac{P \text{ (aged 20–24) } 1880^{\text{USA}}}{P \text{ (aged 10–14) } 1870^{\text{USA}}} \right)$$
$$\times P \text{ (aged 10–14) } 1870^{\text{Ohio}}$$

will yield a different result than

(ii) *Reverse survival method:*

$$M \text{ (aged 20–24 in 1870) } 1870\text{–}1880^{\text{Ohio}}$$
$$= P \text{ (aged 20–24) } 1880^{\text{Ohio}} \times \left(\frac{P \text{ (aged 10–14) } 1870^{\text{USA}}}{P \text{ (aged 20–24) } 1880^{\text{USA}}} \right)$$
$$- P \text{ (aged 10–14) } 1870^{\text{Ohio}}$$

because the survival ratio is applied to P 1880 rather than P 1870. The problem is that a forward ratio in this case measures deaths in 1870 and therefore misses deaths of immigrants 1870–80. The reverse method measures all immigrant deaths but overstates them because it assumes they were all there in 1870. The reverse is true for out migrants. This problem is not great for the young age groups but with ageing populations it can be serious. In order that states could be compared and that the net internal migration for the whole country should be nil in each period, one method only was used.[27]

Other characteristics of the study were as follows:

1. US (national) census survival rates rather than calculated life table data was used as it was more realistic.
2. It was assumed that these rates could be equally applied in all states (i.e. that there were few age-specific causes of death peculiar to particular states).
3. It was assumed under-enumeration was constant from state to state. Then by using census survival ratios under-enumeration errors can be partly self-corrected.

The only attempt to show interstate flows of migrants was a calculation of the 'birth residence indices' of the then forty-eight US states for each census 1870–1950, i.e.

P Wisconsin $1870^{\text{all other states}} - P$ all other states $1870^{\text{Wisconsin}}$

$$= \text{Birth residence index } 1870$$

but since time periods are not distinguished this type of analysis is only of limited use for historical purposes. Inter-censal change in the indices will, however, predict the main migratory movements.

The Brinley Thomas method of showing flows by county of origin into Glamorgan and the big Pennsylvania study cannot seem to be superior to the methods described earlier. These methods can have the disadvantage, however, that a total study is needed to gain partial information which with some loss of accuracy could well be produced by simpler means.

9. CONCLUSION

Most social historians will probably prefer to present the data as simply as possible unless they are building complicated economic models, which need *indices* of migration flows. It would, therefore, seem that to show the actual *numbers* of inter-censal migrants is sufficient, although some indication of the mid-year population of their county of origin (and destination?) should be given so that the relative importance of each flow can be judged. Friedlander and Roshier used a map with arrows, the direction of which showed the main non-adjacent flows and their thickness the relative importance to the particular counties. Their gross index was calculated by the formula:

$$\text{Gross index of migration flow} = \frac{M \text{ Herts.} \rightarrow \text{Bucks. } 1861\text{--}70^{\text{Herts.}}}{P \text{ Herts. } 1861 \times P \text{ Bucks. } 1861}.$$

If the aim is simply to show variations in movement over time, a simple graph of the proportion of native migrants to the total home county population for each decade may be used.

The methods described above have many disadvantages for the historian. With the exception of the 'Pennsylvania' study, none are appropriate for British data after 1911, because place of birth is no longer given in the census (until 1951) and the national county units bear less and less reality. Thus the attempt by Friedlander and Roshier to extend their analysis to 1951 by *estimating* the 1931 place of birth enumeration has no historical validity. The enforced choice of the county as the basic unit in Britain, the lack of information outside census years, the scarcity of data on marital status, ages and occupations all leave many important questions unanswered. In effect, the more comprehensive the method employed the less is the degree of disaggregation possible. It is, of course, possible to complement aggregative methods with detailed local studies from other sources and these will yield much additional information. The 'macro' methods will, however, suggest lines of enquiry and the areas of greatest interest. The final choice of method to adopt must depend on the purpose to which the results are to be put. For example, the primary purpose of my study was to examine internal and external migration flows over time to isolate changes in direction and rate. I was, therefore, able (among other things) to examine the relationship between domestic and foreign investment and internal and external migration. For this purpose a country-wide study was essential, and the cost was the loss of much important information.

The use of the county as a unit is a source of much 'leakage' of information. It is neither a completely arbitrary unit (of common area, shape or size, density and spread of population etc.) nor is it often a meaningful social and economic unit – which many American states are (though many are not). County boundaries often run through heavily urban areas and many rural areas because of topography or merely the shape of the county, are tributary to an urban area in another county. However, *any* chosen area can be studied by using the census enumerators' books. And, it is possible by using such sources to distinguish a person's birthplace, age, occupation and marital condition which will obviously yield enormously valuable results.[28] Unfortunately, to trace persons the investigator has to match names[29] from one census to another. But outmigrants can never be isolated, because sufficient names could never be matched in the subsequent census and via registration data, to eliminate births and deaths and to relate two groups of whom it could be said that all of those not enumerated in the second census had migrated, or that all the new names were new migrants. Some interesting case histories could be assembled but a systematic migration study over several decades is probably impossible. An alternative is to trace the birth and marriage certificates and the birth certificates of children of known emigrants.[30] But although interesting in itself tracing those in Britain known to have emigrated is unlikely to tell us much about migration in *general* since such a group is obviously not a sample of the general population. The expense[31] and labour of such sampling on a county-wide scale is probably too great to justify the likely returns.

There is much that can be learnt from nineteenth-century government publications, particularly the various reports on agricultural distress and reports of the Poor Law authorities. It was a report by this body on emigration in the six months prior to the census of 1841 (published in the census tables) that Redford used.[32] Finally, local newspapers can be an invaluable source of material as long as the investigator remembers that newsprint was expensive in the nineteenth century and that what is common is not necessarily newsworthy.

In conclusion there is still an enormous amount of local work to do before the process of nineteenth-century migration can be fully understood. Despite the qualifications noted above, it must be re-emphasised that detailed national estimates are an essential prerequisite for the study of migration. For example (after 1861) with no increase in total error, the mobility of males and females can be distinguished (although Friedlander and Roshier did not do this). This is important in emigration studies since the known national preponderance of male emigrants (particularly for a large number of counties, or all of them) is a reasonable check on the accuracy of the data. It was also held in the late nineteenth century that domestic service increased female relative to male mobility. And it is possible to infer further details. For example, emigration can be seen alongside net native outflow (they are not strictly comparable).[33] This could be held to show rates of turnover of population, in say industrial compared with agricultural counties. Inaccurate as they obviously are, inferences of this type are important to those who wish to stress the ebb and flow of migration rather than its net effects.

8. Criminal statistics and their interpretation

V. A. C. Gatrell and T. B. Hadden

PART 1. STRUCTURE AND INTERPRETATION

INTRODUCTION

Annual statistical returns relating to criminal behaviour in England and Wales have been published in the parliamentary papers since 1805. In the early decades of the century they were limited in scope, but from 1857 onwards they contained the several distinct types of information which form the basis of criminal statistics even today: the numbers of indictable offences known to the police, the numbers of people committed to trial for indictable and summary offences respectively, and the numbers and personal characteristics of the people imprisoned upon conviction. These returns enable us to plot across a period of years the long-term trends and the short-term fluctuations in the incidence of criminal activity of different kinds, in England and Wales as a whole and in different parts of the country, and to say something also, with a fair degree of certainty, about the kinds of people who came before the courts.[1]

Of the several kinds of numerical data on nineteenth-century social behaviour at our disposal, the criminal statistics are among the most comprehensive and copious. Since the incidence of criminal activity in certain forms, at different periods, and in different parts of the country can sometimes be explained in terms of the impact of social and economic conditions on the population at large, the records of crime may reflect directly on the degree of security which the English social and economic system assured or failed to assure to the mass of its people at a time of rapid urban and industrial growth.

Of course in this context there is a real danger of over-simplification. It cannot be maintained, for example, that all forms of criminal activity, at all times, constituted part of something that could be called a 'social movement'. (Thus there is little reason to ascribe clear-cut social significance to the murder rate.) Some criminologists would argue that the reasons why people commit criminal offences of any kind are more intimately related to the individual's personality and experience than to some 'force' residing in the socio-economic system. And it is certainly true that research directed to discover a single 'root cause' of crime in the social order is likely to be fruitless: the concept has involved criminologists in circuitous debate for nearly a century.

But it does not follow that because any aggregate index of mass behaviour

336

must mask the circumstances of the individual case, the aggregate is merely a statistical artifact, a mere average of probability. For the historian aggregate crime rates retain a peculiar interest and importance. Provided the individual cases of which they are constituted are sufficiently numerous, the trends and fluctuations in the rates through a period of time, or in regions with different demographic and social structures, are not random phenomena. They are what Durkheim in another context called social facts, *sui generis*, and their examination is a proper task for the historian and the sociologist alike.[2]

Approached in this way, the official returns can be exploited to illuminate more than a few of the dark areas of nineteenth-century social history, two of which we may suggest at once. It is possible, first, that the study of trends and fluctuations in certain forms of criminal behaviour, and especially in that directed against property, will further the debate about the qualitative changes in the nineteenth-century standard of living. If, for example, we could detect an overall increase in the incidence of property offences during the first half of the nineteenth century, or a correlation between their higher incidence and economic depression in any one year, we might be able to approach some definition of the dislocating effects of urban and population growth and economic hardship at a level which has not hitherto been examined. If, conversely, it could be shown that the rate of property offences decreased from mid-century onwards, or that the clarity of their correlation with economic depression diminished, this could be related not merely to the increasing efficiency of the forces of law and order, but also to a real change in the standard of living, and to a wider acceptance of the standards of respectability, which enabled and encouraged proportionately more people to keep clear of the courts. An analysis along these lines could be further developed by comparing the regional differences in crime rates, to illustrate how different population groups were variously affected by conditions operating in manufacturing and agricultural counties respectively. Such a comparison would also considerably deepen our understanding of those regional variations in living standards.

Secondly, a similar examination of the relationship between criminal activity and socio-economic conditions may help us to measure the depth and extent of contemporary social tensions and unrest. The political or quasi-political movements to which historians of the early nineteenth century have usually directed their attention in this context, were after all merely the more dramatic and 'directed' manifestations of social unrest, and in any case they affected only a very small proportion of the population at any one time. Unemployment, hunger, and urbanisation, also provoked what we may call an 'undirected' response in many more people than those who happened to voice a political or near-political creed or goal. Since this response frequently took the form of 'ordinary' criminal behaviour, the incidence of certain kinds of criminal activity may in certain periods constitute a more sensitive index of the extent and depth of social and economic frustrations than any other available to us.

Many commentators in the 1830s and 1840s were more consistently aware of the potential importance of analyses of this kind than recent historians have shown themselves to be.[3] A new statistical consciousness in those years, and a widespread alarm at the apparent increase in crime over the previous quarter century, generated a sizeable criminological literature in which a direct relationship between crime and the impact upon the population of economic and social conditions was largely taken for granted. Indeed, the varying incidence of crime, from year to year and from county to county, was frequently regarded as a legitimate index of a pattern of social dislocation in the country at large. But if these writers anticipated our hypotheses, they did not develop them fully, and tended to be unsatisfactory in their statistical methods. And by the late 1850s, as police control grew more effective and the political climate changed, the focus of attention turned from general questions about the total incidence of various types of crime to the consideration of particular problems such as juvenile delinquency or drunkenness.

In this century research based on the early criminal statistics has been no more conclusive: no adequate study of the long-term or short-term trends in different forms of crime and their relationship to social conditions throughout the nineteenth century has yet been published.[4] This is not because the significance of aggregate indices of criminal behaviour is underestimated. Many modern criminologists have accepted Durkheim's argument and applied themselves to the statistical analysis of twentieth-century criminal activity, to define, for example, the difference between the rates of offences committed by people of different economic status, and the degree to which the incidence of different kinds of offence is affected by depression and affluence or by changing patterns in the age structure of the population.[5] But this kind of analysis has not been extended back into the nineteenth century.

There is good reason for this. The early statistical tables, published in over 100 separate blue books, are cumbersome and inconvenient in arrangement, while many series are incomplete. And since there is a valid case for arguing that even the best of modern criminal statistics are in many respects defective, it is naturally assumed that those for the nineteenth century, and particularly for the early nineteenth century, must be much more so. Given the numerous developments in the organisation of the police and the courts which are likely to have caused serious distortions in the nineteenth century returns, this assumption is not unreasonable. As a result, those who have written about nineteenth century criminal behaviour have relied almost exclusively on the contemporary literature on the subject. Their decision is an attractive one. By comparison with the statistics, the literary sources are readily accessible and easily digested, and they possess an immediacy of reference which the statistics inevitably lack. They are also especially valuable where they reflect the writer's intimate experience of local conditions. Considerations of this sort account for Tobias's claim, in the most recent study based on the literary sources, that 'the criminal statistics have little to tell us about crime and criminals in the nineteenth century', and that 'when they point to a conclusion opposed to that based on contemporary description they can perhaps be disregarded without much anxiety'.[6]

The position adopted by writers like Tobias, however, is not as strong as it may seem, for total dependence on the literary sources can be seriously misleading. In the first place, it was very seldom that contemporary commentators resisted the temptation of venturing beyond the anecdotal description of their personal experience of criminals to assert their own interpretation about the trends in and causes of criminal behaviour, and it is precisely such assertions that modern historians tend to find the most appealing in their reconstruction of the past.

The real difficulty, however, arises from the fact that few contemporaries were either in a position or had the inclination to attempt an extended survey of the records over a period of several decades; nor were they always critically aware of the dangers inherent in the figures which all modern commentators must recognise. Thus even when they did use the official statistics their conclusions were often based upon incomplete and ill-assimilated evidence. More than this, the discussion of crime was fraught with presupposition and prejudice then as it is now. It was commonly loaded with moral judgement, and no less frequently biased in favour of certain prior assumptions. By judicious selection of data it was as possible for one writer to demonstrate the 'criminality' of rural counties as it was for another to demonstrate the depravity of industrial counties. And from the 1850s onwards the growing preoccupation with the problems of drunkenness and juvenile delinquency tended to preclude a balanced assessment of criminal activity as a whole.

If then, we are not to abdicate entirely from a systematic examination of nineteenth century criminal behaviour, it is only by returning to the official statistics that we can hope to attain a wider perspective than contemporary observers, to avoid repeating their prejudices, and to arrive at conclusions based on a greater awareness of the possible distortions in the criminal records than that which they usually exhibited. Even our preliminary work on the statistics demonstrates that some contemporary conclusions – about the relationship between crime and economic conditions, or between crime and drunkenness; about the activities of juveniles or of the 'criminal class', about the distinctive criminality of the manufacturing districts – are grossly oversimplified or even palpably wrong.

For these reasons it is desirable to undertake a statistical analysis of nine-teenth-century criminal behaviour *de novo*. But it remains true that full account has to be taken of the very real difficulties involved in the use of the official returns. The purpose of this chapter, therefore, is two-fold: in part 1 to explain the structure of the nineteenth-century returns and to discuss the difficulties and dangers in utilising them, showing how they may be circumvented; and in part 2 to illustrate their practical value through a number of basic tabulations and analyses likely to be of immediate interest to the social historian.

By way of introduction, the complex and often unsystematic arrangement of the early returns is discussed in section 1, which will serve also as a guide to their contents. Section 2 discusses their deficiencies: those inherent in all criminal statistics, and those peculiar to the nineteenth-century returns. None of these deficiences, in our view, seriously impedes the sensitive exploitation of the returns, or invalidates the examination of the more important hypotheses relevant to the historian, though they undoubtedly complicate the work of analysis immensely.

These methodological points will be given substance in the illustrative analyses which make up the second part of the chapter. Careful tabulation and interpretation of the data allows us to establish trends and correlations which often present a rather different picture from that which has come down to us from contemporary commentators. Section 3 contains a comprehensive tabular and graphical description of the incidence of different categories of serious crime in England and Wales throughout the century, an interpretation of the most conspicuous trends, and a necessarily brief discussion of the apparent relationship between criminal behaviour and economic conditions. It also illustrates how a comparable analysis may be conducted for an individual county through a discussion of the incidence of serious crimes in Lancashire. Section 4 illustrates how the compendious information on the character of offenders may be utilised through an examination of the changes which took place across the century in respect of their literacy, age structure, and criminal records.

Some of the findings presented in this chapter perhaps go as far as the published figures permit. Others are clearly tentative. In almost every case they may be further refined both by reference to local literary sources and by a much more detailed examination of the county statistics than can be attempted here. Some of the further possibilities open to those prepared to use the official statistics with care are suggested in the concluding section.

1. THE AVAILABLE MATERIAL

At their most comprehensive, English criminal statistics contain four kinds of information upon which any detailed examination of criminal behaviour will have to be based. They may be listed as follows.

(a) The numbers of males and females, in each county and in England and Wales as a whole, committed to trial for an indictable offence (that is an offence tried before a jury in the superior courts of assize or quarter sessions). These are referred to as *indictable committals*, and in the nineteenth century they were published in the set of returns headed Judicial Proceedings or Criminal Offenders from 1805 onwards.

(b) The numbers of males and females in each county and in England and Wales, *committed to prison* after conviction, either on an indictable or on a summarily tried offence, together with their ages, degrees of instruction, previous records, etc. These were published in the set of returns headed Gaols and Prisons, from 1836 onwards.

(c) The numbers of males and females, in each police district and county, and in England and Wales as a whole, brought before a magistrate on summary jurisdiction for less serious offences. These are referred to as *summary committals*, and they were published in the set of returns which appeared from 1857 onwards headed Police Returns.

(d) The numbers of *indictable offences known to the police* to have been committed in each police district or county and in England and Wales as a whole, whether or not the offender was actually traced and brought to trial. These were also published in the Police Returns from 1857 onwards.

The continuity of these series was affected by two major reorganisations in 1833–4 and in 1856–7 and to a lesser extent by a third in 1893. To describe the contents of the criminal statistics in more detail, therefore, it is convenient to isolate the three periods marked off by these dates (1805–33, 1834–56, and 1857–92) and to treat them separately.

FIRST PERIOD 1805–33: *indictable committals*

The stimulus for the collection of the first committal returns was the contemporary debate on the death penalty, which caused the Home Secretary in 1805 to direct the clerks of each court or circuit to make an annual return of the numbers of indictable committals for trial, of capital convictions, and of executions.[7] In 1810 the House of Commons passed a motion proposed by Romilly for the collection of much fuller returns covering both indictable and summary offences, but though no summary returns were collected in this period, the motion did secure the publication of the figures collected for 1805–9, and thereby established the standard format of the committals statistics up to 1834.[8] For this period, then, figures are available for the number of persons in England and Wales as a whole, and in each county respectively, (i) committed for trial on an indictable offence, (ii) discharged on 'no true bill' being found, (iii) acquitted and (iv) convicted. This information was given for each of an alphabetical list of some fifty major offences, covering most forms of homicide, robbery, housebreaking, larceny, and the more serious political offences such as riot and machine-breaking.

These first statistics were thus no more than court records of all those dealt with for a restricted group of offences defined as 'serious' only in terms of legal history. But they can be used for the study of long-term trends in certain forms of criminal behaviour from the start of the century.

SECOND PERIOD 1834–56: (a) *Indictable committals and* (b) *Commitments to prison*

(a) *Indictable committals*

In 1833 Samuel Redgrave, the Criminal Registrar, reorganised the presentation of the returns for indictable committals by replacing the old alphabetical list of fifty or so indictable offences with a new and expanded classification. Seventy-five offences were now rearranged under the following six main headings which have survived with minor variations in their content until the present day:

- (i) offences against the person (homicide, wounding etc., including for the first time simple assaults and assaults on police officers);
- (ii) offences against property involving violence (robbery, burglary, house-breaking etc.);
- (iii) offences against property not involving violence (larceny etc.);
- (iv) malicious offences against property (arson, machine-breaking, rick-burning etc.);
- (v) offences against the currency (forgery, coining etc.);
- (vi) miscellaneous offences (including notably treason, sedition, riot etc.)

Apart from this rearrangement, the returns of persons in each county committed to trial, acquitted, and convicted, for each of the seventy-five offences thus categorised, were continued much as before, together with a statement of the sentences imposed. Thus by linking these returns with those for 1805–34, it is relatively easy to construct a general table for the incidence of indictable committals in the first half of the century, both regionally and nationally.

For the brief period 1834–49 there was one exceptional addition to the contents of the committal returns – probably in response to the growing interest in the characteristics of offenders fostered by the statistical societies established in the 1830s. This was the provision of data on the 'character' of those committed for indictable offences: their ages, sex, and degree of instruction. This series was discontinued in 1849 since it more or less duplicated the comparable information given for prisoners in the Prison Returns; and it was in any case reasonably argued that prison officials were better placed to compile reliable returns of character than the officials of the courts.

(b) *Commitments to prison*

An unsatisfactory series of Prison Returns had been published since 1820, for the most part containing only written reports from each county on the conditions of individual gaols. From 1836, the information relating to gaols and prisoners was systematised in tabular form in an annual digest. Until 1856 this was published as an appendix to the report of the inspector of prisons for the Home Counties, and thereafter it was brought within the composite volume of Statistics to which we have already referred.

The importance of these new returns is twofold. First, they contain comprehensive information on the character of offenders, and this was published in a similar form thoughout the century. From the start the Prison Returns gave the age, sex, degree of instruction, and number of previous commitments to gaol of all prisoners, distinguishing between those imprisoned for indictable and for summary offences respectively. Secondly, the distinction drawn between committals to prison for indictable and for summary offences respectively makes the Prison Returns our only source for the number of summary offences committed in the period before 1857. It is, however, an indirect and necessarily inaccurate one: the different kinds of summary offences for which the prisoners were gaoled were not fully specified; and in any case many offences tried summarily would not be included in the total because many petty offenders might merely be discharged with a caution or fined.

THIRD PERIOD 1857–1892: (a) *Indictable committals*, (b) *Commitments to prison*, (c) *Summary committals* and (d) *Indictable offences known to the police*

In 1856–7 Redgrave undertook a thoroughgoing reorganisation of the official returns following on the Police Act passed in 1856 'to render more effectual the police in the counties and boroughs of England and Wales'.[9] This marks the main turning point in the structure of the statistics for three reasons.

First, the existing returns from the courts and from the prisons were supplemented by a new set of Police Returns from the newly-constituted police districts, now based on boroughs as well as on counties. For each district the Police Returns now provided two kinds of information hitherto lacking: the number of offenders tried summarily for each offence and the number of indictable offences in the existing classification known to the police to have been committed. Secondly, all this information, relating to indictable committals, to prisons and prisoners, to summary committals, and to indictable offences known to the police, was henceforth brought together in one annual volume. Thirdly, each volume from 1859 onwards was prefaced by a full review written by the Criminal Registrar. This contained a number of useful summaries and analyses of the information in the subsequent tables, as well as occasional further information not otherwise published. In these prefaces, moreover, Redgrave and his successors maintained a running commentary on the effects of legal changes on the statistics, and speculated with varying degrees of perceptivity on the causes of the changes in the patterns of criminal behaviour observed from year to year and decade to decade. The prefaces written towards the end of the century naturally tended to be more sophisticated than those written earlier; but in all cases they are worth consulting, not merely for their useful synopses, but also in their own right, in so far as they exemplify the thinking of perhaps the most professional of all nineteenth-century criminologists.

Redgrave himself described the new structure of the returns as follows:

The principle of arrangement adopted has been that the three separate heads shall form one document, and that under each such facts shall be included, among others, as more peculiarly appertain to it. Thus under the head *Police* will be found such particulars as can be obtained relative to the crimes committed, the numerous petty offences punished summarily, and the antecedents and previous habits and character of the offenders. The head *Criminal Proceedings* will be chiefly confined to an accurate definition of the offences, result of trial, and punishments of those charged with indictable crimes; and the *Prisons* portion will contain more full information as to the ages of prisoners, their state of instruction, number of previous convictions, and such other particulars as the gaol officers have the best means of ascertaining, but in no case has an attempt been made to obtain information not properly within the knowledge of the officers making the returns, and upon which reliance may not be placed.[10]

The contents and significance of the new series may be summarised as follows.

(a) *Indictable committals*

These were continued without alteration under the classification introduced in 1834. Thus the analyses which are possible on the earlier returns can be carried through to the end of the century without difficulty. One interesting addition to the tables published under this heading related to the number of juvenile offenders committed to the reformatories and industrial schools established from the 1850s onwards. The number of these juveniles, however, was always included in the returns for indictable or summary committals as the case might be; and since every juvenile sent to one of these institutions had to serve a brief time in prison beforehand, they are included in the Prison Returns as well. Thus the development of differential treatment for juveniles involved no distortion of the main statistical records.

(b) *Commitments to prison*

The Prison Returns were also continued without major alteration, although information on the occupations and birthplaces of prisoners was added to that given in the earlier period on their ages, sex, literacy, and previous records.

(c) *Summary committals*

The importance of the new information given in the Police Returns should not be underestimated. That relating to summary offences enables us to allow for the appreciable extension from the 1820s onwards in the summary jurisdiction of magistrates' courts over offences which had previously been considered indictable and reserved for the superior courts.[11] Naturally this process seriously affected the long-term comparability of the records both of indictable committals and of indictable offences known to the police, since indictable offences which were in fact tried summarily were normally deducted from the total of indictable offences. More direct and comprehensive information than that previously obtainable from the Prison Returns about each type of offence dealt with summarily is thus essential if these distortions are to be corrected. In any case it is obviously advisable to include in any index of 'serious' crime the incidence of the more important larcenies and assaults which were in the event tried summarily. Even some of those offences which were not 'serious', such as drunkenness and disorderliness, are clearly of interest in their own right.

(d) *Indictable offences known to the police*

The publication of these figures in the Police Returns after 1857 is perhaps of even greater importance than the publication of the figures for summary committals. They constitute what is generally recognised as the best available indication of the 'actual' incidence of various kinds of criminal activity in the society at large, since they are less subject than all other figures to the distorting effects of local differences in police practice or of national developments in police efficiency, prosecution practice, and court procedure. On the basis of these figures, moreover it is possible to attempt a very approximate estimate of police efficiency in tracing offenders, by comparing the numbers of offences known with the numbers of people committed to trial for those offences.

Apart from the information on (c) and (d) above, the Police Returns contain two further kinds of data of rather less importance. First, tables are given on the size, expense, and ratio of individual police forces to the populations of their districts. This enables us to estimate the differing strength of police forces across the country, a process which for the period before 1857 could be attempted only from local sources and occasional parliamentary papers.[12] Secondly, tables were provided on the size in each district of the 'criminal class', defined as known thieves and depradators, receivers of stolen goods, suspicious characters, etc.

1893 AND AFTER

Although this chapter is primarily concerned with the nineteenth-century returns, it may be helpful to give a brief description of the changes which took place in 1893 following the recommendations of the Select Committee to Revise the Criminal Portion of the Judicial Statistics.[13] They were quite straightforward and can be simply listed. Whereas hitherto annual police and prison returns had been based on the year ending 30 September and 31 March respectively, all returns from 1893 onwards were standardised on the calendar year. All figures were given as ratios per 100,000 of the population, whether male or female, in order to allow easier comparison with rates in earlier years. Certain elementary illogicalities in the previous returns were rectified: thus the practice of excluding from the returns all reported cases of simple larceny involving less than five shillings, except where an arrest took place, was discontinued;[14] and the figures for indictable offences which were in the event tried summarily were no longer deducted from those for indictable offences known to the police. The enumera-

M

tion of offences was slightly altered, but the basic categories introduced in 1834 were retained. The returns for summary committals were transferred from the Police to the Judicial Returns. Finally, the Criminal Registrar's introductory reports were considerably expanded and simplified. Henceforth they contained clearer and more detailed analyses of the incidence of various types of crime over periods of twenty years, maps showing the geographical distribution of certain offences, and precise accounts of the effects of legal reforms on the continuity of the statistical records.

Though the organisation of the returns was rationalised and their use made correspondingly less time-consuming, the information they contained was not seriously altered, and the possibility of carrying analyses and comparisons into the twentieth century is not, therefore, unduly affected.

It will be clear from this discussion that to exploit fully the information contained in the official returns across the whole century is no simple task. To collate and tabulate even a simple series of figures over an appreciable period may involve a considerable amount of cross-reference from one set of returns to another, the format of which in various periods may well be quite different. If only on this account, it is important to be quite clear before beginning to collect figures what combinations of data will provide the best answer to the questions asked of them. One must always bear in mind for instance the advisability of combining figures for summary committals with those for indictable offences, whether these last relate to indictable committals or to indictable offences known to the police.

The simplest of the tables and graphs presented in the later sections of this chapter illustrates the relationship between the incidence of assaults and of drunkenness respectively, and it may serve as an example of several of the processes involved in the use of the returns.[15] For each year covered it was necessary to locate in separate tables in the Police Returns and then to tabulate the numbers of summarily tried assaults and summarily tried offences of drunkenness and disorderliness; a further table in the Police Returns had to be consulted for the number of indictable assaults known to the police; the two figures for assaults had to be added; and both this composite figure, and the figure for drunkenness, had to be reduced to rates per 100,000 of the relevant population. The compilation of other tabulations may be even more complex. If, as is sometimes the case, the difference between male and female behaviour is of importance, the process must be carried out twice. And if regional variations are required it must be repeated for each area, usually from data published in different tables on different pages, and occasionally in a different form, from those containing the national figures. In some cases, moreover, the straight tabulations of the rates thus compiled have to be corrected either numerically or graphically in order to allow for the many distortions in the original figures which derive from the administrative and procedural changes with which we shall be concerned in the next section.

The basic information included in the foregoing general description can be summarised, and in some respects supplemented, in a tabular form, showing for the several different periods the availability and location of the most important material in the returns: table 1 indicates the location and the completeness of the information at various times on the incidence of *offences*, as these are reflected in data on (i) indictable offences known to the police; (ii) committals for trial for indictable offences; and (iii) committals for trial for summary offences; table 2 summarises in a different form the location and extent of the material which is available at various times on *offenders'* characteristics.

Table 1 *The availability of published figures relating to offences: 1805–92**

	Offences known to the police	Committals for indictable offences	Offences tried summarily
1805–08	—	National figures and sex of offenders for each offence (CO)	—
1809	—	National figures and sex of offenders for block totals only (CO)	—
1810–23	—	National figures for each offence; sex of offenders for block total only (CO)	—
1824–34	—	As above (CO)	Some unsystematic county figures for summary offenders imprisoned (PR)
1834–35	—	National and county figures and sex of offenders for each offence under new classification (CP)	As above
1836–51	—	As above	National and county figures for committals to gaol for each main summary offence; sex of offenders for each (PR)
1852–54	—	National and county figures, but not sex of offenders, for each main offence (CP)	As above but sex of offenders for block totals only (PR)
1855–56	—	As above	Block totals only for national and county returns and for sex of offenders (PR)
1857–92	National and police district figures for each main indictable offence (PolR)	National and county figures and sex of offenders for each main offence (CP)	National and (from 1858) county figures for each main offence summarily tried; sex of offenders for national figures, but for block total only for county (PolR)

* Location indicated in brackets: CO = Criminal Offenders; PR = Prison Returns; CP = Criminal Proceedings; PolR = Police Returns.

Table 2 *The availability of published figures on the characteristics of offenders: 1805–92*

	Prison Returns (all prisoners)	Police Returns (summary and indictable)	Criminal Proceedings (indictable committals)
Sex	1836–92*	1857–92	1805–92
Age	1836–92*	—	1834–49
Degree of instruction	1836–92*	—	1834–49
Place of birth	1857–92	—	—
Occupation	1857–92	—	—
Recommittals	1836–92*	—	—
Criminality of offenders	—	1857–92†	—
Known thieves at large	—	1857–92‡	—

* Listed by offence and county from 1834 to 1839, by county only from 1840 to 1856, and by county and police district from 1857; data given separately for prisoners for indictable and summary offenders until 1856, thereafter for all offenders without discrimination.

† Classified as: prostitutes; known thieves; vagrants, tramps and others without visible means of subsistence; suspicious characters; habitual drunkards.

‡ Classified as: known thieves and depredators; receivers of stolen goods; suspected persons. Each group is divided into those above and below the age of 16.

LOCAL AND UNPUBLISHED SOURCES

It is a commonplace that officially published statistics do not always accurately represent the data from which they are compiled. This applies as much to criminal statistics as to a census. We have not ourselves been able to undertake any detailed work on the accuracy of the published figures in this context, but we can at least refer the reader to the largely unpublished information contained in the Public and in individual County Record Offices, upon which the official figures were based. This material is by no means comprehensive; only in a few cases, and then merely for short periods, is it possible to correlate the published returns with the unpublished. But where they do survive, the manuscript sources tend to contain much greater detail than was published, particularly about the characteristics of criminal behaviour in individual magistracies or police districts. And because a great deal of overt political behaviour was considered criminal in the nineteenth century, they also occasionally throw light on the identity and the activities of those who participated in local political and social movements.

The fullest of these sources are the Criminal Registers in the Home Office Papers in the PRO. For each county annually they give the name, the degree of instruction, the age, the offence, and the sentence imposed, for each person committed to trial for an indictable offence. It is easy to use these returns in years and for counties in which there was known political unrest, in order to define the identities of 'political' offenders in some detail.

To this end it may often be even more rewarding to resort to the records in individual County Record Offices. The quality and the quantity of the material which these Offices contain varies immensely, and all we can do here is to give a rough indication of what may be found. The following sources, for example, are the most important among those available in the Lancashire Record Office at Preston:

Riot Depositions 1826–93 for Manchester and Salford: many of these relate to quite minor incidents such as public house brawls, but in years of great unrest, for example 1842, their value is obvious.

Charge Books 1842–54 for Manchester: giving for each person charged the date of his charge, name, occupation, place of residence, age, country of origin, degree of instruction, whether married or single, number of children, and the offence for which arrested.

Calendars of Prisoners 1821 to date: giving name, age, degree of instruction, offence, sentence for each prisoner.

Manchester Gaol Returns 1823–46: containing chaplain's annual reports etc.

In the Kent Record Office at Maidstone, the Process Book of Indictments contains the name, address, marital status, and offence of each person indicted from 1649 to 1792, while similar information is contained in the Calendar of Prisoners from 1649 to 1674, and from 1836 to 1893. In most cases the information is given in a highly abbreviated form – as in this entry in 1842: 'John Amos; 16th July 1842; stealing peas; fined 5/- and 11/- costs' – or in extended legal jargon – as in this case from the Calendar of Prisoners in 1855: 'Mary Streater: Convicted of felony in breaking and entering a dwelling house and stealing therein: Ordered and adjudged to be kept in penal servitude for the term of four years pursuant to the statute in that behalf provided'. In addition, in both Lancashire and Kent, the actual indictment rolls from the mid-seventeenth century to date are available, though the real circumstances of the cases with which they are concerned are all too often hidden in the standard legal forms which reveal in effect only the offenders' name, parish of residence, the date and nature of his or her offence, and the value of the goods involved.[16]

Naturally the level of generalisation permitted by sources of this kind is low, and the information they contain is not always continuous across a number of years. But for certain purposes their use is obvious. It may not be without interest, for instance, that the Manchester Charge Books tell us that those charged for rioting or begging and intimidating on the outskirts of Manchester and in the surrounding districts during the plug plot riots in 1842 included a band of ten unmarried labourers, all English except one, with an average age of 16, only two of them whom could neither read nor write; a group of fifty-seven colliers, mostly illiterate and married and aged well above 25; five 'well-educated' Scots mechanics, all married but one, all over 30. To a limited extent information of this kind may help historians to define those 'faces in the crowd' which would otherwise remain anonymous.[17]

2. PROBLEMS OF SIGNIFICANCE AND INTERPRETATION

So far we have been concerned with the purely practical difficulties likely to be encountered in mastering the arrangement of the criminal statistics. It is necessary now to consider the major factors which may most seriously impair their reliability. For the sake of clarity, these will be discussed under a number of separate heads, though their effects are closely interrelated.

In the first place there is the problem common to all statistics of criminal behaviour: the fact that even under the most effective systems of law enforcement some offences must always escape detection. As a result a certain discrepancy between the 'actual' and the recorded incidence of crime is inevitable.

Secondly, there were a number of legal and administrative changes in the nineteenth century which must have affected the extent of this discrepancy across a long period of time: as the century progressed recorded rates probably drew progressively closer to the 'actual' rates. This clearly impairs the *long-term* consistency in the relationship between them, so that the early returns will not be directly comparable with those for the later part of the century: any long-term statistical or graphical analysis will be correspondingly affected.

We shall also be concerned with the analysis of *short-term*, year-to-year, fluctuations in the incidence of criminal activity. The degree to which these too were affected by the factors already mentioned will also be considered in detail. In this context, the dangers of faulty interpretation will be clear. The reform of the police in any one year, for example, may lead to a marked increase in the number of offenders brought to trial in the following year, and this increase could be wrongly ascribed to social or economic factors. Such factors are clearly of equal importance in dealing with regional or local figures.

In what follows, then, we shall be primarily concerned with (i) the inevitable discrepancy between 'actual' and recorded criminal activity; with the way the statistics were affected (ii) by changes in the degree of public co-operation with the police, (iii) by police reforms, and (iv) by legal developments; and finally (v) with the difficulty of comparing regional crime rates.

(i) 'ACTUAL' AND RECORDED CRIME RATES

In any series of criminal statistics the number of offences officially recorded inevitably falls short of the number of offences actually committed. The real incidence of criminal activity, the so-called 'dark figure', must always remain a matter for informed judgement rather than precise quantification. The difference between actual and recorded incidence of course depends very much on the offence in question. Some crimes are more easily detected than others. Serious crimes are more frequently reported than minor ones: proportionately more murders, for example, are likely to be recorded than larcenies. And in many cases there will be real difficulty in defining what constitutes a separate crime.

But if the actual incidence of crime must in varying degrees remain obscure, the analysis of known offences in terms of the official returns is not thereby ruled out. Other more direct measures of criminal activity which are sometimes resorted to – for instance those based on individual confessions of past offences – are open to equally serious objections. The officially recorded figures are in fact used by modern criminologists on the unproved, though generally uncontested, assumption that they do bear a fairly constant relationship to the real incidence of the offence in question.

In this context, however, it is important to bear in mind that certain figures will always give a closer approximation to the actual incidence of the offence than others, and it is this principle that may be presented as the first law of criminal statistics. The further the record is removed from the actual commission of the offence – in the course of the processes of reporting, of detection, of prosecution, of conviction or acquittal, of imprisonment or discharge – the less directly and accurately will it reflect the incidence of a particular form of criminal activity, rather than the nature of the processes of law enforcement. Thus the number of convictions or the number of offenders imprisoned will constitute less precise indices of the actual number of offences committed than the number of indictable committals; and the number of committals will in turn be a less precise index than the number of offences recorded as known to the police. The numbers of offences known, in short, are for most purposes the best statistics available.[18]

Difficulties arise, of course, when such figures are not available, as in the period before 1857. Then we have no choice but to resort to the statistics for indictable committals. Nonetheless the consequent loss of accuracy in the earlier record need not be too damaging – for certain purposes at least – provided the nature of the figures used is taken into account in any conclusions drawn. In fact, a comparison of the *trends* in the rates for crimes known to the police and in those for committals in the period after 1857 (illustrated in some of the graphs below) shows that the relationship between the two indices was relatively constant. Therefore, we may perhaps use the committal rates for the earlier period without excessive fear that their year-to-year movements, and to a certain extent their long-term movements, will be so distorted as to be meaningless, especially as it is with the explanation of these movements rather than with the more problematic question of the 'real' incidence of crime in society that we should be primarily concerned.

(ii) PUBLIC ATTITUDES AND THE DIMINISHING SEVERITY OF PUNISHMENT

Even as late as 1901 the Criminal Registrar was able to suggest that the growth of public cooperation with the law and the police made the number of crimes reported and known to the police 'now a much better test [of the incidence of criminal activity] than it was twenty or even ten years ago'.[19] Although there was probably a certain amount of truth in this, it need cause us little concern as regards the later decades of the century at least, when this factor is unlikely to have been significant enough to have caused serious distortions in the figures. Changes in public attitudes are likely to have had most effect on the long-term consistency of the relationship between recorded and actual criminal activity in the period between 1805 and about 1850, because it was then that three distinct influences were most conspicuously at work.

First, at a time when the introduction of any form of police control was commonly regarded as a serious infringement of civil liberty, a large proportion of minor offences and some major offences were not reported to the police or to the magistrates at all. Secondly, between 1808 and 1860 more than 190 enactments were repealed, many it is true already obsolete, which imposed the death penalty for particular offences; in the same period the severity of other penalties was correspondingly diminished.[20] There is no lack of evidence that this gradual reduction in the severity of statutory penalties increased the public's readiness to cooperate in prosecutions. Thirdly, there were a number of important administrative and procedural reforms which made the prosecution of offenders both easier and cheaper. In these ways, the disincentives to prosecution by the disaffected, the humane, and the parsimonious were progressively removed.[21]

These processes almost certainly contributed to the marked increase of committal rates in the first half of the century, and they must be taken into account in any interpretation of the long-term movements in criminal behaviour across that period. On the other hand, they do not cause comparable difficulties with regard to the analysis of short-term, year-to-year, fluctuations in the rates, because it is unlikely that public attitudes changed so markedly over a couple of years as to affect the recorded rates at once. The repeal of capital statutes, for example, cannot account for the phenomenal rise in the rate of indictable committals from 1814 to 1819, the most rapid of the whole century, since this rise antedated the most important of these repeals.[22] Nor can it account for the subsequent year-to-year fluctuations in the same rate, such as the significant diminution in committals between 1820 and 1823. In fact the mitigation of the severity of the law, and its effect on public attitudes, probably had less influence on the committal rate than on the rate of convictions to committals, which increased steadily with only very minor variations from 60 per cent in 1805 to 78·5 per cent in 1856.[23] Short-term fluctuations in the committal rates must be explained in other ways.

(iii) THE EXTENSION OF POLICE CONTROL

A much more serious and complex factor which also affects the long-term comparability of the series, and possibly the short-term continuity as well, was the progressive introduction of police forces throughout the country as a result of the legislation of 1829, 1835, 1839 and 1856. The Municipal Corporations Act of 1835 encouraged the establishment of borough police forces on the Metropolitan model instituted in 1829; the County Police Act of 1839 encouraged the similar establishment of county police forces; and the County and Borough Police Act of 1856 compelled JPs to establish county police where they did not already exist, and to consolidate them with the forces of any borough with a population under 5,000. As a result of the 1856 Act, the English police approached something like its modern form, under a centralised inspectoral system.[24]

In the light of the gross inadequacy of the police system in the early decades of the century, the *long-term* effects of these developments were undoubtedly profound, and it would be foolish to underestimate them. The precise impact in each case may be an open question, but it seems likely that their *initial* effect would be to bring more criminals before the courts who might previously have escaped detection; and that, other things being equal, their *subsequent* effect might be reflected in a decline in the rates as the deterrent influence of the new police forces came to be felt.[25] Thus it is clear that any increase in crime rates detectable over the first few years after any single police reform might reflect the consequences of improved police efficiency rather than a real increase in the actual incidence of crime. On the other hand, a long-term decline after the deterrent power of the police might be presumed to have taken effect, will probably reflect a real decline.

The effects of police reforms on the *short-term* year-to-year, fluctuations in national crime rates cause less difficulty, simply because the regional implementation of each Act tended to be spread out over a number of years. This is particularly noticeable in the case of the Acts of 1835 and 1839. The reform of borough police in 1835, for example, was scarcely effective on a national scale even by the 1850s: only 93 out of 171 qualified boroughs had established their own forces within two years of the Act, and the rest followed suit spasmodically during the next 20 years. In any case, the new forces were deficient in many respects. They had no liaison with the county police set up in 1839. Often they failed to police more than the central township of the boroughs under their control. And there were wide variations in their strength: even by 1856 the ratio of police to population in six boroughs was less than 1:1,500, and in eleven more less than 1:940; Liverpool, Manchester and Birmingham were considered to be densely policed with ratios of 1 : 460, 1 : 610, and 1 : 840 respectively. The county police forces encouraged by the Act of 1839 were similarly inadequate. The average ratio of county police to population as late as 1846 was a mere 1 : 2,700, and some counties did not have them at all. It has been pointed out, further, that while both statutes resulted in an increase in arrests for drunkenness and disorderliness, the local rates for indictable offences were scarcely influenced at all.[26] It is thus difficult to argue that these reforms affected the short-term statistical record in any serious way – on a national basis at least. It is true that committal rates rose generally in the period from 1836 to 1842, and might therefore be thought to reflect them. But there is ample evidence that the rates were responding also to quite different influences, which we shall discuss in section 3. It is certainly true that they cannot account for the dramatic fluctuations noticeable in the years after 1842.

The third important police reform effected by the 1856 Act, probably did have more profound long-term effects upon the record than the earlier reforms.[27] But again it is not clear that it is sufficient to account for the year-to-year fluctuations which immediately followed it. In this instance the effects of the Act on the statistics are to some extent camouflaged by the almost simultaneous impact of the Summary Jurisdiction Act of 1855 and the consequent reduction in the number of committals for simple larcenies and assaults. But it is difficult to see why both the committal rates and the rates for crimes known to the police – even when corrected by the addition of the numbers of larcenies now tried summarily – should decline from 1857 to 1860 if they were seriously subject to the effects of the police reform: we should normally expect the rates initially to increase. Equally, the increase in the rates which did take place from 1860 onwards is not easily explained in these terms, since it is around then that we should normally expect the deterrent effects of the new forces to make themselves evident in a decline in the rates. The net effect of this reform in the few years after its implementation is largely imponderable. But there is little doubt that most of the short-term fluctuations from the 1860's onwards will have to be explained by reference to other quite independent factors.

It must be remembered, however, that these points apply with more validity to the analysis of national rates than they do to the analysis of county rates. In the case of regional statistics, the institution in any one year either of several borough police forces or of a county police force is much more likely to affect the record in the short-term; and the only antidote to this is to identify the timing of the effect in the process of analysis, and not to ascribe it to a factor which may be quite irrelevant.

In any consideration of the effects of changes in police efficiency a further but rather different problem relates to the possibility that year-to-year fluctuations in recorded crime may be affected by fluctuations in the rate of police recruitment, or, more seriously, by increased police vigilance at times of social or political unrest. These are real dangers which must qualify the certainty of conclusions, but again they must not be overstated. When the figures available after 1856 for the numbers of police in each borough and county and in the metropolis are reduced to a ratio per 100,000 of the national population, they indicate a short-term increase in recruitment rates only in 1867–8 and 1881–3 (figure 1). This factor might account in part for the increase in committals in those years if it were not for the strong evidence that at times of heavy recruitment police efficiency tended to be disrupted rather than enhanced. The researches of Caroline Pilling, now nearing completion, suggest that police recruited in depressions were unreliable and seldom adequately trained. Police forces at such times also experienced an exceptionally high turn-over.

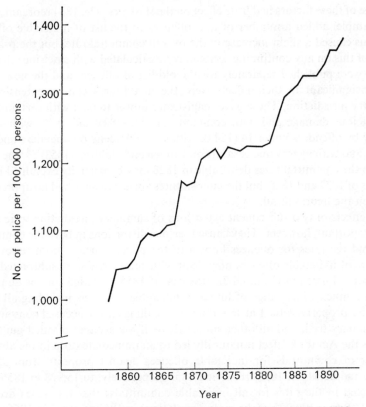

Figure 1   The ratio of police to population in England and Wales, 1857 to 1892. Source: Annual Criminal Statistics (Police Returns).

Two conclusions, then, seem to be valid. The first is that police reforms were of the utmost long-term importance, and that on their account chiefly, though not solely, the relationship between actual and recorded criminal activity over a considerable span of years cannot be assumed to be in any way comparable. The second is that the police reforms did not cause any striking short-term discontinuities, in the national rates at least.

(iv) THE EFFECTS OF LEGAL AND ADMINISTRATIVE CHANGES

The structure of the criminal statistics was further affected by legislative and administrative changes in what was recorded and in the system of recording. In this context two main developments have to be considered: first, the gradual statutory extension in magistrates' powers of summary jurisdiction over previously indictable offences, and secondly the administrative reorganisations of the statistics which took place in 1834 and 1856–7.

Some of these factors had little effect on the statistics. The 1834 reorganisation, for example, added a number of new offences to the list of indictable offences and thus caused a slight increase in the overall committal rate, but the practical result of this on any continuing series may be calculated with ease since the 1834 figures were published separately for the old list of offences and the new. Similarly insignificant in their effects were the first four statutory extensions of summary jurisdiction. These gave magistrates power to deal with certain forms of malicious damage and with common assaults (1827 and 1828) with simple larceny by offenders under 14 (1847), with simple larceny by offenders under 16 (1850), and with aggravated assaults on women and children (1853).[28] The slight drop in the committal rates detectable in 1828 may be partially explained by the statutes of 1827 and 1828, but the later statutes appear to have had no appreciable effect on the figures at all.

The effects of two subsequent extensions of summary jurisdiction were much more important, however. They caused serious distortions in both the committal rates and the rates for offences known to the police, since in both series large numbers of indictable offences now dealt with summarily were subtracted from the record. First, the Criminal Justice Act of 1855 provided for the summary trial of a much wider range of hitherto indictable larcenies, including all thefts involving property valued at less than five shillings if the accused consented to the summary trial, and all other simple thefts if the accused pleaded guilty. As soon as the Act took effect it naturally led to an immediate drop in the absolute number of committals for indictable offences against property from 23,241, 25,677, and 22,347 in 1853, 1854, and 1855 respectively, to 15,928 in 1856. This is reflected in the rates for all indictable committals: that for males dropped from 215·9 (per 100,000 of the male population) in 1855 to 165·7 in 1856; while the female rate dropped from 63·2 to 41·2.

An equally sudden decrease in both the committal rates and the rates for offences known to the police was caused by the Summary Jurisdiction Act of 1879. This statute extended the earlier statutes of 1847, 1850, and 1855 by bringing under summary jurisdiction all children under 12 charged with any indictable offence except murder or manslaughter; all juveniles under 16 consenting to be summarily tried for larceny, embezzlement, obstructing trains etc.; and most important of all, all adults pleading guilty to larceny, embezzlement, etc., or consenting to be tried summarily for larceny, embezzlement etc. in cases where the property involved did not exceed 40 shillings in value.[29] As a result, the number of larcenies tried summarily for males and females together rose from 42,011 in 1879 to 51,025 in 1880; while the committal rates for all indictable offences dropped correspondingly from 106·3 to 95·4 of the male population and from 25·0 to 21·4 of the female population.

The discontinuities in the records of indictable offences directly caused by the Acts of 1855 and 1879 are clearly considerable. Therefore to ensure that over a number of years each series encompasses the same individual offences, both the indictable committal returns and the returns for indictable offences known to the police must be corrected by adding to them those offences (larcenies in particular) which were subtracted from their annual totals by the two Acts in question. In the case of the 1879 Act, this raises no difficulties: the committals series, and that for offences known, can both be adjusted for each year before and after the Act by adding the number of summary larcenies which are given in the annual Police Returns. But to apply a comparable adjustment to the discontinuity in the committals returns caused by the 1855 Act is much more of a problem, since the 'direct' figures for summary larcenies are available in the Police Returns only after 1857. Adjustment is further complicated by the reorganisation of the statistics which took place in 1856–7.

The effect of the 1856–7 reorganisation was more serious than that of 1834 – not on the committal figures, since the existing classification of indictable offences was carried over from the previous series, but on the Prison Returns. By the 1850s the publication of these returns was running a couple of years late, and when the new comprehensive volume of returns was issued for the year 1857, the Prison Returns for 1855 and 1856 which had not yet been published remained unpublished. Redgrave realised the discontinuity this caused and filled in some of the main series in the introduction to the new volume for 1857, but he did not do so for committals to gaol for each kind of summary offence separately.

The relevance of this omission for the correction of the effects of the extension of summary jurisdiction in 1855 will be clear. In the absence of the 'direct' returns on committals for summary larceny published in the Police Returns from 1857, we should normally resort to the admittedly defective but still useful numbers of offenders imprisoned for summary larceny. The absence of these numbers for that offence specifically makes it virtually impossible, in the construction of any series of rates, to bridge the gap between 1854 and 1857 in a fully satisfactory way. Therefore all that can be attempted is an approximate connection of a particular series before 1854 and after 1857 by resorting to the figures available from 1836 in the Prison Returns, supplemented by those in Redgrave's introduction of 1857, for committals to gaol for *all* summary offences. In relying on this process it is assumed that the larceny cases which would previously have been tried on indictment, would constitute the majority of the summary total, and that the sum of these cases and of all committals on indictment is an acceptable guide to the trends in the incidence of all serious offences for these years.[30]

Even when these various numerical adjustments have been made by the use of available data on summary proceedings, there will still be a certain discontinuity in the series before and after the reorganisations of the returns in

1834, and of 1856–7. When the best available composite rates are represented graphically, however, it is relatively easy to allow for known distortions simply by altering the scale so that the various sections of the graph, from 1805 to 1833, from 1834 to 1854, from 1857–92, can be directly related in visual terms. Only in the case of property crimes does this process involve any real loss of accuracy, because the information on prisoners committed to gaol for summary larcenies specifically is lacking in the years 1855–6: thus the two sections of the property graph, 1836–54 and 1857–92 respectively, have to be presented as independent series.

In sum, it will be clear that by careful tabulation of the returns, and by various statistical adjustments, the effects of the legal and structural changes discussed can be largely if not entirely circumvented. They certainly do not impede the construction of continuous series except across the period 1855–7.

(v) THE DIFFICULTIES IN THE WAY OF REGIONAL ANALYSES

There can be no doubt about the importance of the analysis of regional variations in criminal behaviour. Conclusions drawn from national rates can only be generalisations.[31] Not only do they mask wide local variations; they also fail to answer some of the more pressing questions with which the historian is likely to be concerned – how, for example, criminal activity might have differed across the country under the influence of distinct occupational and population structures.

It is unfortunate, then, that a regional analysis raises more difficulties than almost any other. What is at issue is whether county or borough figures are directly comparable with each other, given the fact that individually they may be very much more subject than national figures to the distorting effects of local variations in the practical enforcement of the law. It is clear why this should be so: first, police strength varied from county to county and borough to borough; and secondly, there were wide local discrepancies in the practice of both police and courts. We might add, thirdly, that in the case of a region with a small population and a low incidence of crime, rates may be based on numbers too small to be statistically significant.

We have already given some indication of the wide variations which existed across the country in police strength and efficiency. Further examples only emphasise the point. In 1846 the ratio of county police to population varied from 1:2,300 in Bedfordshire and 1:3,560 in Lancashire, down to 1:4,200 in Shropshire and 1:8,350 in Warwickshire. There were comparable variations even late in the century between the strength of different kinds of police force, as table 3, which is based on the police returns, indicates. And the ratios for a small sample of borough forces in 1861 were as follows: Liverpool 1:422; Bristol 1:510; Manchester 1:515; Hull 1:690; Birmingham 1:785; Norwich 1:826; Leeds 1:908; Oldham 1:2,494. Of course all these differences may simply reflect the fact that in each case the local supply of police was in rough balance with the demand or the need. An index of local police strength possibly more accurate than the ratio of police to population, might be the number per acre of each town. In these terms the variations are less marked: at the end of the century Liverpool had 10 policemen to each acre of the borough, Manchester 12, Oldham 29, Salford 15, Birmingham 18, Cardiff 25 etc.[32] But it will be clear that even these variations must make the comparison of crime rates in different counties, and particularly in different boroughs, a perilous operation.

Table 3   *Average ratios of police to population*

	Borough	County	Metropolitan
1871	1 : 800	1 : 1,348	1 : 419
1881	1 : 792	1 : 1,286	1 : 466
1891	1 : 758	1 : 1,192	1 : 421

Source: Police returns.

It is quite as serious an objection to the feasibility of regional comparisons that it is almost impossible to allow for the many purely administrative factors influencing local figures. Some forces might devote more time than others to the detection of serious rather than of petty crime. Some might be more lax than others in recording those offences for which an offender had not actually been detected and brought to trial. More frequently in some districts than in others, offenders might be dealt with by a simple caution, with the result that the record of their offences would not be included in the returns for summary committals. Again, given two towns with an equal criminal population, the number of crimes reported to the police might be greater in that where the sentences were usually shorter. So too, magistrates varied in their readiness to deal summarily with indictable offences: in large towns they sometimes assumed greater power simply because of the pressure on prison cells and the need for quick administration of justice. And as Tobias has shown in the case of Leeds the rate of arrests might be significantly affected by changes in the upper ranks of the local police force.[33]

This catalogue of objections is a formidable one, and it must rule out a good deal of direct comparative work which might otherwise be desirable. Thus, for example, it is impossible to demonstrate, as many mid-century commentators tried to do,[34] a correlation between the incidence of criminal behaviour and the extent of urbanisation or population density in various counties in terms of their respective committal rates. Urbanised and industrialised counties like Lancashire certainly come high in the order, but so do rural counties like Hereford and Somerset: the pattern is almost meaningless.[35] Rank orders of this kind may be useful for particular purposes, but scarcely to indicate relative levels of criminality. Naturally the same is true of rank orders for boroughs or police districts.

There remains, however, one form of regional study which avoids most of these difficulties. This involves not the direct comparison of one county's rate with another's in one particular year, but (a) the definition of *trends* in an individual county's rate over a *number* of years, and (b) the comparison of these trends with those in comparable rates either in another county or in England and Wales as a whole. This technique permits a reasonably valid assessment of the differential impact of certain social and economic influences on the crime rates in the county or counties in question. It might, moreover, be extended to cover certain groups of counties, to lead to an eventual comparison of rates in several of those which were predominantly rural with rates in several of those which were industrial or heavily populated. We have illustrated the potential of the technique in section 3, where we briefly discuss the differences between the trends in criminal behaviour in Lancashire and in England and Wales respectively.

Even here, however, two cautions are relevant. First, it will be recalled that although the major police reforms are unlikely to have introduced serious discontinuities in the short-term movement of the national criminal rates, this will not be true of rates for individual counties where the reforms might have taken rather more immediate effect. Thus care must be taken over any sudden change in the county rates which coincides with the known introduction of new police forces into that county.

Secondly, it is important to stress that the reliability of any results which may be sought by this technique will depend on the size of the unit or units in question. In counties in which the population, the offences recorded, and the police districts are all numerous, the trends defined are likely to be meaningful. This is because the distorting effects of 'irrelevant' local factors will tend to cancel each other out in the gross total. But the smaller the unit is in these terms, the more likely it is that administrative and other factors of the kind we have discussed will distort the statistical record.

Thus it might be legitimate to apply this method of analysis to Lancashire, while it might not be legitimate to apply it to Dorset. Lancashire had a population ranging from nearly one and a half million in 1834 to nearly four million in 1892; the numbers of crimes known to the police and of summary larcenies combined was about 15–20,000; and as a county it was divided into as many as 14 police districts in 1857 and 22 in 1892. Therefore when the figures for offences are reduced to ratios of incidence to the population, they are unlikely to be seriously influenced by an 'irrelevant' factor such as a change in the personnel of the police force in one district, or even by the establishment of an entirely new police district. The same argument naturally applies with even more force to the national rates. Tobias quite misses the point of this argument when he attempts to discredit the statistics by suggesting that 'the national totals are as strong only as the weakest component; and, at any rate for much of the nineteenth century, the weakest component – say, a newly reorganised borough force – was very weak'.[36] This may be true of a small county like Dorset, though not even then as markedly as Tobias implies. Of the national totals it is not true at all. It would not be true of the totals for a sizeable group of counties. It is not even true of the totals for Lancashire.

CONCLUSION

Two deficiencies in the criminal statistics cannot be circumvented: the fact that they can never reflect the 'actual' extent of criminal behaviour in society, and the fact that legal and police developments must affect the consistency of the relationship between this unknowable figure and the recorded incidence of criminal activity across a period of time. The first problem, however, is less serious than it might be, provided we satisfy ourselves that the fluctuations in recorded offences are meaningful in the particular context of our analysis and are worthy of examination in their own right. If they prove to be so, it follows that recorded rates are sensitive enough to reflect the otherwise unknowable movements in the 'actual' incidence of criminal activity. Secondly, though the analysis of long-term trends is immensely complicated by the effects of a progressive increase in police and court efficiency, and therefore by the increase in the proportion of offences or offenders recorded, certain conclusions are not thereby invalidated. If, for example, certain crime rates *decrease* over a period during which police efficiency is known to have improved, we can safely conclude that this trend reflects a movement in the actual incidence of crime rather than the effect of a purely administrative factor; if other things were equal, of course, we should normally expect rates to increase.

Fewer difficulties are raised in the analysis of year-to-year fluctuations, since across the nation as a whole none of the factors examined seems to have taken effect immediately or simultaneously. Where they did so, in a single county for instance, their influence can usually be identified, and therefore need not invalidate the conclusions drawn from the fluctuations which were not so influenced.

Other problems can usually be resolved satisfactorily in the careful tabulation of data and in its graphical representation. Thus the breaks in the series of indictable returns caused by the two main extensions of summary jurisdiction can be rectified by constructing a composite series of indictable and summary offences together – a technique which will be illustrated in the next section.

It will be clear that for most purposes the value of the nineteenth-century criminal statistics is not seriously affected by the factors discussed above. Certainly they constitute evidence of more considerable importance than has been usually acknowledged. It remains true, however, that they have to be used with caution, and it is appropriate to conclude this section with four general propositions which will summarise the argument so far, and serve as a guide to the statistics' fuller exploitation.

1. The 'first law' of criminal statistics states that figures for the numbers of crimes known to the police, when they are available, are generally to be preferred to those for committals, and those for committals to those relating to convictions and to prisoners.

2. In short-term analyses, the fluctuations of rates from year to year, if not known to be due to legal, administrative or other changes taking immediate effect, are likely to be meaningful reflections of real trends in criminal activity which may occasionally be explained by reference to economic and social circumstances.

3. In long-term analyses, the distortions consequent on improved administrative, police, and legal efficiency, must be taken into account in any conclusions about the increase or decrease in criminal activity across any period longer than a decade. As a general rule, the later the period, the more closely the rate of recorded crime is likely to approximate to the real extent of criminal activity.

4. National crime rates are sensitive to trends in the incidence of criminal activity since local variations in police efficiency and procedure and in legal practice may be expected to cancel themselves out in the gross total. This applies also to rates in counties with a large population, a heavy recorded incidence of crime, and a large number of police districts; the smaller the district with which we are concerned, the more danger there is that figures may reflect changes in local practice rather than in criminal activity. As in the case of any average, however, national and county crime rates may mask important and perhaps contradictory movements in the incidence of criminal activity, often of a very localised character.

PART 2. THE ANALYSIS OF THE STATISTICS

INTRODUCTION: THE INCIDENCE OF CRIMINAL BEHAVIOUR IN THE
NINETEENTH CENTURY

Since there is a danger that the simple enumeration of the difficulties involved in
the use of the criminal statistics may distract attention from their real value, the
rest of this chapter is devoted to certain analyses which will illustrate the application of the principles discussed above, and at the same time initiate a discussion
of the more important themes upon which the official returns can throw some
light. We shall attempt first to establish how far there was a relationship between
the incidence of different kinds of criminal activity and economic conditions,
and to define the long-term trends in crime across the century. We shall be
chiefly concerned with criminal behaviour in England and Wales as a whole,
but wherever possible we shall draw comparisons with its incidence in Lancashire
as well, to show how more detailed analyses might be conducted at the level of
the individual county. A further section will discuss the information on the
changing character of offenders from about mid-century. And we shall conclude
by suggesting some of the lines of research which it may be profitable to pursue
in future.

The graphs and tables which follow are of interest in their own right. Some
of them demonstrate more clearly than any alternative source the long-term
consequences of increasing police and court efficiency in the enforcement of law
and order. But we argued at the beginning of this chapter that the aggregate
incidence of criminal behaviour is likely to be influenced by social and economic
conditions as well. Thus the most interesting effect of these analyses may be to
suggest that changes in the incidence of criminal activity and in the character of
offenders resulted not only from administrative and legal developments in the
processes of law enforcement, but also from qualitative changes in the standard
of living of the population at large. Moreover, the figures impart an added
dimension to the discussion of the social tensions consequent on industrialisation
and urbanisation, and throw light also on the diminution of those tensions as
the century wore on.

3. THE INTERPRETATION OF CRIME RATES

The full tabulation of the data on which the following analyses are based is

Figure 2. Offences against property: England and Wales, 1805–92; Lancashire (total only) 1858–92.

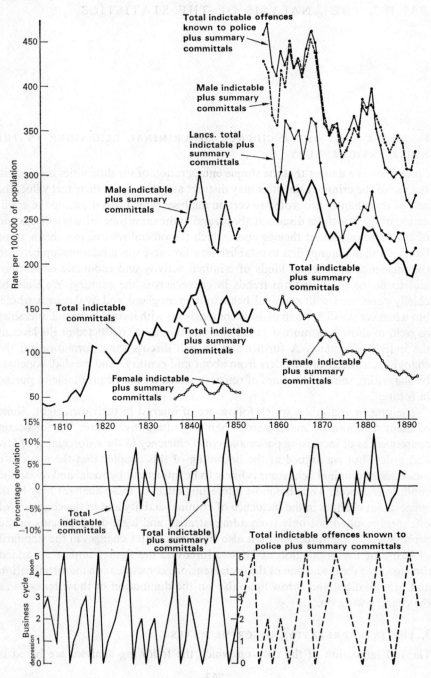

Figure 3. Assaults and drunkenness. England and Wales and Lancashire, 1857–92.

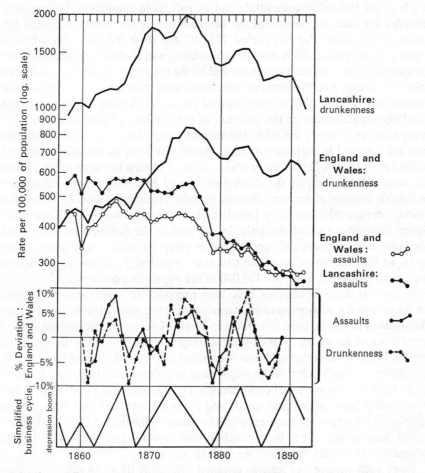

Assaults = Offences against the person tried summarily plus indictable offences against
the person known to police.

Drunkenness = Offences of drunkenness and disorderliness tried summarily.

reproduced in the appendix. In most cases the figures consist of composite totals which summarise and combine in different forms the much more detailed numerical information published annually in the blue books. In each tabulation, for example, the best available information on the relevant summary offences has been added to the basic data on indictable offences. Where possible this has been done for males and females separately. Thus for the period 1834–54 the totals of all indictable committals and of indictable committals for property offences are each supplemented by the addition of the numbers gaoled for summary larcenies. For the period 1857–92 the totals of indictable offences known to the police, all indictable committals, and indictable committals for property offences, are each supplemented by the total of committals to summary trial for larceny. And the totals of indictable committals for offences against the person, and of indictable offences against the person known to the police, are similarly supplemented by the addition of the numbers of committals to summary trial for summary assaults. The various composite series arrived at in this way are designed in each case to approximate as closely as possible to the real incidence of those offences upon which we have chosen to concentrate, and at the same time to correct the distortions caused by the subtraction from the indictable returns of certain offences (usually larcenies) which by successive statutes came under summary jurisdiction. As far as possible the Lancashire figures have been treated similarly. In the case of the counties, however, data for individual summary offences was never given for males and females separately, so that the series cover the two sexes together. In all cases, the figures have been reduced to rates per 100,000 of the population concerned.[37]

In the text these tabulations have been presented in simple graphical form. In the graphs for offences against property and for assaults (figures 2 and 3), the fluctuations have also been illustrated in terms of percentage deviations from a secular trend based on a seven-year moving average. To allow direct visual comparisons between the incidence of criminal activity and changes in economic conditions, a rough index of the major turning points in the trade and business cycle has been superimposed on all the main graphs on a five-point scale.[38] The relationship between criminal trends and the trade cycle has been presented in simple visual terms, in preference to the more sophisticated statistical correlation tests which might be applied to the figures, since this method quite adequately illustrates the points we wish to make.

Since each category of serious criminal offence is likely to exhibit its own unique response to the conditions influencing its rate of incidence over a number of years, we shall examine three of these categories separately: (a) property offences; (b) offences involving violence and/or drunkenness; (c) offences involving an element of political or social protest. The selection of any group of offences of course depends on the particular issue or hypothesis to be investigated: we have simply chosen those which are likely to be of most interest to the historian. In these three cases we shall be concerned chiefly with the short-term,

year-to-year, fluctuations in their rates, and with their relationship to simultaneous fluctuations in the trade cycle. Nonetheless, the long-term trends in
criminal behaviour across a number of decades or across the whole century are
of considerable importance, and despite the difficulties involved in their interpretation they cannot be ignored. They are dealt with in section (d) which
discusses the rate of incidence of all serious offences together. In section (e) we
shall briefly compare the incidence of criminal activity in England and Wales
as a whole with its incidence in Lancashire. Finally, in (f), we shall discuss the
significance of these analyses in more general terms, and the light they throw
on the main features in the incidence of criminal behaviour throughout the
nineteenth century.

(a) PROPERTY OFFENCES

In every year of the century the incidence of all forms of theft (from burglary,
housebreaking, and robbery to simple larceny) made up the bulk of all serious
offences committed.[39] Until 1857 roughly 80 per cent of all indictable committals
were for non-violent offences against property. After 1857 this proportion fell
to between 60 per cent and 70 per cent, chiefly due to the increase in the powers
of summary jurisdiction over simple larcenies. If summary larcenies are added,
the proportion of property offences recorded after 1857 in fact rises to about
90 per cent of the sum total of offences (see appendix, table 1).

For those years for which statistical data is available, the graphs in figure 2,
illustrating the incidence of property offences, are composed as follows:

   (i)   1805–38: all committals to trial for indictable offences against property
             (total only);

   (ii) 1836–51: committals to trial for indictable offences against property
             (male, female, and total separately) *plus* committals to prison
             for summary larcenies (male, female, and total separately);

   (iii) 1852–54: committals to trial for indictable offences against property
             plus committals to prison for summary larcenies (totals only);

   (iv) 1855–56: data not published;

   (v) 1857–92: (a) committals to trial for indictable offences against pro-
                  perty (male, female, and total separately) *plus* committals
                  to trial for summary larcenies (male, female, and total
                  separately); comparable figures for Lancashire, totals
                  only;
               (b) indictable offences against property known to the police
                  plus all committals to trial for summary larcenies.

The national total rates above have been presented graphically not only in
direct visual terms, but also in terms of percentage deviations from a secular
trend calculated on a seven-year moving average.[40] By smoothing the graphs,

this process obviates possible distortions in year-to-year movements in the incidence of the offences in question, and serves also to clarify their relationship with the movements of the trade cycle superimposed on figure 2.

The particular significance of these graphs resides in the light they throw on two theories of criminal behaviour. First, it was assumed by one school of nineteenth-century criminologists that the incidence of criminal activity was unconnected with economic hardship and could be better explained in terms of the irremediable depravity of the habitually drunk or of the so-called criminal class. This view has been restated by Tobias, who quotes an ample number of contemporary literary sources to support his own claim that depression had little effect in increasing the incidence of 'crime' and that 'crime was not as a rule the result of want'.[41] Secondly, on the basis of extensive statistical analysis it has been established by present-day criminologists that twentieth-century property offences tend to increase in times of affluence and to diminish in times of depression – a conclusion which would seem if anything to corroborate the theories of nineteenth-century observers. Our examination of the nineteenth-century statistics disproves the earlier theories and in some measure qualifies the modern. The rates for property offences – which constituted the vast preponderance of all serious crimes committed – entirely contradict the interpretation put forward by the sources on which Tobias has chiefly relied. And they imply further that whatever the case may be in this century, it was quite different in the past: far from being of universal application, the sociological explanation for the incidence of property offences must change with time. Figure 2 shows that fairly consistently, in nearly every decade of the nineteenth century, the year-to-year movements in the incidence of property offences were inversely correlated with the fluctuations of the trade cycle. They increased in times of depression and diminished in times of prosperity: more people stole in hard times than in good.

It is true that in the first decades of the century, and for different reasons in the last, this pattern is rather obscure. The rapid increase in offences between 1814 and 1817, for example, began well before the depression of 1816: but this can be explained quite simply in terms of the disruptive effects of war on the economy and the population at large. Certainly the high rate of crime in the post-war years accords well with our knowledge of the political and social climate of the time. A similar imprecision in the correlations begins to manifest itself from the 1880s onwards. The increase in the rates which we should normally expect to result from the depression beginning in the late 1870s took three years to manifest itself, and the same was true of the effects of the depression of 1886. To be sure, this may merely reflect the fact that the effects of the so-called 'great depression' were complex: it is hardly likely in this period that the crude trade cycle reproduced in the figures would be sensitive enough to reflect the movement in wages, prices and employment indices upon which the aggregate rates of criminal activity seem to depend. Alternatively it may be that these years betray the first indications of the shift from poverty-based to prosperity-based offences against property which characterises the fluctuations of the twentieth century rates: the high peak of 1882 nearly coincides with the prosperity peak in the trade cycle in 1883, and the depression of 1886 actually coincides with a trough in the rates.

These qualifications apart, the rule that nineteenth-century property crime increased in depression and diminished with prosperity holds true, allowing for the occasional disjunction in the graphical correlations, and for a slight diminution in the clarity of the association in later years of the century compared with earlier.[42] In the period 1819–36, the fluctuations for male and female offences combined are not dramatic, but they still reflect the movements in the trade cycle fairly closely, especially in the years 1826–36. This is certainly clear in the graph for those years showing their percentage deviation from the secular trend. Very much more conspicuous are the fluctuations in the incidence of property offences committed by males in the periods 1836–51 and 1857–80. Here six major peaks (1837, 1842, 1848, 1863, 1868, 1880) correspond with troughs in the trade cycle (1837, 1842, 1848, 1862, 1869, 1879). Conversely the major troughs in the graph for male offences (1845–6, 1860, 1866, 1872–3) all correspond with peak years of prosperity or with years of rising prosperity.[43] Similar correlations are less marked in the case of the female index, since the actual number of offences committed by women was always rather low in comparison with those committed by men: but they are detectable nonetheless. If female offences were presented in terms of their deviation from their secular trend, the correspondence between their movement and that of male offences would be evident at once. No less than men, women stole more frequently in times of depression than they did in times of prosperity.

Finally, it will be clear from figure 2 that the rate of incidence of property offences in Lancashire was considerably higher than it was in England and Wales as a whole, but followed much the same pattern. In the 1860s, however, when the cotton famine was at its worst, it increased much more rapidly than the national rate, and in the 1870s its decline was correspondingly more acute.

(b) CRIMES OF VIOLENCE AND OF DRUNKENNESS

The incidence of crimes of violence was much lower than that of property offences. Offences against the person constituted about one tenth of all indictable committals in the period from 1834 to 1856 and just more than a tenth of all indictable offences known to the police thereafter. After 1828 minor common assaults, and after 1853 aggravated assaults on women and children, could be dealt with summarily. From 1857, when more accurate figures on summary committals became available, these offences (together with assaults on the police) represented about 15 per cent of all summary convictions (see appendix).

The trends in crimes of violence were quite unrelated to those for crimes against property. They appear also to have been related to economic conditions in a quite different way. Table II of the appendix shows for the period 1857–92 the incidence of all recorded crimes of violence – indictable offences against the person known to the police as well as assaults dealt with by summary jurisdiction.[44] In the graphs in figure 3 the fluctuations in these composite rates for violent crime are compared with those for summary committals for drunken and disorderly behaviour, for England and Wales and for Lancashire respectively.[45] And for both sets of *national* rates the annual percentage deviations from the secular trend, calculated upon a seven-year moving average, have been superimposed upon a simplified figure which illustrates the major turning points in the trade cycle.

The *long-term* trends in assaults and in drunkenness in the nation at large and in Lancashire specifically are best clarified in their 'direct' graphical representation. The county rates closely followed the pattern of the national, though it is noticeable that for most of the period the Lancashire drunkenness rates were almost double those of England and Wales as a whole. From 1858 to 1876 the incidence of drunkenness in both cases more than doubled, and they rose with particular rapidity after 1867 – a rise which provoked the licensing statutes of 1869 and 1872 but whose continuity was not apparently affected by them. One historian has referred to the 'frightening burst of debauchery' which was caused by the boom of the 1870s.[46] The propriety of the phrase is amply borne out by the official rates. The passage of the 1856 Police Act notwithstanding, this overall increase is too marked to be explicable solely or even chiefly in terms of developments in police efficiency. On the other hand, the decline in drunkenness from 1876 onwards must represent a real decline, since, if other things were equal, the tendency of police developments would be to inflate the rates from year to year. The same argument holds true, of course, for the decline in the incidence of assaults which is detectable from the mid 1860s onwards. There will be room for debate in interpreting these trends in detail; but the long-term movements in drunkenness can probably best be explained in terms of cyclical advances and recessions in the standard of living of the population at large, and possibly also, in the latter decades, in terms of the development of new standards of respectability and temperance. The decline in criminal violence was probably more directly an achievement of the deterrent effects of police control.[47]

The *short-term* fluctuations in these offences are of particular interest, and they are best brought out in the diagram representing their annual percentage deviations from the secular trends. Here two kinds of correlation are immediately visible: the first between the rate of assaults and of drunkenness, and the second between the troughs and peaks in both kinds of behaviour and the troughs and peaks in the trade cycle. It is true that in the latter case there is a certain disjunction between the correlations, although this is probably because the economic index is too crude to reflect the precise timing of the qualitative and quantitative changes in economic conditions which might have affected the criminal rates. It would require a much more sensitive analysis than is possible here, for example, to explain why the troughs and peaks in the rates preceded the trade cycle turning points of 1862, 1866, and 1868 by a year, and why they lagged behind by a year or more in 1873, 1879, 1883, and 1886. But the overall pattern is clear enough. In times of depression the incidence of assaults and drunkenness declined, and in times of prosperity they increased. The likely implications of this pattern need not be laboured: high wages and high employment led to a higher consumption of liquor, and this in turn contributed to a higher incidence in violent crime in the year in question.

This analysis leads to a considerable qualification of an opinion which was widespread in the later nineteenth century, and which Tobias has revived in support of his conclusion that 'crime was not as a rule the result of want'. It was commonly argued that the ultimate cause of 'crime' was drink rather than poverty, and that if there was a relationship between criminal activity and economic conditions it manifested itself in the overall increase in crime in good years when the consumption of liquor was high.[48] Though as a general statement valid of all criminal activity this might have been true in a very local context, as one of Tobias's sources claimed of Birmingham in 1857, it was certainly not true of the nation as a whole, or even of that county in which public intoxication was exceptionally prevalent. The statement can apply only to crimes of violence. Other offences, and especially property offences, reacted to economic conditions in a quite different way.

(c) PROTEST OFFENCES

The figures for offences involving some element of political protest, listed under the categories 'malicious offences against property' and 'miscellaneous', are so small that they cannot meaningfully be reduced to a ratio of the population. Nor can any distinct trend be perceived across the century. Actual committals for arson and other forms of industrial and agricultural sabotage in the disturbed period 1834–56, for example, averaged a mere 170 per annum with a maximum of 302 in 1844 and a minimum of 79 in 1841. Figures for the number of these same offences known to the police in the period 1857–92 averaged only 425 per annum, varying between a maximum of 641 in 1864 and a minimum of 274 in 1877. The incidence of cases of 'riot and sedition', a classification introduced by Redgrave in 1839 to record Chartist activities, was noticeably spasmodic: their totals in each year of incidence across the century were as follows: 1839, 231; 1840, 212; 1841, 5; 1842, 962; 1843, 60; 1844, 2; 1848, 253; 1849, 3; 1855, 1; 1884, 23; 1886, 10; 1892, 1. And the annual average of committals for the less serious offences of riot and breach of the peace from 1834 to 1892 was only 411, many of which were public house brawls. Finally, in the whole period from 1834 to 1892 there were only 64 committals for high treason.

Figures of this order form a sufficient basis for only one conclusion: that while explicitly political or semi-political responses of this kind may be the most dramatic, they are quantitatively the least important recorded indices of discontent.[49] Nonetheless the figures are of some value. The incidence of the offences can be traced to the county and after 1857 to the police district in which they occurred; and by going further into the local manuscript sources upon which they are based some degree of identification can be made of those who participated in this kind of 'directed' activity which has found its way into the records.

(d) ALL SERIOUS OFFENCES

The importance of examining the incidence of different categories of offence individually will now be sufficiently clear: each type exhibited its own characteristic relationship to economic conditions and other factors affecting its rate of incidence. For certain purposes, however, it is still desirable to consider the movements of *all* serious offences together. Only on this basis can an unbroken series be presented for the whole century, since in the earliest decades, and for a few years in mid-century, the lack of data either on male and female offences separately, or on summary jurisdiction, makes it impossible to define the incidence of individual categories of crime with accuracy. In any case, the long-term movements in the rates for all serious crimes throughout the century provide the clearest indication of the impact of increasing police and court efficiency in dealing with criminal activity as a whole. Such an index may also reflect on the real justification for certain contemporary attitudes towards criminal behaviour and social disorder, which in all periods are usually formed with reference to a composite index of this nature.

The composition of the graphs in figure 4 is as follows:

  (i)   1805–36: committals to trial for all indictable offences;
 (ii)   1836–54: committals to trial for all indictable offences *plus* committals to prison for summary larcenies;
(iii)   1857–92: (a) committals to trial for all indictable offences *plus* committals to trial for summary larcenies;
             (b) all indictable offences known to the police *plus* committals to trial for summary larcenies.

In all instances except (iii) (b), rates have been calculated for males and females separately. These composite graphs thus indicate the incidence of all forms of serious crime in England and Wales from 1805 to 1892.

In view of the vast preponderance of property offences in the total, it is not surprising that their *short-term* fluctuations confirm the conclusions drawn from the rates for property offences alone. We need not repeat those conclusions here. It is with *long-term* trends that we are chiefly concerned in this figure, and these are much more difficult to assess. At first glance the graph for offences committed by males, for example, would seem to show a peak of criminal activity in the 1840s and a subsequent decline throughout the rest of the century. But any conclusions drawn from this overall pattern must take account of the long-term distortions which have already been discussed. Given developments in police efficiency, in public co-operation with the police, and in the simplification of trial procedures, it is probable that the official figures for the latter part of the century will provide a better indication of the real incidence of offences than those for the earlier part. It follows that crime rates in the two periods, or even from one decade to another, are not strictly comparable. But despite these difficulties, it is still possible to draw some tentative conclusions from the graphs.

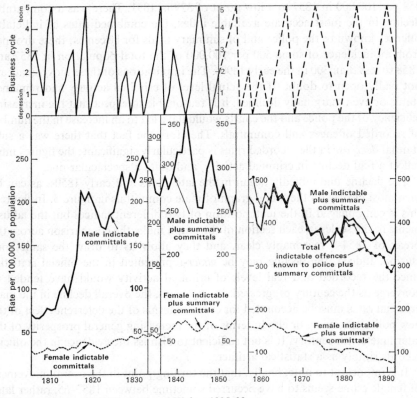

Figure 4   Crime rates in England and Wales: 1805–92.

It is clear that the increase from a minimum rate of 66 male committals in 1807 to a maximum of 326 in 1842 (or of 360 if committals for summary larceny are added) must in part be an artificial one, assisted by institutional developments discussed in section 2. The cumulative effects of these factors were not in themselves sufficient to account for the *total* increase in recorded criminal activity which characterizes this period. The cliff-face ascent in the period 1815–17, for example, coincides with the release from active service of large numbers of men, as well as with known economic hardship and political tensions. And, in any case, there is an *a priori* reason for assuming that, because of the disruptive effects of urban and industrial growth criminal activity was likely to increase in this period. Nonetheless it remains true that for these years the statistical record can only substantiate, rather than authoritatively confirm, historians' expectations of what might have happened.

We are on much safer ground in dealing with the long-term downward trend in crime rates in the latter part of the century. The composite rate for male committals and summary trials for larceny declined from a high point of some 459 per 100,000 in 1857 to a low point of 329 in 1891. There was a comparable decline in the most accurate available index, the combined rates of indictable offences known to the police and of summary trials for larcenies; these dropped from an incidence of some 500 per 100,000 of the total population in 1857 and 1858 to less than 300 in the early 1890s. The implications of these movements are not really open to doubt. If the actual level of criminal activity had remained stable or even marginally declined, it is reasonable to expect that the increasing efficiency of the police and the courts would have led to an increase in the number of recorded offences and committals. Therefore the fact that there was a substantial *decrease* in the recorded rates is particularly significant: the figures must reflect a real decline in criminal activity, and quite a spectacular one.

The decline undoubtedly began in the late 1840s and early 1850s, as can be seen most clearly on the 'pure' graph of male committals in figure 5. In figure 4 this is camouflaged in the juxtaposition of two different indices but the adjustments in the scales in each section of the graph make the comparison across the break of 1854–7 reasonably clear, and they allow us to draw the same conclusion. Indeed, the decline may be *under*-represented in the official statistics since the recorded and real levels of criminal activity would have tended to converge as the century progressed. In any event, the overall decline in the male criminal rates must be accounted for either in terms of the deterrent effect of the new police efficiency, or else in terms of the increasing general prosperity of the later nineteenth century. It is not sufficient to dismiss the evidence in the official records simply as a statistical artifact.

It is important to note, finally, that the turning-point in the overall movement of female crime seems to have occurred sometime between 1857–65, rather later than it did in the case of the male rates. Even the 'pure' rates of female indictable committals alone demonstrate this. There was a higher rate of female committals in England and Wales in 1854 than there was even in the 1840s (figure 5). The highest composite rate for all indictable committals plus summary committals for larceny occurred as late as 1861 (figure 4). The reasons for this gentle increase in female crime over a period when male crime was on the decrease are not immediately apparent.

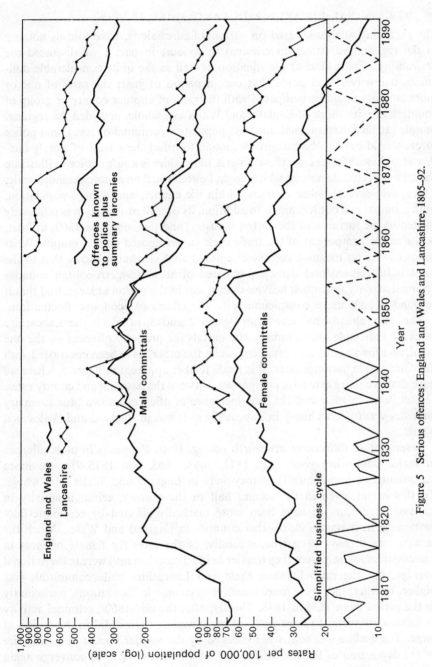

Figure 5 Serious offences: England and Wales and Lancashire, 1805–92.

(e) CRIMINAL BEHAVIOUR IN LANCASHIRE 1834–92

The preceding analyses, based on national figures alone, have told us nothing of the regional variations in criminal behaviour. In part 1 we discussed the desirability of this kind of examination as well as the quite considerable difficulties it involves, and noted that over a period of years the rates of one or more counties could be compared with the rates of another county or group of counties, or with those of England and Wales as a whole, provided the regional sample satisfied certain conditions: its population, criminal offences, and police forces would have to be numerous enough to offset the effects of purely incidental and local factors. By these criteria Lancashire is a safe choice to illustrate the type of regional analyses which might be attempted on a more extended scale. There were several police districts within the county, and a large population, both criminal and non-criminal. In addition, its overall prosperity was intimately related to the fortunes of the cotton industry, and this, until the 1860s at least, was a major component of the trade cycle superimposed on our graphs. What follows is by no means a complete regional analysis, but it shows that in the most industrialised and densely-populated of all extra-metropolitan counties criminal activity was much heavier than it was in the nation at large, and that it responded even more conspicuously to the effects of economic fluctuations.

This may already be clear from figures 2 and 3, in which the Lancashire rates for indictable and summary committals for property offences on the one hand, and for assaults and drunkenness on the other, have been contrasted with the comparable national rates. It is made further apparent in figure 5, where we have drawn a more extensive comparison between the national and county rates. In fact between 1858 and 1867 the incidence of offences known plus summary larcenies was twice as heavy in Lancashire as it was in England and Wales as a whole.

Several other differences are worth noting. First, the peaks in male offences in major depression years (e.g. 1842, 1848, 1863, and 1875–9) were more accentuated in Lancashire than they were in England and Wales as a whole. To this extent, even in the second half of the century, criminal activity in Lancashire appears to have been more markedly affected by economic fluctuations than it was in most other counties in England and Wales. Much the same seems to have been true, secondly, of the rates for female offences in Lancashire. Not only were they heavier in incidence than they were in the national average, but the ratio between them and Lancashire male committals was higher. Further, they were more sensitive to economic fluctuations, particularly in the period from 1834 to 1848. Thirdly, after the mid-1860s, criminal activity in Lancashire seems to have declined more rapidly than it did in the nation at large. The decline was somewhat checked by the heavier impact in Lancashire of the depression of the late 1870s, but the two rates began to converge again after about 1882.

(f) GENERAL CONCLUSIONS

The feature common to all the series examined, but best illustrated in the graphs indicating the incidence of all serious crimes, is their long-term increase until mid-century, and their subsequent long-term decline. About the real degree of their increase there is room for debate, since the criminal record would have been artificially swollen by the factors discussed in section 2. But there can be no doubt that their decrease reflected a real decline in criminal activity. For this there are probably two explanations, the most obvious and convincing of which must refer to the effects of increasing police and administrative efficiency in maintaining law and order. Indeed, this decrease is probably the clearest quantitative index we can hope for of the degree to which later Victorian society had succeeded in controlling the disruptive forces consequent on social and demographic change. By 1890, it is clear that Britain had become what may properly be called a 'policed' society:[50] in that year only about 300 indictable offences were known to the police in England and Wales for every 100,000 of the population, a rate considerably lower than that prevalent today.

The other possible explanation for the long decline in criminal activity lies in the growing prosperity of the population in the second half of the century. Even allowing for the unequal distribution of the expanding wealth, it is probable that on the whole it enabled proportionately more and more people to maintain a degree of respectability which kept them out of the courts. The importance of this factor can of course be argued at length in terms of wage, price, and employment indices, and at this level the analysis of the statistics merges into the debate about the much more complex changes and regional variations in the nineteenth century standard of living. In most cases, however, the criminal rates can reflect these changes and variations only indirectly. To explain why Lancashire rates were in all cases heavier than the national, for example, we can only refer to known features of the local society which by their very nature are beyond the purview of the official records. And a similar problem arises in considering the relationship between the long-term decline in criminal activity and overall improvements in the standard of living. Given the direct relationship between the higher incidence of property crime and a wide experience of economic hardship, we may be justified in concluding that a decrease in property crime in the long-term would in some way be related to an overall increase in prosperity. But this must be argued chiefly on *a priori* grounds, since there is no statistical method by which the effects of this factor can be distinguished from the effects of police and court developments.

The long-term trends by themselves cannot explain the relationship of prosperity to the decline in criminal activity, but some aspects of the decline can be illustrated by some quite different evidence. The analysis of the changing character of the prison population which follows in the next section of this chapter demonstrates that in the later decades of the century prisoners were on

N

average older than they had been in earlier decades, that more of them had been previous offenders, and that as many were illiterate in the 1870s and 1880s as in the 1840s and 1850s – despite great improvements in national educational standards in the intervening years. This evidence is slender, but it does imply that prisoners later in the century were drawn from a hardened criminal class which was relatively less numerous, and less representative of the population as a whole, than that from which most offenders had been drawn earlier in the century. This may be taken to imply further that fewer 'potentially honest' people, who earlier in the century might have been driven to commit an offence because of want, were now brought before the courts.

A further feature which has emerged from our analyses is perhaps the most suggestive of all: the coincidence in varying degrees throughout the century, but particularly in the first half, of increases in property offences and waves of popular agitation and discontent. Of course it would be foolish on account of this phenomenon to suggest that criminal activity of this kind was in any conscious sense part of a 'social movement'. This may have been true of offences like riot, arson, machine-breaking, seditious libel etc.; but we have seen that their incidence even in years of great unrest was slight. Nonetheless the coincidence of depression, a high rate of property crime, and of working-class political unrest, was of more than incidental importance. If it can be agreed that the increase in property offences in those years constitutes an index of the pressure of poverty and hunger on large numbers of people, the way in which their miseries, thus defined, might have amplified protest movements needs no emphasis. It suggests indeed, that political protests were merely the surface manifestations of social tension and frustration which can be quantitatively assessed in terms of the incidence of certain kinds of criminal activity.

Finally, our analysis of the short-term fluctuations in the incidence of property offences reveals a pattern of great interest. It is now almost a criminological truism that increases in serious property crime in the twentieth century are associated with the effects not of poverty and depression but rather of prosperity. This association has been explained in various ways. In Mertonian terms, crime is seen as a natural outlet for those whose aspirations in the modern consumer society cannot be legitimately fulfilled because of their social position.[51] Others more simply suggest that crime is a consequence of the erosion of traditional rules of conduct. Theories of this kind have an obvious relevance today. But what criminologists have often ignored in their peremptory dismissal of nineteenth-century theories of criminal behaviour is the possibility that the sociological explanation for some kinds of offence is likely to change over time, and that the discovery of a positive correlation between poverty and property crime in the nineteenth-century need not conflict with the more generally accepted twentieth-century theories.

It would be desirable to explain the gradual change which must have taken place from poverty-based offences to prosperity-based offences, and which in fact begins to manifest itself in the period with which we have been chiefly concerned. A close examination of the graphs in figures 2 and 4 will show that from 1819 to 1848 the year-to-year coincidence of high criminal rates with the major depressions in the trade cycle was precise in six cases out of seven – the only exception being that of 1826 when it was a year out. In the second half of the century, by contrast, the coincidence was inexact in many more cases (most notably in 1862, 1869, and 1879), and in one, 1886, there was the reverse of the normal pattern. It is not appropriate here, but there is clearly scope for a more ambitious study of the changing relationship between crime and economic and social conditions in each of the stages of the development of modern industrial society, beginning in the early years of the nineteenth century.

4. PRISONERS AND OFFENDERS

The information in the Prison and Police Returns relating to prisoners' and offenders' ages, standards of literacy, previous records, nationalities, and occupations, is probably the least reliable material in the official statistical records.[52] The standards and methods of classification on the part of prison officials and police were quite unsystematic, and in some cases there is no guarantee that they did not vary both regionally and over a period of years.

But for all its defects, the information does throw some light on the character of those responsible for the incidence of crime, and also serves to amplify some of the conclusions outlined above. Even a preliminary examination of the data, for example, suggests that offenders towards the end of the century were less representative of the character of the rest of the population than they had been earlier. Their average literacy improved less than that of the population at large; a higher proportion of those imprisoned had previous gaol records; and their average age increased sharply. These factors suggest – though in default of closer analysis they do no more than suggest – that a significant improvement had taken place in the economic and social conditions which in earlier years had caused the hypothetical 'ordinary' man to break the law, and particularly to steal. By the 1880s and 1890s those who stole by habit or who had to steal to survive were more and more conspicuously the most depressed and the least literate in the population: and the increase in their average age and in the percentage who had past records suggests also that those who came before the courts were hard-core, confirmed criminals, in a new sense. Working men and women with some aspirations towards respectability, and very many more juveniles than hitherto, were now able to keep clear of the police.

(a) LITERACY OF PRISONERS

The reliability of the information on prisoners' educational standards is questionable. We have found no Home Office directive to prison chaplains (who usually compiled the information for their own prisons) on the criteria to be applied, and it is highly likely that they changed over time, just as they probably varied from prison to prison. In any case, as the headings in table 4 demonstrate, the classifications used were vague and imprecise. The category of total illiteracy, however, presents relatively little difficulty. Its incidence among prisoners throws light on the points mentioned above and further defines the strata from which the prison population – and most offenders – were drawn. Table 4 gives the national percentages of male and female prisoners respectively (for both indictable and summary offences together), classified under each of the five customary headings, for sample years 1840–90. Those who wish to examine prisoners' literacy more closely can draw on comparable information for individual counties and prisons, and distinguish between prisoners convicted of indictable and summary offences respectively.

Table 4   *Degree of instruction: male and female prisoners (percentages)*

Year	Neither read nor write		Read only, or read and write imperfectly		Read and write well		Superior instruction		Not known	
	M	F	M	F	M	F	M	F	M	F
1840	36·5	44·2	54·6	53·3	6·7	1·9	0·0	0·0	2·2	0·6
1845	31·3	41·8	61·5	56·2	6·9	1·8	0·0	0·0	0·3	0·2
1850	33·3	44·7	60·7	52·9	5·4	2·0	0·3	0·1	0·3	0·3
1855	30·6	36·4	54·6	48·7	3·9	1·2	0·3	0·1	10·6	13·6
1860	32·2	38·5	61·7	58·9	5·1	1·8	0·4	0·1	0·6	0·7
1865	34·9	37·6	60·4	59·8	3·7	1·9	0·2	0·0	0·8	0·7
1870	32·1	39·1	63·8	59·2	3·7	1·6	0·2	0·0	0·2	0·1
1875	31·0	39·4	64·0	58·7	4·7	1·8	0·2	0·0	0·2	0·1
1880	30·9	40·3	65·1	57·0	3·5	2·4	0·2	0·1	0·3	0·2
1885	26·2	36·2	70·5	58·7	2·8	4·4	0·1	0·6	0·4	0·1
1890	21·4	34·8	75·5	63·8	2·9	1·3	0·1	0·0	0·1	0·1

The table makes it clear that the majority of prisoners came from the most illiterate sections of the population. Furthermore, it shows that even though standards of literacy among the population at large were improving throughout the century, the percentage of totally illiterate prisoners remained remarkably stable until at least the 1880s. Certainly it declined somewhat thereafter, while the percentage of prisoners who could read only, or read and write imperfectly, marginally increased. But there had been a rapid rise in national literacy rates after the 1840s, and particularly after the Education Act of 1870,[53] which is not reflected in these figures. Though there is obvious scope for further research on the figures at a local level and for different types of offence, it is reasonable to conclude that on average prisoners later in the century were of a lower educational status *vis-à-vis* the rest of the population than they had been earlier.

(b) PREVIOUS CHARACTER OF OFFENDERS

From 1857 onwards there are two main sources of information about the previous criminal records of offenders, although each is untrustworthy for any purpose other than that of broad generalisation. First, the police returns recorded the numbers of persons out of all those committed to summary or indictable trial in each police district whom the police deemed to belong to what was called the criminal class. And secondly, the prison returns published the number of times prisoners gaoled for summary or indictable offences had been previously committed to prison.

The reliability of the prison returns must have depended on the variable efficiency of prison authorities, but they are probably marginally more trustworthy than the police returns on the criminal class. As the Criminal Registrar pointed out in 1895, these last might 'merely represent the varying extent of the knowledge which the police possess of the character of individuals according to the circumstances of the Metropolis, of smaller towns, and of country districts'.[54] Doubtless, too, the concept of the criminal class allowed free play for the prejudices of the police, while respectable contemporaries discovered in it – 'this dismal substratum, this hideous black band of society', as one commentator called it – a convenient scapegoat for the palpable lawlessness of the great towns.

Table 5 *The criminal class 1860–90*

	1860	1865	1870	1875	1880	1885	1890
	Percentage of indictable committals						
Criminal class	57·5	51·8	51·5	44·1	48·1	49·3	44·6
Known thieves specifically	21·7	19·2	20·7	19·2	21·0	21·9	22·4
	Percentage of summary committals						
Criminal class	29·5	26·4	27·1	20·4	21·9	21·3	17·9
Known thieves specifically	3·7	3·9	2·9	1·6	2·2	2·2	2·0

Some kind of criminal class certainly existed, but it tended disproportionately to dominate a great deal of nineteenth century criminological thought, often to the detriment of an objective assessment of other factors contributing to the general incidence of criminal behaviour. As early as 1839, for example the Royal Commission on Constabulary referred to the criminal class to justify the claim that property crimes were 'ascribable to one common cause, namely, the temptations of the profit of a career of depredation,' rather than to the effect of economic conditions. 'The notion that any considerable proportion of the crimes against property are caused by blameless poverty or destitution we find disproved at every step.' That this comfortable point of view is mistaken will be clear from our earlier analysis of the very close relationship between the incidence of property offences and the fluctuations of the trade cycle. What is more in question, however, is whether all or even most of the 'suspicious characters' or drunkards or vagrants whom the police included within the criminal class were in fact the latter-day Fagins most commentators had in mind when they were discussing them. If so, according to the Police Returns, they were responsible for a quite phenomenal average of about 50 per cent of all indictable committals in the period 1860–90, and for about 25 per cent of all summary committals. It might be more realistic to ascribe a habitual criminal intent to a more specific group within the criminal class, that is, to those whom the police returned as 'known thieves'. These accounted for between 19 and 22 per cent of all indictable committals and for only 2 to 4 per cent of all summary committals (see table 5).

Since summary larcenies made up the majority of property offences, the conclusion is inescapable that their higher incidence in depressed years (especially early in the century) still has to be attributed to the fact that at such times quite ordinary people (the hypothetical 'hitherto honest') were frequently obliged to steal in order to survive.

To the extent that there was a hard core of criminals, it was by one criterion at least more in evidence later in the century than earlier. The percentages of men and women who had been gaoled previously for indictable and summary offences together are presented in table 6 for sample years between 1860 and 1890.

Table 6 *Prisoners previously committed to gaol (percentages)*

Year	Male	Female
1860	26·1	42·4
1865	35·3	45·5
1870	35·1	45·8
1875	36·1	51·4
1880	36·9	53·2
1885	41·9	62·2
1890	45·6	63·0

It is true that the increase in the percentages over this period partly reflects the consequences of a gradual diminution in the length of customary sentences: in 1890, for example, a prisoner might have been released earlier than he would have been had he been imprisoned for a comparable offence in 1860, and so might have had an earlier opportunity (or necessity) to commit a further offence. Equally, more first offenders may have been fined where previously they might have been imprisoned. But the increase is too large to be wholly explicable in these terms, and it reflects also a change in the kind of man who typically broke the law. He was, to put it at its simplest, more 'hardened' than his earlier counterpart: he had been to gaol more frequently: the rate of imprisonment of 'respectable' men (and women) diminished.[55]

(c) AGES OF OFFENDERS

Tobias plausibly suggests that 'discussion of the effect of want on the entry into crime of the honest poor must again be divided, this time on the basis of age'. There are two prongs to this argument. It is proposed first that the adult poor 'remained honest despite appalling suffering and often great temptation'; and secondly, that when criminal behaviour did increase with depression, the increase was generally to be ascribed to the activity of juveniles – especially in towns where there was little demand for their labour.[56] Although again this theory is advanced without reference to the available statistics, at first sight it is not unreasonable. If juveniles were more affected by depression than adults, it is quite possible that the sensitivity of trends in property crime to economic conditions in the earlier nineteenth century is to be accounted for chiefly by an exceptional incidence in that period of juvenile crime. It is equally possible that the diminution in that sensitivity later in the century may be accounted for by the increase in social welfare facilities, reformatories, and industrial schools, which took delinquents, orphans, deserted children and runaways off the streets. If this were so, our conclusions ventured in section 3 would have to be modified. An initial examination of the statistics for juvenile crime, however, does not support this theory. At *no* period does the incidence of juvenile crime appear to have been of sufficient quantitative importance to account alone either for the long-term trends or for the short-term fluctuations in criminal activity.

Two kinds of information on the ages of offenders can be used to assess this theory. From 1834 to 1849 the Judicial Returns give the ages of those committed for trial for indictable offences; and from 1834 to 1892 the Prison Returns give the ages of those committed to prison for both indictable and summary offences.

The first kind of information is specially convenient for our purposes, since it covers the period in the 1830s and 1840s when juvenile delinquency was discovered to be a major social problem: it was only towards the end of the 1840s and in the 1850s that attempts were made to combat it in the Juvenile Offenders Acts of 1847 and 1850 (which provided for the summary trial of larcenies by juveniles) and in the establishment of reformatories and industrial schools by statutes of 1854 and 1857. The figures in table 7 thus reflect the age distribution of those committed to trial for indictable offences in the period when the rate of juvenile offences was at its peak and had yet to be controlled by remedial legislation. The average annual percentages of committals in each age group are given for two periods, 1834–41 and 1842–7, this division being necessitated by the adjustments made in the committal returns to correlate the age groupings with those of the 1841 census. For the sake of comparison the percentage age distribution of the total population at the 1841 census is appended as well.

Table 7   *Age distribution of offenders*

Average annual age distribution of those committed for indictable offences				Age distribution of total population	
1834–41		1842–7		1841	
Age	(%)	Age	(%)	(%)	
12 and under	1·7				
13–16	9·8	under 15	6·0	36·0	
17–21	28·8	15–19	23·5	9·9	
22–30	31·5	20–9	38·8	17·7	
31–40	14·7	30–9	16·1	12·9	
41–50	6·9	40–9	8·3	9·6	
51–60	3·1	50–9	3·6	6·4	
61 upwards	1·4	60 upwards	1·8	7·2	
Not known	2·1	Not known	1·9	0·3	
	100·0		100·0	100·0	

Table 7 makes it clear that even in this period juveniles accounted for only about a tenth of all serious offences, while adolescents accounted for about a quarter, and adults for perhaps two-thirds. It can scarcely be argued therefore that the extent of juvenile crime by itself accounted for the sensitivity of the crime rate to economic conditions, though it is of course possible that it was of disproportionate influence in the worst years. Nor is there evidence here that it was a peculiarity of the adult poor to remain honest whatever their hardships.

The extent of juvenile and adult crime in subsequent years can be estimated only through the prison returns. The percentage of prisoners in each age group (for indictable and summary committals together) is represented for the census years from 1841 to 1891 in table 8.

Table 8   *Age distribution of prisoners, male and female separately (percentages)*

Year	Under 17		17–20		21–29		30 and over	
	Male	Female	Male	Female	Male	Female	Male	Female
1841	12·4	9·9	23·1	24·3	33·4	34·6	30·1	31·2
1851	12·0	7·5	23·1	22·4	32·1	34·1	30·8	36·1
	Under 16		16–20					
1861	9·2	4·5	21·3	21·1	31·6	36·2	37·3	37·6
1871	7·2	2·8	18·7	17·7	31·7	33·4	42·2	46·0
1881	3·7	1·6	17·4	13·3	31·2	33·1	47·5	51·9
1891	3·2	1·0	17·0	9·4	29·0	30·2	50·8	59·4

This makes two points clear. First, the proportion of juvenile prisoners decreased markedly, from 12·4 per cent (males) and 9·9 per cent (females) in 1841 to 3·2 per cent and 1·0 per cent in 1891. This is a real decrease, which cannot be explained by the growing numbers of juveniles sent to reformatories and industrial schools, since before being sent there juvenile offenders were committed for a brief period to the regular prisons, and were thus included within the numbers of prisoners given annually in the returns. Secondly, there was a marked increase in the percentage of prisoners aged thirty years and over: from 30·1 per cent (males) and 31·2 per cent (females) in 1841 to 50·8 per cent and 59·4 per cent in 1891. Nor can this last increase be explained wholly as a reflection of the decrease in the proportion of juvenile prisoners. It must reflect also a real upward movement in the age composition of the prison population and probably therefore in the criminal population as well. And this indirectly confirms the conclusion that proportionately more offenders later in the century came from a hardened and perhaps an experienced criminal class than was the case in earlier decades – notwithstanding the preoccupation of Dickens' contemporaries with the Fagins of the urban slums.

5. CONCLUSION – SOME GENERAL REMARKS ON RESEARCH POSSIBILITIES

We began this chapter by stating that our own initial objective was to show the possibility of relating the incidence of criminal activity in the nineteenth century to economic and social conditions. This is simply one theme upon which extended research seemed to be advisable. It may be of interest, therefore, to mention the further possibilities which seem to be worth pursuing in any research based on the official returns.

In the first place we have suggested that as the century progressed the incidence of property offences ceased to be positively associated with economic depression. There is clearly a need for a more precise examination of this change from 'poverty-based crime' to what was perhaps 'prosperity-based crime'. This examination should be concerned with the timing of the change, its relevance to different types of offences, and the possible regional or urban/rural differences which might apply in both respects. It might well involve the continuation of the relevant analyses far beyond our present termination point of 1892.

Related to this is the question of the changing nature of the criminal class, as the century progressed. On this issue our analysis of the available material has not been as full as we should have wished, and we suspect that there is a good deal more that may be done to supplement and correct the full account which Tobias has given from the literary sources. It is important in this context to make every possible analysis in terms of the ages or criminal career patterns of each group of offenders. The material is not always precise, and to attempt to trace individual offenders would be extremely laborious. But an accurate conclusion on this issue is basic to any real understanding of the nature of nineteenth century criminality.

Thirdly, although we have tried to make this exploratory chapter as comprehensive as possible, anyone who consults the published returns with care will discover information (on developments in sentencing practice, on the changing ratio of convictions to committals, on prison conditions, on seasonal variations in criminal activity, and on the structure and strength of police forces, to name the most important) with which we have not dealt in detail. Some sources we have referred to but not ourselves thoroughly examined. Perhaps the most profitable is that contained in the Criminal Registrar's annual reports. These were a sustained and impressive form of criminological writing in their own right – not least because they exhibited an uncommon concern for the statistical verities.[57]

Fourthly, there are very many questions which may be answered by more comprehensive regional analyses than that which we have attempted for Lancashire: we have suggested some of the more obvious. In this context, we might recall also the possibility of tracing back certain of the offences recorded in the published returns to their earliest manuscript record in local record offices, which may identify the offender with considerable precision.

Finally, and much more generally, there is clearly scope for comparisons of criminal behaviour in England and Wales and in other societies, either in the nineteenth century, or at a similar stage in the processes of industrialisation or urbanisation, to throw light on the types of criminality which characterised them. This is merely part of the more theoretical study of the nature of law and the extent of its breach and observance in any type of society. It has been strangely neglected since the pioneering work of Durkheim and his immediate followers. It is well worth resurrection.

Appendix

NINETEENTH-CENTURY CRIMINAL RATES

Table I   Offences against property
   II   Offences against the person (and drunkenness)
   III All 'Serious' offences

Rates presented in terms of incidence of offences per 100,000 of the population in question (national or county; male, female or total).
Data for England and Wales: 1805–92; for Lancashire 1835–92.

Table I Offences against property

I(a) 1805-37 *England and Wales (Indictable committals)*

Total			Total			Total		
Year	Indictable committals to trial	Rate	Year	Indictable committals to trial	Rate	Year	Indictable committals to trial	Rate
1805	4,196	44·1	1816	8,144	72·7	1827	16,194	122·0
1806	3,933	40·7	1817	12,451	109·4	1828	14,836	110·4
1807	3,989	40·7	1818	12,267	106·2	1829	17,003	124·8
1808	4,279	32·1	1819	n.k.	—	1830	16,546	121·4
1809	n.k.	—	1820	12,176	102·3	1831	16,849	120·4
1810	4,561	44·8	1821	11,646	96·2	1832	18,836	133·0
1811	4,752	46·0	1822	11,077	89·9	1833	18,102	126·3
1812	5,647	53·9	1823	10,992	87·7	1834	18,070	124·4
1813	6,246	58·6	1824	12,397	97·5	1835	16,832	114·3
1814	5,601	51·8	1825	13,089	101·4	1836	17,477	117·1
1815	6,932	63·0	1826	14,647	112·0	1837	20,284	134·3

(Property offences continued)
I(b) 1834–56 *England and Wales (Indictable committals plus summary committals to prison)*

Year	Males (i) Indictable committals to trial	Males (ii) Summary committals to prison	Males Combined rate (i+ii)	Females (iii) Indictable committals to trial	Females (iv) Summary committals to prison	Females Combined rate (iii+iv)	Total rate (i+ii+iii+iv)
1834	14,977	n.k.	—	3,070	n.k.	—	—
1835	13,840	n.k.	—	2,992	n.k.	—	—
1836	14,160	2,303	225·2	3,317	365	48·3	134·9
1837	16,560	1,981	250·8	3,724	341	52·7	149·7
1838	16,086	1,694	237·7	3,730	422	53·2	143·5
1839	16,500	2,292	247·7	4,175	487	58·8	151·2
1840	18,325	2,448	270·2	4,643	520	64·2	164·9
1841	19,185	2,134	273·8	4,705	409	62·8	165·9
1842	21,194	2,726	303·2	4,979	444	65·8	181·9
1843	20,040	1,594	270·8	4,788	219	60·0	163·1
1844	17,806	1,679	240·8	4,378	248	54·8	145·8
1845	16,448	1,430	218·1	4,529	119	54·4	134·6
1846	16,764	1,064	214·8	4,778	190	57·5	134·5
1847	19,879	2,157	250·4	5,424	370	66·2	156·4
1848	20,896	2,075	270·2	5,196	421	63·4	164·7
1849	19,276	1,957	246·8	4,853	395	58·6	150·8
1850	18,430	1,553	229·5	4,837	254	56·2	141·1
1851	18,938	2,127	239·1	5,028	169	56·6	146·0
1852	*	1,361	—	*	225	—	136·7
1853		1,338	—		266	—	135·0
1854		1,590	—		369	—	148·5
1855		n.k.	—		n.k.	—	n.k.
1856		n.k.	—		n.k.	—	n.k.

* Male and female indictable committals published only as combined totals: 1852, 23,284; 1853, 23,241; 1854, 25,677; 1855, 22,347; 1856, 15,928.

(Property offences continued)

I(c) 1857–92 England and Wales (Indictable and summary committals to trial; Indictable offences known to the police)

Year	Males			Females			Total	Known to police	
	(i) Indictable committals to trial	(ii) Summary committals to trial	Combined rate (i+ii)	(iii) Indictable committals to trial	(iv) Summary committals to trial	Combined rate (iii+iv)	Combined rate (i+ii+iii+iv)	(v) Total	Rate (KTP+summary committals) (v+ii+iv)
1857	12,791	27,230	429·8	3,615	11,330	159·8	285·4	49,868	458·3
1858	10,680	28,405	415·4	3,296	11,821	151·7	278·4	51,341	470·3
1859	9,811	25,460	367·1	3,216	11,879	149·8	255·3	45,603	421·3
1860	9,635	24,918	356·1	3,204	11,937	148·5	249·7	45,216	412·4
1861	11,282	29,718	418·3	3,383	13,474	163·4	287·6	45,304	439·9
1862	12,590	27,051	399·5	3,440	12,402	151·6	272·4	46,937	424·1
1863	12,630	32,701	451·2	3,643	13,084	158·1	300·9	45,212	441·2
1864	11,726	31,114	421·2	3,529	12,703	·151·5	282·9	44,503	422·9
1865	11,896	32,413	430·2	3,548	12,495	147·9	285·4	45,543	428·2
1866	11,729	31,444	414·1	3,382	11,794	138·1	272·5	44,819	411·3
1867	12,094	33,809	434·8	3,200	12,535	141·5	284·3	49,642	442·8
1868	12,640	35,877	453·9	3,299	12,772	142·7	294·3	52,857	462·5
1869	12,184	35,300	438·8	3,062	12,413	135·7	283·3	52,166	449·4
1870	10,903	33,426	404·6	3,050	11,331	124·6	260·9	46,252	404·5
1871	9,701	30,763	364·8	3,073	11,119	121·3	239·8	39,783	358·4
1872	8,778	30,091	345·7	2,772	11,257	118·3	229·0	39,012	347·9
1873	8,888	31,607	355·4	2,860	11,739	121·5	235·4	40,004	356·1
1874	8,792	31,925	352·6	2,701	11,128	113·6	229·9	42,033	358·6
1875	8,411	29,101	320·5	2,448	9,849	99·6	207·1	41,118	333·0
1876	9,371	29,454	327·3	2,733	10,028	102·0	211·7	43,511	340·6
1877	9,457	31,341	339·3	2,726	10,304	102·8	217·9	45,114	351·3
1878	9,719	33,335	353·3	2,685	10,316	101·2	223·9	48,085	366·5
1879	10,103	32,351	343·8	2,668	9,660	94·7	215·9	46,847	350·2
1880	8,689	39,577	385·6	2,237	11,448	103·7	240·9	46,058	377·5
1881	8,643	39,049	376·3	2,139	11,750	103·9	236·4	45,093	368·2
1882	8,821	39,990	379·3	2,177	11,783	103·2	238·4	52,781	397·0
1883	8,514	38,940	366·6	2,122	11,436	99·1	229·1	43,439	352·3
1884	8,247	38,142	354·0	1,846	10,757	91·1	219·1	40,400	331·7
1885	7,610	36,819	336·0	1,691	10,105	84·3	206·6	37,364	309·7
1886	7,630	35,969	326·3	1,616	9,790	80·6	199·9	37,879	303·9
1887	7,475	37,465	332·8	1,564	9,758	79·1	202·2	35,508	297·3
1888	8,060	38,957	344·5	1,521	9,602	76·8	206·6	36,669	302·9
1889	7,011	39,327	335·9	1,387	10,132	78·6	203·4	34,814	296·2
1890	6,626	36,115	306·6	1,374	9,833	75·6	187·6	32,147	271·5
1891	6,468	36,584	305·9	1,321	9,436	71·1	185·0	31,024	264·9
1892	7,142	39,275	325·7	1,231	9,887	73·3	199·6	32,356	277·1

(Property offences continued)

I(d) 1857–92 Lancashire (Indictable and summary committals to trial)

Year	(i) Male Indictable committals to trial	(ii) Female Indictable committals to trial	(iii) Male and Female Summary committals to trial	Total Combined rate (i+ii+iii)
1857	1,982	1,010	n.k.	—
1858	1,774	940	6,248	389·3
1859	1,581	875	5,377	334·2
1860	1,474	857	4,627	291·5
1861	1,642	824	4,904	303·4
1862	1,946	850	6,085	360·1
1863	1,988	912	5,954	353·9
1864	1,766	823	6,090	341·7
1865	1,893	887	6,247	350·0
1866	1,708	754	5,890	319·3
1867	1,710	726	6,630	340·2
1868	1,706	709	7,388	363·7
1869	1,701	668	7,470	359·6
1870	1,481	708	6,529	313·9
1871	1,312	647	5,877	278·0
1872	1,272	680	5,698	266·0
1873	1,336	688	5,947	271·5
1874	1,346	639	5,955	265·0

Year	(i) Male Indictable committals to trial	(ii) Female Indictable committals to trial	(iii) Male and Female Summary committals to trial	Total Combined rate (i+ii+iii)
1875	1,255	595	5,186	230·0
1876	1,581	739	5,245	242·5
1877	1,743	738	5,267	243·3
1878	1,765	697	5,539	246·2
1879	2,018	770	5,588	252·6
1880	1,700	684	6,562	264·4
1881	1,598	682	6,711	260·2
1882	1,699	724	7,374	280·1
1883	1,625	642	6,651	251·6
1884	1,533	598	6,403	237·7
1885	1,374	550	6,453	230·5
1886	1,326	546	6,537	228·4
1887	1,239	459	6,729	225·9
1888	1,409	485	6,992	235·2
1889	1,252	434	7,288	234·4
1890	1,202	465	6,590	213·0
1891	1,150	405	6,749	211·5
1892	1,248	415	7,024	217·3

Table II Violent offences against the person, and drunken and disorderly behaviour 1857–92 *England and Wales, Lancashire*

| | England and Wales | | | | | Lancashire | | | | |
| | Offences against person | | | Drunkenness | | Offences against person | | | Drunkenness | |
Year	(i) Indictable known to police	(ii) Summary committals	Combined rate (i+ii)	(iii) Summary committals	Rate (iii)	(iv) Indictable known to police	(v) Summary committals	Combined rate (iv+v)	(vi) Summary committals	Rate (vi)
1857	n.k.	76,029	n.k.	75,859	393·9	n.k.	n.k.	n.k.	n.k.	n.k.
1858	2,709	83,086	440·6	85,472	438·9	501	12,190	551·1	21,313	925·4
1859	2,579	83,933	439·4	89,903	456·6	492	13,231	585·5	23,752	1013·3
1860	2,200	77,290	339·4	88,361	443·9	451	11,748	511·1	24,238	1015·4
1861	2,473	76,681	393·4	82,196	408·5	552	13,431	575·7	23,979	987·2
1862	2,536	79,374	402·1	94,908	465·8	508	13,095	551·6	27,105	1099·1
1863	2,966	86,723	434·8	94,745	459·3	691	12,168	513·9	27,935	1116·5
1864	3,091	94,374	466·7	100,067	479·1	569	13,542	555·6	28,911	1138·2
1865	3,123	98,776	481·9	105,310	498·0	621	14,111	571·2	29,372	1139·0
1866	2,861	93,318	449·2	104,368	487·4	597	14,212	566·1	30,923	1182·1
1867	2,799	90,158	428·8	100,357	462·9	655	14,484	570·2	35,978	1355·1
1868	2,964	92,978	437·1	111,465	507·8	652	14,739	571·1	39,687	1472·6
1869	2,956	94,520	438·6	122,310	550·3	584	14,938	567·3	46,850	1712·4
1870	2,707	90,431	413·9	131,870	586·0	618	13,983	525·8	50,108	1804·4
1871	2,626	93,271	420·8	142,343	624·6	549	14,201	523·2	49,898	1770·1
1872	2,586	96,759	430·1	151,034	653·9	602	14,188	514·3	47,860	1664·1
1873	2,542	95,964	420·8	182,941	781·5	623	14,384	511·1	50,066	1705·2
1874	2,881	101,602	440·4	185,730	782·8	688	15,465	539·2	56,482	1885·2
1875	3,219	101,611	436·0	203,989	848·3	888	15,876	548·6	61,088	1999·0
1876	3,236	100,422	425·4	205,567	843·5	891	16,335	552·3	60,437	1937·7
1877	3,006	94,565	395·0	200,184	810·4	709	15,232	500·7	55,259	1735·5
1878	2,869	91,167	375·6	194,549	777·1	576	14,137	452·8	52,693	1621·3
1879	2,579	80,713	328·3	178,428	703·2	533	11,884	374·5	46,075	1389·5
1880	2,855	82,964	333·7	172,859	672·2	570	12,252	378·9	46,241	1366·5
1881	2,879	83,294	330·8	174,481	669·8	537	11,570	350·5	48,292	1398·1
1882	3,237	87,407	344·2	189,697	720·3	756	11,737	357·1	53,020	1515·7
1883	2,809	82,497	320·4	192,905	724·4	618	11,428	339·9	54,276	1531·5
1884	3,165	87,691	336·6	198,274	736·4	667	11,851	348·7	55,234	1538·6
1885	3,073	82,842	315·6	183,221	673·1	615	11,155	323·8	51,066	1404·8
1886	3,626	77,317	294·1	165,139	600·1	643	10,329	298·0	44,607	1211·5
1887	3,470	75,873	281·5	162,772	584·9	692	10,667	304·4	45,936	1231·2
1888	3,567	74,571	277·7	166,366	591·2	770	10,217	290·8	47,903	1267·9
1889	3,424	76,893	282·3	174,331	612·8	718	9,961	279·0	47,947	1252·5
1890	3,513	79,509	288·6	189,746	659·6	751	9,852	273·6	47,889	1253·5
1891	3,352	77,857	279·2	187,293	643·9	583	9,606	259·5	43,955	1119·3
1892	3,461	79,169	280·9	173,929	591·1	644	9,806	261·4	39,147	979·4

Table III   All 'serious' offences*
III (a) 1805–34 England and Wales (Indictable committals)

Year	Males		Females		Year	Males		Females	
	Indictable committals to trial	Rate	Indictable committals to trial	Rate		Indictable committals to trial	Rate	Indictable committals to trial	Rate
1805	3,267	70·6	1,338	27·4	1820	11,595	198·4	2,115	34·9
1806	3,120	66·4	1,226	24·7	1821	11,173	187·9	1,942	31·5
1807	3,159	66·3	1,287	25·6	1822	10,369	171·4	1,872	29·9
1808	3,332	69·0	1,403	27·6	1823	10,342	168·1	1,921	30·1
1809	3,776	77·1	1,554	30·1	1824	11,475	183·7	2,223	34·3
1810	3,733	75·3	1,413	27·0	1825	11,889	187·7	2,548	38·8
1811	3,859	76·8	1,478	27·9	1826	13,472	209·9	2,692	40·4
1812	4,891	95·9	1,685	31·3	1827	15,154	233·1	2,770	41·1
1813	5,433	104·7	1,731	31·7	1828	13,832	209·8	2,732	39·9
1814	4,826	91·4	1,564	28·2	1829	15,552	232·8	3,119	44·9
1815	6,036	112·3	1,782	31·7	1830	15,135	223·7	2,972	42·2
1816	7,347	134·2	1,744	30·5	1831	16,600	242·0	3,047	42·7
1817	11,758	211·2	2,174	37·4	1832	17,486	251·8	3,343	46·3
1818	11,335	200·3	2,232	37·9	1833	16,804	239·3	3,268	44·7
1819	12,075	210·1	2,179	36·5	1834	16,815	236·3	3,353	45·3

* I.e. all indictable offences, in certain periods combined in rates with summary offences against property.

(All 'serious' offences continued)

III(b) 1834-56 England and Wales (Indictable committals and Committals to prison for summary offences against property)*

Year	Males (i) Indictable committals to trial	Rate (i)	Combined rate (i+summaries*)	Females (ii) Indictable committals to trial	Rate (ii)	Combined rate (ii+summaries*)	Total Combined rate (i+ii+summaries*)
1834	18,880	265·3	—	3,571	48·2	—	—
1835	17,275	239·5	—	3,456	46·0	—	—
1836	17,248	236·0	267·5	3,736	49·0	53·8	158·4
1837	19,407	262·5	289·3	4,205	54·5	58·9	171·7
1838	18,905	252·8	275·4	4,189	53·6	59·0	164·9
1839	19,831	261·4	291·6	4,612	58·2	64·3	175·5
1840	21,975	285·8	317·6	5,212	64·8	71·3	191·7
1841	22,560	289·8	317·2	5,200	63·9	68·9	190·2
1842	25,740	326·4	360·9	5,569	61·6	72·9	213·8
1843	24,251	303·5	323·5	5,340	64·0	66·6	192·3
1844	21,549	266·3	287·0	4,993	59·1	62·1	172·2
1845	19,341	236·0	253·4	4,962	58·1	59·5	154·4
1846	19,850	239·2	252·0	5,257	60·8	63·0	155·1
1847	22,903	272·6	298·3	5,930	67·8	72·0	182·9
1848	24,586	289·1	313·5	5,763	65·1	69·8	189·2
1849	22,415	260·5	283·2	5,401	60·3	64·7	171·8
1850	21,548	247·5	265·3	5,265	58·1	64·8	163·1
1851	22,391	254·9	278·3	5,569	60·7	62·5	168·2
1852	21,885	245·6	260·9	5,625	60·6	63·0	159·9
1853	20,879	231·7	246·6	6,178	65·8	68·6	155·7
1854	22,723	249·4	266·9	6,636	69·8	73·7	168·2
1855	19,890	215·9	—	6,082	63·2	—	—
1856	15,425	165·7	—	4,012	41·2	—	—

* Committals to prison for summary offences against property taken from table I(b).

(All 'serious' offences continued)

III(c) 1857-92   *England and Wales* (*Indictable committals; Indictable offences known to police; summary committals for offences against property**)

Year	Males (i) Indictable committals to trial	Males Rate (i)	Males Combined rate (i+summaries*)	Females (ii) Indictable committals to trial	Females Rate (ii)	Females Combined rate (ii+summaries*)	Total Combined rate (i+ii+summaries*)	(iii) Indictable offences known to police	Combined rate (KTP (iii) +summaries*)
1857	15,970	169·7	459·1	4,299	43·7	158·7	305·5	57,273	497·7
1858	13,865	145·8	444·5	3,990	40·1	158·7	298·3	57,868	504·0
1859	12,782	133·1	398·1	3,892	38·6	156·5	274·4	52,018	453·9
1860	12,168	125·4	382·2	3,831	37·6	154·6	265·6	50,405	438·5
1861	14,349	146·4	449·6	3,977	38·5	169·1	305·8	50,809	467·2
1862	15,896	160·2	432·8	4,105	39·3	158·0	291·9	53,225	455·0
1863	16,461	163·8	489·3	4,357	41·2	164·9	322·9	52,211	475·1
1864	15,398	151·4	457·3	4,108	38·4	156·9	303·2	51,058	454·3
1865	15,411	149·6	464·4	4,203	38·8	154·0	305·1	52,250	459·5
1866	14,880	142·7	444·3	3,969	36·1	143·5	290·0	50,549	438·9
1867	15,208	144·1	464·3	3,763	33·8	146·6	301·3	55,538	470·0
1868	16,197	151·5	487·2	3,894	34·6	148·0	313·2	59,080	490·4
1869	15,722	145·3	471·5	3,596	31·5	140·4	301·6	58,441	477·7
1870	14,010	127·9	433·0	3,568	30·9	129·1	277·0	51,972	429·9
1871	12,640	114·0	391·3	3,629	31·0	126·1	255·2	45,149	381·9
1872	11,467	102·0	369·7	3,334	28·1	123·1	243·1	44,191	370·4
1873	11,490	100·8	378·2	3,403	28·3	126·0	248·8	45,214	378·3
1874	11,912	103·2	379·6	3,283	27·0	118·4	245·5	47,824	383·1
1875	11,662	99·6	348·3	3,052	24·7	104·5	223·2	47,045	357·6
1876	12,711	107·2	355·5	3,367	26·9	107·1	228·0	49,320	364·4
1877	12,536	104·3	364·9	3,354	26·5	107·7	232·9	50,843	344·5
1878	13,104	107·5	381·1	3,268	25·4	105·7	239·8	54,065	382·4
1879	13,130	106·3	368·3	3,258	25·0	99·2	230·2	52,447	372·3
1880	11,943	95·4	411·6	2,827	21·4	108·2	255·9	52,427	402·3
1881	12,058	95·2	403·3	2,728	20·4	108·3	251·8	51,193	391·6
1882	12,430	97·1	409·3	2,830	20·9	108·0	254·5	52,180	394·7
1883	11,963	92·4	393·2	2,696	19·7	103·3	244·2	49,534	371·1
1884	11,952	91·4	382·9	2,455	17·7	95·5	235·1	47,089	356·5
1885	11,318	85·6	364·1	2,268	16·2	88·4	222·2	43,962	333·9
1886	11,763	88·0	357·2	2,211	15·6	84·8	217·0	44,925	329·5
1887	11,162	82·7	360·1	2,130	14·9	83·0	217·5	42,391	322·0
1888	11,678	85·6	371·0	2,072	14·3	80·6	221·5	43,336	326·6
1889	10,192	73·9	359·0	1,907	13·0	82·2	216·4	41,285	319·0
1890	10,075	72·3	331·3	1,899	12·8	79·2	201·4	38,650	294·1
1891	9,837	69·8	329·4	1,858	12·4	75·3	198·4	37,252	286·3
1892	10,492	73·6	349·2	1,724	11·4	76·5	208·6	39,021	299·7

* Summary committals to trial for offences against property taken from table I(c).

(All 'serious' offences continued)

III(d) 1834-56 Lancashire (*Indictable committals*)

Year	Males		Females		Year	Males		Females	
	Indictable committals to trial	Rate	Indictable committals to trial	Rate		Indictable committals to trial	Rate	Indictable committals to trial	Rate
1834	2,203	316·5	575	78·6	1846	2,246	250·1	826	87·8
1835	2,027	284·7	627	83·8	1847	2,574	281·0	882	91·9
1836	1,704	234·1	561	73·3	1848	2,876	307·9	902	92·2
1837	2,171	291·4	638	81·7	1849	2,471	259·3	819	82·0
1838	2,030	266·4	555	69·5	1850	2,390	245·9	950	93·2
1839	2,219	284·9	682	83·6	1851	2,440	246·2	1,019	98·0
1840	2,679	336·1	827	99·2	1852	2,465	244·5	933	88·1
1841	3,060	375·5	927	108·8	1853	2,265	221·0	931	82·2
1842	3,550	427·9	947	109·0	1854	2,493	239·3	961	80·1
1843	2,830	334·1	847	95·5	1855	2,270	214·2	881	78·6
1844	2,204	255·1	689	76·2	1856	2,180	202·2	778	68·1
1845	2,154	244·5	698	75·6					

(All 'serious' offences continued)

III(e) 1857–92 Lancashire (Indictable committals; Indictable offences known to the police; Summary committals for offences against property)*

Year	Males (i) Indictable committals to trial	Males Rate	Females (ii) Indictable committals to trial	Females Rate	Total Combined rate (i+ii+summaries*)	(iii) Indictable offences known to police	Combined rate (KTP (iii) + summaries*)
1857	2,433	222·0	1,157	99·4	n.k.	17,535	n.k.
1858	2,229	200·0	1,112	93·7	416·4	16,812	1,001
1859	1,993	175·7	1,010	83·5	357·5	14,308	840
1860	1,759	152·4	942	76·5	307·0	14,440	799
1861	2,051	174·9	908	72·3	323·7	14,509	799
1862	2,422	203·4	967	75·8	384·2	15,658	882
1863	2,556	211·6	1,052	81·3	382·2	14,802	830
1864	2,196	179·1	908	69·1	362·0	15,283	841
1865	2,321	186·6	984	73·7	370·4	15,825	856
1866	2,081	164·9	838	61·9	336·7	14,969	797
1867	2,114	165·2	833	60·6	359·4	15,917	849
1868	2,163	166·5	789	56·5	383·7	16,774	897
1869	2,083	158·0	747	52·7	376·5	15,007	822
1870	1,877	140·3	808	56·2	331·8	13,488	721
1871	1,699	125·1	764	52·3	295·8	11,195	606
1872	1,682	121·4	772	51·8	283·4	10,812	574
1873	1,714	121·1	793	52·1	287·9	11,269	586
1874	1,910	132·3	806	51·9	289·4	12,228	607
1875	1,852	125·6	734	46·4	254·3	12,612	582
1876	2,265	150·5	914	56·6	270·1	13,051	587
1877	2,293	149·2	935	56·8	266·8	12,759	566
1878	2,302	146·7	845	50·3	267·3	13,042	572
1879	2,484	155·1	919	53·6	271·1	12,996	560
1880	2,181	133·4	814	46·5	282·4	12,932	576
1881	2,092	125·3	809	45·3	278·2	12,779	564
1882	2,267	134·1	886	49·0	300·9	13,051	584
1883	2,094	122·3	760	41·5	268·2	12,445	539
1884	2,083	120·2	703	37·9	256·0	11,808	507
1885	1,903	108·5	659	35·0	248·0	11,330	489
1886	1,852	104·3	657	34·5	245·7	11,714	496
1887	1,746	97·1	575	29·8	242·6	9,867	445
1888	1,890	103·8	612	31·3	251·3	9,156	427
1889	1,715	93·0	542	27·3	249·3	9,343	434
1890	1,701	91·2	575	28·6	228·7	9,241	408
1891	1,549	82·0	491	24·1	223·8	8,413	386
1892	1,683	86·9	401	19·5	227·9	8,131	379

* Summary committals to trial for offences against property taken from table I(d)

9. The incidence of education in mid-century

B. I. Coleman

The standard histories of education are remarkably uninformative on the prevalence of education in nineteenth-century England, and particularly on its variation between different areas, social groups and age-groups. The textbooks either ignore these questions or confine themselves to summarising the very limited findings of the contemporary enquiries.[1] This paucity probably owes something to the real or supposed inadequacies of the evidence, but more perhaps to the tendency for educational history to separate itself from general historical studies and remain the preserve of educationists whose interests lie primarily in the theory and methods of education or in the development of the public system of instruction. The latter preoccupation indeed gives a special perspective to the history of education in England. The period before 1870 is studied as the prelude to Forster's Act, and the specialists are rarely interested enough in the antediluvium itself to venture much beyond the proposition that before 1870 the mass of the population was grossly uneducated or at least under-educated.

The pattern of education before the 1870s deserves closer attention than this, for voluntary provision and attendance must have reflected social conditions far more than the subsequent system of board schools and compulsory attendance could do. Its obvious relevance to problems of literacy and social mobility provides further justification for studying the educational structure of the earlier period.

For these purposes the interest lies less in the provision of educational facilities, on which the standard histories have tended to concentrate, than in their utilisation. For instance educationists have usually dismissed as scarcely worth attention the common private schools which proliferated, especially in the towns, alongside the schools of the great education societies.[2] But however ineffective most of the private schools were in giving instruction they obviously existed to meet a demand which could not be satisfied elsewhere, and the extent of the demand and its variations are of significance. Whoever provided the schools and whatever instruction they gave, one also wants to know what numbers and sorts of children were attending them (or were not) and for what periods of their lives.

This chapter considers ways of charting the incidence of education in different districts and among different social categories from the most complete (though not the only) bodies of evidence, namely the various official enquiries and the census returns.

I

The first figures produced to satisfy the contemporary appetite for educational statistics were collected by Brougham's Select Committee on the Education of the Lower Orders in 1818. Enquiries were sent out to the parochial clergy, though many of the returns were completed by curates, churchwardens or overseers. The parochial returns arranged under counties were printed in full, together with summaries of the salient information for each parish and summary tables for each county.[3] In keeping with the committee's terms of reference, private schools of a superior character were omitted from the summaries, though they were sometimes listed in the detailed parochial returns. The returns themselves were unreliable, being apparently much less complete for the larger urban parishes, particularly as to dissenting and private schools, than for the countryside. The committee admitted that they were reliable only for the endowed schools and were particularly inadequate for London and the large towns.[4] Some pattern of school enrolment could be obtained by combining the 1818 figures with the population figures of the 1821 census, at least for the more rural counties and districts, but the failure of the 1818 enquiry to distinguish between male and female pupils in its summaries and most of its returns makes it of limited value and difficult to compare profitably with later and more complete enquiries.

The returns collected at the request of the Commons in 1833 escaped the last failing but shared some of the other inadequacies of the 1818 figures. Circulars were sent to the overseers of every parish and copies of the questions were circulated for the use of schoolteachers, some of whom completed the forms which the overseers then forwarded to London. Again the answers were printed in extenso together with summary tables of attendances at day and Sunday schools in each county, distinguishing schools supported by dissent and schools established since 1800.[5] The returns had the appearance of greater completeness than those of 1818 and were probably fairly reliable for the rural districts, but they were scarcely so for the larger towns, where many common private schools escaped the net, either through their multiplicity and obscurity or through the refusal of their teachers to cooperate.[6] A survey by the Manchester Statistical Society in 1834 revealed 10 Sunday schools and 177 day schools, mostly small private schools, which had evaded the Manchester overseers in 1833.[7] The larger urban parishes apart, however, the 1833 figures provide some sort of picture of the patterns of educational provision and attendance.

The survey conducted in conjunction with the 1851 census was more thorough. Unlike the concurrent survey of religious worship, the educational enquiry attracted little comment, partly because the subject had been officially investigated before, partly because its findings were less controversial and their interpretation less questionable. The census enumerators, who were anyway required to visit every building in their districts, left the educational questionnaire wherever they found any description of school, a procedure which probably traced most of the small private schools which had previously been so elusive. Of 44,836 day schools and 23,173 Sunday schools discovered by the enumerators, only 1,206 day and 377 Sunday schools failed to complete a form of enquiry much more detailed than any earlier one,[8] but as the returns themselves have not survived we have only the printed summaries of the information they contained. The census report on education gives the enrolment and attendance figures for male and female pupils respectively at day schools (distinguishing 'public' from 'private') and at Sunday schools in England and Wales, the metropolitan district, each registration county and registration district, and 197 municipal cities and boroughs.[9] Table 1 presents the figures for England and Wales as percentages of the population aged under 20, a crude method which nevertheless has certain advantages in comparability with the figures considered in section II below. In the census report more detailed tables, though providing only enrolment figures, break down the 'public' schools into four classes and various subclasses for England and Wales, each county and registration district, London and forty-four cities and principal towns.[10]

Table 1   *1851 Census of schools. Enrolment and attendances for England and Wales as percentages of the population (male and female respectively) under 20*

	Enrolment		Attendance	
	M	F	M	F
All day Schools	23·9	20·4	20·0	16·9
Public	16·7	13·0	13·4	10·1
Private	7·2	7·4	6·6	6·8
Sunday schools	24·7	25·0	18·7	19·0

Although it does not specify the denominational character of endowed schools or differentiate between the various grades of private schools, the 1851 schools census provides the period's most detailed picture of educational provision. To illustrate some of its possibilities, table 2 shows the enrolment and attendance figures, again as percentages of the population under 20, for day schools in Warwickshire and its registration districts. (A similar set of figures could be provided for Sunday schools.) It shows an incidence of schooling rather higher in the county than the national average; generally lower, though not to a uniform degree, among girls than among boys; and tending to be lower in the more urbanised districts like Birmingham, Aston and Coventry. The highest figures occur in registration districts containing ancient boroughs and market towns. Everywhere the difference between enrolment and attendance is sizeable, though tending to be rather less for girls than for boys. The more detailed summary

Table 2   *1851 Census of schools: day scholars as percentages of the population under 20*

Registration district	Enrolment		Attendance	
	M	F	M	F
Birmingham	24·6	21·0	20·4	16·6
Aston	19·2	18·4	15·4	14·8
Meriden	27·3	25·0	21·7	19·0
Atherstone	33·1	27·5	28·4	23·9
Nuneaton	27·1	24·2	22·4	19·3
Foleshill	17·9	12·1	14·6	9·8
Coventry	21·5	13·0	18·5	11·1
Rugby	39·5	32·4	32·0	26·7
Solihull	27·8	26·8	21·2	20·9
Warwick	32·2	28·3	26·8	23·6
Stratford	30·6	30·1	24·7	24·4
Alcester	20·2	16·4	15·1	11·8
Shipston	29·3	29·8	24·3	24·4
Southam	31·0	28·7	25·5	25·6
Birmingham (borough)	22·6	19·8	18·6	15·3
Warwickshire (registration county)	25·7	22·0	21·0	17·8
Warwickshire less Birmingham (borough)	28·5	24·6	23·3	20·1

Table 3   *1851 Census of schools: percentage of population under 20 in private and in public schools*

Registration district	In private schools	In public schools[a]	
		class II	class III
Birmingham	8·9	2·1	10·0
Aston	8·2	0·5	10·0
Coventry	6·9	2·6	7·0
Rugby	7·1	14·2	14·4
Warwick	7·4	4·4	16·2
Stratford	8·5	3·1	18·2
Shipston	3·7	12·2	12·9

[a] See note 10 of this chapter.

tables allow the deficiency of schooling in the more recently and heavily populated areas to be pinpointed as far as the types of school are concerned. The selection of registration districts in table 3 suggests that the proportion of the child population attending private schools was fairly constant and that the major variations were in the numbers attending denominational and endowed schools.

The insufficiency of these schools in the populous districts, however, explains the lower incidence of schooling only so far as attendance was regulated by the supply of school-places rather than by an autonomous demand for them, and the summaries provide little to help establish the relationship between school attendance and social structure. They illuminate the pattern of school provision rather than the social distribution of schooling. There is no information on parents' occupations, and, except for the counties,[11] there is no breakdown of the aggregates of scholars into age-groups. The summaries do not even establish clearly the extent of schooling in an area as small as a single registration district, for, like any survey of schools rather than households, the educational census disguised the extent to which districts of plentiful school provision drew pupils from less favoured districts, an important consideration where a single conurbation contained a number of registration districts, like London, and perhaps even in less populous places. The degree of variation among the Warwickshire registration districts in table 2 could be misleading. The summaries show the numbers of children attending school *in* each district, not the numbers *from* each district who did so. The high figures for Rugby, for example, are partly attributable to the number of endowed schools in the town, some of them, particularly the boarding schools, presumably drawing their pupils from a much wider area. The summaries of the schools census are probably dependable enough for counties or even clusters of registration districts, but for smaller areas their margin of unreliability is considerable.

The census of schools was not repeated, but there were two other major, though less complete, surveys before the board school system was established. In 1858 the Newcastle Commission collected returns of the enrolment at public schools (as defined in 1851), evening schools and Sunday schools, though omitting all consideration of private schools. Summary figures for each county distinguishing the different types of schools, though with a classification slightly different from and less detailed than that of 1851, were printed in the commission's report.[12] More detailed statistics were obtained for a number of specimen districts which permit fairly close comparison with the 1851 figures for the same localities,[13] though even these figures omit superior private schools and so fall short of a complete survey of school provision and attendance.

Under the provisions of Forster's Act in 1870 local authorities provided returns of all schools where fees did not exceed ninepence a week, and summaries were printed for all parishes outside municipal boroughs and the London School Board area giving the numbers in attendance on the day of the return in 'public', 'private' and 'adventure' schools respectively (categories different from those of either 1851 or 1858) and the number of schools (though without their attendance figures) associated with each denomination.[14] For additional details and for information on schools in the municipalities one needs to consult the accommodation notices, the inspectors' reports and the original returns kept in the Public Record Office.[15]

Despite their value to students of other aspects of educational history, for present purposes the surveys of schools are vitiated by their various individual defects as well as by the limitations inherent in the mode of enquiry. Even the most complete of them, the 1851 schools census, is best considered as supplementary to the other material to be considered here, namely the occupational returns of the census.

II

Although in 1841 the census returns achieved the form to which they have approximated ever since, the 1851 census was the first in which scholars were listed in the occupational returns. The 1851 householder's schedule instructed the recipient: 'Against the names of children above five years of age, if daily attending school, or receiving tuition under a master or governess at home, write "Scholar," and in the latter case add "at home". ' The accompanying specimen of a completed return gave an example.[16] Similar instructions were given in 1861 and 1871, though the exclusion of children below five (widely ignored in practice in 1851) was dropped and scholars taught at home were no longer distinguished from those at school.[17] The enumerators' books and the printed occupational summaries of the three censuses thus provide a picture of the incidence of education for the 20 years before the board schools. The advantages of a survey of households over the surveys of schools considered above are obvious. It shows the residential distribution of pupils and allows the pattern of school attendance to be related to the social character of districts and of definable groups within them. The only major limitation is that, as a record only of the residents in each household on the census night, the census does not list with their families children attending boarding schools, which is presumably a serious drawback for the study of some localities and social groups. The censuses have the further advantage of being directly comparable with each other, for, unlike the schools enquiries, they were all taken at the same time of the year and by a standardised procedure.[18]

The reliability of the returns is difficult to estimate. The census officials were convinced that scholars were under-registered. A footnote to the printed occupational summaries for 1861 and 1871 stated: 'It is probable that a considerable number of the children here returned were under tuition, although not described as "scholars" in the householders' schedules.' The view is given some justification by the nature of the returns in some of the enumerators' books. Some list no scholars at all and very few occupations of any kind for children, which suggests either that the enumerators misunderstood their instructions or that they failed to ensure that householders completed their schedules in those respects. In one Bethnal Green enumerator's book for 1861 all the members of each family are returned as following the occupation of its head. If scholars were under-registered in some districts, however, the total of scholars in the occupational returns of

1851 was higher than that produced by the census of schools in the same year, though, as table 4 indicates, the difference was not uniform. In the predominantly rural counties the occupational figures for male scholars were rather below the school enrolment figures, a pattern that might seem reasonable on the assumption that some children remained on the books after they had ceased to attend. In those counties, however, the occupational figures for female scholars were relatively higher, and in many cases they were above the enrolment figures. London and the West Riding fitted the same pattern, but in several other heavily urbanised counties the occupational returns of scholars, both male and female, were considerably higher than the enrolment, one possible explanation being that numbers of obscure schools in the towns had escaped the notice of the enumerators. Explanations are less easily found for other features, like the much closer approximation of the figures for male and female scholars respectively in the occupational returns than in the schools returns.

Table 4   *1851 Classification of scholars*

	A		B		C	
	M	F	M	F	M	F
England and Wales	1148·1	1096·0	1139·3	969·3	99·2	88·4
London	131·0	123·4	140·8	113·4	107·5	91·9
Hampshire	27·9	27·8	29·9	27·7	107·2	99·6
Bedfordshire	7·2	5·9	7·9	5·9	109·7	100·0
Dorset	11·9	12·8	12·6	11·8	105·9	92·2
Lincolnshire	26·8	25·7	28·1	24·0	104·9	93·4
Yorks. W. Riding	86·8	80·3	89·3	74·4	102·9	92·7
Yorks. E. Riding	18·9	17·7	18·7	16·2	98·9	91·5
Lancashire	134·7	124·2	123·6	104·3	91·7	83·9
Cheshire	30·0	27·2	28·0	23·3	93·3	85·6
Warwickshire	30·1	30·0	27·7	24·0	92·0	80·0

Note: Column A shows the total of scholars in the occupational returns (excluding those under tuition at home) and column B the totals of enrolled scholars returned in the schools census, both sets of figures in thousands. Column C shows the enrolment figures as index numbers on a base of 100 provided by the occupational figures.

However disconcerting the discrepancies, the occupational returns of the census remain uniquely valuable. They survive in two forms – the original enumerators' books, which are considered later in the chapter, and the summaries printed in the census reports in the parliamentary papers. The printed summaries provide an outline of the geographical pattern of schooling and of its age distribution which could be obtained from the enumerators' books only with immense labour, and so allow the more detailed and localized information extracted from the latter to be related easily to general conditions and trends.

In the printed summaries for 1851 the domestic class of the occupational classification distinguished between scholars attending school, scholars under tuition at home, and people returned as only 'children or relatives'. The county summaries contained detailed occupational totals for each quinquennial age-group of the population under 20, though regrettably the summaries for the separate registration districts included only the adult population. The cities and principal towns, however, had occupational summaries for their total population under 20 as well as for that over 20. The summaries for 1861 followed the same pattern, except that scholars under tuition at home were no longer distinguished from those attending school. In the 1871 summaries scholars aged 0–14 were listed in a new class of 'scholars and children not engaged in any directly productive occupation', while students aged 15–19 were placed in the professional class. Occupational summaries of the population under 20 were no longer provided for the cities and principal towns.

It is therefore possible to estimate the numbers of scholars in each of the first four quinquennial age-groups for England and Wales, the metropolitan district and each county in the three census years of 1851, 1861 and 1871. Table 5 shows the percentage figures for Warwickshire, omitting the last and least significant quinquennium. The numbers of children at work can also be obtained from the occupational summaries and could be used to explore the nature of the relationship between the prevalence of schooling and that of child employment, though only the 10–14 quinquennium is significant for this purpose.

Table 5 *Occupational summaries: scholars as percentages of total numbers in each age-group (Warwickshire)*

	0–4		5–9		10–14	
	M	F	M	F	M	F
1851	11·9	11·4	62·9	59·0	34·9	39·1
1861	16·9	15·5	69·1	66·1	40·8	50·1
1871	14·1	13·9	71·2	68·9	48·3	53·2

For the cities and principal towns there are only the aggregate figures of scholars under 20 for 1851 and 1861, and they are probably best presented as percentages of the total population in the same age-group, as for the five towns and cities in table 6. The figures for the towns can also be subtracted from those for their respective counties to make possible a comparison between the towns in question and the rest of the county area. The results can sometimes be suggestive. For example, the figures for Hampshire and Warwickshire in table 7 show a tendency for the county areas to have a higher proportion of scholars than the fast-growing industrial towns but a lower one than the older towns with a slower increase of population, but the method itself is crude and potentially misleading and can be recommended only, as here, *faute de mieux*. The quinquennial figures for the counties show that similar percentages of scholars within the 0–19 age-group can disguise very different patterns of age distribution. In 1851 Warwickshire and the metropolitan district had similar percentages for this age group, but London's figures were markedly lower than Warwickshire's for the 5–9 age-group and equally decidedly higher for 10–14.

Table 6 *Occupational summaries: scholars under 20 as percentages of total population under 20*

	1851		1861	
	M	F	M	F
Dudley	24·4	24·6	28·1	30·4
Leeds	30·3	28·9	36·2	36·2
Liverpool	33·1	30·7	37·3	37·4
Oldham	26·1	23·3	28·7	28·3
Sheffield	27·1	28·4	30·0	31·5

Table 7 *Occupational summaries: scholars under 20 as percentages of total population under 20*

	1851		1861	
	M	F	M	F
Hampshire (less three				
towns below)	30·3	32·7	36·7	41·1
Portsmouth	33·3	31·5	40·1	43·5
Southampton	34·4	30·9	37·3	37·1
Winchester	36·5	31·8	41·1	41·5
Warwickshire (less two				
towns below)	30·3	29·8	36·9	38·3
Birmingham	26·2	26·9	31·0	32·9
Coventry	30·1	28·0	31·0	27·1

Several reservations must be made about the occupational summaries. First the aggregates of scholars included children in boarding schools on the census night, a factor which is probably discountable for areas as large as most of the counties but which could have distorted the figures for some of the towns. The second limitation the summaries share with the enumerators' books. The nature of the instructions on the 1851 householder's schedule probably caused scholars under five to be under-registered in that year, with consequently a slight underestimate of scholars in the whole 0–19 age-group. Lastly, in the case of the 1871 summaries it is impossible to know how far the implementation of the 1870 Education Act, or the anticipation of its implementation, distorted the pattern of schooling and the character of the occupational returns of scholars in April 1871, though a close study of particular localities might provide some indications.

Despite these reservations, and despite the crudity of the occupational summaries and some of the figures derived from them, the summaries well repay attention by providing both an overall picture of the incidence of schooling and a framework for more detailed local studies.

III

Under the 'hundred-year rule' applied to census returns, the enumerators' books for 1851 and 1861 are currently available to scholars in the Public Record Office. As the books and methods of extracting and utilising the information they contain are described elsewhere in this volume and in its predecessor, I will cover the same ground only as present purposes require.[19]

The enumerators' books have several distinct advantages over the printed summaries of the occupational returns. They permit the examination of smaller and more precisely defined localities and enable the incidence of schooling to be related to other social characteristics. The books also make possible the elimination of any bias in the figures from the presence of boarding schools, though they do not overcome the associated difficulty that boarding pupils were listed with their schools and not with their parental households. At the same time the smaller the district being studied the more the picture is liable to distortion by variations in the nature and completeness of the returns in the enumerators' books.

The extent of the information which one takes from the books and the size of the sample must be determined by the nature of the questions one wishes to answer. Among the variables to which the incidence of schooling could be related and for which the books contain the requisite information are the ages of children, the occupations and the birthplaces of parents, the size of the family (or at least such of it as resided in the household on census night) and the child's order in the family. The size of the sample (for the numbers will usually be too great for a complete listing of households) must depend not only on the population of the chosen district, but also on which of the variables, singly or in combination, one wishes to consider, remembering that the more variables taken in conjunction the larger the sample must be to remain representative. As the crucial 5–14 age-group was usually from one-fifth to one-quarter of a district's population, a sample, to include significant numbers of such children, must embrace a larger proportion of households than it would need for some other purposes.

These points are illustrated by the results of a sample taken from the 1851 enumerators' books for the first registration district of Bethnal Green. It was not in any sense a representative metropolitan district. Bethnal Green was distinguished as the centre of the declining Spitalfields silk-weaving industry, though furniture workers and labourers of various sorts were also prominent in the

Notes

INTRODUCTION

1 Drake, *Population and society in Norway*, 15–16.
2 See Fleury and Henry, *Nouveau manuel de dépouillement et d'exploitation de l'état civil ancien*, and Wrigley (ed.) *Introduction to English historical demography*, ch. 4.
3 The fact that access to state records of vital registration (births, deaths and marriages) is denied to historians is a severe handicap to the development of this type of research.
4 Anderson, *Family structure in 19th century Lancashire*, is an excellent example of what is possible.
5 See, for example, Henry, *Anciennes familles genevoises* and the many other family reconstitutions carried out by INED; Hollingsworth, *Population Studies* (1964); Wrigley, *Economic History Review* (1966) and *Daedalus* (1968).

CHAPTER 1

1 Cited in *The Times*, 21 April 1851, p. 5, col. 6 (subsequently abbreviated to 5f).
2 *Hansard*, 26 George II, Debate in the Commons on the Bill for Registering the Number of the People, 8 May 1753, 1350–1.
3 *Ibid*. 1355–6.   4 *Ibid*. 1326.   5 *Ibid*. 1365.
6 Williams, *Life and letters of John Rickman*, 40.
7 *Ibid*. 38.   8 James, *The travel diaries of T. R. Malthus*,
9 *The Times*, 24 July 1811, 3e.   10 *The Times*, 18 October 1850, 4c.
11 *The Times*, 9 June 1891, 11a.   12 *The Times*, 13 June 1891, 14f.
13 *The Times*, 18 June 1851, 5b.   14 *The Times*, 4 July 1851, 4d.
15 *Ibid*.   16 *The Times*, 10 August 1811, 3c.
17 *The Times*, 4 June 1853, 6e.   18 *The Times*, 3 February 1880, 9c.
19 *The Times*, 20 March 1851, 5d.   20 *The Times*, 15 April 1861, 8c.
21 *The Times*, 18 October 1850, 4c.   22 *The Times*, 25 February 1851, 4c.
23 *Hansard*, 26 George II, Debate in the Commons on the Bill for Registering the Number of the People, 1320.
24 *The Times*, 25 January 1870, 10d.
25 *The Times*, 30 March 1871, 10e. See also *The Times*, 17 June 1851, 5a; 13 November 1860, 4b; 3 January 1901, 5a.
26 Add. MSS. British Museum 35345f, 3–4. Letter of John Rickman to W. Poole, 18 July 1803.
27 *Hansard*, 26 George II, Debate in the Commons on the Bill for Registering the Number of the People, 1318.
28 *The Times*, 27 August 1840, 6a.   29 *The Times*, 18 October 1850, 4c.
30 *The Times*, 9 July 1850, 3e.
31 *The Times*, 8 May 1860, 8d. See also Caird's intervention on the committee stage of the census bill on 11 July 1860 – reported in *The Times*, 12 July 1860, 6b.
32 *The Times*, 8 May 1860, 8d.   33 *The Times*, 13 July 1860, 8c.
34 For example the government used this argument to oppose a religious census in 1871

411

(*The Times*, 10 August 1870, 6a; against a religious census, enquiries into sickness or injuries and wage rates in 1881 (*The Times*, 13 July 1880, 6a); and against a quinquennial census (*The Times*, 10 December 1888, 6b).

35   *The Times*, 28 July 1870, 7d.   36   *The Times*, 29 July 1870, 8c.
37   *The Times*, 25 July 1870, 9c.
38   *The Times*, 27 July 1870, 7f. The matter was also raised in 1880. Alfred H. Huth, in a letter to *The Times* (20 July 1880, 6c.), alleged there were 'probably about 97,000' marriages in existence in England and Wales where the partners were first cousins and double that number where the blood relationship was less direct.
39   *The Times*, 27 July 1870, 7f.   40   *The Times*, 2 February 1880, 12a.
41   *The Times*, 3 February 1880, 9c.   42   *The Times*, 27 August 1888, 3c.
43   *The Times*, 21 April 1871, 11b.   44   *The Times*, 5 May 1871, 12e.
45   *The Times*, 24 May 1871, 12c.   46   *The Times*, 27 August 1888, 3c.
47   *The Times*, 29 August 1888, 8b.   48   *The Times*, 10 December 1888, 6b.
49   *Ibid.*
50   *Ibid. The Times* was in error in noting that the past eighty-seven years had witnessed 'eight decennial censuses'. The figure was, of course, nine.
51   *The Times*, 9 June 1891, 11a.   52   *The Times*, 15 June 1891, 6f.
53   *The Times*, 15 June 1901, 11c.   54   *The Times*, 26 November 1901, 14f.
55   *The Times*, 12 August 1880, 10e.   56   *The Times*, 13 July 1880, 6a.
57   *The Times*, 12 December 1888, 10a.   58   *The Times*, 18 December 1888, 13f.
59   *Report of the committee appointed by the Treasury to enquire into . . . the taking of the Census . . .* , *PP* 1890, LVIII, 13.
60   *Ibid.*   61   *The Times*, 21 July 1890, 7e.   62   *Ibid.*
63   *Ibid.*   64   *The Times*, 27 November 1899, 12f.   65   *Ibid.*
66   *The Times*, 15 March 1851, 2c.   67   *Ibid.*   68   *Ibid.*
69   *Ibid.*   70   *Ibid.*   71   *Ibid.*
72   *The Times*, 28 March 1851, 2b.   73   *Ibid.*   74   *Ibid.*
75   *Ibid.*   76   *The Times*, 29 March 1851, 5a.
77   *The Times*, 7 June 1860, 12c.   78   *The Times*, 2 July 1860, 10f.
79   *The Times*, 12 July 1860, 6b.   80   *Ibid.*   81   *Ibid.*
82   *Ibid.*   83   *Ibid.*   84   *Ibid.*
85   *Ibid.*   86   *The Times*, 27 July 1870, 7f.
87   *The Times*, 3 August 1870, 6a.   88   *The Times*, 10 August 1870, 6a.
89   *The Times*, 13 July 1880, 6a.   90   *Ibid.*
91   *The Times*, 3 September 1880, 4f.   92   *The Times*, 23 July 1890, 6d.
93   Martin, *A sociology of English religion*, 26, 44.
94   *The Times*, 1 March 1875, 9d.   95   *The Times*, 20 May 1872, 8b.
96   *The Times*, 16 July 1881, 6a.   97   *Ibid.*
98   *The Times*, 3 July 1891, 8e.
99   I have discussed this question at some length in my book *Population and Society in Norway, 1735–1865*, chapter 1.
100   Hansard, 26 George II, Debate in the Commons on the Bill for Registering the Number of the People, 1320.
101   *The Times*, 16 June 1841, 3b.   102   *The Times*, 10 June 1841, 6f.
103   *The Times*, 24 July 1811, 3e and 12 June 1821, 3d.
104   *The Times*, 22 February 1900, 15d.   105   *The Times*, 16 June 1841, 3b.
106   *The Times*, 9 April 1891, 7c.   107   *The Times*, 17 October 1894, 14b.
108   *The Times*, 6 January 1894, 12a.   109   *The Times*, 24 March 1881, 9d.
110   *History of the census of 1841*, 73.   111   *The Times*, 8 June 1841, 6e.
112   *The Times*, 22 October 1841, 6c.   113   *The Times*, 22 November 1841, 5a.
114   *The Times*, 2 July 1851, 8f.   115   *The Times*, 7 April 1851, 5d.
116   *The Times*, 3 April 1901, 15c.   117   *The Times*, 5 April 1901, 9d.
118   *History of the census of 1841*, 75–6.   119   *The Times*, 2 April 1881, 12b.
120   *The Times*, 5 March 1901, 5f.   121   *The Times*, 8 February 1871, 12c.
122   *The Times*, 14 July 1801, 3b.   123   *The Times*, 23 April 1802, 3a.
124   *The Times*, 14 July 1801, 3b.

125 *Minutes of evidence . . . population bill*, Parliamentary Papers, 1840, xv, 471.
126 Hansard, 26 George II, Debate in the Commons on the Bill for Registering the Number of the People, 1325.
127 *Minutes of evidence . . . population bill*, Parliamentary Papers, 1840, xv, 471.
128 *History of the census of 1841*, 40.
129 *Ibid.* 40.   130 *Ibid.* 1.   131 *Ibid.* 3.
132 *Ibid.* 3.   133 *Ibid.* 5.   134 *Ibid.* 4.
135 *Ibid.* 4.   136 *Ibid.* 5.   137 *Ibid.* 26–7.
138 *Ibid.* 17.   139 *The Times*, 16 May 1860, 9a.
140 *The Times*, 5 February 1860.   141 *The Times*, 8 April 1861, 9e.
142 *Report of the committee appointed by the Treasury to enquire into . . . the taking of the census* . . . , Parliamentary Papers, 1890, LVIII, p. 30, Question 33.
143 *Ibid.* 31, Question 47.   144 *Ibid.* 21.   145 *Ibid.* 32, Question 81.
146 *Ibid.* 21.   147 *Ibid.* 33.   148 *Ibid.* 21.
149 *Ibid.* 71.   150 *History of the census of 1841*, 15.
151 *Ibid.* 13, 17.   152 *The Times*, 3 July 1871, 12d.
153 *History of the census of 1841*, 32.   154 *Ibid.* 33.
155 *The Times*, 5 February 1861, 10c.   156 *The Times*, 20 March 1871, 5d.
157 *The Times*, 20 May 1871, 7e.   158 *The Times*, 5 March 1891, 3a.
159 *The Times*, 3 January, 1901, 5a.
160 Hansard, 26 George II, Debate . . . on the Bill for Registering the Number of the People, 1333.
161 *The Times*, 16 April 1841, 6e.
162 *The Times*, 4 April 1891, 12e, and 27 July 1891, 6f.
163 *The Times*, 10 September 1841, 6b.
164 *The Times*, 12 September 1844, 4c.
165 *Ibid.*
166 *The Times*, 16 September 1844, 6f.
167 *The Times*, 23 July 1870, 7f.
168 *Report of the committee appointed by the Treasury to enquire into . . . the taking of the census* . . . , Parliamentary Papers, 1890, LVIII, 34.
169 *The Times*, 15 April 1861, 8c.
170 In 1880, *The Times* commented (3 February, 9c): 'The volumes of the census have, since they assumed their recent bulk, been a chaos through which only a few profound experts can pick their way.'

CHAPTER 2

1 Dahrendorf, *Daedalus* (1964), 257.
2 Mayhew's *London labour and the London poor*, for example, is mainly about London costermongers, a distinctive minority if only because hardly any of them were legally married to their 'spouses' (Mayhew, I, 20). This does not, however, stop Young and Willmott citing him for evidence on family behaviour 'in the old days' (Young and Willmott, *Family and kinship*, 8).
3 Goode, *World revolution*, 6–7. Note how little hard statistical data on the family of the past is used by, for example, Rosser and Harris in *The Family and social change*, or in Young and Willmott's *Family and kinship*. Cf. for a similar criticism of Rosser and Harris's book Sharf, *Population Studies* (1968), 286.
4 E.g. Rosser and Harris, *Family and social change*; Young and Willmott, *Family and kinship*; Hoggart, *The uses of literacy*.
5 *Ibid.*
6 Laslett, *World we have lost*; Laslett and Harrison, *Clayworth and Cogenhoe*. Note also e.g. Williams, *Ashworthy*, esp. 140–4, 217–9.
7 For a list of some of the studies that have been done see footnotes 9–16 below. Note also McGregor, *British Journal of Sociology* (1961). There are also a number of studies mainly with a demographic focus (e.g. Banks, *Prosperity and parenthood*) or studies of certain processes or limited aspects of family behaviour (e.g. McGregor, *Divorce in England*).

8   Sample data on Preston suggest that the earlier that men could support a wife and family at their customary standard of living, or reached their peak earning capacity, whichever came first, the earlier they married.

9   Habakkuk, in *The family.*

10 Collier, *Family economy.*

11 Smelser, *Social change*, esp. ch. 9–13.

12 Hewitt, *Wives and mothers*, and *Effect of married women's employment.*

13 Pinchbeck, *Women workers.*

14 Particularly important of those known to me are those of Armstrong (reported in *Urban history*) and Drake.

15 Crozier, *Sociological Review* (1965).

16 Firth, *Sociological Review Monograph* No. 8.

17 Foster, *Capitalism and class consciousness.*

18 Anderson, *Family structure.*

19 For Lancashire, for example, much useful material can be gleaned from Davies, *North country bred.*

20 *Select Committee on education*, Parliamentary Papers, 1837–8, VII, 102.

21 Crozier, *Sociological Review* (1965).

22 Three thought-provoking discussions are by Back in *Social structure and the family*; Goode, *Current Sociology* (1963–4); and Lancaster, *British Journal of Sociology* (1961).

23 Cf. e.g. 'Labour and the poor', *Morning Chronicle Supplements*, 28–9.

24 This topic is discussed more fully in Anderson, *Family structure*, ch. 7.

25 *Ibid.* esp. ch. 8 and 9.

26 *Ibid.* esp. ch. 4 and 6.

27 Cf. Back in *Social structure and the family*, and Lancaster, *British Journal of Sociology* (1961).

28 Cf. for a useful discussion of this point Fox, *Kinship and marriage*, 15.

29 One example of the use of this perspective is the paper by Townsend in *Social structure and the family.*

30 In Scotland, the enumerators' books for the whole of the nineteenth century are already open to public inspection.

31 Hewitt's *Wives and mothers* and *Effect of married women's employment* are partly based on data obtained in this way.

32 Dyos and Baker's paper in *Urban History* discusses data obtained in this way (see the footnote on page 93 for details).

33 Michael Drake's team at the University of Kent at Canterbury have already made considerable strides in the development of techniques for this purpose.

34 See the discussion in Smelser, *Social change*, ch. 9.

35 See pages 90–105 in this volume for a discussion of this problem. The inconsistencies between the two censuses in this matter seriously reduce the value of comparisons between the years 1851 and 1861.

36 This can, to some extent, be verified by reference to the published census tables of occupations, birthplaces and ages for the town compared with others in the area. A careful search of contemporary descriptive literature also helps to verify points such as this. Nevertheless, it is obvious, and this should always be pointed out, that data assembled on this basis have no statistically valid claim to representativeness.

37 It is, however, well worth while to check before committing oneself too heavily to a region, that the data have not been destroyed or become illegible, and also that special events – strikes, fairs and the like – were not affecting the region at the time the census was taken. Local newspapers and directories will often be useful here.

38 Armstrong in *English historical demography*; Tillott in chapter 3.

39 See chapter 5 for a further detailed discussion of sampling techniques.

40 For the precise definition of this term and the problems involved in this area, see chapter 4.

41 This can only be positively known for a small number of cases, and guessed at for some others, and may well not be worth including in future investigations.

42 See below, table 1, p. 58, for the categories used for this variable.

43 For details see p. 63.   44 For details see pp. 59–61.
45 For details see pp. 61–2.
46 The sample of villages is a specially stratified one and should *not* be considered as in any
    way a random sample of villages of this kind in this area. It is, however, in certain ways
    comparable with the Preston sample. For full details see Anderson, *Family structure*,
    ch. 1, 3 and 4.
47 See footnote 46 for the limitations of this sample.
48 Blalock, *Social statistics*, 163–5.
49 See Rosser and Harris, *Family and social change*, 158. The figures are not exactly com-
    parable, those for Preston being, in fact, for co-residing groups (see pp. 140–3).
50 For modern uses of this variable and its justification see e.g. Lomsing and Kish, *American
    Sociological Review* (1957); Hill in *Social structure and the family*; Rowe in *Emerging
    conceptual frameworks*.
51 For a fuller discussion see Anderson, *Family structure*, ch. 3, 7 and 9.
52 This has been done by, for example, Foster in *Capitalism and class consciousness*.
53 Rowntree, *Poverty*, 110.
54 The most useful wages source for Lancashire is Chadwick, *Journal of the Statistical
    Society* (1860). Another very useful source is *Reports of Factory Inspectors to 31st
    October 1848*, Parliamentary Papers, 1849, xxii.
55 Wood estimates a fall in retail prices of 8–10 per cent from 1851 to 1898–1900 (Mitchell
    and Deane, *British historical statistics*, 343–4).
56 London best coal prices, for example, were 5–47 per cent higher in 1898–1900 (Mitchell
    and Deane, *British historical statistics*, 483).
57 Rowntree's rent of 5s 6d for a family of seven is somewhat higher than most of the sums
    cited in contemporary literature on working class accommodation in Lancashire.
58 Such information is, indeed, rarely found in historical sources. One exception is the
    Cardington listings (Tranter, *Population Studies* (1967)). Some relevant questions were
    also asked in the Irish census of 1841 (*Census of Ireland 1841, Report*, Parliamentary
    Papers, 1843, xxiv, xiii), and some similar information was also sought at later Irish
    censuses.
59 For example, before one can estimate how many of the native born children who are
    recorded in the census as living apart from their parents had in fact left home deliberately
    or been separated for some reason from their parents, one must be able to suggest at
    least roughly the proportion who were separated from parents because their parents
    were both dead. In Preston, on the assumption that a child was born when its parents
    were 32 and that parental mortality was the same as that of the population as a whole in
    the same age-group, the Preston mortality table suggests that no fewer than 31 per cent
    of the children aged 15–19 would have lost one or other parent. On the assumption that
    the mortality of one parent was independent of the mortality of the other, this means that
    (by the binomial) 9·4 per cent would have been total orphans. If the correct equivalent
    age was not 32 but 35, these figures would be 34 per cent and 12 per cent respectively. On
    the same assumptions, the proportion who would have lost a parent by age 15 would be
    26 per cent where children were born to parents aged 32, and 30 per cent where parents
    were aged 35. Young and Willmott found that 29 per cent of the members of their sample
    born before 1891 had lost a parent before the age of 15. This seems a roughly comparable
    figure and certainly suggests that the Preston figure is unlikely to be too low (Young and
    Willmott, *Family and kinship*, 7.)
60 Reproduced among other places in McCulloch, *Statistical account of British Empire*, 419.
61 Farr, *English life tables*.
62 *Appendix to Ninth Annual Report of Registrar General*, Parliamentary Papers, 1849,
    xxi.
63 *Census, 1911*, xiii, 'Fertility of marriage', 416–17.
64 A more detailed calculation based on estimated age of marriage data derived from pro-
    portions unmarried at different ages at the 1861 census, and calculated for each age of
    marriage group separately, gave very similar results to those given here.
65 It will appear below that, because, on the assumptions used here, as the number of
    children in a family increases, the likelihood of being left in old age with no children alive

decreases rapidly, grouping of larger family sizes into groups will therefore introduce minimal bias into the results.

66 This figure is obtained as follows: Of 100 marriages, both the partners of 53 per cent, one partner of 39 per cent, and neither partner of 8 per cent would have survived to age 45. This means that, of the original 200 partners, 145 would have survived to age 45. Of this 145, 106 (53 + 53), or 73 per cent would have had an original spouse still alive.

67 Stehouwer, in *Social structure and the family*, 145.

68 On this point cf. Hubert, *International Social Science Journal* (1965).

69 See n. 33 above.

70 In the area of Preston which I surveyed, only 14 per cent of the 1861 male population of over 10 years of age were living in the same house in 1851. Cf. for other areas in the nineteenth century e.g. Booth, *Life and labour*, III, 61, and *Fourth report on settlement and poor removal*, Parliamentary Papers, 1847, XI, 552.

71 26 per cent of the Preston men aged over 10, excluding those who were living in the same house, were, in 1861, living within 200 yards of their 1851 addresses.

72 In Preston rather over half of all men aged over 10 in 1861 were traced in the 1851 enumerators' books. For further details see Anderson, *Family structure*, 88–92.

73 The assumptions used were: age 5–9 becoming 15–19: 2·5 per cent marrying; 10–14 becoming 20–4: 20 per cent; 15–19 becoming 25–9: 65 per cent; 20 and over becoming 30 and over: 65 per cent. These marriage rates are rough estimates derived from the proportions of population married at the 1861 census.

74 *Census, 1851, Population Tables I*, II, Division VIII, 50.

75 The fact that some of the areas of the town were predominantly middle-class renders this assumption a slightly generous one, but no ready alternative suggests itself.

76 Kendall and Babington Smith, *Random numbers*.

77 A Smirnov test applied to these data give a chi² value at 2 d.f. of 15·101. If the assumptions for chi² were fully met, this would give $p < 0.001$. For the Smirnov test (which has considerable use in this kind of research, being more powerful than chi² when its assumptions are met) see e.g. Blalock, *Social statistics*, 203–6.

78 *Census, 1851, Population Tables II*, Report CXIX.

79 *Committee on census*, Parliamentary Papers, 1890, LVII, *passim*.

80 See also pp. 26–7.

81 This figure is, of course, a minimum, because some single individuals in particular will have been missed because age was one of the criteria used to identify individuals. For the criteria used see above, pp. 72–3.

82 Qualifications similar to those noted in note 81 are also, of course, applicable here.

83 Cf. also the examples given by Tillott, pp. 109–12.

84 For details see Anderson, *Family Structure*, esp. ch. 6.

85 Cf. for this usage *Poor inquiry, Ireland, App. A*, Parliamentary Papers, 1835, XXXII, 288n; Gaskell, *Mary Barton*, 133, 164; and, in a modern context, Humphreys, *New Dubliners*, 127; Lancaster, *British Journal of Sociology* (1961), 324–5.

86 For an important discussion of the uses, problems, and limitations of descriptive data, see also Angell in *The use of personal documents*.

87 It can, for example, fairly easily be established that, in spite of the outcry at the time, and in spite of the fact that almost all the literature seems to imply that it was widespread, at any one point in time, 2 per cent at an absolute maximum of all infant children in the industrial districts of Lancashire were being left during the day with professional child-minders, with all the social problems which were alleged to ensue. (For a full discussion see Anderson, *Family structure*, 182–3; the figures are partly based on Hewitt, *Effect of married women's employment*, 271, 275.)

88 E.g. *Employment of children in factories: first report*, Parliamentary Papers, 1833, XX, D2, 3; *State of the population of Stockport*, Parliamentary Papers, 1842, XXXV, 7.

89 For further discussion see Anderson, *Family structure*, 267–72.

90 *Ibid.* 287–303.   91 *Ibid.* ch. 5.

92 It may, I think quite fairly be asserted that Smelser, whose *Social change in the industrial revolution* is based almost wholly on descriptive data, has not been as cautious as he might in drawing conclusions from them. This is particularly the case when he is dis-

cussing changes in the proportion of children in factories employed and recruited by relatives. On the basis of some limited statistical evidence I gathered in my Lancashire study, it would seem that he has definitely exaggerated the size of the change. (See Anderson, *Family structure*, ch. 6.)

93 Among the more useful introductions to content analysis is Berelson's paper in *Handbook of social psychology*. For a critical discussion of some of the difficulties and restrictions of content analysis and, consequently of all use of qualitative materials in historical sociology (particularly for the imputing of motives or affective states) see Cicourel, *Method and measurement*, ch. 6.

94 For useful discussions of this topic in modern times see e.g. Litwak, in *Social structure and the family*, 290–303; Loudon, *British Journal of Sociology* (1961); Young, *Human Relations* (1954).

95 On this topic, Mrs Gaskell might be a good example of a writer of this kind.

96 For a full discussion see Anderson, *Family structure*, 101–5, 216–30.

CHAPTER 3

1 Dyos, *The study of urban history*, 87–112.

2 *Ibid.* 67–85; and see also Wrigley (ed.), *English historical demography*.

3 Tillott, *The Local Historian* (1968).

4 Much of the work was done by classes held by the Department of Extramural Studies in the University of Sheffield; my own work in the comparative study of census material has been generously assisted by a grant from the research fund of the University.

5 See chapter 9.

6 Lathrop, *Migration into East Texas*, 3–11; 'relationship to head', however, is missing until 1880 and birthplaces are by state.

7 Individual adult students, however, have analysed communities of up to 5,000 using a card index method and manual sorting.

8 Wrigley (ed.), *English historical demography*, 211–17 and references cited there.

9 Such information is not publicly available but conversations with enumerators reveal the difficulties encountered and similar information may be obtained impressionistically from sub-postmasters, social welfare workers, doctors etc. For the mid-nineteenth century, analagous amateur documentation – traders' bills, parochial registers, highway and poor law accounts – demonstrate the variable treatment of repetitive data.

10 *Census, 1851 Report*, pt. I, xiv.   11 *Ibid.* xv–xvi.

12 See below, p. 88.   13 *Census, 1851, Report*, pt. I, xviii.

14 *Census, 1851 Report*, pt. II, xcix.   15 *Ibid.* xxiv–xxv.

16 For work (as yet unpublished) on the Sheffield Directory I am indebted to a member of a Sheffield Extramural class, Mrs M. Furey.

17 For the exploitation of poll books see Vincent, *Poll books*; Vincent, however, does not use the enumerators' books to supplement his material.

18 A study of north west Lincolnshire, using the census material referred to in the appendix 1, together with poll books and directories, by Mr G. Stevenson of Lady Spencer-Churchill College of Education, Oxford, is in progress.

19 The experiment is being conducted by a Sheffield Extramural class at Tickhill (Yorks. W.R.); of the eighty-six households so far examined none has been found where their young children known from the registers fail to appear in the census, nor have discrepancies of relationship, occupation, or birthplace been found for those adults who appear in the census. The check is limited to those born, married or buried in the parish and by incomplete or inadequate registration. For a discussion of ages in the census see below, pp. 108–9.

20 S/G/190; S/N/20; for an explanation of these abbreviations see appendix 1 of this chapter.

21 Taylor, *British Medical Journal* (1951).

22 S/L/89; it was not, of course, humbug but simply unfamiliar to the enumerator; bishops of the Catholic Apostolic Church were known as 'angels'.

P

23 W/c/94.   24 *Census, 1851, Report*, pt. I, xv.
25 *Ibid.* xviii.   26 W/b/28 and 58.   27 D/2/101.
28 See below p. 124.   29 *Census, 1851, Report*, pt. I, xxxviii.
30 *Ibid.* xxxvi.   31 See p. 91.
32 *Census, 1851, Report*, pt. I, xxxv.   33 GRO and COI, 1966.
34 *Census, 1851, Report*, pt. I, cxlii.   35 *Ibid.* cxxxviii.
36 *Ibid.*, cxxxvii.   37 *Ibid.* cxliii.   38 *Ibid.*
39 *Ibid.* cxliv.   40 *Ibid.* cxlv.   41 *Ibid.* clii, cliv.
42 S/T/130, 131; S/T/191, 192; S/P/61–2; one page of the Bradfield enumeration omits
     lines altogether: Brad/3/20–2.
43 Sheffield Crookes and Doncaster districts, 1851, *passim*. See chapter 4 for a full descrip-
     tion of correct procedure in doubtful cases.
44 S/K/18; son of head: Brigg/C/44.
45 *Ibid.*; S/K/135.   46 S/M/3, 35; S/S/15; S/U/41.
47 Public institutions such as schools, workhouses, prisons, hospitals etc. containing 200
     or more persons were to be enumerated by the Masters or Keepers of those institutions
     (*Census, 1851, Report*, Pt. I, cxxxv, cxxxix) though the rule of 200 was not always strictly
     adhered to. Wesley College (S/G/143) housed 162 persons in 1851; the enumerator omit-
     ted two schedule numbers and began the next househould as no. 146.
48 In this and in the other variations mentioned enumerators may not even be consistent
     within their district.
49 See chapter 4.   50 W/c/115 and 116.
51 See below, pp. 112–16.   52 S/Q/70 and 71.   53 S/Q/72 and 73.
54 App/53 and 54, 63 and 64, 75 and 76, 78 and 79.
55 *Census, 1861, Report*, Vol. II, 10.
56 Hath/61/5/12 and so throughout the '61 returns.
57 T/61/S/80–2.   58 Hath/61/5/72–4.   59 S/K/12; S/U/61.
60 S/U/106, 111; S/O/155; S/T/208.   61 D/5/125; Bu/11.
62 D/1/19.   63 T/51/Wg/31.   64 W/c/7.
65 Alk/51/37.   66 Hath/51/a/14 and 15.   67 S/G/201.
68 See Anderson's discussion of this issue in chapter 4.
69 S/N/110.   70 W/b/61.
71 D/2/120; Bu/26; S/K/65; T/61/Wg/99.
72 S/L/23; S/H/101; D/5/130; D/6/4; W/a/2.
73 *Census, 1851, Report*, pt. II, lxxxii.   74 S/b/52; W/c/120.
75 *Census, 1851, Report*, pt. II, lxxviii.
76 The problems of occupational classification are discussed in chapter 6.
77 *Census, 1851, Report*, pt. I, cxxxviii.
78 Ash/46; WH/10 and 17.
79 I am grateful to Mr G. S. Stevenson who has drawn together these figures from the work
     of a Sheffield Extramural class at Scunthorpe. Earlier studies will be found in Sheppard,
     Agricultural History Review (1961), 143–54; and Thomas, *Welsh Historical Review*, III,
     no. 1, 63–73.
80 *Census, 1851, Report*, pt. I, cxxxviii.   81 *Ibid.*, cxlvii.
82 Hath/51/a and b; T/61/Ng/4; F/s/14.
83 Hath/51/c/31; Wham/a/47 and 49; Ash/12 etc.
84 D/1/2.   85 D/1/11; Hath/51/a/19.
86 *Census, 1851 Report*, pt. II, lxxxviii–ix.
87 S/H/68 and 92.
88 *Census, 1851 Report*, pt. I, cxxxviii, cxlvii.
89 *Ibid.*   90 T/61/S/57; Sk/b/93.   91 Wham/a/3.
92 *Census, 1851, Report*, pt. II, tables xxv, xxvi, xxvii.
93 D/15/124.
94 Bu/15; D/1/81 etc., D/4/47 etc.; D/15 *passim*; Sk/a/*passim*.
95 Wham/b/29.   96 S/P/41; S/V/80; Norm/N/19.
97 D/15/17; Norm/T/41.   98 D/3/4; D/5/130; Ap/45.
99 Sk/b/76; T/61/S/70; Ash/6.   100 D/5/135; Alk/51/99.

101 D/6/2; W/a/56; S/H/73; D/1/8; Wham/b/27; and 29; S/U/120.
102 *Census, 1851, Report*, pt. I, cxxxviii, cxlvii.
103 Wham/b/6; D/2/31; Bu/5 and 12.
104 D/15/83; D/1/41, 58 and 61; D/6/38 and 50.
105 Webb, *English Poor Law History*, pt. II, 1, 142ff.

HAPTER 4

1 In particular, W. A. Armstrong, P. M. Tillott and E. A. Wrigley have made important suggestions and contributions to this chapter, though I, of course, retain responsibility for any errors which may remain. This chapter is best read in conjunction with the relevant sections of chapter 3.
2 For the exact definition of a 'census family' see below, section IV.
3 *Census, 1851 Report*, pt. I, cxlii.
4 See Stacey, *Comparability in social research.*
5 See for full details section III.
6 *Census, 1851, Report*, pt. I, cxlv.   7 *Ibid.* xxxviii.
8 *Census, 1861, Report (Scotland)*, xxvii. Cf. *Census, 1871 Report (Scotland)*, xxx–xxxi.
9 *Census, 1881, Report (Scotland)*, x.
10 *Census, 1851, Report*, pt. I, cxlv. The full instructions to enumerators are reproduced on p. 141.
11 *Census, 1861, Report (England and Wales)*, 7.
12 For further information on this subject see chapter 3, appendix 1.
13 Since there are usually only one workhouse, one prison, and one or two boarding schools in any one community, the inclusion of the inmates in a randomly drawn sample in which these institutions happen to fall will seriously bias the sample in any direction in which the institution has a predominance of members (e.g. in the case of workhouse, the old and unmarried mothers). It will usually be necessary, however, to include a proportion of the inmates which corresponds to the sampling fraction employed, in all tabulations relating to individual characteristics and purporting to cover the whole population. Another problem with inmates is that data on relationships between them is not usually given. For further discussion of sampling problems, see chapter 5.
14 The instructions are reproduced in full on pages 91–2.
15 *Census, 1851, Report*, pt. I, cxlv.
16 *Census, 1851, Report*, pt. I, cxlii.
17 For further inconsistencies that sometimes arise see pages 90–105.
18 As reproduced in *Census, 1851, Report*, pt. I, cxxxvii.
19 *Census, 1861, Report (England and Wales)*, 10.
20 Ibid., 76.
21 *Census, 1871, Report (England and Wales)*, 170.
22 One indication of the practical results of this change of instructions is that the mean number of families per inhabited house in England and Wales jumped from 1·13 in 1851 to 1·20 in 1861, the mean number of persons per family fell from 4·83 in 1851 to 4·47 in 1861, while the mean number of persons per inhabited house hardly changed at all (5·36 in 1851 and 5·46 in 1861). See also the comments and data in *Census, 1861, Report (England and Wales)*, 10.
23 In fact it seems that very many fewer single young men and women were given separate 'family' status in 1861 than might have been expected from a close reading of the instructions.
24 *Census, 1861, Report (Scotland)*, xxvii.
25 Problems do, however, arise here as elsewhere because sometimes a shortage of data storage capacity may force investigators to amalgamate categories. This is particularly likely to be the case where cards are used, though many investigators seem unduly suspicious of double, treble, or even quadruple punching of columns, which greatly increases the amount of data that can be stored on a card, without any great increase in tabulation problems.

CHAPTER 5

1 This is perhaps overstating the case; several textbooks written for social scientists provide good introductions to sampling using materials which are more like those encountered by historians. (See, for example, Blalock, *Social Statistics*.) But there are still substantial differences in subject matter and emphasis between these accounts and the requirements of historians. The most comprehensive treatment of sampling methods is Yates, *Sampling methods*, but unfortunately almost all the examples are drawn from agricultural research.

2 See below, pages 177–82.

3 Yates, *Sampling methods*, 12.

4 Most collections of statistical tables, and many standard textbooks, contain a table of random numbers. See, for example, Lindley and Miller, *Statistical tables*; Blalock, *Social statistics*.

5 Technically this method of drawing a sample is known as sampling *without replacement*. Sometimes, as with sampling with probability proportionate to size, items are replaced and can feature more than once in the sample. See below, pages 181–2.

6 If more than one item is taken from each page, or other larger unit, the sample is no longer a simple random sample, and special formulae should be used in making the sample estimates. See Cochran, *Sampling techniques*, ch. 11.

7 See, for example, Armstrong in *Introduction to historical demography*, 217–31.

8 For a discussion of the possibility of bias of this kind in the sampling scheme recommended in Armstrong in *Introduction to historical demography*, 217–31, see Floud and Schofield, *Economic History Review* (1968), 607–9, and Armstrong, *ibid.*, 609–13.

9 Systematic samples are discussed in Cochran, *Sampling techniques*, ch. 8.

10 Cochran, *Sampling techniques*, 207–8.

11 The example is, of course, unrealistic; the population is small enough for every item to be studied.

12 Cochran, *Sampling techniques*, ch. 8.7.

13 An alphabetical list of surnames is not in itself in a random order – Scotsmen tend to dominate the 'M's and Irishmen the 'O's. It will only be in a virtually random order providing the characteristics being studied have nothing to do with ethnicity.

14 Cochran, *Sampling techniques*, ch. 8.5.

15 An exception, where a systematic sample yields an estimate which is more precise than that given by a random sample, is the case in which the population is listed so that the values of the items being estimated from a linear trend. Cochran, *Sampling techniques* ch. 8.6.

16 See below, page 172.

17 Cochran, *Sampling techniques*, 9–12, chs. 2.3, 2.13. This is always true if the population items are themselves normally distributed, and approximately true if the population items are not normally distributed, providing the sample sizes are large. For an informed definition of the normal distribution, see below note 74.

18 See, for example, Yule and Kendall, *Introduction to statistics*, 181–9, appendix table 2.

19 Most statistical textbooks contain tables of the normal distribution, from which other percentage points can be derived. See, for example, Yule and Kendall, *Introduction to statistics*, appendix table 2.

20 In certain circumstances the assumption that all possible sample results are normally distributed does not hold, and alternative action should be taken, as described below, pages 159–60.

21 Cochran, *Sampling techniques*, chs. 2.4, 2.6.

22 See below, pages 173–5.

23 Cochran, *Sampling techniques*, chs. 3.1, 3.2.

24 *Ibid.* chs. 2.3, 2.4, 2.6.   25 *Ibid.* ch. 3.3.

26 If the skewness is produced by a few extreme items, it may be possible to isolate them either to be fully enumerated or to be sampled separately (see below, pages 166–72). Otherwise the standard error can be calculated from a formula given in Cochran, *Sampling techniques*, ch. 2.14.

27 Fisher and Yates, *Statistical tables*, table VIII. 1.
28 Cochran, *Sampling techniques*, ch. 3.6.
29 *Ibid.* ch. 2.7. Most statistical textbooks contain a table of the distribution of Student's *t*.
30 All formulae for standard errors given subsequently in the text will contain the finite population correction.
31 Cochran, *Sampling techniques*, ch. 4.4.   32 *Ibid.*
33 *Ibid.* ch. 4.5. The required sample size for an estimate of the sum total of the values of the population items, $n_0 = (NS)^2/V$.
34 Sample sizes can be estimated for other kinds of sample estimate on the basis: $n_0 =$ the variance of the population items (i.e. the standard deviation squared) divided by V.
35 Cochran, *Sampling techniques*, ch. 4.6.
36 If items are drawn which have already been included in the pilot sample, they should be disregarded and the next random number taken instead.
37 Cochran, *Sampling techniques*, chap. 4.8. The sample size may be reduced by the finite population correction.
38 Stratification is discussed in Cochran, *Sampling techniques*, chs. 5, 5A.
39 *Ibid.*, ch. 5.5.   40 *Ibid.*, ch. 5.7.
41 The following simple procedure gives good results. Draw up a grouped frequency table of the distribution of the population items. Take the square root of the frequency corresponding to each size interval and add up the square roots of the frequencies cumulatively. Divide the range covered by the cumulative square roots into as many equal parts as there are strata required. Take as stratum boundaries the original size intervals which most nearly correspond to the equal divisions on the cumulative square root scale. Cochran, *Sampling techniques*, ch. 5A.6. The following example illustrates how five size intervals, each containing the number of population items given below under the heading 'frequency', can best be divided into three strata.

Size interval	frequency	$\sqrt{(frequency)}$	cumulative $\sqrt{(frequency)}$
0–9	9	3	3
10–19	25	5	8
20–29	36	6	14
30–39	16	4	18
40–49	4	2	20

Dividing the cumulative $\sqrt{(frequency)}$ range (20) into three equal parts indicates divisions on the cumulative $\sqrt{(frequency)}$ scale at 6·7 and 13·3. The nearest figures on this scale are 8 and 14, so the stratum boundaries are drawn as follows:
   Stratum 1: 0–9, 10–19.
   Stratum 2: 20–29.
   Stratum 3: 30–39, 40–49.
42 Cochran, *Sampling techniques*, 102.
43 *Ibid.* ch. 5A.7.
44 Or because systematic samples are being drawn. See below, page 172.
45 Cochran, *Sampling techniques*, ch. 5A.14.
46 *Ibid.* ch. 5A.2.
47 Yates, *Sampling methods*, 23–5.
48 Cochran, *Sampling techniques*, ch. 5A.8.
49 *Ibid.* ch. 5.1.   50 *Ibid.* ch. 5.10.
51 If any N_h is small, the standard error should be estimated using the formula

$$S_{(\hat{P}_{st})} = \sqrt{\left\{ \frac{1}{N^2} \sum_{h=1}^{\Sigma} \frac{N_h{}^2(N_h - n_h)}{N_h - 1} \frac{p_h q_h}{n_h - 1} \right\}}$$

(Cochran, *Sampling techniques*, ch. 5.10.)
52 *Ibid.*, ch. 5.9.   53 *Ibid.*, ch. 5.12.
54 *Ibid.*, chs. 8.11, 5A.11.
55 *Ibid.*, ch. 3.2.   56 *Ibid.*, chs. 2.3, 2.4.

57 Yule and Kendall, *Introduction to statistics*, 443-5.
58 Snedecor and Cochran, *Statistical methods*, 124-5.
59 Cochran, *Sampling techniques*, ch. 2.9.
60 See below, note 66.
61 Yule and Kendall, *Introduction to statistics*, ch. 9, 497-9.
62 Many editions of statistical tables contain a table of the z transformation of the correlation coefficient. See, for example, Lindley and Miller, *Statistical tables*, table 4.
63 Cochran, *Sampling techniques* chs. 2.9, 6.1-6.6.
64 The summary pages of the 1851 census enumerators' returns contain details of the number of occupiers and the number of persons. For difficulties over the interpretation of occupier and household see chapters 4 and 6. For deficiencies in the arithmetic of these summary pages see chapter 3.
65 Cochran, *Sampling techniques*, ch. 6.8.
66 *Ibid.* chs. 6.3-6.6, 6.9. Alternative, but more tedious, methods for calculating the confidence limits for ratio estimates, which avoid the restrictions mentioned in the text, are given in Cochran, ch. 6.7. In certain circumstances another method of deriving the population estimate, which is based on the regression of the y values on the x values rather than on the ratio between them, gives better results. Regression estimates are discussed in Cochran, ch. 7. Formulae for ratio and regression estimates in stratified samples are given in Cochran, chs. 6.10-6.15, and 7.7-7.8, respectively.
67 *Ibid.* ch. 9.   68 *Ibid.* chs. 3.12, 9.7.
69 *Ibid.*
70 Direct methods, however, are more precise in the rare situation where the total value of each clustered item bears no relation to the number of elements it contains. Both direct and ratio estimates are discussed in Cochran, *Sampling techniques*, ch. 9.8. For ratio estimates in stratified sampling see Cochran ch. 6.10.
71 In both cases the finite population correction has been omitted from the calculations.
72 Cochran, *Sampling techniques*, chs. 9.8-9.10, 9.12. For stratified samples see ch. 9.13.
73 An unusually lucid and helpful account of the logic underlying significance testing can be found in Siegel, *Nonparametric statistics*, chs. 1-3.
74 See, for example, Yule and Kendall, *Introduction to statistics*, 487-95, Snedecor and Cochran, *Statistical methods*, ch. 4. Slight deviations from normality can be tolerated. The normal distribution is defined in all statistical textbooks. Informally, in a normal distribution the values of the items of the population are distributed symmetrically about the mean value, becoming progressively less frequent the more extreme their value, so that a range of one standard deviation either side of the average value includes about 68 per cent of the items, a range of two standard deviations includes about 95 per cent of the items, and a range of three standard deviations either side of the average value includes almost all the items.
75 Siegel, *Nonparametric statistics* presents a clear account of a number of these tests.
76 In the interests of precision, historians should renounce their customarily casual use of words and expressions which have acquired a well-defined technical meaning. It is not helpful, for example, to describe as a 'random sample' what is patently a judicious selection of a few items particularly favourable to the argument being presented.

CHAPTER 6

1 Ashton, *Economic history of England*, 17.
2 Relevant census volumes are: *1801, Enumeration abstract*, pt. I, 496-7; *1811, Preliminary observations*, ix-x; *1821, Preliminary observations*, vi, and *Enumeration abstract*, 427, 486; *1831, Enumeration abstract*, pt. I, ix-x; pt. II, 1042-51.
3 *Census, 1841, Occupations abstract*, 31-45.
4 *Census, 1851, Population tables*, pt. II (1), lxxxii-c.
5 Relevant census volumes from 1861 onward are: *1861, Population tables*, II, xl-lxv; *1871, Population tables*, III, xxxv-xlviii; and IV; xxxviii-liv; *1881*, III (Ages, condition as to marriage etc.), vi-xxiii; and IV (General Report), 25-50; *1891*, III (Ages, condition as to

marriage etc.), vii–xxxi; and IV (General Report), 35–60; *1901, General Report with appendices*, 72–132, 245–69; *1911*, x (Occupations and Industries), pt. I, v–cli, 1–25, 524–57.

6   *Census, 1891*, IV (General Report), 35.

7   The existence of such occupational dictionaries is noted in *Census, 1911*, x (Appendix), Classified and alphabetical lists of occupations etc., ii. Copies of these classified lists entitled *Instructions to the clerks employed in classifying the occupations and ages of the people* have come to light for the censuses 1871–1901, and I have briefly examined them. That of 1871 lists 6–7,000 occupations, 1881 and 1891 some 8–9,000 and the list for 1901 covers about 10,000.

8   *Census, 1911*, x (Occupations and Industries, pt. I), vii–viii.

9   *Census, 1921, Industry tables*, iii.

10 *Census, 1951*, Classification of industries, iii–iv; *Census, 1961, Industry tables*, pt. I, xi, and appendix D.

11 The evolution of census procedure is usefully discussed in Marsh, *Changing social structure*, especially ch. V–VI.

12 Mlle Daumard's case is argued in two articles, in the *Revue Historique*, (1962), and the *Revue d'histoire moderne*, (1963).

13 For a recent attempt to apply similar categories to the printed census data for London in 1851, see Bédarida, *Annales E.S.C.* (1968). Using an eighty-category socio-professional code Bédarida groups the data in differing combinations to produce (a) an industrial classification (primary, secondary, tertiary, with sub-divisions within the secondary category), (b) a social classification, based on the Registrar-General's allocations. Further references to this important study will be made below.

14 See J. Dupâquier, in *L'histoire sociale; sources et méthodes*, 157–67, and a critical review of Mlle Daumard's work in *Revue d'histoire moderne* (1963), by J. Y. Tirat.

15 *L'histoire sociale*, 170.

16 For example the industrial classification adumbrated by J. M. Bellamy with reference to Hull. In *Population Studies* (1953) she drew attention to certain omissions in the *Guide to Official Sources No. 2, Census reports of Great Britain*; and in *Yorkshire Bulletin* (1952) explored the principal changes in employment structure for Hull between 1841 and 1931. Occupational data from successive censuses were reclassified into the 23 orders introduced in 1891, and these in turn were numbered on the basis of the 1931 Industry Tables. A list of all local occupations and industries recorded in the census volumes is given in appendix II with details of allocation.

17 These introductory remarks are based largely on a reading of Briggs, in *Essays in labour history*; Laslett, *World we have lost*, ch. 2; and Tawney, *Equality*, ch. 3.

18 Phrases used by Cobbett and Southey respectively. They were however 'praising the past in order to condemn the present', according to Professor Briggs.

19 Marx and Engels, *Communist manifesto*, 46, 53–4. Marx, *Capital*, II, chs XV–XXXIII, elaborates this view. See also F. Engels, *Condition of the working class in England*.

20 Hobsbawn, *Age of revolution*, 207.

21 Thompson, *Making of the English working class*, 11, 251–61.

22 Pollard, *Genesis of modern management*, 2–3, 250.

23 Clapham, *Economic history of Britain*, II, 22–5.

24 Briggs, *Essays in labour history*, 73.

25 Rosser and Harris, *Family and social change*, 93.

26 The sociological literature on class is immense. Valuable introductions, inter alia, are Mayer, *Class and society*; Bendix and Lipset, *Class, status and power*; Tumin, *Social stratification*.

27 Usually basing themselves on a classic distinction made by Weber. (See Gerth and Mills, *From Max Weber*, 180–95.) Though we are not unaware of the value of this conceptual distinction, it will not be employed in this context, since the Registrar-General's stratification system, which will be recommended in a modified form, clearly blends class and status criteria defined in Weber's sense.

28 Thernstrom, *Poverty and progress*, 84, quoting Carlsson, *Social mobility and class structure*, 44–5. Rosser and Harris, *Family and social change*, 89–90, observe that 'though there

appear to be as many views of social class and as many ingenious methods of classification as there are sociologists, it does appear to be generally agreed among sociologists that the most useful piece of information to have about a man to place him in a social context, is to know what sort of a job he does'.

29   Hall and Jones, *British Journal of Sociology* (1950).
30   There were 13 such groups in 1951, 17 in 1961. See *Census, 1961, Socio-economic group tables*, vii–viii.
31   *Census, 1951, Classification of Occupations*, vii. The best critique of the Registrar-General's scheme of social classification is probably Cole, *Studies in class structure*. In essence of course, the five-class scheme is the Whitehall civil servants' view of the social hierarchy.
32   *Registrar-General's Decennial Supplement*, 1911, xl, xli, 73–87.
33   *Registrar-General's Decennial Supplement*, 1921, pt. II, viii.
34   Stevenson, *Journal of the Royal Statistical Society* (1928), 213–4.
35   *Registrar-General's Decennial Supplement*, 1931, pt. IIa, 7–8.
36   Which we shall refer to subsequently as the 1951 classification.
37   *Census, 1951, Classification of occupations*, vii.
38   Using the volume entitled '*Classification of occupations, 1950*' for the 1951 allocations, and two separate volumes for those of 1921, viz. *Census, 1921, Classification of occupations*, (for occupational code numbers), and the *Registrar-General's Decennial Supplement*, 1921, ciii–cxiv, for the social class of each coded occupation.
39   Hobsbawm, *Labouring men*, 274, appears to give some support to this view, but for a contrary opinion see Lockwood, *Blackcoated worker*.
40   Armstrong, *Social structure of York, 1841–51*.
41   For examples, see Mayhew, *London Labour and the London poor*.
42   *Census, 1851, Population tables*, II, (1), lxxviii.
43   *Census, 1891*, IV General Report, 36.
44   See Dyos, *Study of urban history*, 71, 78–81.
45   Armstrong, *Social structure of York* 163. Data in table 2 from the same source, 164. Mr R. Smith, a research student at Nottingham University has found a similar distribution of domestic servants when classifying Nottingham and Radford household heads on this basis.
46   Dyos, *Study of urban history*, 146–9; Cole, *Studies in class structure*, 150–1, also addresses himself to this problem. Bédarida, *Annales ESC.*, 290, deals with the excessive size of Class III by the expedient of dropping large numbers of 'rarely qualified' young men and women (aged under 20), from Class III to Class IV, as well as all female workers in clothing and upholstery, etc. This leads to approximately similar sizes for Classes III and IV in the final analysis.
47   England and Wales (1951) figures from Marsh, *Changing social structure*, 194.
48   Dyos, *Study of urban history*, 147.
49   Although categories based on those of the Registrar-General are also used by Bédarida. However, his purpose was to depict the social structure of London globally, in statistical terms, while our concern has been rather with formulating categories of analysis for empirical research. In its general aims, Bédarida's exercise is more comparable with that of Cole, *Studies in class structure*, ch. 6.
50   Notably in that no relationships to household heads are stated, and exact ages are not given for those aged over 15.
51   The census authorities' comments on the information elicited on the numbers of farmers and distribution of farm size are in *Census, 1851, Population tables*, II, (1), lxxviii–lxxxi.
52   Sheppard, *Agricultural History Review* (1961), 44. Any such distinction is bound to be quite arbitrary.
53   The best introduction is Norton, *Guide to directories*, which discusses their origin, development, authorship and methods of compilation, as well as giving a detailed list of directories by counties (with locations). Directories may often be useful even after detailed census occupational data is available. For example, they might be used for checking statuses implied in the census enumerators' books: for indications of the scale of

businesses: for details of transport and other services: and for a variety of topographical and descriptive information not always readily available elsewhere.

54 *Census, 1911, General Report*, 97–8.
55 Central Statistical Office, *Standard Industrial Classification*.
56 Carr-Saunders, Jones and Moser, *Survey of social conditions*, 92.
57 Deane and Cole, *British economic growth*, 143, 147.
58 Booth, *Journal of the Statistical Society* (1886), 314–435.
59 *Ibid.* 324.   60 *Ibid.* 322–3.
61 As I have already mentioned in note 7 above, internal occupational directories survive from 1871, and perhaps in Booth's time, the first such directory (1861), was still extant. It is not certain whether or not Booth took any account of these directories, but it seems highly improbable since they were not published and Booth at no point mentions their existence. Evidently there are opportunities for further enquiry into the census office procedures and the implications of changes in the detailed composition of census 'occupations' for Booth's aggregative calculations, but this would be a major undertaking and is beyond the scope of the present study.
62 Deane and Cole, *British economic growth*, 142.
63 Booth, *Journal of the Statistical Society* (1886), 350.
64 The column headings should presumably have been –14, 15–19, 20–, 25–, 65– for males, and –14, 15– for females.
65 All classes of students and scholars (other than art, theological, law or medical) were placed by Booth in the 'indefinite' class if aged 20 plus, or in the dependent class if below that age.
66 *Census, 1891*, IV, General Report, 36–7.
67 *Ibid.*
68 It will be noticed that where the splitting of an 1891 occupation is necessary, we have, like Booth, standardized on 1881. To do otherwise would entail extensive revision without the prospect of commensurate improvements.
69 *Census, 1911*, x, Occupations and Industries, pt. I, xxv.
70 Booth, *Journal of the Statistical Society* (1886), 323.
71 The sex ratios given are those for the two boroughs, but data on marital status was not given for the principal towns in 1861, and the proportions married relate to the registration districts of Sheffield and Bath.
72 In 1841 occupational data was given for counties and 183 selected boroughs, large towns or important parishes in England and Wales. In 1851 and 1861 the occupations were given for each registration county and principal towns, and data for those aged 20 and over in all registration districts. In 1871 the range of occupational data was the same, except that for principal towns the coverage was now confined to the 20 plus age group. 1881 and 1891 saw some reduction in local detail, covering only registration districts and urban sanitary districts with a population exceeding 50,000 (all ages).
73 See for example the list of occupations actually found in York in 1841–51, in appendix A of this chapter. A rapid check suggests that only 'ordnance surveyor' and 'perfumer' would cause any difficulty.
74 In addition to the obvious modern reference works such as the *Oxford English Dictionary*, various nineteenth-century encyclopaedic dictionaries and early histories and descriptions of various trades and industries might be pressed into service. Clapham, *Economic History of Modern Britain*, I and II, cites a good many such works in footnotes and the British Museum's catalogue of printed books attests to the existence of many more.

CHAPTER 7

1 I am indebted to many friends and colleagues for valuable criticism and particularly to Dr C. J. Erickson who first suggested this approach and to Dr E. A. Wrigley.
2 For instance in the *Preliminary Report* of the Census of 1961.
3 These estimates can of course establish the *components* of population growth. See, for example, Cairncross, *Manchester School* (1949).

4   See, for example, Smith, *Geographical Journal* (1951), and Osborne, *Advancement of Science* (1956).
5   'Birthplaces of the People', In *General Report* of Census of England and Wales, 1851–1901.
6   *Annual Reports* of the Registrar General 1837–1901 and *Decennial Supplements* to same.
7   A good account is given in *The Census Reports of Great Britain 1801–1931*. See also Taylor, *British Medical Journal* (1951). I am grateful to Mr J. Gillingham for advice on the medieval origins of counties.
8   Mitchell, *Abstract of British historical statistics*, 20–3.
9   A complete summary of the exact coverage of the various censuses is contained in *The Census Reports of Great Britain 1801–1931*.
10 Mainly Greenwich which is in both intra-metropolitan Surrey and intra-metropolitan Kent. Its population has to be divided on the basis of the known 1871 distribution.
11 Glass, *Population Studies* (1951–52).
12 If desired, the numbers used by the nineteenth-century census for each county could be used instead of the county names. Cornwall, for example, was 28 and Devon 27. So Devon-born migrating to other English and Welsh counties from Cornwall 1861–70 would be $M28 \rightarrow OC$ 1861–70[27].
13 Earlier methods will be discussed below.
14 I hope to publish a preliminary analysis in the *Economic History Review*.
15 Friedlander and Roshier, *Population Studies* (1966).
16 It will be remembered from the discussion above that the application of decade birth and death rates presents no problems. The Registrar General's department merely summed births, deaths and marriages and divided by 10, then expressed the rate as a number per 1,000 of the average population for the decade $(P1861 + P1871)/2$.
17 Ravenstein, *Journal of the Royal Statistical Society* (1885) and (1889), Bowley, *Journal of the Royal Statistical Society* (1914), and *Census, 1911, General Report*, 61 ff are the most useful early studies.
       More recent important studies are, Hill, *Internal migration and its effects upon the death rates*, Newton and Jeffery, *Internal migration*, Carrier and Jeffery *External migration*, and Thomas, *Research memorandum on migration differentials*. There is a useful summary of much of the evidence in Saville, *Rural depopulation in England and Wales 1851–1951*, 98–125.
18 The age distribution of the migrant group was given for Carmarthen, Glamorgan, Monmouth (and some towns in those counties), Birmingham, Bradford, Liverpool, Manchester Middlesbrough, Swindon and London.
19 In the late nineteenth century county age-specific mortality rates were very similar, with the exception of infant mortality which was often one and a half times to twice as high in urban than in rural areas.
20 Longstaff, *Studies in statistics*. He estimated migration of English (net) to Scotland and Ireland as follows:

	English to Scotland	English to Ireland
1861–70	27,100	28,800
1871–1880	37,600	15,200

21 Friedlander and Roshier, *Population Studies* (1966).
22 At the moment of writing this data is not in a suitable form for analysis.
23 Thomas, *Economica* (1930).
24 The assumption that the migrant population was aged 35–44 in 1861 is not adhered to in this method, because they are reduced by the 35–44 death rate in 1861–70, when in fact they were 40–49. The true assumption is that the migrant groups were 30–39 in 1861.
25 Shannon, *Economic History Review* (1935).
26 Lee, Miller, Brainerd and Easterlin, *Population redistribution and economic growth*.
27 For a detailed statistical discussion of the problems involved in applying survival ratios to estimate net migration see Hamilton and Henderson, *Journal of the American Statistical Association* (1944); Price, *Journal of the American Statistical Association* (1955); Lee and

Lee, *Journal of the American Statistical Association* (1960); Zachariah, *Journal of the American Statistical Association* (1962).

28 A good example of such a detailed local study is Lawton, *Transactions of the Historic Society of Lancashire and Cheshire* (1955).

29 The operation of the 'hundred-year rule' precludes any such analysis of the 1871 or subsequent censuses because they can only be examined with the names blocked out which makes matching totally impossible.

30 See Duncan, *Economic History Review* (1963).

31 Search fees have to be paid at Somerset House for each certificate.

32 Redford, *Labour Migration in England*.

33 Because emigration is net movement of Cornwall born out of *all* English counties overseas.

CHAPTER 8

1 We shall not attempt to deal in detail with the period after 1893, when the basic structure of the criminal statistics as they now are was settled, nor at all with the separately published returns for Scotland and Ireland. These were organised on an entirely different basis, and would therefore require a detailed analysis of their own.

2 Durkheim had to insist on the autonomous existence of 'social reality' at greater length than may be necessary now, but his denial that aggregate indices of social behaviour were no more significant than the parts of which they were composed is worth quoting nonetheless. Acknowledging that the motives which prompt people towards suicide can be understood in terms of temperament, character, antecedents and private history, he went on as follows:

> That [suicides] may be seen in an entirely different light is certain. If, instead of seeing in them only separate occurrences, unrelated and to be separately studied, the suicides committed in a given society during a period of time are taken as a whole, it appears that this total is not simply a sum of independent units, a collective total, but is itself a new fact *sui generis*, with its own unity, individuality, and consequently its own nature – a nature, furthermore, dominantly social . . .
>
> The suicide-rate is therefore a factual order, unified and definite, as is shown by both its permanence and its variability. For this permanence would be inexplicable if it were not the result of a group of distinct characteristics, solidary with one another, and simultaneously effective in spite of different attendant circumstances; and this variability proves the concrete and individual quality of these same characteristics, since they vary with the individual character of society itself. Each society is predisposed to contribute a definite quota of voluntary deaths. This predisposition may therefore be the subject of a special subject belonging to sociology.

The same argument of course is directly applicable to the study of criminal behaviour. See *Suicide*, 37–8, 46–51, 306–20.

3 For a bibliography of nineteenth-century criminological literature, see Tobias, *Crime and industrial society in the 19th century*.

4 A brief survey of the correlation between criminal activity and economic conditions in the period 1857–1913 is contained in Thomas, *Social aspects of the business cycle*. But she concerns herself exclusively with the records for indictable offences, and thus fails to correct the distortions caused in those records by the gradual extension of summary jurisdiction. This is a problem we discuss below in section 2.

An unpublished statistical study covering the early years of the century is Macnab's *Aspects of the history of crime in England and Wales between 1805–60*. Failure to extend his analysis into the later nineteenth century somewhat qualifies the value of Macnab's work; and he, too, rather disregards the dangers inherent in the analysis of the statistics with which we shall be concerned shortly. But the thesis is excellent in its treatment of legislative changes in the period in question, and many of his conclusions have been substantiated in our analysis in part 2 of this chapter.

5   See Sutherland and Cressey, *Principles of criminology*, 189–95, for a discussion and assessment of recent work in this direction.

6   Tobias, *Crime and industrial society*, 21, 235. For his general discussion of the deficiencies in the statistics, see chapter 2 and appendix, pages 256–67.

7   See the minutes of evidence of the Select Committee on Criminal Laws, *PP* 1819, VIII, 19 and 21. (Radzinowicz, *History of English criminal law*, Vol. I, 526–66.) As early as 1778 Jeremy Bentham had suggested that the returns of the number of crimes committed would be 'a measure of excellent use in furnishing data for the legislator to work on . . . a kind of political barometer by which the effect of every legislative operation relative to the subject may be indicated and made palpable'. Bentham did in fact begin to 'sketch out a plan for a collection of documents . . . to be published under the name of *bills of delinquency* with analogy to the bills of mortality', but soon abandoned the project. See Radzinowicz, *History of English criminal law*, Vol. I, 355 ff, 497–525.

8   Macnab, *Aspects of the history of crime*, 34–43. Certain minor amendments were effected on the recommendation of the Select Committee on Criminal Laws 1819. There were in addition a number of supplementary returns made by special direction, for example of all those proceeded against for treason in 1817. These may be traced in the *Index to the Parliamentary Papers*.

9   19 and 20 Vict. c. 69. See Hart, *Journal of Public Administration* (1956), and on earlier police reforms, *English Historical Review* (1955).

10 *PP* 1857, XVV, V.

11 For a fuller discussion of this process and its consequences, see below, pages 355–8.

12 For a detailed bibliography see Radzinowicz, *History of English criminal law*, Vol. IV. From 1857 onwards annual reports of the Inspectors of Constabulary to the Home Office were also published. These relate to three district regions (Northern Counties; South-east England and South Wales; Eastern Counties, Midlands and North Wales), and contain the Inspectors' commentaries on the efficiency and strength of the forces in each district, and much localised information on the prevalence of certain types of minor crime.

13 *PP*, 1895, CVIII.

14 This rule was introduced in 1867 to ensure uniformity in the returns: previously some forces had habitually included all cases reported to them involving goods valued at 1s or less.

15 See section 3(b) of this chapter, pages 369–71.

16 See *Kentish sources: crime and punishment*.

17 An extensive illustration of the way in which local criminal records may be thus exploited in provided in Hobsbawm and Rudé, *Captain Swing*. See especially pp. 77–81. Note, however, the dangers of suggesting that all 'crime', even in agricultural counties 'was almost entirely economical – a defence against hunger': see pages 369–71 below. Note also that the use of committal returns for a single county (Norfolk) raises the problems we discuss on pages 358–61.

18 See the fuller discussion of this 'law' in Sellin, *The Law Quarterly Review* (1951), 496–504; and in Sellin and Wolfgang, *The measurement of delinquency*, ch. 3. The general difficulties relating to criminal indices are discussed more briefly in Sutherland and Cressey, *Principles of criminology*, 25–30.

19 *PP* 1901, LXXXIX.

20 The most significant of these reforms were enacted between 1831 and 1841, when coining and forgery, housebreaking with larceny, larceny in a dwelling house to the value of £5, riot, rape, the theft of farm stock etc., all ceased to be capital offences. By 1846 the death penalty was reserved for murder, attempted murder and treason.

21 For full accounts of these and similar changes in public attitudes to prosecution, see Macnab, *Aspects of the history of crime*, ch. IV passim; Tobias, *Crime and industrial society*, 223–7; Radzinowicz, *History of English criminal law*, vol. I, pt v.

22 In this discussion and in the following, reference is made to the graphs in section 3 of this chapter, and to the rates upon which they are based, which are published in full in the appendix.

23 Macnab, *Aspects of the history of crime*, 182. These ratios may be calculated from the committal returns.

24   1835: 5 and 6 *Will.* IV, c. 76; 1839: 2 & 3 Vict. c. 93; 1856: see note 9 above.

The fullest discussion of the earlier reforms of 1835 and 1839 – as well as the reform of the metropolitan police in 1829 – is contained in Macnab, *Aspects of the history of crime*, 164–294. He concludes that their effects 'were manifested so slowly that they had no perceptible effect on the records of detected crime' and that 'the reforms of the police did not automatically cause an increase in the efficiency of the police, because the actual consequences of the reforms were not as sweeping as the theoretical scope of the reforms would indicate' (288–9).

For a further discussion of these reforms and that of 1856 see Hart, *English Historical Review* (1955), *Journal of Public Administration* (1956) and Parris, *Public Law* (1961). Our account draws on these sources.

25   'Deterrence has probably been the main element in the preventive influence exercised by the modern constabulary': Criminal Registrar, *PP* 1896, XCIV, 21.

26   Macnab, *Aspects of the history of crime*, 264, 269. Figures in this paragraph from Police Reports, and Hart.

27   'Within two years of the passing of the 1856 Act . . . all the counties but one, and the great majority of boroughs, had efficient forces. The greater success of this measure [as compared with the earlier] may be fairly attributed to the administrative machinery which it set up.' Parris, *Public Law* (1961), 230.

28   See Tobias, *Crime and industrial society* 227–8 for a comprehensive list of these statutes.

29   Discussed and described in the Criminal Registrar's Report, *PP* 1898, CIV, 11–13.

30   It is perhaps reasonable to postulate that the less serious cases would not have been dealt with at all under the old system. The figures for all summary offences show that roughly one in five of those charged and about one in three of those convicted were actually committed to gaol in the period in question, but the corresponding figures for larcenies previously triable on indictment only, but tried summarily in 1857, show that 90 per cent of those convicted were committed to gaol.

On this basis there was a very slight increase in the rate per 100,000 between 1854 and 1857 for both male and female offenders, compared with a sharp decline in the rates for committals for trial. The actual figures for England and Wales, reduced to rates per 100,000 are as follows:

Date	Rate of committals for trial (indictable offences)		Rate of committals for trial added to committals to gaol and summary conviction (all offences)	
	Male	Female	Male	Female
1854	249	70	817	274
1855	216	63	781	274
1856	166	41	741	288
1857	170	44	830	293

31   Nobody has better expressed the degree to which national rates may mask local variations than the Criminal Registrar, in the introduction to the Criminal Statistics for 1899:

> The county is a useful, and for some purposes, an inevitable unit. But within the same county may be the most diverse conditions: a high rate of criminality and a low; a population very dense in some parts, sparse in others, and very different rates of marriages and births, mortality, and amount of school accommodation. Certain towns affect the returns for the whole county; outside them or their zone of influence the criminal returns may be very different. Even the city or town may, for many purposes, be too large an area. Within the same town may be classes living in wholly different conditions . . . Already there is some evidence that 'crime spots' coincide with the maximum of overcrowding and disease. (*PP* 1901, LXXXIX, 68).

32 These figures are calculated from the annual Police Returns.
33 Tobias, *Crime and industrial society*, 256–67. For a contemporary discussion of the
    difficulties in the way of local comparisons see the Criminal Registrar's 'Notes on the
    Criminal Statistics of some Large Towns' in the introduction to the Criminal Statistics
    for 1899 (*PP* 1901, LXXXIX, 68–78). As a further example of the extent of these local
    variations here are the standard rates for certain categories of crime in five large *boroughs*
    in 1899, when the differences in police strength and practice might be expected to have been
    of less importance than they were earlier. It is almost impossible to assess how meaningful
    the differences are.

Rate per 100,000 of population

	Total offences known to police	Offences against the person known to police	Offences against property known to police	Summary drunk and disorderly
Birmingham	392	12	367	724
Cardiff	222	20	192	770
Leeds	225	11	205	403
Liverpool	553	22	512	642
Metrop. London	277	14	252	847

34 See, for example, Plint, *Crime in England – 1801–48*. A full bibliography of contempor-
    ary exercises in criminological analysis is contained in Tobias, *Crime and industrial society*.
35 The twelve counties with the heaviest committal rates for the sample years 1841, 1851
    and 1861 are given in the following table:

1841		*1851*		*1861*	
Surrey	507	Surrey	540	Surrey	326
Monmouth	272	Monmouth	234	Kent	144
Warwick	260	Cheshire	225	Worcester	134
Lancashire	239	Worcester	216	Monmouth	122
Cheshire	238	Berkshire	215	Cheshire	122
Worcester	228	Gloucs.	210	Lancashire	122
Somerset	227	Hereford	210	Warwick	119
Hereford	217	Kent	198	Gloucs.	118
Leicester	216	Oxford	189	Hampshire	114
Kent	215	Suffolk	187	Somerset	102
Staffs.	208	Warwick	182	Shropshire	102
Hertford	203	Cambs.	175	Hereford	98

36 Tobias, *Crime and industrial society*, 19.
37 For intercensal years the male and female population for England and Wales has been
    taken from Mitchell and Deane, *Abstract of British historical statistics*, who adjusted
    their figures to give the best estimate of mid-year population. In the case of Lancashire
    we have used a simpler logarithmic interpolation. The effect of the differences in tech-
    nique on the resulting crime rates are marginal and can be safely ignored.
38 The trade cycle for the period 1805–50 is taken from Gayer, Rostow and Schwartz,
    The growth and fluctuation of the British economy 1790–1850, Vol. 1, 355. It is as authori-
    tative as possible under the circumstances, designed as it is by the authors 'to fit . . .
    accurately our full judgement – statistical and qualitative – on the cyclical pattern'.
    About the simplified cycle pattern reproduced for the period 1851–93 there may be more
    dispute, since no cycle with an authority comparable to that of the earlier one has so far
    been published. It is, however, adequate for the purposes of our discussion. The turning
    points are taken from Rostow, *British economy of the nineteenth century*, 33.

39 The offences included in these categories (2 and 3) are set out in full in table 1 on pages 387–90. It would of course be possible to regard Category 4 (offences against the currency) and Category 5 (malicious offences against property) as 'property offences'; but for our purposes the less comprehensive definition is preferable, covering only cases of robbery, breaking, theft, and fraud.

40 It will be remembered that there is a gap in the figures from 1852 to 1856 due to changes in the form of the returns and the failure to publish the prison returns for 1855 and 1856. This makes it impossible to provide an index of the secular trend between 1850 and 1860.

41 Tobias, *Crime and industrial society*, 150–2.

42 On account of this change we have not attempted an overall statistical analysis of the degree of correlation. The high correlation in the early years of the century would be offset by the lower correlation later in the century, and the results might lead one to conclude that the relationship between property crime and depression throughout the century was considerably less than in fact in some years it was. There is a real danger in placing too much emphasis on statistical 'verifications' of trends and correlations in cases where the nature of the correlation changes through time.

43 The initially surprising graphical convergence of the figures for male offences and those for offences known to the police plus summary larcenies, in this graph as in those which follow, is due simply to the fact that the rates per 100,000 of the latter are worked out for the total population as opposed to the male population only.

44 Before 1857 the only available summary figures with which a graph of violent crime could be constructed are those relating to the number of persons imprisoned after summary conviction for assault. The total rates of these together with indictable committals for violent offences reveal no obvious correlations of the type we have been considering.

45 In the case of individual *counties*, it is not possible to isolate *summary* offences of specific kinds for female and male offenders separately – though this can of course be done for the national figures. If, therefore, we are to attempt a comparison of national and county rates respectively, it must be done in terms of the rates for the total population, regardless of sex.

46 Checkland, *The rise of industrial society in England 1815–85*, 233.

47 See the Criminal Registrar's retrospective discussion of the incidence of violence and drunkenness in the introduction to the Criminal Statistics for 1899 (*PP* 1901, LXXXIX, 17–18).

48 Tobias, *Crime and industrial society*, 150–2.

49 As Macnab points out, *Aspects of the history of crime*, 182, the fact that only 202 persons were committed for Luddite offences in 1812 and 1813 is one dramatic index of this. This is an interesting comment on the competence of the repression of early working class movements, especially since only 21 of those committed were actually convicted.

50 The point is discussed at some length by Silver, in *The police: six sociological essays*.

51 See Merton, *Social theory and social structure*, 147.

52 The least reliable material of this kind relates to prisoners' occupations, and we do not intend to discuss it further. The Criminal Registrar himself pointed out in 1857 that 'as it would be desirous [for prisoners] to claim some honest employment, the numbers classed as in employment would probably be overstated'. More useful is the data on prisoners' nationality. This establishes the disproportionate responsibility of the Irish in the commission of offences. The information on prisoners' occupations and nationalities (for each prison in each county and in England and Wales as a whole) is available in the prison returns only after 1857.

53 'After 1840, especially in the south, there was rapid improvement, so that by the death of Queen Victoria illiteracy had been virtually eliminated throughout all England and Wales, for women as well as men.' Stone, *Past and Present* (1969), p. 125.

54 *PP* 1895, CVIII, 23.

55 That the percentage of female recommitments to prison was even higher than the male is to be accounted for by the number of prostitutes who made up a large proportion of female prisoners (whence the Criminal Registrar's belief in 1860 that the figures showed 'the incorrigible nature of confirmed female depravity').

56 Tobias, *Crime and industrial society*, 152–3ff.

57 Representative of the best of these introductions is that published for the year 1896. The occasion of Victoria's Jubilee inspired the Criminal Registrar to discuss more broadly than was his wont the incidence of criminal behaviour since the beginning of the reign and the way in which, in the long-term, it had been affected by what he called 'civilising influences'. He was inclined to take an optimistic view of their achievement. (*PP* 1898, CIV, 11–31.)

CHAPTER 9

1 The most detailed summaries are by Adamson, *English education*, 27–9, and ch. 8; and Smith, *History of English elementary education*, 114–19, 132–4, 151–2 and 219 ff.

2 Contemporary educationists were similarly scornful. See *Report of the Manchester Statistical Society*, *PP* 1835, VII, 869.

3 *Digest of parochial returns*, *PP* 1819, IX A–C. Corrected and improved summary tables for the counties were printed in *PP*, 1820, XII, 341 ff. The parochial summary tables give the number of schools and scholars in each parish, distinguishing endowed and unendowed schools respectively, Sunday schools, dame schools and schools on the 'new' (monitorial) system. The county summary tables differentiate between free and paying pupils. Neither set of tables distinguishes male and female scholars.

4 *Preface to parochial returns*, *PP* 1819, IX C.

5 *Abstract of answers and returns*, *PP*, 1835, XLI–XLIII.

6 The overseers of St Martin's and St Philip's, Birmingham, wrote: 'That this statement is very defective as regards the private schools, the above number not being more than half the real amount, on account of the masters and mistresses declining to make returns'. *Ibid.* XLIII, 991.

7 *Report of the Manchester Statistical Society*, *PP* 1835, VII. It also found that some of the returns had been erroneous.

8 The form of enquiry for day schools is printed in *Census: Education*, *PP* 1852–3, XC, cii–civ.

9 *Census: Education*, *PP* 1852–3, XC. Public schools were defined as 'schools supported in any degree from other sources than the payments by the scholars, and which are established in any degree for other objects than pecuniary profit to the promoters'. *Ibid.* xcvi.

10 The four classes of public schools were: I, supported by general or local taxation; II, supported by endowments; III, supported by religious bodies; IV, other public schools. These classes were variously subdivided, the differentiation of the schools in class III according to denomination being particularly useful. Sunday schools were similarly classed under their denominations.

11 *Census: Education*, 1852–3, XC, cxxxiii, table H, gives the numbers of scholars in each quinquennium below the age of 20, male and female respectively, in each registration county and in England and Wales. The figures refer only to the 1,450,000 children, about two-thirds of the scholars in the country, whose ages were supplied by the school returns.

12 *Newcastle Report*, vol. I, *Statistical Report*, *PP* 1861, XXI, part 1, 553 ff.

13 The figures are included in the assistant commissioners' reports on the specimen districts in vols. II–V of the *Newcastle Report*.

14 *Return of all civil parishes*, *PP* 1871, LV, 329 ff.

15 The returns for London and the municipal boroughs are among the Ministry of Education records Ed. 3 and Ed. 16 in the Public Record Office. See *Guide to . . . the Public Record Office*, II, 111.

16 *Census, 1851, Population Tables*, pt. 1, cxxxvii–viii, form of householder's schedule.

17 *Census, 1861, General Report*, 76–7. Most enumerators' books in 1851 returned scholars under five, and the printed occupational returns distinguished scholars in the 0–4 age-group.

18 The census nights were 30 March 1851, 7 April 1861 and 2 April 1871.

19 See especially Armstrong in Wrigley (ed.), *Introduction to English historical demography* and Anderson's and Tillott's chapters in this volume.

20 Public Record Office, HO 107/1539/21.1.1 – 21.1.33 (Bethnal Green, Hackney Road registrar's district).
21 Details which might have been recorded for relating to the incidence of schooling included the ages of heads of families, the birthplaces of children (which might serve as a crude index of recent migration), and the sole or shared occupation of dwellings. See also Schofield's chapter for further discussion of sampling problems.
22 For these modifications and for Armstrong's general discussion of the classification, see chapter 6.
23 An interesting though inconclusive example is provided by the report on education in Westminster in the *Journal of the Statistical Society of London*, i (1839), 469.

Bibliography

This does not represent an attempt to provide a full bibliography. The works listed are those to which reference is made in the footnotes. They are divided into three main sections.

1. Books and articles, alphabetically by author's name.
2. Parliamentary Papers (*PP*).
3. Other sources.

There is a detailed list of census publications covering England, Wales and Scotland 1801–91 in Appendix 1 of chapter 1.

BOOKS AND ARTICLES

Adamson, J. W., *English education* (Cambridge, 1930).

Anderson, M., *Family structure in nineteenth century Lancashire*, unpublished PhD thesis (Cambridge, 1969).

Angell, R., 'A critical review of the development of the personal document method in sociology, 1920–1940', in Gottschalk, L., Kluckhohn, C., and Angell, R., *The uses of personal documents in history, anthropology and sociology* (New York, 1947).

Armstrong, W. A., 'Social structure from the early census returns', in Wrigley, E. A. (ed.), *An introduction to English historical demography* (London, 1966).

Armstrong, W. A., *The social structure of York, 1841–51*, unpublished PhD thesis (Birmingham, 1967).

Armstrong, W. A., 'The interpretation of the census books for Victorian towns' in Dyos, H. J. (ed.), *The study of urban history* (London, 1968).

Armstrong, W. A., 'Social structure from the early census returns: a rejoinder', *Economic History Review*, 2nd series, xxi, no. 3 (1968), 609–13.

Ashton, T. S., *An economic history of England: the eighteenth century* (London, 1955).

Back, K. W., 'A social psychologist looks at kinship structure', in Shanas, E., and Streib, G. F. (eds.), *Social structure and the family, generational relations* (New Jersey, 1965).

Banks, J. A., *Prosperity and parenthood* (London, 1954).

Bédarida, F., 'Londres au milieu du XIXe siècle: une analyse de structure sociale', *Annales*, xxiii, no. 2 (1968), 268–95.

Bellamy, J., 'A note on occupation statistics in British censuses', *Population Studies*, vi, no. 3 (1953), 306–8.

Bendix, R., and Lipset, S. M., *Class status and power: a reader in social stratification* (London, 1954).

Berelson, B., 'Content analysis', in Lindzey, G. (ed.), *Handbook of social psychology*, vol. 1 (Reading, Mass., and London, 1954).

Blalock, H. M., *Social statistics* (New York, 1960).

Booth, C., 'Occupations of the people of the United Kingdom, 1801–1881', *Journal of the Statistical Society*, XLIX (1886), 314–444.

Booth, C. (ed.), *Life and labour of the people in London*, 9 vols (London, 1892–7).

Bowley, A. L., 'Rural population in England and Wales. A study of the changes in density, occupations and ages', *Journal of the Royal Statistical Society*, LXXVIII (1914), 597–645.

Briggs, A., and Saville, J., *Essays in labour history* (London, 1960).

Cairncross, A. K., 'Internal migration in Victorian England', *Manchester School*, XVII (1949), 67–87.

Carlsson, G., *Social mobility and the class structure* (Lund, 1969).

Carrier, N. H., and Jeffery, J. R., *External migration*, General Register Office, Studies on medical and population subjects, no. 6 (HMSO, 1953).

Carr-Saunders, A. M., Jones, D. C. and Moser, C. A., *Survey of social conditions in England and Wales* (Oxford, 1958).

Chadwick, D., 'On the rate of wages in Manchester and Salford, and the manufacturing districts of Lancashire, 1839–59', *Journal of the Statistical Society*, XXIII, pt. 1 (1860), 1–36.

Checkland, S. G., *The rise of industrial society in England 1815–1885* (London, 1964).

Cicourcel, A. V., *Method and measurement in sociology* (London, 1964).

Clapham, J. H., *An economic history of modern Britain*, 3 vols (Cambridge, 1926–38).

Cochran, W. G., *Sampling techniques*, 2nd ed. (New York, 1963).

Cole, G. D. H., *Studies in class structure* (London, 1955).

Collier, F., *The family economy of the working classes in the cotton industry 1784–1833* (Manchester, 1965).

Connell, K. H., *The population of Ireland, 1750–1845* (Oxford, 1950).

Crozier, D., 'Kinship and occupational succession', *Sociological Review*, new series XIII, no. 1. (1965), 15–43.

Dahrendorf, R., 'Recent changes in the class structure of European societies', *Daedalus*, XCIII, no. 1 (1964), 225–70.

Daniel, G. H., 'Labour migration and age composition', *Sociological Review*, XXXI (1939), 281–308.

Daumard, A., 'Structures sociales et classement socio-professionnel', *Revue historique*, CCXXVII (1962), 139–54.

Daumard, A., 'Une référence pour l'Etude des sociétés urbaines en France aux XVIIIe et XIX siècles. Projet de code socio-professionnel', *Revue d'histoire moderne*, X (1963), 185–210.

Davies, C. S., *North country bred* (London, 1963).

Davies, J. B., 'Una teoria general de los determinantes de la edad de casarse', *Revista mexicana de sociologia*, XXVI, no. 1 (1964), 191–219.

Deane, P., and Cole, W. A., *British economic growth, 1688–1959* (Cambridge, 1962).

Drake, M., *Population and society in Norway, 1735–1865* (Cambridge, 1969).

Duncan, R., 'Case studies in emigration: Cornwall, Gloucestershire and New South Wales, 1877–1886', *Economic History Review*, 2nd series, XVI, no. 2 (1963), 272–89.

Dupâquier, J., 'Problèmes de la codification socio-professionelle', in *L'histoire sociale. Sources et méthodes* (Paris, 1967).

Durkheim, E., *Suicide, a study in sociology* (London, 1968).

Dyos, H. J. (ed.), *The study of urban history* (London, 1968).

Dyos, H. J., and Baker, A. B. M., 'The possibilities of computerising census data', in Dyos, H. J. (ed.), *The study of urban history* (London, 1968).

Engels, F., *The condition of the working class in England*, trans. and ed. by Henderson, W. O., and Chaloner, W. H. (Oxford, 1958).

Farr, W., *English life tables* (London, 1864).

Firth, R., 'Family and kinship in industrial society', in Halmos, H. J. (ed.), *The development of industrial societies*, Sociological Review Monograph no. 8 (Keele, 1964).

Fisher, R. A., and Yates, F., *Statistical tables for biological, agricultural, and medical research*, 5th ed. (Edinburgh, 1957).

Fleury, M. and Henry, L., *Nouveau manuel de dépouillement et d'exploitation de l'état civil ancien* (Paris, 1965).

Floud, R. C., and Schofield, R. S., 'Social structure from the early census returns: a comment', *Economic History Review*, 2nd ser., XXI, no. 3 (1968), 607–9.

Foster, J. O., *Capitalism and class consciousness in earlier nineteenth century Oldham*, unpublished Ph.D. thesis (Cambridge, 1967).

Fox, R., *Kinship and marriage* (London, 1967).

Friedlander, D., and Roshier, D. J., 'A study of internal migration in England and Wales', *Population Studies*, XIX, no. 3 (1966), 239–79 and XX, no. 1 (1966), 45–59.

Gaskell, E. C., *Mary Barton* (London, 1897).

Gayer, A. D., Rostow, W. W., and Schwartz, A. J., *The growth and fluctuation of the British Economy 1790–1850*, 2 vols. (Oxford, 1953).

Gerth, H. H., and Mills, C. W., *From Max Weber: essays in sociology* (London, 1948).

Glass, D. V., 'A note on the under-registration of births in the nineteenth century', *Population Studies*, V (1951–2), 70–88.

Goode, W. J., 'The process of role bargaining in the impact of urbanisation and industrialisation', *Current Sociology* XII, no. 1 (1963), 1–13.

Goode, W. J., *World revolution and family patterns* (New York, 1963).

Habakkuk, H. J., 'Family structure and economic change in nineteenth century Europe', in Bell, N. W., and Vogel, E. F. (eds), *A modern introduction to the family* (New York, 1960).

Hajnal, J., 'European marriage patterns in perspective', in Glass, D. V. and Eversley, D. E. C. (eds), *Population in history* (London, 1965).

Hall, J. and Jones, D. C., 'Social grading of occupations', *British Journal of Sociology*, I (1950), 31–55.

Hamilton, C. H. and Henderson, F. M., 'Use of the survival method in measuring net migration', *Journal of the American Statistical Association*, XXXIX (1944), 197–206.

Hart, J. M., 'Reform of the borough police 1836–56', *English Historical Review*, LXX (1955), 411–27.

Hart, J. M., 'The County and Borough Police Act 1856', *Journal of Public Administration*, XXXIV (1956), 405–17.

Henry, L., *Anciennes familles genevoises* (P.U.F., 1956).

Hewitt, M., *The effect of married women's employment in the cotton textile districts on the home in Lancashire, 1840–1880*, unpublished PhD thesis (London, 1953).

Hewitt, M., *Wives and mothers in Victorian industry* (London, 1959).

Hill, A. B., *Internal migration and its effects upon the death rates with special reference to the county of Essex* (Medical Research Council, 1925).

Hill, R., 'Decision making and the family life cycle', in Shanas, E. and Streib, G. F. (eds), *Social structure and the family, generational relations* (New Jersey, 1965).

Hobsbawm, E. J., *The age of revolution* (London, 1964).

Hobsbawm, E. J., *Labouring men* (London, 1964).

Hobsbawm, E. J. and Rudé, G., *Captain Swing* (London, 1969).

Hoggart, R., *The uses of literacy* (London, 1957).

Hollingsworth, T. H., 'The demography of the British peerage', *Population Studies*, supplement to vol. XVIII, no. 2 (1964).

Hubert, J., 'Kinship and geographical mobility in a sample from a London middle class area', *International Journal of Comparative Sociology*, VI, no. 1 (1965), 61–80.

Humphreys, A. J., *New Dubliners* (London, 1966).

James, P. (ed.), *The travel diaries of T. R. Malthus* (Cambridge, 1966).

Kendall, M. C. and Babington Smith, B., *Tables of random sampling numbers* (Cambridge, 1939).

Lancaster, L., 'Some conceptual problems in the study of family and kin ties in the British Isles', *British Journal of Sociology*, XII, no. 4 (1961), 317–33.

Laslett, P., *The world we have lost* (London, 1965).

Laslett, P. and Harrison, J., 'Clayworth and Cogenhoe', in Bell, H. E. and Ollard, R. L. (eds.), *Historical essays 1600–1750 presented to David Ogg* (London, 1963).

Lathrop, B. F., *Migration into East Texas, 1835–60* (Austin, 1949).

Lawton, R., 'The population of Liverpool in the mid-nineteenth century', *Transactions of the Historic Society of Lancashire and Cheshire*, CVII (1955), 89–120.

Lee, E. S. and Lee, A. S., 'Internal migration statistics for the United States', *Journal of the American Statistical Association*, LV (1960), 664–97.

Lee, E. S., Miller, A. R., Brainerd, C. P. and Easterlin, R. A., *Population redistribution and economic growth, United States 1870–1950*, vol. 1 (Philadelphia, 1957).

Lindley, D. V. and Miller, J. C. P., *Cambridge elementary statistical tables* (Cambridge, 1964).

Litwak, E., 'Extended kin relations in an industrial democratic society', in Shanas, E. and Streib, G. F. (eds), *Social structure and the family, generational relations* (New Jersey, 1965).

Lockwood, D., *The black-coated worker* (London, 1958).

Lomsing, J. B. and Kish, L., 'Family life cycle as an independent variable', *American Sociological Review*, XXII, no. 5 (1957), 512–19.

Longstaff, G. B., *Studies in statistics, social, political, medical* (London, 1891).

Loudon, J. B., 'Kinship and crisis in South Wales', *British Journal of Sociology*, XII, no. 4 (1961), 333–50.

McCulloch, J. R., *A descriptive and statistical account of the British Empire* (London, 1847).

McGregor, O. R., *Divorce in England* (London, 1957).

McGregor, O. R., 'Some research possibilities and historical materials for family and kinship study in Britain', *British Journal of Sociology*, XII, no. 4 (1961), 310–17.

Macnab, K. K., *Aspects of the history of crime in England and Wales between 1805–60*, unpublished PhD thesis (Sussex, 1965).

Marsh, D. C., *The changing social structure of England and Wales, 1871–1951* (London, 1958).

Martin, D., *A sociology of English religion* (London, 1967).

Marx, K., *Capital. A critical analysis of capitalist production*, trans. Moore, S., and Aveling, E., and ed. Engels, F. (London, 1909).

Marx, K. and Engels, F., *Manifesto of the Communist party* (Moscow, 1959).

Mayer, K. B., *Class and society* (New York, 1955).

Mayhew, H., *London labour and the London poor*, 2 vols (London, 1851).

Merton, R. K., *Social theory and social structure* (Glencoe, 1957).

Millerson, G., 'Criminal statistics and the Perks Committee', *Criminal Law Review* (1968), 478–89.

Mitchell, B. R. and Deane, P., *Abstract of British historical statistics* (Cambridge, 1962).

Newton, M. P. and Jeffrey, J. R., *Internal migration*, General Register Office, Studies on medical and population subjects, no. 5 (HMSO, 1951).

Norton, J. E., *Guide to the national and provincial directories of England and Wales published before 1856*, Royal Historical Society, Guides and handbooks, 5 (London, 1950).

Osborne, R. H., 'Internal migration in England and Wales, 1951', *Advancement of Science*, XII (1956), 424–34.

Parris, H., 'The Home Office and the provincial police in England and Wales, 1856–70', *Public Law* (1961), 230–55.

Perkin, H., *The origins of modern English society* (London, 1969).

Petersen, W., *The politics of population* (New York, 1965).

Pinchbeck, I., *Women workers and the industrial revolution* (London, 1930).

Plint, T., *Crime in England, 1801–48* (London, 1851).

Pollard, S., *The genesis of modern management* (London, 1965).

Price, D. O., 'Examination of two sources of error in the estimation of net external migration', *Journal of the American Statistical Association*, L (1955), 689–700.

Radzinowicz, L., *A history of English criminal law and its administration from 1750*, 4 vols (London, 1948–68).

Ravenstein, E. C., 'The laws of migration', *Journal of the Royal Statistical Society*, XLVIII (1885), 162–235 and LII (1889), 241–301.

Reader, W. J., *Professional men: the rise of the professional classes in nineteenth century England* (London, 1966).

Redford, A., *Labour migration in England 1800–1850* (Manchester, 1926).

Rosser, C. and Harris, C. C., *The family and social change* (London, 1965).

Rostow, W. W., *British economy of the nineteenth century* (Oxford, 1948).

Rowe, C. P., 'The developmental conceptual framework to the study of the family', in Nye, F. I. and Berardo, F. M. (eds), *Emerging conceptual frameworks in family analysis* (New York, 1965).

Rowntree, B. S., *Poverty: a study of town life* (London, 1901),

Saville, J., *Rural depopulation in England and Wales 1851–1951* (London, 1957).

Sellin, T., 'The significance of records of crime', *Law Quarterly Review*, LXVII (1951), 489–504.

Sellin, T. and Wolfgang, M. E., *The measurement of delinquency* (New York, 1964).

Shannon, H. A., 'Migration and the growth of London 1841–1891', *Economic History Review*, V (1935), 78–86.

Sharf, B. R., review of Rosser, C. and Harris, C. C. (see above), *Population Studies*, XXII, no. 2 (1968), 285–6.

Sheppard, J. A., 'East Yorkshire's agricultural labour force in the mid-nineteenth century', *Agricultural History Review*, IX (1961), 43–54.

Siegel, S., *Nonparametric statistics for the behavioral sciences* (Tokyo, 1956).

Silver, A., 'The demand for order in civil society', in Bordua, D. (ed.), *The police: six sociological essays* (New York, 1967).

Smelser, N. J., *Social change in the industrial revolution* (London, 1959).

Smith, C. T., 'The movement of population of England and Wales in 1851 and 1861', *Geographical Journal*, CXVII (1951), 200–10.

Smith, F., *History of English elementary education 1760–1902* (London, 1931).

Snedecor, G. W. and Cochran, W. G., *Statistical methods*, 6th ed. (Ames, Iowa, 1967).

Stacey, M. (ed.), *Comparability in social research* (London, 1969).

Stehouwer, J., 'Relations between generations and the three generation household in Denmark', in Shanas, E. and Streib, G. F. (eds.), *Social structure and the family, generational relations* (New Jersey, 1965).

Stevenson, T. H. C., 'The vital statistics of wealth and poverty', *Journal of the Royal Statistical Society*, XCI (1928), 207–30.

Stone, L., 'Literacy and education in England 1640–1900', *Past and Present*, 42 (1969), 69–139.

Sutherland, E. H. and Cressey, D. R., *Principles of criminology*, 6th ed. (Chicago, 1960).

Tawney, R. H., *Equality* (London, 1964).

Taylor, A. J., 'The taking of the census, 1801–1951', *British Medical Journal*, I (1951), 715–20.

Thernstrom, S. A., *Poverty and progress* (Harvard, 1964).

Thomas, B., 'Migration into the Glamorganshire coalfield 1861–1911', *Economica*, XXX (1930), 275–94.

Thomas, D. S., *Social aspects of the business cycle* (London, 1925).

Thomas, D. S., *Research memorandum on migration differentials*, Social Science Research Council, Bulletin no. 43 (New York, 1938).

Thomas, S., 'The agricultural labour force in some south-west Carmarthenshire parishes in the mid-nineteenth century', *Welsh History Review* III, no. 1 (1967), 63–73.

Thompson, E. P., *The making of the English working class* (London, 1964).

Tillott, P. M., 'The analysis of census returns', *Local Historian*, VIII, no. 1 (1968), 2–10.

Tirat, J. Y., 'Problèmes de méthode en histoire sociale', *Revue d'histoire moderne*, X (1963), 211–18.

Tobias, J. J., *Crime and industrial society in the nineteenth century* (London, 1967).

Townsend, P., 'The effects of family structure on the likelihood of admission to an institution in old age', in Shanas, E. and Streib, G. F. (eds), *Social structure and the family, generational relations* (New Jersey, 1965).

Tranter, N. L., 'Population and social structure in a Bedfordshire parish: the Cardington listing of inhabitants, 1782', *Population Studies*, XXI, no. 3 (1967), 261–82.

Tumin, M. M., *Social stratification: the forms and functions of inequality* (Englewood Cliffs, 1967).

Vincent, J. R., *Pollbooks: how Victorians voted* (London, 1967).

Webb, S. and B., *English local government*, 9 vols (London, 1906–29).

Williams, O., *The life and letters of John Rickman* (London, 1911).

Williams, W. W., *A West country village: family, kinship and land. Ashworthy* (London, 1963).

Wrigley, E. A. (ed.), *An introduction to English historical demography* (London, 1966).

Wrigley, E. A., 'Family limitation in pre-industrial England', *Economic History Review*, 2nd series, XIX, no. 1 (1966), 82–109.

Wrigley, E. A., 'Mortality in pre-industrial England: the example of Colyton, Devon, over three centuries', *Daedalus*, XCIII, no. 2 (1968), 246–80.

Yates, F., *Sampling methods for censuses and surveys*, 3rd ed. (London, 1960).

Young, M., 'The role of the extended family in a disaster', *Human Relations*, VII, no. 3 (1954), 383–91.

Young, M. and Willmott, P., *Family and kinship in East London* (London, 1957).

Yule, G. U. and Kendall, M. G., *Introduction to the theory of statistics*, 14th ed. (London, 1950).

Zachariah, K. C., 'A note on the census survival ratio method of estimating net migration', *Journal of the American Statistical Association*, LVII (1962), 175–83.

PARLIAMENTARY PAPERS

Report from the Select Committee appointed to consider of so much of the criminal law as relates to capital punishment in felonies, PP, 1819, VIII.

Digest of parochial returns to the Select Committee on the education of the poor, PP, 1819, IX, A–C (improved tables in *PP*, 1820, XII, 341 ff.).

First report of the Commissioners appointed to inquire into the employment of children in factories, PP, 1833, XX.

Report of the Manchester Statistical Society on the state of education in the borough of Manchester in 1834, PP, 1835, VII, 867 ff.

Poor inquiry, Ireland: Appendix A, PP, 1835, XXXII.

Abstract of answers and returns on education, PP, 1835, XLI–XLIII.

Report from the Select Committee on the education of the poorer classes in England and Wales, PP, 1837–8, VII.

Evidence taken, and report made, by the Assistant Poor Law Commissioner sent to inquire into the state of the population of Stockport, PP, 1842, XXXV.

Census of Ireland, 1841, Report, PP, 1843, XXIV.

Fourth report from the Select Committee on settlement and poor removal, PP, 1847, XI.

Reports of the Inspectors of Factories for the half year ending 31st October 1848, PP, XXII.

Report of the Commissioners appointed to inquire into the state of popular education, PP, 1861, XXI, parts 1–6.

Return of all civil parishes not within municipal boroughs and the district of the School Board of London, PP, 1871, LV, 329 ff.

Census of England and Wales, 1911, vol. X, 'Occupations and industries', PP, 1913, LXXVIII, 321–, LXXIX.

Census of England and Wales, 1911, General Report with Appendices, PP, 1917–18, XXXV.

Census of England and Wales, 1911, vol. XIII, 'Fertility of marriage', part I, PP, 1917–18, XXXV.

In addition the following series may be noted:

Registrar General: Annual reports, 1837–.

Crime and outrage, criminal offenders, etc., 1805–56
    Returns of offenders committed to trial, etc.

Gaols and prisons, 1836–56
    Reports from district inspectors of prisons, in annual digests.

Judicial statistics, 1867–92
    Combined returns, comprising (1) Police and constabulary, (2) Criminal proceedings, (3) Prisons.

OTHER SOURCES

The census reports of Great Britain 1801–1931, Guides to official sources, no. 2 (HMSO, 1951).

History of the census of 1841 (GRO) MS. in library of General Register Office, Somerset House.

Guide to the contents of the Public Record Office, 2 vols (HMSO, 1963).

Hansard, 26 George II, May 1753.

L'histoire sociale: sources et méthodes, Colloque de l'Ecole Normale Supérieure de Saint-Cloud, 1965 (Paris, 1967).

Instructions for census enumerators (GRO and COI, 1966).

Kentish sources: crime and punishment (Kent Record Office, 1969).

Morning Chronicle Supplements, 'Labour and the poor', 1849–50.
Standard industrial classification (CSO, 1948).
The Times (London, 1800–).
'Second report of the Statistical Society of London on the state of education in Westminster', *Journal of the Statistical Society of London*, i (1839), 193–215.

Index

Bold type indicates key information presented in tabular form

social class (*cont.*)
    Registrar-General's classification of,
    203–5
Solihull, 400
Somerset, 29, 359, 430
Somerset House, 31, 315, 427
Southam, 400
Southampton, 13, 405
Southey, R., 8, 423
Spain, census of, 12
Spitalfields, 22, 406
Stacey, M., 419
Staffordshire, 312, 430
standard deviation, of sample distribution,
    155–6, 173
standard error, of sample, 156–61, 169, 170–1,
    173, 174, 176, 178, 179, 180, 181
standard of living, 63; of families, 61–2
Statistical Society, 11, 12, 14, 21, 232
Statistik des Deutschen Reichs, 1
Stehouwer, J., 69, 416
Stevenson, G. S., 417
Stevenson, T. H. C., 424
Stone, L., 431
Stratford, 400
stratified sampling, *see* sampling
Stockport, 312
Stourport, 312
Suffolk, 430
Summary Jurisdiction Act: of 1855, 354, 357,
    of 1879, 356, 357
Sunday schools, *see* education
Surrey, 312, 426, 430
Sutherland, E. H., 428
Swansea, 59
Swindon, 426
Switzerland, 27
systematic sampling, *see* sampling

Tawney, R. H., 423
Taylor, A. J., 417, 426
Thernstrom, S., 202, 423
Thomas, B., 331, 333, 426
Thomas, D. S., 426, 427
Thomas, S., 418
Thompson, E. P., 199, 423
Thornton, W., 7, 20, 30
Tickhill, 96, 106, 109, 118, 119, 124, 125, 417
Tillott, P. M., 2, 55, 139, 414, 417, 419, 432
Times, The, 8, 9, 10, 12, 13, 14, 15, 16, 20, 21,
    26, 29, 31

Tirat, J. Y., 423
Tobias, J. J., 338, 339, 359, 360, 361, 368, 371,
    383, 385, 427, 428, 429, 430, 431
Tonna, 79
Tower Hamlets, 14
Townsend, P., 414
trade cycle, and criminal behaviour, 5, 368–9,
    370–1, 376, 378–9
Tranter, N. L., 415
Truro, 28
Tumin, M. M., 423

under-registration, in London, 22
unemployed, reporting of in enumerators'
    books, 126–7
United States, 69, 332, 339; census of, 15

Vincent, J. R., 417
visitors, reporting of in enumerators' books,
    112–16, 132, 144

Wales, 82, 109, 239, 314; household in, 92
Warwick, 400, 430
Warwickshire, 358, 399, 400, 401, 403, 404,
    405, 430
Webb, S. and B., 127, 419
Weber, M., 423
Westmeath, 21
Westminster, 22, 28, 433
Westmorland, 29
White's Directory, 85
Whitechapel, 22
Williams, O., 411
Williams, W. W., 413
Willmott, P., 413, 415
Winteringham, 103, 126, 127
Winterton, 88, 99, 106, 113, 116
Wolfgang, M. E., 428
Wood, G. H., 415
Worcester, 430
Wrexham, 201
Wrigley, E. A., 411, 417, 419, 425, 432
Wycomb, 28

Yates, F., 420, 421
York, 206, 209, 211, 212, 215, 425
Yorkshire, 82, 119, 248, 403, 417
Young, M., 413, 415, 417
Yule, G. U., 420, 422

Zachariah, K. C., 427